P9-DBJ-227

PUBLIC PAPERS OF THE PRESIDENTS
OF THE UNITED STATES

PUBLIC PAPERS OF THE PRESIDENTS

OF THE UNITED STATES

Gerald R. Ford

Containing the Public Messages, Speeches, and

Statements of the President

AUGUST 9 TO DECEMBER 31, 1974

1974

UNITED STATES GOVERNMENT PRINTING OFFICE

WASHINGTON : 1975

Published by the
Office of the Federal Register
National Archives and Records Service
General Services Administration

For sale by the Superintendent of Documents, U.S. Government Printing Office
Washington, D.C. 20402 - Price $16
Stock Number 022-003-00913-2

FOREWORD

THE SPEECHES, messages, press conferences and major statements contained in this volume speak for themselves. They record not only the words and policies of a new Presidential Administration but the momentous events of a critical period in American history. No past Administration has begun its tenure in office under more unusual circumstances than this one. At no time in history has America faced quite the same mixture of problems, challenges and opportunities as during the period covered in these pages. This volume shows how they were met. Hopefully, it will help future generations to put into historical perspective the many issues and events of this period.

The reader will find not one, but many stories: the story of a peaceful, Constitutional transfer of power at the end of a long political ordeal; the story of a foreign policy which, despite some setbacks, has succeeded in keeping American prestige high and the chances for world peace strong; the story of a nation grappling with the twin economic menaces of inflation and recession—a battle partially won though still very real today.

But it is both my hope and my firm belief that there runs through all of these varied themes an underlying note of American stability, character and strength: stability in the midst of political shock and change; character in the preservation of basic American values and institutions despite economic pressures and political conflicts; and strength as America's resolve and diplomatic commitment successfully passed through a time of testing at home and abroad.

As this is written, the story still unfolds. America, on the threshold of her third century, faces many new challenges, many new opportunities. But, as these pages clearly show, our people—and our institutions—still possess the idealism, the vitality and the basic soundness which has seen us through difficult times before and which can make the years ahead as great as any in our history.

Gerald R. Ford

PREFACE

IN THIS VOLUME are gathered most of the public messages and statements of the 38th President of the United States that were released by the White House during the period August 9–December 31, 1974. Volumes covering the Administrations of Presidents Truman, Eisenhower, Kennedy, Johnson, Nixon, and the first year of President Hoover are also available.

The series was begun in 1957 in response to a recommendation of the National Historical Publications Commission. An extensive compilation of the messages and papers of the Presidents, covering the period 1789 to 1897, was assembled by James D. Richardson and published under Congressional authority between 1896 and 1899. Since then, various private compilations have been issued but there was no uniform publication comparable to the *Congressional Record* or the *United States Supreme Court Reports*. Many Presidential papers could be found only in mimeographed White House releases or as reported in the press. The National Historical Publications Commission therefore recommended the establishment of an official series in which Presidential writings and utterances of a public nature could be made promptly available.

The Commission's recommendation was incorporated in regulations of the Administrative Committee of the Federal Register issued under section 6 of the Federal Register Act (44 U.S.C. 1506). The Committee's regulations, establishing the series and providing for the coverage of prior years, are reprinted as *Appendix E*.

Content and Arrangement

The text of this book is based on Presidential materials that were White House press releases, on material issued by the White House Press Office, and on transcripts of news conferences. Where available, original source materials, including tape recordings, have been used to protect against errors in transcription.

The dates shown at the end of item headings are White House release dates. In instances where the date of the document differs from the release date, that fact is shown in the note immediately following the item. Textnotes, footnotes, and cross references have been supplied only where needed for purposes of identification or clarity.

Remarks or addresses were delivered in Washington, D.C., unless otherwise indicated, and all times shown are local time. Similarly, statements, messages, and letters were released from the White House in Washington unless otherwise indicated.

The items published in this volume are presented in chronological order, rather than being grouped in classes. Most needs for a classified arrangement are met by the subject index. For example, a reader interested in the President's speeches will find them listed in the index under "addresses and remarks."

Appendixes have been provided to deal with special categories of Presidential issuances and actions, as noted below.

White House releases not included as items in this volume and not appearing in later appendixes are listed in *Appendix A*.

A complete listing by number and subject of all Proclamations, Executive orders, and similar documents required by law to be published in the *Federal Register* appears in *Appendix B* for the period covered by this volume.

The President is also required by law to transmit numerous reports to the Congress. Those transmitted during the period covered by this volume are listed in *Appendix C*.

Appendix D is the condensed transcript of an interview with the President as published in Newsweek magazine on December 9, 1974. It is printed here in order to provide more complete coverage of the Presidency in 1974.

This series is under the direction of Fred J. Emery, Director, and Ernest J. Galdi, Deputy Director, of the Office of the Federal Register. Chief Editor of the present volume was William R. Minning, assisted by Kenneth R. Payne and other members of the Presidential Documents Division.

White House liaison was provided by Paul A. Theis, Executive Editor, White House Editorial Office. Photography was under the direction of David Hume Kennerly, Personal Photographer to the President, assisted by picture editor Sandra Eisert.

The typography and design of this volume was developed under the direction of Robert J. Worley, Acting Superintendent of Typography and Design, United States Government Printing Office.

James B. Rhoads
Archivist of the United States

Jack Eckerd
Administrator of General Services
December 1975

CONTENTS

LIST OF ITEMS

CABINET

Secretary of State	Henry A. Kissinger
Secretary of the Treasury	William E. Simon
Secretary of Defense	James R. Schlesinger
Attorney General	William B. Saxbe
Secretary of the Interior	Rogers C. B. Morton
Secretary of Agriculture	Earl L. Butz
Secretary of Commerce	Frederick B. Dent
Secretary of Labor	Peter J. Brennan
Secretary of Health, Education, and Welfare.	Caspar W. Weinberger
Secretary of Housing and Urban Development.	James T. Lynn
Secretary of Transportation	Claude S. Brinegar

Gerald R. Ford

1974

1

Remarks on Taking the Oath of Office. *August 9, 1974*

Mr. Chief Justice, my dear friends, my fellow Americans:

The oath that I have taken is the same oath that was taken by George Washington and by every President under the Constitution. But I assume the Presidency under extraordinary circumstances never before experienced by Americans. This is an hour of history that troubles our minds and hurts our hearts.

Therefore, I feel it is my first duty to make an unprecedented compact with my countrymen. Not an inaugural address, not a fireside chat, not a campaign speech—just a little straight talk among friends. And I intend it to be the first of many.

I am acutely aware that you have not elected me as your President by your ballots, and so I ask you to confirm me as your President with your prayers. And I hope that such prayers will also be the first of many.

If you have not chosen me by secret ballot, neither have I gained office by any secret promises. I have not campaigned either for the Presidency or the Vice Presidency. I have not subscribed to any partisan platform. I am indebted to no man, and only to one woman—my dear wife—as I begin this very difficult job.

I have not sought this enormous responsibility, but I will not shirk it. Those who nominated and confirmed me as Vice President were my friends and are my friends. They were of both parties, elected by all the people and acting under the Constitution in their name. It is only fitting then that I should pledge to them and to you that I will be the President of all the people.

Thomas Jefferson said the people are the only sure reliance for the preservation of our liberty. And down the years, Abraham Lincoln renewed this American article of faith asking, "Is there any better way or equal hope in the world?"

I intend, on Monday next, to request of the Speaker of the House of Representatives and the President pro tempore of the Senate the privilege of appearing before the Congress to share with my former colleagues and with you, the American people, my views on the priority business of the Nation and to solicit your views and their views. And may I say to the Speaker and the others, if I could meet with you right after these remarks, I would appreciate it.

Even though this is late in an election year, there is no way we can go forward except together and no way anybody can win except by serving the people's urgent needs. We cannot stand still or slip backwards. We must go forward now together.

To the peoples and the governments of all friendly nations, and I hope that could encompass the whole world, I pledge an uninterrupted and sincere search for peace. America will remain strong and united, but its strength will remain dedicated to the safety and sanity of the entire family of man, as well as to our own precious freedom.

I believe that truth is the glue that holds government together, not only our Government but civilization itself. That bond, though strained, is unbroken at home and abroad.

In all my public and private acts as your President, I expect to follow my instincts of openness and candor with full confidence that honesty is always the best policy in the end.

My fellow Americans, our long national nightmare is over.

Our Constitution works; our great Republic is a government of laws and not of men. Here the people rule. But there is a higher Power, by whatever name we honor Him, who ordains not only righteousness but love, not only justice but mercy.

As we bind up the internal wounds of Watergate, more painful and more poisonous than those of foreign wars, let us restore the golden rule to our political process, and let brotherly love purge our hearts of suspicion and of hate.

In the beginning, I asked you to pray for me. Before closing, I ask again your prayers, for Richard Nixon and for his family. May our former President, who brought peace to millions, find it for himself. May God bless and comfort his wonderful wife and daughters, whose love and loyalty will forever be a shining legacy to all who bear the lonely burdens of the White House.

I can only guess at those burdens, although I have witnessed at close hand the tragedies that befell three Presidents and the lesser trials of others.

With all the strength and all the good sense I have gained from life, with all the confidence my family, my friends, and my dedicated staff impart to me, and with the good will of countless Americans I have encountered in recent visits to 40 States, I now solemnly reaffirm my promise I made to you last December 6: to uphold the Constitution, to do what is right as God gives me to see the right, and to do the very best I can for America.

God helping me, I will not let you down.

Thank you.

NOTE: The President spoke at 12:05 p.m. in the East Room at the White House following administration of the oath of office by Chief Justice Warren E. Burger. The oath of office and the President's remarks were broadcast live on radio and television.

The White House announced that Richard Nixon's letter of resignation as 37th President of the United States was tendered to Secretary of State Henry A. Kissinger in his White House office by Assistant to the President Alexander M. Haig, Jr., at 11:35 a.m.

2

Remarks Announcing Appointment of J. F. terHorst as Press Secretary to the President. *August 9, 1974*

Good morning:

Number one, it is a nice opportunity this morning to get reacquainted with many of you who suffered with me when I was over here with Ev Dirksen and subsequently with Hugh Scott. So, let me say that I look forward to meeting the new faces, and it is a pleasure to see those that I have known before.

I have two profound announcements to make.

We will have one of yours as my Press Secretary, Jerry terHorst. We will, of course, have Paul Miltich and Bill Roberts with Jerry. We haven't worked out all the titles and responsibilities, but that will be our team, and I hope and trust that they can work with you as well as Paul and Bill have worked with the people that I have been working with.

The second one is—the second very profound announcement—I understand that where many of you are standing there is a swimming pool, and you know my great interest in aquatic activity. [*Laughter*]

I haven't made a firm decision yet. I don't know whether we should solicit your recommendations or whether we should just confine it to the National Security Council or some other very important body. [*Laughter*]

Let me say again, I do look forward to working with you. We will have, I trust, the kind of rapport and friendship which we had in the past. And I don't ask you to treat me any better than I would expect in reverse.

We will have an open, we will have a candid Administration. I can't change my nature after 61 years.

So, all I can say is thank you for your kindnesses in the past, your reporting, good and bad, mistakes and maybe a few pluses. And I say again, good luck to you, and thanks for the opportunity of seeing you this morning.

I should tell you that Jerry terHorst was, along with several others, responsible for my first political success. He and another very fine reporter from

Grand Rapids connived to help me get a little extra space in the Grand Rapids Press, and I am just delighted to have Jerry with us here on this occasion.

NOTE: The President spoke at 1:04 p.m. in the Briefing Room at the White House. His remarks were broadcast live on radio and television.

3

Memorandums on the Transition of the Presidency. *August 10, 1974*

MEMORANDUM FOR MEMBERS OF THE VICE PRESIDENTIAL STAFF

On a number of occasions in the past, I have told you that I was only the "front man" in our efforts. Behind the scenes, each of you worked, sometimes day and night, and often all weekend, to facilitate our joint efforts. Some have been with me longer than others, but all of you have combined in a short time to perform at a singular level of excellence.

As I assume the new responsibilities of the Presidency, I want you to know how mindful I am of your past labors—and how grateful and indebted I am to you. You have contributed indispensably to the successful operation of the Office of the Vice President and to my ability to assume my new responsibilities. Our staff has been close to one another, much as a family, and I hope all of you understand the depth of my appreciation and affection. Although I am moving to another office, my loyalty and esteem for you remain unchanged.

I have asked some old friends to come in and help us during this difficult period, which we all hoped would not come. I hope you will render all possible cooperation to those who will be here to facilitate the transition, as well as to those of Mr. Nixon's staff for whom this time is even more difficult than it is for us.

With heartfelt thanks,

GERALD R. FORD

MEMORANDUM FOR THE HEADS OF DEPARTMENTS AND AGENCIES

Just as President Nixon kept up the business of government so long as he was President, I know each of you has worked diligently to carry out the responsibilities you hold. I am sure you have a feeling of sorrow, as I do, but you can also take pride in the many constructive accomplishments made by the Nixon Administration.

Some of you may now want to pass your responsibilities on to others. But I need your help. I ask each of you to continue to carry on the mission of your agency and to give me the advice I need as I take on my new responsibilities.

I have asked some friends whose counsel I respect to help me with the transition. They will form a bridge for me to my Vice Presidential staff office and to the officials of the Executive Branch until a permanent organization is established. I ask your help and cooperation for them as well as myself.

President Nixon fought long and with all his might to serve the American people well, ending his Presidency with a selfless and courageous act. You can still serve him and the Nation by helping me to carry on the essential functions of the Presidency. I will hold a Cabinet meeting Saturday morning at 10:00 a.m. I will meet with heads of other government agencies and with the sub-cabinet as soon as my schedule permits.

GERALD R. FORD

NOTE: The texts of the memorandums, dated August 9, 1974, were released August 10. The text of the following memorandum, dated August 9, was released August 10:

MEMORANDUM FOR THE WHITE HOUSE STAFF
FROM: The Vice President

I know this has been a difficult and confusing time for each of you. You must have feelings of sorrow, as I do, but you also should be proud—proud of the President you served and of your efforts for him and the country.

Many of you will want to go on to other pursuits now that your service to him has ended. I understand and respect that, but I also need your help. I ask each of you to stay on long enough to assure a steady and informed transition of the Presidency.

I have asked some friends whose counsel I respect to help me with the transition. They will form a bridge for me to my Vice Presidential staff office and to the officials of the Executive Branch until a permanent organization is established. I ask your help and cooperation for them as well as myself.

President Nixon fought long and with all his might to serve the American people well, ending his Presidency with a selfless and courageous act. You can still serve him and the Nation by helping me to carry on the essential functions of the Presidency. I will meet with the senior officials of the White House in the Roosevelt Room soon after I take the oath of office to discuss transition arrangements and responsibilities.

4

Statement on Portuguese Recognition of the Independence of Guinea-Bissau. *August 12, 1974*

THE GOVERNMENT and the people of the United States welcome the agreement in principle reached on August 9 between the Portuguese Government and representatives of Guinea-Bissau. We extend our congratulations to the leaders of both governments. We look forward to a productive and friendly relationship with Guinea-Bissau.

I have instructed our representatives at the United Nations to support the application of Guinea-Bissau for membership in the United Nations.

NOTE: The statement was read by Press Secretary J. F. terHorst at his news briefing at the White House on August 12, 1974.

5

Statement on a General Motors Price Increase for 1975 Automobiles and Trucks. *August 12, 1974*

I WAS very disappointed, and I hope that the General Motors action will not be viewed as a signal by other auto companies or other industries. In this critical period, the President of the United States cannot call on others to sacrifice if one or more parts of the economy decide to go it alone. It is essential at this time, particularly, that all segments of the economy, industry and labor, exercise restraint in their wage and price actions.

NOTE: On August 9, 1974, General Motors Corporation had announced an average price increase of 9.5 percent on its 1975 models.

The statement was read by Press Secretary J. F. terHorst at his news briefing at the White House on August 12, 1974.

6

Address to a Joint Session of the Congress. *August 12, 1974*

Mr. Speaker, Mr. President, distinguished guests, and my very dear friends:

My fellow Americans, we have a lot of work to do. My former colleagues, you and I have a lot of work to do. Let's get on with it.

Needless to say, I am deeply grateful for the wonderfully warm welcome. I can never express my gratitude adequately.

I am not here to make an inaugural address. The Nation needs action, not words. Nor will this be a formal report of the state of the Union. God willing, I will have at least three more chances to do that.

It is good to be back in the People's House. But this cannot be a real homecoming. Under the Constitution, I now belong to the executive branch. The Supreme Court has even ruled that I *am* the executive branch—head, heart, and hand.

With due respect to the learned Justices—and I greatly respect the judiciary—part of my heart will always be here on Capitol Hill. I know well the coequal role of the Congress in our constitutional process. I love the House of Representatives. I revere the traditions of the Senate despite my too-short internship in that great body. As President, within the limits of basic principles, my motto toward the Congress is communication, conciliation, compromise, and cooperation.

This Congress, unless it has changed, I am confident, will be my working partner as well as my most constructive critic. I am not asking for conformity. I am dedicated to the two-party system, and you know which party I belong to.

I do not want a honeymoon with you. I want a good marriage.

I want progress, and I want problemsolving which requires my best efforts and also your best efforts.

I have no need to learn how Congress speaks for the people. As President, I intend to listen.

But I also intend to listen to the people themselves—all the people—as I promised last Friday. I want to be sure that we are all tuned in to the real voice of America.

My Administration starts off by seeking unity in diversity. My office door has always been open, and that is how it is going to be at the White House. Yes, Congressmen will be welcomed—if you don't overdo it. [*Laughter*]

The first seven words of the Constitution and the most important are these: "We the People of the United States . . . ." *We the people* ordained and established the Constitution and reserved to themselves all powers not granted to Federal and State government. I respect and will always be conscious of that fundamental rule of freedom.

Only 8 months ago, when I last stood here, I told you I was a Ford, not a Lincoln. Tonight I say I am still a Ford, but I am not a Model T.

I do have some old-fashioned ideas, however. I believe in the very basic decency and fairness of America. I believe in the integrity and patriotism of the Congress. And while I am aware of the House rule that no one ever speaks to the galleries, I believe in the first amendment and the absolute necessity of a free press.

But I also believe that over two centuries since the First Continental Congress was convened, the direction of our Nation's movement has been forward. I am here to confess that in my first campaign for President—of my senior class in South High School in Grand Rapids, Michigan—I headed the Progressive Party ticket, and lost. Maybe that is why I became a Republican. [*Laughter*]

Now I ask you to join with me in getting this country revved up and moving.

My instinctive judgment is that the state of the Union is excellent. But the state of our economy is not so good. Everywhere I have been as Vice President, some 118,000 miles in 40 States and some 55 press conferences, the unanimous concern of Americans is inflation.

For once all the polls seem to agree. They also suggest that the people blame Government far more than either management or labor for the high cost of everything they have to buy.

You who come from 50 States, three territories, and the District of Columbia, know this better than I do. That is why you have created, since I left, your new Budget Reform Committee. I welcome it, and I will work with its members to bring the Federal budget into balance in fiscal year 1976.

The fact is that for the past 25 years that I had the honor of serving in this body, the Federal budget has been balanced in only six.

Mr. Speaker, I am a little late getting around to it, but confession is good for the soul. I have sometimes voted to spend more taxpayer's money for worthy Federal projects in Grand Rapids, Michigan, while I vigorously opposed wasteful spending boondoggles in Oklahoma. [*Laughter*]

Be that as it may, Mr. Speaker, you and I have always stood together against unwarranted cuts in national defense. This is no time to change that nonpartisan policy.

Just as escalating Federal spending has been a prime cause of higher prices over many years, it may take some time to stop inflation. But we must begin right now.

For a start, before your Labor Day recess, Congress should reactivate the Cost of Living Council through passage of a clean bill, without reimposing controls, that will let us monitor wages and prices to expose abuses.

Whether we like it or not, the American wage earner and the American housewife are a lot better economists than most economists care to admit. They know that a government big enough to give you everything you want is a government big enough to take from you everything you have.

If we want to restore confidence in ourselves as working politicians, the first thing we all have to do is to learn to say no.

The first specific request by the Ford Administration is not to Congress but to the voters in the upcoming November elections. It is this, very simple: Support your candidates, Congressmen and Senators, Democrats or Republicans, conservatives or liberals, who consistently vote for tough decisions to cut the cost of government, restrain Federal spending, and bring inflation under control.

I applaud the initiatives Congress has already taken. The only fault I find with the Joint Economic Committee's study on inflation, authorized last week, is that we need its expert findings in 6 weeks instead of 6 months.

A month ago, the distinguished majority leader of the United States Senate asked the White House to convene an economic conference of Members of Congress, the President's economic consultants, and some of the best economic brains from labor, industry, and agriculture.

Later, this was perfected by resolution [S. Res. 363] to assemble a domestic summit meeting to devise a bipartisan action for stability and growth in the American economy. Neither I nor my staff have much time right now for letterwriting. So, I will respond. I accept the suggestion, and I will personally preside.

Furthermore, I propose that this summit meeting be held at an early date, in full view of the American public. They are as anxious as we are to get the right answers.

My first priority is to work with you to bring inflation under control. Inflation is domestic enemy number one. To restore economic confidence, the Government in Washington must provide some leadership. It does no good to blame the public for spending too much when the Government is spending too much.

I began to put my Administration's own economic house in order starting last Friday. I instructed my Cabinet officers and Counsellors and my White House Staff to make fiscal restraint their first order of business, and to save every taxpayer's dollar the safety and genuine welfare of our great Nation will permit. Some economic activities will be affected more by monetary and fiscal restraint than other activities. Good government clearly requires that we tend to the economic problems facing our country in a spirit of equity to all of our citizens in all segments of our society.

Tonight, obviously, is no time to threaten you with vetoes. But I do have the last recourse, and I am a veteran of many a veto fight right here in this great chamber. Can't we do a better job by reasonable compromise? I hope we can.

Minutes after I took the Presidential oath, the joint leadership of Congress told me at the White House they would go more than halfway to meet me. This was confirmed in your unanimous concurrent resolution of cooperation, for which I am deeply grateful. If, for my part, I go more than halfway to meet the Congress, maybe we can find a much larger area of national agreement.

I bring no legislative shopping list here this evening. I will deal with specifics in future messages and talks with you, but here are a few examples of how seriously I feel about what we must do together.

Last week, the Congress passed the elementary and secondary education bill, and I found it on my desk. Any reservations I might have about some of its provisions—and I do have—fade in comparison to the urgent needs of America for quality education. I will sign it in a few days.

I must be frank. In implementing its provisions, I will oppose excessive funding during this inflationary crisis.

As Vice President, I studied various proposals for better health care financing. I saw them coming closer together and urged my friends in the Congress and in the Administration to sit down and sweat out a sound compromise. The comprehensive health insurance plan goes a long ways toward providing early relief to people who are sick.

Why don't we write—and I ask this with the greatest spirit of cooperation—why don't we write a good health bill on the statute books in 1974, before this Congress adjourns?

The economy of our country is critically dependent on how we interact with the economies of other countries. It is little comfort that our inflation is only a part of a worldwide problem or that American families need less of their paychecks for groceries than most of our foreign friends.

As one of the building blocks of peace, we have taken the lead in working toward a more open and a more equitable world economic system. A new round of international trade negotiations started last September among 105 nations in Tokyo. The others are waiting for the United States Congress to grant the necessary authority to the executive branch to proceed.

With modifications, the trade reform bill passed by the House last year would do a good job. I understand good progress has been made in the Senate Committee on Finance. But I am optimistic, as always, that the Senate will pass an acceptable bill quickly as a key part of our joint prosperity campaign.

I am determined to expedite other international economic plans. We will be working together with other nations to find better ways to prevent shortages of food and fuel. We must not let last winter's energy crisis happen again. I will push Project Independence for our own good and the good of others. In that, too, I will need your help.

Successful foreign policy is an extension of the hopes of the whole American people for a world of peace and orderly reform and orderly freedom. So, I would say a few words to our distinguished guests from the governments of other nations where, as at home, it is my determination to deal openly with allies and adversaries.

Over the past 5½ years in Congress and as Vice President, I have fully supported the outstanding foreign policy of President Nixon. This policy I intend to continue.

Throughout my public service, starting with wartime naval duty under the command of President Franklin D. Roosevelt, I have upheld all our Presidents when they spoke for my country to the world. I believe the Constitution commands this. I know that in this crucial area of international policy I can count on your firm support.

Now, let there be no doubt or any misunderstanding anywhere, and I emphasize anywhere: There are no opportunities to exploit, should anyone so desire. There will be no change of course, no relaxation of vigilance, no abandonment of the helm of our ship of state as the watch changes.

We stand by our commitments and we will live up to our responsibilities in our formal alliances, in our friendships, and in our improving relations with potential adversaries.

On this, Americans are united and strong. Under my term of leadership, I hope we will become more united. I am certain America will remain strong.

A strong defense is the surest way to peace. Strength makes détente attainable. Weakness invites war, as my generation—my generation—knows from four very bitter experiences.

Just as America's will for peace is second to none, so will America's strength be second to none.

We cannot rely on the forbearance of others to protect this Nation. The power and diversity of the Armed Forces, active Guard and Reserve, the resolve of our fellow citizens, the flexibility in our command to navigate international waters that remain troubled are all essential to our security.

I shall continue to insist on civilian control of our superb military establishment. The Constitution plainly requires the President to be Commander in Chief, and I will be.

Our job will not be easy. In promising continuity, I cannot promise simplicity. The problems and challenges of the world remain complex and difficult. But we have set out on a path of reason, of fairness, and we will continue on it.

As guideposts on that path, I offer the following:

—To our allies of a generation in the Atlantic community and Japan, I pledge continuity in the loyal collaboration on our many mutual endeavors.

—To our friends and allies in this hemisphere, I pledge continuity in the deepening dialog to define renewed relationships of equality and justice.

—To our allies and friends in Asia, I pledge a continuity in our support for their security, independence, and economic development. In Indochina, we are determined to see the observance of the Paris agreement on Vietnam and the cease-fire and negotiated settlement in Laos. We hope to see an early compromise settlement in Cambodia.

—To the Soviet Union, I pledge continuity in our commitment to the course of the past 3 years. To our two peoples, and to all mankind, we owe a continued effort to live and, where possible, to work together in peace, for in a thermonuclear age there can be no alternative to a positive and peaceful relationship between our nations.

—To the People's Republic of China, whose legendary hospitality I enjoyed, I pledge continuity in our commitment to the principles of the Shanghai communique. The new relationship built on those principles has demonstrated that it serves serious and objective mutual interests and has become an enduring feature of the world scene.

—To the nations in the Middle East, I pledge continuity in our vigorous efforts to advance the progress which has brought hopes of peace to that region after 25 years as a hotbed of war. We shall carry out our promise to promote continuing negotiations among all parties for a complete, just, and lasting settlement.

—To all nations, I pledge continuity in seeking a common global goal: a stable international structure of trade and finance which reflects the interdependence of all peoples.

—To the entire international community—to the United Nations, to the world's nonaligned nations, and to all others—I pledge continuity in our dedication to the humane goals which throughout our history have been so much of America's contribution to mankind.

So long as the peoples of the world have confidence in our purposes and faith in our word, the age-old vision of peace on Earth will grow brighter.

I pledge myself unreservedly to that goal. I say to you in words that cannot be improved upon: "Let us never negotiate out of fear, but let us never fear to negotiate."

As Vice President, at the request of the President, I addressed myself to the individual rights of Americans in the area of privacy. There will be no illegal tappings (tapings), eavesdropping, buggings, or break-ins by my Administration. There will be hot pursuit of tough laws to prevent illegal invasion of privacy in both government and private activities.

On the higher plane of public morality, there is no need for me to preach tonight. We have thousands of far better preachers and millions of sacred scriptures to guide us on the path of personal right-living and exemplary official conduct. If we can make effective and earlier use of moral and ethical wisdom of the centuries in today's complex society, we will prevent more crime and more corruption than all the policemen and prosecutors governments can ever deter. If I might say so, this is a job that must begin at home, not in Washington.

I once told you that I am not a saint, and I hope never to see the day that I cannot admit having made a mistake. So I will close with another confession.

Frequently, along the tortuous road of recent months from this chamber to the President's House, I protested that I was my own man. Now I realize that I was wrong.

I am your man, for it was your carefully weighed confirmation that changed my occupation.

The truth is I am the people's man, for you acted in their name, and I accepted and began my new and solemn trust with a promise to serve all the people and do the best that I can for America.

When I say all the people, I mean exactly that.

To the limits of my strength and ability, I will be the President of black, brown, red, and white Americans, of old and young, of women's liberationists and male chauvinists—[*laughter*]—and all the rest of us in-between, of the poor and the rich, of native sons and new refugees, of those who work at lathes or at desks or in mines or in the fields, of Christians, Jews, Moslems, Buddhists, and atheists, if there really are any atheists after what we have all been through.

Fellow Americans, one final word: I want to be a good President. I need your help. We all need God's sure guidance. With it, nothing can stop the United States of America.

Thank you very much.

NOTE: The President spoke at 9:06 p.m. in the House Chamber at the Capitol, after being introduced by Carl Albert, Speaker of the House of Representatives. The address was broadcast live on radio and television.

7

Veto of Legislation To Reclassify and Upgrade Deputy United States Marshals. *August 13, 1974*

To the House of Representatives:

I am today returning to the Congress without my approval H.R. 5094, a measure that would require the reclassification and upgrading of deputy United States marshals.

A bill substantially similar to this legislation was passed by the Congress and then pocket vetoed by President Nixon in October, 1972. Since that time various departments of the executive branch have consistently argued that such legislation would be unwise and discriminatory.

That opposition has been based upon the view that by singling out deputy United States marshals for significant salary increases, the Government would be creating serious pay inequities with other Federal law enforcement personnel, thus violating fundamental principles of fairness. In addition, H.R. 5094 would severely disrupt existing grade and pay relationships among the deputy marshals themselves. In some cases, under this legislation, junior marshals would be paid $1,150 a year more than their senior colleagues. Some deputies doing identical work would be placed in different pay grades, while deputies performing different jobs would be placed in the same pay grade.

I fully appreciate the fine service performed by our deputy U.S. marshals, and I am aware that the Congress was prompted by a desire to ensure that their pay matched the increasing responsibilities they have assumed in recent years. But I also believe that this legislation would run directly counter to the principle of equal pay for equal work that underlies our civil service system. Our policy has been and must continue to be one of fundamental fairness to all Federal employees. For that reason, I am returning this legislation without my approval.

GERALD R. FORD

The White House,
August 12, 1974.

NOTE: The text of the veto message was released August 13, 1974.

8

Message to the Congress Transmitting Annual Report on Special International Exhibitions. *August 13, 1974*

To the Congress of the United States:

As required by law, I transmit to the Congress the Eleventh Annual Report on Special International Exhibitions conducted during fiscal year 1973 under the authority of the Mutual Educational and Cultural Exchange Act of 1961 (Public Law 87–256).

This report covers exhibitions presented abroad by the U.S. Information Agency at international fairs and under East-West Cultural Exchange agreements, as well as exhibitions and labor missions presented abroad by the Department of Labor.

GERALD R. FORD

The White House,
August 13, 1974.

NOTE: The 43-page report is entitled "Special International Exhibitions—FY-73 Eleventh Annual Report, United States Information Agency" and is based on material prepared by the Department of Labor and the United States Information Agency.

9

Veto of Animal Health Research Legislation. *August 15, 1974*

To the House of Representatives:

I am returning today without my approval H.R. 11873, an act authorizing the Secretary of Agriculture to encourage and assist States in carrying out programs of animal health research.

I believe, as do proponents of this bill, that veterinary research has helped to make American livestock the healthiest and most productive in the world. We must continue to maintain high standards of research.

But I also believe that this bill adds little to the existing programs of the Department of Agriculture and other agencies.

We are presently spending over $40 million on programs involving animal health research, and nearly every land grant college and colleges of veterinary medicine in the United States is participating in these programs.

This bill, however, would establish a new categorical grant program that would authorize an expenditure of an additional $47 million annually and would be duplicative of many programs that already exist. The overlapping would be especially true of programs in fish and shellfish research and predator control.

Because this bill would add further to the Federal taxpayers' burdens without significantly meeting national needs and would only add to inflationary pressures within the economy, I feel that I must withhold my approval.

GERALD R. FORD

The White House,
August 14, 1974.

NOTE: The text of the veto message was released August 15, 1974.

10

Message to the Congress Transmitting an Amendment to the Agreement Between the United States and the United Kingdom on Uses of Atomic Energy. *August 15, 1974*

To the Congress of the United States:

Pursuant to the Atomic Energy Act of 1954 as amended, I am submitting to the Congress an authoritative copy of an amendment to the Agreement between the Government of the United States of America and the Government of the United Kingdom of Great Britain and Northern Ireland for Cooperation on the Uses of Atomic Energy for Mutual Defense Purposes of July 3, 1958, as amended. The Amendment was signed at Washington on July 22, 1974.

The Agreement as previously amended includes a provision (Paragraph A of Article III *bis*) under which the Government of the United States agrees to transfer to the Government of the United Kingdom for its atomic weapons program prior to December 31, 1974 in such quantities and on such terms and conditions as may be agreed non-nuclear parts of atomic weapons and atomic weapons systems as well as source, by-product and special nuclear material. A second provision of the existing Agreement (Paragraph C of Article III *bis*) stipulated that the Government of the United Kingdom agrees to transfer to the Government of the United States for military purposes such source, by-product and special nuclear material, and equipment of such types in such quantities, at such times prior to December 31, 1974 and on such terms and conditions as may be agreed.

Under the Amendment submitted herewith the period during which the provisions of Paragraph A and C of Article III *bis* of the Agreement for Cooperation remain in force would be extended for five years so that transfers could be made any time prior to December 31, 1979. The continued authorization of the two Governments to cooperate with each other in these respects would contribute to our mutual defense, particularly in the North Atlantic Treaty area.

The Amendment also would delete references in the preamble and Article XI (H) of the Agreement to the UK Atomic Energy Authority, since that Authority no longer has any direct responsibility in the field of nuclear defense.

I am also transmitting a copy of the Secretary of State's letter to me accompanying authoritative copies of the signed Amendment, a copy of a joint letter from the Chairman of the Atomic Energy Commission and the Secretary of

Defense recommending approval of this Amendment, and a copy of my memorandum in reply thereto, setting forth my approval.

GERALD R. FORD

The White House,
August 15, 1974.

NOTE: The amendment to the agreement was referred to the Joint Committee on Atomic Energy.

11

Letter Accepting Honorary Chairmanship of the American National Red Cross. *August 16, 1974*

Dear Mr. Chairman:

I have your letter of August 9, and it is with great pleasure that I accept the invitation you have extended on behalf of the Board of Governors to be the Honorary Chairman of the American National Red Cross.

Through the years, the American Red Cross has maintained an outstanding record of voluntary humanitarian services, fulfilling with high dedication and skill the obligations of its Congressional Charter. In the time ahead, I look forward to the opportunity of working with you, the Board of Governors and the Red Cross volunteer leadership across the Nation as we continue to meet the emergency and humanitarian needs of all our people.

With personal best wishes,

Sincerely,

GERALD R. FORD

[The Honorable Frank Stanton, Chairman, The American National Red Cross, Washington, D.C. 20006]

NOTE: The text of letter was issued by the White House.

12

Toasts of the President and King Hussein of Jordan. *August 16, 1974*

Your Majesties, Mr. Prime Minister and Mrs. Zaid Rifai, honorable guests:

May I, Your Majesty, on behalf of all of us here and on behalf of all of us in America, wish you a very, very warm welcome on this occasion.

And may I say on a very personal note that it is a great honor and privilege for me to have you as the first chief of state to visit our country during the new Administration.

During the fine tenure of your being head of your country, we have had, as I recollect, some five national administrations in the United States, some Democrat and some Republican, but during this period of time there have been some changes. Those changes I will make a comment or two about subsequently, but we, regardless of the administration in the United States, have never changed our view concerning yourself and your country, and we are proud of our long friendship and association.

Those changes that have taken place—and there are some changes in recent months—have been encouraging because they seem to have opened the door to progress for peace. They seem to have given us all hope that there will be greater improvement as we move ahead. Those changes, I think, in many respects can be attributed to you because of your courage, the great risks that you have taken during your lifetime and your superb understanding of the problems of the Middle East and your desire to work for peace for all peoples.

There has been progress in this process of change. More recently we can see it in the two disengagements that have taken place in the last few months, in the continuing consultation in the diplomatic area, and speaking of the diplomatic, may I say that for myself and our country, I pledge, on behalf of the American people, full support for the continuing diplomatic initiatives which are so essential for the goals that we seek.

Those goals, those hopes, of course, are the peace on a just, on a permanent basis that have for so many years, many centuries, eluded all of those in that area and the world at large. But it seems to me that as we look ahead, with the foundation that has been built, that with your continuing leadership, your continuing effort, with your continuing courage, and with the cooperation of ourselves and many others, we can achieve what has been the hope and aspirations of people throughout the world, as well as in the Middle East.

And if I might, in closing, may I congratulate you on your leadership, your dedication, your wisdom, and your cooperation. You have set an example for all of us to follow and to use as a guidepost for people not only in the Middle East but elsewhere.

So, may I ask that all join with me in a tribute to His Majesty and to the Kingdom of Jordan.

To you and to your country.

NOTE: The President spoke at 9:51 p.m. in the State Dining Room at the White House. King Hussein responded as follows:

Mr. President, Mrs. Ford, my good friends:

It is a source of pride to me, sir, that over the years, the many years that have passed, I have been a firm believer in the great mutual benefits of relations that have happily developed, not only between my country and the United States but recently in the period of change that you so kindly refer to between many countries in our part of the world and the United States of America.

To me, it has been an honor to have visited this great Nation's Capital many a time, to have found friendship, understanding, sympathy, not only for myself but for my country and for a common cause to which I am proud to say we have always been dedicated, the cause of an honorable, just peace.

On this visit, sir, I am most proud to convey to you and to Mrs. Ford the feelings of not only my wife and those who have accompanied me from Jordan but my government and the people of Jordan, their wishes to you, sir, for every future success. I am sure these are the feelings of all in the United States and the very many throughout the world.

I am proud indeed, sir, to have had the privilege of knowing you before this visit and most proud, sir, that you consider me a friend. I am so touched, sir, by the kind words, but more so the sincerity that I know you possess, sir, which endears you to all your people, all the people of the United States, and so many who have had the privilege of knowing you and who will have this privilege.

It is really a source of pride to us to have had this very close cooperation between our nations, to have seen in the recent past some basic steps taken for the establishment of a just and durable peace in our part of the world, largely through the efforts of our friends in the United States, the patience, the patient effort, the perseverance, the determination that has resulted in the first few steps materializing.

We know, sir, that you are dedicated to the cause of peace with justice. We are not only comforted but confident that the United States will contribute her full share for the achievement of this worthy objective under your wise leadership.

We will be ever proud to play our role, if enabled, to the fullest possible extent that we someday feel that will present the generations after us with a better life, with a better future, with a better world than possibly that in which we have had to live.

I would like to thank you and Mrs. Ford once again for your very, very great kindness and wish you every success. May God be with you, and I am sure, sir, that the hopes of so many in the United States and in the world as a whole under your great leadership will be fully justified.

Ladies and gentlemen, my good friends, I would very much indeed like you to join me in drinking a toast to the President of the United States and Mrs. Ford for every continued success.

To the President.

13

Statement on Signing the Forest and Rangeland Renewable Resources Planning Act of 1974. *August 17, 1974*

I AM signing today S. 2296, the Forest and Rangeland Renewable Resources Planning Act of 1974.

One of the essential lessons of the recent energy crisis is that if we are to prevent shortages of natural resources in the future, we must plan for the future today. Our resources, however abundant, are not inexhaustible. They must be conserved and replenished.

The Forest and Rangeland Renewable Resources Planning Act provides us the means for planning national programs now which will assure future generations of adequate supplies of forest and related resources.

The great naturalist, John Muir, once said of our Nation's forests: "The forests of America, however slighted by man, must have been a great delight to God; for they were the best He ever planted." This act proves that Americans intend never again to slight our forests.

I would be less than candid if I did not admit that certain provisions of this act disturb me, especially those provisions relating to Presidential discretion in formulating annual budget requests for our national forestry programs. But the benefits of this legislation far outweigh any potential drawbacks, and I am confident that the Congress and the executive branch, working together, can and will manage, develop, and improve our priceless natural legacy of forests and rangelands.

NOTE: As enacted, S. 2296, approved August 17, 1974, is Public Law 93–378 (88 Stat. 476).

14

Joint Statement Following Discussions With King Hussein of Jordan. *August 18, 1974*

HIS MAJESTY King Hussein I of Jordan paid a visit to Washington August 15–18, at the invitation of the President. The President and His Majesty conferred at the White House and the President hosted a dinner in honor of His Majesty and Queen Alia. The President expressed his pleasure that His Majesty was the first Head of State to visit Washington in the new administration. His Majesty also conferred with the Secretaries of State and Defense and met with members of Congress. His Majesty was accompanied by the Prime Minister of Jordan, Mr. Zaid Rifai.

The talks were held in the atmosphere of friendship and understanding traditional in relations between the United States and Jordan. The President and His Majesty pledged that the two countries will continue to work closely together for the achievement of a just and lasting peace in the Middle East. The President stressed the continuity of United States' policy in this regard as in all other aspects of American foreign policy and affirmed his commitment that the United States would continue its determined efforts to help bring a peace settlement in the Middle East. The discussions between His Majesty and the President and Secretary of State were a constructive contribution to the consultations now underway looking toward the next stage in negotiations for a just and durable peace in the Middle East. It was agreed that these consultations will continue with a view to addressing at an appropriately early date the issues of particular concern to Jordan, including a Jordanian-Israeli disengagement agreement.

The President and His Majesty reaffirmed the close ties of friendship between the United States and Jordan and pledged to continue their efforts to strengthen the bonds which join the two countries in mutually beneficial cooperation.

Specifically, His Majesty and the President recalled that the joint U.S.-Jordanian statement issued June 18 at the end of President Nixon's visit to Amman announced that Jordan and the United States agreed to establish a Joint Commission to oversee and review at a high level the various areas of cooperation between the two countries. In fulfilling this agreement, the U.S. and Jordan have pledged to make every effort to expedite the development of an effective structure of cooperation and have agreed on the following concrete steps:

The United States and Jordan have established a general Jordan-United States Joint Commission under the chairmanship of the Jordanian Prime Minister and the U.S. Secretary of State. The first meetings of this Commission were held during the Prime Minister's visit to Washington August 5–8 and August 16–17 during which promising areas of mutual interest were identified.

The Commission will sponsor a meeting on economic development, trade and investment before the end of the year to review plans for Jordan's economic development and identify additional areas in which the United States can be of assistance. Work will begin immediately in Amman and Washington to prepare for this meeting. The Commission will also explore possibilities for increased American private participation in Jordan's economic development and ways of increasing trade between the two countries. Mr. Daniel Parker will head the American Delegation to the economic meeting, which will also include representation from various government agencies. The Jordanian Economic Delegation will be headed by Dr. Khalil Salem, President of the National Planning Council.

The Commission will arrange meetings on military assistance and supply problems at a mutually acceptable date to review implementation of continuing U.S. assistance to the Jordanian Armed Forces and to advance planning for future assistance. Jordan's Chief of Staff, Major General Zaid bin Shaker, and the Assistant Secretary of Defense for International Security Affairs, Ambassador Robert Ellsworth, will head the respective delegations.

It was further agreed that Jordan and the United States will give attention to the means by which educational, cultural, and scientific cooperation between the two countries can be enhanced.

Finally, the President and His Majesty agreed that they would remain in close contact with each other with a view to giving their full support to the efforts being made to achieve peace in the Middle East and to the further strengthening of the ties between their two countries.

His Majesty expressed the hope that the President would be able to visit Jordan at some future date. The President said he would be happy to do so.

15

Remarks on Arrival at Chicago, Illinois. *August 19, 1974*

THIS IS a wonderful, wonderful day in Chicago, and Betty and I are deeply grateful for all of you coming out to visit us on our first trip out of Washington since a week or 10 days ago. Thank you so, so very much.

Now, let me just add a word, if I might. I have said it several times, but all of you can contribute so much. We have got a lot of work to do. That includes me as well as you and our fellow Americans. We are going to do that work, and we are going to accomplish what has to be done, both at home and abroad.

There is, I think, a great opportunity for America, for what we can do at home and what we can do abroad. It will take a little belt tightening and sacrificing, but with the spirit that I know exists in America, and you exemplify it here this morning by your warm welcome, I am sure we can do the job, with God's help.

Thank you so very, very much.

NOTE: The President spoke at 9:30 a.m. at O'Hare Field.

16

Remarks to the Veterans of Foreign Wars Annual Convention, Chicago, Illinois. *August 19, 1974*

Commander Ray Soden, Governor Walker, my former Members or former colleagues of the United States Congress, my fellow members of the Veterans of Foreign Wars:

Let me express my deepest gratitude for your extremely warm welcome, and may I say to Mayor Daley and to all the wonderful people of Chicago who have done an unbelievable job in welcoming Betty and myself to Chicago, we are most grateful.

I have a sneaking suspicion that Mayor Daley and the people of Chicago knew that Betty was born in Chicago. Needless to say, I deeply appreciate your medal and the citation on my first trip out of Washington as your President. I hope that in the months ahead I can justify your faith in making the citation and the award available to me.

It is good to be back in Chicago, among people from all parts of our great

Nation, to take part in this 75th annual convention of the Veterans of Foreign Wars.

As a proud member of Old Kent Post VFW 830, let me talk today about some of the work facing veterans—and all Americans—the issues of world peace and national unity.

Speaking of national unity, let me quickly point out that I am also a proud member of the American Legion and the AMVETS.

In a more somber note, this morning we all heard the tragic news of the killing of our American Ambassador to Cyprus.[1] He, too, gave his life in foreign wars. Let us offer our prayers and our condolences to his loved ones for his supreme sacrifice on behalf of all Americans.

As President and as a veteran, I want good relations with all veterans. We all proudly wore the same Nation's uniform and patriotically saluted the same flag. During my Administration, the door of my office will be open to veterans just as it was all my 25 years as a Member of the Congress.

Today, I am happy to announce my intention to send the Senate the nomination of my personal friend and former Congressional colleague Dick Roudebush of Indiana—it seems to me you know what I am going to say—[*laughter*]—but I will finish the sentence—to be Administrator of the Veterans Administration.

As past national commander of the VFW, Roudy has served well as Deputy Administrator of the VA. He is a man who gets things done and, I am confident, will do a first-class job.

It seems to me that we should recognize the veteran is a human being, not just a "C" number to be processed by a computer system. We all know that the Government knew our name when we were called into service. This Administration is going to see to it that we still know your name and your problems. A veteran is a person, not just a digit in a computer system which more often than not goofs up.

I propose the VA take the best of our technology and the very best of our human capabilities and combine them. As President, I want no arrogance or indifference to any individual, veteran or not. Our Government's machinery exists to serve people, not to frustrate or humiliate them.

---

[1] Ambassador Rodger P. Davies was killed by a sniper during a demonstration at the American Embassy in Nicosia on August 19.

On the same day, the White House issued the following statement by Press Secretary J. F. terHorst:

"The President was shocked and deeply saddened by the death of Ambassador Davies in Nicosia today. This tragic incident emphasizes the urgent need for an end to the violence on Cyprus and an immediate return to negotiations for a peaceful settlement."

I don't like redtape. As a matter of fact, I don't like any kind of tapes.

Our great veterans hospitals, which will not lose their identity, must be the very best that medical skill and dedication can create. VA hospitals have made many great medical breakthroughs in the past. One of America's great challenges today is the older veteran. The VA medical and nursing care system for older people must become a showcase for the entire Nation. We can work together to achieve that end and humanize the VA.

But to achieve such progress, I intend to improve the management of the VA. We must get the most for our tax dollars. While supporting the new Administrator in maximum efforts to make the best use of funds available, I want Roudy to take a constructive new look at the VA's structure and the services that it renders to our veterans.

I think it is about time that we should stop thinking of veterans in terms of different wars. Some may march at a different pace than others. But we all march to the same drummer in the service of our Nation. I salute the men of many campaigns—of World War I, World War II, Korea, and Vietnam.

As minority leader of the House and recently as Vice President, I stated my strong conviction that unconditional, blanket amnesty for anyone who illegally evaded or fled military service is wrong. It *is* wrong.

Yet, in my first words as President of all the people, I acknowledged a Power, higher than the people, Who commands not only righteousness but love, not only justice but mercy.

Unlike my last two predecessors, I did not enter this office facing the terrible decisions of a foreign war, but like President Truman and President Lincoln before him, I found on my desk, where the buck stops, the urgent problem of how to bind up the Nation's wounds. And I intend to do that.

As a lawyer, I believe our American system of justice is fundamentally sound. As President, I will work within it.

As a former naval reservist, I believe our system of military justice is fundamentally sound. As Commander in Chief, I will work within it.

As a former Congressman who championed it, I believe the concept of an all-volunteer armed force is fundamentally sound and will work much better than peacetime conscription.

Accordingly, in my first week at the White House, I requested the Attorney General of the United States and the Secretary of Defense to report to me personally, before September 1, on the status of some 50,000 of our countrymen convicted, charged or under investigation, or still sought for violations of [the]

Selective Service [Act] or the Uniform Code of Military Justice—offenses loosely described as desertion and draft-dodging.

These two Cabinet officers are to consult with other Government officials concerned and communicate me their unvarnished views and those of the full spectrum of American opinion on this controversial question, consolidating the known facts and legal precedents.

I will then decide how best to deal with the different kinds of cases—and there are differences. Decisions of my Administration will make any future penalties fit the seriousness of the individual's mistake.

Only a fraction of such cases I find in a quick review relate directly to Vietnam, from which the last American combatant was withdrawn over a year ago by President Nixon.

But all, in a sense, are casualties, still abroad or absent without leave from the real America.

I want them to come home if they want to *work* their way back.

One of the last of my official duties as Vice President, perhaps the hardest of all, was to present posthumously 14 Congressional Medals of Honor to the parents, widows, and children of fallen Vietnam heroes.

As I studied their records of supreme sacrifice, I kept thinking how young they were.

The few citizens of our country who, in my judgment, committed the supreme folly of shirking their duty at the expense of others, were also very young.

All of us who served in one war or another know very well that all wars are the glory and the agony of the young. In my judgment, these young Americans should have a second chance to contribute their fair share to the rebuilding of peace among ourselves and with all nations.

So, I am throwing the weight of my Presidency into the scales of justice on the side of leniency. I foresee their earned re-entry—*earned* re-entry—into a new atmosphere of hope, hard work, and mutual trust.

I will act promptly, fairly, and very firmly in the same spirit that guided Abraham Lincoln and Harry Truman. As I reject amnesty, so I reject revenge.

As men and women whose patriotism has been tested and proved—and yours has—I want your help and understanding. I ask all Americans who ever asked for goodness and mercy in their lives, who ever sought forgiveness for their trespasses, to join in rehabilitating all the casualties of the tragic conflict of the past.

Naturally, I am glad to see the VFW at this convention install a veteran of the Korean war, John Stang, as your new national commander-in-chief. And I compliment you and congratulate you as well as John.

We have struggled for years in America to overcome discrimination against younger Americans, against older Americans, against Americans of various creeds, religions, races and, yes, against women. I will not tolerate any discrimination against veterans, especially those who served honorably in the war in Vietnam.

I am deeply concerned about employment opportunities for the Vietnam-era veterans. We have had some success in placing veterans in the age span of 20 to 34, but the facts and figures show us that there are some tough problems in this category.

As of last month, the rate of unemployment for veterans between 20 and 24 was nearly 10 percent, much too high. The rate of unemployment for these young veterans who are members of minority groups was 19 percent. And far, far too many disabled veterans are still without jobs.

I can assure you, without hesitation or reservation, that this Administration puts a very high priority on aiding the men who bore the brunt of battle. If we can send men thousands and thousands of miles from home to fight in the rice paddies, certainly we can send them back to school and better jobs at home.

I am consequently considering the veterans education bill in this light. But your Government, of necessity, has to be constrained by other considerations as well. We are all soldiers in a war against brutal inflation. The veterans education bill more than likely will come before me very shortly for action. It comes when I am working hard, along with others from the Congress, labor, management, and otherwise, on a nonpartisan battle against excessive Government spending.

America today is fighting for its economic life. The facts are that uncontrolled inflation could destroy the fabric and the foundation of America, and I will not hesitate to veto any legislation to try and control inflationary excesses. I am open to conciliation and compromise on the total amount authorized so that we can protect [veteran] trainees and all other Americans against the rising cost of living.

I commend not only the past service of veterans but also the continuing involvement of many of you in the National Guard and Reserve forces. With current manpower reductions in the active duty Army, Navy, Air Force, and Marines, the Commander in Chief must, of necessity, place continuing reliance on the readiness of our National Guard and Reserves. And I intend to put muscle into this program.

Peace—it depends upon the strength and readiness of our defenses. And I will support every sensible measure to enhance the morale and the combat readiness of our Armed Forces.

The United States, our allies, and our friends around the world must maintain strength and resolve. Potential adversaries obviously watch the state of our readiness and the strength of our will. I will offer them no temptations.

America is not the policeman of the world, but we continue to be the backbone of a free world collective security setup.

Just as America will maintain its nuclear deterrent strength, we will never fall behind in negotiations to control—and hopefully reduce—this threat to mankind. A great nation is not only strong but wise, not only principled but purposeful. A fundamental purpose of our Nation must be to achieve peace through strength and meaningful negotiations.

Our good will must never be construed as a lack of will. And I know that I can count on you and the families of each and every one of you. Peace and security require preparedness and dedication.

You have experienced war firsthand. I want to make certain and positive that Washington never sends another tragic telegram. The list of mourners is already far too long. So is the list of those who wait and wonder—the families of those missing in action. I will never forget them.

Together we are going forward to tackle future problems, including the scourge of inflation which is today our Nation's public enemy number one. Our task is not easy. But I have faith in America. Through our system of democracy and free enterprise, the United States has achieved remarkable, unbelievable progress. We have shared our plenty with all mankind.

This is the same Nation that transcended inflations and recessions, slumps and booms, to move forward to even higher levels of prosperity and productivity. This is the same Nation that emerged from the smoke of Pearl Harbor on December 7, 1941, to change its own destiny and the history of the world—and for the better.

During the first few months that I was Vice President, I traveled some 118,000 miles and visited 40 of our great States. What I saw and what I heard gave me renewed inspiration. It made me proud, proud of my country. It sustains me now.

Our great Republic is nearly 200 years old, but in many, many ways we are just getting started. Most Americans have faith in the American system. Let us now work for America, in which all Americans can take an even greater pride.

I am proud of America. You are proud of America. We should be proud to be Americans.

Thank you very much.

NOTE: The President spoke at 11:38 a.m. at the Conrad Hilton Hotel. Prior to his remarks, the President was presented the VFW Citizenship Gold Medal Award by Ray R. Soden, commander-in-chief of the Veterans of Foreign Wars.

17

Remarks on Intention To Nominate Nelson A. Rockefeller To Be Vice President of the United States. *August 20, 1974*

Mr. Speaker, members of the leadership of the House and Senate, members of the Cabinet:

After a great deal of soul searching, after considering the advice of Members of the Congress, Republicans as well as the Democratic leadership, after consulting with many, many people within the Republican Party and without, I have made a decision which I would now like to announce to the American people.

This was a difficult decision, but the man that I am selecting as nominee for Vice President is a person whose long record of accomplishment in the Government and outside is well known. He comes from a family that has long been associated with the building of a better America. It is a family that has contributed significantly to many accomplishments, both at home and abroad, for the American people.

His achievements in Government are well, well known. He served in the Department of State under former President Franklin Delano Roosevelt. He served under the Presidency of Harry Truman. He served in the Department of HEW under President Eisenhower.

He has served as Governor of the great Empire State, the State of New York, for 15 years, the longest period of time in the history of the State of New York. He is known across the land as a person dedicated to the free enterprise system, a person who is recognized abroad for his talents, for his dedication to making this a peaceful world.

It was a tough call for a tough job. The number of people who were considered by me in the process were all men and women of great quality. They came from those suggested to me who serve in the Congress, the Senate and the House of Representatives.

The names included individuals who had served their respective States with great credit. The names included individuals who were in government, but not in Washington. The names included individuals who were not connected with government.

But after a long and very thoughtful process, I have made the choice, and that choice is Nelson Rockefeller of New York State. It is my honor and privilege to introduce to you a good partner for me and, I think, a good partner for our country and the world.

So, I now announce officially that I will send the name of Nelson Rockefeller to the Congress of the United States for confirmation.

NOTE: The President spoke at 10:04 a.m. in the Oval Office at the White House. His remarks were broadcast live on radio and television.

Vice President-designate Rockefeller responded as follows:

Mr. President, Mr. Speaker and leaders of the Congress, Mr. Secretary of State and members of the Cabinet, and friends:

Mr. President, your nomination of me to be Vice President of the United States under the 25th amendment of the Constitution makes me very humble. If I am confirmed, it will be my great honor to serve you and through you to serve all of the people of this great country.

As you pointed out in your moving message to the Congress, these are very serious times. They are times, as you pointed out, that require the closest cooperation between the Congress of the United States and the executive branch of Government. They also require the dedication of every American to our common national interest.

You, Mr. President, through your dedication and your openness have already reawakened faith and hope, and under your leadership, we as a people and we as a nation have the will, the determination, and the capability to overcome the hard realities of our times. I am optimistic about the long-term future.

Thank you, sir.

18

Remarks at a News Conference for Vice President-designate Rockefeller. *August 20, 1974*

Good morning.

I think all of you have probably heard by now that my nominee for Vice President is Governor Nelson Rockefeller. I told him I was going to bring him over to all of my friends to have some discussion, and so if you would like, I just want to reiterate the fact that I stated, that after I looked at all of the choices, and they were difficult, after I looked at all of the people, there were many, but the one that in good judgment under all of the circumstances was Nelson Rockefeller.

I think he will make a great teammate. I think he will be good for the country, I think he will be good for the world, and I am looking forward to working with him.

So, Nelson.

NOTE: The President spoke at 10:20 a.m. in the Briefing Room at the White House. His remarks and Vice President-designate Rockefeller's news conference were broadcast live on radio and television.

Following the President's remarks, Vice President-designate Rockefeller made an opening statement and participated in a question-and-answer session with reporters. His opening statement follows:

Well, needless to say, ladies and gentlemen, I am deeply honored, and should I be confirmed by the Congress, I will look forward to the privilege and honor of serving the President of the United States and, as I said in the other room, through him all of the people of this great country.

I am fully cognizant of the fact that the responsibilities of the Vice President are to preside over the Senate of the United States and to otherwise simply carry out any assignment that he or she may receive from the President.

I will look forward to that opportunity of serving him in any way that can be useful to him, and I think and feel very strongly that already his own dedication and openness has reawakened hope and faith and that under his leadership, we as a people and we as a nation have the capacity, the will, and the ability to face the tough realities—and overcome them—that exist in our country and in the world today. And I am optimistic about the long-term future.

19

Statement Following Congressional Action on Legislation To Establish a Wage and Price Monitoring Agency. *August 20, 1974*

THIS MORNING I had a very fine meeting with the bipartisan leadership of the Congress. I thanked them for their prompt action on legislation currently before the Congress to provide a wage and price monitoring agency. At the same time, I advised them as emphatically as I could, I do not expect to ask for any legislation for either standby or mandatory wage and price controls. Recent experience makes it clear that, under current conditions, compulsory wage and price controls would be most undesirable. It was the unanimous opinion of the leaders present that, as a practical matter, this Congress would not approve such legislation. Since both business and labor also have indicated their opposition, it is clear that there will be no Federal mandatory wage and price controls. I, therefore, ask labor and business leaders in this country to act on that basis. They can do so with the assurance that I will do my best to see that the new price and wage monitoring agency works effectively to combat inflation.

20

Message to the Congress Reporting on the Balance of Payments Deficit Incurred Under the North Atlantic Treaty. *August 20, 1974*

To the Congress of the United States:

In accordance with Section 812(d) of the Department of Defense Appropriation Authorization Act, 1974 (Public Law 93–155), I am pleased to submit a report to Congress on our progress toward offsetting the balance of payments deficit resulting from the deployment of U.S. forces in NATO Europe.

President Nixon reported to the Congress on May 16, 1974 that the offset agreement concluded in April 1974 with the Federal Republic of Germany had a dollar value of approximately $2.22 billion over fiscal years 1974 and 1975. Of that amount, the fiscal year 1974 portion will total approximately $1.1 billion and will be directly applicable toward meeting the requirements of Section 812.

Since President Nixon's last report, the NATO Economic Directorate has concluded a study showing the payments for military-related items from the United States by allies other than the Federal Republic of Germany should amount to approximately $1 billion. When the amount is added to the fiscal year 1974 portion of the offset agreement with Germany, it becomes clear that the United States should be able to offset the $2.1 billion military foreign exchange expenditures resulting from the deployment of our forces in NATO Europe during fiscal year 1974. Accordingly, I can report to the Congress that the requirements of Section 812 should be met.

GERALD R. FORD

The White House,
August 20, 1974.

21

Remarks at a Reception Honoring Senate Majority Leader Mike Mansfield. *August 20, 1974*

LET ME say that it is great to be back up on Capitol Hill and to see Senator Mansfield and the Democratic and Republican leadership in this end of the Capitol and also great to see the Speaker and the others from the other end of the Capitol.

But I am here primarily, in fact exclusively, to pay tribute to a person that I have known all of my almost 26 years in Washington, 25 of them being in the Congress—Mike Mansfield.

When I came in January of 1949, Mike had been here 4 or 6 years, and I quickly developed a great respect and admiration for him as a Member of the House. And when he went to the Senate, that admiration and respect increased.

Anybody that can be a leader, particularly in the majority, for 13 years, I think deserves the greatest congratulations and compliments. I think it proves a couple of things: that bullies don't always prevail. You have to have some of that very fine quality of working with people without twisting their arm. I think it proves that people who can negotiate survive better than those who take a flat, adamant attitude.

But I think you can sum it up better than any way by going along in opposition to a statement that Leo Durocher is alleged to have said, that good guys always finish last. Mike Mansfield is a good guy and he has finished first for a long, long time.

NOTE: The President spoke at 4:50 p.m. in the Senators' conference room at the Capitol.

Senator Mansfield was being honored for having served longer than any other Senator as majority leader. He was elected to the position on January 3, 1961.

22

Remarks at a Ceremony Honoring the Slain United States Ambassador to Cyprus. *August 21, 1974*

Secretary Kissinger, Dana and John, and members of the family, distinguished guests:

This is a very sad occasion for all Americans, as we gather here to pay tribute to a great patriot, one of our most admired and one of our most respected diplomats. Rodger Davies leaves behind many friends and many, many accomplishments in the career that he selected.

He possessed the full measure of many of those attributes which are so invaluable as a person and in the career that he sought. He had judgment, he had dignity, he had wisdom, and he had humor, and all of these are necessary ingredients for the job that he chose for his full life.

As the Secretary has mentioned, Rodger Davies was a professional in the fullest sense. His services to our country embodied the best of time, of effort, and competence. He loved and worked for peace, and he lost his life in the search for peace for all America and all the world.

On Monday of this past week I had the opportunity to make some remarks to a group who had served their country in uniform, and I had the sad occasion to announce to that group the loss of life by Rodger Davies. And I said to them and I repeat here today, some serve in uniform, some serve in other capacities. The loss of life in either case means as much to America.

And, therefore, it is appropriate on this occasion that we pay a very special tribute to a great Ambassador, highly respected by his friends, a person who gave his full life to the career that he sought. So, I say it is an honor for me on this occasion to present, on behalf of all Americans, the flag to Dana, the Ambassador's flag, to which your father, as my personal representative in the service of his country, brought such great distinction.

NOTE: The President spoke at 11:40 a.m. at Andrews Air Force Base, Md., where he and Secretary of State Henry A. Kissinger met the plane bearing Ambassador Davies' children, Dana and John, and the body of the slain Ambassador.

On the same day, the President signed Executive Order 11801 directing the flag to be flown at half-staff on the day of interment as a mark of respect for Ambassador Davies.

Prior to the President's remarks, Secretary Kissinger spoke as follows:

Mr. President, Excellencies, ladies and gentlemen:

A professional Foreign Service officer has come home. He returns not to joy, but to sadness; not to parades, but to solemn ceremony.

Rodger Davies embodied the qualities and spirit which mark an American. He chose an unusual profession, a profession which required that to serve his country he leave his home but never forget it.

Wherever he went, the heritage of America was in his heart. He remembered the dignity of the individual where individuals had lost their dignity. He remembered the rights to liberty and justice where these rights were under attack. He remembered peace where there was war. In that sense, Rodger Davies never left home.

In the diplomatic entrance at the Department of State, the American Foreign Service Association maintains plaques which list the names of those members of the Foreign Service who gave their lives under heroic or tragic circumstances in the service of their country. It is not a short list, and now tragically another name will be added.

I am today awarding to Ambassador Davies the highest award of the Department of State, the Secretary's Award. The citation reads as follows:

"For inspiring leadership, outstanding courage, and dedication to duty for which he gave his life, Nicosia, August 19, 1974."

Awards and names on plaques are little comfort to those who loved and admired Rodger Davies. To his children, Dana and John, I would only repeat my remarks of Monday that Ambassador Davies was beloved, admired, and respected by his colleagues. He was a professional in the fullest and best sense of the word.

Dana and John, your father leaves behind a legacy of which any man should be proud. Even more important, he leaves a multitude of friends whose lives were enriched by knowing him.

Ladies and gentlemen, it is now my honor to introduce a man who in less than 2 weeks has given hope to America and inspired confidence in the world, the President of the United States.

23

Statement on a General Motors Announcement of a Reduction in 1975 Price Increases. *August 21, 1974*

I AM encouraged by General Motors' announcement today that it is reducing the amount of the price increases previously announced for its 1975 model cars and trucks. The consumer will save money, and the economy will benefit.

I am confident that this action will be but one of many examples of restraint by management and labor as we all join in the fight against inflation.

NOTE: The average price increase for automobiles and trucks was reduced to 8.5 percent.

The statement was read by Press Secretary J. F. terHorst at his news briefing at the White House on August 21, 1974.

24

Remarks on Signing the Education Amendments of 1974. *August 21, 1974*

Secretary Carlucci, distinguished administrators and employees of the Department of Health, Education, and Welfare, my former colleagues in the House and the Senate, fellow Americans:

It is really a great privilege and pleasure for me to be here. I know all of us wish that Secretary Weinberger were here, but he is off on a very important responsibility, and I am sure he is here in spirit, if not in person.

I suspect this is the first Federal aid to education bill that has ever been signed by a left-handed President. I attach no significance to that, but it was difficult with a person with a short name to use so many pens. [*Laughter*]

President Eisenhower once said, in discussing education, and I quote: The Federal role should be merely to facilitate, never to control education.

Now, striking the right balance between helping on the one hand and dominating on the other is never an easy task. And those of you who participated in the preparation of the submission in the first instance to the Congress, and those of you who have labored so hard in both the House and the Senate to find a balance in 1974, in my judgment all deserve a great deal of commendation and congratulation.

I don't think any one faction or any one party dictated the contents of that very substantial and very important piece of legislation. I know from some personal experience on the periphery, when I was in the House and subsequently as Vice President, how much hard work, how many long hours, how many compromises were made between, in the first instance, the legislative and the executive branches and between various points of view, legitimate, well-motivated differences philosophically.

I don't believe anyone who labored so long and so hard would say this is a perfect piece of legislation, but I think it is a good law; it justified the final action by the Congress; and it fully justified my signature representing approval by the executive branch.

It does provide, in my opinion, for a more effective distribution of Federal funds to help elementary and secondary schools so that our Federal tax dollars can be more appropriately and efficiently and economically utilized to improve education throughout our 50 States.

The legislation also provides for better Federal administration of the various programs under the more or less direct control of Federal officials, and this better management of Federal programs will help States and localities so they will have a better and more effective input into the management of these Federal programs.

I think it is fair to say that this legislation places reasonable and equitable restrictions upon the problem of busing, and in conjunction with the Supreme Court decision will hopefully relieve that problem and make the solution far more equitable and just.

It is my judgment that H.R. 69 represents the kind of an approach that in this day and age we must follow if we are to do the right thing in education, in housing, and in a multitude of other highly essential programs for the benefit of our country as a whole.

This legislation itself does represent the way to solve disagreements, but if we approach other problems as we have approached this one, with candor on the one hand, cooperation on another, compromise on a third, I think we can march together, the executive, the legislative, Democrats, Republicans, liberals, and conservatives in working together to make our country what we all want it to be, a better America.

Thank you very kindly.

NOTE: The President spoke at 2:15 p.m. in the auditorium at the Department of Health, Education, and Welfare. In his opening remarks, the President referred to Frank C. Carlucci, Under Secretary of Health, Education, and Welfare.

As enacted, H.R. 69 is Public Law 93–380 (88 Stat. 484).

25

Statement on the Education Amendments of 1974. *August 21, 1974*

I TAKE special pleasure today in signing H.R. 69, an omnibus education bill.

As the first major legislation to become law during my Administration, this bill symbolizes one of my greatest hopes for the future—the hope that a new spirit of cooperation and compromise will prevail between the legislative and executive branches. Enactment of this bill was possible only because the two branches settled their policy differences in that spirit. If it continues, I am confident that we can make equally effective progress on other pressing issues.

While I would have preferred different provisions in some sections of this bill, the overall effect of H.R. 69 should be a significant step forward in our quest for more effective distribution of Federal education funds and for better administration of Federal education programs.

Federal funding will be improved through a new formula for distributing Federal assistance for training educationally deprived children. Under the old formula, assistance was directed to States and localities which needed help several years ago, but may no longer need it. Under the new formula, it will be directed to those areas where help is definitely needed today. This change should make the distribution of funds more effective and more equitable.

The Congress has also acted wisely to improve the administration of Federal programs by consolidating a number of categorical programs supporting libraries, educational innovation, and other services. For the first time, State and local education officials will have an important degree of authority over Federal funds in these areas. I hope that this consolidation will become the trend of the future.

Another positive feature of this bill is that it provides for advanced funding of certain education programs. This provision should help to end much of the uncertainty that local school boards have had over the continuity and prospective funding levels of Federal education programs. In the near future, I will send to the Congress a supplementary appropriations request to carry out this advance funding provision.

I am also pleased that H.R. 69 provides new safeguards to protect the privacy of student records. Under these provisions, personal records will be protected from scrutiny by unauthorized individuals, and, if schools are asked by the Government or third parties to provide personal data in a way that would invade the student's privacy, the school may refuse the request. On the other hand, records will be made available upon request to parents and mature students. These provisions address the real problem of providing adequate safeguards for individual records while also maintaining our ability to insist on accountability for Federal funds and enforcement of equal education opportunity.

Much of the controversy over H.R. 69 has centered on its busing provisions. In general, I am opposed to the forced busing of schoolchildren because it does not lead to better education and it infringes upon traditional freedoms in America.

As enacted, H.R. 69 contains an ordered and reasoned approach to dealing with the remaining problems of segregation in our schools, but I regret that it lacks an effective provision for automatically re-evaluating existing court orders. This omission means that a different standard will be applied to those districts which are already being compelled to carry out extensive busing plans and those districts which will now work out desegregation plans under the more rational standards set forth in this bill. Double standards are unfair, and this one is no exception. I believe that all school districts, North and South, East and West, should be able to adopt reasonable and just plans for desegregation which will not result in children being bused from their neighborhoods.

Another troublesome feature of this bill would inject the Congress into the process of administering education laws. For instance, some administrative and regulatory decisions of the Department of Health, Education, and Welfare would be subjected to various forms of Congressional review and possible veto. As a veteran of the Congress, I fully appreciate the frustrations that can result in dealing with the executive branch, but I am equally convinced that attempting to stretch the constitutional role of the Congress is not the best remedy. The Congress can and should hold the executive branch to account for its performance, but for the Congress to attempt to administer Federal programs is questionable on practical as well as constitutional grounds. I have asked the Attorney General for advice on these provisions.

Closely related to this issue is my concern about substantially increased Federal funding for education, especially at a time when excessive Federal spending is already fanning the flames of inflation. I hope the Congress will exercise restraint in appropriating funds under the authorizing legislation included in H.R. 69 and will carefully avoid increasing the budget.

In conclusion, I would re-emphasize that this bill shows us the way for further legislative and executive branch cooperation in the future. I congratulate all of those who participated in this endeavor. Today, and for generations to come, America will benefit from this law which expresses our national commitment to quality education for all of our children.

26

Remarks in the Chamber of the United States Senate. *August 21, 1974*

Mr. President, Senator Mansfield, Senator Scott, Members of the United States Senate:

I wanted to stop by today just to say hello to those with whom I had an opportunity to get better acquainted and to officially inaugurate Pennsylvania Avenue as a two-way street.

It is wonderful to be back in a chamber where so much of America's history for almost 200 years has been written, and, I say without any hesitation, one of the greatest experiences of my life was the privilege of presiding here, though for a relatively short period of time.

Although my tenure was quite short, I think it was long enough to convince me that the U.S. Senate is one of the greatest legislative bodies in the history of mankind.

I think in the days and months ahead all of us must draw upon the great traditions of the Senate. Our job, both in the legislative as well as the executive branch, is to restore the people's faith in the history and tradition of our American Government. No single man and no single woman can possibly do this all alone. It is a job for all of us working together to achieve.

As Governor Rockefeller said yesterday, we must deal with some very hard and somewhat harsh realities. We are not always going to be on the same side. It would not be America if we were. I do not think that really matters. It only matters if we end up by being on the best side for America from one State to another.

I would be very, very remiss if I did not express my appreciation for the Senate and the House going more than halfway on several measures of major importance in the last week or so.

I speak here specifically of the Cost of Living Council proposal, some actions taken on appropriation matters, the action on housing, the action on pension legislation, and the legislation affecting education.

I think what has taken place and transpired in these various proposals is indicative that we can march toward the center in achieving some good results for our country as a whole.

Now, I do not intend to talk specifically about any prospective legislation. I think I would probably be out of order, and I certainly shall respect the rules or traditions of the Senate in that regard.

As we go ahead, we must look not only at our problems at home but also at our problems abroad.

I believe we have a good team in the executive branch of the Government, and I can assure you that that team will be working with this team, the House and the Senate, in the months ahead.

Thank you very much.

NOTE: The President spoke at approximately 2:40 p.m. His remarks as printed above follow a text printed in the Congressional Record.

27

Remarks in the Chamber of the United States House of Representatives. *August 21, 1974*

Mr. Speaker and my former colleagues of the House of Representatives:

You do not know how much it means to me to come back and see all of you and to be so warmly welcomed. It makes one's political life a great, great experience to know that, after all of the disagreements we have had and all of the problems we have worked on, there are friends such as you. It is a thing that in my opinion makes politics worthwhile. I am proud of politics, and I am most grateful for my friends.

Mr. Speaker, I was glad to see that the rules of the House of Representatives have been changed. I was expecting, knowing that the House was considering a bill from the Committee on Banking and Currency, that I would have to go to my old friend, the chairman of the Committee on Banking and Currency [Representative Wright Patman], and get a couple of minutes.

But let me say after 10 days of the honeymoon, Mr. Speaker—and I recall the old adage, "out of sight, out of mind"—I just wanted to drop by my old home to say "hello."

Mr. Speaker, as most of you know, my wife, Betty, and I packed up our belongings and moved across the Potomac earlier this week. We were reminded of what Harry Truman said when he moved out of the White House in 1953: "If I had known how much packing I would have to do, I would have run again."

I did better than Harry did. I went to Chicago.

It is a beautiful house down there, as all of you know, not only beautiful in appearance inside and out, but it has great, great traditions.

But, Mr. Speaker, let me say that our—and when I say "our" I mean my wife Betty and the family and myself—our affections for the White House will never surpass our love for the House of Representatives and for the fine men and women who work here.

You have all been extremely generous in your support, extremely generous in your good will, and you have been extremely generous in your advice. But it has all been good, and I hope you keep the flow going.

I said on the other side of the Capitol, in the other body, a few moments ago, that I was making a few remarks as an inauguration of Pennsylvania Avenue as a two-way street.

I have asked your help in the past when I was in the House, and I am going to ask it now. This is a standard procedure for Presidents, but I am not making, I hope and trust, a pro forma gesture when I ask your help in the remaining days of the Congress. You know and I know that I do not believe in gestures. I never have and I never will. So when I ask your help, I mean it.

I want to reiterate, the help I have sought in the last 10 days has been responded to in a beautiful way, and, Mr. Speaker, your leadership in this has made it much, much easier for me, and for that I am deeply grateful.

Together we have got a big job ahead, and I emphasize "we" on the basis of togetherness, for if we do work together as we have in recent days, we can get the job done.

I want to express my appreciation for the response that has come already in the Cost of Living Council monitoring legislation; the action taken in reference to some of our spending problems; the action taken in housing, in education, and in pension reform. These are all landmark pieces of legislation. This is a good achievement for the Congress, and this is legislation that I am proud of and privileged to sign as President of the United States.

I will be coming back when you return from your much-deserved recess, and I will be coming back to ask your help in the future. I think we can continue to work together, and if we do, it will be the best for the country, and the best for you, and certainly the best for me.

I have noted in my contacts throughout the country that the public wants us to work together, and we can prove that such togetherness will be beneficial.

Let me conclude by simply saying that I think we have a good team in the executive branch, and it can work as a team with a good team on Capitol Hill, the House and the Senate. With that kind of partnership, a good team in the legislative and a good team in the executive, America cannot help but move ahead for the betterment of all.

Thank you very much.

NOTE: The President spoke at approximately 3:10 p.m. His remarks as printed above follow a text printed in the Congressional Record.

28

Message to the Senate Transmitting the United States-Australian Treaty on Extradition. *August 22, 1974*

To the Senate of the United States:

With a view to receiving the advice and consent of the Senate to ratification, I transmit herewith the Treaty on Extradition between the United States of America and Australia, signed at Washington on May 14, 1974. I transmit also, for the information of the Senate, the report of the Department of State with respect to the Treaty.

The Treaty will, upon entry into force, terminate, as between the United States and Australia, the Treaty on Extradition between the United States and Great Britain of December 22, 1931, as made applicable to Australia. This new Treaty represents a substantial modernization with respect to the procedural aspects of extradition.

The Treaty includes in the list of extraditable offenses several which are of prime international concern, such as aircraft hijacking, narcotics offenses, and conspiracy to commit listed offenses.

The Treaty will make a significant contribution to the international effort to control narcotics traffic. I recommend that the Senate give early and favorable consideration to the Treaty and give its advice and consent to ratification.

GERALD R. FORD

The White House,
August 22, 1974.

NOTE: The text of the treaty and accompanying papers are printed in Senate Executive F (93d Cong., 2d sess.).

29

Remarks on Signing the Housing and Community Development Act of 1974. *August 22, 1974*

Secretary Lynn, my former colleagues in the House and Senate, distinguished guests:

It is a great privilege to be here on this landmark day in the field of housing legislation. It is landmark in that it has a new impact on community development and housing legislation generally. I think it was Chairman Sparkman who said that this new legislation is the most significant community development legislation since the 1949 act. He had added, however, that this legislation is the most significant in the field of housing legislation since the 1934 act.

There seems to be almost universal agreement that very significant progress has been made. I think we can say without any reservation that the move from the narrow programs of the past in community development to programs that are very broad gauged, a consolidation of programs such as Model Cities and urban development, will give a real impetus to local decisionmaking, local action, and local responsibility, and I am confident that the mayors, the Governors, the other local officials will assume that decisionmaking, that action, and that responsibility.

In the field of housing, there are some innovative efforts. There are some extensions of existing programs. The housing industry needs a shot in the arm, and this bill, I think, can be extremely helpful in this area.

I would be very remiss if I did not pay tribute to the long and, I think, skillful efforts of those both in the executive branch and those in the Congressional field for what has been accomplished.

I know how hard Jim Lynn has worked, how hard Jim Mitchell has worked, but I think those in the Congress, particularly those who were on the conference, deserve a very special tribute.

I know at times it seemed like an impossible obstacle to overcome the vast differences between the House and the Senate versions, but by patience, by understanding, by the kind of give-and-take and compromise we—not just myself and a few—but we, the American people, are the beneficiaries.

I think that Chairman Patman, Bill Widnall, Chairman Sparkman, Senator Tower deserve very special commendation. We are very grateful for what they did, but if I might be a little provincial or parochial, it seems to me that the Middle West, from which some of us come, deserves a little pat on the back.

Congressman Lud Ashley did a fine job. My former colleague from Michigan, Garry Brown, did a superb job, and then in addition, Jim Lynn and Jim Mitchell.

So, when we add it all up, that document right there will, I think, write new pages of history in community development and housing production. I said a moment ago, we are all the beneficiaries of the dedication, the service, the patience, the understanding of this group of men and many others.

I thank them on behalf of all of you and many, many millions of others throughout our country. Congratulations.

I should add a postscript. I have shaken hands, I think, in the last 24 hours with virtually every Member of the House and Senate, not once but several times. We are going to have a reception, and I won't feel offended in the least if the Members of the Congress avoid me and go to the State Dining Room, and we will have a reception when this breaks up.

Real nice to see you all.

NOTE: The President spoke at 2:15 p.m. in the East Room at the White House. In his remarks, the President referred to James L. Mitchell, Under Secretary of Housing and Urban Development; Senators John J. Sparkman, chairman, and John G. Tower, ranking minority member, Senate Committee on Banking, Housing, and Urban Affairs; and Representatives Wright Patman, chairman, William B. Widnall, ranking minority member, Thomas L. Ashley, and Garry E. Brown, House Committee on Banking and Currency.

As enacted, the bill (S. 3066) is Public Law 93–383 (88 Stat. 633).

30

Statement on the Housing and Community Development Act of 1974. *August 22, 1974*

IT IS with great pleasure today that I am signing into law S. 3066, the "Housing and Community Development Act of 1974."

This bill is of far-reaching and perhaps historic significance, for it not only helps to boost the long-range prospects for the housing market but also marks a complete and welcome reversal in the way that America tries to solve the problems of our urban communities. In urging passage of this bill on the Senate floor, Chairman Sparkman said that "it is probably . . . the most important legislation on community development since the passage of the Housing Act of 1949."

This bill climaxes years of efforts to replace the rigid programs of the past with a more flexible approach by sweeping away seven categorical grant programs such as urban renewal and Model Cities and replacing them with a single "block grant" program for community development. This new approach will put Federal funds to work on behalf of our cities and towns far more effectively than before by:

—providing communities with greater certainty about the level of Federal funding they can expect;

—distributing Federal funds to communities according to what they need rather than who they know;

—replacing Federal judgments on local development with the judgments of the people who live and work there; and,

—allowing local officials to concentrate on comprehensive programs for community betterment instead of grant applications for individual projects.

In a very real sense, this bill will help to return power from the banks of the Potomac to people in their own communities. Decisions will be made at the local level. Action will come at the local level. And responsibility for results will be placed squarely where it belongs—at the local level.

I pledge that this Administration will administer the program in exactly this way. We will resist temptations to restore the redtape and excessive Federal regulation which this act removes. At the same time, of course, we will not abdicate the Federal Government's responsibility to oversee the way the taxpayers' money is used. In particular, we will carefully monitor the use of funds to assure that recipients fully comply with civil rights laws prohibiting discrimination.

This act will also provide significant assistance to the mortgage market and those who depend on it—home buyers, homebuilders, and mortgage lenders. The act makes FHA mortgage insurance available to a greater number of families by reducing required downpayments, expanding the limits on mortgages eligible for Federal insurance, and enabling FHA on an experimental basis to tailor plans for loan repayment to the unique circumstances of individual home buyers. Other sections of the act broaden the lending and investment powers of federally regulated financial institutions, making more credit available for mortgage loans, and thereby providing some needed help for the housing sector.

By prohibiting discrimination on the basis of sex in making mortgage loans, this measure will also enable millions of hardworking women and married couples to obtain the mortgage credit to which their economic position clearly entitles them. I fully support these efforts to eliminate discrimination based on race or sex.

Finally, S. 3066 authorizes a more flexible approach to assisting low- and moderate-income families obtain adequate housing. This new lower income housing assistance program should also help increase the supply of housing in areas where vacancies are unreasonably low.

No one expects this bill to bring substantial immediate relief to the housing market, but over the long haul it should provide the foundations for better housing for all Americans.

This act is important not only for what it does but for how it came about. Like any omnibus bill, S. 3066 has minuses as well as pluses. But it is the product of significant cooperation and compromise by the legislative and executive branches of this Government, and, as such, it is an important example of how the Congress and I intend to approach the Nation's problems in the future.

31

Letter to the Chairmen of the Conference Committee Considering Freedom of Information Act Amendments. *August 23, 1974*

I APPRECIATE the time you have given me to study the amendments to the Freedom of Information Act (H.R. 12471) presently before you, so that I could provide you my personal views on this bill.

I share your concerns for improving the Freedom of Information Act and agree that now, after eight years in existence, the time is ripe to reassess this profound and worthwhile legislation. Certainly, no other recent legislation more closely encompasses my objectives for open Government than the philosophy underlying the Freedom of Information Act.

Although many of the provisions that are now before you in Conference will be expensive in their implementation, I believe that most would more effectively assure to the public an open Executive branch. I have always felt that administrative burdens are not by themselves sufficient obstacles to prevent progress in Government, and I will therefore not comment on those aspects of the bill.

There are, however, more significant costs to Government that would be exacted by this bill—not in dollar terms, but relating more fundamentally to the way Government, and the Executive branch in particular, has and must function. In evaluating the costs, I must take care to avoid seriously impairing the Government we all seek to make more open. I am concerned with some of the provisions which are before you as well as some which I understand you may not have considered. I want to share my concerns with you so that we may accommodate our reservations in achieving a common objective.

A provision which appears in the Senate version of the bill but not in the House version requires a court, whenever its decision grants withheld documents to a complainant, to identify the employee responsible for the withholding and to determine whether the withholding was "without (a) reasonable basis in law" if the complainant so requests. If such a finding is made, the court is required to direct the agency to suspend that employee without pay or to take disciplinary or corrective action against him. Although I have doubts about the appropriateness of diverting the direction of litigation from the disclosure of information to career-affecting disciplinary hearings about employee conduct, I am most concerned with the inhibiting effect upon the vigorous and effective conduct of official duties that this potential personal liability will have upon employees responsible for the exercise of these judgments. Neither the best interests of Government nor the public would be served by subjecting an employee to this kind of personal liability for the performance of his official duties. Any potential harm to successful complainants is more appropriately rectified by the award of attorney fees to him. Furthermore, placing in the judiciary the requirement to initially determine the appropriateness of an employee's conduct and to initiate discipline is both unprecedented and unwise. Judgments concerning employee discipline must, in the interests of both fairness and effective personnel management, be made initially by his supervisors and judicial involvement should then follow in the traditional form of review.

There are provisions in both bills which would place the burden of proof upon an agency to satisfy a court that a document classified because it concerns military or intelligence (including intelligence sources and methods) secrets and diplomatic relations is, in fact, properly classified, following an *in camera* inspection of the document by the court. If the court is not convinced that the agency has adequately carried the burden, the document will be disclosed. I simply cannot accept a provision that would risk exposure of our military or intelligence secrets and diplomatic relations because of a judicially perceived failure to satisfy a burden of proof. My great respect for the courts does not prevent me from observing that they do not ordinarily have the background and expertise to gauge the ramifications that a release of a document may have upon our national security. The Constitution commits this responsibility and authority to the President. I understand that the purpose of this provision is to provide a means whereby improperly classified information may be detected and released to the public. This is an objective I can support as long as the means selected do not jeopardize our national security interests. I could accept a provision with an express presumption that the classification was proper and with *in camera* judicial review only after a review of the evidence did not indicate that the matter had been reasonably classified in the interests of our national security. Following this review, the court could then disclose the document if it finds the classification to have been arbitrary, capricious, or without a reasonable basis. It must also be clear that this procedure does not usurp my Constitutional responsibilities as Commander-in-Chief. I recognize that this provision is technically not before you in Conference, but the differing provisions of the bills afford, I believe, grounds to accommodate our mutual interests and concerns.

The Senate but not the House version amends the exemption concerning investigatory files compiled for law enforcement purposes. I am concerned with any provision which would reduce our ability to effectively deal with crime. This amendment could have that effect if the sources of information or the information itself are disclosed. These sources and the information by which they may be identified must be protected in order not to severely hamper our efforts to combat crime. I am, however, equally concerned that an individual's right to privacy would not be appropriately protected by requiring the disclosure of information contained in an investigatory file about him unless the invasion of individual privacy is *clearly unwarranted*. Although I intend to take action shortly to address more comprehensively my concerns with encroachments upon individual privacy, I believe now is the time to preclude the Freedom of Information Act from disclosing information harmful to the privacy of individuals. I urge that you strike the words "clearly unwarranted" from this provision.

Finally, while I sympathize with an individual who is effectively precluded from exercising his right under the Freedom of Information Act because of the substantial costs of litigation, I hope that the amendments will make it clear that corporate interests will not be subsidized in their attempts to increase their competitive position by using this Act. I also believe that the time limits for agency action are unnecessarily restrictive in that they fail to recognize several valid examples of where providing flexibility in several specific instances would permit more carefully considered decisions in special cases without compromising the principle of timely implementation of the Act.

Again, I appreciate your cooperation in affording me this time and I am hopeful that the negotiations between our respective staffs which have continued in the interim will be successful.

I have stated publicly and I reiterate here that I intend to go more than halfway to accommodate Congressional concerns. I have followed that commitment in this letter, and I have attempted where I cannot agree with certain provisions to explain my reasons and to offer a constructive alternative. Your acceptance of my suggestions will enable us to move forward with this progressive effort to make Government still more responsive to the People.

Sincerely,

GERALD R. FORD

NOTE: This is the text of identical letters addressed to the Honorable Edward M. Kennedy, United States Senate, and the Honorable William S. Moorhead, United States House of Representatives. The texts of the letters, dated August 20, 1974, were issued by the White House August 23.

32

Remarks on Signing the Council on Wage and Price Stability Act. *August 24, 1974*

THANK YOU very much, Mr. Speaker, for coming, along with Mr. Rhodes and Mr. Arends and members of the White House Staff and the Cabinet and others.

I appreciate your coming down here on a Saturday morning for this signing which I think probably best indicates the cooperation that exists before the Congress and the White House.

I was just noticing that less than 2 weeks ago, Mr. Speaker, I asked for the help of the Congress in one important piece of legislation, namely, the one I am about to sign, and within that short span of time the House and Senate responded—responded, I think, in a very constructive way.

Not that this particular piece of legislation is going to be an instant answer or an immediate panacea, but it is important. It was so indicated by the Republican Administration and concurred in by the Democratic leadership and the Democratic Congress. I think it is indicative of the recognition that we have to work together, not only in this instance but in others, in meeting the problem of inflation which plagues us, which is our public enemy number one.

Now we have got some other things that have to be done. I have said very emphatically, and I think it has been generally agreed to, that this legislation is not the forerunner of any wage and price controls. This is a monitoring piece of legislation to give guidance in very broad terms to management and labor so they don't take advantage of a free economy in this critical situation.

I am not going to ask for wage and price controls, and we generally agreed last week that the Congress in 1974 would not respond to any wage and price control recommendation.

We are going to do some other things, and I think all of this ought to be encouraging to the American people and to our friends around the world. We are going to hold the line on spending. The target, of course, is a figure in this fiscal year of under $300 billion. We can do it. We are going to do it. And that ought to be reassuring, I think, to the American people.

There will be some other things that will undoubtedly come out of the economic summit which is being put together by cooperation with the Congress and with the White House.

This battle has to be won, and it will be won, and the cooperation that I have gotten from not only the Congress but from some in industry, and I hope from those in labor, should absolutely reassure the American people that inflation can be licked here as well as abroad.

So, with those remarks I would like to sign this bill which I appreciate and I think the American people will be glad to have on the statute book.

Thank you very much. I appreciate everybody being here, and now we are going back to work without any further ado.

Thank you very much.

NOTE: The President spoke at 11:07 a.m. in the Cabinet Room at the White House. In his remarks, the President referred to Representatives John J. Rhodes, House minority leader, and Leslie C. Arends, House minority whip.

As enacted, the bill (S. 3919) is Public Law 93–387 (88 Stat. 750).

33

Statement on the Council on Wage and Price Stability Act. *August 24, 1974*

ONE OF my first acts as President was to ask the Congress to reactivate a wage and price monitoring agency before its Labor Day recess. Today—less than 2 weeks later—I am gratified to sign the legislation authorizing me to create such a council, and I hereby announce its creation without further delay.

It is certainly encouraging to me, as it must be to all Americans, to know that the Government can act so swiftly on the inflation front. Prompt and aggressive action against inflation is precisely what America needs, and that is the kind of leadership that must be provided by the Federal Government.

This new Council on Wage and Price Stability will provide us with one means of identifying and exposing some of the causes of inflation. It will bring into sharper focus the critical developments of industrial performance, wage and productivity performance, and the effect on inflation of actions taken by the Federal Government.

I must reemphasize that the Council should not be a steppingstone back to mandatory wage and price controls. We have learned from experience that in today's economy, controls lead to disruptions and new troubles.

It would also be unrealistic to expect this Council to bring any immediate relief from inflation. Establishment of the Council is but one step along a difficult road that all of us must travel in the months ahead. We in the Federal Government must hold to a firm, responsible policy of fiscal and monetary restraint. Industry and labor will have their work cut out for them in exercising every responsible restraint in price and wage increases. We face an uphill road, and we will make it through only if we all pull together.

I will announce shortly the membership of the Council so that it can convene promptly and develop an agenda for action in the immediate future.

Once again, I commend the Members of Congress for their quick and responsible action in helping to establish this Council.

34

Statement on Signing the Small Business Amendments of 1974. *August 24, 1974*

LATE yesterday I signed into law S. 3331, the "Small Business Amendments of 1974."

Most of the provisions of this bill are essential to the ongoing programs of the Small Business Administration or are desirable amendments to existing law.

This legislation, for instance, raises ceilings on the SBA's loan programs. It increases the agency's flexibility to establish interest rates on guaranteed loans purchased from financial institutions. It expands the authority to carry out lease guarantee and surety bond guarantee programs. And it authorizes disaster loans with terms of up to 30 years for small business concerns affected adversely by energy shortages.

Each of these provisions was either requested or supported by the executive branch. Their enactment is welcome evidence that the executive branch and the Congress can work together to meet the needs of small business. In the Congress, I have long supported small business as the backbone of our American enterprise system. As President, I intend to encourage small business in every way I can.

There is one provision in this bill which disturbs me. That provision would require SBA to make direct loans under its regular business loan program in an aggregate amount of at least $400 million during fiscal year 1975. The 1975 budget, however, provides only $40 million for this direct loan program. Thus, in the absence of reprograming, the effect of S. 3331, if fully funded, would be to increase Federal budget outlays by $360 million this year.

At a time when both the Congress and the Administration are committed to fighting inflation by reducing Federal spending, outlays of this magnitude would be excessive. Therefore, I do not intend to request additional appropriations to carry out the $400 million authorization for fiscal year 1975. The present 1975 budget request of $40 million, combined with the continuing success of SBA's loan guarantee program, should ensure an adequate level of assistance for small businessmen.

In sum, the bill is generally responsive to the needs of small businesses. I commend the Congress for enacting it.

NOTE: As enacted, S. 3331, approved August 23, 1974, is Public Law 93–386 (88 Stat. 742).

35

Remarks to the Michigan Republican State Convention. *August 24, 1974*

Governor Milliken, Members of Congress, State candidates, and delegates to the State Convention:

Greetings from Betty and me from the White House. You know I would have liked to greet you in person as I have done so many times in the past at our State conventions. However, the very sudden change in circumstances has made that impossible at this time.

But I want you to know that I am thinking about my many, many good Michigan friends gathered in Detroit. I want you to know, too, that there are many good Michiganders who are helping greatly here in Washington in moving the Ford Administration through the very difficult transition period. It is tough, demanding work, but it is accomplishing our great goal.

The transition is going very smoothly. I can assure you that the Ford Administration is moving and moving strongly to meet the Nation's needs, both at home and abroad.

But a President must have help to get his policies and plans into operation. That is where you are needed and needed very badly. One of the most important of our Republican concepts is to reverse the concentration of power in Washington. With the revenue sharing and such important new programs as the Housing and Community Development Act which I signed into law this week, we are beginning to see a transfer of power back to the people.

You, at State and local levels, are getting the power to decide where and how your tax dollars are to be spent in more and more areas of human need. I think that is a great trend in exactly the right direction. It is a trend that must continue, and with your help in electing candidates who support such programs, the power of the people will continue to grow.

You have a fine Governor. Bill Milliken has done an outstanding job. He has a fine record of performance in office. You have an equally fine group of candidates for Congressional and for State office.

I have a particular interest in our Congressional candidates. Our candidates for the Congress are worthy of your full support. We need them in the House of Representatives in Washington, D.C. Our legislative candidates in Lansing also need your full support. Governor Bill Milliken must have help in the State legislature.

You have a lot going for you during the coming campaign in our State. But there has to be one additional factor, the dedicated efforts of Republican workers. You—the key people in the Republican Party of Michigan—must give the leadership and show the way.

It is time for all of us to get down to hard work. With your very real effort, we together can show those who despair the future just how wrong they are. Join with me in helping to build a better America.

Thank you very much.

NOTE: The President's remarks were recorded for use at 12 noon at the convention in Detroit, Mich.

36

Remarks to Members of the Little League World Series Teams. *August 26, 1974*

LET ME welcome all of you on behalf of myself and the American people. We are very grateful to have the teams from the countries that came from abroad. We congratulate all eight teams for participating in the Little League World Series—and I mean really world series. All of you should be congratulated.

Of course, we will congratulate the team from the Republic of China, which won. I can't help but admire—where is Mr. Lin [Wen-hsiang]? Here he is. I watched on television one of those home runs. What was it, five in three ball games? A .727 batting average. I wish I had that good a batting average. [*Laughter*]

But I do want to congratulate every one of you individually, congratulate you as a team, and congratulate those who were the sponsors and the coaches. I wish to welcome all of you from foreign lands.

It is my impression that competitive athletics, whether it is in little league baseball or whether it is in the Olympics or whether it is in any other sport, contributes very significantly to a better world for all of us, those here in the United States, those who come from foreign lands.

The exchange of relationships, the exchange of ideas, the friendships that you make are of invaluable benefit to everybody in the world. And at your young age, you are making a tremendous contribution to better world understanding by the fact that you have participated in this world championship.

I congratulate you again, and I hope that I will have an opportunity to not only say hello in this way but perhaps we can shake hands as I leave the room.

Good luck, and God bless each and every one of you.

NOTE: The President spoke at 2:07 p.m. in the State Dining Room at the White House. The group included the eight teams which competed in the Little League World Series in Williamsport, Pa. The teams were from Red Bluff, Calif.; Tallmadge, Ohio; New Haven, Conn.; Jackson, Tenn.; Republic of China (Taiwan); Maracaibo, Venezuela; Victoria, Canada; and a team made up of children of American military and embassy staff in Athens, Greece.

37

Statement on the Death of Charles A. Lindbergh. *August 26, 1974*

FROM THE MOMENT that the *Spirit of St. Louis* landed in Paris on May 21, 1927, Charles A. Lindbergh had earned a place in history. For a generation of Americans and for millions of other people around the world, the "Lone Eagle" represented all that was best in our country—honesty, courage, and the will to greatness.

In later years, his life was darkened by tragedy and colored by political controversy. But, in both public and private life, General Lindbergh always remained a brave, sincere patriot. Nearly half a century has passed since his courageous solo flight across the Atlantic, but the courage and daring of his feat will never be forgotten. For years to come, we will also remember the selfless, sincere man himself, Charles A. Lindbergh, one of America's alltime heroes and a great pioneer of the air age that changed the world.

On the occasion of his death, Mrs. Ford and I extend our sincere condolences to Mrs. Lindbergh and the family.

NOTE: General Lindbergh, 72, died at his home on the island of Maui, Hawaii.

38

Remarks at a Farewell Party for Herbert Stein, Chairman of the Council of Economic Advisers. *August 26, 1974*

Herb and Mrs. Stein and all of your many, many friends, both professionally and socially and politically and otherwise:

I think all of us are here tonight to say goodby to a trusted friend and a very valued adviser.

Herb, as most of you know, has been with the Council, I think, since 1969, and both economically and politically Herb has been through periods of both good times and bad. It is obvious to a non-economist like myself that economics is something of an inexact science.

I think an economist has been described as a person who tells you there will definitely not be a hurricane and then shortly thereafter helps you repair and rebuild the roof. [*Laughter*]

But through fair weather or foul, Herb Stein, in my judgment, from my view, when I was in the House as minority leader, when I was Vice President, and now as President, has been a model helpmate, adviser to public servants. He has advised Presidents to the very best of his outstanding ability, and on occasions when Herb's advice was not necessarily taken, he stayed loyal to a constituent, the only one under the law that he had, the President of the United States. And to me that kind of loyalty is invaluable.

Herb came to the Government, as I recollect, when the economy was going through a very difficult time. Obviously he is leaving when the economy is going through a very difficult time. But I think we shouldn't lose sight of the fact that while Herb was here the economy went through an enormous expansion and remained the most powerful and most productive and certainly the richest economy in the world today.

One fact that impressed me during Herb's tenure: since 1968, employment, civilian employment, has increased by some 12 million, the largest increase in any 5-year period in the history of the United States. I think that is a tremendously favorable statistic that we can all be proud of.

Real per capita income, after taxes—and that has an impact on all of us—during that same span of time, has increased 15 percent.

In both cases, the gain in employment, the gain in real per capita income, this is indicative of substantial progress. And I think despite the problems we face, the dark clouds that may be on the horizon, we are going to make the same kind of progress in the battle against inflation, with your help, with the help of the American people.

I think we will miss Herb's sense of the dramatic. And I have seen several instances of it. Who can ever forget that economic conference a few years ago when Herb pulled a rib roast out of his briefcase. He said that 2 years ago Mildred had bought that rib roast, and now anybody could buy it for a lot less money. You know why? Have you ever tasted a rib roast that had been in Herb's briefcase for 2 years? [*Laughter*]

Although I will not have the benefit of Herb's advice in person, I am looking forward to getting up each morning, making my own breakfast, and then reading his opinions in the Wall Street Journal and other newspapers. I suspect it will be very appropriate. His views are just about as hardboiled as the eggs that I will cook. [*Laughter*]

But Herb, you brought to Government a wealth of knowledge, experience, and deep insight. I think you leave us with a little more in each category. Your students will be the beneficiaries at the University of Mich—Virginia. [*Laughter*] A few have gone back there. I don't want you to crowd Paul McCracken and the others. But your readers will be the beneficiaries of what you learned down here in the trenches far from that ivory tower. I ask only one thing: Just remember the trenches a bit when you get back up to that ivory tower.

We do, all of us, including myself, wish you the very best of luck. I speak for the White House Staff, your associates in the Council, the Cabinet, the Members of Congress. We will miss your wit, and we will miss your fortitude, and we will miss your loyalty. And we extend to you and to Mildred our very, very best wishes for a happy and successful tenure away from the trenches.

Thank you.

NOTE: The President spoke at 7:19 p.m. in the Atrium at the John F. Kennedy Center for the Performing Arts.

Dr. Stein had served as a member of the Council since February 1969, and as its Chairman since November 1971. He responded to the President's remarks as follows:

Well, Mr. President, Mildred and I and all our friends here are tremendously honored by your presence on this occasion, by your willingness to be seen in public with an economist, and particularly with this economist. [*Laughter*]

You have shown that you are prepared to go the last mile to bring the country together and to establish stability in the American economy. [*Laughter*]

We, of course, wish you every success. Mildred and I are about to join the 98 percent of the American public whose troubles are all caused by the 2 percent who work in the Government. In fact, one can say that their troubles are all caused by four or five people who meet at 8 or 8:30 in the morning in the White House. [*Laughter*]

So when things are not as good as they might be, we will know where to look. [*Laughter*]

But we are sure that they will be as good as they might be. We have every confidence in the program on which you have embarked, on the staff of advisers that you will have working with you and although we know—God knows we know—that there will be ups and downs and trials and tribulations, we have confidence in you and in the American economy to swim through these things which are after all, in the end, only minor ripples—I guess I have said this before; they didn't believe it when I said it before, but I am left with it—[*laughter*]—minor ripples on the rising tide of economic welfare.

So again, let me thank you very much for coming here to join us and our friends.

39

The President's News Conference of *August 28, 1974*

THE PRESIDENT. Good afternoon.

At the outset, I have a very important and a very serious announcement. There was a little confusion about the date of this press conference. My wife Betty had scheduled her first press conference for the same day. And obviously, I had scheduled my first press conference for this occasion. So, Betty's was postponed.

We worked this out between us in a calm and orderly way. She will postpone her press conference until next week, and until then, I will be making my own breakfast, my own lunch, and my own dinner. [*Laughter*]

Helen [Helen Thomas, United Press International].

QUESTIONS

IMMUNITY OR PARDON FOR FORMER PRESIDENT NIXON

[1.] Q. Mr. President, aside from the Special Prosecutor's role, do you agree with the bar association that the law applies equally to all men, or do you agree with Governor Rockefeller that former President Nixon should have immunity from prosecution? And specifically, would you use your pardon authority, if necessary?

THE PRESIDENT. Well, let me say at the outset that I made a statement in this room a few moments after the swearing in. And on that occasion I said the following: that I had hoped that our former President, who brought peace to millions, would find it for himself.

Now, the expression made by Governor Rockefeller, I think, coincides with the general view and the point of view of the American people. I subscribe to that point of view, but let me add, in the last 10 days or 2 weeks I have asked for prayers for guidance on this very important point.

In this situation, I am the final authority. There have been no charges made, there has been no action by the courts, there has been no action by any jury. And until any legal process has been undertaken, I think it is unwise and untimely for me to make any commitment.

POLITICAL PHILOSOPHY

[2.] Q. Mr. President, you have been in office 19 days now, and already some of your natural, conservative allies are grumbling that you are moving too far to the left. Does this trouble you?

THE PRESIDENT. I don't think I have deviated from my basic philosophy nor have I deviated from what I think is the right action. I have selected an outstanding person to be the Vice President. I have made a decision concerning amnesty, which I think is right and proper—no amnesty, no revenge—and that individuals who have violated either the draft laws or have evaded selective service or deserted can earn their way or work their way back. I don't think these are views that fall in the political spectrum right or left.

I intend to make the same kind of judgments in other matters because I think they are right and I think they are for the good of the country.

PUBLIC SERVICE PROGRAM

[3.] Q. Mr. President, may I follow that with one more example, possibly; that is, there is a report that the Administration is considering a $4 billion public works program in case the inflation rate gets higher than it is, say 6 percent. Is that under consideration?

THE PRESIDENT. I think most of you know that we do have a public service employment program on the statute books which is funded right today, not for any major program, but to take care of those areas in our country where there are limited areas of unemployment caused by the energy crisis or any other reason.

There is a recommendation from some of my advisers saying that if the economy gets any more serious, that this ought to be a program—a broader, more expensive public service program. We will approach this problem with compassion and action if there is a need for it.

1976 PRESIDENTIAL CAMPAIGN

[4.] Q. Sir, two political questions: Do you definitely plan to run for President in 1976, and if so, would you choose Governor Rockefeller as your running mate or would you leave that choice up to the convention's free choice?

THE PRESIDENT. I will repeat what has been said on my behalf, that I will probably be a candidate in 1976. I think Governor Rockefeller and myself are a good team, but, of course, the final judgment in this matter will be that of the delegates to the national convention.

POSSIBILITY OF PARDON FOR FORMER PRESIDENT NIXON

[5.] Q. May I just follow up on Helen's question. Are you saying, sir, that the option of a pardon for former President Nixon is still an option that you will consider, depending on what the courts will do?

THE PRESIDENT. Of course, I make the final decision. And until it gets to me, I make no commitment one way or another. But I do have the right as President of the United States to make that decision.

Q. And you are not ruling it out?

THE PRESIDENT. I am not ruling it out. It is an option and a proper option for any President.

ACTION BY THE SPECIAL PROSECUTOR

[6.] Q. Do you feel the Special Prosecutor can in good conscience pursue cases against former top Nixon aides as long as there is the possibility that the former President may not also be pursued in the courts?

THE PRESIDENT. I think the Special Prosecutor, Mr. Jaworski, has an obligation to take whatever action he sees fit in conformity with his oath of office, and that should include any and all individuals.

PREVENTION OF FURTHER "WATERGATES"

[7.] Q. What do you plan to do as President to see to it that we have no further Watergates?

THE PRESIDENT. Well, I indicated that, one, we would have an open Administration. I will be as candid and as forthright as I possibly can. I will expect any individuals in my Administration to be exactly the same. There will be no tightly controlled operation of the White House Staff. I have a policy of seeking advice from a number of top members of my staff. There will be no one person, nor any limited number of individuals, who make decisions. I will make the decisions and take the blame for them or whatever benefit might be the case.

I said in one of my speeches after the swearing in, there would be no illegal wiretaps, there would be none of the other things that to a degree helped to precipitate the Watergate crisis.

CODE OF ETHICS

[8.] Q. Do you plan to set up a code of ethics for the executive branch?

THE PRESIDENT. The code of ethics that will be followed will be the example that I set.

CONTROL OF INFLATION

[9.] Q. Mr. President, do you have any plans now for immediate steps to control and curtail inflation, even before your summit conference on the economy?

THE PRESIDENT. We have announced that as far as fiscal control is concerned, we will spend less in the Federal Government in the current fiscal year than $300 billion. That is a reduction of $5,500 million at a minimum.

This, I think, will have two effects: Number one, it will be substantially beneficial, it will make our borrowings from the money market less, freeing more money for housing, for the utilities to borrow, and, in addition, I think it will convince people who might have some doubts that we mean business.

But in the meantime, we are collecting other ideas from labor, from management, from agriculture, from a wide variety of the segments of our population to see if they have any better ideas for us to win the battle against inflation.

WAGE AND PRICE CONTROLS

[10.] Q. Mr. President, as you know, a number of people have questioned your opposition to a return to wage and price controls. Gardner Ackley, a University of Michigan economist that you have listened to in the past, recently testified before Congress that if we are really frightened about inflation, we ought to think about returning to wage and price controls.

Can you foresee any circumstances under which you would be willing to do that and make them work?

THE PRESIDENT. I foresee no circumstances under which I can see the reimposition of wage and price controls. The situation is precisely this: This past week I had a meeting with the Democratic and Republican leadership, plus my own advisers in the field of our national economy. There was an agreement, number one, that I would not ask for any wage and price control legislation. There was agreement by the leadership on both sides of the aisle that there was no possibility whatsoever that this Congress in 1974 would approve any such legislation. Number three, labor and management almost unanimously agree that wage and price controls at the present time or any foreseeable circumstances were unwise.

Under all of those circumstances, it means wage and price controls are out, period.

DUTIES OF THE VICE PRESIDENT

[11.] Q. Can you give us your present thinking on how best you might use Mr. Rockefeller as Vice President once he is confirmed?

THE PRESIDENT. I have a lot of ideas. Until Congress confirms Mr. Rockefeller, we are sort of in a honeymoon period. I really shouldn't make any commitments until we actually get married.

But to be serious, if I might, I think Governor Rockefeller can be extremely important in the new Administration as my teammate in doing effective work in the area of the Domestic Council. We have to prepare legislative proposals that will go to the Congress when the new Congress comes back in January.

I believe that Governor Rockefeller will take over my responsibilities heading the subcommittee of the Domestic Council on privacy. Governor Rockefeller, with his vast experience in foreign policy, can make a significant contribution to some of our decisionmaking in the area of foreign policy. Obviously, in addition, he can be helpful, I think, in the political arena under certain guidelines and some restrictions.

WAGE AND PRICE CONTROLS

[12.] Q. Mr. President, you just ruled out wage and price controls, but I just would like to ask you why Mr. Nixon, when he was President, felt he was compelled to go back to them because the situation was getting out of hand? Can you just reinforce what you told Mr. Brokaw [Tom Brokaw, NBC News], why you think the situation is not that much out of hand yet?

THE PRESIDENT. I can only refer you to the circumstances and the decision of President Nixon in August of 1971. That was a decision he made under quite different circumstances. We are in totally different circumstances today. We have gone through a 3-year period, more or less. I think we have learned a few economic lessons that wage and price controls in the current circumstances didn't work, probably created more dislocations and inequities. I see no justification today, regardless of the rightness or wrongness of the decision in 1971, to reimpose wage and price controls today.

ECONOMIC ADVISERS

[13.] Q. Mr. President, you are still working with the same team of economic advisers who advised your predecessor. As a matter of putting your own stamp on your own Administration, perhaps spurring confidence, do you plan to change the cast of characters?

THE PRESIDENT. There is one significant change, just within the last 48 hours. Herb Stein, who did a superb job for President Nixon, is going back to the University of Virginia, and Alan Greenspan is taking over, and he has been on board, I think, 2 days. That is a distinct change.

I think Mr. Greenspan will do an excellent job. We are soliciting, through the economic summit, the views of a great many people from the total spectrum of the American society. Their ideas will be vitally important in any new, innovative approaches that we take. So, I think, between now and the 28th of September, when I think the second day of the summit ends, we will have the benefit of a great many wise, experienced individuals in labor, management, agriculture, et cetera, and this will give us, I hope, any new approaches that are wise and beneficial.

OIL PRICES AND PRODUCTION

[14.] Q. Some oil governments and some commercial cartels, notably Aramco [Arabian-American Oil Company] in Saudi Arabia are restricting oil production in order to keep oil prices artificially high. Now the U.S. can't do anything about Venezuela, but it can conceivably vis-a-vis cartels like Aramco. What steps and actions do you plan to take in this regard?

THE PRESIDENT. I think this points up very vividly the need and necessity for us to accelerate every aspect of Project Independence. I think it highlights the need and necessity for us to proceed with more oil and gas drilling, a greater supply domestically. I believe it points up the requirement that we expedite the licensing processes for new nuclear reactors. I think it points up very dramatically the need that we expand our geothermal, our solar research and development in the fields of energy.

In the meantime, it seems to me that the effort that was made several months ago to put together a group of consumer-industrial nations requires that this group meet frequently and act as much as possible in concert, because if we have any economic adverse repercussions because of high oil prices and poor investment policies, it could create serious economic problems throughout the industrial world. So it does require, I believe, the short-term action by consumer nations and the long-term actions under Project Independence.

COMMUNICATIONS WITH THE SPECIAL PROSECUTOR

[15.] Q. Mr. President, to further pursue Helen's inquiry, have there been any communications between the Special Prosecutor's office and anyone on your staff regarding President Nixon?

THE PRESIDENT. Not to my knowledge.

ADVICE TO WAGE EARNERS

[16.] Q. Mr. President, the beneficial effects of budget cutting on inflation will take some time to dribble down to the wage earner. What advice would you give the wage earner today who is having trouble stretching his dollar over his needs?

THE PRESIDENT. I think every wage earner has to realize we are going through a serious economic problem with inflation in double digits, not as bad as people in many Western European countries, but it will require him or her to follow the example of their Federal Government which is going to tighten its belt and likewise for an interim period of time watch every penny.

INDIAN OCEAN NAVAL BASES

[17.] Q. Mr. President, you said last March in an interview, I think in Sea Power magazine, that you came down quite strongly in favor of establishing a U.S. Indian Ocean fleet with the necessary bases to support it. Do you still stand by that and do you favor the development of Diego Garcia? [1]

THE PRESIDENT. I favor the limited expansion of our base at Diego Garcia. I don't view this as any challenge to the Soviet Union. The Soviet Union already has three major naval operating bases in the Indian Ocean. This particular proposed construction, I think, is a wise policy, and it ought not to ignite any escalation of the problems in the Middle East.

Yes, Sarah [Sarah McClendon, McClendon News Service].

VETERANS BENEFITS LEGISLATION

[18.] Q. I want to ask you about this new veterans benefits bill which Congress passed in the last hours. I understand this is a bill that you favored and maybe have spurred the Congressmen to pass. It saves $200 million.

Now my question is: Is that a real savings when it gives the disabled man less money than an able man and disrupts completely the veterans going to college in September?

[1] Diego Garcia, an island approximately 1,000 nautical miles south of India, was part of the British Indian Ocean Territory. The United States Navy maintained a communications station on the island.

The President. I had no part in just how that House action was taken. I did discuss, coming back from the VFW meeting in Chicago, with a number of Members of the House and Senate, the problem that I faced with the bill that came out of conference, which would have added $780-some million over and above the budget for this year and a substantial increase for a number of succeeding years.

But that particular compromise was put together and brought to the floor of the House without any participation by me. I think there are some good provisions in that particular House action. It does tend to equalize the benefits for Vietnam veterans with the benefits that were given to World War II and to Korean veterans.

There are some, I think, inequities, and you probably pointed out one. I hope when the Congress reconvenes within a week or so that they will go back to conference, take a good look, and hopefully eliminate any inequities and keep the price down because it is inflationary the way it was and it may be the way it was proposed by the House.

ANTI-INFLATION MEASURES AND THE FEDERAL BUDGET

[19.] Q. Mr. President, concerning the Federal budget, will the domestic social programs have to bear the whole brunt of the anti-inflation fight or can some money come out of the defense budget, and if so, how much?

The President. No budget for any department is sacrosanct, and that includes the defense budget. I insist, however, that sufficient money be made available to the Army, the Navy, and the Air Force so that we are strong militarily for the purpose of deterring war or meeting any challenge by any adversary. But if there is any fat in the defense budget, it ought to be cut out by Congress or eliminated by the Secretary of Defense.

In the meantime, all other departments must be scrutinized carefully so that they don't have any fat and marginal programs are eliminated.

Mrs. Tufty [Esther Van Wagoner Tufty, Tufty News Service].

DOMESTIC PRIORITIES

[20.] Q. Mr. President, you have given top priority to inflation. Do you have a list of priorities, and if so, what is number two?

The President. Well, of course, public enemy number one, and that is the one we have to lick, is inflation. If we take care of inflation and get our economy back on the road to a healthy future, I think most of our other domestic programs or problems will be solved.

We won't have high unemployment. We will have ample job opportunities. We will, I believe, give greater opportunities to minorities to have jobs. If we can lick inflation, and we are going to try, and I think we are going to have a good program, most of our other domestic programs will be solved.

OFFICE OF ECONOMIC OPPORTUNITY

[21.] Q. Do you have any plans to revive the Office of Economic Opportunity, and if so, in what areas?

THE PRESIDENT. As I am sure you know, the old poverty program has been significantly changed over the last several years. The Headstart program has been taken out of OEC [OEO] and turned over to the Department of HEW. The health aspects of the old poverty program are also over in HEW.

The Congress just approved, and Mr. Nixon approved, a Legal Services Corporation, which was another part of the old poverty program. So, we end up really with just the CAP program, community action program.

Now I think most people who have objectively looked at the community action program and the Model Cities program and maybe some of the other similar programs—there is duplication, there is overlapping.

And under the new housing and urban development bill, local communities are given substantial sums to take a look at the Model Cities programs and related programs, and they may be able to take up the slack of the ending of the community action programs.

ISRAELI CAPITAL

[22.] Q. Mr. President, my question applies to a 1972 statement in which you said that an impediment to a regional peace settlement is an impediment to preserve the fiction that Jerusalem is not the capital of Israel. My question, sir, is would you, now that you set foreign policy, request that the embassy be shifted from Tel Aviv to Jerusalem along with 17 other national embassies?

THE PRESIDENT. Under the current circumstances and the importance of getting a just and lasting peace in the Middle East, I think that particular proposal ought to stand aside. We must come up with some answers between Israel and the Arab nations in order to achieve a peace that is both fair and durable.

POLICY TOWARD CUBA

[23.] Q. Mr. President, do you contemplate any changes in our policy with Cuba?

THE PRESIDENT. The policy that we have toward Cuba today is determined by the sanctions voted by the Organization of American States, and we abide by those actions that were taken by the members of that organization.

Now if Cuba changes its policy toward us and toward its Latin neighbors, we, of course, would exercise the option, depending on what the changes were, to change our policy. But before we made any change, we would certainly act in concert with the other members of the Organization of American States.

POSSIBILITY OF PARDON FOR THE FORMER PRESIDENT

[24.] Q. Mr. President, you have emphasized here your option of granting a pardon to the former President.

THE PRESIDENT. I intend to.

Q. You intend to have that option. If an indictment is brought, would you grant a pardon before any trial took place?

THE PRESIDENT. I said at the outset that until the matter reaches me, I am not going to make any comment during the process of whatever charges are made.

ECONOMIC POLICIES

[25.] Q. Mr. President, two questions, related: How long will the transition last, in your opinion, and, secondly, how soon would it be proper and fair for Democrats on the campaign trail this fall to hold you accountable for the economic policy and the economic problems the country faces?

THE PRESIDENT. Well, I can't judge what the Democrats are going to say about my policies. They have been very friendly so far and very cooperative. I think it is a fair statement that our problems domestically, our economic problems, are the joint responsibility of Government. As a matter of fact, I think the last poll indicated that most Americans felt that our difficulties were caused by Government action and that, of course, includes the President and the Democratic Congress. So, we are all in this boat together, along with labor and management and everybody else. I don't think making partisan politics out of a serious domestic problem is good politics.

FEDERAL PAY RAISE

[26.] Q. Mr. President, in your fight against inflation, what, if anything, do you intend to do about the next Federal pay raise?

THE PRESIDENT. I have made no judgment on that yet, the recommendation has not come to my desk.

SALT TALKS

[27.] Q. Mr. President, when do you expect the SALT talks to resume, and is there a disagreement over our position in the Pentagon and State Department and other agencies?

THE PRESIDENT. At the present time, there is an effort being made to bring the Department of Defense, the State Department, and any others together for a resolution of our, the United States, position regarding SALT Two. This decision will be made in a relatively near future. I don't think there are any basic difficulties that cannot be resolved internally within our Government. I believe that Secretary Kissinger is going to be meeting with representatives from the Soviet Union in the near future, I think in October, if my memory is correct, and we, of course, will then proceed on a timetable to try and negotiate SALT Two. I think a properly negotiated, effective strategic arms limitation agreement is in the best interests of ourselves, the Soviet Union, and a stable international situation.

FRANK CORMIER (Associated Press). Thank you, Mr. President.

NOTE: President Ford's first news conference began at 2:30 p.m. in the East Room at the White House. It was broadcast live on radio and television.

40

Statement on Signing the Public Works for Water and Power Development and Atomic Energy Commission Appropriation Act, 1975. *August 29, 1974*

I HAVE signed H.R. 15155, a public works appropriations bill for fiscal year 1975 providing funds for water and power development, the Atomic Energy Commission, and related agencies and commissions.

The bill raises for one of the first times the question of how well the executive and legislative branches can cooperate in carrying out the new Congressional Budget Act of 1974. Under that act, a President who signs an appropriations bill but wishes to avoid spending all of the funds may either seek a rescission of appropriations or seek a deferral. In either case, the President's action requires the concurrence of the Congress.

This public works bill is troublesome because it would increase the 1975 outlays by $80 million above the budget and would commit us to major outlay increases in future years. I am strongly opposed to those increases because they would intensify our number one problem—inflation.

Nonetheless, I also recognize that this bill is the product of much hard work and deliberation and contains funds for many worthy projects. A veto would commit us to the time-consuming process of reformulating a public works appropriations bill at a time when our energies should be focused on more pressing matters.

After discussions with Congressional leaders, I have therefore decided to sign this bill with the hope and expectation that under the budget act, the Congress will work in cooperation with the executive branch to defer for one full year the expenditure of that amount of appropriated funds which would contribute excessively to inflationary governmental spending.

I am totally committed to close cooperation between the Congress and the Executive, and I know that this spirit will continue to prevail as we work together to halt the inflationary spiral.

NOTE: As enacted, H.R. 15155, approved August 28, 1974, is Public Law 93-393 (88 Stat. 782).

41

Statement Announcing Appointment of Chairman and Members of the Council on Wage and Price Stability. *August 29, 1974*

LAST SATURDAY, when I signed the legislation creating a Council on Wage and Price Stability, I said that Washington must provide prompt and aggressive action in the fight against inflation.

Today I want to move forward in that fight by appointing the members of the new Council and asking them to begin work as quickly as possible. I am asking Mr. Kenneth Rush, my Counsellor for Economic Policy, to serve as Chairman of the Council. I am also asking seven other members of the Administration to serve as members of the group:

William Simon, Secretary of the Treasury
Earl Butz, Secretary of Agriculture
Frederick Dent, Secretary of Commerce
Peter Brennan, Secretary of Labor
Roy Ash, Director of the Office of Management and Budget
Virginia Knauer, Special Assistant to the President for Consumer Affairs, and
Anne Armstrong, Counsellor to the President

In the near future, I also intend to set up an advisory committee to the Council, drawing upon the best talent we can find in labor and industry.

One of my first acts as President was to ask that this Council be established.

It is a tribute to the Congress that the necessary legislation reached my desk in less than 2 weeks. That is the kind of responsible leadership we can and must provide. Let me reemphasize, however, that the new wage and price council is not a forerunner of new wage and price controls. Americans have learned from experience that controls are not the answer to our economic troubles.

In the next few weeks, as we engage in a series of economic summit meetings here in Washington, I hope we can determine just what the best answers are. But one thing is already clear: There will be no instant miracles. This is an uphill struggle. We're all in it together. We must be tough with ourselves, we must be ready for sacrifices, and we must be prepared to stick it out over the long haul.

But I am certain that if we work together and if we summon the same courage and wisdom that built America, then we can lick inflation and put our economic house in order.

42

Remarks at Ohio State University, Columbus, Ohio. *August 30, 1974*

President Enarson, President Fleming, Governor Gilligan, Senator Metzenbaum, Congressman Sam Devine, Congressman Chalmers Wylie, Mr. Mayor, honored graduates, members of your family, and friends and guests:

It is a very great privilege and an exceedingly high honor to participate in this wonderful graduation ceremony. And at the outset, may I congratulate each and every one of the graduates.

But if I might add, I think, appropriate congratulations to the members of your family—husbands, wives, mothers, fathers, and others who have done so much to make it possible for you to be here on this wonderful occasion.

And I think it is appropriate also that we add a special tribute to the members of the faculty who have likewise contributed to this very wonderful occasion.

So much has happened in the few months since you were so very kind to ask me to participate on this occasion. I was then America's first instant Vice President—and now, America's first instant President. The United States Marine Band is so confused they don't know whether to play "Hail to the Chief" or "You've Come a Long Way, Baby." [*Laughter*]

Obviously, it is a very great honor for me to be at Ohio State University, sometimes known as the "Land of the Free and the Home of Woody Hayes." [1] I met

[1] Head coach of the Ohio State University football team.

Woody at the airport. We just had our picture taken together, and when the picture appears in today's [Columbus] Dispatch, I am pretty sure what the caption will say: "Woody Hayes—and Friend." [*Laughter*]

As many of you know, I have had a great interest in football for a good many years. I played center for the University of Michigan, and I still remember my senior year back in 1934. The Wolverines played Ohio [State] in Columbus, and we lost 34 to 0. And to make it even worse, we lost seven out of our eight ball games. But what really hurt was that my teammates, after the end of the season, voted me the most valuable player. I didn't know whether to smile or sue. [*Laughter*]

But I want you to know that I have a great feeling of kinship with this graduating class. I understand that you have all taken your final examinations this week. As your new President, I feel like I am just beginning mine. They are tough, both at home and abroad, but we will make it. Instead of dwelling on how my team lost here in Columbus in 1934, I would prefer to advance the clock to 1974 and talk about winning against the odds that confront today's graduates and all America.

The first of these problems is summed up by the editor of your campus newspaper. She reports that the one dominant question in the minds of this year's graduates is very simple: How can I get a job that makes sense as well as money?

Your professors tell you that education unlocks creative genius and imagination and that you must develop your human potential. And students have accepted this. But then "Catch 22" enters the picture: You spend 4 years in school, graduate, go into the job market, and are told that the rules have changed, there is no longer a demand for your specialty—another educational discipline is now required.

And so one or two more years of study inevitably follows, and you again return to the job market. Yes, what you now offer is salable except that competition is very tough. To succeed you must acquire further credentials so you go back to the university and ultimately emerge with a master's or even a Ph. D.

And you know what happens next? You go out and look for a job and now they say you are overqualified.

In one form or another, this is a "three shell game." Our society has been playing tricks with our greatest natural energy source—that is, you. And this has got to stop.

Although this Administration will not make promises it cannot keep, I do want to pledge one thing to you here and now. I will do everything in my power to bring education and employers together in a new climate of credibility—an atmosphere in which universities turn out scholars and employers turn them on.

Ever since President Abraham Lincoln initiated the concept of land grant colleges, set up to bring educators closer to the people and students closer to the land, the Federal Government has been interested in the practical application of education.

Take the example of Project Independence. Frankly, I am not satisfied with the progress we are making toward energy independence by 1980. However, this is a problem that I can appropriately discuss at a Labor Day weekend commencement. It concerns both the academic community and our great labor organizations.

I am not speaking of gasoline for a Labor Day trip to the lake or the seashore. I am speaking of fuel and raw materials for our factories which are threatened by shortages and high costs. Skills and intellect must harmonize so that the wheels of industry not only hum but sing.

I propose a great new partnership of labor and educators. Why can't the universities of America open their doors wide to working men and women, not only as students but as teachers? Practical problemsolvers can contribute much to education, whether or not they hold degrees. The fact of the matter is that education is being strangled—by degrees.

I want to see labor open its ranks to researchers and problemsolvers of the campuses whose research can give better tools and methods to the workman. I want to see a two-way street speeding the traffic of scientific development, speeding the creation of new jobs, speeding the day of independence in energy, and speeding an era of increased production for America and the world.

What good is training if it is not applied to jobs? What good are factories if they are shut down? What good is business and industry without those who solve their problems, perform their jobs, and spend their paychecks?

Next year, I will ask Congress to extend two laws which are expiring. One provides for higher education, the other for vocational education. Both are essential because we need new jobs and we need new skills, academically as well as vocationally.

Your Government will help you create a vocational environment responsive to our needs, but the Government cannot achieve personal fulfillment for each of you. You, in this case, are the essential ingredient. Your determination, your dedication, your will, will make the signicant difference.

For you, the time has come to test the theories of the academic world in the laboratory of life. As President, I invite students and graduates and faculties to contribute their energies and their genius to the solution of massive problems facing America. I invite your ideas and your initiatives in fighting inflation, in providing realistic education, in making sure our free enterprise system continues to give freedom as well as enterprise.

Show us how to increase productivity. Show us how to combine new lifestyles with old responsibilities. Show us how universities can work with industry and labor unions to devise a whole new community of learning across this great land. Show us how work-study programs can become a part of the ongoing educational process. Show us how new skills can improve technology while humanizing its use.

A French statesman once observed that war is much too important to be left to generals. Our Nation's future is far to important to be left only to Presidents or other officials of the Federal Government.

I like the phrase of a former great President, Theodore Roosevelt: "The Government is us; we are the Government, you and I." Oh yes, your vote and your voice are essential, as essential as mine, if each American is to take individual responsibility for our collective future.

As you move into that job that makes sense and money to you—and you will find it—you move from a position of strength. With the war over and the draft ended, your duty now to your country is to enlist in the campaigns currently being waged against our urgent domestic threats, especially inflation which is public enemy number one.

Abroad, we are seeking new peaceful relationships, not only with the Soviet Union and the People's Republic of China but with all peoples—industrial, underdeveloped nations, every nation, if we possibly can. There will be continuity in our foreign policy and continued realism in our self-defense.

At home the Government must help people in doing things they cannot achieve as individuals. Accordingly, I have asked the Secretaries of Commerce, Labor, and HEW to report to me new ways to bring the world of work and the institutions of education closer together. For your Government as well as you, the time has come for a fusion of the realities of a work-a-day life with the teachings of academic institutions.

As a starter, the Department of Labor will shortly announce a pilot program to improve occupational information for graduates and others in making career choices. There will be grants for State and local initiatives to provide data on occupations available and to help channel the potential employees into positions which are not only personally satisfying but financially rewarding.

The States have always assumed the primary responsibility for public education. That tradition in my judgment is very sound and Ohio State University and my alma mater, the University of Michigan, are excellent examples. But there is now too much confusion about which level of Government is to play which role in post-secondary education.

I am directing the responsible agencies of the Federal Government to make a new evaluation of where we are, where we want to go, and where we can reasonably expect to be 5 years from now.

Discussions will be held with Governors, State legislators, academic leaders, Federal officials, and the consumers of education.

Our goal of quality education is on a collision course with the escalating demands for the public dollar. Everyone must have a clearer understanding and a clearer agreement on who is responsible for the specific aspects of the direction and the financing of a college education.

Oftentimes our Federal Government tries to do too much and unfortunately achieves too little. There are, for example, approximately 380 separate Federal educational programs beyond the high school level, some duplicating others, administered by some 50 separate executive agencies. The result inevitably is a bureaucracy that often provides garbled guidelines instead of taut lifelines to good and available jobs.

But let us look for a moment beyond the campus and beyond Washington. In 1972, I was fortunate to visit the People's Republic of China. With four times the population of the United States, a nation growing at the rate of two New York City's every 12 months, that vast nation is making very significant technological progress. From a personal observation as well as by records, you can see the Chinese productivity is gaining momentum, and the majority of the Chinese on the mainland today are young people, highly motivated, extremely well disciplined.

As fellow human beings, we celebrate the rising capacities of the Chinese nation, a people with a firm belief in their own destiny.

However, as Americans, motivated by free competition, we see a distant challenge. And I believe all Americans welcome that challenge.

We must compete internationally not only to maintain the balance of trade in our standard of living but to offer to the world's impoverished, examples and opportunities for a better life. We should do that for humane and for perhaps even self interest.

Let this peaceful competition, however, animate the last quarter of the 20th century. And I am confident that America's youth will make the difference.

You are America's greatest untapped source of energy. But energy unused is energy wasted.

It is my judgment that we must make extraordinary efforts to apply our know-how, our capital, our technology, and our human resources to increase productivity at a faster rate. Unfortunately, inflation is creating a national state of public anxiety. Productivity, yours as well as mine, must improve if we are to have less of an inflationary economy. In the long run, it is the only way that we can raise wages without inflationary price increases. It is essential in creating new jobs and increasing real wages. In a growing economy, everyone—labor, management, and the consumer—wins when productivity expands.

At this very moment of America's history, we have the knowledge and the material resources to do almost anything that any one of us, or all of us collectively, can imagine. We can explore the depths of the oceans. We can put a man on the Moon. We can reach for the stars.

But great problems confront us here on Earth. To face these problems, we need even more than technology, we need more than programs. We need a belief in ourselves. We need the will, the dedication, the discipline to take action.

Let us take a new look at ourselves as Americans. Let us draw from every resource available. Let us seek a real partnership between the academic community and the rest of our society. Let us aspire to excellence in every aspect of our national life.

Now, may I close with a word between friends? Sometimes deep feelings can get lost in words. I don't want that to happen here today. And so, I would like to share with you something that I feel very deeply: The world is not a lonely place. There is light and life and love enough for all of us. And I ask you, and all Americans, to reach out to join hands with me—and together we will seek it out.

Thank you very much.

[At this point, Dr. Harold Enarson, president of Ohio State University, conferred an honorary Doctor of Laws degree upon the President. Dr. Enarson then presented the President with two tickets for the Michigan-Ohio State football game on November 23, 1974. The President then resumed speaking.]

President Enarson, obviously I am deeply grateful and most indebted to you. I won't tell this audience who I will be rooting for. I don't want to go from the White House to the doghouse so quickly. [*Laughter*]

Somehow I learned indirectly, and I don't know the source, that I might be the beneficiary of Ohio State's generosity this morning, and this information came to me late, late yesterday afternoon, just as Henry Kissinger and I were breaking up a meeting talking about some foreign policy matter, and I told

Secretary Kissinger that I was coming out to Columbus for this game. And I could see a light sort of get in his eye, and I said, "Well, Henry, would you and Nancy like to join us?"

And I'll tell you the answer came very quickly.

I told that to President Enarson this morning and he said he would try to scrounge up a couple of extra tickets. But you know there might be an extra dividend. Having Henry here on November 23 might give a very unique opportunity. If Henry Kissinger can successfully negotiate the long-standing disputes between the Israelis and the Arab nations, he might have an opportunity to do it between Woody Hayes and [Michigan head coach] Bo Schembechler.

Thank you.

NOTE: The President spoke at 10:11 a.m. at summer commencement exercises in St. John Arena. In his opening remarks, the President referred to Robben W. Fleming, president of the University of Michigan, and Tom Moody, mayor of Columbus, Ohio.

43

Special Message to the Congress Proposing a Reduction in Federal Civilian Employment and Deferral of Federal Pay Increase. *August 31, 1974*

To the Congress of the United States:

At a time when inflation is the main concern of every American, the Federal Government has a special obligation to take those actions which begin to stop inflation.

In this spirit and with the knowledge that the action I am taking will help to hold down the cost of living for all Americans, I now recommend a ninety-day deferral in the pending pay adjustment for Federal employees. At the same time, I am also ordering the Director of the Office of Management and Budget to proceed with a reduction of 40,000 Federal civilian positions from those planned for the current fiscal year.

Therefore, as required by law, I am transmitting to the Congress a plan to defer Federal pay raises for ninety days. This is intended to meet both the needs of those who serve the Government and the common interest of the general public, all of whom must bear the burden of increased inflation.

Under this plan, a pay increase for all Federal employees based upon an appropriate comparability adjustment would become effective on the first pay period beginning on or after January 1, 1975. The level of the comparability adjustment will be determined during the next few weeks.

I regret asking for this postponement of a Federal pay increase, but I am convinced of its necessity. Federal employees who I am asking to make a sacrifice are the foundation of sound, effective and efficient Government. I am more conscious than ever of their contributions to our country.

Nevertheless, at this critical time in the economic health of our Nation, I must call on all Americans without exception to make sacrifices in order to hold down wages and prices. Federal employees, as one of the largest groups of workers in the country, have a special role to play in the fight against inflation because we in Government set the example. As we seek a noninflationary budget, it is especially important this year that Federal spending be held to a minimum.

I urge the Congress to support this action, because it is in the best interest of all Americans.

The plan to defer Federal pay raises by ninety days is attached. As required by law, the plan represents an alternative to the October effective date which would otherwise occur.

In addition, the Office of Management and Budget has now determined the specific reductions in civilian positions from those budgeted for the current fiscal year. The agencies will shortly be informed of these reductions by letters from OMB. Wherever possible, these reductions will be accomplished through normal attrition.

It is extremely important that the Federal establishment hold employment to the absolute minimum needed to get the job done. Effective use of human talents is a wise use of the tax dollar.

The pay raise deferral and the reduction in civilian positions together will reduce the 1975 budget by about $1 billion. Thus, the Federal Government is taking an essential first step in holding down the Federal budget and showing the way for restraint by all Americans.

GERALD R. FORD

The White House,
August 31, 1974.

NOTE: The President's Federal pay comparability alternative plan was included with the message and is printed in the Weekly Compilation of Presidential Documents (vol. 10, p. 1083).

44

Labor Day Statement. *September 2, 1974*

I SALUTE the working men and women of America on the 80th anniversary of labor's special day. Their strength of mind, heart, and hand continues to guide our destiny.

As American society has changed in modern times, the role and needs of labor have also changed. A need for organization arose and was filled.

Today, therefore, we salute not only the 93 million men and women in the labor forces but also the organizations which represent labor so well. The goals of those organizations were eloquently summed up by Samuel Gompers 81 years ago, when he said that labor wants "more school houses and less jails; more books and less arsenals; more learning and less vice; more constant work and less crime; more leisure and less greed; more justice and less revenge; in fact, more of the opportunities to cultivate our better natures. . . ."

The organized efforts of America's working men and women have been instrumental in helping move this Nation a long way towards those goals. Today, the Nation needs their support in a new struggle for productivity—for more purchasing power and less inflation. I am confident that the men and women of the American labor movement know that the struggle against inflation is a joint venture by all segments of the American people and that they will do their part.

On this Labor Day, I say to my fellow Americans who have provided us with so much in the past and from whom we expect even more in the future—thank you.

45

Remarks on Signing the Employee Retirement Income Security Act of 1974. *September 2, 1974*

Mr. Speaker, my former colleagues in the Congress, Secretary Brennan, Secretary Dent, distinguished leaders in the labor movement, distinguished leaders in business:

It is a great privilege and pleasure for me to have the opportunity of participating in the signing of that massive bill. I think this is really an historic Labor Day—historic in the sense that this legislation will probably give more benefits and rights and success in the area of labor-management than almost anything in the history of this country.

I think it is historic, too, because that tremendous document is indicative of the kind of cooperation between the House and Senate, the House Committee on Ways and Means, and the Senate Committee on Finance, the House Committee on Education and Labor, and the Senate Committee on Labor and Public Welfare.

I think it is indicative of the kind of cooperation that can be achieved between labor and management. I know how hard and how long many people in the labor movement and management have worked to make sure that we came up with the right kind of legislation.

I think it is a good reflection on the relationship between the executive branch on the one hand and the legislative branch on the other. So, when you add it all up, even though this is an extremely complicated piece of legislation, it has been the long labors of many, many people that have produced the kind of result that is good for America and, primarily, for those who will be the ultimate beneficiaries of the legislation.

This legislation will alleviate the fears and the anxiety of people who are on the production lines or in the mines or elsewhere, in that they now know that their investment in private pension funds will be better protected, they have a vested right. They are certain, obviously, of better management of those funds.

It certainly will give to those 30-plus million American workers a greater degree of certainty as they face retirement in the future.

I do want to extend to all of you my congratulations and compliments. I do not think I have had a happier day than the opportunity today to see so many people who have worked so long on legislation of such great significance, and to have it happen on Labor Day is a tribute to the American process, a process which is good for all of us.

Thank you very, very much.

NOTE: The President spoke at 11:40 a.m. in the Rose Garden at the White House.

As enacted, the bill (H.R. 2) is Public Law 93–406 (88 Stat. 829).

46

Statement on the Employee Retirement Income Security Act of 1974. *September 2, 1974*

DRAMATIC growth in recent years has thrust private pension plans into a central role in determining how older Americans live in their retirement years.

From 1960 to 1970, private pension coverage increased from 21.2 million employees to approximately 30 million workers. During this same period, assets of these private plans increased from $52 billion to $138 billion. And they are now increasing at a rate of $12–15 billion a year. It will not be long before such assets become the largest source of capital in our economy.

Yet, this same growth in pension plans has brought with it a host of new problems. Many workers have ultimately lost their benefits—even after relatively long service—because when they left jobs, they thereby gave up rights to hard-earned pension benefits. Others have sustained hardships because their companies folded with insufficient funds in the pension plan to pay promised pensions. In addition, some pension funds have been invested primarily for the benefit of the companies or plan administrators, not for the workers. It is essential to bring some order and humanity into this welter of different and sometimes inequitable retirement plans within private industry.

Today, with great pleasure, I am signing into law a landmark measure that may finally give the American worker solid protection in his pension plan.

Under this law, which is entitled the Employee Retirement Income Security Act of 1974, the men and women of our labor force will have much more clearly defined rights to pension funds and greater assurances that retirement dollars will be there when they are needed. Employees will also be given greater tax incentives to provide for their own retirement if a company plan is unavailable.

It is certainly appropriate that this law be signed on Labor Day, since this act marks a brighter future for almost all the men and women of our labor force.

There are seven essential parts to this legislation:

—first, it establishes major standards for employee participation in private retirement plans, standards which encourage earlier participation by workers, and longer periods over which benefits can be earned;

—second, and perhaps most important to those already under private pension plans, the new law establishes equitable standards for the "vesting" of retirement benefits. The standards under this law will assure to the greatest possible extent that a worker who participates in a plan actually receives some benefits from that plan and does not lose them because of punishing forfeiture standards or inadequate pension fund resources;

—third, the act requires that the fiduciaries who control the pension funds act as reasonable and prudent men, discharging their duties solely in the interests of protecting the beneficiaries of the fund;

—fourth, the law will impose a high standard upon the operation of plans by making mandatory full disclosure of all information concerning the operations of the employer's retirement plan;

—fifth, the tax laws will be revised to provide more nearly equal treatment to different kinds of plans. The new law will encourage the self-employed to provide for their retirement by raising the limits on the amount of their income which may be contributed on a deductible basis to a retirement fund. It will also allow the one-half of American employees not covered by private pension plans to enjoy equivalent tax advantages if they set up individual retirement accounts;

—sixth, as a final backstop to private pension plans, a federally sponsored, privately financed Pension Benefit Guaranty Corporation will be set up to pay an adequate retirement benefit to those whose private pension funds have foundered and are not adequate for the beneficiaries; and,

—seventh, the act will establish a limited form of portability of pension benefits by allowing workers to transfer some of their pension benefits to other plans or to their individual retirement accounts.

Together these seven points add up to a better deal for American workers than they have ever known before in private pension plans.

I believe this act is a model of what can be done by the Government to improve the lives of Americans within the private sector without harming the dynamics of our free enterprise system.

I also believe that its passage is a model of cooperation and hard work between the executive and the legislative branches.

The act has its genesis in a message to the Congress by President Nixon on December 8, 1971. The legislation was and is extraordinarily complicated. It was worked on relentlessly by four Congressional committees: House Ways and Means, House Education and Labor, Senate Labor and Public Welfare, and Senate Finance.

Individual members have devoted enormous effort to this bill. I believe we can all be proud that the Government has now taken action to make workers' lives more secure.

47

Statement on Signing Youth Conservation Corps Legislation. *September 3, 1974*

I AM signing today S. 1871 which amends the Youth Conservation Corps Act of 1970.

The Youth Conservation Corps program provides summer work-education experiences for young people aged 15 through 18, of all income classes, on Federal lands administered by the Departments of Interior and Agriculture. This year, most of the States and territories established YCC programs on State lands under a pilot grant program.

This act establishes a program to expand the participation of young people in activities on Federal and State lands. It makes the State grant program permanent. It also would permit use of Corps members on projects on Federal lands administered in other Federal agencies.

Though I have some concerns about the cost of this program at a time when inflation is our number one domestic problem, this act is not inconsistent with the 1975 budget, and thus I am pleased to be able to sign it.

NOTE: As enacted, S. 1871, approved September 3, 1974, is Public Law 93–408 (88 Stat. 1066).

48

Remarks on Signing a National Hispanic Heritage Week Proclamation. *September 4, 1974*

LET ME sign this declaration or proclamation, and then I will make sure that you all get a pen, Joe.

In 1968, the Congress passed a resolution [H.J. Res. 1299] which provided for the recognition of Hispanic Americans, that we should have a week once a year where their contribution to the American society would be fully appreciated and totally recognized.

This week begins on September 10 and runs through the 17th [16th], and this proclamation is predicated on that resolution which was approved 6 years ago.

It is a pleasure for me to be in the company of the Members of Congress who are here, and I understand that Congressman Manuel Lujan is flying in from New Mexico but will be a few minutes late, but he will be joining us very shortly.

In the group here are some leaders of the Spanish-speaking Americans who will be here to give me the benefit of their observations and comments and recommendations as to how we can very appropriately and properly recognize the many, many contributions that have been made, from the very beginning of our Nation's history, to the great accomplishments of America.

I think history shows that before Plymouth Rock there were Spanish-speaking individuals who had made settlements in not only Florida but New Mexico and Puerto Rico and possibly California, I am not sure.

I think it illustrates the fact that Spanish-speaking Americans were in the very vanguard of the settlement of the new world, and they have contributed significantly with their deep religious convictions. They have contributed unbelievably to a better America by their dedication to an outstanding family life.

We believe, in this Administration, as others have, that this important growing part of our American population should be recognized for what they can do for all of us and for what they have done for America over the 200 years, nearly, of our Nation's history.

So, it is a pleasure for me to sign this proclamation in the presence of not only Members of Congress who are representative of the Hispanic Americans but the others who are here from private life.

So, without any fanfare, I will undertake this. I have learned how, Ed, to do this with a few letters instead of doing it with one pen.

NOTE: The President spoke at 11:10 a.m. in the Cabinet Room at the White House. In his remarks, the President referred to Senator Joseph M. Montoya of New Mexico and Representative Edward R. Roybal of California.

Following the signing ceremony, the President met with Hispanic-American Members of Congress and Administration officials to discuss the problems and needs of Hispanic Americans.

49

Proclamation 4310, National Hispanic Heritage Week, 1974. *September 4, 1974*

By the President of the United States of America a Proclamation

Our country's Hispanic heritage reaches back more than four centuries. When the Pilgrim Fathers landed at Plymouth Rock, Hispanic civilization was already flourishing in what is now Florida and New Mexico. Since then the Hispanic contribution to America has been a consistent and vital influence in our country's cultural growth.

More than ten million Americans of Hispanic origin today contribute to our national diversity, enriching the quality of American life in the arts, the sciences, sports, religion and the small but important things of everyday living.

Now, Therefore, I, Gerald R. Ford, President of the United States of America, do hereby proclaim the week beginning September 10, 1974, and ending September 16, 1974, as National Hispanic Heritage Week. I call upon all the people of the United States, especially the education community and those organizations concerned with the protection of human rights, to observe that week with appropriate ceremonies and activities.

In celebrating this occasion, I also call upon my fellow Americans to rededicate themselves to the principle of full and equal opportunity for all citizens, and to seize upon the broad spectrum of skills and abilities of those individuals of Hispanic heritage who have so significantly contributed to our Nation's growth and prosperity.

In Witness Whereof, I have hereunto set my hand this fourth day of September, in the year of our Lord nineteen hundred seventy-four, and of the Independence of the United States of America the one hundred ninety-ninth.

Gerald R. Ford

NOTE: The full text of this proclamation is included as an example of the proclamations the President issues. All the proclamations issued by President Ford in 1974 are listed in Appendix B.

50

Message to the Congress Transmitting Annual Reports on Highway, Traffic, and Motor Vehicle Safety Programs. *September 4, 1974*

To the Congress of the United States:

The 1950's and early 1960's were marked by enormous growth in the Nation's highway systems—the number of vehicles which used them and the miles which they traveled nearly doubled. We developed a modern, flexible form of transportation. It was also deadly. Deaths rose from 34,700 in 1950 to top 53,000 in 1966, when the Congress determined that a national effort was needed to contain the runaway slaughter and passed the Highway Safety and National Traffic and Motor Vehicle Safety Acts. The attached reports, which I am transmitting in accordance with the reporting requirements in those acts, describe the various traffic safety programs, with emphasis on activities during 1973.

Without question, the seven-year-old national traffic safety effort has proved beneficial. As will be seen by figure 1 in the motor vehicle safety report, annual deaths among passenger car occupants, which were rising throughout the early 60's, have since leveled off and remained fairly constant in face of a rise through 1972 in traffic deaths. This is in spite of large increases in mileage driven, number of vehicles, drivers, average speed, and alcohol consumption—to name some of the factors which we know contribute to highway accidents. The overall growth in traffic fatalities is attributable to motorcycle, pedestrian, and bicycle accidents. There is little doubt that our motor vehicle safety standards are saving lives and reducing the severity of injuries.

Improvements in the Nation's highways are also making a major contribution to progress in traffic safety. Since 1967 the death rate per 100 million miles traveled has declined steadily on our modernized roadways.

Although total traffic fatalities remain shockingly high, the fatality rate has declined from 5.5 per 100 million vehicle miles to 4.3—a significant decrease of 22 percent since 1967. Had the 1967 fatality rate continued, almost 72,000 Americans would have been killed in highway accidents in 1973, instead of the estimated total of just over 56,000. This estimated saving of 16,000 lives in a single year represents an enormous financial saving to society in terms of wages, medical costs, legal expenses, and property damage, not to mention human suffering. Such savings would not have come about without the combined efforts of Federal, State, and local officials involved in this national emphasis, as well as private citizens who have supported the program.

In 1973, the lowering of speed limits and other effects of the energy shortage situation had a dramatic impact on highway fatality statistics. During the last two months of the year, as States reduced their speed limits and motorists voluntarily limited their driving, the number of fatalities declined by as much as 25 percent below the November/December 1972 totals in some States. As a result, the Nation as a whole ended the year having lost 2,000 fewer lives than had been projected.

The saving in lives during the past year provides an added incentive for the Government and the Nation to persist in the endeavor to make our vehicles, our highways, and our drivers safer. I am confident that well-managed programs and well-managed use of our resources will continue to have a positive effect in improved highway safety.

GERALD R. FORD

The White House,
September 4, 1974.

NOTE: The reports are entitled:

"Traffic Safety '73, A Report on the Activities of the National Highway Traffic Safety Administration and the Federal Highway Administration Under the Highway Safety Act of 1966" (Government Printing Office, 48 pp. plus appendixes).

"Traffic Safety '73, A Report on the Activities of the National Highway Traffic Safety Administration Under the National Traffic and Motor Vehicle Safety Act of 1966" (Government Printing Office, 60 pp. plus appendixes).

51

Statement on the Death of Gen. Creighton W. Abrams, Jr. *September 4, 1974*

GEN. CREIGHTON ABRAMS was an American hero in the best tradition. In the heat of battle and in the gray corridors of the Pentagon, he proved that he was that rare combination—a man of action who was also a first-class administrator.

He was also a colorful, courageous leader who won the admiration and respect of enemies as well as allies and subordinates. His 38-year military record spanned three wars, as he rose from first lieutenant in 1936 to Chief of Staff in 1972. He has left us an example of service and a memory of heroism that future generations of Americans, in and out of uniform, will long cherish. We will miss him very much.

Mrs. Ford joins me in extending to his wonderful wife and family our deepest condolences.

NOTE: General Abrams, 59, died at Walter Reed Army Medical Center, Washington, D.C.

On the same day, the President signed Executive Order 11802 directing the flag to be flown at half-staff until the day of interment as a mark of respect for General Abrams.

On September 6, 1974, the President attended funeral services for General Abrams at the Memorial Chapel, Ft. Myer, Va.

52

Remarks at the Swearing In of Alan Greenspan as Chairman of the Council of Economic Advisers. *September 4, 1974*

THIS IS a very, very auspicious occasion. It is my first opportunity to participate in the swearing in of a Chairman of the Council, and, of course, I am pleased and honored to have the opportunity to do it with a man as outstanding as Alan Greenspan.

And it is so nice to have you here and to participate as well. If my recollection is correct, about the time I came to the Congress, our distinguished guest, who is about to be sworn in, was an accomplished clarinetist in and around New York City.

Well, he gave up that occupation at a subsequent date and became a very, very outstanding economist in the private field as well as an adviser to the Federal Government.

But now, as the ninth Chairman, he has a new responsibility to try and stop playing the blues and curing the blues. [*Laughter*]

I was told the other day that being a clarinetist or a musician in Washington was not necessarily bad. Len Garment was an accomplished musician and has done extremely well here in Washington.

Somebody mentioned to me the other day that they wondered why it took me so long to make a choice for Vice President. Well, I will make this observation and comment. I had a hard time deciding between Nelson Rockefeller and Benny Goodman. [*Laughter*]

I am delighted to have an opportunity to participate in this swearing in of Alan because, not only his talents are superb and his education and reputation are of the finest but I like his approach. He is recognized as an optimist in the field of economic policy, and I happen to believe that despite some of the problems we face, we have to be optimistic about what we can do about them.

And Alan Greenspan has that reputation. I believe in being an optimist, and I think that attitude is helpful and beneficial as we face some of the difficult problems and the hard decisions ahead.

So, Alan, I congratulate you and wish you well, and it has been a pleasure to get to know you better, to have the benefit of your recommendations, and I think the country is going to be far better off with your counsel and advice as we move ahead in these very difficult times.

NOTE: The President spoke at 5:47 p.m. in the Cabinet Room at the White House. In his remarks, the President referred to Assistant to the President Leonard Garment.

53

Remarks at a Reception for Members of the National Council on the Arts. *September 4, 1974*

WHEN I am surrounded by Betty on the one hand, who is an expert in her own right and her own background, and Nancy on the other, I am a completely helpless individual.

I have been delighted to have a part to some extent in promoting the council of arts and all of the things that are related thereto. I would be, I think, off on the wrong track if I took any credit for any significant gains. But it has been a very wonderful experience for me to go from one who had little or no appreciation or support for the arts to one who has learned that the arts can be very important, very vital in a community and, I think, in the Nation.

So, I am a converted individual, and I don't apologize for it. And converts oftentimes are known as more ardent advocates than those who were brought up in an environment or in a religion.

It has been a great experience for me to see over the last 4 or 5 years the tremendous increase not only in money from the Federal Government but the interest throughout the Nation.

I have traveled a good bit, as some of you may know, and I have seen from community to community, including my own community in Grand Rapids, Michigan—go from a rather placid interest to an interest of broad-based public support.

And the National Council and all those associated with it can take a great deal of credit. I wish to compliment the Congress because the Congress in this span of time has really contributed very significantly. I doubt if there is a program in the Government in the last 5 or 6 years that has grown in dollars percentagewise as rapidly as this program, and I think that it is a compliment to the program from its inception to the program under Nancy. I think Roger [1] and you have been the only two heads of the department, or organization, and I think when you can go from Roger to Nancy and have this kind of progress, it is a tribute to both of them.

My home of Grand Rapids, Michigan, is the honored place where one of Alexander Calder's wonderful mobiles—is that the proper——

MRS. FORD. No, that is not a mobile; it is a stabile.

THE PRESIDENT. ——stabile, all right—is and will be a hallmark of the arts as far as we are concerned. I point it out to all the visitors who come, including the Secret Service. [*Laughter*] I tell them that it is nothing they should be worried about. [*Laughter*] It is stimulating, it is a great attraction as far as the community is concerned, and I am proud of it.

And I have yet to find out with any specificity or any great deal of definitiveness what he was trying to tell us, but nevertheless it is a great attraction and a

[1] Roger L. Stevens, Chairman of the John F. Kennedy Center for the Performing Arts, was Chairman of the National Council on the Arts from its establishment in 1965 to March 1969.

wonderful addition to our community. And I think it is indicative of what can be done and will be done in the months and years ahead under the leadership of the Council of Arts and the leadership of Nancy, because you have to have a broad-based public, I think, range of activities, ranging from those that I know best to those that others know far better than I.

And the arts are an important and integral part of our better society. And I compliment you all, those on the Council at the present, those who have been there in the past, and those who will be assuming responsibilities in the future.

I think it is a great addition to our society here in the United States, and we can be as proud as any of our old countries in what we have done in America, and we are going to do infinitely better.

Thank you very much.

NOTE: The President spoke at 7:55 p.m. in the Atrium at the John F. Kennedy Center for the Performing Arts, after being introduced by Nancy Hanks, Chairman of the National Council on the Arts.

54

Remarks Opening the Conference on Inflation. *September 5, 1974*

Good morning:

It is a pleasure to be here with the distinguished Members of the Congress, both Democratic and Republican, and the very eminent group of economists and guests.

I look forward to a very beneficial and fruitful meeting this morning. This meeting marks the start of our national Conference on Inflation. I have called this series of working conferences in response to a bipartisan recommendation by the United States Senate and with the cooperation of concerned citizens representing all elements of our American society.

Our purpose is to find ways by which we, the American people, can come to grips with our economic difficulties and surmount them.

This has been called a summit conference. Maybe that title is a bit misleading. Recent summit conferences have been held between leaders of international adversaries with the hope of reducing their differences. Around this table there are no adversaries. We come together as allies to draw upon, or to draw up, I should say, a battle plan against a common enemy, inflation. Inflation is our domestic enemy number one.

Battle strategies are usually devised in secret. At my insistence, this is a typically American open meeting. Some skeptics have warned me that putting 28 of our most distinguished economists and eight Members of Congress, both Democratic and Republican, on public display with live microphones would produce a spectacle something like professional wrestlers playing ice hockey. [*Laughter*] But I am ready to referee this opening match.

It is not widely known, but I started out in college very much attracted to economics. Later I switched to the law, probably because the legal profession seemed a better path to success in politics.

Having come this far, I can see why no economist would ever dream of wanting to be President.

But if we succeed in the job cut out for us, I can promise you there will be statues of each of you in every city park throughout the United States. Economics will never again be called a dismal science, nor will politicians, if we succeed, dare again to hide behind the old alibi that the people just don't understand economics. The people understand economics very, very well, and they are sick and tired of having politics played with their pocketbooks.

This Conference on Inflation is a joint enterprise of the legislative and executive branches of our Government which can become a monument to politics in the very best sense of the word. It unites Republicans and Independents and Democrats in an election year against a deadly enemy that doesn't recognize one political party from another.

The President cannot lick inflation. The Congress cannot lick inflation. Business, labor, agriculture, and other segments of America cannot lick inflation. Separately we can only make it worse, but together we can beat it to its knees.

These meetings are not going to be empty exercises in economic rhetoric, neither are they going to reveal any quick miracles. There is no quick fix for what ails our economy. I, for one, refuse to believe that the very best brains in America and the smartest, hardest working workers in the world cannot find a workable way to get the productive machinery of this great country back on the track and going full speed ahead.

Let me say, or set out, if I might, a few ground rules at the outset. We can't waste time stating and restating the problems. The problems are obvious, painful, and perplexing.

What we want are some right answers, not a long list of alternative answers, theoretical and hypothetical, good and bad. We need to have attainable answers sharply defined and carefully sorted out with the pluses and the minuses of each clearly stated.

We are looking for action that is practical, possible, and as rapid in its effect as we can reasonably expect.

I don't have to tell all of you experts that there are many answers, most of which have been tried at some historic time. But before this conference ends, I would like to see and to have set before the American people a consistent and considered package of the most promising answers that you can find, some of which, or all of which, will restore economic stability and sustain economic growth in these United States.

If our country is economically healthy, the whole world will be economically healthier. Inflation is a world-wide epidemic and we will quarantine it in collaboration with our friends abroad.

As you test your answers against the hard rock of economic law, as you discard beguiling, instant cures for reliable remedies, as you try to treat the cause rather than the symptom, I ask you to bear in mind that no solution will work without a lot of willpower and individual sacrifice. America has plenty of both—a capacity for both.

Sacrifice is easy to ask of others. It is harder to demand of ourselves. Burdens never fall equally on everybody's shoulders, but we must seek to share them as widely as the prosperity we hope will follow. The burdens of battle against inflation will be lighter if every American, all 210 million of us, lends a hand.

There will be 10 more specialized meetings over the next few weeks culminating in a final 2-day session on Sepetember 27 and 28. When we are done, there will be some things we can agree on.

I hope these areas of agreement will be greater than the areas of disagreement. But it is a fact that our economic system, like our political system, is based on competition in the honest conflict between different interests and different opinions. So there will be some things about which we cannot reach a consensus.

This would be a dull country without dissenters. But fortunately that is not a foreseeable danger in this case. Where we disagree, it will be necessary for the President and the Congress to make some very hard decisions. Our political system is designed to do exactly that, relying in the end on the ultimate good sense of the American people.

That is why these conferences must be open to the public. After all, it is their business we are really talking about.

So, ladies and gentlemen, let's get to work.

At this point I would like to ask our newly sworn-in Chairman, Mr. Alan Greenspan, to give his outlook on the economy.

NOTE: The President spoke at 9:32 a.m. in the East Room at the White House. His remarks and both the morning and afternoon sessions of the conference were broadcast live on public television.

Subject areas for subsequent meetings included labor, State and local government, agriculture and food, transportation, natural resources and recreation, business and manufacturing, housing and construction, banking and finance, and health, education, and welfare.

55

Message for the Jewish High Holy Days. *September 5, 1974*

ON THE occasion of the High Holy Days, it is my pleasure to send special greetings to my fellow Americans of the Jewish Faith. Your inheritance of accumulated wisdom and moral precepts makes you strong guardians of the ideals of righteousness, justice and human dignity. This has given you a special sensitivity to the social needs of each generation. And this has also been the guiding force behind your impressive contributions to the vitality of our American democracy.

These solemn days of worship which you celebrate have a message for all Americans. They exhort us to search our souls, to render an inner accounting, and a self-examination of the standards we profess and the actions we perform. They invite us to a return to righteousness and truth and to a rebirth in the spirit of neighborliness and brotherhood. They remind us that we are in God's hands and that He has given us our lives in trust to use in His service.

At a time which urgently tests our will as a people to put humanity's interest above self-interest, we can be greatly sustained and guided by the traditions of valor and resilience that mark the history of the Jewish people.

GERALD R. FORD

NOTE: The text of the message was issued by the White House.

56

Remarks Concluding the First Meeting of the Conference on Inflation. *September 5, 1974*

LET ME reiterate my appreciation for all of you being here.

I must confess that when I first heard of the resolution [S. Res. 363] that was proposed in the Senate, I was somewhat apprehensive about an undertaking of this kind. But in the first few hours of this Administration, I reanalyzed the suggestion in relationship to the economic problems that have been well-displayed here. And it seemed to me, as I tried to say in the opening statement, this isn't a problem that only a President can solve. It is not a problem that only the Congress can solve. And it certainly is not a problem that any one element in our society can solve.

So, in response to the recommendation of a bipartisan effort in the Senate, I determined that it should be undertaken, that it should be in the open so the American people could see firsthand the consensus as well as the divergencies. And this was the first group, and I shared the apprehension that some have expressed, that men of high academic standing and great intellect couldn't sit in a gathering such as this and give a topflight presentation of the problem and some responsible suggestions.

But I think you gentlemen and ladies have set a very high example for those meetings that shall follow. And I happen to believe that with this outstanding gathering, and the things that have been done, those that will follow will likewise be of the same caliber and high quality.

So, I thank you not only for what you have contributed but the performance that I think has been superb.

And with those words, I think we probably ought to conclude the afternoon session and the day's labors and retire for a bit of relaxation and a reception, and I cordially invite you all to come to the dining room for such a purpose.

Thank you very, very much.

NOTE: The President spoke at 5:30 p.m. in the East Room at the White House. His remarks were broadcast live on public television.

57

Remarks on the United Way Campaign. *September 6, 1974*

TONIGHT I would like to talk with you about the special challenge this year's United Way campaign in your community faces. And I am speaking as one who has worked as a United Way volunteer in my own hometown, as one who knows what the United Way campaign can do in your community.

The one annual campaign for your community agencies may still be called the United Fund or the Community Chest. But this year a new symbol for such campaigns has been adopted. We call it the United Way. This one effort each year to raise funds to help people in need is one of vast importance to you and to your community, and to the Nation as well.

The United Way symbolizes the very best in each of us and in each of our communities. It brings together men and women from every part of the community, all working together to help those who need help.

This is the way to handle community problems—a uniquely American way. We care about our less fortunate neighbors. We are willing to work to make our communities better and you in your community know far better than anyone in Washington which of your neighbors needs help and what is needed to make your community better.

That is why the United Way serves so very well, because it is an effort with a special goal and a special campaign, designed for the community involved.

It is impossible for me to discuss each of those community campaigns and problems individually, but tonight I want to talk with you about the urgent need for your support for your community's campaign.

The national goal for the United Way campaign this year is more than $1 billion—the largest goal of any campaign in our history.

But it is a critical goal this year. Last year your United Way pledge, with those of other Americans, helped 34 million families. That is a tremendously impressive total, but we can't help that many families this year with the amount of money we all pledged last year. I think you know the reason why.

The same problem that put the squeeze on your family budget and which is the number one concern of this Administration has hit the United Way, too. Inflation has taken its toll in the voluntary sector as well.

Last year, for example, in a typical community, the United Way could provide professional care for a retarded child for a little more than $6 a day. This year it costs $10 a day to provide the same professional care to the same child.

Last year a typical day care center could care for a child for $24 a week. This year it costs $30.

Last year a hot-meal program for senior citizens cost $1. Now that same meal costs $1.25.

The problem is where inflation causes you to cut back for the same sick and aged and the dependent young, there is nothing left to cut. They cannot afford to lose the help they are now receiving. Your pledge to United Way in your community provides the most effective, the most economical and efficient way to provide that help. The volunteer effort of the United Way workers insures that more of your dollars go to serve people. Your pledge to the United Way campaign in your community is an investment in a better community. It is an investment in a better Nation and a better world.

I ask you to join in, to give your fair share to make the United Way work for our fellow human beings this year, just as it has worked so well in the past.

Thank you for thinking of others.

NOTE: The President's remarks were filmed on September 3, 1974, for broadcast on television.

58

Remarks at a Dinner Concluding the Reconvening of the First Continental Congress in Philadelphia, Pennsylvania. *September 6, 1974*

GOVERNOR SHAPP, let me say at the outset, I am deeply grateful for your overly generous and very kind remarks. I accept the invitation for July 4, 1976.

Mayor Rizzo, distinguished Governors, my beloved and wonderful former colleagues in the United States Senate and House of Representatives, distinguished guests, ladies and gentlemen:

It is a great privilege and a very high honor to have the opportunity of participating in this function tonight.

Philadelphia, the City of Brotherly Love, was the cradle of American liberty. "Love" and "liberty" are two pretty good words with which to start a nation.

I learned in school a good many years ago that the first shots of the American Revolution were fired at Concord and the last at Yorktown. But it was in Philadelphia that 56 patriots from 12 of the original 13 colonies convened two centuries ago to protest the military coercion of Massachusetts and the united economic action against the mother country. I am sure that the history books will show, in addition, that both George Washington and John Adams slept here. [*Laughter*]

"The . . . Congress," John Adams wrote home to his wife Abigail, "is tedious beyond expression. The assembly is like no other that ever existed. Every man is a great man, an orator, a critic, a statesman; and therefore every man upon every question must show his oratory, his criticism, and his political abilities."

"The consequence of this," Adams concluded wearily, "is that business is drawn and spun out to an immeasurable length."

Speaking as a former Congressman, I can assure you that more than once in the last 25 years—especially after a long, long debate in the House of Representatives—I have found myself saying pretty much the same to my wife, Betty. Only the names have changed—that and the fact that John Adams never had to fix his own breakfast. [*Laughter*]

Yes, there was plenty of pessimism in the land in 1774 when the First Continental Congress gathered in the City Tavern over there someplace. And, the problems they faced were enough to drive the bravest patriots to a tavern.

Individually and collectively, the 13 colonies were divided by class, by tradition, by religion, by ethnic origins, and by economic interests. And as for a central structure of government, they had to make that up as they went along.

On the opening day of the First Continental Congress when the countdown to our independence began, Patrick Henry struck, I think, an appropriate and common chord. In his opening address, he declared, and I quote: The distinctions between Virginians, Pennsylvanians, New Yorkers and New Englanders are no more. I am [not] a Virginian, but I am an American.

This, I think, is a unique insight into the attitude of the Congress: their determination of all for one and one for all. The punitive acts that were directed at Massachusetts and the closing of Boston Harbor would have diverted trade and commerce to other ports—to New York, to Philadelphia, to Baltimore, and to Norfolk. Yet unselfishly, even in that day, all the colonies knew that any such benefits would only be temporary—the cause of Boston in that day was the cause of all of them.

America has a sense of unity today. The cause of the South is the cause of the North; the cause of the West is the cause of the East. We are today, as our forefathers were, bound together in the great American experiment—the greatest experiment in the history of man governing himself.

Yet the American Revolution remains a lesson as to what a few, a very few, dedicated people can do. Today we number 50 States and span a continent. We reach northward to the Pacific and Alaska, and west to the islands of Hawaii. Our people number more than 211 million.

Two hundred years ago our population in those 13 sparsely populated colonies were 2½ million. Historians estimate that of that number only one-third—one-third out of 2½ million—provided the strength and the fiber and the dedication of the Revolution. We can call them the patriots. Another third felt very deeply their allegiance to the Crown. Some served in the King's army; some fled to England, Canada, or other British colonies. They were the loyalists. The other one-third sat on the fence. I guess today we would call them mugwumps. But history fortunately has long forgotten the timid.

Last December, the Congress created a Federal American Revolutionary Bicentennial Administration to coordinate and facilitate Bicentennial activities. The new Administration is now hard at work on a nonpartisan basis, with the

Congress and the Bicentennial organizations in each of the 50 States, the territories, the District of Columbia, and the Commonwealth of Puerto Rico.

Already some 1,300 cities, towns, villages, counties, some Indian tribes, embracing more than a third of our total population, have met the qualifications for the official "Bicentennial Communities" designation. Our new director of the Bicentennial, John Warner, tells me that the list is growing phenomenally, month by month. Thousands of programs, thousands of events are crowding the Bicentennial calendar.

It is interesting to note that a growing number of foreign governments are planning to participate in our Bicentennial. I think this is welcome news, because there is no nation which is not a great part of our American heritage. The blood of all peoples flows in our veins. Whatever we are or have been able to accomplish, we owe in larger measure to our richly diverse heritage from around the world.

If I remember my Bible correctly, I think this quote is appropriate: The beauty of Joseph's coat is its many colors.

But may I offer my own idea on how best to commemorate the Bicentennial. Let us all, during the coming months, study carefully the character, study the qualities of the men who founded this Nation. Let us try to grasp the stuff that was inside of each of them and all of them collectively. And then, let us release, if we can, the same spirit within ourselves. We have the same capacity for unity, discipline, and sacrifice. Let us show the world that the character and quality of the American people has not changed in 200 years.

What we are really doing, as we celebrate our Nation's 200th birthday, is actually laying the cornerstone of America's third century. And every citizen of this great Nation should have his or her name inscribed on that imaginary stone so that all who come after us can say, as we say of the 56 who labored here for us, "They gave of themselves. They cared."

I am especially glad to note that we are launching the celebration of our Bicentennial right here in the great city of Philadelphia where the first of my two predecessors as Presidents labored as members of the First Continental Congress. I am glad that this period of national rededication, which will extend to July 4, 1976, begins on this almost forgotten day, when the colonial delegates wrestled with their common problems of skyrocketing prices, shrinking purchasing power, shortages, hoarding, and financial speculation.

It was interesting to me to find, in reading the document which recorded what was said here, that the men and women of 1774 were inflation fighters before they took up arms against the British redcoats. Actually, they met voluntarily to wage economic warfare for their future freedom and prosperity, even before the Liberty Bell tolled the birth of a new nation.

The spirit of 1774 was a sudden quickening of American unity in the face of common calamity, of confidence, of patriotism, and determination of the people themselves, and of mutual willingness to take risks and to make sacrifices for the good of all.

In my judgment, there are two very important things to remember about our American Revolution. It was not a revolution to tear down what the colonists had, but to preserve the freedoms, to preserve the rights of free Englishmen, and to expand the material prosperity that they already enjoyed for generations on this bountiful continent. It was not a revolution to make life better for themselves, but to make sure that these blessings would continue for their children and their children's children.

The men who gathered here 200 years ago put it in these words, and I quote: "It is a duty," they wrote in this fabulous document, "which we owe to God, our country, ourselves, and posterity . . . to maintain, defend and preserve those civil and religious rights and liberties, for which many of our fathers fought, bled and died, and to hand them down [entire] to future generations."

What beautiful words—words which they made into deeds.

In short, the inflation fighters of 1774 were not much different from the inflation fighters of 1974 who started a series of conferences in Washington yesterday. Then as now there are no easy answers. Then as now they had to depend very heavily on popular understanding and public support.

For example, John Rutledge of South Carolina might have given the very same speech at the opening of the White House conference yesterday that he gave precisely in this point 200 years ago. And with your indulgence, let me quote from John Rutledge in Philadelphia 200 years ago: We have no legal authority; and obedience to our determinations will only follow the reasonableness, the apparent utility and necessity of the measures we adopt. We have no coercive or legislative authority. Our constituents are bound only in honor to observe our determination.

What are some of these determinations? I have been browsing through this journal of the First Continental Congress, and I must say to my former colleagues in the Congress, it reads a lot easier than the Congressional Record when I was a contributor to that document. But except for the elegant language and the more eloquent age, it deals with the very real problems that are amazingly contemporary. And let me now ask you to listen to this:

"Resolved, that all manufactures of this country be sold at reasonable prices, so that no undue advantage be taken of a future scarcity of goods."

I continue the quote from this document: Such as are vendors of goods or merchandise will not take advantage of the scarcity of goods, that may be occasioned by this association, but will sell the same at the rates we have been respectively accustomed to for the last 12 months past.

And then follows some good advice, and I quote again: And if any vendor of goods or merchandise shall sell any such goods on higher terms, . . . no person ought, nor will any of us deal with any such person, or his or her factor or agent.

I hope you noticed the last phrase in that last quote, and I say this to our liberated women: Please note, "His or her factor or agent." [*Laughter*]

We have heard an awful lot—a lot of talk about our Founding Fathers. Let's not forget our Founding Mothers. Obviously they didn't.

But these resolutions continue, and again I quote: That a committee be chosen in every county, city, and town, by those who are qualified to vote for the representatives of the state legislature, whose business it shall be attentively to observe the conduct of all persons touching this association.

It goes on, and again I quote: We will, in our several stations, encourage frugality, economy, and industry, and promote agriculture, the arts, and the manufactures of this country . . . and will discountenance and discourage every species of extravagance and dissipation.

These are the conclusions of the First Continental Congress. These were chosen at random, but they convey the sense of urgency and unity which existed here, right here, two centuries ago.

I happen to believe there is the same sense of urgency and unity in America today. I have encountered it in Washington and throughout our country. I know it is the reason for this distinguished gathering here tonight in the shadow of Independence Hall.

You who are Governors, Senators, Representatives, mayors, and other public officials elected by the people have told me individually and collectively that you share this sense of urgency, this sense of unity. So, I have come here tonight to ask your help and the help of some 211 million Americans, not only in celebrating what is right about America but in correcting what is wrong about America.

The tyranny of the British Parliament and Crown in 1774 animated our ancestors. The tyranny of double-digit inflation is our common enemy in 1974. I think everybody in this wonderful audience tonight knows as well as I do that inflation is the cruelest kind of taxation without representation.

I have decided that the first priority for us as a nation, domestically, is an all-out war against inflation. Like the patriots who met here some 200 years ago, we may seem to be moving cautiously and too deliberately. But I hope no one will underestimate the generalship or fighting ability of all Americans today the same way they did in 1774. I warn you, as wise old Ben Franklin did, that if we do not all hang together, we certainly will hang separately. But we will not hang separately, nor will we fall divided. We are going after—one and all, Democrats, Independents, and Republicans—we are going after what I term public enemy number one, inflation, in 1974, and we will lick it by July 4, 1976.

I think we must recognize, to be honest, that we will have our Valley Forges, our summer soldiers and sunshine patriots. But we are the descendants, we are the heirs, spiritually if not genealogy—*genealogically,* excuse me—of the patriots who assembled here 200 years ago tonight.

I told my wife Betty that I knew this speech backwards, and I think that is the way I am doing it. [*Laughter*]

And we may truly say, as Joseph Warren of Massachusetts wrote in the Suffolk Resolves, delivered to the First Continental Congress by Paul Revere, and again I quote: On the fortitude, on the wisdom and on the exertions of this important day, is suspended the fate of this new world, and of unborn millions.

We must not let them down.

With your help, we will—we will win our battle against inflation.

What better way can we begin our third century of independence as a nation of liberty under God and brotherly love for all.

Thank you very much.

NOTE: The President spoke at 9:44 p.m. at Independence Mall. Prior to the President's remarks, Governor Milton Shapp of Pennsylvania invited the President to visit Philadelphia on the Nation's Bicentennial, July 4, 1976.

Participants in the 2-day reconvening of the First Continental Congress included Governors and legislative leaders from the original 13 States.

59

Remarks at the Alexandria Police Association Picnic in Fairfax, Virginia. *September 7, 1974*

WELL, thank you very, very much for the invitation to be here and the warm reception that I have received.

I wanted to come out here because it was one way that I could express my appreciation for the warm and kind things that were done by so many of the

Alexandria Police Department, not only during those hectic weeks when I was Vice President and the even more hectic 8 or 10 days while we couldn't move out of where we were into where we are now.

But it was the wonderful opportunities that I and my wife and our four children had to live in Alexandria, to get to know the police department, the school system, the many nice people.

We have many fond memories of living in Alexandria, and we aren't going to sell our home. We are going to come back there. I don't know how soon. We like it and we like the people, and we are deeply grateful to the members of the Alexandria Police Force for all of the nice and many kind things that were done on our behalf.

And we apologize for the inconveniences, the extra hours, and any of the other problems that you went through.

When I decided to come out and have an opportunity to join with you in the crabfest, my schedule was put before me, and it indicated that I was to welcome some very distinguished guests from the Soviet Union who are here with me now, along with three of our American astronauts.

They are Soviet Union cosmonauts who have been in space and the American astronauts have likewise had that experience. And next July, in 1975, the cosmonauts, the two, and the three American astronauts will take off, the Soviet Union cosmonauts from their country, and our three from our country. And within 2 days, or whatever the time is, they will join up in space and will spend 2 days with their two space vehicles joined, and they will move back and forth between their spaceship and our spaceship.

This is not only a tremendous technological achievement but it is, I think, far broader in its implications and ramifications as far as the world is concerned.

We, as Americans, are very proud of our country; our friends from the Soviet Union are very proud of their country. And our two countries in very recent years have sought to work together in space, in the environment, in medicine, in many fields, including an effort to resolve differences in strategic arms.

I think all of us agree that the broader we can make our relationships in health, in environment, in space, and many other areas, the better it is for us here in America and for our friends in the Soviet Union.

So, I am honored to have the Ambassador from the Soviet Union, Mr. Anatoli Dobrynin, and his cosmonauts here this afternoon. They are your guests and I would like, Mr. Ambassador, for you, because I am not the best spokesman in the Russian language, if you would introduce—well, I will try, but if I don't do very well, then he will have to correct me.

First, this is the Ambassador from the Soviet Union, Mr. Anatoly Dobrynin. And the next is Major General Vladimir Shatalov—General Shatalov. And Colonel Aleksei Leonov—Colonel Leonov. And Mr. Valery Kubasov—Mr. Kubasov.

I think your warm welcome to them is indicative of the kind of friendship we have between peoples from the Soviet Union and the United States.

Now, I would like to introduce our three astronauts. First, Brigadier General Tom Stafford. Secondly, Deke Slayton. Where is Deke? And then Vance Brand. Where is Vance?

So, next July, I want you young people to understand this, next July the people you have met—one group being launched from the Soviet Union and the other group being launched from the United States of America—will meet way up in the heavens some place—where is it going to be? They are going to meet over Spain—I am sure for some technical reason, not for any other.

We have some other guests here. General Brent Scowcroft, who is the Deputy Director of the National Security Council, and Mr. Low, who is the deputy director of our National Aeronautics and Space Agency.[1]

Well, we enjoy the opportunity to be here. We look forward to some of that good crab. He said he would open the shells, or whatever you call them. Out in Michigan, we don't have crab. We have a few crabby people but not any crabs. [*Laughter*]

SGT. JOHN V. STREETER (picnic chairman). Mr. President, we have an officer on our police department that is a very talented artist. It is Officer Ned Thompson, and he has taken the time to draw this for you. If I may describe it to the people out here, because they have not seen it either.

It shows President Ford. He is standing there, and there is a poor, sad little fellow there with a sign. In one hand, he is holding the world, and it is all cracked up. And then in the other hand, he is holding a sign that says, "Fix it." [*Laughter*]

Mr. President, God bless you, sir.

THE PRESIDENT. Thank you very much.

Well, I hope all you young people, particularly, will get to know our astronauts and the Soviet cosmonauts. The astronauts have learned to speak some

[1] George M. Low was Deputy Administrator of the National Aeronautics and Space Administration.

Russian and the cosmonauts have learned to speak some English, so you can either talk to them in Russian or English, either way you want. [*Laughter*]

Thank you very much, and we look forward to having a bite to eat.

NOTE: The President spoke at 3:35 p.m. at the Northern Virginia Police Academy.

60

Remarks on Signing a Proclamation Granting Pardon to Richard Nixon. *September 8, 1974*

Ladies and gentlemen:

I have come to a decision which I felt I should tell you and all of my fellow American citizens, as soon as I was certain in my own mind and in my own conscience that it is the right thing to do.

I have learned already in this office that the difficult decisions always come to this desk. I must admit that many of them do not look at all the same as the hypothetical questions that I have answered freely and perhaps too fast on previous occasions.

My customary policy is to try and get all the facts and to consider the opinions of my countrymen and to take counsel with my most valued friends. But these seldom agree, and in the end, the decision is mine. To procrastinate, to agonize, and to wait for a more favorable turn of events that may never come or more compelling external pressures that may as well be wrong as right, is itself a decision of sorts and a weak and potentially dangerous course for a President to follow.

I have promised to uphold the Constitution, to do what is right as God gives me to see the right, and to do the very best that I can for America.

I have asked your help and your prayers, not only when I became President but many times since. The Constitution is the supreme law of our land and it governs our actions as citizens. Only the laws of God, which govern our consciences, are superior to it.

As we are a nation under God, so I am sworn to uphold our laws with the help of God. And I have sought such guidance and searched my own conscience with special diligence to determine the right thing for me to do with respect to my predecessor in this place, Richard Nixon, and his loyal wife and family.

Theirs is an American tragedy in which we all have played a part. It could go on and on and on, or someone must write the end to it. I have concluded that only I can do that, and if I can, I must.

There are no historic or legal precedents to which I can turn in this matter, none that precisely fit the circumstances of a private citizen who has resigned the Presidency of the United States. But it is common knowledge that serious allegations and accusations hang like a sword over our former President's head, threatening his health as he tries to reshape his life, a great part of which was spent in the service of this country and by the mandate of its people.

After years of bitter controversy and divisive national debate, I have been advised, and I am compelled to conclude that many months and perhaps more years will have to pass before Richard Nixon could obtain a fair trial by jury in any jurisdiction of the United States under governing decisions of the Supreme Court.

I deeply believe in equal justice for all Americans, whatever their station or former station. The law, whether human or divine, is no respecter of persons; but the law is a respecter of reality.

The facts, as I see them, are that a former President of the United States, instead of enjoying equal treatment with any other citizen accused of violating the law, would be cruelly and excessively penalized either in preserving the presumption of his innocence or in obtaining a speedy determination of his guilt in order to repay a legal debt to society.

During this long period of delay and potential litigation, ugly passions would again be aroused. And our people would again be polarized in their opinions. And the credibility of our free institutions of government would again be challenged at home and abroad.

In the end, the courts might well hold that Richard Nixon had been denied due process, and the verdict of history would even more be inconclusive with respect to those charges arising out of the period of his Presidency, of which I am presently aware.

But it is not the ultimate fate of Richard Nixon that most concerns me, though surely it deeply troubles every decent and every compassionate person. My concern is the immediate future of this great country.

In this, I dare not depend upon my personal sympathy as a long-time friend of the former President, nor my professional judgment as a lawyer, and I do not.

As President, my primary concern must always be the greatest good of all the people of the United States whose servant I am. As a man, my first consideration is to be true to my own convictions and my own conscience.

My conscience tells me clearly and certainly that I cannot prolong the bad dreams that continue to reopen a chapter that is closed. My conscience tells me that only I, as President, have the constitutional power to firmly shut and seal this book. My conscience tells me it is my duty, not merely to proclaim domestic tranquillity but to use every means that I have to insure it.

I do believe that the buck stops here, that I cannot rely upon public opinion polls to tell me what is right.

I do believe that right makes might and that if I am wrong, 10 angels swearing I was right would make no difference.

I do believe, with all my heart and mind and spirit, that I, not as President but as a humble servant of God, will receive justice without mercy if I fail to show mercy.

Finally, I feel that Richard Nixon and his loved ones have suffered enough and will continue to suffer, no matter what I do, no matter what we, as a great and good nation, can do together to make his goal of peace come true.

[At this point, the President began reading from the proclamation granting the pardon.]

"Now, therefore, I, Gerald R. Ford, President of the United States, pursuant to the pardon power conferred upon me by Article II, Section 2, of the Constitution, have granted and by these presents do grant a full, free, and absolute pardon unto Richard Nixon for all offenses against the United States which he, Richard Nixon, has committed or may have committed or taken part in during the period from July (January) 20, 1969 through August 9, 1974."

[The President signed the proclamation and then resumed reading.]

"In witness whereof, I have hereunto set my hand this eighth day of September, in the year of our Lord nineteen hundred and seventy-four, and of the Independence of the United States of America the one hundred and ninety-ninth."

NOTE: The President spoke at 11:05 a.m. in the Oval Office at the White House, where he signed Proclamation 4311 granting the pardon.

61

Proclamation 4311, Granting Pardon to Richard Nixon. *September 8, 1974*

By the President of the United States of America a Proclamation

Richard Nixon became the thirty-seventh President of the United States on January 20, 1969 and was reelected in 1972 for a second term by the electors of forty-nine of the fifty states. His term in office continued until his resignation on August 9, 1974.

Pursuant to resolutions of the House of Representatives, its Committee on the Judiciary conducted an inquiry and investigation on the impeachment of the President extending over more than eight months. The hearings of the Committee and its deliberations, which received wide national publicity over television, radio, and in printed media, resulted in votes adverse to Richard Nixon on recommended Articles of Impeachment.

As a result of certain acts or omissions occurring before his resignation from the Office of President, Richard Nixon has become liable to possible indictment and trial for offenses against the United States. Whether or not he shall be so prosecuted depends on findings of the appropriate grand jury and on the discretion of the authorized prosecutor. Should an indictment ensue, the accused shall then be entitled to a fair trial by an impartial jury, as guaranteed to every individual by the Constitution.

It is believed that a trial of Richard Nixon, if it became necessary, could not fairly begin until a year or more has elapsed. In the meantime, the tranquility to which this nation has been restored by the events of recent weeks could be irreparably lost by the prospects of bringing to trial a former President of the United States. The prospects of such trial will cause prolonged and divisive debate over the propriety of exposing to further punishment and degradation a man who has already paid the unprecedented penalty of relinquishing the highest elective office of the United States.

Now, Therefore, I, Gerald R. Ford, President of the United States, pursuant to the pardon power conferred upon me by Article II, Section 2, of the Constitution, have granted and by these presents do grant a full, free, and absolute pardon unto Richard Nixon for all offenses against the United States which he, Richard Nixon, has committed or may have committed or taken part in during the period from January 20, 1969 through August 9, 1974.

In Witness Whereof, I have hereunto set my hand this eighth day of September, in the year of our Lord nineteen hundred and seventy-four, and of the Independence of the United States of America the one hundred and ninety-ninth.

Gerald R. Ford

62

Statement on Signing the Juvenile Justice and Delinquency Prevention Act of 1974. *September 8, 1974*

LATE SATURDAY, I signed into law S. 821, the Juvenile Justice and Delinquency Prevention Act of 1974.

This is the first piece of legislation to reach my desk for action in the field of prevention and reduction of crime among our youth. Its passage by very strong majorities in both bodies of the Congress represents a continuation of our national commitment to reduce juvenile delinquency in the United States, to keep juveniles from entering the treadmill of the criminal process, and to guarantee procedural and constitutional protection to juveniles under Federal jurisdiction.

This national commitment is one of partnership with State and local governments through which, together, we spend over $10 billion per year for criminal justice programs.

During the course of this bill's passage through the Congress, the executive branch voiced serious reservations with regard to several of its provisions for organizational change and fund authorizations. I continue to be concerned about these provisions—especially the threat they carry with regard to increased Federal spending at a time when the economic situation demands across-the-board restraint, especially in the Federal budget.

Therefore, I do not intend to seek appropriations for the new programs authorized in the bill in excess of amounts included in the 1975 budget until the general need for restricting Federal spending has abated. In the interim, the estimated $155 million in spending already provided under current programs will provide a continuation of strong Federal support.

This bill represents a constructive effort to consolidate policy direction and coordination of all Federal programs to assist States and localities in dealing with the problems of juvenile delinquency. The direction of our Federal programs has been fragmented for too long. This restructuring of present operation and authority will better assist State and local governments to carry out the responsibilities in this field, which should remain with them. Hopefully, the result will be greater security for all citizens and more purpose, sense, and happiness in the lives of young Americans.

NOTE: As enacted, S. 821, approved September 7, 1974, is Public Law 93–415 (88 Stat. 1109).

63

Statement on Signing Legislation Revising Federal Employees' Compensation Benefits. *September 8, 1974*

ON SATURDAY, I signed into law H.R. 13871, the 1974 amendments to the Federal Employees' Compensation Act. This act provides workers' compensation benefits for Federal employees injured or killed in the performance of duty. Since the law was last amended over 8 years ago, a number of social and economic developments have made it necessary to update and revise the requirements regarding compensation benefits for injured Federal workers. I feel this new legislation meets those changing conditions.

This bill will provide for improved protection against rising costs for Federal employees and survivors who receive benefits. It also guarantees reemployment rights at the same or an equivalent position upon recovery within certain time limitations. Finally, the bill increases compensation benefits for survivors.

Therefore, I am pleased to sign this bill which will assure quality protection for a very deserving group of workers—the Nation's Federal employees.

NOTE: As enacted, H.R. 13871, approved September 7, 1974, is Public Law 93–416 (88 Stat. 1143).

64

Statement on the Resignation of J. F. terHorst as Press Secretary to the President. *September 8, 1974*

I DEEPLY regret Jerry terHorst's resignation. I understand his position. I appreciate the fact that good people will differ with me on this very difficult decision. However, it is my judgment that it is in the best interest of our country. I think Jerry did an outstanding job in a controversial period of transition. I thank him for his service.

NOTE: The statement was issued by the White House.

Regarding his decision to resign as a result of the President's pardon of Richard Nixon, news accounts quoted Mr. terHorst as saying, "It was simply after a great deal of soul-searching that I decided I couldn't in good conscience support the President's decision on former President Nixon, even though I knew he took that action in good conscience."

65

Remarks to the Sixth International Conference on Urban Transportation, Pittsburgh, Pennsylvania. *September 9, 1974*

Will Rockwell, Senators Scott and Schweiker, my former colleagues in the House of Representatives, Governor Shapp, Mayor Flaherty, distinguished local officials, ladies and gentlemen:

It is a very great privilege and an exceedingly high honor for me to participate in this conference on urban transportation, and I am especially grateful to be participating here in the Golden Triangle in the area where the city of Pittsburgh has done so much in the field of urban transportation.

And may I also express my appreciation for the Secretary of Transportation, Mr. Claude Brinegar, and Mr. Russell Train of the Environmental Protection Agency for joining me on this trip on this occasion.

I am told that some people in Europe heard about my nomination of Governor Rockefeller and concluded that we had solved our transportation problems in America. The Europeans said that we now have a combination of a Ford, who makes automobiles, and a Rockefeller, who makes gasoline.

In any event, you are international authorities on—all of you are international authorities on urban transportation. You know better than I that we have too many automobiles at the wrong place and at the wrong time, and not enough gasoline at the right place at the right time.

So, it is essential that you in this conference proceed, move ahead with the problems that you see and the problems that must be solved.

Even though I am not in the transportation business, I am dedicated to the revival of efficient transportation in our great urban centers here in the United States. Pittsburgh, where we are meeting, in the Golden Triangle, has done an effective and efficient job, and I compliment the citizens and public officials who have made this possible.

Your theme of this conference—"Marketing Urban Renaissance"—is appropriate, appropriate not only for those of us in America but, I think, worldwide. And all of our cities obviously will be observing the work, the recommendations, the proposals that come from this conference.

The relationship between urban regeneration and urban transportation is extremely close. Among our most pressing urban problems—and your presence here highlights it—is transportation, especially the automobile. For the last 25 years, two decades and a half, automobiles have been the most important factor in shaping urban centers and expanding suburbs. The statisticians tell me that there are some 100 million automobiles on nearly 4 million miles of American streets and highways. That makes one automobile for every two Americans, and most of those 100 million cars are in our way when any one of us tries to go downtown.

Many Americans have moved to suburbs where there is less and less traffic. My wife Betty and I can vouch for the very restful suburban life, and we picked it for reasons that most Americans select it. We raised our family in Alexandria, Virginia, just outside of Washington, D.C., and on a personal note, I miss it, especially my backyard swimming pool.

In the last two decades, suburban population grew far faster than our central city population. And in some instances, the population growth in our suburbs resulted in an actual numerical decline in our central cities. Americans, as a result, by the millions on a day-to-day basis, drive to and from work. Most took the road or the highway or the street, approximately at the same time of day as everybody else. Frankly, I admire the fortitude and the driving skill of the millions of Americans who are on time going to work without police and Secret Service escorts. And may I thank the Governor and the mayor for the State and local police in Pittsburgh for their fine courtesy and efficiency this morning.

I am sure everyone, everyone here especially, along with thousands, or literally millions of other Americans have been caught in rush-hour traffic jams. I know I have for a number of years while serving in the House of Representatives and living in Alexandria. Sitting in bumper-to-bumper traffic has become a way of life to far too many Americans.

As a Congressman, I was in New York City about 10 years ago, and I asked a New York City policeman the best way to get to Brooklyn, and he was very blunt in his answer. "Buddy," he said, "the best way to get to Brooklyn is to be born there." [*Laughter*]

Obviously, America must have better solutions. That is what this conference is all about. Solutions must be found for the growing problems of congestion and pollution, challenges now complicated very severely by our energy conservation.

As a Michigander with the name of Ford, you can be sure I am not going to say anything unkind about automobiles. But it is self-evident that excessive use of cars in dense urban areas increases pollution levels, causes unbelievable traffic jams, massive headaches, and bumper-to-bumper tie-ups which burn too much scarce and expensive fuel.

I think last winter's serious energy crisis drove home a message to our fellow Americans. The net result is we must make major progress in improving urban transit. We must move promptly, we must have a well-planned, a well-coordinated action, an action program.

Priorities at the local level must be very carefully laid out. If there is to be a renaissance of urban transportation, that renaissance must be built on solid, defendable concepts.

We must, in this conference, address ourselves to the high priority need for action to halt the decline which has developed over the past decade in existing or traditional urban transit systems. And time is of the essence.

Progress, fortunately, is being made. The approximately 750 separate capital grants, totaling more than $3 billion since 1970, which the Federal Urban Mass Transportation Administration made to our cities to buy buses and to add urban and commuter rail systems has certainly helped.

It was encouraging, I think, to find that mass transit ridership in the United States this past year has risen above last year's level. And I think it should be even more encouraging, this is the first time such an increase has taken place since the end of World War II.

Our Nation has to develop urban mass transit systems that people want to use. Until we develop those systems that offer convenience, comfort, and reliability expected from the automobiles that Americans have been traditionally using, transit service, even in our most congested urban areas, will continue to be underused.

That is why I believe this conference, with its accent on transit marketing, is exactly on the right target.

We know that most Americans for a wide variety of reasons have simply not bought the concept of public transit. Unlike the appealing and heavily used mass transit of cities like London, Paris, Montreal, Munich, and Moscow, public transportation in America is considered by most of our fellow Americans as a painful last resort.

There is a terrible reluctance to go from what they were brought up to use, to something that is new and different. There has to be something extra if we are going to achieve a viable mass transit system in most of our urban metropolitan areas.

But let's take a look, or a leaf, I should say, from the book of the automotive industry. They have done quite well with the product that they have promoted in our country. We must compete with the automakers in the effective promotion of products, in their imagination, enterprise, and marketing skills.

I don't think there is a group of men and women better qualified to carry out that mission than all of you here today. But I quickly add, I don't minimize the challenge that you are faced with.

Now, as we move to improve our transit systems, we must not lose sight of one very important fact: The automobile is and will continue to be our chief transportation vehicle. The automobile fits America's traditional lifestyle.

No matter how plush the bus, no matter how comfortable the train, Americans, to one degree or another, will continue to drive their automobiles. The car will be with us for a long, long time to come.

But what we must do is to learn how best to live with them in the urban scene. We have to develop, to achieve the end that you seek, and we must have, we must develop and come forth with sound planning procedures, transit programs, and policies that are sufficiently flexible to match the diversity of our many, many cities.

I think diversity of the community is the key, and it does require some flexibility in our planning for an adequate, usable, desirable transit system.

Because of this diversity, there is no one best transit solution that will fit all of our cities. Some are better suited for bus systems, others for subways, fixed guideway systems, or for a combination of such services.

And in developing these systems, long-term considerations require that transportation and land-use planning be closely coordinated. And this, of course, can only be done, in my judgment, wisely and well at the local level.

There is a legitimate and major role to be played by the Federal Government in assisting urban mass transit systems. But I emphasize here that role must be carried out in complete and total partnership with States and localities. The heavy hand of the Federal Government must not be the dictator that tells how Pittsburgh or other communities should utilize their systems or the funding.

Obviously, we will help with urban planning, although under the new better communities legislation recently approved, local planning and decisionmaking will be controlling.

The Federal Government will assist with important technological development, yet it should be clearly understood that the chief objective of the Department of Transportation grant programs is to help cities solve their transportation problems. It is not a program primarily aimed at the restructuring and rebuilding of our cities in America.

Federal assistance, as I see it, must be primarily directed at finding cost-efficient solutions to the problem of moving people. It must only secondarily be viewed as a means to stimulate urban area economic growth or to increase central-city density.

Federal taxpayers just can't afford to pay for the whole package, and I won't ask them to do so.

Washington, obviously, has to help with the funding, but that funding must have realistic restraints. This is especially true as the Congress, Members of the House and the Senate, join with the White House as inflation fighters in a policy of fiscal responsibility. Investments in local mass transit systems must have reasonable cost-to-benefit ratios or relationships. The House-passed Federal Mass Transit Act of 1974 proposes an $11 billion spread over a 6-year period and, I add emphatically, an absolute upper dollar limit.

In addition, I have a problem with the program structure in the House bill and its treatment of Federal operating assistance for public transit. A committee of the Senate will be considering a transit bill whose program structure is similar to the Administration's transit proposal. I am confident that this problem, or this conflict between the House and Senate versions, can be overcome in a House and Senate conference.

It is probably known to many here, I have opposed in the past transit operating subsidies, particularly out of the Highway Trust Fund, because of my strong belief that such a program would lead to the Federal Government in the local day-to-day transit operating matters. And also, I have learned, from my experience with other Federal categorical grant programs for operating expenses, that these funds often do not result in better or more service. Instead, they simply result in greater cost and less efficiency.

It is my conclusion, however, that our current inflexible urban mass transit grant program encourages States, encourages cities to adopt what you can call capital-intensive solutions, such as subways, as a response to their transportation problems.

Accordingly, as a compromise for my own long, deeply held previous convictions, I am supporting some limited Federal operating assistance such as the proposal I mentioned a few moments ago, submitted in February and currently being considered by the Senate.

I recognize that this change will allow a limited portion of Federal urban transit funds to be used for operating expenses as an integral part of a comprehensive transit program and as a result, primarily, of decisions by local and State officials.

The key here, therefore, is that Federal officials are not involved in the capital operating tradeoff. Local officials will make that decision.

And although the operating assistance provisions of the House bill do not meet these standards, the Senate will have, and I hope does, correct this deficiency, and I trust the final version will contain that specific provision.

I am convinced that with enough imagination, with enough determination, with enough flexibility, and with careful ordering of your local priorities, we can achieve our national transportation goals. I am determined to do so without further feeding the fires of inflation or busting the Federal budget.

Let me leave you with one final thought. From the early days of this Nation, we have been a mobile people. We have carved canals out of the countryside to carry our commerce. We journeyed west following the only roadmaps we knew, the wagon ruts of those who had gone before.

Today, with modern methods of movement, we have achieved miracles of mobility in America and in many, many parts of the world. But we have to maintain and expand the avenues of movement for all Americans, young and old, rich and poor.

The wheels of this Nation cannot stop turning, whether they are on cars or trucks or buses or trains or planes. If we are to continue to be a great nation, and I think we will, as Americans we must move forward together in the future.

With your dedicated, inspired efforts here this week, I think you can contribute very significantly to make this journey a memorable one in the years ahead.

Thank you very much.

NOTE: The President spoke at 11:35 a.m. at the Pittsburgh Hilton Hotel. In his opening remarks, the President referred to Willard F. Rockwell, Jr., general conference chairman.

66

Remarks of Welcome to Prime Minister Yitzhak Rabin of Israel. *September 10, 1974*

Mr. Prime Minister and Mrs. Rabin:

It is a very real pleasure for me to have the opportunity of welcoming both of you to the United States.

You are returning as the leader of a great country. You are returning to meet many of your friends over the years that you knew so well during your service here as Ambassador to the United States.

I trust that you and Mrs. Rabin will thoroughly enjoy this visit back to the United States.

The United States, Mr. Prime Minister, has been proud of its association with the State of Israel. We shall continue to stand with Israel. We are committed to Israel's survival and security.

The United States for a quarter of a century has had an excellent relationship with the State of Israel. We have cooperated in many, many fields—in your security, in the well-being of the Middle East, and in leading what we all hope is a lasting peace throughout the world.

Many of our people have a close personal relationship and association with your citizens, your fellow citizens in Israel, and we hope and trust that this relationship will grow and expand.

Over the last few months, there has been movement in the Middle East for a lasting and durable peace. Israel has cooperated; Israel has been helpful. And we hope and trust that in the months ahead, the foundation which has been laid will be built upon.

We want, you want, and others throughout the world want a lasting and durable peace in the Middle East.

The first steps have been taken; others will follow. And I am certain and positive that, as we meet here during the next several days, we can contribute to the building of a better and finer peace in the Middle East.

I hope that you and Mrs. Rabin will have a delightful and warm welcome, which you so richly deserve, in the United States.

NOTE: The President spoke at 3:10 p.m. on the South Lawn at the White House where Prime Minister Rabin was given a formal welcome with full military honors. Prime Minister Rabin responded as follows:

Mr. President, Mrs. Ford, I am grateful to you for your kind invitation to come to Washington and for your warm words of welcome.

As you know, Mr. President, I am not a complete stranger in this country nor, indeed, in this city. But this is the first time that I come here in my capacity of Prime Minister of Israel.

You, Mr. President, have very recently undertaken new and awesome responsibilities, and I feel certain, therefore, that you can appreciate the weighty load that rests on my shoulders.

I represent a country which is faced—which is facing manifold problems, great challenges, but also great and new opportunities for internal progress and for peace with her neighbors.

In the performance of my new duties, I am encouraged, as all my predecessors have been, by their binding friendship and by the ever-deepening ties which bind the people of Israel with the people of this, the greatest democracy, and with its leaders.

Ever since the renewal of Jewish independence in the land of our forefathers, after long generations of suffering and martyrdom, Israel has enjoyed generous aid and support on the part of the United States. Our gratitude for this sustenance will be recorded forever in the annals of our people.

During all these times since 1948, Israel has seen periods of trials and hardships. Yet she never swerved, even for a moment, from her supreme national goal, which is the quest for peace with her Arab neighbors.

So far, to our nation's deep sorrow, this goal has eluded us. Despite the recent test of arms, Israel is prepared to continue to seek progress towards peace.

We have in recent months demonstrated that we have taken risks for peace to see whether new efforts may possibly bring us nearer to its achievement.

I know, in this quest for peace in our region, we have in you, Mr. President, and in your colleagues in the Government of the United States, a strong and determined partner.

Indeed, you, Mr. President, pronounced the commitment of the United States to the quest of world peace as the central theme in your inaugural address only a few weeks ago.

The people of Israel stand united in the conviction that war is futile, that it cannot solve problems, that only human suffering is brought in its wake. As far as our part of the world is concerned, we are convinced that there is no issue, however complicated it may now appear, that it cannot be resolved by patient negotiations.

What is needed is an equal measure of desire and determination on all sides to achieve peace.

Much depends at this stage on what other governments in the area are prepared to do. At any rate, we in Israel are ready for the peacemaking effort.

I must, however, with a full sense of responsibility, add this: As you, Mr. President, assumed high office you conveyed to your people and to the world the message that a strong America is a paramount guarantee for peace in the world. This is true in the same measure as far as Israel and her own region are concerned. Only a strong Israel which has the capacity to deter aggression and to defend herself successfully by her own strengths, has a chance of winning peace.

I cannot underline strongly enough our conviction that the constant maintenance of Israel's strength is an absolute prerequisite for the attainment of solutions to the problems of our troubled region.

On these and other matters of common interest and concern, I shall be exchanging views with you, Mr. President, and your colleagues, within the next few days. I look forward to doing so in the spirit of confidence and of the cultivation of a good future which has linked our governments and our people for so many years.

I am confident that I shall return to Jerusalem assured of the United States' determination to support the well-being of Israel within a Middle East that we hope that will finally be advancing on the road towards a just and durable peace which assures security and progress for all its people.

Thank you very much.

67

Remarks to the Conference on Inflation. *September 11, 1974*

LET ME at the outset wish you all a good morning and to express my deep appreciation for your attendance at this very important and very critical meeting.

Naturally, I am very pleased to have in attendance the distinguished Members of the House and the Senate—both Democratic as well as Republican—and I am especially pleased to see so many outstanding labor leaders in the United States. And I warmly welcome each and every one of you.

Obviously, we have gathered here to deal with inflation and the immediate danger that is threatening every American, young and old, poor and well-to-do.

It is a very critical issue. I think the future of labor union members and all other Americans depends upon what we can achieve together in this campaign against inflation. And I wish to reemphasize my appreciation for your participation.

Some of you have generously accepted an additional burden by agreeing to participate in such other meetings. By so doing, you have indicated that you share with me the conviction that inflation is the most critical national domestic issue facing the United States.

I am grateful for your willingness to work together with me on a problem that transcends America's many special interests, whether Republican or Democratic, labor or business, urban or rural.

I think it also goes beyond any divisions based on age, sex, race, color, or creed.

The enlistment of trade unionists in the war against inflation is consistent with the patriotic involvement of American labor in every great challenge that our Nation has faced. Without the productive dedication of American labor, World War II might have ended very differently.

Labor built America, and labor is America. Together we must now preserve and enhance the economic base of our existence from everybody's enemy, the scourge of inflation. I have described it as public enemy number one in America, and it might be expanded actually to say that it is a worldwide problem.

We need your advice and we need your guidance on this issue of such overwhelming concern to all your members. I want your ideas on steps which can help the individual as well as the Nation.

Today's meeting is a part of the series that culminates in the [summit] Conference on Inflation on September 27 and 28. Since this is only a 1-day session, let's get directly to the point. Let's dispense with formality. Let's be frank. Let us also try to keep our comments brief and specifically on target.

I should say that the meeting we held last week with 28 outstanding economists was, by all standards, a success.

I must confess I was dubious that we could get that many divergent economists together and have them come up with a superb performance, which they did, and I am confident in this room we can have the same constructive results.

I will certainly welcome, however, any detailed statement that anyone wishes to make in the form of a written proposal, and please submit these directly to me, if you will, within the next several days. This will give us adequate time to consider them before the conclusion of the designated time frame.

You are aware of the severity of inflation although inflation is unfortunately no novelty in our economic history.

Its present form is the worst we have experienced in 27 years. Consumer prices are increasing at an unacceptable annual rate of 11 percent. Statistics alone are inadequate to describe the inflation in human terms; cold and impersonal numbers and percentages cannot describe the impact on individuals' lives.

While everyone is hit by inflation, some obviously are hit much harder. I am thinking of families in the low- and moderate-income levels, of older people who are struggling, trying to live on modest incomes, or young people whose initial experience with the employment scene may not generate real confidence in our economic system. These are very real human problems which must guide the actions of Government as well as the decisions in the private sector.

Government has a particular obligation to act responsibly, and we will. We will make a concerted effort to cut the budget and reduce our expenditures to show our willingness to sacrifice. But we shall wield our budgetary knife ever so carefully so as not to sacrifice the meat while trimming the fat.

Within our general budgetary restraint, we shall be mindful of the need to increase what we allocate to the essential, while we decrease what we apportion to programs which are to some extent discretionary.

We also must exercise care to prevent our recently overheated economy from cooling off too rapidly. We must, at all costs, avoid a damaging recession.

We are now making a cooperative effort, in response to the initiative of the distinguished majority leader of the United States Senate and other Members of the Congress, on a bipartisan basis. The legislative and executive branches are working together, and this is evidenced by the people who are here from both political parties to seek short-term answers to short-term problems and long-term answers to long-term problems.

In May 1973, the Administration requested enactment of the job security assistance act. This proposal is an important part of our policy to assist in a period of rising unemployment. It would modernize the unemployment compensation system without violating the relationship between the States and the Federal Government.

I recognize the concern of many that unemployment might rise because of the policies we must follow to fight inflation. I am watching the unemployment rate very, very closely. This Administration, as I said the other day, will act with compassion. We will not permit the burden of necessary economic restraint to fall on those members of society least able to bear the cost.

The unemployment rate in August, announced last Friday, was 5.4 percent. But we certainly cannot be complacent about any American lacking work. The present situation calls for full use of currently available tools and dollars. As a consequence, I have instructed the Department of Labor to accelerate the obligation of currently available funds under the Comprehensive Employment and Training Act [CETA].

The Secretary of Labor will immediately disburse $65 million to those communities in which unemployment is at the highest level. By the end of the month, he will make available another $350 million under the CETA title II program. This $415 million will finance some 85,000 public sector jobs in State and local governments.

Added to the almost $550 million obligated for public service employment in June from the FY 1974 appropriation, and about $50 million in prime sponsorship under CETA title I as allocated for this purpose, currently available resources will provide approximately 170,000 public service jobs this coming winter.

The effect of these actions, based on the tools and the dollars we have, will be to double the number of federally funded public service jobs. In addition, $1.3 billion will be available to State and local governments for manpower programs.

Beyond this, drawing on the outcome of the Conference on Inflation, and your suggestions, we will develop contingency plans against the possibility that unemployment might give evidence of rising to substantially higher levels.

If the employment statistics demonstrate the need in the future, we will be ready to present such plans to the Congress and work together to assure a mutually satisfactory course of action before the end of this session.

To the leaders of our labor organizations and to the captains of industry, I make a sincere appeal for restraint. It must be a self-imposed restraint. As I have said before, there will be no controls imposed on wages and prices, as far as I am concerned. Settlements at the bargaining table are the sole responsibility of the participants, so long as they respect the public interest.

We need your help today, not merely for my Administration but for the whole Nation. I hope this discussion will not only be productive of ideas to preserve the American dollar but will demonstrate that in a time of crisis we remain a nation united.

With those opening observations and comments, I would like to move now to some observations and comments.

First, I would like to call on my friend [AFL–CIO president] George Meany, who will make his comments.

NOTE: The President spoke at 9:47 a.m. in the East Room at the White House. His remarks and both the morning and afternoon sessions of the conference were broadcast live on public television.

At the conclusion of the morning session of the meeting, the President hosted a luncheon for the participants in the State Dining Room.

68

Statement on Presidential Clemency and Pardons. *September 11, 1974*

THE ANNOUNCEMENT yesterday by Mr. Hushen concerning study of the entire matter of Presidential clemency and pardons was prompted by inquiries to the White House Press Office concerning Mrs. John Dean's reported statement in reference to pardoning of her husband and similar public statements on behalf of others.

Such a study is, of course, made for any request concerning pardon of an individual.

However, no inference should be drawn as to the outcome of such study in any case. Nor is my pardon of the former President, under the unique circumstances stated by me in granting it, related to any other case which is or may be under study.

NOTE: The statement was read by Senator Hugh Scott at the White House at a news briefing by Senator Scott and Representative John J. Rhodes following the President's first meeting with the Republican Congressional leadership.

The statement refers to Deputy Press Secretary John W. Hushen's answer to a reporter's question at his news conference at the White House on September 10, 1974. The exchange follows:

"Q. Mrs. Dean is now talking about a pardon for John Dean; what is the President's feeling about pardon for any of the other people involved in the whole Watergate thing?

"MR. HUSHEN. I am authorized to say that that entire matter is now under study."

69

Remarks at Pope Air Force Base, North Carolina. *September 11, 1974*

THANK YOU very, very much for coming out in such great numbers. I am very, very grateful.

It is a particular pleasure to be here in the great State of North Carolina. It is a pleasure to be—or have come down with me, Senator Jesse Helms, and it is always nice to see an old friend of mine like Congressman Earl Ruth, who I knew a long, long time ago back in the days when both he and I were in the Navy. I guess that is not a good thing to say here with all of you. [*Laughter*]

As a matter of fact, I got to know Congressman Ruth when we were both stationed here in the Navy over at Chapel Hill. So, I spent a bit of my military career in Chapel Hill before going to sea with the Navy.

It is nice to be in North Carolina because I have had the privilege and pleasure of knowing so many, many good people from this State.

But in addition—and this is the main point I would like to make—this air base, which is so vitally important, is not one that just belongs to the State of North Carolina but it belongs to all of us.

I come from the State of Michigan. We are as proud as all of the North Carolinians are of Pope Air Force Base and the people who are here, and Fort Bragg and the others.

We feel that the contribution made by the Defense Department—the 2,200,000, roughly, men and women in the Army, Navy, Air Force, and Marines, the people who are civilians and work for the Defense Department are an extremely vital part of our security and the security of the free world.

And when we talk about security today, we are talking not only about security from attack but we are talking about a deterrence against war. And one major part of my service in the Presidency is to be sure that the Defense Department is strong enough to deter war and to protect our great country from any aggression.

I know there are people who think that we can slash the money for the Army, the Navy, the Air Force, Marines, and spend money for other programs. I don't think we can hurt our military establishment without hurting our security.

And so, to the extent that I have any influence, I am going to make sure that we have adequate funding for the weapons system, research and development, operations and maintenance, personnel, so that all of you feel that the service you are performing is with the best of equipment, in the best of environment, and for the best interests of every one of 211 million Americans.

Thank you very, very much.

NOTE: The President spoke at 1:47 p.m.

70

Remarks at a Ceremony Opening the World Golf Hall of Fame in Pinehurst, North Carolina. *September 11, 1974*

Honored inductees, Governor Jim Holshouser, Lieutenant Governor Hunt, ladies and gentlemen:

Back in late July of this year, I participated in the induction ceremonies for four or five professional football players in Canton, Ohio, at their Hall of Fame.

It was a little more logical for me to participate in that even though I was never good enough on the gridiron to play professional football, but I did play at the University of Michigan and coached at Yale, and it was a very important part of my life for a substantial part of my youth.

Shortly after that, I got a letter of invitation, while I was still the first instant Vice President, to come and participate in these ceremonies. Well, I think my record is clear. I have no background that would justify my professional appearance here, but I thought maybe by coming, it would be helpful to me to get a little rub-off from some of the people who are inductees and others who are participating.

I can only say, regardless of which sport, I think, whether it is golf, professional or college football, or any one of the other wonderful athletic areas of competition, so much is added to America's society by the things that you learn and the things that you do.

So, I am always a willing participant in anything that involves athletics. I think it is great and wholesome, not only for the United States but the world.

And, naturally, I wish to compliment and congratulate Don and Bill [1] and those who had the vision and the foresight. I am sure you realize what a thrill it is for a weekend golfer like myself to walk the same fairways today with Byron Nelson, Gene Sarazen, Ben Hogan, Sam Snead, Arnold Palmer, Jack Nicklaus, Gary Player, Patty Berg.

I always have idols in athletics, and I don't apologize for it now. These are the kind of idols that I think are good and wholesome for America.

And then, of course, there are the immortals who are not here today. They are here in spirit: Walter Hagen, Harry Vardon, Francis Ouimet, Babe Didrikson Zaharias, and that great statesman of golf, of course, Bobby Jones.

I think it is fair to say that there is another great golfer who I know is actually watching us here today. He wasn't a professional, but his love for golf was profound, and I think he did as much as any man in this century to make golf one of the world's number one participant sports. And I, of course, on this occasion refer to Ike Eisenhower.

Ike would be deeply honored that some of his golfing gear is to be included in the World Golf Hall of Fame here in Pinehurst.

As President Eisenhower knew so very well, golf is a very special game, and it is not hard to understand its popularity. Fortunately, golf is a game that crosses all borders and is played in virtually every country in the world.

Today we are dedicating the World Golf Hall of Fame, and I think the word "world" is vitally important.

This is an international event, and participating with my good friend, Jim Holshouser, who has proclaimed the "Grand Week of Golf," are, of course, athletes from all over the world. The list is long, and I won't read it at the present time.

I think Americans sometimes lose sight of the fact that many things we value most have been bequeathed to us by other nations. Golf, for instance, has a cen-

[1] Donald C. Collett, president, and William H. Maurer, board chairman, World Golf Hall of Fame.

turies-old history and is just as popular in scores of other countries throughout the world. And I think that is why history's most spectacular chip shot struck such a responsive chord among people in so many nations. No one will ever forget that moment when Alan Shepard, swinging his homemade six-iron, lofted a ball off the surface of the Moon.

That was a great chip shot for all mankind. [*Laughter*]

And in conclusion, let me say, we made it to the Moon because of a technology built upon the knowledge and the discoveries by all the nations of the Earth. We made it to the Moon because of the shared experiences of the human race.

And that chip shot symbolized all that in one of the most natural languages shared by all—the language of golf.

Congratulations to the inductees and thank you all for being here.

NOTE: The President spoke at 3:28 p.m.

71

Remarks at a Dinner Honoring Inductees Into the World Golf Hall of Fame. *September 11, 1974*

Thank you very, very much Governor Jim Holshouser, my good golfing partner, the Governor of South [*North*] *Carolina, Senator Jesse Helms, my old friend Earl Ruth:*

But I do wish to acknowledge and pay special tribute to the inductees who I tremendously admire and greatly respect. And I have really enjoyed listening to the stories that each of them have given. And it is an awfully hard act to follow after the tales they have told and the incidents that they have related.

It has always been one of the great things that I have admired—excellence. And I have spent a great deal of time in the last few years on Saturday afternoons and Sunday afternoons watching various tournaments.

I usually take with me—and sit in front of the television and take a pile of work, and in between this shot and that shot, I try to concentrate. But I really am more interested in the excellence that they demonstrate to the American people. I admire excellence. I respect it.

And it seems to me that this is what we want in this country and what we want in the world. And to be here this afternoon and this evening, and to get better acquainted with those I have known, and to meet others that I have not known in the sport of golf has been a great and an exhilarating day for me.

And I compliment and congratulate every one of them because they epitomize excellence in probably one of the most competitive areas of athletic competition that I have ever seen.

And I just hope that they, through their example, give to all Americans the kind of spirit, the kind of drive, the kind of dedication that is so essential if we are to achieve what is the best for everybody in this country and throughout the world.

If I may, I would like to tell you the most memorable golfing experience I ever had. I was at the Burning Tree course, which is one of those courses in Washington, D.C. I was playing with Ben Hogan, and Arnold Palmer, and Byron Nelson. And they came up to me, and they said they were looking for another great, great golfer to join them. I said, "Well, here I am." And they said, "Good. Can you help us look for one?" [*Laughter*]

I didn't mind that so much, but what really hurt me was when Arnold Palmer asked if I would not wear his slacks except under an assumed name. [*Laughter*]

I do appreciate the honor of the invitation from Don and Bill, but as I stand before all of you golfing immortals, one thought keeps running through my mind. I have an 18 handicap, and I guess I played it that way today in between the first and 18th hole. You need me as a good golfer like Sam Snead needs another tomato can. [*Laughter*]

They say you can always tell a good player by the number of people in the gallery. You have heard, and we have all heard, of Arnie's Army.[1] My group is called Ford's Few. [*Laughter*]

I figured it out, that my problem is I have a very wild swing, and I demonstrated it on a number of occasions for Patty [Berg] and some of the others this afternoon. Back on my home course in Grand Rapids, Michigan, they don't yell "Fore," they yell "Ford." [*Laughter*]

And you know, all of these fine Secret Service men you have seen around me today, and elsewhere—when I play golf, I am told they qualify for combat pay. [*Laughter*]

But I try to keep my hand in whenever I can. Personally, I thoroughly enjoy playing golf with Henry Kissinger. Henry is undoubtedly one of the greatest, one of the finest, and one of the very best diplomats the world has ever known, and fortunately for us, he has been carrying out that responsibility on behalf of our country. I will tell you why I say that: Last week, I was in a sand trap, which

[1] Fans of Arnold Palmer.

I frequently find myself in. There was a water hazard beyond that, and then some 95 feet or more to the pin, and Henry conceded the putt. [*Laughter*]

But this afternoon, I had one of the greatest thrills of my lifetime, the chance to play a few holes with the superstars of world golfing, and I thoroughly enjoyed it and they were most considerate of my difficulties.

I can't tell you how I felt out there surrounded by such legendary names as Berg, Hogan, Nelson, Nicklaus, Palmer, Player, Sarazen, Snead. And in all honesty, it was something like being in a golfer's heaven, and I appreciate the opportunity to be there.

But as the cliché goes, tonight I have good news and some bad news. The good news, that four of our honorees—Jack Nicklaus, Arnold Palmer, Gary Player, and Sam Snead—will be competing in the World Open beginning tomorrow.

The bad news is today they shared the course with me. And I will tell you what I mean.

In 1972, I played with Sam Snead in the Pro-Am before the Kemper Open, and he didn't win. In 1973, I played with Miller Barber before the Kemper Open, and he didn't win. And this year, I played with Tom Weiskopf before the Kemper Open, and then I played with Dave Stockton up at Pleasant Valley in the Pro-Am, and neither of them won the tournament.

Now, you know why, I am sure, in Washington I am known as the President of the United States, and in golf I am sort of known as the jinx of the links. [*Laughter*]

Frankly, I figured it out, that Snead, Barber, Weiskopf, and Stockton blew about $165,000 in prize money by their performance with me in the several pro-amateurs that I indicated. But if you think they are unhappy, you should see the Internal Revenue Service. [*Laughter*]

As you undoubtedly know by now, I thoroughly enjoy golf, not only the competition but the people. I enjoy the exercise it provides, the competitive challenge, the good fellowship before and after each game.

But if I had to single out one attribute of golf above all others, it would be found in the very simple statement from the Encyclopaedia Britannica, and I quote: Golf is played on the honor system. A player is expected to count his own strokes even though he may miss the ball completely, to acknowledge the fact promptly if he violates a rule and incurs a penalty, and to avoid interfering in any way with his opponent's or his fellow competitor's play.

Golf is one of the few games where honor is more important than the rules. Without good sportsmanship, golf could not exist. Without trust, another name for good sportsmanship, governments cannot exist.

But there is still one more lesson to be learned from golf. And I have never seen a tournament, regardless of how much money, or how much fame, or prestige, or emotion was ever involved, that didn't end with the victor extending his hand to the vanquished.

I have enjoyed sitting there watching on television the pat on the back, the arm around the shoulder, the praise for what was done right, and the sympathetic nod for what wasn't. These are as much a part of golf as life itself, and I would hope that understanding and reconciliation are not limited to the 19th hole.

Before I leave—and let me express to Don and Bill my great enjoyment to be with all of you—I would like to thank them and you for asking me. It was a delightful day, after a few kind of tough ones.

This afternoon for a few hours, quite unsuccessfully, I tried to make a hole in one. Tomorrow morning I will be back in Washington trying to get out of one. [*Laughter*]

And thank all of you for making this a most welcome "mini" vacation.

Thank you, and good night.

NOTE: The President spoke at 10:35 p.m. at the World Golf Hall of Fame in Pinehurst, N.C.

72

Message to the Congress on Legislative Priorities. *September 12, 1974*

To the Congress of the United States:

In my first address before a Joint Session of Congress, I spoke of "communication, conciliation, compromise and cooperation." The Congress responded. We have communicated, conciliated, compromised, and cooperated.

I thank the bipartisan leaders and all Members for this working partnership. So far, despite some spats, we have had a good marriage.

Landmark bills in the fields of *Education, Housing-Community Development,* and *Pension Reform* were passed. For these examples of cooperation of real benefit to so many Americans, I am grateful.

I had serious objections to the *SBA loan legislation, Public Works Appropriations,* and *D.C. Medical School bill.* Recognizing congressional interest in particular elements of each measure, I signed them.

No effort was made to override measures that I had to veto. Congress responded promptly to my request for a *Council on Wage and Price Stability.*

Of the specific proposals I am singling out today, some are in the conference stage. Others have passed only one body. A few have passed neither. But virtually all have been the subject of hearings and are in the mark-up phase.

Nominations

Of utmost importance for Congress in its fall term is the consideration of *Nelson Rockefeller* as my nominee for Vice President of the United States. The Administration will assist the Congress in all appropriate ways to expedite this nomination. The precedent for this procedure under the 25th Amendment to the Constitution has been established. I am sure there will be no inordinate delay in moving forward Governor Rockefeller's nomination.

There are other nominations before the Senate, some pending since last January. There are other candidates for Federal office in varying stages of clearance. I expect to be able to submit them to the Senate within a few days. I would hope Congress could expedite action on all these nominees so that none will have to be held over to 1975.

Reducing 1975 Spending

Responding to the initiative of the distinguished majority leader of the Senate and other members of the Congress, I have convened bi-partisan summit meetings on the issue of inflation. Many of you are participating. The legislative and executive branches are working together.

We are seeking short-term answers to short-term problems and long-term answers to long-term problems.

A concerted effort must be undertaken to bring spending down to manageable proportions. An important first step in this effort is to bring Federal outlays under control in 1975, making possible a balanced budget in 1976.

I need the help of the Congress in reducing 1975 spending below $300 billion. Several important cooperative steps by the Congress will be required to achieve this difficult target.

First, the Congress must resist temptations to add to spending totals on legislation now being considered. Responsible action calls for agreements on cuts, not increases. I solicit suggestions on any programs that might be curtailed or stopped. Let me know about any spending that seems unnecessary or inflationary.

In the same vein, I would hope the Congress could pass specific legislation proposed in the February Budget submission that would reduce 1975 spending by almost $700 million.

Immediate action should be taken on the rescissions that I am proposing in my first message to the Congress under the newly-enacted *Budget and Impoundment Control Act.* Moreover, the deferrals transmitted to Congress under the same Act should be supported. Overturning these actions could increase spending by as much as $600 million in 1975 and by far more in 1976 and future years.

As a matter of highest priority, I need your support of my recommendation to defer the next *Federal pay raise* from October to January. It will be my intention to deal fairly with the just concerns of Federal workers. But I am asking them to join in the sacrifice I want all Americans to share. This action will reduce 1975 outlays by $700 million. It will also set an example of wage restraint for the private sector. Let us practice what we preach.

These efforts are essential if our cooperation is to keep spending under $300 billion. We simply cannot afford to fail.

Appropriations

Eight of fourteen regular appropriations bills have been enacted. These measures in total represent a reduction of $532 million from the Administration's Budget in spending authority and $144 million in outlays for the current fiscal year. These are helpful moves in the right direction. I urge that this momentum be maintained.

There are seven money bills that require action during the balance of the session.

The *Agriculture* money bill was vetoed on the basis of excessive funding; the *Defense* appropriation is in conference with very sharp reductions. Levels below the House bill would be extremely unwise. *State-Justice-Commerce* is also in conference and undoubtedly will show a reduction in the Budget; *Labor-HEW* appropriations, however, appear to be moving in the direction of exceeding the Budget substantially.

Appropriations for *Military Construction* and *Foreign Assistance* have not yet passed the House of Representatives.

There is ample time to consider the remaining appropriations bills before adjournment. In addition, I will be sending essential but carefully limited *Supplemental Requests* for fiscal year 1975. I trust they will be considered an urgent priority.

Legislation

It is unnecessary to submit a complete list of Administration legislative initiatives to this Congress. Leaders and Members know them as well as I do. I recognize that the inevitable consequence of any legislative Message in the twilight of the 93rd Congress is to suggest deferment of some desirable legislation in favor of imperatives that are realistic in the time we have left.

The *Trade Reform bill* has passed the House of Representatives but remains pending before the Senate Finance Committee. Efforts are underway to find a reasonable and mutually acceptable compromise to restrictive language that would deny Most Favored Nation status and Export-Import credits to the Soviet Union. I want to emphasize the importance I attach to the granting of Most Favored Nation status to the USSR. Careful attention should also be given to the importance of Title V concerning tariff preferences for developing countries and providing appropriate limits for Trade Adjustment Assistance. This legislation is close to enactment. It would be a tragedy not to pass it.

In the area of foreign policy, Congress should enact the *Export-Import Bank Authorization, Asian and African Development Bank Authorizations,* and the *Foreign Assistance Act.*

I know that a troublesome piece of legislation for me—and perhaps one of the most important for the Nation—is the Foreign Assistance Act. I am disturbed over the deep cuts in many essential and worthwhile programs which contribute to our overall efforts to attain peace and stability in the world. In addition, the bill contains several restrictions on the Executive which would reduce my ability to meet obligations to American security and that of our friends abroad. I respect and strongly support the role of Congress in the area of foreign policy. But under the Constitution, the Executive is the spokesman for the Nation and must have adequate freedom of action. I may recommend changes in our approach to foreign aid in the coming year and will propose realistic programs in the national interest. I strongly urge this Congress to continue the current programs unencumbered by amendments which prevent the effective implementation of policy.

There are several significant problems in the *State Department Authorization.* I have requested Secretary of State Kissinger to work with appropriate leaders in an effort to resolve these differences.

The *USIA Authorization* has been passed by both bodies and should be finally considered by a conference committee. The House version is preferred.

Both bodies have passed an extension of the *Defense Production Act.* I hope the differing versions will be reconciled and sent to me for signature.

To promote more effective management of the Government's approach to our national energy resources, the Administration recommended creation of an *Energy Research and Development Administration.* This key legislation has now passed both Houses and hopefully will soon be considered by a conference committee. In its consideration of this legislation, I recommend to the conference committee that the provision calling for an Energy Policy Council be deleted and several other undesirable provisions be revised in accordance with current discussions.

To increase the availability of clean natural gas through competitive pricing of newly developed gas supplies, I urge this Congress to enact the *Natural Gas Supply bill.* As we enter the winter months, our energy resources must be effectively utilized for the benefit of all Americans. Gas deregulation which would increase supply is a vital part of the Administration's response to the energy shortage.

Of major importance to our ability to provide sufficient energy in the years ahead is a proposal for the Federal Government to grant permits for construction, licensing and operation of *Deepwater Ports* beyond the three-mile limit. The House has passed a bill. Hopefully, the Senate will also move forward on this key measure.

Among the many energy-related bills before Congress, is the important *Energy Tax Package.* This measure imposes a windfall profits tax on the selling price of domestic crude oil, eliminates the percentage depletion deduction for U.S. taxes on foreign production of oil and gas, and limits foreign tax credits available to U.S. oil and gas companies operating in foreign lands.

We learned from the recent oil embargo that we must be better prepared to reduce the impact of any future supply interruptions. At the time of the embargo our Naval petroleum reserves, set aside through the foresight of the Congress for the specific purpose of assuring adequate supplies of essential fuels, could not be used in time to contribute to our national defense requirements.

In a moment of need, oil in the ground is useless. We must have authority to produce and deliver our emergency petroleum reserves to the user. Presently, the *Navy Petroleum Reserves at Elk Hills,* California, have proven reserves of approximately one billion barrels. The *Navy Petroleum Reserves in Alaska,* although unexplored, have estimated reserves of up to 33 billion barrels. I intend to consult with the Congress on the best way to assure that the reserve capacities of these fields are in a state where they can contribute effectively to our national security in any future energy crisis.

The House and Senate conferees are now addressing the difficult issues involved in striking a balance between the environmental effects of surface coal mining under the proposed *Surface Mining Act* and the nation's need for coal as an essential source of energy. This issue has been under consideration throughout this Congress. It would greatly reduce the problem of opening new coal mines and increasing production if acceptable mined area legislation can be enacted. I am asking Secretary of the Interior Morton to continue discussions with legislative leaders in an effort to reach an agreement over troublesome provisions in this measure.

The *Illegal Aliens* legislation is necessary to establish clear guidelines regarding the law for employment of aliens who work in this country. The House has already passed a bill. I would hope the Senate could consider this measure during the fall term.

Real progress was made on the House floor when the Conference report on the *Veterans Education Bill* was substantially reduced in terms of Federal expenditures. I hope the Senate will now act in the same spirit. This can be done by reducing the benefit limit to the original Senate bill. It provided a substantial increase—18.2 percent. But cost-of-living increases for our veterans in school are necessary. I urge the Senate to reaffirm its original rate increase and send the bill to me so benefits can begin.

In May of 1973, the Administration proposed the *Job Security Assistance Act.* This measure is an important part of our policy to assist in a period of rising unemployment. It would modernize the unemployment compensation system without violating the relationship between the States and the Federal government.

I recognize the concern of many that unemployment might rise because of the policies we must follow to fight inflation.

I am watching the unemployment rate very closely. This Administration will act with compassion. We will not permit the burden of necessary economic restraint to fall on those members of society least able to bear the costs.

The unemployment rate in August, announced last Friday, was 5.4 percent. While we certainly cannot be complacent about any American lacking work, we are thankful that the number is not larger.

The present situation calls for full use of available tools and dollars.

I have asked Secretary of Labor Brennan to accelerate the obligation of currently available funds under the *Comprehensive Employment and Training Act.*

The Secretary will immediately disperse $65 million to those communities in which unemployment is highest. By the end of the month he will make available another $350 million under CETA Title II. This $415 million will finance some 85,000 public sector jobs in State and local governments. Added to the almost $550 million obligated for public service employment in June from the FY 1974 appropriation, and about $50 million in other funds, currently available resources will provide 170,000 public service jobs this coming winter. The effect of these actions will be to double the number of federally funded public service jobs. In addition, $1.3 billion will be available to State and local governments for manpower programs.

Beyond this, I have requested the Secretary of Labor, in consultation with my economic advisors, and drawing on the outcome of the Conference on Inflation, to develop contingency plans against the possibility of substantially increased unemployment. If future unemployment statistics demonstrate the need, we will be ready to present plans to the Congress and to work together to assure a mutually satisfactory course of action.

There are several health authorizations that require extension this year. They are the *Health Manpower Act, Health Services Act* and the *Health Resources Planning Act.* All are necessary but, unfortunately, each currently has objectionable features in program provisions and excessive authorizations. I have requested Secretary of Health, Education, and Welfare Weinberger to cooperate fully with appropriate committees in an effort to enact reasonable legislation. I will continue to seek a sound compromise on the *Comprehensive Health Insurance Plan.*

The House recently passed the *Federal Mass Transportation Act.* While the funding was kept to a level which I can support, certain structural changes in that bill are necessary. I am asking Secretary of Transportation Brinegar to work closely with the Senate in an effort to develop an acceptable bill.

The Administration's proposal to improve the *regulatory climate in the surface transportation industry* is presently before the Congress. This bill, with certain modifications to ensure greater reliance on competitive market forces, would contribute substantially to the efficiency and vitality of this Nation's private sector transportation system. I urge the Congress to act promptly to complete its work on this important legislation.

The *Amtrak Authorization* legislation is now ready for Conference. Since major problems exist with the Senate version, I hope the Conference will adhere as closely as possible to the House measure and soon present it for my signature.

I assume the Congress will pass the *Military Construction Authorization bill,* including expansion of the support facility at Diego Garcia.

The *Export Administration Act* is ready for conference action and should be reported soon.

Legislation to restore financial integrity to the *Railroad Retirement system* has not been enacted by either House. I urge legislation be adopted to accomplish this objective without resorting to a subsidy from either the Social Security System or the general taxpayers.

Court congestion impairs fair and speedy trials. The Administration supports legislation to create new *Federal District Court Judgeships*. While this measure has been slow to move, I would hope Congress could expedite consideration in order to alleviate overcrowded court calendars.

A bill to renew my authority to submit *Executive Reorganization Plans* has been sent to the Congress. During the past 25 years all Presidents have used this authority to improve management in the executive branch. I would like my Administration to be able to utilize this effective tool of good government. I urge prompt bipartisan consideration of this bill.

It is apparent that I have referred to some legislative matters and omitted reference to others. This is not an inventory of my total legislative concerns. I will send the traditional message to the Congress in January covering the broad spectrum of legislative programs. This will afford me an interim opportunity for detailed study and review.

The 93rd Congress, in which I am proud to have served, has an opportunity to join with the Executive Branch at this turning point of history. We can respond together in the constructive harmony that ought to exist between Republicans and Democrats, between Federal and local governments, between the Executive and Legislative branches, and between America and other nations. A momentous challenge confronts me as well as the 93rd Congress. Together, we can summon forth the reserves of energy, imagination, and devotion necessary to generate a new and proud era of American achievement. We cannot and will not fail the American people.

GERALD R. FORD

The White House,
September 12, 1974.

73

Message to the Senate Transmitting the United States-Bulgarian Consular Convention. *September 12, 1974*

To the Senate of the United States:

I am pleased to transmit for the Senate's advice and consent to ratification the Consular Convention between the United States of America and the People's

Republic of Bulgaria, with an Agreed Memorandum and a related exchange of letters, signed at Sofia on April 15, 1974. I transmit also, for the information of the Senate, the report of the Department of State with respect to the Convention.

The signing of this Convention is a significant step in the gradual process of improving and broadening the relationship between the United States and Bulgaria. Consular relations between the two countries have not previously been subject to formal agreement. This Convention will establish firm obligations on such important matters as free communication between a citizen and his consul, notification to consular officers of the arrest and detention of their citizens, and permission for visits by consuls to citizens who are under detention.

I welcome the opportunity through this Consular Convention to strengthen the ties between the United States and Bulgaria. I urge the Senate to give the Convention its prompt and favorable consideration.

GERALD R. FORD

The White House,
September 12, 1974.

NOTE: The text of the convention and accompanying papers are printed in Senate Executive H (93d Cong., 2d sess.).

74

Message to the Senate Transmitting the United States-Canadian Treaty on Extradition. *September 12, 1974*

To the Senate of the United States:

With a view to receiving the advice and consent of the Senate to ratification, I transmit herewith the Treaty on Extradition between the United States of America and Canada, signed at Washington on December 3, 1971, as amended by an exchange of notes of June 28 and July 9, 1974.

The Treaty is one of a current series of extradition treaties being negotiated by the United States and contains provisions regarding extradition for the offenses of aircraft hijacking, narcotics and conspiracy to commit listed offenses.

The Treaty will facilitate the mutual efforts of the United States and Canada in combating international crime. In addition, modernization of the extradition relations between the United States and Canada is especially important in light of the ease of travel between the two countries. I recommend that the Senate give early and favorable consideration to the Treaty as amended and give its advice and consent to ratification.

GERALD R. FORD

The White House,
September 12, 1974.

NOTE: The text of the treaty and accompanying papers are printed in Senate Executive G (93d Cong., 2d sess.).

75

Toasts of the President and Prime Minister Rabin of Israel. *September 12, 1974*

Mr. Prime Minister, Mrs. Rabin, and honored guests:

It is a great privilege and honor for Mrs. Ford and myself to be host to the two of you on this occasion and to warmly welcome you back to the United States in this capacity as the Prime Minister of your great country.

But I would also like to extend our warm welcome for all of your friends who are here and the many, many friends throughout the whole United States who are also good and firm friends of the two of you and to extend to you, representing your country, the depth and the warmth of the feeling that we in the United States have for Israel.

As I was sitting here chatting with you and talking to Mrs. Rabin, I couldn't help but note that 1948 was a somewhat significant year as far as your country is concerned, and it just happened that it was quite a year as far as the Fords were concerned. It was the year that we were married——

MRS. RABIN. And the Rabins.

THE PRESIDENT. Oh! [*Laughter*]——and the year that I got elected to Congress but, more importantly, certainly, the year that Israel gained its independence.

And I am pleased to note that our country was the first of all countries in the world at that time to recognize Israel. And we were proud to do it then, and we are proud that it was done by America at that time.

It is especially nice to have the opportunity of meeting with you yesterday, and today, and tonight, tomorrow, a person who is a soldier, a diplomat, and a political leader, and to know that you represent your country so effectively and so well.

The American people have a great deal of understanding and sympathy and dedication to the same kind of ideals that are representative of Israel. And, therefore, I think we in America have a certain rapport and understanding with the people of Israel.

We, as two nations who believe in peace, have sought by joint action in conjunction with others a durable and stable peace in the Middle East which I think all of us agree is in the best interest of your country and the Middle East—the world as a whole.

We, as a country, are proud to be associated with Israel in this mutual effort to move and to continue to move in the direction of an even better, more stable, and more equitable peace in the Middle East.

I can't tell you how pleased that we are to have the opportunity of expressing our gratitude for all of the things that our countries have done together and all of the things that I hope that our two countries can continue to do in the future.

We have mutual aims and objectives. We have a friendship that is durable and growing. We have the kind of relationship that I think, if expanded worldwide, would be beneficial to all mankind.

And so if I may, Mr. Prime Minister, I would like to ask all of our guests here tonight to stand and to offer a toast to your President, and to you and Mrs. Rabin.

To the President.

NOTE: The President spoke at 9:58 p.m. in the State Dining Room at the White House. Prime Minister Rabin responded as follows:

Mr. President, Mrs. Ford, distinguished guests:

In the name of my wife and myself, I would like to thank you very much for inviting us and taking care of us during our visit here.

I remember, Mr. President, meeting you while you were the minority leader in the House. I had many talks then with you; I learned very much to admire you. And I know that by assuming the responsibilities of the President of the United States, you have taken upon yourself tremendous—tremendous role not only for this country but I believe that the President of the United States is the leader of the free world and has to bear in mind, if you would allow me to say so, not only the well-being of this country but the well-being of all countries that strive for freedom, for democracy; because in the world that we live today, it is not always possible to a small country to do it against odds.

The relations between the United States and Israel started many years ago. When our country was reborn we faced many problems. The first one was the absorption of many newcomers, immigrants, the remnants of the holocaust of Europe, the Second World War, the refugees that came from the Arab countries. I believe that we were a country that half of its population were refugees.

And then the United States offered Israel economic aid, technical aid that made it possible to us to absorb these people, our brothers, in a way that the transformation from refugees to be part of our creative society was very much facilitated by your help.

During the years other problems appeared. The threat from outside became more apparent, and the United States added also military aid in terms of supplying us arms to be able to defend ourselves by ourselves.

I think that 26 years from 1948 have proved that your support to us was used in the best way for the well-being of our people and for preservation of a democracy and the free country in that part of the world.

And I would like to thank you, to thank everybody in this country that has made it possible till today.

I don't know, Mr. President, if you have seen it. I have given a small present to you. It is a sculpture, a sculpture that describes the struggle between David and Goliath. I believe it is not only a story from the Bible, it is a story that started then and continues on till the present days.

And if there is something that symbolizes Israel today, it is the spirit of David facing Goliath. And the meaning of the spirit is, on the one hand, to seek peace, to believe in peace. We are a Jewish state, and we believe that part of being a Jew means to seek peace, to search peace, but on the other hand, to realize that peace is attainable only for those who are ready to take risks to dare to withstand Goliaths.

I believe that this is what is significant to Israel today, the spirit of David seeking peace and, at the same time, being ready and capable to meet some Goliaths.

I hope and I believe, Mr. President, that under your leadership the relations between our two countries will continue, will be strengthened in the unique spirit that was so significant till today, the search of peace and the understanding that strength helps to achieve peace.

Allow me, Mr. President, to raise my glass to the President of the United States.

76

Remarks to the Radio and Television Directors' Association Conference. *September 13, 1974*

I WOULD very much rather be giving you this greeting in person than on film. It has been far too long since I have had a chance to meet with you and your organization.

I well remember that 1968 conference in Los Angeles when you asked me to discuss the legislative plans of the newly elected Republican administration. A lot has happened since then.

And unpredictable as the future can be, I can tell you one thing for sure about my new job. To the very best of my ability to make it so, this will be an open Administration, and that means open to all newsmen.

You and your organization can perform a very vital service for those of us in government through your questions and your reports.

We get a wealth of information fed back to us about what people are thinking, what their concerns are, and their hopes and aspirations. And this is even more important to me as President than it has been in the past.

The members of your organization know so well the communities and the people they serve. Over the years I was able to pay particular attention to the work of two of your members, the late Dick Cheverton at WOTV, and that of Jack Hogan at WZZM–TV, both stations in Grand Rapids, Michigan.

Their work and their involvement in the community problems and projects provide eloquent testimony to the dedication of your members.

I believe the news media's concern with community affairs is vitally important. Half jokingly, I have urged Washington correspondents to go back to their hometowns occasionally, for 6 months or so each year, to get reacquainted with what the people are thinking and doing.

By the same token, I suggest it might be profitable for you who work outside Washington to spend a few months in our Capital every so often. We all would benefit from such an exchange of ideas, attitudes, and experiences.

As you may know, most of our White House press staff are experienced journalists. One of them, Bill Roberts, served as president of your organization. I know that to the best of their abilities they will do what they can to help you.

And while some people say that government and the news media are in a sense adversaries, I hope we can always remain friendly adversaries.

I trust your conference will prove stimulating and professionally helpful. I congratulate your president, Tom Frawley, on completion of a successful year, and wish your new president and officers well in meeting and surmounting the challenges and the concerns of the broadcast journalists.

Thank you very much.

NOTE: The President's remarks were recorded for use at the conference in Montreal, Canada, on September 13, 1974.

77

Remarks Announcing a Program for the Return of Vietnam Era Draft Evaders and Military Deserters. *September 16, 1974*

Good morning:

In my first week as President, I asked the Attorney General and the Secretary of Defense to report to me, after consultation with other Governmental officials and private citizens concerned, on the status of those young Americans who have been convicted, charged, investigated, or are still being sought as draft evaders or military deserters.

On August 19, at the national convention of Veterans of Foreign Wars in the city of Chicago, I announced my intention to give these young people a chance to earn their return to the mainstream of American society so that they can, if they choose, contribute, even though belatedly, to the building and the betterment of our country and the world.

I did this for the simple reason that for American fighting men, the long and divisive war in Vietnam has been over for more than a year, and I was determined then, as now, to do everything in my power to bind up the Nation's wounds.

I promised to throw the weight of my Presidency into the scales of justice on the side of leniency and mercy, but I promised also to work within the existing system of military and civilian law and the precedents set by my predecessors who faced similar postwar situations, among them Presidents Abraham Lincoln and Harry S. Truman.

My objective of making future penalties fit the seriousness of each individual's offense and of mitigating punishment already meted out in a spirit of equity has proved an immensely hard and very complicated matter, even more difficult than I knew it would be.

But the agencies of Government concerned and my own staff have worked with me literally night and day in order to develop fair and orderly procedures and completed their work for my final approval over this last weekend.

I do not want to delay another day in resolving the dilemmas of the past, so that we may all get going on the pressing problems of the present. Therefore, I am today signing the necessary Presidential proclamation and Executive orders that will put this plan into effect.

The program provides for administrative disposition of cases involving draft evaders and military deserters not yet convicted or punished. In such cases, 24 months of alternate service will be required, which may be reduced for mitigating circumstances.

The program also deals with cases of those already convicted by a civilian or military court. For the latter purpose, I am establishing a clemency review board of nine distinguished Americans whose duty it will be to assist me in assuring that the Government's forgiveness is extended to applicable cases of prior conviction as equitably and as impartially as is humanly possible.

The primary purpose of this program is the reconciliation of all our people and the restoration of the essential unity of Americans within which honest differences of opinion do not descend to angry discord and mutual problems are not polarized by excessive passion.

My sincere hope is that this is a constructive step toward a calmer and cooler appreciation of our individual rights and responsibilities and our common purpose as a nation whose future is always more important than its past.

At this point, I will sign the proclamation [4313] that I mentioned in my statement, followed by an Executive order [11803] for the establishment of the Clemency Board, followed by the signing of an Executive order [11804] for the Director of Selective Service, who will have a prime responsibility in the handling of the matters involving alternate service.

Thank you very much.

NOTE: The President spoke at 11:21 a.m. in the Cabinet Room at the White House.

78

Proclamation 4313, Announcing a Program for the Return of Vietnam Era Draft Evaders and Military Deserters. *September 16, 1974*

By the President of the United States of America a Proclamation

The United States withdrew the last of its forces from the Republic of Vietnam on March 28, 1973.

In the period of its involvement in armed hostilities in Southeast Asia, the United States suffered great losses. Millions served their country, thousands died in combat, thousands more were wounded, others are still listed as missing in action.

Over a year after the last American combatant had left Vietnam, the status of thousands of our countrymen—convicted, charged, investigated or still sought for violations of the Military Selective Service Act or of the Uniform Code of Military Justice—remains unresolved.

In furtherance of our national commitment to justice and mercy these young Americans should have the chance to contribute a share to the rebuilding of peace among ourselves and with all nations. They should be allowed the opportunity to earn return to their country, their communities, and their families, upon their agreement to a period of alternate service in the national interest, together with an acknowledgement of their allegiance to the country and its Constitution.

Desertion in time of war is a major, serious offense; failure to respond to the country's call for duty is also a serious offense. Reconciliation among our people does not require that these acts be condoned. Yet, reconciliation calls for an act of mercy to bind the Nation's wounds and to heal the scars of divisiveness.

Now, THEREFORE, I, GERALD R. FORD, President of the United States, pursuant to my powers under Article II, Sections 1, 2 and 3 of the Constitution, do hereby proclaim a program to commence immediately to afford reconciliation to Vietnam era draft evaders and military deserters upon the following terms and conditions:

1. *Draft Evaders*—An individual who allegedly unlawfully failed under the Military Selective Service Act or any rule or regulation promulgated thereunder, to register or register on time, to keep the local board informed of his current

address, to report for or submit to preinduction or induction examination, to report for or submit to induction itself, or to report for or submit to, or complete service under Section 6(j) of such Act during the period from August 4, 1964 to March 28, 1973, inclusive, and who has not been adjudged guilty in a trial for such offense, will be relieved of prosecution and punishment for such offense if he:

(i) presents himself to a United States Attorney before January 31, 1975,

(ii) executes an agreement acknowledging his allegiance to the United States and pledging to fulfill a period of alternate service under the auspices of the Director of Selective Service, and

(iii) satisfactorily completes such service.

The alternate service shall promote the national health, safety, or interest. No draft evader will be given the privilege of completing a period of alternate service by service in the Armed Forces.

However, this program will not apply to an individual who is precluded from re-entering the United States under 8 U.S.C. 1182(a)(22) or other law. Additionally, if individuals eligible for this program have other criminal charges outstanding, their participation in the program may be conditioned upon, or postponed until after, final disposition of the other charges has been reached in accordance with law.

The period of service shall be twenty-four months, which may be reduced by the Attorney General because of mitigating circumstances.

2. *Military Deserters*—A member of the armed forces who has been administratively classified as a deserter by reason of unauthorized absence and whose absence commenced during the period from August 4, 1964 to March 28, 1973, inclusive, will be relieved of prosecution and punishment under Articles 85, 86 and 87 of the Uniform Code of Military Justice for such absence and for offenses directly related thereto if before January 31, 1975 he takes an oath of allegiance to the United States and executes an agreement with the Secretary of the Military Department from which he absented himself or for members of the Coast Guard, with the Secretary of Transportation, pledging to fulfill a period of alternate service under the auspices of the Director of Selective Service. The alternate service shall promote the national health, safety, or interest.

The period of service shall be twenty-four months, which may be reduced by the Secretary of the appropriate Military Department, or Secretary of Transportation for members of the Coast Guard, because of mitigating circumstances.

However, if a member of the armed forces has additional outstanding charges pending against him under the Uniform Code of Military Justice, his eligibility to participate in this program may be conditioned upon, or postponed until after, final disposition of the additional charges has been reached in accordance with law.

Each member of the armed forces who elects to seek relief through this program will receive an undesirable discharge. Thereafter, upon satisfactory completion of a period of alternate service prescribed by the Military Department or Department of Transportation, such individual will be entitled to receive, in lieu of his undesirable discharge, a clemency discharge in recognition of his fulfillment of the requirements of the program. Such clemency discharge shall not bestow entitlement to benefits administered by the Veterans Administration.

Procedures of the Military Departments implementing this Proclamation will be in accordance with the guidelines established by the Secretary of Defense, present Military Department regulations notwithstanding.

3. *Presidential Clemency Board*—By Executive Order I have this date established a Presidential Clemency Board which will review the records of individuals within the following categories: (i) those who have been convicted of draft evasion offenses as described above, (ii) those who have received a punitive or undesirable discharge from service in the armed forces for having violated Article 85, 86, or 87 of the Uniform Code of Military Justice between August 4, 1964 and March 28, 1973, or are serving sentences of confinement for such violations. Where appropriate, the Board may recommend that clemency be conditioned upon completion of a period of alternate service. However, if any clemency discharge is recommended, such discharge shall not bestow entitlement to benefits administered by the Veterans Administration.

4. *Alternate Service*—In prescribing the length of alternate service in individual cases, the Attorney General, the Secretary of the appropriate Department, or the Clemency Board shall take into account such honorable service as an individual may have rendered prior to his absence, penalties already paid under law, and such other mitigating factors as may be appropriate to seek equity among those who participate in this program.

IN WITNESS WHEREOF, I have hereunto set my hand this sixteenth day of September in the year of our Lord nineteen hundred seventy-four, and of the Independence of the United States of America the one hundred and ninety-ninth.

GERALD R. FORD

79

Remarks at a Luncheon for Members of the Republican National Committee and Republican National Finance Committee. *September 16, 1974*

Thank you very, very much, Nelson. Mary Louise, Dick, George, Senator Bill Brock, Congressman Bob Michel, members of the National Republican Committee, members of the Finance Committee, and others:

It is really a great privilege and a high honor to have an opportunity of participating with all of you on this fine occasion.

At the outset, let me congratulate Mary Louise on being unanimously selected this morning. That is a lot better than I did before the Congress, and I suspect it might be a little better than what Nelson will do. [*Laughter*]

I also wish to congratulate all of you on the selection of Dick Obenshain. As Nelson said, it reflects in this team the recognition that we wish to give as a political party to the women throughout the country who over the years have done as much, if not more, to make our political system work by working in the grassroots, unselfishly dedicating themselves to the necessary efforts that had to be made the length and the breadth of our country.

And Mary Louise, I am positive, will end up being an outstanding chairman of the Republican National Committee.

We have been a long time working on trying to make the Republican Party a viable, effective party in all 50 States. When I came to the Congress 26 years ago, the Republican Party was practically prohibited from having an impact politically in a number of our States in the South.

Patiently, constructively, and effectively, today the Republican Party is viable. It is constructive in every one of our 50 States. And the Republican Party can only expand and broaden that total effort by making certain that the voices in that area of our country are heard, and heard at the highest level.

And in Dick Obenshain we have a man who will represent that overall viewpoint and represent it well, as he has in the State of Virginia, where now we have a second Republican Governor elected, one after another, where we now have more Republican Congressmen on our side of the aisle than the opposition does on their side of the aisle.

We want this kind of effort made in every State, and Mary Louise and Dick, in my judgment, make that kind of a team.

But let me say, speaking of a team, I believe that Nelson Rockefeller and myself will make a good team, reflecting your views and the views of the Republicans and Independents and, I trust, a good many Democrats, in trying to head the executive branch of the Government.

At the time that I made the announcement of Nelson's selection, I said I picked a strong man for a tough job. And I am even more convinced today that his selection is in the best interests of this country, and he will be a great person.

The Governor is going to be given plenty of work to do politically, within the executive branch of the Government, in the field of domestic as well as foreign policy, and it is a pleasure for me to see the way it has all worked so far, and I am sure that this team will do the best job we possibly can in the months ahead, primarily for the country but also reflecting our political philosophy.

May I say also that the White House at the present time has in my judgment one of the finest members of the White House team to concentrate exclusively on the problems relating to politics. Dean Burch, a Counsellor with Cabinet status, is in charge of the White House political activities and relationships.

A former chairman of the national committee, an outstanding and long-dedicated Republican, a person who performed superbly on the Federal Communications Commission—I think we are lucky to have Dean, and if you have any political problems, talk to Dean. He has an open door to my office and always will.

Dean has an assistant, one of you from the Republican National Committee, and here I speak of Gwen Anderson, who was my political adviser while I was Vice President.

So again, in Dean, from the great State of Arizona, and Gwen, from the great State of Washington—they make a broad and effective Republican organization, operating in the White House.

Now, we all hate to say goodby to George Bush, our new U.S. representative to the People's Republic of China. George, as all of you know, was a hard campaigner when he was first campaigning for the House of Representatives. He served extremely well in the House. He was a strong representative of our Government at the United Nations. He has been, I think, an excellent national chairman in a most difficult time.

And so, with all that background, with all the wonderful personality and talent that he has, along with Barbara, our country will be extremely well represented in the People's Republic of China, and I just know they will enjoy it and do an extremely good job for all of us in that great responsibility.

A few months ago, when Ray Bliss [1] asked me to come out to make a speech in Chicago to a regional gathering of Republicans, I went and made some remarks that I won't dwell on this morning, but I would like to say that what I said there is the criteria by which we will meet the campaign problems of 1976. The campaign will be in the hands of the Republican National Committee.

But that is all I am going to say about 1976, because we have a more important job in 1974.

A few months ago there were dire predictions about the fate of the Republican candidates from Governor down through local offices, from candidates for the United States Senate, candidates for the House of Representatives in the Federal Congress.

I can remember some great predictions by some of our adversaries who said we were going to have a net loss of 100 or a net loss of 50, and there was great glee on the part of some of our adversaries that they were going to have a veto-proof Congress.

Well, we took on that challenge, and we pointed out what a veto-proof Congress would mean. It would mean a Congress that would spend more and more—and I repeatedly alerted people around the country that if we had a veto-proof Congress, they better tighten their seatbelts because they were going right through the sky in spending. They backed off from that, and we on the other side have coined, I think, a better campaign slogan, because it involves our number one public enemy domestically: inflation.

What we want to elect to Congress—Senators and Members of the House—is an *inflation-proof* Congress, and we will get it with Republican candidates.

And I am quite frank to tell you that those Members of Congress who support our efforts to win the battle against inflation will get my wholehearted endorsement.

But we need strong and tall candidates who will stand up and fight the battle of inflation in fiscal policy and in any other of those policies that involve saving this country from the ravages of inflation.

So, urge your incumbents who are running for reelection, urge your candidates who are seeking the high office of the Congress, to campaign, to vote for economy, for strength in our battle against inflation.

You can have a big impact. Your influence can be significant. And we have got some tough votes coming up right soon in the Senate and in the House. Let

---

[1] Ray C. Bliss, chairman of the Republican National Committee 1965–69.

them hear from you, that you want them to vote for economy, to hold down the lid.

And if we win some of these battles—and I hope we can—with the help of Republicans, the help of a necessary number of Democrats, then I think we will have defeated our public enemy number one.

But there are some other issues which I think we can affirmatively talk about. We can honestly say that we have turned a great deal of the power that was accumulating in Washington away and sent it back to our local units of government, to our States.

We have revenue sharing. It is a most important part of New Federalism. I can remember 5, 6, 7 years ago, maybe longer, talking to Nelson Rockefeller when he was Governor, working with him when he was active in the Governors' Conference.

I can recall vividly working with Bill Brock and Bob Michel and other Members of the Congress on trying to get the Congress to undertake a general revenue sharing program.

It is now law. It is about halfway through. Approximately $16 billion of Federal money has gone back to States and local units of government so that they can establish at the local or State level that priorities that vary from New York to California, or Michigan to Florida, or communities in one State or another, have totally different problems.

And this vast amount of Federal money going without restriction for decisionmaking at the local and State level, I think, is a great achievement for a Republican administration. And this Administration is going to continue it.

We want the legislation extended so that this effort will get even stronger in the months ahead.

So, I think we can take credit as Republicans for a program that is very meaningful and very substantial. But there are other things that have to be done, and they involve the area of foreign policy.

I always said and I believed then that America and the world was fortunate to have a great statesman in Henry Kissinger as our Secretary of State. And I have learned to an even greater degree how effective, how able, what a great teammate he is as he and I work on the problems involving peace throughout the world.

We have peace at the present time. We have peace for several reasons. One, we have peace because the United States is strong militarily. And we are not going to weaken our national security, despite the pressure from some sources.

Peace is related to strength. Weakness inevitably brings on war. History tells us that story.

In the interim while we are keeping strong, we are going to make conscientious efforts to negotiate with the Soviet Union, broadening our détente, seeking to make our total effort one of negotiation, not necessarily confrontation.

We are going to be working intimately with the problems of the Middle East, trying to move forward the successful efforts of disengagement which took place last fall.

We will concentrate in seeking to obtain a just and durable peace in that very difficult area of the world, but that is not the only area where we must concentrate. The Pacific, where over a period of about 10 years almost 60,000 Americans lost their lives—that was a great sacrifice, a sacrifice for an objective that many administrations, not just one, felt was in the best interests of the United States and the world at large.

We cannot afford to throw away the sacrifices of those people. So, we must maintain our own strength and help our allies who are trying to retain the gains that were made in Vietnam and elsewhere in the Pacific.

We have the problem of Western Europe. The key to peace in the minds of many is the strengthening of NATO. We are working to keep better cooperation, stronger military and economic policies moving ahead.

I am encouraged, and we are going to be meeting from time to time, Secretary Kissinger and others, with those who can have a meaningful impact on the NATO organization, keeping it strong militarily, economically, diplomatically, and otherwise.

When you look at the other areas—Latin America, we are not going to neglect Latin America. We are going to work for greater cooperation there, and the activities of Dr. Kissinger in this area in the last 5 or 6 months have been significant.

We are not going to neglect Africa. We have and we will continue to work with those nations in that area of the world.

So anyplace you go, our broad policy of global peace will get our first and top attention, because if we are going to keep peace, we can solve more easily our problems at home.

As I close, let me just thank all of you for the wonderful job you did in endorsing Mary Louise and Dick. Let me thank George for his tireless efforts, effective ones, and let me thank the Republican leadership in the House, Hugh Scott, John Rhodes, and their associates, and let me express to my staff that have been so helpful to me that I am grateful, and we are moving, and we are going to move with the Republican workers throughout the country. It is vital for us to carry our banner high, because I think we can do a great job for the country as a whole.

Thank you very kindly.

NOTE: The President spoke at 12:13 p.m. at the Mayflower Hotel. Earlier in the day, the President held a breakfast meeting with members of the nominating committee of the Republican National Committee at the White House.

Prior to the luncheon, members of the Republican National Committee had elected Mary Louise Smith chairman, and Mrs. Smith had appointed Richard D. Obenshain cochairman.

Senator Bill Brock was chairman of the Republican Senatorial Campaign Committee, and Representative Robert H. Michel was chairman of the National Republican Congressional Committee.

80

The President's News Conference of *September 16, 1974*

THE PRESIDENT. Ladies and gentlemen, this press conference is being held at a time when many Americans are observing the Jewish religious New Year. It begins a period of self-examination and reconciliation. In opening this press conference, I am mindful that the spirit of this holy day has a meaning for all Americans.

In examining one's deeds of the last year and in assuming responsibility for past actions and personal decisions, one can reach a point of growth and change. The purpose of looking back is to go forward with a new and enlightened dedication to our highest values.

The record of the past year does not have to be endlessly relived, but can be transformed by commitment to new insights and new actions in the year to come.

Ladies and gentlemen, I am ready for your questions.

Mr. Cormier [Frank Cormier, Associated Press].

QUESTIONS

PARDON FOR FORMER PRESIDENT NIXON

[1.] Q. Mr. President, some Congressional Republicans who have talked to you have hinted that you may have had a secret reason for granting President Nixon a pardon sooner than you indicated you would at the last news conference, and I wonder if you could tell us what that reason was?

THE PRESIDENT. At the outset, let me say I had no secret reason, and I don't recall telling any Republican that I had such a reason.

Let me review quickly, if I might, the things that transpired following the last news conference.

As many of you know, I answered two, maybe three, questions concerning a pardon at that time. On return to the office, I felt that I had to have my counsel undertake a thorough examination as to what my right of pardon was under the Constitution. I also felt that it was very important that I find out what legal actions, if any, were contemplated by the Special Prosecutor.

That information was found out, and it was indicated to me that the possibility exists, the very real possibility, that the [former] President would be charged with obstructing justice and 10 other possible criminal actions.

In addition, I asked my general counsel to find out, if he could, how long such criminal proceedings would take, from the indictment, the carrying on of the trial, et cetera. And I was informed that this would take a year, maybe somewhat longer, for the whole process to go through.

I also asked my counsel to find out whether or not, under decisions of the judicial system, a fair trial could be given to the former President.

After I got that information, which took 2 or 3 days, I then began to evaluate, in my own mind, whether or not I should take the action which I subsequently did.

Miss Thomas [Helen Thomas, United Press International].

Q. Throughout your Vice Presidency, you said that you didn't believe that former President Nixon had ever committed an impeachable offense. Is that still your belief, or do you believe that his acceptance of a pardon implies his guilt or is an admission of guilt?

THE PRESIDENT. The fact that 38 members of the House Committee on the Judiciary, Democrat and Republican, have unanimously agreed in the report that was filed that the former President was guilty of an impeachable offense, I think, is very persuasive evidence.

And the second question, I don't——

Q. Was it an admission of guilt?

THE PRESIDENT. Was the acceptance of the pardon by the President an admission of guilt? The acceptance of a pardon, I think, can be construed by many, if not all, as an admission of guilt.

Yes, Mr. Nessen [Ron Nessen, NBC News].

Q. What reports have you received on Mr. Nixon's health, and what effect, if any, did this have on your decision to pardon him now?

THE PRESIDENT. I have asked Dr. Lukash, who is the head physician in the White House, to keep me posted in proper channels as to the former President's health. I have been informed on a routine day-to-day basis, but I don't think I am at liberty to give any information as to those reports that I have received.

You also asked what impact did the President's health have on my decision. I think it is well known that just before I gave my statement, at the time that I gave the pardon, I personally wrote in a phrase "the threat to the President's health."

The main concern that I had at the time I made the decision was to heal the wounds throughout the United States. For a period of 18 months or longer, we had had turmoil and divisiveness in the American society. At the same time, the United States had major problems, both at home and abroad, that needed the maximum personal attention of the President and many others in the Government.

It seemed to me that as long as this divisiveness continued, this turmoil existed, caused by the charges and countercharges, the responsible people in the Government could not give their total attention to the problems that we had to solve at home and abroad.

And the net result was I was more anxious to heal the Nation—that was the top priority. And I felt then, and I feel now, that the action I took will do that. I couldn't be oblivious, however, to news accounts that I had concerning the President's health, but the major reason for the action I took related to the effort to reconcile divisions in our country and to heal the wounds that had festered far too long.

Q. Mr. President, after you had told us that you were going to allow the legal process to go on before you decided whether to pardon him, why did you decide on Sunday morning, abruptly, to pardon President Nixon?

THE PRESIDENT. I didn't decide abruptly. I explained a moment ago the process that I went through subsequent to the last press conference. And when I had assembled all of that information that came to me through my counsel, I then most carefully analyzed the situation in the country, and I decided that we could not afford in America an extended period of continued turmoil. And the fact that the trial and all of the parts thereof would have lasted a year, perhaps more, with the continuation of the divisions in America, I felt that I should take the action that I did promptly and effectively.

FORMER PRESIDENT'S TAPES AND DOCUMENTS

[2.] Q. Mr. President, I would like to ask you a question about the decision relating to custody of the Nixon tapes and documents. Considering the enormous interest that the Special Prosecutor's office had in those documents for further investigation, I am wondering why the negotiations with Mr. Nixon's representatives were conducted strictly between the counsel in your office without bringing in discussions with either Mr. Jaworski's representatives or those from the Justice Department?

THE PRESIDENT. In the first place, I did receive a memorandum, or legal opinion, from the Department of Justice which indicated that in the opinion of the Department of Justice, the documents, tapes—the ownership of them—were in the hands of the former President.[1] And historically, that has been the case for all Presidents.

Now, the negotiations for the handling of the tapes and documents were undertaken and consummated by my staff and the staff of the former President. I believe that they have been properly preserved, and they will be available under subpoena for any criminal proceeding. Now, the Special Prosecutor's staff has indicated some concern. I am saying tonight that my staff is working with the Special Prosecutor's staff to try and alleviate any concerns that they have. I hope a satisfactory arrangement can be worked out.

PREVIOUS STATEMENTS ON PARDON

[3.] Q. Mr. President, during your confirmation hearings as Vice President, you said that you did not think that the country would stand for a President to pardon his predecessor. Has your mind changed about such public opinion?

THE PRESIDENT. In those hearings before the Senate Committee on Rules and Administration, I was asked a hypothetical question. And in answer to that hypothetical question, I responded by saying that I did not think the American people would stand for such an action.

Now that I am in the White House and don't have to answer hypothetical questions but have to deal with reality, it was my judgment, after analyzing all

[1] In a news briefing held on September 8, 1974, Counsel to the President Philip W. Buchen announced, in regard to the status of the Presidential materials of Richard Nixon, that Attorney General William B. Saxbe had determined that "such materials are the present property of Mr. Nixon; however, it is also concluded that during the time the materials remain in the custody of the United States, they are subject to subpoenas and court orders directed to any official who controls that custody."

The texts of the Attorney General's legal opinion, dated September 6, 1974, and a September 6 letter of agreement between Mr. Nixon and Administrator of General Services Arthur F. Sampson concerning control of and access to Mr. Nixon's Presidential materials, were released by the White House September 8. They are printed in the Weekly Compilation of Presidential Documents (vol. 10, pp. 1104 and 1105).

of the facts, that it was in the best interest of the United States for me to take the action that I did.

I think if you will reread what I said in answer to that hypothetical question, I did not say I wouldn't. I simply said that under the way the question was phrased, the American people would object.

But I am absolutely convinced, when dealing with reality in this very, very difficult situation, that I made the right decision in an effort—an honest, conscientious effort—to end the divisions and the turmoil in the United States.

Mr. Lisagor [Peter Lisagor, Chicago Daily News].

SAFEGUARDING OF TAPES AND DOCUMENTS

[4.] Q. Mr. President, is there any safeguard in the tapes agreement that was made with Mr. Nixon, first, with their destruction in the event anything happens to him, because under the agreement they will be destroyed, and secondly, should not the tapes be kept in the White House until the Special Prosecutor has finished dealing with them?

THE PRESIDENT. The tapes and the documents are still in our possession, and we are, as I said a moment ago, working with the Special Prosecutor's office to alleviate any concerns they have as to their disposition and their availability.

The agreement as to destruction is quite clear-cut. As long as Mr. Nixon is alive and during the period of time that is set forth, they are available for subpoena by a court involving any criminal proceedings. I think this is a necessary requirement for the protection of evidence for any such action.

THE CIA AND CHILE

[5.] Q. Mr. President, recent Congressional testimony has indicated that the CIA, under the direction of a committee headed by Dr. Kissinger, attempted to destabilize the Government of Chile under former President Allende.

Is it the policy of your Administration to attempt to destabilize the governments of other democracies?

THE PRESIDENT. Let me answer in general. I think this is a very important question.

Our Government, like other governments, does take certain actions in the intelligence field to help implement foreign policy and protect national security. I am informed reliably that Communist nations spend vastly more money than we do for the same kind of purposes.

Now, in this particular case, as I understand it—and there is no doubt in my mind—our Government had no involvement whatsoever in the Allende coup.

To my knowledge, nobody has charged that. The facts are we had no involvement in any way whatsoever in the coup itself.

In a period of time, 3 or 4 years ago, there was an effort being made by the Allende government to destroy opposition news media, both the writing press as well as the electronic press, and to destroy opposition political parties.

The effort that was made in this case was to help and assist the preservation of opposition newspapers and electronic media and to preserve opposition political parties.

I think this is in the best interest of the people in Chile and, certainly, in our best interest.

Now, may I add one further comment.

The 40 Committee was established in 1948. It has been in existence under Presidents since that time. That Committee reviews every covert operation undertaken by our Government, and that information is relayed to the responsible Congressional committees where it is reviewed by House and Senate committees.

It seems to me that the 40 Committee should continue in existence, and I am going to meet with the responsible Congressional committees to see whether or not they want any changes in the review process so that the Congress, as well as the President, are fully informed and are fully included in the operations for any such action.

Mr. Sperling [Godfrey Sperling, Jr., Christian Science Monitor].

FURTHER QUESTIONS ON PARDON DECISION

[6.] Q. In view of public reaction, do you think that the Nixon pardon really served to bind up the Nation's wounds? I wonder if you would assess public reaction to that move.

THE PRESIDENT. I must say that the decision has created more antagonism than I anticipated. But as I look over the long haul with a trial, or several trials, of a former President, criminal trials, the possibility of a former President being in the dock, so to speak, and the divisions that would have existed not just for a limited period of time but for a long period of time, it seems to me that when I had the choice between that possibility and the possibility of taking direct action hoping to conclude it, I am still convinced, despite the public reaction so far, that the decision I made was the right one.

Q. Mr. President, in regard to the pardon, you talk about the realities of the situation. Now those realities, rightly or wrongly, include a good many people who speculate about whether or not there is some sort of arrangement—they even, some of them, call it a deal—between you and the former President, or between your staff and his staff—resignation in exchange for a full pardon.

The question is: Is there or was there, to your knowledge, any kind of understanding about this?

THE PRESIDENT. There was no understanding, no deal between me and the former President, nor between my staff and the staff of the former President, none whatsoever.

ACCESS TO INCOME TAX RETURNS

[7.] Q. Mr. President, sir, there is a bill that the Treasury Department has put forward, I think it is about 38 pages. Under this bill, which deals with getting hold of the returns, Internal Revenue returns, of citizens of the country, you could take action to get those returns whenever you wanted to.

I wonder if you are aware of this and if you feel that you need to get those returns of citizens?

THE PRESIDENT. It is my understanding that a President has, by tradition and practice and by law, the right to have access to income tax returns. I personally think that is something that should be kept very closely held. A person's income tax return is a very precious thing to that individual, and therefore, I am about to issue an Executive order [11805] that makes it even more restrictive as to how those returns can be handled. And I do think that a proposed piece of legislation that is coming to me and subsequently will be submitted, as I recollect, to the Congress would also greatly tighten up the availability or accessibility of income tax returns. I think they should be closely held, and I can assure you that they will be most judiciously handled as far as I am concerned.

OWNERSHIP OF PRESIDENTIAL PAPERS

[8.] Q. Mr. President, looking beyond the Nixon papers and in view of some criticism in Congress, do you believe we may have now reached the point where Presidential White House papers should remain in the Government's hands as the property of the Government?

THE PRESIDENT. As far as I am personally concerned, I can see a legitimate reason for Presidential papers remaining the property of the Government. In my own case, I made a decision some years ago to turn over all of my Congressional papers, all of my Vice Presidential papers, to the University of Michigan archives.

As far as I am concerned, whether they go to the archives for use or whether they stay the possession of the Government, I don't think it makes too much difference. I have no desire, personally, to retain whatever papers come out of my Administration.

Mr. Mollenhoff [Clark R. Mollenhoff, Des Moines Register and Tribune].

THE PARDON DECISION

[9.] Q. Mr. President, at the last press conference you said, "The code of ethics that will be followed will be the example that I set." Do you find any conflicts of interest in the decision to grant a sweeping pardon to your life-long friend and your financial benefactor with no consultation for advice and judgment for the legal fallout?

THE PRESIDENT. The decision to grant a pardon to Mr. Nixon was made primarily, as I have expressed, for the purpose of trying to heal the wounds throughout the country between Americans on one side of the issue or the other. Mr. Nixon nominated me for the office of Vice President. I was confirmed overwhelmingly in the House as well as in the Senate. Every action I have taken, Mr. Mollenhoff, is predicated on my conscience without any concern or consideration as to favor as far as I am concerned.

CONDITIONAL AMNESTY AND THE PARDON DECISION

[10.] Q. If your intention was to heal the wounds of the Nation, sir, why did you grant only a conditional amnesty to the Vietnam war draft evaders while granting a full pardon to President Nixon?

THE PRESIDENT. The only connection between those two cases is the effort that I made in the one to heal the wounds involving the charges against Mr. Nixon and my honest and conscientious effort to heal the wounds for those who had deserted military service or dodged the draft. That is the only connection between the two.

In one case, you have a President who was forced to resign because of circumstances involving his Administration, and he has been shamed and disgraced by that resignation. In the case of the draft dodgers and Army and military deserters, we are trying to heal the wounds by the action that I took with the signing of the proclamation this morning.

REPORTS ON WATERGATE INVESTIGATION

[11.] Q. Mr. President, another concern that has been voiced around the country since the pardon is that the judicial process as it finally unwinds may not write the definitive chapter on Watergate and perhaps with particular regard to Mr. Nixon's particular involvement, however total, however it may have been in truth. My question is, would you consider appointing a special commission with extraordinary powers to look into all of the evidentiary material and to write that chapter and not leave it to later history?

THE PRESIDENT. Well, it seems to me as I look at what has been done, I think you find a mass of evidence that has been accumulated. In the first instance, you have the very intensive investigation conducted by the House Committee on the Judiciary. It was a very well-conducted investigation. It came up with volumes of information.

In addition, the Special Prosecutor's office under Mr. Jaworski has conducted an intensive investigation and the Special Prosecutor's office will issue a report at the conclusion of their responsibilities that I think will probably make additional information available to the American people.

And thirdly, as the various criminal trials proceed in the months ahead, there obviously will be additional information made available to the American people. So, when you see what has been done and what undoubtedly will be done, I think the full story will be made available to the American people.

SUCCESSORS TO GENERAL HAIG AND PRESS SECRETARY TER HORST

[12.] Q. Mr. President, could you give us an idea who will succeed General Haig, and how are you coming on your search for a Press Secretary?

THE PRESIDENT. Do I have a lot of candidates here? [*Laughter*] No shows. [*Laughter*]

I have several people in mind to replace General Haig, but I have made no decision on that. It was just announced today that the NATO countries have accepted him as the officer handling those responsibilities.[2]

I think he is to take office succeeding General Goodpaster on December 15. He assumes his responsibilities as the head of U.S. military forces November 1. In the next few days undoubtedly I will make the decision as to the individual to succeed him.

As far as the Press Secretary is concerned, we are actively working on that, and we hope to have an announcement in a relatively short period of time.

THE FORMER PRESIDENT'S HEALTH

[13.] Q. Mr. President, prior to your deciding to pardon Mr. Nixon, did you have, apart from those reports, any information either from associates of the President or from his family or from any other source about his health, about his medical condition?

---

[2] The President's nomination of Gen. Alexander M. Haig, Jr., to be Supreme Allied Commander, Europe, was approved by the NATO Defense Planning Committee.

The President. Prior to the decision that I made granting a pardon to Mr. Nixon, I had no other specific information concerning his health other than what I had read in the news media or heard in the news media. I had not gotten any information from any of the Nixon family.

The sole source was what I had read in the news media plus one other fact. On Saturday, before the Sunday, a member of my staff was working with me on the several decisions I had to make. He was, from my staff, the one who had been in negotiations on Friday with the President and his staff. At the conclusion of some decisions that were made, I asked him, how did the President look, and he reported to me his observations.

But other than what I had read or heard and this particular incident, I had no precise information concerning the President's health.

Yes, Mr. Joyce [Thomas H. Joyce, Newsweek Magazine].

POSSIBILITY OF A DEPRESSION

[14.] Q. Mr. President, your own economic advisers are suggesting—say the economy is very bad and they're very pessimistic—we are hearing the word "depression" used now. I wonder how you feel about whether we are heading for a depression?

The President. Let me say very strongly that the United States is not going to have a depression. The overall economy of the United States is strong. Employment is still high. We do have the problem of inflation. We do have related problems, and we are going to come up with some answers that I hope will solve those problems.

We are not going to have a depression. We are going to work to make sure that our economy improves in the months ahead.

FOOD AID POLICY

[15.] Q. Mr. President ,in the face of massive food shortages and the prospects of significant starvation, will the United States be able to significantly increase its food aid to foreign countries, and what is our position going to be at the Rome conference on participation in the world grain reserves?

The President. Within the next few days a very major decision in this area will be made. I am not at liberty to tell you what the answer will be because it has not been decided.

But it is my hope that the United States for humanitarian purposes will be able to increase its contribution to those nations that have suffered because of drought or any of the other problems related to human needs.

INTELLIGENCE ACTIVITIES AND INTERNATIONAL LAW

[16.] Q. Back to the CIA. Under what international law do we have a right to attempt to destabilize the constitutionally elected government of another country, and does the Soviet Union have a similar right to try to destabilize the Government of Canada, for example, or the United States?

THE PRESIDENT. I am not going to pass judgment on whether it is permitted or authorized under international law. It is a recognized fact that historically, as well as presently, such actions are taken in the best interest of the countries involved.

ADMINISTRATION OPENNESS AND CANDOR

[17.] Q. Mr. President, last month when you assumed the Presidency, you pledged openness and candor. Last week you decided on the ex-President's pardon in virtually total secrecy. Despite all you have said tonight, there would still seem to be some confusion, some contradiction.

My question is this: Are your watchwords of your Administration still openness and candor?

THE PRESIDENT. Without any question, without any reservation. And I think in the one instance that you cite, it was a sole decision, and, believe me, it wasn't easy. And since I was the only one who could make that decision, I thought I had to search my own soul after consulting with a limited number of people. And I did it. And I think in the long run it was the right decision.

MR. CORMIER. Thank you, Mr. President.

NOTE: President Ford's second news conference began at 8 p.m. in the East Room at the White House. It was broadcast live on radio and television.

81

Address to the 29th Session of the General Assembly of the United Nations. *September 18, 1974*

Mr. President, Mr. Secretary General, your Excellencies:

In 1946, President Harry Truman welcomed representatives of 55 nations to the first General Assembly of the United Nations. Since then, every American President has had the great honor of addressing this Assembly.

Today, with pleasure and humility, I take my turn in welcoming you, the distinguished representatives of 138 nations.

When I took office, I told the American people that my remarks would be "just a little straight talk among friends." Straight talk is what I propose here today in the first of my addresses to the representatives of the world.

Next week, Secretary of State Henry Kissinger will present in specifics the overall principles which I will outline in my remarks today. It should be emphatically understood that the Secretary of State has my full support and the unquestioned backing of the American people.

As a party leader in the Congress of the United States, as Vice President, and now as President of the United States of America, I have had the closest working relationship with Secretary of State Kissinger. I have supported and will continue to endorse his many efforts as Secretary of State and in our National Security Council system to build a world of peace.

Since the United Nations was founded, the world has experienced conflicts and threats to peace, but we have avoided the greatest danger—another world war. Today, we have the opportunity to make the remainder of this century an era of peace and cooperation and economic well-being.

The harsh hostilities which once held great powers in their rigid grasp have now begun to moderate. Many of the crises which dominated past General Assemblies are fortunately behind us. And technological progress holds out the hope that one day all men can achieve a decent life.

Nations too often have had no choice but to be either hammer or anvil, to strike or to be struck. Now we have a new opportunity—to forge, in concert with others, a framework of international cooperation. That is the course the United States has chosen for itself.

On behalf of the American people, I renew these basic pledges to you today:

—We are committed to a pursuit of a more peaceful, stable, and cooperative world. While we are determined never to be bested in a test of strength, we will devote our strength to what is best. And in the nuclear era, there is no rational alternative to accords of mutual restraint between the United States and the Soviet Union, two nations which have the power to destroy mankind.

—We will bolster our partnerships with traditional friends in Europe, Asia, and Latin America to meet new challenges in a rapidly changing world. The maintenance of such relationships underpins rather than undercuts the search for peace.

—We will seek out, we will expand our relations with old adversaries. For example, our new rapport with the People's Republic of China best serves the purposes of each nation and the interests of the entire world.

—We will strive to heal old wounds, reopened in recent conflicts in Cyprus, the Middle East, and in Indochina. Peace cannot be imposed from without, but we will do whatever is within our capacity to help achieve it.

—We rededicate ourselves to the search for justice, equality, and freedom. Recent developments in Africa signal the welcome end of colonialism. Behavior appropriate to an era of dependence must give way to the new responsibilities of an era of interdependence.

No single nation, no single group of nations, no single organization can meet all of the challenges before the community of nations. We must act in concert. Progress toward a better world must come through cooperative efforts across the whole range of bilateral and multilateral relations.

America's revolutionary birth and centuries of experience in adjusting democratic government to changing conditions have made Americans practical as well as idealistic. As idealists, we are proud of our role in the founding of the United Nations and in supporting its many accomplishments. As practical people, we are sometimes impatient at what we see as shortcomings.

In my 25 years as a Member of the Congress of the United States, I learned two basic, practical lessons:

First, men of differing political persuasions can find common ground for cooperation. We need not agree on all issues in order to agree on most. Differences of principle, of purpose, of perspective, will not disappear. But neither will our mutual problems disappear unless we are determined to find mutually helpful solutions.

Second, a majority must take into account the proper interest of a minority if the decisions of the majority are to be accepted. We who believe in and live by majority rule must always be alert to the danger of the "tyranny of the majority." Majority rule thrives on the habits of accommodation, moderation, and consideration of the interests of others.

A very stark reality has tempered America's actions for decades and must now temper the actions of all nations. Prevention of full-scale warfare in the nuclear age has become everybody's responsibility. Today's regional conflict must not become tomorrow's world disaster. We must assure by every means at our disposal that local crises are quickly contained and resolved.

The challenge before the United States [Nations] is very clear. This organization can place the weight of the world community on the side of world peace. And this organization can provide impartial forces to maintain the peace.

And at this point I wish to pay tribute on behalf of the American people to the 37 members of the United Nations peacekeeping forces who have given their lives in the Middle East and in Cyprus in the past 10 months, and I convey our deepest sympathies to their loved ones.

Let the quality of our response measure up to the magnitude of the challenge that we face. I pledge to you that America will continue to be constructive, innovative, and responsive to the work of this great body.

The nations in this hall are united by a deep concern for peace. We are united as well by our desire to ensure a better life for all people.

Today, the economy of the world is under unprecedented stress. We need new approaches to international cooperation to respond effectively to the problems that we face. Developing and developed countries, market and nonmarket countries—we are all a part of one interdependent economic system.

The food and oil crises demonstrate the extent of our interdependence. Many developing nations need the food surplus of a few developed nations. And many industrialized nations need the oil production of a few developing nations.

Energy is required to produce food and food to produce energy—and both to provide a decent life for everyone. The problems of food and energy can be resolved on the basis of cooperation, or can, I should say, [be] made unmanageable on the basis of confrontation. Runaway inflation, propelled by food and oil price increases, is an early warning signal to all of us.

Let us not delude ourselves. Failure to cooperate on oil and food and inflation could spell disaster for every nation represented in this room. The United Nations must not and need not allow this to occur. A global strategy for food and energy is urgently required.

The United States believes four principles should guide a global approach:

First, all nations must substantially increase production. Just to maintain the present standards of living the world must almost double its output of food and energy to match the expected increase in the world's population by the end of this century. To meet aspirations for a better life, production will have to expand at a significantly faster rate than population growth.

Second, all nations must seek to achieve a level of prices which not only provides an incentive to producers but which consumers can afford. It should now be clear that the developed nations are not the only countries which demand and receive an adequate return for their goods. But it should also be clear that by confronting consumers with production restrictions, artificial pricing, and the prospect of ultimate bankruptcy, producers will eventually become the victims of their own actions.

Third, all nations must avoid the abuse of man's fundamental needs for the sake of narrow national or bloc advantage. The attempt by any nation to use one commodity for political purposes will inevitably tempt other countries to use their commodities for their own purposes.

Fourth, the nations of the world must assure that the poorest among us are not overwhelmed by rising prices of the imports necessary for their survival. The traditional aid donors and the increasingly wealthy oil producers must join in this effort.

The United States recognizes the special responsibility we bear as the world's largest producer of food. That is why Secretary of State Kissinger proposed from this very podium last year a world food conference to define a global food policy. And that is one reason why we have removed domestic restrictions on food productions in the United States.

It has not been our policy to use food as a political weapon, despite the oil embargo and recent oil prices and production decisions.

It would be tempting for the United States—beset by inflation and soaring energy prices—to turn a deaf ear to external appeals for food assistance, or to respond with internal appeals for export controls. But however difficult our own economic situation, we recognize that the plight of others is worse.

Americans have always responded to human emergencies in the past, and we respond again here today. In response to Secretary General Waldheim's appeal and to help meet the long-term challenge in food, I reiterate: To help developing nations realize their aspirations to grow more of their own food, the United States will substantially increase its assistance to agricultural production programs in other countries.

Next, to ensure that the survival of millions of our fellow men does not depend upon the vagaries of weather, the United States is prepared to join in a worldwide effort to negotiate, establish, and maintain an international system of food reserves. This system will work best if each nation is made responsible for managing the reserves that it will have available.

Finally, to make certain that the more immediate needs for food are met this year, the United States will not only maintain the amount it spends for food shipments to nations in need but it will increase this amount this year.

Thus, the United States is striving to help define and help contribute to a cooperative global policy to meet man's immediate and long-term need for food. We will set forth our comprehensive proposals at the World Food Conference in November.

Now is the time for oil producers to define their conception of a global policy on energy to meet the growing need and to do this without imposing unacceptable burdens on the international monetary and trade system.

A world of economic confrontation cannot be a world of political cooperation. If we fail to satisfy man's fundamental needs for energy and food, we face a threat not just to our aspirations for a better life for all our peoples but to our hopes for a more stable and a more peaceful world. By working together to overcome our common problems, mankind can turn from fear towards hope.

From the time of the founding of the United Nations, America volunteered to help nations in need, frequently as the main benefactor. We were able to do it. We were glad to do it. But as new economic forces alter and reshape today's complex world, no nation can be expected to feed all the world's hungry peoples.

Fortunately, however, many nations are increasingly able to help. And I call on them to join with us as truly united nations in the struggle to produce, to provide more food at lower prices for the hungry and, in general, a better life for the needy of this world.

America will continue to do more than its share. But there are realistic limits to our capacities. There is no limit, however, to our determination to act in concert with other nations to fulfill the vision of the United Nations Charter, to save succeeding generations from the scourge of war, and to promote social progress and better standards, better standards of life in a larger freedom.

Thank you very, very much.

NOTE: The President spoke at 12:15 p.m. at United Nations headquarters in New York City. The address was broadcast live on radio and television.

In his opening remarks, the President referred to Abdelaziz Bouteflika of Algeria, President of the 29th Session of the United Nations General Assembly, and Kurt Waldheim of Austria, Secretary General of the United Nations.

82

Statement Urging the Senate To Sustain the Deferral of a Federal Pay Increase. *September 18, 1974*

I HAVE LABELED inflation fighting as my number one priority. To win will require the cooperation of all branches of Government and all of the American people.

Tomorrow, the Senate will consider a vital part of this effort—my decision to defer a pay increase for Federal employees from October 1974 to January 1975. This deferral will save the American taxpayers $700 million and will help the Federal Government in its campaign to bring inflation under control.

I realize that I am asking Federal employees to make a sacrifice, but now is the time when all of us must set an example of fiscal restraint for the rest of the Nation.

The Senate can do its part by voting to sustain my action on the 3-month Federal pay deferral. I see this vote as the first test of our common effort to put our economic house in order.

This is one of the most significant votes the Congress is being called upon to take in the fight against inflation. I am confident the Senate will act responsibly and in the best interests of all Americans.

83

Statement on the Release of an American Prisoner in Laos. *September 18, 1974*

WITH ALL Americans, I welcomed the news that Mr. Emmet Kay has been released as part of the prisoner exchange in Laos. This release marks a major positive step in carrying out the Vientiane Accords which ended the war in that country last year. We are encouraged by this development and hope it will be followed by other positive steps to achieve peace and reconciliation in Laos.

At the same time, I remain concerned about the many Americans still unaccounted for in Southeast Asia. As Vice President, and during my time in the Congress, I had the opportunity to meet with the families of a number of our missing men. I have the highest regard for the strength and courage these families have shown in the long period since their loved ones were lost.

It has now been more than 18 months since the Paris Agreement on Vietnam was signed in January 1973. In addition to the return of prisoners, that Agreement contained specific provisions on accounting for the missing and the return of the remains of the dead. The record shows that there has been almost no compliance with these humanitarian provisions. Although the Government of North Vietnam returned the remains of 23 American servicemen who died in captivity, there has been no progress on accounting for the missing and no further arrangements for the return of the remains of the dead.

The Communist side has refused to permit searches in areas under their control for crash sites, graves, and other information on the MIA's. We are prepared to carry out such searches by unarmed American teams, and we stand ready to discuss arrangements for the conduct of such searches by teams from neutral countries, the International Red Cross, other humanitarian organizations, or by local authorities. The important thing is that we get on with this job now.

The families of our men have waited too long already, and I am sure that families of those of other nationalities who remain unaccounted for have a similar desire to know the fate of their loved ones. There should be no political or military controversy about this humanitarian problem, and I call for renewed efforts to resolve it.

NOTE: Emmet James Kay, a civilian pilot on contract with the Agency for International Development, was released by the Pathet Lao on September 18, after 16 months of captivity.

84

Remarks at a Meeting of the Washington Press Club. *September 18, 1974*

Thank you very much, Wauhillau, Miriam, Ron, Betty, all of you:

Obviously, it is a great privilege and a great pleasure for me to be here tonight.

When I received the printed invitation for this affair this evening, one phrase in particular caught my attention. It said, "Come honeymoon with us."

You people sure know how to hurt a fellow. [*Laughter*]

As you might imagine, I don't agree with those who have called me the Evel Knievel [1] of politics, but I do think beyond a doubt, beyond a shadow of a doubt, you don't need to have a pool at the White House to get in deep water. [*Laughter*]

Really, I didn't realize how much the honeymoon was over until this morning when the Metro [subway system] started to build a new station in the Oval Office. [*Laughter*]

When I first said yes to being here tonight, I was then Vice President and had a lot more time on my hands. You know, people say a lot of nice things about Vice Presidents. But it is almost like being the best man at a wedding—you never get a chance to prove it. [*Laughter*]

As all of you know, on August 9 I became President, and I wasn't sure that my schedule would allow me enough time to be here with all of you tonight. But then 3 weeks ago, Maggie Hunter—she cornered me at Ron Nessen's Sunday pool party, and who can say no to Maggie Hunter in a bathing suit? [*Laughter*]

And frankly, I am very glad she did ask me, because it is a real pleasure to be here and see so many familiar faces in the audience.

[1] A motorcycle stuntrider.

For instance, I saw, as I came in, my very good friend, Sarah McClendon. Some people say that Sarah is very outspoken. Not by anyone that I know. [*Laughter*]

But anybody in public life is well aware of how important the judgments of the press are. I am firmly convinced that if the good Lord had made the world today, He would have spent 6 days creating the heavens and the Earth and all the living creatures upon it. But on the seventh day, He would not have rested. He would have justified it to Helen Thomas. [*Laughter*]

I also want to say a special hello to all my fellow survivors of Air Force Two who are here tonight, and I see many in the audience. Be honest, now, all of you who flew with me in Air Force Two. Don't you really miss it? This is the only plane that the Air Force has that has to stop for red lights. [*Laughter*]

When Governor Nelson Rockefeller saw this plane, he was really in a state of shock. As a matter of fact, I think he thought about reconsidering the nomination.

He said, "Is this Air Force Two? I have something that goes much faster."

And I said to Nelson, "Is it a jet?"

Nelson said, "No, it is a lawnmower." [*Laughter*]

Before closing, I would like to congratulate the very popular Ron Sarro on the occasion of his being elected to the presidency of the Washington Press Club. I understand that Ron really put his heart and his soul into this campaign. He was even going to set up a campaign organization called "The Committee to Reelect Ron President" until somebody pointed out that is CREEP spelled sideways. [*Laughter*]

But when it comes to a reporter's intuition, and really being ahead of his time, you just can't beat Ron Sarro. Do you know that in 1970—that is quite a while ago—Ron wrote a book called "Are You Safe From Burglars?" [*Laughter*]

I don't know how many people bought it—obviously not enough—but I do deeply appreciate your asking me to be here tonight on this very historic occasion, the inauguration of the first male president of the Washington Press Club.

As one President to another, Ron, I salute you, and I also salute the members of the Washington Press Club for breaking down the barriers of sexual discrimination.

I think all of you know where I stand on this issue. As I prove every morning at breakfast time, I certainly don't believe that a woman's place is in the kitchen. [*Laughter*]

If our country is to survive and to prosper, we need the best efforts of all Americans—men and women—to bring this, I think, proper attitude and atmosphere and results in America.

And besides, as one of the great philosophers once said—and it was Henry A. Kissinger—"Nobody will ever win the battle of the sexes. There is just too much fraternizing with the enemy." [*Laughter*]

Thank you very much.

NOTE: The President spoke at 7:50 p.m. at the Sheraton-Carlton Hotel, prior to administering the oath of office to Ronald A. Sarro, a reporter for the Washington Star-News. In his remarks, the President referred to Wauhillau LaHay, former president of the Washington Press Club, Miriam Ottenberg, chairman of the club's inaugural party committee, and Marjorie Hunter, a reporter for the New York Times.

85

Message to the Senate Transmitting the Protocol to the United States-Soviet Antiballistic Missile Treaty. *September 19, 1974*

To the Senate of the United States:

I transmit herewith the Protocol to the Treaty between the United States of America and the Union of Soviet Socialist Republics on the Limitation of Anti-Ballistic Missile Systems. This Protocol was signed in Moscow on July 3, 1974. I ask the Senate's advice and consent to its ratification.

The provisions of the Protocol are explained in detail in the report of the Department of State which I enclose. The main effect of the Protocol is to limit further the level and potential extent of ABM deployment permitted by the 1972 ABM Treaty. The Protocol furthers fundamental United States objectives set forth in President Nixon's message to the Senate of June 13, 1972 transmitting the Agreements reached at SALT ONE.

The ABM Treaty prohibits the deployment of operational ABM systems or their components except at two deployment areas, one centered on a Party's national capital area and the other in a separate area containing ICBM silo launchers. The Protocol would amend the Treaty to limit each Party to a single ABM deployment area at any one time, which level is consistent with the current level of deployment. However, each side would retain the right to remove its ABM system and the components thereof from their present deployment area and to deploy an ABM system or its components in the alternative deployment area permitted by the ABM Treaty. This right may be exercised only once.

This Protocol represents a further advance in the stabilization of the strategic relationship between the United States and the Soviet Union. It reinforces the ABM Treaty provision that neither Party will establish a nationwide ABM defense or a base for such a defense.

I believe that this Protocol strengthens the ABM Treaty and will, as an integral part of the Treaty, contribute to the reduction of international tension and a more secure and peaceful world in which the security of the United States is fully protected. I strongly recommend that the Senate give it prompt and favorable attention.

GERALD R. FORD

The White House,
September 19, 1974.

NOTE: The text of the protocol and accompanying papers are printed in Senate Executive I (93d Cong., 2d sess.).

86

Message to the Congress Transmitting Annual Report on United States Participation in the United Nations. *September 19, 1974*

To the Congress of the United States:

I am pleased to send to the Congress the 28th annual report on United States participation in the work of the United Nations.

This report, covering Calendar Year 1973, encompasses the wide range of activities carried on by the United Nations and its subsidiary organizations. It demonstrates the growing conviction of United Nations members that many problems of international concern are best resolved through multilateral action, utilizing the machinery of mature international institutions.

In the fall of 1973 the United Nations demonstrated once again its ability to foster peace by the crucial role it played in the Middle East. Following the outbreak of war, the Security Council arranged a ceasefire and deployed United Nations troops to supervise disengagement agreements between Israel and Egypt and, later, between Israel and Syria. We cannot know what might have happened in the absence of such United Nations action. However, it is clear that the efforts of the United Nations, combined with bilateral diplomacy, are still crucial to promoting a just and lasting settlement of the Middle East dispute.

One area of increasing concern is the production and distribution of adequate supplies of food. Our concern with feeding the world can no longer be limited to relief activities in aid of victims of natural disasters. Population growth and better living standards have increased the total demand for food which in turn has increased the demand for energy sources and fertilizer. The pressure of these interlocking demands has pushed against limited supplies and caused spiraling prices. This is a worldwide problem requiring worldwide action for its solution. Secretary Kissinger proposed to the United Nations General Assembly in September 1973 that the organization sponsor a World Food Conference. The General Assembly acted favorably on this proposal and the Conference will be held in Rome in November 1974. The United States also took an active participation in the preparation for the first United Nations Conference on World Population, convened in Bucharest in August 1974.

The Third United Nations Conference on the Law of the Sea, which convened an organizational session in December 1973, is another example of how the United Nations can be utilized to attack contemporary world problems. The goal of the Law of the Sea Conference is a comprehensive international convention to govern man's use of the oceans. We need new understandings to govern international navigation, rational management of the ocean's living and non-living resources, and the protection of the life-sustaining processes of the marine environment. Success in the efforts to resolve conflicting claims over ocean jurisdiction would remove a major and growing source of conflict from the international arena.

The regular economic and social activities of the United Nations' family of organizations continued to absorb over 90 percent of its funds and personnel during 1973. In addition to the traditional operational programs, many special conferences during the year provided opportunities for nations to enlarge their understanding of and work toward consensus on such major international economic and social issues as development assistance, the role of multinational corporations, commodity agreements, and the economic rights and duties of states. Perhaps the most important series of negotiations were those held to carry out the first biennial review and appraisal of the progress toward the goals of the Second United Nations Development Decade. In these negotiations delegations from all parts of the world worked for months to formulate a report that refined the broad measures necessary to improve the world's economic and social situation. The United States played a leading role in these negotiations.

Unfortunately, not all international problems dealt with by the United Nations were successfully approached in 1973. For example, it is generally believed in the United States that terrorism against innocent third parties, including the hijacking of aircraft, is a matter of international concern that calls for international solutions. The divergence of political views among member states, however, has made it impossible to agree on either a general definition of terrorism or a remedy for it. Despite the limit thus placed on the effectiveness of the

United Nations forum in dealing with the problem, a start was made in 1973 with the adoption by the General Assembly of the Convention on the Prevention and Punishment of Crimes Against Internationally Protected Persons, Including Diplomatic Agents. On the other hand, neither the International Conference on Air Law nor the Assembly of the International Civil Aviation Organization, which met simultaneously, made progress on measures to improve security for aircraft passengers.

An important part of the United Nations record in 1973 was the admission to membership of the Federal Republic of Germany, the German Democratic Republic, and The Bahamas—admissions the United States supported. The United Nations has thus become still more representative of the world community.

Our participation in the United Nations reflects our fundamental belief that to assure a peaceful world it is necessary to cooperate with other nations in a multilateral framework on mutually agreed upon activities. This report records the successes and failures, the hopes and frustrations of many of those activities. Above all it records what we tried to accomplish through the United Nations to further the many interests that our citizens and our country share with the world community.

GERALD R. FORD

The White House,
September 19, 1974.

NOTE: The 416-page report is entitled "U.S. Participation in the UN, Report by the President to the Congress for the Year 1974."

87

Statement on Senate Action Disapproving Deferral of a Federal Pay Increase. *September 19, 1974*

WHILE disappointed in today's Senate vote, I am in agreement with the Congress that Federal employees deserve this pay increase. It was painful for me to ask the Congress to defer this raise for 3 months. I know I had asked the Congress to do a difficult thing. But there was a compelling reason. I refer to the inflationary momentum which I regard as domestic public enemy number one. That is why I had requested the Congress and the Federal employees to cooperate.

Now that the Congress has acted, I will proceed to reach a decision as quickly as possible, within the prescribed discretionary limits, on the precise amount of the raise.

The need to reduce Federal spending continues. I sincerely hope that the Congress will join with me in this effort.

88

Remarks at a Reception for Representative Stanford E. Parris in Alexandria, Virginia. *September 19, 1974*

I THINK MOST of you know I was originally scheduled to get together and help Stan, if he thought it might be helpful, before I got this new job and this new responsibility. I wanted to do it then, and I am here now because the Fords lived in Stan's Congressional district a good part of the time in the last several years, and we thought as a constituent of Stan's that he did a first-class job.

We talked with our neighbors. That was their impression, and of course, it fortified my own deep conviction that Stan was an outstanding Member of the Congress.

I had an opportunity to work with him following his swearing in. I was impressed not only with his background when he served all of you so well, I was impressed with Stan's willingness to look at an issue and to decide it on its merits.

He was independent when he thought he was right and I was wrong. It didn't happen too often. [*Laughter*] But when he agreed with me, he was a strong and staunch ally and was very effective in helping to get others to join us in whatever the issue was.

So, on the basis of his experience, on the basis of Stan's willingness to be a real teamplayer, and yet on the respect that I had for him to be independent when he thought it was the right thing to do, I am delighted to be here and to show to all of you and to any others that might be interested that I think Stan Parris has done a great job, and I surely hope he is reelected.

It was a wonderful thing for me to meet, as I came to the door, your fine Governor, Mills Godwin. I said to Mills, when he was campaigning last fall, that I envied the State of Virginia when he was a Democratic Governor because I thought he did a great job. And I was so pleased to contribute to a very minor degree last fall when he was a candidate, because I think he has proven to all of us that the State of Virginia is lucky to have him as a Governor.

I see some of my former House colleagues here. They are the kind of people that, in my judgment, make a good representative in the House of Representatives.

Bob, it is nice to see you. Is anybody else here? Dan? Is Kenny here? Well, those are the kind of people that I think are first-class.

I did see Dick Obenshain, and I think you know how strongly I feel about him. He is our new cochairman of the Republican Party in the United States, and we are fortunate to have Dick joining us in trying to broaden our party's representation on a nationwide basis.

I just would like to conclude by expressing my appreciation for all of you being here to show your support for Stan. Stan is a first-class Member of the House of Representatives, and I am going to rely on him in this session, and I know that he will be back so I can rely on him in the next Congress.

Thank you very, very much.

NOTE: The President spoke at 6:45 p.m. at the Belle Haven Country Club. In his remarks, the President referred to Representatives Robert W. Daniel, Jr., W. C. (Dan) Daniel, and J. Kenneth Robinson.

89

Special Message to the Congress Transmitting Budget Deferrals and Proposed Rescissions. *September 20, 1974*

To the Congress of the United States:

The recently enacted Congressional Budget and Impoundment Control Act of 1974 provides new procedures for executive reporting and congressional review of actions by the executive branch affecting the flow of Federal spending. It thereby serves to make the Congress a full partner in the continuing struggle to keep Federal spending under control.

The new law provides that the executive branch may seek to alter the normal course of spending either through deferrals of spending actions or by asking the Congress to rescind authority to spend. The use of funds may be deferred unless either House of the Congress enacts a resolution requiring that they be made available for spending. For executive rescission proposals to take effect, the Congress must enact rescission bills within 45 days of continuous session.

Following these procedures, I am today reporting the first in a series of deferrals and proposed rescissions.

As is often the case in the institution of new procedures, and in the implementation of new laws, there are questions as to what the law may require of the executive branch and what the Congress may expect. In this instance, the Attorney General has determined that this act applies only to determinations to withhold budget authority which have been made since the law was approved.

However, I am including in today's submission to the Congress reports on some actions which were concluded before the effective date of the act. While these items are not subject, in the Attorney General's opinion, to congressional ratification or disapproval as are those addressed in the recent law, I believe that it is appropriate that I use this occasion to transmit this information to the Congress.

Reasonable men frequently differ on interpretation of law. The law to which this message pertains is no exception. It is particularly important that the executive and legislative branches develop a common understanding as to its operation. Such an understanding is both in keeping with the spirit of partnership implicit in the law and essential for its effective use. As we begin management of the Federal budget under this new statute, I would appreciate further guidance from the Congress. The added information on the status of funds not subject to Congressional action is being made available with this in mind. It will also permit a better understanding of the status of some funds reported previously under the earlier impoundment reporting law.

Virtually all of the actions included in this report were anticipated in the 1975 budget, and six of them were taken before July 12, when the new procedures came into effect. Failure to take these actions would cause more than $20 billion of additional funds to become available for obligation. The immediate release of these funds would raise Federal spending by nearly $600 million in the current fiscal year. More significantly, outlays would rise by over $2 billion in 1976 and even more in 1977, the first year in which the new procedures for congressional review of the budget will be in full effect.

The deferrals of budget authority being reported today total $19.8 billion. The major deferrals are:

—Grants for waste treatment plant construction ($9 billion). Release of all these funds would be highly inflationary, particularly in view of the rapid rise in non-Federal spending for pollution control. Some of the funds now deferred will be allotted on or prior to February 1, 1975.

—Federal aid highway funds ($4.4 billion for fiscal year 1975 and $6.4 billion for fiscal year 1976). Release of these funds would also be highly inflationary and would have to be offset by cuts in higher priority programs. Some of the funds are being withheld pending resolution of court cases concerning the environmental effects of proposed highway construction.

—Various programs of the Department of Health, Education, and Welfare ($39.6 million). Pending enactment of the 1975 appropriations, HEW funds are being provided under a continuing resolution. Amounts available under the continuing resolution above the budget request are deferred to preserve the flexibility of the Congress and the Administration in arriving at a final decision on the funding levels for these programs.

The larger of the two rescissions which I am proposing would write off the $456 million of budget authority provided for rural electric and telephone loans at a 2 percent interest rate. The release of these funds would be inconsistent with the legislation enacted in 1973, which limits the availability of 2 percent loans to cases of special need. Loans to borrowers who meet the specified criteria can be financed out of funds provided by the pending Agriculture Appropriations Act.

The deferrals and rescissions covered in this first report are those believed to be of particular interest to the Congress and which would have significant impact on budget spending if released. They are summarized in the attached table. A second report of a series on additional deferrals and rescissions will be submitted to the Congress soon.

Budgetary restraint remains a crucial factor in our efforts to bring inflation under control. In today's environment, we cannot allow excess Federal spending to stimulate demand in a way that exerts further pressures on prices. And we cannot expect others to exercise necessary restraint unless the Government itself does so.

The responsible apportionment of congressional appropriations and other Federal budget authority is an essential—though often controversial—element of budget execution. Sound management principles and common sense dictate that Federal agencies spend money in an orderly fashion and only to the extent necessary to carry out the objectives for which the spending authority was provided. Current economic conditions require extra care to assure that Federal spending is held to the minimum levels necessary.

The deferrals and rescissions described in the attached report represent an essential step toward the goal of reducing spending and achieving the balanced budget we seek by fiscal year 1976. These actions, by themselves, will not be enough. However, failure to take and sustain this important step would jeopardize our ability to control Federal spending not only during the current fiscal year but, more importantly, for several years to come.

GERALD R. FORD

The White House,
September 20, 1974.

NOTE: A summary of the deferrals and proposed rescissions was included with the message and is printed in the Federal Register of September 23, 1974 (39 F.R. 34225).

For a complete listing of special messages to the Congress transmitting budget deferrals and proposed rescissions in 1974, see Appendix B.

90

Memorandum on Budget Deferrals and Proposed Rescissions. *September 20, 1974*

MEMORANDUM TO THE HEADS OF DEPARTMENTS AND AGENCIES
SUBJECT: Budget Rescissions and Deferrals

I have today sent to the Congress my first special message under Title X of the recently enacted Congressional Budget and Impoundment Control Act of 1974. A copy of that message is attached.

The package I have submitted contains reports on budget authority totalling $20.3 billion. Included among these items are some which are not covered by the new Act, but release of virtually any of them would lead to spending above that contemplated by the FY 1975 Budget.

Gaining congressional support for the items contained in this transmittal, and for those I will be sending up in the future under this Act, is absolutely vital if we are to make any headway against inflation by controlling Federal expenditures. This Government must set an example of fiscal restraint for the people of America and the world.

Each of you knows my position on cutting back below 1975 Budget levels. I need your strong assistance in supporting this first critical step, and the others that follow, to meet our budgetary goals. I know I can count on you to work closely with the Congress in order to gain the necessary acceptance of the deferrals and rescissions I propose today and in the future.

GERALD R. FORD

91

Memorandum on the Career Civil Service. *September 20, 1974*

MEMORANDUM FOR HEADS OF DEPARTMENTS AND AGENCIES

Whatever else, recent experience has proven one thing about the Federal Government: It can continue to function and move ahead even under the most difficult circumstances. This is due chiefly to more than two million career civil servants who, day-in and day-out, give of themselves in a thoroughly dedicated and efficient manner to assure this continuity.

These men and women act in the best traditions of the career civil service which has demanded from them for more than 90 years the highest degree of professionalism and competence. In return, it has assured them of a competitive system free from political considerations either in their appointments or in their promotions.

I intend to keep it that way—and I call upon you to see to it that the merit principles contained in the Civil Service Act and the personnel laws and regulations are fully and effectively carried out in your department or agency. Appointments and promotions in the career service must not be made on the basis of either politics, race, creed or sex.

I have informed the Chairman of the United States Civil Service Commission of my determination to keep the Federal career service just that—a career service in which men and women can be accepted in the first place on their ability and promoted on their merit. I ask you to make sure your agency fully complies with both the letter and the spirit of the law in this regard.

GERALD R. FORD

92

Remarks Announcing Appointment of Ron Nessen as Press Secretary to the President. *September 20, 1974*

THIS is an opportunity for me to make a very, very pleasing announcement. I think I am very, very fortunate on this occasion to have the opportunity of announcing to all of you and to others, in fact, that Ron Nessen is going to be my Press Secretary.

Ron, as you know, has a superb reputation—standing—in the electronic media, but I was pleased to find out in my discussions with him that he has a background in the writing press.

So, we are very fortunate to have someone like Ron who not only knows the writing but also the electronic press.

I had the opportunity of getting acquainted with Ron in the many, many trips that he took with me on Air Force Two. I think the number is some 57. So, in that luxurious aircraft—[*laughter*]—in the many travels we made around the country, I was given the opportunity of getting to know Ron very well.

I admired his skill and objectivity as a reporter. I enjoyed his company. I was greatly impressed with his ability and overall approach to the problems that I faced and others did.

So, when I asked Ron if he would take the job, I couldn't have been more pleased.

I must say that this announcement comes at a somewhat unique time. I just spent 2½ hours with one of the leading Communists, and now I am about to meet with one of the most wealthy and influential capitalists.[1] So in between those two meetings, it is my privilege and pleasure to indicate to all of you that Ron Nessen will be my Press Secretary, and I couldn't be more pleased.

MR. NESSEN. Thank you, Mr. President.

THE PRESIDENT. Fine, Ron. You are the boss.

MR. NESSEN. My wife said to tell you that this entitles you to one free dancing lesson. [*Laughter*]

THE PRESIDENT. I need it. [*Laughter*]

MR. NESSEN. Thank you very much for the trust you put in me, and I will try to live up to it.

THE PRESIDENT. I have no doubt about it, Ron.

So, I will turn the job over to Ron. He has my full backing and support, and I think I am very lucky to have somebody like him handling the job.

MR. NESSEN. You are not going to leave me out here all alone, are you?

THE PRESIDENT. You better get used to it. No, I am going to stand here until you finish your remarks.

MR. NESSEN. Well, I did want to say a couple of things.

I hope the White House press corps is ready for another Ron. I am a Ron, but not a Ziegler, I can tell you that.

I do want to say a couple of things. One is that I will never knowingly lie to the White House press corps. I will never knowingly mislead the White House

---

[1] The President was referring to his meetings with Soviet Foreign Minister A. A. Gromyko and David Rockefeller.

press corps, and, I think, if I ever do, you would be justified in questioning my continued usefulness in this job.

My concept of the job is that a Press Secretary does not always have to agree with the decisions of the President. I think a Press Secretary's job is to report to you the actions of the President, why he has taken the actions, how he has arrived at the action.

I don't think that the Press Secretary and the press are natural antagonists. I think we really both have the same aim. I have been out on the other side for a long time, and now I am on this side, but I think we have the same aim, which is to get as much news as possible about what goes on in this place to the American people.

Obviously, the Press Secretary needs to know what is going on to do that job, and I have been assured that I will know what is going on.

I don't expect to be a salesman for the President. I am not going to try to sell his programs to you.

I am apolitical. Like most of you, I have worked on covering most of the political campaigns of the last 15 years. The last time I voted, I am ashamed to say, was in 1960, when I voted for John Kennedy. Other than that, I have no affiliation with any political party.

I think my models in trying to do this job will be Bill Moyers for his knowledge and his honesty and the amount of information that he put out, Pierre Salinger for the good humor and the good fellowship and the grace that he brought to this job, and I would hope to be able to earn as much respect from you as Jerry terHorst had.

I think it is probably too late to go back to a honeymoon, but maybe we could have a trial reconciliation.

Thank you very much, Mr. President.

THE PRESIDENT. Thank you, Ron. We are very proud to have him, and we look forward to working together.

I will leave you to your friends.

Thank you very much.

NOTE: The President spoke at 1:45 p.m. in the Briefing Room at the White House. Following the President's remarks, Press Secretary Nessen participated in a question-and-answer session with reporters.

93

Statement on Signing the Alcohol and Drug Abuse Education Act Amendments of 1974. *September 21, 1974*

I AM today signing into law H.R. 9456, the Alcohol and Drug Abuse Education Act Amendments of 1974.

I share the concern of the Congress and the people about the problem of alcohol and drug abuse among our Nation's youth. At the Federal level, this concern has been expressed over the past 5 years in greatly increased efforts to find effective ways of dealing with the problem. The 1975 budget proposed Federal spending of over $600 million to support alcohol and drug abuse prevention and treatment—apart from law enforcement activities.

This act improves the overall program a number of ways. It includes alcohol education explicitly as a part of the program. It provides for comprehensive school and community demonstration activities which focus on the causes rather than on the symptoms of drug and alcohol abuse. Most important, it consolidates scattered activities under the Office of Education. This will provide more economical and higher quality development of educational and demonstrational materials. It will provide more effective thrust and more effective management.

In signing this bill into law, I wish to reemphasize my determination to keep the overall budget in line, in this area as in other areas of Federal activity. This act provides a means and a commitment for more effective management; it does not represent a commitment to greater spending.

NOTE: As enacted, H.R. 9456, approved September 21, 1974, is Public Law 93-422 (88 Stat. 1154).

94

Remarks to the Ninth World Energy Conference, Detroit, Michigan. *September 23, 1974*

President Groza, Steve Bechtel, Walker Cisler, Governor Milliken, Senator Griffin, Mayor Young, Minister Macdonald of Canada, other distinguished guests from abroad, and all participants in this special World Energy Conference:

On behalf of the American people, on behalf of my home State of Michigan, on behalf of the city of Detroit, it gives me a very great privilege and pleasure to welcome you to the city which some blame for the energy crisis.

But I hasten to add this, if I might: This is also a city [to] which we, along with the world's other great industrial nations, look for significant solutions that I know are possible. This is a "can do," a problem-solving city and State.

It was here in Detroit that the internal combustion engine was transformed from a plaything of the rich into basic transportation on which people all over the world now depend.

The whole structure of our world society rests upon the expectation of abundant fuel at reasonable prices. I refer to cities and suburbs, farms and factories, shopping centers and office buildings, schools and churches, and the roadways that connect them all.

The expectation of an assured supply of energy has now been challenged. The repercussions are being felt worldwide. There is widespread uncertainty and deep and serious apprehension. Today, at the opening of this conference, we are determined to provide guidance to a world in crisis.

Many people became aware that there was an energy problem for the first time last October, when the oil embargo was imposed. But those who were well-informed about the energy situation had known for some time that a crisis was coming. With burgeoning demand all over the world, they knew that we could not forever expect a steady supply of low-priced fuel. The embargo merely brought to a head what experts had known for many years—that energy sources must be expanded and wasteful use eliminated to keep pace with the needs of a growing and modernizing world.

Everyone can now see the pulverizing impact of energy price increases on every aspect of the world economy. The food problem, the inflation problem, the monetary problem, and other major problems are directly linked to the all-pervasive energy problem.

The American response to the oil embargo and recent oil price increases, along with production decisions, has taken the form of a program for action under the general title "Project Independence." This integrated domestic energy program will seek in many, many different ways to reduce American consumption and to increase production of energy.

Officials of my Administration will more fully describe to this conference our determination to achieve energy independence. We will take tough steps to obtain the degree of self-sufficiency which is necessary to avoid disruption of our economy. We will make sure there is heat for our homes and power for the people who work in our plants. Realistically, this does not mean zero imports.

In the immediate future, we will expand our efforts to increase our energy efficiency. This will reduce the growing dependence on foreign petroleum.

Project Independence will also require us to increase the output of existing domestic resources.

In mobilizing to achieve long-term goals, we will fully exploit one of our most powerful natural resources—U.S. technology. We are moving in this direction.

Last year, for example, the United States Government funding for energy research and development was approximately $1¼ billion. This year, we will spend over $2¼ billion. These funds, together with those provided by private industry, will support a growing national effort. In terms of joint private and public resources, it will mean a commitment in excess of the successful one made by John F. Kennedy to put a man on the Moon in the last decade.

I mention this highly successful Moon landing to dramatize the magnitude of the energy task before us, the dedication with which we approach it, and the national mobilization of attention and talent it will require.

We are also moving to improve the organization of the U.S. Government for carrying out our energy programs. A key step now awaiting final action by the Congress is the creation of an Energy Research and Development Administration. It will provide coordination and leadership, in cooperation with private industry, in developing the necessary technology to fulfill our long-range energy requirements.

Even if there had been no political interference in the production and distribution of petroleum, nations today would still be facing the problem of finding enough fuel at reasonable prices to continue the modernization of our world. Our needs then and now for energy are increasing much, much faster than our ability to produce it. But, in addition, most industrialized nations experienced the direct impact of the oil embargo which, obviously, greatly intensified the problem. All nations have been adversely affected by price increases.

When nations use their resources as political weapons against others, the result is human suffering. It is then tempting to speculate on how much better off man would be if nature had distributed vital resources more evenly around the world, making every nation self-sufficient. But perhaps nature had a better idea. Because vital resources are distributed unevenly, nations are forced to choose between conflict and cooperation.

Throughout history, nations have gone to war over natural advantages such as water, or food, or convenient passages on land and sea. But in the nuclear age, when any local conflict may escalate to global catastrophe, war brings unacceptable risks for all mankind.

Now, more than any time in the history of man, nations must accept and live peacefully with the fact that they need each other. Nations must turn to international cooperation as the best means for dealing with the uneven distribution of resources.

American foreign policy rests on two obvious new facts: First, in the nuclear age, there is no rational alternative to international cooperation. Second, the more the world progresses, the more the world modernizes, the more nations need each other.

As you know, a theme of the foreign policy of this Administration is "international cooperation in an interdependent world." Stressing interdependence, you may ask why is our domestic energy program called Project Independence? As I see it, especially with regard to energy, national sufficiency and international interdependence fit together and actually work together.

No nation can be part of the modern world and live unto itself. No nation has or can have within its borders everything necessary for a full and rich life for all its people. Independence cannot mean isolation.

The aim of Project Independence is not to set the United States apart from the rest of the world; it is to enable the United States to do its part more effectively in the world's effort to provide more energy. Project Independence will seek new ways to reduce energy usage and to increase its production. To the extent that we succeed, the world will benefit. There will be much more energy available for others.

As America expands existing sources and develops new ones, other nations will also benefit. We especially want to share our experience and our technology with other countries in efforts to increase their own energy supplies. We are also aware that in some respects other countries are ahead of us, and we will seek to learn from them.

Sovereign nations try to avoid dependence on other nations that exploit their own resources to the detriments of others. Sovereign nations cannot allow their policies to be dictated, or their fate decided, by artificial rigging and distortion of world commodity markets.

No one can foresee the extent of damage, nor the end of the disastrous consequences, if nations refuse to share nature's gifts for the benefit of all mankind. I told the United Nations assembly last Wednesday, and I quote: The attempt by any country to use one commodity for political purposes will inevitably tempt other countries to use their commodities for their own purposes.

There are three ways, fortunately, that this danger can and must be avoided:

—first, each nation must resolve not to misuse its resources;

—second, each nation must fully utilize its own energy resources; and

—third, each nation must join with others in cooperative efforts to reduce its energy vulnerability.

In doing so, we emphasize that our actions are not directed against any other nations, but are only taken to maintain the conditions of international order and well-being.

The quest for energy need not promote division and discord; it can expand the horizons of the world's peoples. I envision a strong movement towards a unifying cooperation to ensure a decent life for all.

I welcome the development in Brussels last Friday of a new international energy program by the Energy Coordinating Group of the Washington Energy Conference. We were pleased to participate in that meeting. The 12 nations reached an ad referendum agreement on a far-reaching cooperative plan to deal with such emergencies as embargoes by sharing available oil and by cutting consumption and using stocks on an equitable basis. While seeking conservation, we and the other nations will work for expanded production of both conventional and nonconventional fuels. The cooperating countries are also creating an international agency to carry out this program.

The United States welcomes this demonstration of international action rather than words.

Just as Americans are challenged by Project Independence, the world faces a related challenge that requires a "Project Interdependence." No single country can solve the energy problem by itself. As President, I offer America's partnership to every other nation willing to join in a common effort to expand the spirit flowing from the Washington Energy Conference. A start has been made in Brussels. The momentum must be continued if true interdependence is to be achieved.

The economy of the world is facing unprecedented challenges. Old remedies are inadequate for new problems. New and appropriate solutions must be found without delay, and I am absolutely convinced that they will be found.

I firmly believe that the unselfishness of all nations is in the self-interest of each nation. We all depend on each other in so many ways that there is no way in today's world for any nation to benefit at the expense of others—except for the very short term and at a very great risk.

Without having planned it, we find ourselves in the strange situation in which the most selfish individual can figure out that it is profitable to live by what we call the Golden Rule: We can help ourselves only if we are considerate and only if we are helpful to others.

The energy crisis is the clearest example of the world's interdependence. The industrialized nations need the oil produced by a few developing nations, and all developing nations need the technology, the services, and the products of industrialized nations.

The opportunity for a great advance for the whole world is tantalizingly apparent, but so is the danger that we will throw away this very, very rare opportunity to realize mankind's hopes. Let us build and implement a global strategy for energy.

If I may, I call on this World Energy Conference and other international organizations to accept the challenge of formulating Project Interdependence, a comprehensive energy program for the world to develop our resources, not just for the benefit of a few but for all mankind.

This task is surely monumental, but the United States believes that it is possible, that it is essential. To help you in the beginning to take the first steps, let me propose some principles that could guide a global approach:

First, all nations must seek to increase production, each according to its resources and its level of technology. Some can develop known and available resources; others can try to improve methods of extraction or intensify exploration; and others are capable of developing new sources of energy appropriate to their own circumstances. But all nations can and should play a part in enlarging and diversifying the sources of usable energy. Diversification can help deter nations from resorting to monopolistic prices or practices.

Next, the rate of increase in consumption of energy must be reduced and waste eliminated. Americans will do their part in this necessary effort. But all nations can contribute to discovering new ways to reduce the energy we consume, partly through common sense, partly through self-discipline, and partly through new technological improvements. Whatever energy-saving methods are developed anywhere must be communicated quickly to all concerned. Energy-saving possibilities are promising, especially for the short term, as production increases.

Third, a cooperative spirit, a cooperative conduct are essential to success in a global energy program. Nothing, in my judgment, could be more harmful than policies directed against other nations. If we lapse into confrontation of exporters on the one hand and consumers on the other, or an unseemly scramble of consumers being played off one against another, all hopes for a global solution will be destroyed.

Fourth, we must be especially attentive to the situation of the poorest nations which will suffer drastically if the energy problem does not come under control.

Actually, they are the chief victims, even now, of the uncontrolled inflation driving world prices up, far beyond their reach for all the goods and all the services they must import to survive.

Finally, a global strategy must seek to achieve fuel prices which provide a strong incentive to producers, but which do not seriously disrupt the economies of the consumer. We recognize the desires of the producers to earn a fair share or a fair price for their oil as a means of helping to develop their own economies. But exorbitant prices can only distort the world economy, run the risk of a worldwide depression, and threaten the breakdown of world order and world safety.

It is difficult to discuss the energy problem without lapsing, unfortunately, into doomsday language. The danger is clear. It is very severe. Nevertheless, I am very optimistic. The advantages of cooperation are as visible as the dangers of confrontation, and that gives me hope as well as optimism.

But good intentions will not be enough. Knowledgeable people, like all of you at this important conference, are needed to give understanding, analysis, technical competence, and solutions for the people and the leaders to consider.

I call on all of you to respond to the challenge and to propose to the world your recommendations for a global energy strategy. Whether you call it Project Interdependence or some other name is not the essential point. What is essential is the challenge be accepted and the job be done quickly and well.

Ladies and gentlemen, I now declare the Ninth World Energy Conference officially open, and thank you very, very much.

NOTE: The President spoke at 10:40 a.m. in Cobo Hall. In his opening remarks, the President referred to Octaviani Groza, president of the conference; Stephen D. Bechtel, Jr., chairman of the conference's organizing committee; Walker Cisler, chairman of the board of Detroit Edison Company; and Donald S. Macdonald, Canadian Minister of Energy, Mines, and Resources.

95

Message to President Oswaldo Lopez Arellano of Honduras About Hurricane Disaster. *September 23, 1974*

Dear General Lopez:

On behalf of the Government and people of the United States, I extend our profound sympathy to you and the Honduran people on the tragic loss of life and suffering caused by the hurricane which struck your country. The close bonds of friendship between our countries evoke particularly strong feelings of solidarity with the Honduran people at times like these. You may be assured of our continuing interest in and support for the courageous efforts which you and your people are making to alleviate human distress and initiate recovery from this tragedy.

Sincerely,

GERALD R. FORD

NOTE: The text of the message was issued by the White House, together with details on relief efforts. Hurricane Fifi struck Honduras on September 18, 1974.

96

Remarks to the Annual Convention of the International Association of Chiefs of Police. *September 24, 1974*

Chief Looney, distinguished guests, members of the International Association [of Chiefs] of Police:

It is a great privilege and a very high honor to have an opportunity of participating with you here this morning.

Frankly, if there had been enough room, I really wanted to bring the United States Marine Corps Band with me, but it might have been a little embarrassing. Can you imagine if they played "Hail to the Chief" and all 3,000 of you stood up? [*Laughter*]

But frankly, I have to admit being a little worried and a little concerned about standing up here this morning. You can imagine how it feels to be facing 3,000 of the most capable, the most diligent, the most conscientious police officers in the world—and right outside, I am parked in front of a fire hydrant. [*Laughter*]

Six weeks ago, I told the American people and the Congress that we all have a lot of work to do. We have a long national agenda, and I stress today that the control of crimes, especially violent crime, is one of the top items on that agenda.

I think it is fair to say that all Americans can agree on some conclusions about crime. There is far too much of it. It can no longer be ignored. It can no longer be rationalized away. The time has come for all of us to act.

The point in dispute is precisely how crime can be reduced. I have some proposals that I will spell out later to both the Nation and to the Congress.

Crime is scarcely a new concern in this country. For more than 50 years, its level has steadily increased. Crime is still on the rise. In fact, most of our statistics seem to be on the increase. Prices are up; unemployment is up. In addition, we face some serious shortages.

One shortage particularly bothers me. This is the shortage of easy answers. We are faced with growing problems on all fronts, and there is no easy answer to any of them.

We all know that earthy description which President Truman gave to the Oval Office some years ago: "The buck stops here." When it comes to fighting crimes, most of the buck stops at your offices. You are in the frontline; you are the top commanders in the war on crime.

As you well know, most police powers are reserved to the States and largely delegated to local communities. I think this is a good and key feature of our Federal system. It will remain a key feature as long as I have anything to do with it.

The Federal role is essentially supportive. The solution depends upon State and local efforts under the leadership and the guidance of all of you.

As you know, Washington provides direct assistance to States and local communities through the Law Enforcement Assistance Administration. Grants have increased to about $880 million annually and most of it in block grants to the States. That is a lot of money, and I look back to the first year, about 7 or 8 years ago, when it amounted to approximately $50 million in the first instance.

But the total of $880 million, which is roughly the annual appropriation now at the Federal level, it is actually only 5 percent of the total spent on State and local crime justice systems. Actually, Federal money is essentially seed money.

Perhaps the most important activity of the Federal Government in this area is research and development. We have learned very valuable lessons about the nature of crime and its prevention.

We are cooperating with local agencies in pilot development and in testing new law enforcement tools.

In this process we have learned that there is need for better management, particularly the need to concentrate limited resources where they will be most effective.

There is also a need for greater citizen cooperation, particularly as ready and willing witnesses.

For effective management, we first have to have some hard decisions on priorities. As a starter, I would suggest a high priority on violent crime and street crime in the inner city. There is where crime does the most damage to our whole urban structure. There is where crime most hurts the poor who already suffer enough.

One bright spot in the crime scene is the success of your efforts against urban crime. Your concentration on street crime seems to be paying off, and I compliment you and congratulate you. But as we move forward in this area with the success that you have, let's keep the effort moving stronger and stronger.

Another priority as I see it is the habitual offender—the so-called career criminal. Most crime, according to the statistics, is the work of a limited number of hardened criminals. We must take the criminal out of circulation. We must make crime hazardous and very costly. We must ensure that swift and prolonged imprisonment will *inevitably* follow each and every offense. Only then will we deter others from pursuing careers of crime.

Accordingly, I have directed the Department of Justice to undertake, in cooperation with State and local governments, a Career Criminal Impact program. It will target and keep track of professional criminals. This program will also assign priority to cases of habitual criminals and expedite the process by which they are brought to justice.

Here in the District of Columbia we have already seen dramatic results in a very short time. Perhaps this can be adopted as a similar program in other urban areas.

In the U.S. Attorney's office, a special group known as the Major Violators Unit has been established. This unit tracks the cases of major repeat offenders. It ensures that these cases receive the most urgent attention of prosecutors. This unit has dramatically reduced the ability of case-hardened offenders to escape through the loopholes of the criminal justice system.

As I indicated, the results are already very impressive. For example, in the first month of operation, the Major Violators Unit substantially increased the conviction rate for serious cases. The average time from arrest to trial has been reduced by at least 3 weeks. The career criminal now realizes that serious cases will no longer simply slip through the cracks in the system.

In this area, you know better than I that all this cannot be done by the police in isolation. Effective anticrime management requires the close cooperation of police, prosecutors, courts, and corrections. Where they work together, you not only will obtain a better conviction rate but you will save unbelievable hours—police hours—that are now, unfortunately, wasted.

But to reduce the crime rate, we need the cooperation of one other party—namely, the public. Crime statistics, shocking as they are, often show us only the top of the iceberg. Too much crime goes unreported. A lot of witnesses never show up, especially after the fourth or fifth continuance.

A study in the District of Columbia shows that noncooperation of witnesses was by far the most common reason for losing major cases. Throughout this Nation, nearly half the victims of assault, robbery, burglary, and larceny above

$50 failed to report the incident to the police. In larcenies below $50, about 80 percent did not report.

I think it is reasonable to ask the question why, and according to a survey, the results show that most victims are frustrated, fearful, and pessimistic about results. Even victims, unfortunately, do not want to get involved with all the paperwork, interrogations, and repeated visits to the courthouse in cases that after several continuances may be dropped anyway. And sometimes—you know better than I—the victim fears reprisal.

Now, what can be done? First of all, we go back to good management. Fast action and better conviction rate of major crimes can help restore public confidence in the system. Better scheduling, better notification of witnesses, and fewer continuances will serve to cut down the terribly frustrating waste of the witness' time.

There are many other, many other things law enforcement professionals can do to encourage citizen cooperation and citizen initiative. Some communities have already launched very successful programs, and I congratulate each and every one of you in those instances.

LEAA has the information, the ideas, and some block-grant money to help you launch a program in your community—a program to overcome the sense of futility, frustration, and fear, and get the man on the street turned back to cooperation with the police.

Of course, the police can't do everything to win the war on crime, although you have done a magnificent job under most difficult circumstances. The police, plus the prosecutors, plus the courts, plus the prisons, cannot do the whole job. The community and, particularly, the family can be of tremendous help.

I think we on the outside recognize how difficult your job is. Under our constitutional system, the Federal Government, as I indicated earlier, can only give you limited aid and limited support, but I commit to you that this Administration will continue the kind of support that is needed and necessary for your job and the protection and the benefit of our fellow citizens.

Progress is slow, but it is my honest judgment that I think we are on the right track. We are beginning, as we move in the decade of the seventies, to learn how to fight modern crime more effectively. And as we move together, I think the results will be increasingly evident.

In the District of Columbia, for example, there has been a fortunate combination of good management methods, very ample resources, and outstanding leadership from Chief Jerry Wilson, who, unfortunately, is retiring this year.

Reported crime in the District of Columbia shows a 40 percent drop during his tenure in office, spanning the last 5 years.

It was here in Washington that a sad but heroic chapter of police history was made last week. Officer Gail Cobb became the first policewoman in the United States killed in the line of duty. I commend this brave officer who gave her life to protect her community. To honor her memory, I ask this convention to stand in silent tribute to Officer Cobb, whose funeral is taking place at this very moment.

[At this point, a moment of silence was observed in memory of District of Columbia Police Officer Gail A. Cobb who was killed on September 20, 1974. The President then resumed speaking.]

Thank you very much.

This latest tragedy has a vital lesson for every American. Whatever the insufficiencies and inadequacies of our criminal justice system, the officer on the beat is laying his or her life on the line every single day to make our respective communities a better place in which to live.

The police officer, from the top to the bottom, deserves the respect and cooperation of every American, and as I close, I pledge you my full cooperation here today.

Thank you very much.

NOTE: The President spoke at 10:28 a.m. in the International Ballroom at the Washington Hilton Hotel. In his opening remarks, the President referred to Francis B. Looney, deputy commissioner of the New York City Police Department, who was president of the association.

97

Message to the Congress Transmitting First Annual Report of the Director of the National Heart and Lung Institute. *September 24, 1974*

To the Congress of the United States:

The "National Heart, Blood Vessel, Lung, and Blood Act of 1972" created a National Heart and Lung Institute and required the Director in consultation with the National Heart and Lung Advisory Council to prepare and submit to the President for transmittal to the Congress an annual report and a plan for the next five years.

This report is enclosed. It is a detailed and thorough description of what is being done in research and treatment of heart and lung diseases, with a thoughtful plan for what might be done in the next five years. The keynote of the report is the same as that of the NHLI's first program plan: "to marshall national resources for promoting and restoring health, and for preventing and treating disease more effectively. . . ."

That part of the report which deals with the future proposes certain expenditures for fiscal years 1976 through 1980 which are in excess of what has been requested in the 1975 budget. The report, of course, frankly says that it represents a parochial, although important, point of view, and does not take into account the competing claims on the Federal budget at any time.

There is no conflict, however, about the depth of this administration's commitment to find cures and preventions for diseases of the heart, blood vessels, lungs, and blood. From a commitment of $182 million in 1971 to a proposed commitment of $309 million in 1975, the Federal Government's concern and determination on this matter has grown steadily greater. My administration reaffirms that commitment.

This report shows that the money spent by the NHLI has been well spent. I hope that the NHLI's accomplishments will be further milestones in our progress for our Nation and for mankind against those diseases which wreak so much heartbreak, death, and misery.

GERALD R. FORD

The White House,
September 24, 1974.

NOTE: The 150-page report is entitled "National Heart, Blood Vessel, Lung, and Blood Program—First Annual Report of the Director of the National Heart and Lung Institute."

98

Remarks at a Reception for Republican Congressional Staff Members. *September 24, 1974*

NEEDLESS to say, I am very grateful for the warm reception, and today we are paying tribute, as I look at it, to the unsung heroes and heroines of our Republican staff organization on Capitol Hill and, I might add, their long-suffering spouses.

Frankly again, nobody has ever been able to really pin down the exact duties, as I see it, of a good staff assistant. But somebody did come up with a pretty good definition the other day as I was talking to someone about this prospective meeting, and he said, and I will quote: A good staff assistant is someone who gets half the pay, a quarter of the office, and all of the blame. [*Laughter*]

Maybe this is telling tales out of school—and I have been accused of that before—but I once overheard a lady who was trying to get in to see her Senator, without too much success. The administrative assistant was, you know, as they always do, trying to smooth the obviously unhappy constituent. He said, "Madam, perhaps I could help you. I am his AA." She gave him a sympathetic nod and said, "Don't feel bad. If I worked for him, I would drink, too." [*Laughter*]

Needless to say, in closing, I do want to thank all of you most sincerely for the wonderful job you have done over the years that I had something to do with the Republican Party on Capitol Hill. Your talents, your cooperation, your dedication, the endless hours that all of you have given so freely, I deeply appreciate.

And I have found that words alone don't very adequately express this appreciation, and so I have written a little poem. It is called "A Toast to Congressional Staffers." It goes like this:

A toast to Congressional staffers:
They listen, write and edit.
They work and work and work and work,
And we take all the credit. [*Laughter*]

So, let me thank all of you again. I have done it on many occasions, but I say it most sincerely tonight, because I know firsthand the effort, the result, and all of the good things that flow from what you have done for me and all others in the Republican leadership and the principles for which we stand.

I thank you very, very much.

NOTE: The President spoke at 5:49 p.m. in the East Room at the White House.

99

Remarks at the Unveiling of a Portrait of Representative Leonor K. Sullivan, Chairman of the House Merchant Marine and Fisheries Committee. *September 24, 1974*

Dick, Mr. Speaker, our honored guest, Leonor, my many, many former colleagues and friends:

I have been accused of coming up to Capitol Hill so frequently lately that some people have suggested I was trying to build up my attendance record. [*Laughter*]

I think all of us know that my friendship with Leonor Sullivan goes back a long, long way. I had the privilege and honor of serving with her husband, John Sullivan, from 1948 until 1952. Leonor became a Member, as all of you know, in 1952, and ever since then, for 22 years, Leonor, we have been good friends. And I have valued and have been most grateful for that friendship.

We have discussed legislation on the floor of the House, and we have discussed it in the corridors, and we have discussed it in committee. We have shared thoughts and ideas on many other matters in the Longworth Building and in the Members dining room.

And so, after all these years, I come to this ceremony with a very special message. And Leonor, let me put it this way: Leonor, we can't go on meeting like this; Betty is getting suspicious. [*Laughter*]

But in this very busy day, I am particularly proud to be here, and I have looked forward to attending this ceremony, this very special and very well deserved occasion in your honor.

I think most of you know that I don't pretend to be an expert in the field of art. In fact, back in my hometown of Grand Rapids, Michigan, we have a very large, modernistic piece of sculpture by the great Alexander Calder. He has several here in the District of Columbia. And every time I try to describe it to somebody or interpret it for somebody, poor Mr. Calder doesn't know whether to smile or sue. [*Laughter*]

But you don't have to be an expert to appreciate this wonderful portrait of Leonor. I have been impressed by what I have seen on the program, and I can't help but admire it in reality.

I have heard that a good painting is a mirror held to the soul of the subject. And Charles Fox, the portrait painter, has certainly captured the richness of Leonor Sullivan's character and her wonderful personality.

I understand that Mr. Fox has previously painted three Presidents—Eisenhower, Kennedy, and Nixon—as well as many other very prominent people in public life, and I know that his portrait of Leonor will be a credit to his career as much as the career of Leonor Sullivan has been a credit to the Congress of the United States.

I don't have to repeat here all of the achievements, the accomplishments, the superb record of Leonor. She has been an outstanding chairman of the Committee on Merchant Marine and Fisheries.

I think it is significant to point out, however, that—I think it was last year, Leonor—when the American maritime industry awarded her for her dedication, her success on behalf of the maritime industry, and made her an admiral of the ocean seas. This, I think, is unbelievable for someone who comes from the heartland of America to be so recognized by the maritime industry, an industry that, I am sure, watches and husbands that award for only those who have done superb work on behalf of our merchant marine.

So, what I would like to say is, Leonor, whether it was on the Committee on Banking and Currency, or whether it was on the Committee on Merchant Marine and Fisheries, or whether it was on the floor of the House, there have been no other Members who I think enjoys the respect and admiration, Democratic or Republican, more than you.

But most of all, I am proud to call you a friend and to wish you the very best as you leave the Congress at the end of this session.

NOTE: The President spoke at approximately 6:30 p.m. in the Hearing Room of the Ways and Means Committee at the Longworth House Office Building. In his opening remarks, the President referred to Representative Richard Bolling of Missouri.

The President later stated that he had been mistaken in his concluding remarks, in that Mrs. Sullivan was not planning retirement at the end of the session.

100

Remarks of Welcome to President Giovanni Leone of Italy. *September 25, 1974*

Mr. President, and ladies and gentlemen:

Mr. President, I warmly welcome you to the United States of America. I warmly welcome you on behalf of all Americans who are deeply grateful for the gifts of genius and beauty your country has given to all mankind. On behalf of the millions and millions of Americans who are proud to claim Italy as their ancestral homeland, I welcome you with a very special family affection.

You, Mr. President, are an honored leader of one of America's truest allies. In the past three decades, America has been very, very proud to have been associated with Italy in your successful efforts to build a democratic industrial society. I assure you, Mr. President, of America's continued commitment to a stable, free, and democratic Italy.

I also wish to restate most emphatically our intention to work closely with your country in strengthening Atlantic cooperation and Atlantic security. I think we must all admit that the road will not be easy. The problems of inflation and of assuring equitable access to fairly priced resources, for example, threaten the stability of every economy and the welfare of people in developed as well as in developing countries alike. The very nature of these problems defies solution by unilateral measures.

Mr. President, I look forward to our discussions over the next 2 days. I am confident that our talks will contribute to our mutual efforts to secure peace for all nations of the world. There is no doubt that they will serve to reinforce the ties that have bound our friendship over the many years.

Mr. President, you are most welcome to America.

NOTE: The President spoke at 11:09 a.m. on the South Lawn at the White House where President Leone was given a formal welcome with full military honors.

President Leone spoke in Italian. His remarks were translated by an interpreter as follows:

Mr. President, I thank you for the invitation that you extended to me immediately after taking over your high office as President of the United States of America, thus confirming an invitation I had received last year. Thank you for the warm welcome you have given me and for the kind words of welcome that you have just spoken.

It is a great honor for me to represent Italy on this official visit to this great country, which is striking in its vitality and creative capacity, which is in the vanguard of progress, which is strong in its democratic institutions which date back to the birth of a free nation.

And it is precisely to celebrate with just pride the birth of a free nation that you are about to celebrate the Bicentennial of the Declaration of Independence, which also carries the signature of an Italian, Guglielmo Paca.

It is an historic and solemn document which prepared the Constitution of the United States of America, among whose inspirers may I recall with pride the name of a great Neapolitan lawyer, Gaetano Filangieri.

The relations between our two nations have deep and longstanding roots, embodied by those millions of Italians, who at all times in every capacity, with their work and their intelligence and their thought, have made substantial contribution to the well-being and progress of this country.

Those relations are sustained by our common dedication to the principles of democracy and freedom and to the cause for peace.

Our common efforts, within the purview of our respective possibilities, are aimed at a constant quest for peace. The Atlantic Alliance is conceived and experienced by the United States, by Italy, and by all its members as an instrument for security and peace.

The commitment that Italy is pursuing with constancy, energy, and firmness is to achieve a unity that is not only economic but also political, so as to convey and channel the considerable resources of the old continent, in the light of its great traditions, to the service of the well-being of nations and the consolidation of peace.

The work of détente that Italy, like the United States and other countries, has been pursuing for years with constancy and firmness in close cooperation with its allies, knowing that we have the will of the peoples of the world behind us.

And it is in the same spirit that we think we must study and tackle the great economic problems which beset the world and the even greater problems posed by modern civilization, problems which affect very closely our social and private lives.

The vastness and urgency of the task and the importance of the resources that it requires are such as to call for a global answer resulting from the joint efforts of all.

I feel certain, Mr. President, that our talks will consolidate the friendship between the people of America and of Italy, and that they will develop our already excellent relations.

And I should like to extend to you also, on behalf of the Italian Government represented here by our Foreign Minister, Signor Moro, my warmest greetings and my good wishes to you for your Presidency, and I should like also to extend those greetings on behalf of my wife to Mrs. Ford and to your children.

And in conclusion, Mr. President, it is with great pride that I bring the fraternal greetings of the people of Italy to the great and generous people of the United States of America.

101

Message to the Congress Transmitting Final Report of the Advisory Council on Intergovernmental Personnel Policy. *September 25, 1974*

To the Congress of the United States:

It is a privilege for me to transmit to the Congress the final report of the Advisory Council on Intergovernmental Personnel Policy.

This report, which supplements earlier work by the Council, addresses three issues of importance to Government at all levels: equal employment, labor management relations, and the development of workforce policies by State and local governments. Because the members of the Council have expressed themselves forcefully and forthrightly on these matters, their work should serve as a useful reference point for public officials everywhere. All of us should be indebted to the Council members for their dedicated service and wisdom.

GERALD R. FORD

The White House,
September 25, 1974.

NOTE: The 63-page report is entitled "More Effective Public Service—The Supplementary Report to the President and the Congress by the Advisory Council on Intergovernmental Personnel Policy."

102

Message to the Congress Transmitting Annual Report on the Food for Peace Program. *September 25, 1974*

To the Congress of the United States:

I am pleased to transmit to the Congress the 1973 annual report on agricultural export activities carried out under Public Law 480 (Food for Peace). This has been a successful program. It has provided a channel for humanitarian assistance, promoted economic development and, in general, supported foreign policy objectives of the United States.

Throughout the year, the Food for Peace program demonstrated its flexibility in a changing agricultural situation. Because of the tight commodity supply situation in the United States, shipments during the year were somewhat restricted. This was especially true of wheat and wheat product shipments. However, our food contributions to the drought-stricken African countries, including

Ethiopia, were substantial. In both East and West Africa, United States food aid represented about 40 percent of the total supplied by the international community. The level of U.S. contributions to the World Food Program and the U.S. voluntary agencies was maintained and the Title I concessional sales programs continued in such high-priority countries as Bangladesh, Bolivia, Cambodia, Israel, Pakistan, and Vietnam.

The Food for Peace program continues to be the primary U.S. food aid activity. Concessional sales programs continued to encourage recipient countries to establish self-help objectives and also support economic development projects. The program retains its emphasis on improving the nutrition of pregnant and nursing mothers, babies, and pre-school children, the most nutritionally significant periods of human life. Although most programs have aspects of agricultural market development, specific programs for trade expansion have been limited because of strong commercial demand. Such programs could be resumed under changed supply conditions.

As 1973 legislation authorized the extension of the Public Law 480 program through 1977, it will go on playing its vital role in terms of development assistance, trade expansion, and promotion of our foreign policy objectives.

GERALD R. FORD

The White House,
September 25, 1974.

NOTE: The report is entitled "The Annual Report on Activities Carried Out Under Public Law 480, 83d Congress, as Amended, During the Period January 1 Through December 31, 1973" (Government Printing Office, 115 pp. plus tables).

103

Memorandum on the Combined Federal Campaign. *September 25, 1974*

MEMORANDUM FOR FEDERAL EMPLOYEES AND MILITARY PERSONNEL:

Those of us who work for the Federal Government have a special responsibility to demonstrate our generosity and compassion toward fellow citizens and concern for our communities.

Through the Combined Federal Campaign, we have an opportunity to meet these commitments in a positive, productive way by supporting the services of voluntary health and welfare agencies, including the United Way, the American

Red Cross, national health agencies, and international service agencies—organizations concerned with the welfare of human beings.

In supporting the Combined Federal Campaign, we are participating voluntarily as citizens in a uniquely American project, helping our neighbors—especially the aged, the infirm, the handicapped, the ill, and families in distress—through these voluntary charitable organizations.

By bringing the helping hand of voluntary organizations to those in need, whether at home or abroad, we strengthen what is best in our Nation and realize what is best in ourselves as a people. The amount you give must be a personal and voluntary decision. But I ask each of you to join with me in supporting this most worthy effort to the fullest possible extent.

GERALD R. FORD

104

Toasts of the President and President Leone of Italy. *September 25, 1974*

MR. PRESIDENT, it is wonderful to have you and Mrs. Leone and your three sons with us this evening. As I said this morning, at the time you came and joined us, the United States has a great debt of gratitude and a great sense of friendship for Italy because of the many, many people in this United States who have an ancestral background from Italy.

As I read and listen and look around our country, some 10 percent of our people have a background from Italy. We have superb artists, we have outstanding individuals in science, we have some very renowned athletes, we have many, many people in public life who have had a background from your country. And we are proud of them and their contributions to our country.

But I think, Mr. President, the broadest relationship that we have is what Italy has contributed to the United States, without personal identification, in the field—in those areas that one could describe as grace, humanity, tolerance, and an awareness of beauty.

We have a great American writer by the name of Mark Twain who once wrote—and he wasn't very complimentary to foreigners—but in one of his nicer moments, he wrote: The Creator made Italy from the designs of Michelangelo. And that was a nice comment. It was probably the best he ever made about any foreigners.

But to be serious, Mr. President, in all of the time that I had the privilege of serving in the Congress, the United States and Italy were building together. We were building in the process of reconstruction following the war. We were building in the process of Europe as a whole in the reconstruction period.

This 25-year span led, of course, to our alliance, where we have developed a friendship and an agreement for diplomatic, military, economic, and cultural expansion and reciprocity.

We dealt with Italy on a personal basis, and we have worked together in our relationships with our allies in Western Europe. And the net result has been a better relationship between us as people and our Governments on behalf of our people.

But, Mr. President, it was a pleasure for me to meet you this morning and to be reassured of your willingness to talk in a frank and candid way about our mutual problems. And from one who spent a good share of his life in the political arena in the United States, I was greatly impressed with your wise statesmanship and your great knowledge of the problems in Europe and the rest of the world.

And so, it was a privilege and a pleasure for me to meet you and to discuss these matters with you and to help in the process of building a better relationship between Italy and the United States.

And if I might, may I ask all of you to stand and join with me in a toast to the President of the Republic of Italy.

NOTE: The President spoke at 10:03 p.m. in the State Dining Room at the White House.

President Leone spoke in Italian. His remarks were translated by an interpreter as follows:

For the second time today, Mr. President, I take my set speech and I set it aside. I am putting it back into my pocket, because I want to speak from my heart. The set speech, the written paper, will remain. It will perhaps go into the archives of state, but my speech will spring from my heart.

You, Mr. President, have said some very nice things about me and about my country. Now the things you said about me, I am sure, were totally undeserved, and they merely stemmed from your very great kindness. But what you said about my country makes me very proud indeed.

You recalled the contribution that Italy has made to arts and to civilization. We present this heritage to you, which is the heritage of centuries. We present it to you as our friendly ally, not with pride—which might perhaps be justified—but as a sort of visiting card for you to understand us better.

Italy has inherited the greatest legal tradition of all times, and Italy is the mistress of the arts. It can, therefore, only pursue ideals of democracy and freedom for all. And what other nation can better support us in these ideals than the United States?

Your Constitution, Mr. President, the first written constitution that ever existed, has laid the foundations of the free world. And we are making this visit to this great country with the Foreign Minister, Mr. Moro, who is an authoritative representative of my Government, to reassert four things: The first is the faithful, loyal, and constant friendship between our two nations which is based, as you said, in part also on our common ancestry.

The second point is the Atlantic Alliance. That is the second point we want to reassert. As I said this morning, it is seen by Italy, by the United States, and by all the member countries, as an instrument for détente and peace.

And we want to reassert, thirdly, our firm belief in the need to build a united Europe which will be complementary to the Atlantic Alliance and which will not be against America, but with the United States of America.

And, fourthly, we want to tell you how very much we support your policy of détente, in which you have the great cooperation of your Secretary of

State, which policy of détente expresses the will of the peoples of the world that thirst for peace and justice.

Now, if these four points are confirmed—and they have already been confirmed, indeed, by our talks this morning with you, Mr. President, and this afternoon with your Secretary of State, and I am sure they will be reconfirmed again in the meeting you were kind enough to arrange with me tomorrow—if they are reconfirmed, Mr. President, then I can only say that I thank God for allowing me to represent Italy in this great country.

And, Mr. President, you were good enough to extend your greetings to my whole family, and this is somewhat unusual, because in Italy we tend to hide our families away. And I have broken away from this tradition; I have brought my wife and children with me to present to you a typical Italian family, one that is a sound family, that is respectful of moral values, and that is united.

Mr. President, may I take this opportunity to say how satisfied I am with the talks that we have had, and how very glad I am that you have accepted my invitation to come and visit us in Italy. This has already made a favorable impression outside.

And I hope that the burden that is now weighing on your shoulders—but you have very square shoulders, indeed; I know that you are an athlete; I am not referring only to your physical strength—I hope that burden will yet give you some time to come to Italy where I can assure you of a very warm and affectionate welcome from the people of my country. And I hope that Mrs. Ford will be able to come with you.

And so I say to you, God bless you. And I invoke the blessings of God upon you as I do upon my own family.

And so I want to say now, thank you to the United States of America, and thank you very much for the music that you provided tonight. It was a touch of sentiment that I very much appreciated. I appreciated the Neapolitan song that was played.

I told you, Mr. President, in our private talk that Naples is my hometown. It is very beautiful, generous, and poor. And many parts of Italy are poor, and that causes us some concern.

I am mentioning this not with cup in hand at all, but merely as a matter of interest.

And so now, Mr. President, ladies and gentlemen, I give you the toast: the health and prosperity of President Ford and his family, and the success and well-being of the people of America, and the consolidated friendship of the peoples of Italy and the United States of America.

105

Joint Statement Following Discussions With President Leone of Italy. *September 26, 1974*

PRESIDENT Giovanni Leone of Italy made a State visit to the United States of America September 25–29, 1974, at the invitation of President Gerald R. Ford of the United States of America. Accompanying the President were Mrs. Leone, Minister of Foreign Affairs Aldo Moro, and other Italian officials.

During the visit, President Leone and President Ford held extensive and cordial discussions on a wide variety of international questions in which Minister of Foreign Affairs Aldo Moro and Secretary of State and Assistant to the President for National Security Affairs Henry A. Kissinger also participated. Minister Moro and Secretary Kissinger also held detailed talks on current issues of mutual interest.

President Ford and President Leone expressed their mutual satisfaction with the results of the talks. It was agreed that frequent consultations in the spirit of the Atlantic Declaration signed in Brussels on June 26 were a most desirable means of achieving better understanding of problems of common interest and possible solutions. They were in full agreement that such consultations should in no way prejudice other existing obligations. As a result of their exchanges of views, the two Presidents noted the broad agreement between them with respect to their policies in numerous areas:

1. They noted that their policies will continue to be guided by their desire for the maintenance of peace, adherence to the principles of the United Nations Charter, and promotion of a stable structure of peace which reflects the diverse nature and needs of the nations of the world. In this connection, both sides emphasized their commitment to overcoming the sources of tension and conflict which are divisive factors in the international community.

2. There was full agreement on the importance of the North Atlantic Alliance as an instrument which has guaranteed the security of its members, strengthened international stability, enhanced confidence among peoples, and thus has permitted them growing and fertile contacts with all the peoples of the world and provided the indispensable basis for the process of détente.

3. They reemphasized in this connection the importance they attach to the Atlantic Declaration and their determination to seek the fulfillment of the principles set forth in the Declaration in concert with their other NATO allies. President Ford underlined the importance the United States attaches to Italy's continuing valuable contributions to the Alliance.

4. They recognized the importance attached by the Nine members of the European Community to their efforts toward European union, and welcomed the reciprocal undertaking by the members of the Community and the United States to strengthen their relations on the basis of enhanced consultations within the broad framework of Atlantic cooperation. President Ford welcomed particularly the constructive role played by Italy in strengthening this cooperation.

5. They noted their determination that current negotiations in furtherance of détente on matters related to security and cooperation in Europe must result in enhanced stability in the relationships among all nations concerned. They also emphasized their continuing commitment to achieving balanced and effective international arms control agreements resulting in undiminished security for all nations.

6. They noted their concern with developments in the Mediterranean Basin and pledged their efforts to achieve equitable solutions. The United States noted in this connection that it looks to Italy, as a Mediterranean nation which has made a signal contribution to world civilization, to play a leading role in the common pursuit of lasting peace in that area.

7. They expressed their conviction that only international cooperative efforts can overcome the trade and financial problems confronting the nations of the world. They recognized that the solutions to national problems have their impact on the international community as a whole. While individual nations have primary responsibility for their own problems, the two Presidents recognize that the solutions required in a modern and complex interdependent world may go far beyond individual capabilities and require cooperation among members of the international community. In this regard, the United States has taken careful note of Italy's major efforts to meet its own domestic economic and financial problems and the responsiveness of the international community to these efforts. President Ford stated that the United States is prepared to play an appropriate, constructive and responsible role in a return to economic equilibrium in Italy.

8. They recognized the great importance of industrial, technical, and cultural cooperation among all nations and the imperative need for the equitable distribution of world resources among all nations. They agreed to facilitate initiatives in this regard in appropriate forums.

9. Finally, the two Presidents particularly noted the extraordinarily broad human ties between Italy and the United States of America, and the shared values and goals which bind together the Italian and American peoples.

10. President Leone extended to President Ford an invitation to visit Italy in the near future. President Ford accepted with pleasure.

106

Remarks Opening the Summit Conference on Inflation. *September 27, 1974*

Mr. Speaker, Senator Mansfield, Senator [Hugh] Scott, distinguished Members of the Congress of the United States, members of the Cabinet, participants, observers, ladies and gentlemen:

At the first session of the Conference on Inflation, I asked that we get to work on a battle plan against public enemy number one. Important work has been done throughout the country. Today, the climax of our efforts is at hand. I welcome the many distinguished Members of the Congress and citizens from all sectors of American society. I deeply appreciate your commitment and your involvement.

I am also very pleased to welcome representatives from many foreign lands. This is, as we all know, an interdependent world. Inflation is an international problem. The efforts of each nation can become more effective if concerted action is achieved. The United States Government will consult with friends abroad as we move to combat an international threat.

I look forward to a productive series of discussions today and tomorrow morning.

In the great tradition of the American town hall, this conference includes the widest range of views and opinions. Inflation concerns all Americans. This is a joint executive-legislative undertaking in response to a bipartisan recommendation of the Congress. It demonstrates that Americans can still come together in an effective way to confront an immediate danger threatening every citizen.

There has been much talk at the various sessions throughout the country, but there has been action and a generation of ideas that will be used as tools for us on this occasion today and tomorrow.

We have taken a good look at many, many options, and we have already narrowed some of the options to those which would appear to be most effective and command the widest support.

I appreciate your willingness to work with me on the inflationary problem which transcends America's many special interests, whether Republican or Democratic, labor or business, urban or rural. Nor does inflation respect age, sex, race, color, or creed. And inflation certainly punishes most cruelly those least able to cope with it.

Today's conference, like others that preceded it, is wide open. All views and opinions are invited. This Administration's commitment to visible and responsive Government remains intact. I might not like everything I hear, but it is my solemn duty as President of the United States to give fair consideration to all views and to carefully weigh the possible courses of action.

At the outset of this session, a word about expectations is appropriate. In searching for the very best policies, let us recognize that there are no quick or easy solutions. No miracle cure has emerged from the pre-conference meetings. Inflation is a problem which we must deal with patiently and persistently. In this battle, there is no substitute for candor and hard work.

Spokesmen from the specialized meetings will report areas of general agreement. I have also asked them, and I think this is important, to report areas of disagreement and alternatives which the Congress and I must consider in making difficult decisions.

I, like all of you, have unlimited confidence in America. The battle against inflation will not be an easy one. It will require sacrifice and a strong common effort. It will require discipline, but I am certain and positive that we as Americans can and will win.

This Administration will seek to ensure that burdens are distributed equally. No group should be called upon to carry an unfair share of the burden.

America's traditional resourcefulness and ingenuity helped build the Nation and provide an abundance unknown by most other peoples of the world. Although Americans must increase their productive capacity, this by itself will not eliminate the scourge of inflation. Other actions and hard decisions are required. We cannot hope to satisfy all, but we will seek to act in the best interest of all.

I intend to constantly reassess policies and to change those that are not working. My actions will not be set in concrete. As President, I will continue to listen with all the openness with which I am capable and acting with all the decisiveness at my command. Together, with great confidence in America's capacity, let us begin.

NOTE: The President spoke at 9:07 a.m. in the International Ballroom at the Washington Hilton Hotel. His remarks and both the conference's morning and afternoon sessions were broadcast live on public television.

At the conclusion of the afternoon session, the President hosted a reception at the White House for participants.

107

Remarks at Groundbreaking Ceremonies for the LBJ Memorial Grove. *September 27, 1974*

Mrs. Johnson, the Johnson family, Mr. Speaker, my former colleagues in the Congress, distinguished public officials, friends of Lyndon Johnson:

It is really a great honor and privilege for me to participate in this auspicious occasion today, to participate not only as President but as an old friend of the man we honor here on this occasion.

I think it is appropriate, before we talk about the man, to say a few words about another person. And I would like to make a comment or two, if I might, about our former First Lady who I am delighted to see here on this occasion.

I don't think there is an American in our society today, or maybe historically, who has done more to beautify America than Lady Bird Johnson. We all know there are countless trees, literally millions and millions of flowers that were planted across this land thanks to her efforts and are a true reflection—as I know her and many of you know her infinitely better than I—a true reflection of her warm, wonderful personality, who was a very great First Lady.

Lyndon Baines Johnson, long before he entered the White House, had already made his mark—his mark on history as a very great Member of the House of Representatives, subsequently the United States Senate, not only a Member but an inspirational and effective leader of the United States Senate.

As Senate minority and subsequently as Senate majority leader during former President Eisenhower's administration, whenever America's welfare was concerned, Lyndon B. Johnson always put his country above his party.

His cooperation with the Eisenhower administration—and I knew it somewhat intimately—on matters of foreign policy and national security was an outstanding one. It seems to me as I recollect—and I sought to last night—it was a model of bipartisan statesmanship.

But aside from his skill and his achievements in the field of the Congress and his relationship to a President, we all knew Lyndon Johnson as a big man, a strong man. And it was that strength, coupled with his faith in himself and his even stronger faith in America, that saw him through his Presidency.

Now, as much as Lyndon Johnson loved his great State of Texas, Mr. Governor, and as much as he loved that great land, his ranch along the Pedernales, I think part of his heart and a part of his spirit, that indomitable spirit, never left Washington, D.C.

Now it has a home in this beautiful setting overlooking Washington, adjoining the Potomac. From this peaceful, inspiring location, we can see the great dome of the Capitol where Lyndon Johnson rose to his first prominence. We can see the Jefferson Memorial, a monument to the great author of the Declaration of Independence. We can see the Lincoln Memorial, the shrine of a man of vision, a vision of freedom, a vision of human dignity. For all of this was an integral part of Lyndon Baines Johnson's own life.

One of the great heroes of the War Between the States, General Stonewall Jackson, expressed the feeling, I think, of this very moment. He expressed this feeling that we can use in this very occasion, and it was something like a hundred years ago, and let me quote: "Let us cross over the river," Stonewall Jackson said, "and rest under the trees."

For those of us who knew the former President personally, this will always be a very special place. But for millions of Americans of this and, more importantly, future generations who never knew him in life, this grove will be a grove, a place of pleasure, rest, as well as comfort—a place where they can pay an appropriate silent tribute, a silent respect, to the memory of a President who served his country and his countrymen very well.

Thank you very much.

NOTE: The President spoke at 12:24 p.m. at the LBJ Memorial Grove, located on the west bank of the Potomac River on a site in Lady Bird Johnson Park.

In his remarks, the President referred to Gov. Dolph Briscoe of Texas.

108

Statement on Signing Legislation Extending the Public Works and Economic Development Act. *September 27, 1974*

IT IS with great pleasure that I sign today H.R. 14883, the 2-year extension of the Public Works and Economic Development Act.

From the time the Administration's proposed Economic Adjustment Act was sent to the Congress last February, significant debate has occurred regarding the proper Federal role in the economic development and adjustment process. This legislation has benefited greatly from the debate and incorporates many improvements which will enable the Economic Development Administration and the Regional Action Planning Commissions to be more effective in overcoming or preventing problems of economic distress. I believe this legislation is a fine example of the beneficial results of consultation and compromise between the Congress and the executive.

Perhaps the most noteworthy provisions of the act are the changes that have been made in title III and in the addition of the new title IX. The improvements in title III should strengthen State capacities to plan for and assist economic development, while preserving a strong development role for local areas and economic development districts. Title IX marks a new direction in our approach to economic adjustment and development. It permits States and local areas to develop comprehensive and flexible responses to actual or threatened severe unemployment problems. It will permit early action to adjust to economic dislocation problems, to minimize personal hardships, and improve the chances of an effective long-range solution to the problems of the communities.

In conjunction with the other titles of the act and coupled with the Comprehensive Employment and Training Act, which contains provisions for special distribution of funds to areas of high unemployment, this title provides another tool available to States and communities to increase employment opportunities and offset particular local unemployment problems.

Despite these desirable new features in this bill, it does not provide for the comprehensive reform in our economic development and adjustment programs which I believe is necessary. It retains too much direct Federal control over the allocation of the assistance funds. This reduces the ability of States and communities to realistically plan and manage their programs. It continues undue emphasis on public works as the solution to problems of unemployment and low income, and it continues to encourage a narrow categorical approach to the problems of distressed areas.

Although this act represents substantial progress in the design of an effective Federal role in assisting economic development and adjustment, much remains to be done. During the next several months, and certainly before the expiration of this legislation, the Congress and the Administration must begin to consider changes to further improve the design of economic development and adjustment assistance. This extension, while valuable in itself, should be viewed as a transition period in which new approaches to relieving the burdens of unemployment and low incomes may be developed.

NOTE: As enacted, H.R. 14883, approved September 27, 1974, is Public Law 93–423 (88 Stat. 1158).

109

Remarks Concluding the Summit Conference on Inflation. *September 28, 1974*

Ladies and gentlemen, companions in this conference, and my fellow Americans:

Just one personal note, if I might. I just returned from the hospital where I saw Betty as she came from the operating room. Dr. Lukash has assured me that she came through the operation all right.[1]

It has been a difficult 36 hours. Our faith will sustain us, and Betty would expect me to be here.

I thank each and every one of you for your contributions to this summit. For most summits, there is no way to go except down. From this summit, we are going to start going up. This is not the end, but it is the beginning of a battle against inflation and waste which will not end until it is won.

I have vowed and asked all of you to resolve here that we will celebrate our

[1] Mrs. Ford underwent surgery for breast cancer at Bethesda Naval Hospital on September 28. Rear. Adm. William M. Lukash was Physician to the President.

Nation's 200th birthday with our economy healthy and strong, with prosperity as well as peace that brings the solid realities of a great republic.

Thousands and thousands of dedicated men and women have come together in this series of inflation conferences to map the strategies and the tactics of our all-out war against America's domestic enemy number one. All of you will be the Founding Fathers—if we succeed. If we fail, then certainly we will all hang separately.

General George Washington's words at the start of our Nation are equally appropriate at this time, and I quote: Let us raise a standard to which the wise and honest can repair; the rest is in the hands of God.

And God helps those who help themselves. On this principle, Americans in two centuries have astonished the world and, time and time again, have confounded the pessimists and the cynics who said it couldn't be done.

You have discussed many ideas. You have spoken candidly. And as a result, I, along with other Americans, have gained a far better understanding of our economic problems. Perhaps we have caught glimpses of the political problems, and we understand those, but even in our controversies, we have all developed a super sense of direction. You have done your homework well. Now it is my turn.

In the days immediately ahead, I will offer to the American people and to the Congress a program of action which will help bring balance and vitality to our economy. This program could not be formulated without your participation and without the support of millions of other Americans who have given us their ideas. I think all agree on one point: Inflation must be stopped. But this Administration will respond not with words but with action and with programs.

As your President, the only special interest I have, the only special interest I represent is the American people—housewives struggling with rising grocery prices, workers whose real purchasing power has eroded because of inflation, businessmen trying to control rising costs, families needing new homes but unable to find mortgage money to buy them, those thousands of unemployed who want work, the elderly locked into pension programs earned years ago—indeed, all 213 million Americans.

I pledge to you that I will not shrink from the hard decisions needed to meet the problems facing each and every one of us. This is a critical hour in America's history. It requires that Americans once again rise above petty partisanship or factional interests in any segment of our society. The very future of our political and economic institutions, indeed our whole way of life, is literally at stake.

A fundamental fact of human history is precisely this: Nations which cannot impose on themselves a disciplined management of their fiscal and monetary affairs are doomed to economic disorder and widespread inflation. Such discipline is imperative, it is urgent if we are to achieve a stable and expanding economy.

The American people have repeatedly demonstrated their ability to submerge personal and group interests to the general welfare. When they know the chips are down, they are really down—and they have done it in the past, and they will do it again—they will respond as they always have.

As part of the demanded discipline, I will send to the Congress a plan of action to keep Federal outlays for fiscal year 1975 at or under $300 billion. Every dollar the Federal Treasury must borrow is a dollar not available to the home buyer or the businessman trying to expand or other citizens who may be borrowers for good and sufficient reasons.

A coherent national policy on energy is essential for economic stability. It must encourage prudent use of available energy. There must be an assured future energy supply to enable consumers and businessmen to plan in a confident and orderly way. I will soon propose a national energy program aimed at assuring adequate internal supplies while reducing dependence on external sources. At this very minute, Secretaries Kissinger and Simon are exploring with their counterparts from four major industrial nations a coordinated plan to cope with a world energy crisis and world economic dislocations.

Today, I can announce three actions I have just taken:

First, I have directed the consolidation by Executive order [11808] of all the Federal Government economic efforts, domestic and international, under a new [President's] Economic Policy Board. The Secretary of the Treasury, Bill Simon, will serve as Chairman of this Board and as my principal spokesman on matters of economic policy.

I have appointed Bill Seidman, who has done so well with this conference, to serve as my Assistant for the coordination and the implementation of economic affairs and also as Executive Director of the new Economic Policy Board.

In addition to Secretary Simon and Bill Seidman, I have appointed eight Cabinet officers as members of this Board. They include Henry Kissinger, Rog Morton, Earl Butz, Fred Dent, Pete Brennan, Caspar Weinberger, Jim Lynn, and Claude Brinegar.

In addition, membership includes the Director of the Office of Management and Budget, Roy Ash; the Chairman of the Council of Economic Advisers, Alan Greenspan; and the Executive Director of the Council on International Economic Policy, William Eberle. Dr. Arthur Burns, Chairman of the Board of Governors of the Federal Reserve System, will attend meetings of this Board, which will start work immediately.

Second, I have established by Executive order [11809] a White House [President's] Labor-Management Committee whose counsel and recommendations will not only be sought by me but given to me man-to-man and face-to-face. Eight distinguished labor leaders and eight distinguished business executives comprise its membership. The objective of this Committee is not only to serve as advisers to me on major economic policies but to help assure effective collective bargaining, promote sound wage and price policies, develop higher standards of living, boost productivity, and establish more effective manpower policies.

Dr. John T. Dunlop, a dedicated public servant and professor of economics at Harvard University, has agreed—and we are very thankful—to serve as coordinator of this Committee.

Representing labor on this Committee will be President George Meany of the AFL–CIO; Secretary-Treasurer Lane Kirkland of the AFL–CIO; President I. W. Abel of the United Steel Workers of America; President Murray H. Finley of the Amalgamated Clothing Workers of America; President Paul Hall of the Seafarers International Union of North America; President Frank Fitzsimmons of the Teamsters International Union; and President Leonard Woodcock of the United Auto Workers; and President Arnold Miller of the United Mine Workers.

Representing management on the Committee will be John Harper of the Aluminum Company of America; Reginald H. Jones of General Electric; Steve Bechtel of the Bechtel group; Richard Gerstenberg of General Motors; Rawleigh Warner of the Mobil Oil Company; Walter Wriston of the First National City Bank; Arthur Wood of Sears, Roebuck and Company; and R. Heath Larry of U.S. Steel.

I am proud to announce this group of 16 distinguished, outstanding Americans.

A third announcement: The Council on Wage and Price Stability, recently established by Congress at my request and with my deep appreciation, is another arm I will use in the fight on inflation. I have asked Dr. Albert Rees, a distinguished economist and professor of economics at Princeton, to direct the Council's work. We are fortunate to have Dr. Rees with us.

And may I express to all the people—those that I have mentioned and others that will help—their willingness to step in and help the country and 213 million people.

But nobody knows better than I that councils and committees cannot win this war. The most important weapon in the fight against inflation is the spirit of the American people. This spirit is no secret weapon; it is renowned all over the world. And I call on each of you in this room, but more urgently, on each of you at home watching on television and all the other Americans across this vast land who either hear or read my words, I urge them, as I know they will, to join with all of us in a great effort to become inflation fighters and energy savers.

I know all across our country the question everyone asks me is, "What can I do to help?"

I will tell you how we can start. Right now, make a list of some 10 ways you can save energy and you can fight inflation. Little things that become habits—they do become habits—they don't really affect, in some instances, your health and happiness. They are habits that you can abandon if we are all faced with this emergency.

I suggest that each person exchange your family's list with your neighbors, and I urge you and ask you to send me a copy. Some of the best ideas come from your home rather than from the White House. The success or failure of our fight against inflation rests with every individual American. Our country is above all a union, and you and I can make it a more perfect union as our fathers did.

One of our delegates yesterday, Sylvia Porter, the well-known newspaper columnist on economics, has kindly consented to help me get this voluntary citizens program organized and underway, and I thank you very, very much, Sylvia.

It was dramatically pointed out here yesterday that inflation strikes our society very unevenly. Government must concern itself with those on whom the burden falls excessively. For instance, we must provide productive work for those without jobs. We must adjust our tax system to encourage savings, stimulate productivity, discourage excessive debt, and to correct inflation-caused inequities. And I can assure the American people that the executive branch and the Congress working together will effectuate and implement such a program.

May I add a very special word to our distinguished foreign guests. What you heard here yesterday and today may remind each of you of the current problems of your own country's economy. The problems of people are not very different in these days wherever they live and work.

The whole world suffers from inflation. I assure you the United States is seeking honest solutions that will help, not hinder, other nations' efforts to advance or to restore their economic health. I will have extensive consultations with leaders of other governments aimed at strengthening international institutions and to assure that we never again experience worldwide and interacting inflations and deflations.

There are more difficult decisions ahead for me and for the Congress. From the many alternative policies which we have heard here, given in good faith, listened to in good faith, we can and will fashion a coherent and consistent program. I will present my recommendations to the Nation and to the Congress within the next 10 days.

Finally, you will understand my two compelling reasons for canceling all but my most essential appointments and travel plans in order to be here in Washington. I will devote every minute that I can to forge the mass of evidence and the evaluations generated by this conference into concrete action—into concrete plans and legislative proposals.

A great leader of this country—of this century, I should say—in whom the unbeatable willpower of his American heritage combined with English eloquence, rallied his embattled countrymen from almost certain defeat by a blunt promise of blood, toil, tears, and sweat.

I trust we can avoid blood and tears, and we will. But I do offer you plenty of toil and plenty of sweat. I will roll up my sleeves and work every bit as hard as you do, starting this weekend, until every American is enlisted as an inflation fighter and as an energy saver until this job is done.

Thank you and God bless you.

NOTE: The President spoke at 12:37 p.m. in the International Ballroom at the Washington Hilton Hotel. His remarks were broadcast live on radio and television.

110

Remarks at the Annual Meeting of Boards of Governors of the International Monetary Fund and the World Bank Group. *September 30, 1974*

Secretary Simon, distinguished officials, representatives of many, many governments, ladies and gentlemen:

It is a very great privilege and a very high honor to have the opportunity of making some preliminary remarks on this gathering here in the Nation's Capital of our country.

I extend to each and every one of you a very, very warm welcome. I and all Americans want your continuing friendship, and we welcome your constructive and thoughtful observations and recommendations. And I assure you at the outset that we will reciprocate in every way in order to make progress in this very vital area for each and every one of us.

We come together at an unprecedented time of challenge in our world's economy. But that makes my welcome to all of you—those of you who must solve these serious problems—an even warmer welcome.

The serious problems that confront us today are extremely complex and, I presume, in some respects controversial. We do this at a time of worldwide inflation at a rate far, far in excess of what any one of us can tolerate.

We come here today at a time of unparalleled disruptions in the supply of the world's major commodity. We are here today at a time of severe hindrances to the real growth and the real progress of many nations, including, in particular, some of the poorest and most unfortunate among us.

We in America view these problems very soberly and without any rose-tinted glasses. But we believe at the same time the spirit of international cooperation which brought about the Bretton Woods Agreement a generation ago can resolve the problems today effectively and constructively.

My very capable Secretary of the Treasury, Bill Simon, will speak in greater detail on how we, the United States, view these problems and how we think they can be solved. But I think I can sum up in general our thinking quite briefly.

We in this country want solutions which serve very broad interests, rather than narrow, self-serving ones. We in America want more cooperation, not more isolation. We in America want more trade, not protectionism. We in America want price stability, not inflation. We in America want growth, not stagnation. We want for ourselves, as you want for yourselves and we all want for the world, a better life for ourselves and for those generations that follow.

You will help, and I am sure you will come forth with the kind of recommendations that will be beneficial. We want to help decide how this can best be done. The United States is fully prepared to join with your governments and play a constructive leadership role.

I say as I close, as I said at the outset, we want your friendship, your cooperation, and we, as a country, will maximize to reciprocate in every way possible.

Again, welcome to our Capital, Washington, D.C., and the very, very best in this period of serious deliberation.

Thank you very, very kindly.

NOTE: The President spoke at 10:08 a.m. at the Sheraton-Park Hotel to members of the Boards of Governors of the International Monetary Fund, International Bank for Reconstruction and Development (World Bank), International Development Association, and International Finance Corporation.

111

Veto of Legislation Providing for the Sale of United States Phosphate Interests in Florida. *September 30, 1974*

To the House of Representatives:

I return herewith, without my approval, H.R. 10626, a bill that directs the Secretary of the Interior to convey all phosphate interests of the United States in approximately 40 acres in Polk County, Florida to John Carter and Martha B. Carter upon payment of administrative costs and the fair market value of the phosphate interests.

Present law provides that phosphate interests of the United States shall be disposed of under a leasing system. The Congress and the Executive Branch have developed an alternative policy of selling phosphate and other mineral interests when the surface is not owned by the United States and when at least one of two criteria is met. The criteria are that the mineral interests have no value or that they interfere with development of the surface that is more beneficial than mineral development. This policy is carried out through private legislation on a case-by-case basis, and it is solely for the benefit and convenience of surface owners.

The instant case meets neither of the two criteria. The land is prospectively valuable for phosphates, and we know of no proposed use of the surface with which the mineral interest would interfere. The land is presently being used for grazing cattle.

At least six private bills have been enacted to convey reserved mineral interests in the 93rd Congress, and every one of them has met one of the criteria. There are presently several private bills still pending before this Congress. Also pending is the Administration's proposed "National Resource Lands Management Act", and a similar Senate-passed proposal, S. 424, which would give the Secretary of the Interior general authority to convey mineral interests to surface owners when one of the criteria is met. It is therefore clear that enactment into law of H.R. 10626 would conflict with established policy and would confuse our action on similar proposals in the future.

For these reasons I feel that the approval of H.R. 10626 would not be desirable.

GERALD R. FORD

The White House,
September 30, 1974.

112

Letter to the Chairman of the Subcommittee on Criminal Justice of the House Judiciary Committee Offering To Testify Concerning the Pardon of Richard Nixon. *September 30, 1974*

Dear Bill:

This is to advise you that I expect to appear personally to respond to the questions raised in House Resolutions 1367 and 1370.

It would be my desire to arrange this hearing before your Subcommittee at a mutually convenient time within the next ten days.

Thank you for your help and assistance in this matter.

Sincerely,

GERALD R. FORD

[Congressman William Hungate, U.S. House of Representatives, Washington, D.C.]

NOTE: The text of the letter was issued by the White House.

113

Statement on Senate Action To Suspend United States Military Assistance to Turkey. *October 1, 1974*

LAST NIGHT, the Eagleton amendment to the continuing resolution authority was passed by the Senate. Today, the continuing resolution itself will be brought to a Senate vote.

It is my conviction that approval of the continuing resolution, containing the Eagleton amendment or similar language, would destroy any hope for the success of the initiatives the United States has already taken or may take in the future to contribute to a just settlement of the Cyprus dispute. This view is shared by Secretary of State Kissinger, who is now in New York where he is making a major effort in his talks with Greek and Turkish representatives to bring about progress.

If the Eagleton amendment or similar language is adopted by the Congress, the United States will have lost its negotiating flexibility and influence. It thus hurts the very countries and objectives it purports to help.

It is my intention, therefore, to withhold my consent to any continuing resolution which reaches my desk containing language such as that found in the Eagleton amendment. I can, however, accept, and indeed endorse, the language relating to military assistance to Turkey contained in the continuing resolution as reported to the full Senate by the Senate Appropriations Committee.

I deeply appreciate the constructive efforts of the Democratic and Republican leadership in both the Senate and House of Representatives in their support for an amendment which would assist the diplomatic efforts of Secretary Kissinger in seeking an equitable solution to the Cyprus question. I hope a majority of the Senate will respond to this bipartisan leadership effort.

114

Statement on Signing the Defense Production Act Amendments of 1974. *October 1, 1974*

I HAVE signed S. 3270, the Defense Production Act Amendments of 1974.

The Defense Production Act was first passed in 1950 at the beginning of the Korean war, as a means of expanding the Nation's industrial capacity and enabling the Federal Government to produce and allocate critical materials in times of national emergency and for national security and other purposes. Since 1950, the act has provided ongoing authorization for the Government to assure that we have the productive capacity that would be needed for wartime mobilization.

The legislation I have signed extends the Defense Production Act until June 30, 1975. It also makes two significant changes in that act.

First, S. 3270 completely revises the financing mechanisms for loan and purchase activities under the act. All such activities will no longer be funded through Treasury borrowing, but through regular, more straightforward appropriations process.

Secondly, S. 3270 creates a National Commission on Supplies and Shortages. This Commission will study our supply picture and make recommendations on those institutional adjustments which may be needed to ensure that we can respond quickly and effectively to potential resources and commodity shortages.

For the last 6 months, a special Administration task force has been at work identifying and assessing potential threats to our imports of critical, nonfuel raw materials. The findings of this task force are completed, and they will be discussed with the new Commission on Supplies and Shortages and should be of significant help to the Commission in carrying out its mandate.

NOTE: As enacted, S. 3270, approved September 30, 1974, is Public Law 93–426 (88 Stat. 1166).

115

Statement Announcing Federal Civilian and Military Pay Increases. *October 1, 1974*

THE LAW on pay rates for Federal employees requires that they be paid salaries comparable with private enterprise and provides for an annual review process by which this comparability shall be determined and maintained.

Under that process, the Director of the Office of Management and Budget and the Chairman of the Civil Service Commission serve jointly as the President's agent for Federal pay.

Acting as my agent, Mr. Ash and Mr. Hampton have completed their review of pay comparability and have concluded that an average increase of 5.52 percent is justified this year. Accordingly, I have determined that Federal employees will receive a pay hike of that amount, and I have directed that it be placed in effect as of the beginning of the next applicable pay period.

In making this determination, I have also received two other recommendations. One was from the representatives of the Federal employees, who proposed an increase of 8.4 percent. The second was from an Advisory Committee on Federal Pay, consisting of three distinguished nongovernment experts in labor relations and pay policy.

I met with this second group and listened to a well-reasoned preparation of their views. In brief, they agree with the method used by my agent to arrive at the 5.52 percent figure but feel that an extra 1.7 percent should be added to make a total increase of 7.22 percent. This additional sum is based on a special study which was made at the direction of the Advisory Committee and covered increases that have occurred in the private sector since the completion of the annual BLS [Bureau of Labor Statistics] survey upon which the agent's recommendation is based.

I have given careful and sympathetic consideration to both of these additional proposals. Federal employees, like all other citizens, are suffering financially from the current high level of inflation. However, the comparability law requires that my sympathy for Federal employees be balanced by concern for the taxpayers who pay the bills. In today's economy, it is clear that one of the best services we can render to the taxpayer as well as the Federal worker is to keep the Federal budget within bounds to help alleviate current economic problems.

After weighing these considerations, I have concluded that I should not go beyond the clearly justified increase recommended by my agent. This increase gives full weight to the findings of the full-scale BLS survey made this year in the traditional manner. To depart from past practice by use of a special survey to support a higher increase than can be justified by normal methods does not seem to me to be the right thing to do at this time.

NOTE: On October 7, 1974, the President signed Executive Orders 11811 and 11812, providing for an increase in Federal civilian and military pay.

116

Message to the Congress Transmitting the Cost of Living Council's Final Quarterly Report on the Economic Stabilization Program. *October 1, 1974*

To the Congress of the United States:

In accordance with section 216 of the Economic Stabilization Act of 1970, as amended, I am hereby transmitting to the Congress the final quarterly report of the Economic Stabilization Program. This report covers the first three months of 1974 as well as the month of April, 1974—the last month before legislative authority for the program expired.

When the Economic Stabilization Program was begun in 1971, President Nixon emphasized his hope that it would be temporary. This objective has now been met, as all mandatory wage and price controls have been lifted, except for those on petroleum which have been mandated separately by the Congress.

Looking back, I believe this program gave all Americans a better appreciation of how powerful the forces of inflation are in our economy and how difficult it is to harness them. It also gave us convincing proof that wage and price controls are not the right way to solve the long-range problems of our economy. In retrospect, this may have been the program's greatest lasting value.

GERALD R. FORD

The White House,
October 1, 1974.

NOTE: The report, covering the period January 1 through May 1, 1974, is entitled "Economic Stabilization Program Quarterly Report" (Government Printing Office, 607 pp.).

117

Message to the Congress on Federal Civilian and Military Pay Increases. *October 7, 1974*

To the Congress of the United States:

In accordance with the provisions of section 5305 of title 5, United States Code, I hereby report on the comparability adjustment I am ordering for the Federal statutory pay systems in October 1974.

The Director of the Office of Management and Budget and the Chairman of the United States Civil Service Commission, who serve jointly as my agent for Federal pay, have recommended a 5.52 percent average increase in Federal statutory pay rates. The Federal Employees Pay Council and other employee organizations have proposed an increase of 8.4 percent. The Advisory Committee on Federal Pay has agreed with the method used by the agent to arrive at the 5.52 percent, but has recommended that it be augmented by an additional 1.7 percent, producing a total increase of 7.22 percent. This additional 1.7 percent is based on a special study of pay increases that have occurred in the private sector since completion of the annual Bureau of Labor Statistics survey on which the agent's recommendation is based.

I have decided that I must choose the 5.52 percent increase, without the additional 1.7 percent. The Advisory Committee has made a forceful case for the additional amount, both in their report and in their meeting with me. However, I do not feel that in the context of our current economic situation, I should go beyond the clearly justified increase recommended by my agent. This increase gives full weight to full scale Bureau of Labor Statistics survey findings of this year in the same manner as last year.

The time lag between the annual BLS survey and the resulting pay adjustment has been an integral part of our Federal pay-setting system since the principle of pay comparability was first adopted. The overriding need of the nation at present is clearly to dampen the fires of inflation. To depart from past practice by the use of a special survey to support a higher increase than can be justified by normal methods does not seem to me to be the right thing to do at this time.

I have noted the Advisory Committee's recommendation that the results of the annual survey of private sector pay be made available by July 1 of each year rather than the present date of August 1. I am in full agreement that an earlier arrival of the survey results would be highly desirable, since it would provide more time for all the parties involved in the annual pay comparison to give thorough consideration to the very complex issues involved. Therefore, I shall see what can be done so that the survey results will reach my agent by July 1 of each year.

I am transmitting herewith the reports of my agent and the Advisory Committee, as well as a copy of the Executive order [11811] I have promulgated to put this pay increase into effect. Also transmitted herewith is a copy of an Executive order [11812] I have promulgated to increase basic pay and basic allowances for quarters and subsistence for members of the uniformed services, in accordance with section 1009 of title 37, United States Code, as added by Public Law 93–419 of September 19, 1974.

GERALD R. FORD

The White House,
October 7, 1974.

118

Remarks at a Dinner Honoring Senator George D. Aiken in Burlington, Vermont. *October 7, 1974*

I WAS warned when I came up here that it would be difficult to say anything about George Aiken, but trying to follow him in Vermont is unbelievable.

George and Lola, Senator Stafford, Helen [Stafford], Dick Mallary, distinguished candidates and officeholders, ladies and gentlemen:

It is wonderful to be here; it is a tremendous privilege and pleasure. And let me express three special words of gratitude and appreciation.

Number one, last night I spent an hour or so with Betty at the hospital, and I was telling her that I was coming up to Vermont. And we were talking about the wonderful expressions of sympathy and best wishes she had gotten, some 20,000 from all over the country, and she indicated that there had been some warm and very friendly letters from Vermont and New England.

Let me say to all of you on behalf of those who have wished her well and who have included her in their prayers, I, for her as well as for myself, am very, very thankful.

Number two, I thank the Springfield High School band for doing two things. Number one, you did play the Michigan victory song, which is nice to hear, particularly when we do well, but it is something that I remember with great fondness. And number two, I am a great exponent of Scott Joplin's ragtime, and some of you who heard it I am sure would appreciate it, as I did. Thank you very, very much.

About 35 years ago I was at Yale Law School, and I tried to learn to ski. And I spent a good bit of my time in New England, Vermont particularly, in the old equipment and the old roads and the rope tows and some of the old Harold Burke techniques which I have been trying to forget for the last several years.

But all of you who were there at the time, who were then skiing, I thank you for your hospitality as well as your warm welcome tonight. It is wonderful to be here in Burlington.

Before I begin, I want you to know that I am not exactly a stranger here, not only from the skiing a few years ago but I have been in Vermont, and I was here on this precise campus. As a matter of fact, I was here on a very similar function 9 years ago almost to the day, October 2, 1965.

Now, I know that you Vermonters have a great reputation for being honest, for being direct, but I never knew just how honest and direct you were until that visit.

On that occasion, I gave a little talk and then I was taken to a reception in another part of the town. And at the reception a very sweet, very nice grandmother came up to me and put her gloved hand in mine and said, "I heard you gave a speech here tonight." And trying to be a little modest, I said, "Oh, that was nothing." And she said, "That's just what I heard." [*Laughter*]

So, with that thought of that sweet grandmother that was so kind rather fresh in my mind, I want you to know I am standing here tonight with all the confidence and self-assurance of the man who sells life insurance to Evel Knievel. [*Laughter*]

But it is a real pleasure to be here. I have had many wonderful times in Vermont, and I have thoroughly enjoyed my association with your Members of the Congress that I have known so well.

I do have fond memories of skiing up here a long time ago, and as you know, I pledged an open and honest Administration when I was sworn in, and I have tried to apply that honesty to all aspects of my life. So, I was in a little bit of trouble when Bob Stafford asked me if I was much of a skier. I said, "Well, let's just say I can ski for hours on end," and you know which end I am talking about. [*Laughter*]

I am particularly pleased, and I say this very sincerely, to have an opportunity to participate in "George Aiken Day." There is an old expression—at least we out in Michigan knew, and I think it is pretty widely known in the country:

"Let George do it." And for more than 40 years, the citizens of Vermont have let George do their bidding in the statehouse, in the Governor's mansion, and in the United States Senate.

I say to each and every one of you now, you have been fortunate to have such an outstanding public servant represent you in any and every public office. I congratulate you.

I think you can best summarize it by saying that George was a public servant for all seasons. He has the enviable ability to cut through the chaff and get to the very heart of any and every matter. We who served with him in the Congress, even though I was on the other end of the Capitol, know that he was noted for his strong independence of mind. Some have criticized him for that characteristic. Frankly, I praise him for it, and all of you should, too.

George has given the Nation the benefit of his down-to-earth wisdom, his leadership, and his guidance in many, many areas. You in Vermont know those areas infinitely better than I—education, electric power development, betterment of rural America, and more importantly today, foreign relations. This very different, this wide spectrum of legislative expertise and activity—I think they only suggest the breadth and the depth and the greatness of this man.

Those who served with him a part of the time of this exemplary tenure in the Congress, we are in debt for 34 years of senatorial service to America as well as to Vermont. And I think it is very safe to say, and it ought to be said, that he, George Aiken, is in no one's debt.

I understand it is unbelievable that in George's last campaign 6 years ago, he spent the grand total of $17.04 for his reelection. Can you imagine anyone spending that much for a political campaign in this day and age?

I think George Aiken is the only man that I know who could go to a supermarket today to buy 5 pounds of sugar with a dollar bill and come back with some change. [*Laughter*]

George, with your understanding and forgiveness, I don't think those of us who know her can forget Lola Aiken's service to Vermont in her own right. You know as well as I, and probably better, her great and long service on George's staff, and then his wife who has given her life in dedicated service to the State of Vermont, to your senior Senator. And I think it might be said that whatever Lola wants, Lola gets.

Driving from the airport, George and Lola were in the car with me, and I said to her—which Betty had asked me to indicate to her—how grateful my Betty was for the thoughtful card and note and the kind message that Betty received from

Lola Aiken. It was this expression, which is typical of her, which has made her so popular in Washington and, I think, so popular here in Vermont.

And to you as well as George, Lola, I express heartfelt gratitude not only for Vermont and Washington but for the Nation as a whole, and it is my privilege and honor to be here on this occasion.

But you know, as it has been since the days of Ethan Allen, the Green Mountain State continues to produce outstanding leaders. I have known quite a few in my 25 years in the House and a few months since then.

Bob Stafford came to the House after I had been there a few years. He was a former Governor. He came with a great reputation as an individual who had served so well. And I can only say that it is wonderful to see him rise with deserved recognition in the United States Senate.

Bob, it is nice to be here with you and Helen tonight.

Dick Mallary came a couple of years ago, and he, like Bob, had a wonderful reputation for superb service in your State legislature. A former Speaker, a man who was an expert in fiscal and financial affairs, he was instantly recognized in the House of Representatives for this experience, his integrity, and his skill. And it is a pleasure for me to see that he is your candidate for the United States Senate.

Dick, I look forward to you extending and expanding the contributions that you have made in the past to the future, on behalf of not only Vermont but to the country as a whole. Good luck. It is wonderful to see you coming down the path.

I have to be frank though. I hate to see good people like Bob Stafford leave the House and good people like Dick Mallary leave the House, because my heart really was in the House of Representatives. It was my home for nearly—or over 25 years.

And with the departure of Dick Mallary, I just hope and trust that Jim Jeffords will follow and be in the great image, in the great pattern of people like Charlie Plumley, Bob Stafford, Win Prouty,[1] Dick Mallary. These are the kind of people that you have sent in the past and the kind that I hope you will send in the future, and Jim Jeffords is in that mold. Jim, good luck to you.

Mr. Chairman,[2] it was wonderful that you recognized Jeannette Prouty, a dear friend of Betty's and myself. Just nice to see you, Jeannette.

We have had some other fine people appear on the program. I was delighted to

[1] Charles A. Plumley, United States Representative from Vermont 1933–51, and Winston L. Prouty, United States Senator from Vermont 1958–71.

[2] Richard A. Snelling was chairman of the dinner.

see that there was a Kennedy [3] that I could endorse. I know that he will be a first-class Governor when you elect him on November 5.

Let me, if I might, speak about a problem that I think transcends the borders of Vermont, a problem that is of great importance to people whether they are from the State of Washington or Vermont or Michigan or Florida.

I would like to say a word or two about one of my very chief concerns: the preservation of a two-party system in our country.

In the wake of Watergate, the national polls tend to indicate that the number of Independent voters is growing, and I understand that. There is great disillusionment, for good and sufficient reasons. The number of party voters, both Republicans and Democrats, is shrinking rapidly, tragically. Unfortunately, we in the Republican Party are not doing as well as our Democratic friends.

I am deeply concerned about this, not for the sake of our party or the Democratic Party, but in all sincerity, for the fate of the country. For I am convinced that the future of America is very directly tied to the good aspects of politics in this country, and I use it in the proper context: the politics that have made America grow from 13 poor, struggling colonies almost 200 years ago with some 3 million people primarily on the borders of the Atlantic Ocean, to a nation today with some 213 million people with 48 States within the continental limits, plus Alaska and Hawaii.

I am convinced that politics in the best sense can and will be in the future the salvation of our system. And the politics of America is bound up in the two-party system.

I think most of us know that a two-party system, the one we have had in America, has contributed stability, opportunity, and freedom. These things do not just sort of happen. They do not happen automatically. These very treasured elements—stability, opportunity, and freedom—they are the outgrowth of a political continuity and stability that followed in the development of a two-party system in America.

It seems to me, as I have looked back over the history, that this approach that has been so strong in the development of self-government—it offers diverse people and segments of our population a choice, a choice without chaos.

I think historically a two-party system has worked well in America. It was not envisaged by our Founding Fathers. There is nothing in the Constitution that says we should have two political parties and no others. As a matter of fact, we went through somewhat of an evolutionary process and finally fell into the the pattern of a two-party system.

[3] State Senator Walter L. Kennedy was the Republican candidate for Governor of Vermont.

But as we look back over the last century, the evolution of a two-party system in this country has been the foundation of political balance and strength. This is not just a personal view of my own. It is a lesson that we have learned and relearned, not only in America but in other countries.

As we look around the globe, we find that in those countries where there are many, many political parties—and some countries do have many—there is instability, there is chaos, there is a lack of direction, whether it is in foreign policy or domestic policy. Or if we look at those countries where there is a one-party system—you are familiar with the facts of the extermination of freedom. So, what I am saying is that the alternatives to a two-party system, many, many political parties with chaos, or one political party with a loss of freedom, that is not what we want in America.

Well, you could look in some of these areas of the globe today, not a few but many, where you have a mass of small, regional, or class-oriented splinter groups, and none of those groups are strong enough or imaginative enough to give leadership to the country.

And you can look in the other direction and see where those countries that have a dictatorial, dogmatic kind of government, the people do not really have a chance. What worries me about the extremes on either side, one party or many parties, is there is always the possibility of a man on horseback or a demagog on a pedestal, and tragically the result is too often the same.

What we need in America is two strong political parties—free, vital, broad enough to encompass people from all segments of our society, from all economic portions of our society. This wide spectrum of political diversity can serve as the twin pillars of democracy.

I happen to think this spectrum that we represent is broad enough to have many, many people in the State of Vermont who have a similar political philosophy to those of us in Michigan who belong to the Republican Party, but at the same time, in your State as well as in ours, there is a sufficiently broad spectrum in the public to appeal to those that want to be Democrats.

This competition between two major political parties is healthy. I have often said, and I believe very deeply, that competition in business is good for business and good for the consumer. Competition in the political arena is good for the candidates, but more importantly, it is good for the voters. And we need the two-party system to develop, to maintain, and to stimulate that future in our political structure.

President Eisenhower once outlined what our vision should be as members of one great political party, and he, of course, embraced the Republican Party. Ike said, "We see our party not as an end in itself, but as a magnificent means, a means through which countless thousands of devoted citizens can cooperate in the conquering of problems that beset free men everywhere." I think Ike expressed it about as well as anybody that I know.

Now, at the moment, you are as familiar as I am with the biggest problem that I think our country faces domestically. It is besetting free men everywhere throughout the globe, and I speak very candidly of inflation.

We have inflation here that is serious—double-digit inflation—we do not like, we are not going to tolerate. But it is not just in the United States. And this concern is one of my prime interests in solving, as it is yours.

In the 2 months that I have been privileged to be your President, I probably spent as much, if not more time in listening to people who had ideas, listening to groups that had suggestions, trying to sort out the many, many things that came to us in the Nation's Capital from people all over the United States.

I am sure in the many, many communications that we have gotten and suggestions we have received, Vermont contributed its share. Tomorrow, before a joint session of the Congress, I will outline a comprehensive plan to deal with inflation, and I will recommend a two-pronged attack or a two-pronged undertaking.

First, I will call for strong, broad, and firm legislative action by the Congress in a number of areas, but it will require a responsive action by the Congress with the President if we are going to meet this challenge.

In addition, I will call upon the American people, 213 million of you, to join with me and the Congress in an effort to move ahead to accomplish success, to win the battle over inflation, and at the same time, to maintain a growing economy. And I know that I can call upon the fine legislators like George Aiken, Bob Stafford, Dick Mallary, who worked with me and with their colleagues in the Senate and the House.

We must win this battle—our public enemy number one—if we are going to save the political fabric of this country and the political fabric of countries that believe in freedom around the world.

Yes, I am going to ask every citizen to enlist, every citizen in this country to participate, to make a sacrifice. And I am going to call upon the Federal Government to sacrifice, and State and local units of government to tighten their belts, and others to cooperate in winning the struggle against our public enemy number one.

I am particularly mindful of the unemployed and the retired people living on already small and fixed incomes. And we have to have a program that is designed to protect those who are least fortunate, and there will be a program aimed to be compassionate and helpful.

But it will be a fair program, as I said the other day to some news commentator. I do receive a lot of advice in this area, and I must reveal one thing. I am not going to ask for—and I got this advice from George and Bob and Dick. They said, "Don't ask for any increase in the Federal gasoline tax."

So, let me give you a preview. Let me give you one sneak preview. I am not going to ask for any increase in the gasoline tax, and any speculation to the contrary is untrue.

Now, if I might close with just one final comment. I, as all of you, particularly your Governmental officials, have great faith in our system. I know there are skeptics and pessimists who from time to time wonder whether our system can survive in the competitive world that we face. But every time I listen to a pessimist, I cannot help but recall what Winston Churchill once said when he was asked to comment about a free society. And as I recall—and I am paraphrasing a bit—Winston Churchill said democracy is the worst form of government except it is better than any other that has ever been tried. I believe in that and so do you.

And then they tell the story—and I was in Philadelphia a few weeks ago—that Continental Congress that met for the purpose of writing our Constitution, or I should say our Constitutional Convention—they had representatives from 12 of the 13 States, some 55 of them. They worked long and hard from May until September. When they finished their labors—and there were compromises between the big States and the small States, between the big cities and the rural communities—they finally fashioned probably the greatest document in the history of mankind for the governing of people.

And after they had all signed and left that hall, the last one to leave was Benjamin Franklin. He strolled down those steps and as he got to the cobblestone street, he was asked this question by a bystander: "Mr. Franklin, what have you given us—a monarchy or a republic?" And according to the story, Ben Franklin said, "We have given you a republic—if you can keep it."

I do not have to talk to Vermonters about keeping the Republic. You have done it for 200 years.

But what I am saying is we have done it for 200 years, but we must do it today by sacrifice and vision and wisdom for the next 200 years. And George Aiken represents the kind of leadership that has built and constructed the future for those of us who will carry on.

Thank you very kindly.

NOTE: The President spoke at 9:31 p.m. in Patrick Gymnasium at the University of Vermont.

119

Remarks of Welcome to First Secretary Edward Gierek of Poland. *October 8, 1974*

MR. FIRST SECRETARY, it is a very distinct pleasure for me to welcome you and Mrs. Gierek to the United States. As you know, Mr. First Secretary, the family ties that bind our two peoples together in a very special way are very, very old, indeed older actually than the United States itself.

You have already visited Jamestown, Virginia, where the first Poles arrived in 1608, only 1 year after it was first settled. From that day to this day, large numbers of your countrymen have helped to build this country and to mold our great American traditions.

America treasures these contributions to our growth, to our culture, and to our history. During your stay in this country, Mr. First Secretary, you and Mrs. Gierek will be able to see for yourself the character of our country and the role that men and women from Poland have played in America's history.

Our two nations have thus a fine foundation upon which to build. I have watched with very great interest the substantial growth of our bilateral trade in the last 2 years since the establishment of the joint Polish-American Trade Commission. And continuing expansion of contacts between officials and private citizens, in the fields of such activities as science, technology, and the arts is another evidence of the dynamic development of Polish-American relations.

You, Mr. First Secretary, will surely agree with me that we must not allow our satisfaction with past progress to slow our pace or slacken our efforts in the future. We must use the opportunity your visit affords to seek new avenues of bilateral cooperation in many, many fields, including energy and environmental areas.

In many other areas of common interest, for example, our participation in the Conference on Security and Cooperation in Europe and our participation in the force reduction talks, we are engaged in common endeavors for peace.

Today, economic problems almost everywhere are very, very severe. That stability of the world is in danger, and almost everywhere it develops, as well as in developing countries, the welfare of people on a global basis unfortunately is actually threatened.

Mr. First Secretary, Poland knows too well, perhaps better than any other nation, the fearful experience of war and its very painful consequences. A thorough review of all the dangers to peace for ourselves and the world must surely be a matter of highest priority.

We seek a peaceful world and a more prosperous world. Poland is a world leader in coal production and coal research. Poland has a very major role, a role to play in contributing solutions to the world energy problem, and you, Mr. First Secretary, with a lifetime of expertise, are able to make a very important personal contribution in this specific area. I look forward to exchanging views with you on the energy problem.

Mr. First Secretary, we, all of us in America, are pleased that you and Mrs. Gierek are here. I am confident, Mr. First Secretary, that our meetings will deepen the friendship of our two peoples and broaden the cooperation of our two nations.

Thank you very much.

NOTE: The President spoke at 10:43 a.m. on the South Lawn at the White House where Mr. Gierek, First Secretary of the Central Committee of the Polish United Workers' Party, was given a formal welcome with full military honors.

First Secretary Gierek spoke in Polish. His remarks were translated by an interpreter as follows:

Mr. President, Mr. Secretary of State, ladies and gentlemen:

I wish to thank you for your words of cordiality which you, Mr. President, have addressed to me, to Mrs. Gierek, and to members of my delegation. I take these words of yours as being directed to the people of Poland and to the Polish State on behalf of which and upon your invitation I am visiting the United States.

I am pleased to have made this visit, as it adds new testimony to the friendly ties that have linked our two nations since the times of George Washington and Tadeusz Kosciuszko.

I rest assured that it is the desire of both our peoples not only to preserve these traditional relations but also to strengthen them through closer and broader cooperation in the world of today.

Indeed, Socialist Poland, dynamically developing her new potential and creating as she does new living conditions for her people, is vitally interested in this. I trust that the talks we shall hold and agreements we shall conclude will greatly contribute towards this end, that they will open up broader prospects for cooperation between our countries.

I am pleased to have made this visit, also, because it represents yet another reaffirmation of international détente which my country views as extremely significant and to which we try to make our utmost contribution.

That process which originates from the very essence of the contemporary world, from the need for and necessity of peaceful coexistence among states with differing political systems has been considerably enhanced in recent years.

We of Poland can only welcome it in our profound conviction that it is in the interest of all nations to make that process further extend universal and irreversible. Precisely for this reason there is wide appreciation today that it is you, Mr. President, who is steering the United States policy towards this direction.

I am pleased to have made this visit, as it will enable me to get to know the United States, to acquaint myself with the outstanding accomplishments of the progress of civilization of the American people, whose history and achievements have since the very outset been and continue to be so much enriched by the Americans of Polish extraction.

Mr. President, I am profoundly convinced of the propitious conditions today and the right time for expansion of Polish-American cooperation in its new dimensions and in all fields of endeavor.

Mine is also a firm belief that we can work closer together for the great cause of peace. That is the purpose of my visit here, and I am happy that you too share these aspirations of ours.

Please accept, Mr. President, the best wishes from Poland to the United States, from the Polish people to the American people.

120

Statement on House Action To Suspend United States Military Assistance to Turkey. *October 8, 1974*

YESTERDAY the House of Representatives, once again acting against the almost unanimous advice of its leadership, amended the continuing resolution granting funds for our foreign aid programs. The amendment requires an immediate cessation of all U.S. military assistance to Turkey and is, in my view, a misguided and extremely harmful measure.

Instead of encouraging the parties involved in the Cyprus dispute to return to the negotiating table, this amendment, if passed by the Senate, will mean the indefinite postponement of meaningful negotiations. Instead of strengthening America's ability to persuade the parties to resolve the dispute, it will lessen our influence on all the parties concerned. And it will imperil our relationships with our Turkish friends and weaken us in the crucial Eastern Mediterranean.

But most tragic of all, a cutoff of arms to Turkey will not help Greece or the Greek Cypriot people who have suffered so much over the course of the last several months. We recognize that we are far from a settlement consistent with Greece's honor and dignity. We are prepared to exert our efforts in that direction. But reckless acts that prevent progress toward a Cyprus settlement harm Greeks, for it is the Greek Government and the Greek Cypriots who have the most to gain from a compromise settlement. And it is they who have the most to lose from continued deadlock.

Thus I call upon the Senate to accept the original conference report language on Turkish arms aid and to return the bill to the House of Representatives once again. And I ask the House of Representatives to reconsider its hasty act and, working with the Senate, pass a bill that will best serve the interests of peace.

121

Address to a Joint Session of the Congress on the Economy. *October 8, 1974*

Mr. Speaker, Mr. President, distinguished guests, my very dear friends:

In his first inaugural address, President Franklin D. Roosevelt said, and I quote: The people of the United States have not failed . . . . They want direct, vigorous action, and they have asked for discipline and direction under our leadership.

Today, though our economic difficulties do not approach the emergency of 1933, the message from the American people is exactly the same. I trust that you are getting the very same message that I am receiving: Our constituents want leadership, our constituents want action.

All of us have heard much talk on this very floor about Congress recovering its rightful share of national leadership. I now intend to offer you that chance.

The 73d Congress responded to FDR's appeal in 5 days. I am deeply grateful for the cooperation of the 93d Congress and the Conference on Inflation, which ended 10 days ago.

Mr. Speaker, many—but not all—of your recommendations on behalf of your party's caucus are reflected in some of my proposals here today. The distinguished majority leader of the Senate offered a nine-point program. I seriously studied all of them and adopted some of his suggestions.

I might add, I have also listened very hard to many of our former colleagues in both bodies and of both the majority and the minority, and have been both persuaded and dissuaded. But in the end, I had to make the decision, I had to decide, as each of you do when the rollcall is called.

I will not take your time today with the discussion of the origins of inflation and its bad effect on the United States, but I do know where we want to be in 1976—on the 200th birthday of a United States of America that has not lost its way, nor its will, nor its sense of national purpose.

During the meetings on inflation, I listened carefully to many valuable suggestions. Since the summit, I have evaluated literally hundreds of ideas, day and night.

My conclusions are very simply stated. There is only one point on which all advisers have agreed: We must whip inflation right now.

None of the remedies proposed, great or small, compulsory or voluntary, stands a chance unless they are combined in a considered package, in a concerted effort, in a grand design.

I have reviewed the past and the present efforts of our Federal Government to help the economy. They are simply not good enough, nor sufficiently broad, nor do they pack the punch that will turn America's economy on.

A stable American economy cannot be sustained if the world's economy is in chaos. International cooperation is absolutely essential and vital. But while we seek agreements with other nations, let us put our own economic house in order.

Today, I have identified 10 areas for our joint action, the executive and the legislative branches of our Government.

Number one: food. America is the world's champion producer of food. Food prices and petroleum prices in the United States are primary inflationary factors. America today partially depends on foreign sources for petroleum, but we can grow more than enough food for ourselves.

To halt higher food prices, we must produce more food, and I call upon every farmer to produce to full capacity. And I say to you and to the farmers, they have done a magnificent job in the past, and we should be eternally grateful.

This Government, however, will do all in its power to assure him—that farmer—he can sell his entire yield at reasonable prices. Accordingly, I ask the Congress to remove all remaining acreage limitations on rice, peanuts, and cotton.

I also assure America's farmers here and now that I will allocate all the fuel and ask authority to allocate all the fertilizer they need to do this essential job.

Agricultural marketing orders and other Federal regulations are being reviewed to eliminate or modify those responsible for inflated prices.

I have directed our new Council on Wage and Price Stability to find and to expose all restrictive practices, public or private, which raise food prices. The Administration will also monitor food production, margins, pricing, and exports. We can and we shall have an adequate supply at home, and through cooperation, meet the needs of our trading partners abroad.

Over this past weekend, we initiated a voluntary program to monitor grain exports. The Economic Policy Board will be responsible for determining the policy under this program.

In addition, in order to better allocate our supplies for export, I ask that a provision be added to Public Law 480 under which we ship food to the needy and friendly countries. The President needs authority to waive certain of the restrictions on shipments based on national interest or humanitarian grounds.

Number two: energy. America's future depends heavily on oil, gas, coal, electricity, and other resources called energy. Make no mistake, we do have a real energy problem.

One-third of our oil—17 percent of America's total energy—now comes from foreign sources that we cannot control, at high cartel prices costing you and me $16 billion—$16 billion more than just a year ago.

The primary solution has to be at home. If you have forgotten the shortages of last winter, most Americans have not.

I have ordered today the reorganization of our national energy effort and the creation of a national energy board.[1] It will be chaired with developing—or I should say charged with developing a single national energy policy and program. And I think most of you will be glad to know that our former colleague, Rog Morton, our Secretary of Interior, will be the overall boss of our national energy program.

Rog Morton's marching orders are to reduce imports of foreign oil by 1 million barrels per day by the end of 1975, whether by savings here at home, or by increasing our own sources.

Secretary Morton, along with his other responsibility, is also charged with increasing our domestic energy supply by promptly utilizing our coal resources and expanding recovery of domestic oil still in the grounds in old wells.

New legislation will be sought after your recess to require use of cleaner coal processes and nuclear fuel in new electric plants, and the quick conversion of existing oil plants. I propose that we, together, set a target date of 1980 for eliminating oil-fired plants from the Nation's base-loaded electrical capacity.

I will use the Defense Production Act to allocate scarce materials for energy development, and I will ask you, the House and Senate, for whatever amendments prove necessary.

I will meet with top management of the automobile industry to assure, either by agreement or by law, a firm program aimed at achieving a 40 percent increase in gasoline mileage within a 4-year development deadline.

Priority legislation—action, I should say—to increase energy supply here at home requires the following:

—One, long-sought deregulation of natural gas supplies,

—Number two, responsible use of our Naval petroleum reserves in California and Alaska,

—Number three, amendments to the Clean Air Act; and

—Four, passage of surface mining legislation to ensure an adequate supply with commonsense environmental protection.

Now, if all of these steps fail to meet our current energy-saving goals, I will not hestitate to ask for tougher measures. For the long range, we must work harder on coal gasification. We must push with renewed vigor and talent research in the use of nonfossil fuels. The power of the atom, the heat of the sun and the steam stored deep in the Earth, the force of the winds and water must be main sources of energy for our grandchildren, and we can do it.

Number three: restrictive practices. To increase productivity and contain prices, we must end restrictive and costly practices whether instituted by Gov-

[1] On October 11, 1974, the President signed Executive Order 11814 activating the Energy Resources Council.

ernment, industry, labor, or others. And I am determined to return to the vigorous enforcement of antitrust laws.

The Administration will zero in on more effective enforcement of laws against price fixing and bid rigging. For instance, non-competitive professional fee schedules and real estate settlement fees must be eliminated. Such violations will be prosecuted by the Department of Justice to the full extent of the law.

Now, I ask Congress for prompt authority to increase maximum penalties for antitrust violations from $50,000 to $1 million for corporations, and from $50,000 to $100,000 for individual violators.

At the Conference on Inflation we found, I would say, very broad agreement that the Federal Government imposes too many hidden and too many inflationary costs on our economy. As a result, I propose a four-point program aimed at a substantial purging process.

Number one, I have ordered the Council on Wage and Price Stability to be the watchdog over inflationary costs of all governmental actions.

Two, I ask the Congress to establish a National Commission on Regulatory Reform to undertake a long-overdue total reexamination of the independent regulatory agencies. It will be a joint effort by the Congress, the executive branch, and the private sector to identify and eliminate existing Federal rules and regulations that increase costs to the consumer without any good reason in today's economic climate.

Three: Hereafter, I will require that all major legislative proposals, regulations, and rules emanating from the executive branch of the Government will include an inflation impact statement that certifies we have carefully weighed the effect on the Nation. I respectfully request that the Congress require a similar advance inflation impact statement for its own legislative initiatives.

Finally, I urge State and local units of government to undertake similar programs to reduce inflationary effects of their regulatory activities.

At this point, I thank the Congress for recently revitalizing the National Commission on Productivity and Work Quality. It will initially concentrate on problems of productivity in Government—Federal, State, and local. Outside of Government, it will develop meaningful blueprints for labor-management cooperation at the plant level. It should look particularly at the construction and the health service industries.

The Council on Wage and Price Stability will, of course, monitor wage and price increases in the private sector. Monitoring will include public hearings to justify either price or wage increases. I emphasize, in fact reemphasize, that this is not a compulsory wage and price control agency.

Now, I know many Americans see Federal controls as the answer. But I believe from past experience controls show us that they never really stop inflation—not the last time, not even during and immediately after World War II when, as I recall, prices rose despite severe and enforceable wartime rationing.

Now, peacetime controls actually, we know from recent experience, create shortages, hamper production, stifle growth, and limit jobs. I do not ask for such powers, however politically tempting, as such a program could cause the fixer and the black marketeer to flourish while decent citizens face empty shelves and stand in long waiting lines.

Number four: We need more capital. We cannot "eat up our seed corn." Our free enterprise system depends on orderly capital markets through which the savings of our people become productively used. Today, our capital markets are in total disarray. We must restore their vitality. Prudent monetary restraint is essential.

You and the American people should know, however, that I have personally been assured by the Chairman of the independent Federal Reserve Board that the supply of money and credit will expand sufficiently to meet the needs of our economy and that in no event will a credit crunch occur.

The prime lending rate is going down. To help industry to buy more machines and create more jobs, I am recommending a liberalized 10 percent investment tax credit. This credit should be especially helpful to capital-intensive industries such as primary metals, public utilities, where capacity shortages have developed.

I am asking Congress to enact tax legislation to provide that all dividends on preferred stocks issued for cash be fully deductible by the issuing company. This should bring in more capital, especially for energy-producing utilities. It will also help other industries shift from debt to equity, providing a sounder capital structure.

Capital gains tax legislation must be liberalized as proposed by the tax reform bill currently before the Committee on Ways and Means. I endorse this approach and hope that it will pass promptly.

Number five: Helping the casualties. And this is a very important part of the overall speech. The Conference on Inflation made everybody even more aware of who is suffering most from inflation. Foremost are those who are jobless through no fault of their own.

Three weeks ago, I released funds which, with earlier actions, provide public service employment for some 170,000 who need work. I now propose to the Congress a two-step program to augment this action.

First, 13 weeks of special unemployment insurance benefits would be provided to those who have exhausted their regular and extended unemployment insurance benefits, and 26 weeks of special unemployment insurance benefits to those who qualify but are not now covered by regular unemployment insurance programs. Funding in this case would come from the general treasury, not from taxes on employers as is the case with the established unemployment programs.

Second, I ask the Congress to create a brand new Community Improvement Corps to provide work for the unemployed through short-term useful work projects to improve, beautify, and enhance the environment of our cities, our towns, and our countryside.

This standby program would come alive whenever unemployment exceeds 6 percent nationally. It would be stopped when unemployment drops below 6 percent. Local labor markets would each qualify for grants whenever their unemployment rate exceeds 6.5 percent.

State and local government contractors would supervise these projects and could hire only those who had exhausted their unemployment insurance benefits. The goal of this new program is to provide more constructive work for all Americans, young or old, who cannot find a job.

The purpose really follows this formula: Short-term problems require short-term remedies. I therefore request that these programs be for a 1-year period.

Now, I know that low- and middle-income Americans have been hardest hit by inflation. Their budgets are most vulnerable because a larger part of their income goes for the highly inflated costs of food, fuel, and medical care.

The tax reform bill now in the House Committee on Ways and Means, which I favor, already provides approximately $1.6 billion of tax relief to these groups. Compensating new revenues are provided in this prospective legislation by a windfall tax, profits tax on oil producers, and by closing other loopholes. If enacted, this will be a major contribution by the Congress in our common effort to make our tax system fairer to all.

Number six: stimulating housing. Without question, credit is the lifeblood of housing. The United States, unfortunately, is suffering the longest and the most severe housing recession since the end of World War II. Unemployment in the construction trades is twice the national average.

One of my first acts as President was to sign the Housing and Community

Development Act of 1974. I have since concluded that still more help is needed, help that can be delivered very quickly and with minimum inflationary impact.

I urge the Congress to enact before recess additional legislation to make most home mortgages eligible for purchase by an agency of the Federal Government. As the law stands now, only FHA or VA home mortgages, one-fifth of the total, are covered.

I am very glad that the Senate, thanks to the leadership of Senator Brooke and Senator Cranston, has already made substantial progress on this legislation. As soon as it comes to me, I will make at least $3 billion immediately available for mortgage purchases, enough to finance about 100,000 more American homes.

Number seven: thrift institutions. Savings and loan and similar institutions are hard hit by inflation and high interest rates. They no longer attract, unfortunately, adequate deposits. The executive branch, in my judgment, must join with the Congress in giving critically needed attention to the structure and the operation of our thrift institutions which now find themselves for the third time in 8 years in another period of serious mortgage credit scarcity.

Passage of the pending financial institution bill will help, but no single measure has yet appeared, as I see it, to solve feast or famine in mortgage credit. However, I promise to work with you individually and collectively to develop additional specific programs in this area in the future.

Number eight: international interdependency. The United States has a responsibility not only to maintain a healthy economy at home, but also to seek policies which complement rather than disrupt the constructive efforts of others.

Essential to U.S. initiatives is the early passage of an acceptable trade reform bill. My Special Representative for Trade Negotiations [William D. Eberle] departed earlier this afternoon to Canada, Europe, Japan, to brief foreign friends on my proposals.

We live in an interdependent world and, therefore, must work together to resolve common economic problems.

Number nine: Federal taxes and spending. To support programs, to increase production and share inflation-produced hardships, we need additional tax revenues.

I am aware that any proposal for new taxes just 4 weeks before a national election is, to put it mildly, considered politically unwise. And I am frank to say that I have been earnestly advised to wait and talk about taxes anytime after November 5. But I do say in sincerity that I will not play politics with America's future.

Our present inflation to a considerable degree comes from many years of enacting expensive programs without raising enough revenues to pay for them. The truth is that 19 out of the 25 years I had the honor and the privilege to serve in this Chamber, the Federal Government ended up with Federal deficits. That is not a very good batting average.

By now, almost everybody—almost everybody else, I should say—has stated my position on Federal gasoline taxes. This time I will do it myself. I am not—emphasizing not—asking you for any increase in gas taxes.

I am—I *am* asking you to approve a 1-year temporary tax surcharge of 5 percent on corporate and upper-level individual incomes. This would generally exclude from the surcharge those families with gross incomes below $15,000 a year. The estimated $5 billion in extra revenue to be raised by this inflation-fighting tax should pay for the new programs I have recommended in this message.

I think, and I suspect each of you know, this is the acid test of our joint determination to whip inflation in America. I would not ask this if major loopholes were not now being closed by the Committee on Ways and Means' tax reform bill.

I urge you to join me before your recess, in addition to what I have said before, to join me by voting to set a target spending limit—let me emphasize it—a target spending limit of $300 billion for the Federal fiscal budget of 1975.

When Congress agrees to this spending target, I will submit a package of budget deferrals and rescissions to meet this goal. I will do the tough job of designating for Congressional action, on your return, those areas which I believe can and must be reduced. These will be hard choices and every one of you in this Chamber know it as well as I. They will be hard choices, but no Federal agency, including the Defense Department, will be untouchable.

It is my judgment that fiscal discipline is a necessary weapon in any fight against inflation. While this spending target is a small step, it is a step in the right direction, and we need to get on that course without any further delay. I do not think that any of us in this Chamber today can ask the American people to tighten their belts if Uncle Sam is unwilling to tighten his belt first.

And now, if I might, I would like to say a few words directly to your constituents and, incidentally, mine.

My fellow Americans, 10 days ago I asked you to get things started by making a list of 10 ways to fight inflation and save energy, to exchange your list with your neighbors, and to send me a copy.

I have personally read scores of the thousands of letters received at the White

House, and incidentally, I have made my economic experts read some of them, too. We all benefited, at least I did, and I thank each and every one of you for this cooperation.

Some of the good ideas from your home to mine have been cranked into the recommendations I have just made to the Congress and the steps I am taking as President to whip inflation right now. There were also firm warnings on what Government must not do, and I appreciated those, too. Your best suggestions for voluntary restraint and self-discipline showed me that a great degree of patriotic determination and unanimity already exists in this great land.

I have asked Congress for urgent specific actions it alone can take. I advised Congress of the initial steps that I am taking as President. Here is what only you can do: Unless every able American pitches in, Congress and I cannot do the job. Winning our fight against inflation and waste involves total mobilization of America's greatest resources—the brains, the skills, and the willpower of the American people.

Here is what we must do, what each and every one of you can do: To help increase food and lower prices, grow more and waste less; to help save scarce fuel in the energy crisis, drive less, heat less. Every housewife knows almost exactly how much she spent for food last week. If you cannot spare a penny from your food budget—and I know there are many—surely you can cut the food that you waste by 5 percent.

Every American motorist knows exactly how many miles he or she drives to work or to school every day and about how much mileage she or he runs up each year. If we all drive at least 5 percent fewer miles, we can save, almost unbelievably, 250,000 barrels of foreign oil per day. By the end of 1975, most of us can do better than 5 percent by carpooling, taking the bus, riding bikes, or just plain walking. We can save enough gas by self-discipline to meet our 1 million barrels per day goal.

I think there is one final thing that all Americans can do, rich or poor, and that is share with others. We can share burdens as we can share blessings. Sharing is not easy, not easy to measure like mileage and family budgets, but I am sure that 5 percent more is not nearly enough to ask, so I ask you to share everything you can and a little bit more. And it will strengthen our spirits as well as our economy.

Today I will not take more of the time of this busy Congress, for I vividly remember the rush before every recess, and the clock is already running on my specific and urgent requests for legislative action. I also remember how much Congress can get done when it puts its shoulder to the wheel.

One week from tonight I have a longstanding invitation in Kansas City to address the Future Farmers of America, a fine organization of wonderful young people whose help, with millions of others, is vital in this battle. I will elaborate then how volunteer inflation fighters and energy savers can further mobilize their total efforts.

Since asking Miss Sylvia Porter, the well-known financial writer, to help me organize an all-out nationwide volunteer mobilization, I have named a White House coordinator and have enlisted the enthusiastic support and services of some 17 other distinguished Americans to help plan for citizen and private group participation.

There will be no big Federal bureaucracy set up for this crash program. Through the courtesy of such volunteers from the communication and media fields, a very simple enlistment form will appear in many of tomorrow's newspapers along with the symbol of this new mobilization, which I am wearing on my lapel. It bears the single word WIN. I think that tells it all. I will call upon every American to join in this massive mobilization and stick with it until we do win as a nation and as a people.

Mr. Speaker and Mr. President, I stand on a spot hallowed by history. Many Presidents have come here many times to solicit, to scold, to flatter, to exhort the Congress to support them in their leadership. Once in a great while, Presidents have stood here and truly inspired the most skeptical and the most sophisticated audience of their co-equal partners in Government. Perhaps once or twice in a generation is there such a joint session. I don't expect this one to be.

Only two of my predecessors have come in person to call upon Congress for a declaration of war, and I shall not do that. But I say to you with all sincerity that our inflation, our public enemy number one, will, unless whipped, destroy our country, our homes, our liberties, our property, and finally our national pride, as surely as any well-armed wartime enemy.

I concede there will be no sudden Pearl Harbor to shock us into unity and to sacrifice, but I think we have had enough early warnings. The time to intercept is right now. The time to intercept is almost gone.

My friends and former colleagues, will you enlist now? My friends and fellow Americans, will you enlist now? Together with discipline and determination, we will win.

I thank you very much.

NOTE: The President spoke at 4:02 p.m. in the House Chamber at the Capitol. The address was broadcast live on radio and television.

122

Statement on the Death of Paul G. Hoffman. *October 8, 1974*

PAUL GRAY HOFFMAN's life was not one success story but many. A talented, dynamic businessman, he went on to serve both America and the world as an inspired public servant and a great humanitarian.

His work with the Studebaker Packard Corporation marked him as one of the giants of American industry. At the end of World War II, as the first Administrator of the Marshall Plan, his intelligence and compassion helped to rebuild a Europe that was in ruins. Mr. Hoffman served with equal distinction in important posts at the United Nations and with the Ford Foundation and the Fund for the Republic.

His life was as long as it was eventful. To his wife Anna, a distinguished public servant in her own right, and to the other members of the family, Mrs. Ford and I express our deepest sympathy and regret on the passing of a great and beloved American.

NOTE: Mr. Hoffman, 86, died in New York City. On June 21, 1974, Mr. Hoffman was awarded the Presidential Medal of Freedom.

123

Toasts of the President and First Secretary Gierek of Poland. *October 8, 1974*

Mr. First Secretary and Mrs. Gierek, our wonderful guests:

It is a great privilege and pleasure to have you and Mrs. Gierek here with us this evening. We have had a very delightful dinner, and we had a very helpful and constructive discussion during the day, and I am looking forward to further discussions tomorrow.

Mr. First Secretary, I come from a part of our country where we have roughly 30,000 people with a Polish heritage or background. And as I grew up, Mr. First Secretary, I had many wonderful personal experiences with families that had a Polish background, families that had the same great family strength, families that had a tremendous religious dedication, individuals with a Polish heritage that became leaders in our community, outstanding scholars, athletes, public servants.

And so I had a great exposure to the finest, the best, with individuals who had come from your country to ours.

And then in 1958 or '59, I had the opportunity to go to Poland, and I wondered as I went to Poland whether there would be so many comparable, wonderful people in Poland as I had known in my hometown in Michigan in the United States.

And I found, Mr. First Secretary, that instead of 30,000, there were 30 million. And all of them had the same warmth, friendship, family dedication, deep conviction, and all of them wanted to uplift their community, their state, and make their country a better and finer place in which to live.

So it seemed to me, Mr. First Secretary, that it was very easy for Poland and our country to start building a foundation some years ago which has now developed into a great relationship, a relationship predicated on understanding, a relationship that has a far broader vision.

We want to help one another and we do. But we want to build from our relationship a broader effort to improve world relations between countries that did not understand one another, but who now hopefully will, blocs that did not understand one another, but hopefully will. And the net result is that because of our citizens who came from Poland, settled here, and have become so strong and vital in our society, and yours who are so strong and so vital in Europe, I hope and trust that we can move together in cooperation and economic matters, cultural matters, educational matters, environmental matters, and set an example for all nations because we do understand one another and we can, by history, work together.

And so I ask all of our guests here tonight to rise and join with me in offering a toast to the First Secretary and to Mrs. Gierek and offer them the best from all of us in the United States to the First Secretary, to the Polish people.

NOTE: The President spoke at 10:12 p.m. in the State Dining Room at the White House.

First Secretary Gierek spoke in Polish. His remarks were translated by an interpreter as follows:

Dear Mr. President, ladies and gentlemen:

I thank you, Mr. President, for your kind and friendly words. I thank you for the hospitality you have shown us, which both Mrs. Gierek and I greatly appreciate and sincerely hope to heartily reciprocate.

From the outset of our sojourn on the American soil, we have been accompanied by a good, matter-of-fact, and friendly atmosphere. This gladdens us and reaffirms in our profound conviction that my visit here will prove fruitful.

Our conversations with you, Mr. President, have above all reassured me in this. We have exchanged, in their course, views on the most important issues of Polish-American relations and on the further development of the process of international détente.

We have reached important conclusions which will be set down on our joint documents. I am confident that the results of our meetings will open up a new stage in the mutual relations between both our countries and nations.

I highly value, Mr. President, this direct contact with you, with the leader of the United States, who, by his own deep understanding of and positive approach to issues of the present-day cooperation between our two nations, confirms the willingness to develop it further in the friendly attitude toward Poland.

I am also satisfied over my meetings with the Secretary of State, Dr. Henry Kissinger, and with all eminent associates of yours.

It is my conviction, Mr. President, that there exist very favorable conditions to a significant expansion of Polish-U.S. cooperation which is the common concern of ours. These conditions, as you have pointed out a moment ago, stem from our long-standing tradition of friendly, mutual bonds, dating back to the times of the founding of the United States begun by the participation of Tadeusz Kosciuszko, Pulaski, and other sons of the Polish people who struggled for the independence of the United States.

These bonds were subsequently strengthened by the sympathy toward and interest of the democratic forces of the American nation in the cause of Polish independence. And they were amply reaffirmed in our joint struggle for freedom, greatest in history, as it were, conducted by the great anti-Fascist coalition in the years of World War II.

These traditions have remained alive although their early postwar phase has fortunately become a closed historical chapter.

As a result of its own heroic struggle and its cooperation with all other freedom-loving forces, the people of Poland found its road to durable independence, to enviable security, to dynamic development.

The people of Poland found it in its new Socialist homeland, in its consciously chosen alliance with the U.S.S.R. and other Socialist countries, in its active foreign policy of international security and peaceful cooperation.

Modern Poland, Mr. President, with a more than 1,000-year history and great traditions of love for freedom and progress, is proud of the great historic achievements of the past three decades which have essentially altered the course of our nation's tragic past and verily transformed the country, elevating it onto a new place in Europe and the world at large.

The Poland of today, one of the world's top ten industrial producers, is a country of a dynamic economy, of high cultural and scientific standards, and constantly growing standards of living.

In recent years we have endowed her development with a still greater dynamism and higher quality. We still have much to accomplish. But the decisive stage is behind us and Poland could now enter the phase of accelerated growth of her economy. And the aspirations of my people are indeed in keeping with these vital needs and aspirations of all.

It is from this position and for this purpose that we also desire to eject new impetus and quality to our cooperation with other countries of the world. We are delighted to see considerable progress achieved in Polish-American relations, particularly in recent years. But we take it only as a harbinger of a much broader cooperation.

We therefore attach special importance to development of economic cooperation which establishes most durable of bonds and provides for a material base of cooperation in all other fields.

We conceive of the United States as one of our principal partners in the West. There exist all opportunities that it be so. The essential thing is to create conditions that would make us seize of all those opportunities.

I strongly believe that arrangements we are now adopting and the agreements we are concluding will be a decisive contribution towards this end. In the overall framework of relations between our two countries, a major positive role can no doubt be played by the multi-million strong group of Americans of Polish ancestry as good citizens of the United States and at the same time retaining their emotional ties with their old land.

They have always been one of the important factors of mutual rapprochement between our two nations, and they can further make a substantial contribution to their friendly cooperation.

Mr. President, ladies and gentlemen: Our thoughts constantly turn to the great and common cause of all mankind, the cause of peace.

The Polish nation which paid the highest price for its freedom and is fully cognizant of the value of peace, attaches great importance to the process of détente which has been developing in recent years. We see in it a true road toward the strengthening of international security and development of cooperation among nations on the basis of peaceful coexistence of states with different political systems. This is the prime need and necessity of our time.

Let me say, Mr. President, that Poland fully appreciates the far-reaching and all-around significance of Soviet-American agreements for the cause of world peace and general improvement of international relations.

It was with greatest satisfaction that we welcomed progress already achieved here, and together with other countries we have noted with great appreciation the promise that these propitious trends will be continued.

It is only natural that Poland should attach particular significance to progress of détente and to consolidation of the facts of nearly three decades of peace in Europe. We have been actively cooperating to insure the success of the Conference on Security and Cooperation in Europe. We believe that there exist very realistic conditions for its successful conclusion in the months to come.

We shall continue to make our constructive contribution to the Vienna talks on troops and arms reduction in Central Europe.

We are convinced that the United States is also vitally interested in a lasting peace on our continent and can indeed make a substantial and constructive contribution to that cause. We rest assured of the indivisibility of and the universal need for peace and of the desire common to all nations for security, justice, and a better morale.

I trust that also in the strivings to achieve these great objectives closer cooperation between both our countries is possible and necessary.

My first day in Washington and, above all, the talks I had with you, Mr. President, reaffirm me in my conviction that together we can open up new, broader prospects for the development of Polish-U.S. cooperation. I am reassured in this also by the good climate in which all our meetings are held and which is typical of the friendly relations obtaining between our two peoples.

Mr. President, I should like to propose a toast. To your very good health and all success in steering the affairs of the great United States, for the speediest recovery of Mrs. Ford, to your good health, ladies and gentlemen, to the development of friendly cooperation between our peoples and states, to world peace.

124

Remarks on Departure of Secretary of State Henry A. Kissinger for the Middle East. *October 9, 1974*

IT IS nice to see you all, and I just came out with all the Cabinet members and others in the Administration to express our appreciation to the Secretary of State for going on this vitally important mission and to indicate my full support and the support of the Administration for the, I think, tremendous efforts to bring peace in an area of the world that has been so volatile and controversial that it is important for the world, as well as the countries involved, that the maximum efforts for peace be made.

This country and this Administration are going to work with the skill and imagination of Dr. Kissinger in seeking that result.

We wish you the very best.

NOTE: The President spoke at 12:40 a.m. at Andrews Air Force Base, Md., where Secretary Kissinger departed for a 7-day trip to seven Middle East countries.

Secretary Kissinger responded to the President's remarks as follows:

I appreciate very much, Mr. President, your coming out to see me off. The problem of contributing to peace in the Middle East is a very complicated one, but as I have had occasion to say before, it is a source of pride to all Americans that it is the United States that all parties trust, and that we will attempt to make some progress.

I would like to say to the President that this is the first time in a long time that one can go on these missions with an America that is at peace with itself.

Thank you very much.

125

Statement on Privacy Legislation. *October 9, 1974*

LEGISLATION to protect personal privacy is making significant progress in the Congress. I am delighted about the prospect of House and Senate action at this session.

Renewed national efforts to strengthen protections for personal privacy should begin in Washington. We should start by enacting uniform fair information practices for the agencies of the Federal Government. This will give us invaluable operating experience as we continue to examine and recommend needed actions at the State and local level and in the private sector.

The immediate objective should be to give every citizen the right to inspect, challenge, and correct, if necessary, information about him contained in Federal agency records and to assure him a remedy for illegal invasions of privacy by Federal agencies accountable for safeguarding his records. In legislating, the right of privacy, of course, must be balanced against equally valid public interests in freedom of information, national defense, foreign policy, law enforcement, and in a high quality and trustworthy Federal work force.

Immediately after I assumed the Chairmanship, as Vice President, of the Cabinet-level Domestic Council Committee on the Right of Privacy, I asked the Office of Management and Budget to work jointly with the Committee staff, the executive agencies, and the Congress to work out realistic and effective legislation at the earliest possible time. Substantial progress has been made by both the Senate and the House on bills extending personal privacy protections to tens of millions of records containing personal information in hundreds of Federal data banks.

H.R. 16373, the Privacy Act of 1974, has my enthusiastic support, except for the provisions which allow unlimited individual access to records vital to determining eligibility and promotion in the Federal service and access to classified information. I strongly urge floor amendments permitting workable exemptions to accommodate these situations.

The Senate also has made substantial progress in writing privacy legislation. S. 3418 parallels the House bill in many respects, but I believe major technical and substantive amendments are needed to perfect the bill. I do not favor establishing a separate commission or board bureaucracy empowered to define privacy in its own terms and to second-guess citizens and agencies. I vastly prefer an approach which makes Federal agencies fully and publicly accountable for legally mandated privacy protections, and which gives the individual adequate legal remedies to enforce what he deems to be his own best privacy interests.

The adequate protection of personal privacy requires legislative and executive initiatives in areas not addressed by H.R. 16373 and S. 3418. I have asked executive branch officials to continue to work with the Congress to assure swift action on measures to strengthen privacy and confidentiality in income tax records, criminal justice records, and other areas identified as needed privacy initiatives by the Domestic Council Committee on the Right of Privacy.

126

Statement on Signing the Department of Defense Appropriations Act, 1975. *October 9, 1974*

I AM pleased to have signed H.R. 16243. Although not all Administration recommendations were accepted, I recognize and appreciate bipartisan efforts made by the House-Senate conference committee to produce a defense appropriations bill acceptable to both Houses and sufficient for our national security needs.

The bill has, however, a major drawback. The $700 million funding for South Vietnam is inadequate to provide for all of their critical needs, if South Vietnam's enemies continue to press their attacks. It may, therefore, be necessary to approach the Congress early next year to work out some solutions to meet critical needs which arise.

Each year the President of the United States must sign into law an appropriations bill for our defense. From my experience in Congress, I know all too well the conflicts this defense bill can produce in the name of economy and other national interests. Thus, as I sign such a bill for the first time as President, I want to renew my pledge to build a new partnership between the executive and legislative branches of our Government, a partnership based on close consultation, compromise of differences, and a high regard for the constitutional duties and powers of both branches to work for the common good and security of our Nation.

NOTE: As enacted, H.R. 16243, approved October 8, 1974, is Public Law 93–437 (88 Stat. 1212).

127

The President's News Conference of *October 9, 1974*

THE PRESIDENT. I never promised you a rose garden, but I guess Ron Nessen did. So, I hope you enjoy this new setting and the new format, and I hope I enjoy it, too.

MEETING WITH PRESIDENT ECHEVERRÍA

[1.] I do have one business announcement. I am pleased to announce this afternoon that President Echeverría of Mexico and I have agreed to hold a meeting on the U.S.-Mexican border on Monday, October 21.

I am very much looking forward to this opportunity to meet with President Echeverría in the Nogales area, and we plan to visit both sides of the border. The United States and Mexico have a long tradition of friendly and cooperative relations. It is my hope that our meeting will contribute to maintaining that relationship and to strengthen the good will between our countries over the years to come.

At this meeting, we will discuss, obviously, a wide range of subjects of interest to both countries.

One of the first responses to our WIN program yesterday was John Osborne's [1] signing up, and I have his application right here. Thank you, John.

Well, the first question. Dick Lerner [Richard E. Lerner, United Press International].

QUESTIONS

INFLATION AND RECESSION

[2.] Q. Mr. President, a few things were left unsaid in your economic address yesterday. I was wondering if you could say now if the United States is in a recession, and how soon Americans can expect to see a meaningful reduction of inflation and unemployment?

THE PRESIDENT. I do not think the United States is in a recession. We do have economic problems, but it is a very mixed situation, and that was the reason that we had some 31 specific recommendations in my speech yesterday.

We have to be very, very careful to make sure that we don't tighten the screws

[1] White House correspondent for the New Republic.

too tightly and precipitate us into some economic difficulty. And at the same time, we had to have provisions and programs that would meet the challenge of inflation.

I am convinced if the Congress responds, if the American people respond in a voluntary way, that we can have, hopefully early in 1975, some meaningful reduction in the rate of inflation.

Yes, Mr. Cormier [Frank Cormier, Associated Press].

INCOME SURTAX

[3.] Q. Mr. President, no one that I know of has suggested that inflation can be licked within a year, and yet the surtax you seek is only for one year. Is there a pretty good chance you will next year have to go back and ask for it all over again, assuming you get it this time?

THE PRESIDENT. I do not think that the surtax requested to be applicable in calendar year 1975 will have to be extended beyond December 31, 1975. We are in a temporary situation. And the surtax on both personal and corporate income will provide us sufficient income to meet the additional expenses for our community improvement program and, at the same time, will help to dampen inflation by reducing the amount of money of 28 percent of the taxpayers of this country.

And you might be interested—I checked on it this morning—there has been some criticism of this surtax, both political and otherwise: For a family of four, with a $20,000 gross income, that is wages, the 1-year extra tax will amount to $42, which is 12 cents a day.

For a person on a $15,000-a-year income, family of four, there is no extra tax.

And if you take it to $16,000 a day—a year, I mean—the added cost of the 5 percent surtax is $3, which is less than one cent a day.

FURTHER ECONOMIC MEASURES

[4.] Q. Mr. President, following up on Dick Lerner's question, if your economic program does not have the impact that you hope it will by early 1975, what other measures might be necessary? What proposals do you have in mind to follow on this program if it indeed is unsuccessful?

THE PRESIDENT. I am confident, in the first instance, that if all 31 of the recommendations are implemented, including those that I have asked the Congress to give me, that the program will work. We are going to concentrate on making it work. I, therefore, don't think we should speculate about something that I don't think will take place.

GASOLINE TAXES AND RATIONING

[5.] Q. Mr. President, some people think—a great many people, in fact—think that your proposals were not tough enough, or at least tough on the wrong people. In view of your somewhat apocalyptic vision of what will happen to this country if we don't lick inflation, why didn't you propose mandatory gasoline taxes or gasoline rationing in order to conserve fuel, for example?

THE PRESIDENT. We believe that the surtax charges that we have recommended are a more equitable approach to the achievement of greater income so we could give some relief to the less well-off, the people who are suffering greater hardship.

We took a look at the gasoline tax recommendations, and we found that this might be harmful to people, and it would be more harmful to the people less able to pay. And in balancing out all of the tax proposals, we came to the conclusion that what we have recommended, which affects only 28 percent of the personal income tax payers in this country, was the appropriate way to raise the revenue and dampen inflation.

Q. If the purpose is to conserve fuel, because oil being such a large factor in inflation, why not gasoline rationing now?

THE PRESIDENT. We believe that the American people will respond to our volunteer program. In my recommendations yesterday to the Congress, I said we would cut the foreign importation of fuel by 1 million barrels per day, which is 1 million out of the 6 million that is currently imported per day.

Now, the American people last year, in a much greater crisis where we had the embargo, responded very, very well and did as well, if not better, than we are asking them to do now.

So, I don't think we have to put a tax on gasoline users to achieve our objective. And if we can do it by volunteer action, I think it is far preferable and more in the tradition of the American system.

PROJECT INDEPENDENCE

[6.] Q. Mr. President, in June of last year, President Nixon recommended a program. He called for $10 billion for 5 years in the hope of making the United States self-sufficient in energy.

Now it is 16 months; can you update that for us?

THE PRESIDENT. I must confess that we haven't done as well in Project Independence as I think most of us had hoped. This concerns me, and one of the reasons that I indicated yesterday that I was appointing Secretary of Interior Morton to head up the energy council was to get this moving. We are going to concentrate in this area.

Now all of the blame can't be placed on the executive branch. There have been a number of legislative proposals before the Congress that would increase domestic supplies. Unfortunately, in too many cases the Congress has not responded, so the Congress has to share some of the blame with the executive branch.

But I can assure you that with Rog Morton heading this new organization, we are going to do a better job, and I think we will get the cooperation of the American people.

MEETINGS WITH SOVIET LEADERS

[7.] Q. I am sure you have other questions on economics, but let me ask just one on international affairs. There are reports that you are planning some sort of a summit conference with Chairman Brezhnev of the Soviet Union. Can you give us some details on that?

THE PRESIDENT. When I took the oath of office, I indicated that I would continue our country's efforts to broaden and to expand the policies of détente with the Soviet Union.

Since I have been in office, I have had a number of discussions with responsible leaders in the Soviet Union. About 10 days ago, I met with their Foreign Minister, Mr. Gromyko.

Dr. Kissinger is going to the Soviet Union the latter part of this month to continue these discussions.

Now, as you well know, Mr. Brezhnev has been invited to come to the United States in 1975. If there is a reason for us to meet before that meeting in the United States, I will certainly consider it.

ARMS PROPOSALS FOR SOVIET UNION

[8.] Q. To follow up a little, do you expect the United States to have any kind of a proposal on arms to present to the Soviet Union before the end of the year?

THE PRESIDENT. We are resolving our position in this very important and very critical area. When Dr. Kissinger goes to the Soviet Union the latter part of this month, we will have some guidelines, some specific guidelines, for him to discuss in a preliminary way with the Soviet Union.

WAGES AND PRICES

[9.] Q. If inflation is as serious a problem as you have said, can you point to any of your proposals that would persuade businesses to lower prices now or that would encourage labor unions to moderate their wage demands in forthcoming contracts?

THE PRESIDENT. As I said in my remarks before the Congress yesterday, there is no quick fix or no immediate panacea in the fight against inflation. It has taken us roughly 10 years to get this unfortunate momentum for price increases at its present rate.

We do have in the 31-proposal package that I submitted some recommendations which will increase supply of very important ingredients. And we have in those recommendations some proposals to remove some of the restrictive practices of the Government, of private industry, of labor. And if those restrictive practices are eliminated, I think we can look forward to a reduction in prices both in the private sector and as far as the Government is concerned.

PARDON FOR FORMER PRESIDENT NIXON

[10.] Q. Mr. President, at your last news conference you assured us that there had been no deal made on the Nixon pardon either with the former President or with any of his staff members. Since there have been published reports that the pardon was indeed discussed with former chief of staff Haig, I wonder if you could tell us the nature of that conversation, if those reports are indeed accurate?

THE PRESIDENT. Since this last press conference, I have agreed to appear before the Hungate subcommittee of the House Committee on the Judiciary. I will appear before that subcommittee, and until I do appear, I think it is most appropriate that I defer any comment on that subject.

INFLATION

[11.] Q. Mr. President, two of your main anti-inflation proposals, the tax surcharge and cutting Government spending, are intended to curb inflation by reducing demand. But many economists do not believe that this is a demand inflation. They believe it is a wage-price spiral and a shortage inflation.

In view of that, how can the tax surcharge and the cut in Government spending reduce inflation if they are directed at a kind of inflation that we don't have?

THE PRESIDENT. Let me answer that question in two parts if I might.

If the Federal Government reduces its expenditures, and we are going to do it by roughly $5 billion, it makes money more easily available in the money markets of the United States so that home purchasers will have more money at a better rate of interest to borrow so they can build homes. This will stimulate the homebuilding industry and, I think, provide jobs.

Now, the 5 percent surtax is only on 28 percent of the total personal income tax payers in this United States, the people who are better able to pay these minimal amounts extra. I don't think taking away from a family who is earning $20,000 the sum of $42 a year is going to have any serious adverse impact on the purchasing power of that family.

Q. I am not sure that we are talking about the same thing, Mr. President. I am talking about the fact that these are proposals directed at reducing demand and many economists don't think we have that kind of inflation. You are talking about stimulating homebuilding, and I am forced to repeat my question: Why are we attacking the wrong kind of inflation?

THE PRESIDENT. I respectfully disagree with you. I think, if we stimulate homebuilding because we are reducing Federal expenditures and providing more money in the marketplace, I think we are stimulating production. And I think the people who are being taxed, or I hope will be taxed, aren't going to lose sufficiently of their earned income that they are going to cut down significantly in what they buy in the marketplace.

OIL DEPLETION ALLOWANCES

[12.] Q. This morning, Secretary Simon indicated that the Administration was still supporting oil depletion allowances. You yesterday endorsed the Ways and Means package which calls for the phase-out of oil depletion allowances. How do you reconcile your speech and Secretary Simon's testimony this morning?

THE PRESIDENT. Well, that bill before the Committee on Ways and Means has a number of very good features, and it has some that I don't necessarily embrace in toto, and I am sure that Secretary Simon doesn't. But I do believe that on balance, it is important for me to endorse that bill.

And when you endorse a bill of that magnitude, I think you have to take it as a package because it does close some of the loopholes. It provides a sufficient amount of income so we can grant additional relief to the people in the lowest brackets of income taxpayers.

It is my recollection that that bill does phase out not only foreign oil depletion allowance but it provides for a gradual phase-out of the domestic oil depletion allowance.

I am not going to quibble with the committee in every detail. I think we have to buy a package that has far more good in it than those things that I might object to.

Q. Mr. President, is it your own view that the oil depletion allowance should be phased out?

THE PRESIDENT. The answer is yes.[2]

FEDERAL AID TO EDUCATION

[13.] Q. Mr. President, on another question other than the economy, on a subject you haven't talked about before I don't believe, what is the Federal role in public education as you see it? And I have a follow-up.

THE PRESIDENT. The role of the Federal Government——

Q. How little?

THE PRESIDENT.——in the field of education is about what we are currently doing with the Federal aid to education legislation for primary and elementary schools. And I just signed the new education act. It was a step in the direction of consolidating some 35 categorical grant programs into six or seven. I think this is approximately the role of the Federal Government in primary and secondary education.

In higher eduction, if my recollection is correct, I voted for the existing higher education act. Therefore, I feel that it fundamentally is what the Federal Government should do in this area.

Q. Specifically, what are your views on Federal aid to private and parochial schools?

THE PRESIDENT. Well, I have personally expressed, over a long period of time, that I think a tax credit proposal is a good proposal. The Supreme Court, unfortunately a year or so ago, in effect declared such a program—I think it was in the Pennsylvania case[3]—as unconstitutional. I think that is regrettable because

[2] At his news briefing on October 10, 1974, Press Secretary Ron Nessen said:

"The President, after reviewing the transcript of yesterday's news conference, asked me to state more precisely his position on the oil depletion allowance.

"As long as the price of oil continues to be controlled, the President believes the elimination of the percentage depletion on domestic oil production would be a mistake.

"The President feels that oil should be sold on a free market basis, and he thinks that many oil producers would be glad to trade percentage depletion in order to achieve the important result of a free market for oil.

"As for the foreign oil depletion allowance, the President believes that should be phased out immediately and finally."

[3] *Committee for Public Education and Religious Liberty* v. *Nyquist, Commissioner of Education of New York* (413 U.S. 756).

competition in education, between private and public, is good for the student. There is no reason why there should be a monopoly in education just on the public side. And private education has contributed over a long period of time at the primary, secondary, and graduate levels significantly to a better educated America. And I would hope that we could find some constitutional way in which to help private schools.

ACCESS TO INCOME TAX RETURNS

[14.] Q. In the matter of income tax privacy, Mr. President, can you explain the difference between your Executive order [11805] on White House practices, which is very tough on safeguarding the taxpayers, and the legislation which you sent to the Hill, which Congressional experts say is weaker than what went on under the Nixon Administration when there were reported attempts by the White House to subvert the Internal Revenue Service?

The President. Well, if that legislation is weaker than the Executive order that I issued, we will resubmit other legislation.

Mr. DeFrank [Thomas M. DeFrank, Newsweek].

TRANSITION FUNDS FOR THE FORMER PRESIDENT

[15.] Q. Mr. President, you recently asked Congress to appropriate $850,000 to cover transition expenses of former President Nixon. The House has already cut that figure down to $200,000. The Senate seems likely to do the same.

Some of your aides have said in the last few days that they believe that the cutback from $850,000 to $200,000 is both stingy and punitive, and I use their words.

I am wondering if you agree with them that the cutback is stingy and punitive and whether or not you intend to ask the Congress to restore some of those funds?

The President. A recommendation was made to the Congress for the figure of $850,000 for the transition period. About 10 years ago Congress passed a law which provided for transition expenses for an outgoing President. The amount that was submitted on this occasion was roughly comparable to the amounts that have been made available to other Presidents who were leaving office.

Now, the facts and the figures I think can be shown that what was recommended for Mr. Nixon was comparable to others. The Congress, of course, has the right to take whatever action it wants, but under the circumstances, I am not going to use such language myself. I will let the Congress make its decision, right or wrong.

Q. Mr. President, do you feel then, or are you going to ask the Congress to restore some of that funding, or do you believe they should restore it?

THE PRESIDENT. I haven't the bill before me yet. It is still up on the Hill, and until it comes down here, I don't think I should make any judgment.

GIFTS BY GOVERNOR ROCKEFELLER

[16.] Q. Mr. President, have you inquired into the matter of gifts by Governor Rockefeller, and, if so, does a question of possible impropriety occur in any instance, in your judgment?

THE PRESIDENT. The gifts by Governor Rockefeller to the three individuals that I am familiar with—I have looked into the one that involved Dr. Kissinger—but, I think, to put this in proper perspective you have to recognize that Governor Rockefeller is a very wealthy man and that he has been extremely generous with many, many charities over a good many years, and he obviously has sought to compensate former employees or friends for whatever services they performed.

In the case of Dr. Kissinger, I have been assured that every tax that could be applied has been paid and that all legal problems involving that particular case were solved satisfactorily. Under those circumstances, I do not think there was any impropriety in the relationship between Dr. Kissinger and former Governor Rockefeller.

Q. Since you are familiar only with the Kissinger gift, do you plan to inquire into the others?

THE PRESIDENT. I will, but I haven't as deeply because Mr. Morhouse and Mr. Ronan [4] are or were State employees. But I assume that in those two cases, as I found out in the Dr. Kissinger case, that the law had been adhered to and that there was no impropriety.

MASS TRANSIT LEGISLATION

[17.] Q. Sir, if you accept that mass transit is an essential part of the energy-saving program, can you explain why you did not lend your support to a comprehensive Federal mass transit bill now before Congress, in your very important speech yesterday?

THE PRESIDENT. The answer to that is very simple. I had some considerable part in working out the compromise on the Williams-Minish bill. If you will

[4] L. Judson Morhouse, former New York State Republican chairman, and William J. Ronan, chairman of the New York Port Authority.

recall, I had about 15 mayors from all over the country down here to see me, including some business people.

I told them I wanted to help. Within a day or so, I called Senator Williams. After it was suggested, we worked out a figure and a time and a formula. And as a result, Senator Williams, in conjunction with other Members of the Congress, arrived at a mass transit bill that provides for a little over $11 billion over a period of 6 years with a formula between capital outlays and operating expenses.

I think we made a big step forward, and I compliment the Congress for cooperating. And there was no need for me to mention in that speech yesterday something that was fait accompli the day before.

SECRETARY OF STATE KISSINGER

[18.] Q. Mr. President, in your recent U.N. speech, you added some last-minute remarks praising Secretary of State Kissinger, and last night you made an extraordinary move of going out to Andrews Air Force Base to see him off on his trip abroad.

Are you upset by the criticism that Secretary Kissinger is receiving from the press, the public, and Congress?

THE PRESIDENT. I would put it this way, Mr. Jones [Phil Jones, CBS News]. I am very fond of Dr. Kissinger on a personal basis. I have tremendous respect and admiration for the superb job that he has done since he has been the Director of the National Security Agency (Council) and also as Secretary of State.

I think what he has done for peace in the world, what he is continuing to do for peace throughout the world, deserves whatever good and appropriate things I can say about him and whatever little extra effort I can make to show my appreciation. And I intend to continue to do it.

Q. Sir, do you feel that his effectiveness is being undermined by this criticism?

THE PRESIDENT. I haven't seen any adverse effects so far. We are making headway and, I think, constructively in all of the areas where I think and he thinks it is important for us to do things to preserve peace and build a broader base for peace.

1976 PRESIDENTIAL CANDIDACY

[19.] Q. Mr. President, at your first news conference you told us that you probably would run for a term of your own. Since then there has been what you have termed the surprisingly harsh reaction to the pardon of former President Nixon and the tragic illness of your own wife. Do you still plan to be a candidate in 1976?

THE PRESIDENT. The words that I used, if I recall accurately, were I would probably be a candidate in 1976. I have seen nothing to change that decision, and if and when there is, I will promptly notify you.

BOSTON SCHOOL DESEGREGATION

[20.] Q. Mr. President, Boston's Mayor, Kevin White, has appealed to the Federal Government to send U.S. marshals to help restore order in Boston's school desegregation crisis. And black groups have asked for federalizing the National Guard and sending in Federal troops. As the Chief Executive, what do you plan to do, and what comments do you have on this situation?

THE PRESIDENT. At the outset, I wish to make it very, very direct: I deplore the violence that I have read about and seen on television. I think that is most unfortunate. I would like to add this, however: The court decision in that case,[5] in my judgment, was not the best solution to quality education in Boston.

I have consistently opposed forced busing to achieve racial balance as a solution to quality education, and therefore, I respectfully disagree with the judge's order.

But having said that, I think it is of maximum importance that the citizens of Boston respect the law. And I hope and trust that it is not necessary to call in Federal officials or Federal law enforcement agencies.

Now, the marshals, if my information is accurate, are under the jurisdiction of the court, not directly under my jurisdiction. As far as I know, no specific request has come to me for any further Federal involvement, and therefore, I am not in a position to act under those circumstances.

MR. CORMIER. Thank you, Mr. President.

THE PRESIDENT. Thank you very much.

NOTE: President Ford's third news conference began at 2:31 p.m. in the Rose Garden at the White House. It was broadcast live on radio and television.

[5] *Tallulah Morgan et al.* v. *John J. Kerrigan et al.* (379 F.d. Supp. 410).

128

Exchange of Remarks on Signing Joint Statements With First Secretary Gierek of Poland. *October 9, 1974*

MR. FIRST SECRETARY, we have just put our signatures on landmark documents.

The first, on principles of bilateral relations, recognizes the friendly state of those relations. It underlines our joint determination to not only continue this cooperation, but to further expand it for mutual benefit. We will make a joint contribution to peace and security throughout the world.

The second document is more specifically directed to economic, industrial, and technological cooperation. If it is to succeed, cooperation requires the careful and continuing attention of nations, as I am sure you will agree.

Over the past few years, we have made important advances in our economic and trade relations. We have now pledged our countries to even further advances toward realization of the full potential for cooperation that we both see and we desire. Our peoples will benefit and the economic international community will likewise benefit.

These documents should be reassuring to our friends and associates throughout the world. We discriminate against no one, nor do we prejudice any commitments we have already made to others. Indeed, the respect we show for each other and the cooperation that we seek is part of the international spirit we see emerging. This new spirit seeks to solve problems, not to make new tensions.

Mr. First Secretary, my signature on these documents is yet another expression of the deep interest of the people of the United States in the well-being of your nation and its deserved place in the international community. We welcome these documents for the contributions they will make to the spirit of cooperation and peaceful endeavor throughout the world.

THE FIRST SECRETARY.[1] *Mr. President, ladies and gentlemen:*

I do share, Mr. President, your appraisal of the weight of the documents we have just signed, the fruitful nature of our talks, and the importance of the agreements we have concluded. I greatly appreciate what you have said and wish to express my profound satisfaction over the headway we made and results we achieved during my visit to Washington. I especially enjoyed meeting with you, Mr. President, which I shall cherish in my memories as an important, sincere, and friendly encounter.

---

[1] First Secretary Gierek spoke in Polish and his remarks were translated by an interpreter.

We are opening together a new chapter in relations between the Polish People's Republic and the United States of America. As of now, these new annals will be recording the future of our relations as well as our broader, closer, and more extensive cooperation. We are opening up that new chapter aware of the entire tradition of the friendly mutual relations between the Polish and American peoples, in the desire of tightening the bonds which we have inherited from the past and continue to maintain at present.

In enhancing the progress made in our bilateral relations in recent years, we are likewise creating a groundwork for expanded economic, scientific, and technical cooperation, for cultural exchanges, and various contacts between our respective peoples. Particularly important in this regard is expansion of reciprocally beneficial economic ties, which form the most durable basis for all other mutual relationships.

I firmly believe that the inauguration of a future-oriented phase of Polish-American relations concurs with the interests and wishes of our two peoples. We are doing it in accordance both with the principles and the spirit of peaceful coexistence among states with different systems, for the United States and modern, Socialist Poland are precisely such states. Poland, for 30 years, has been shaping new conditions of life and development of her people. She remains faithful to her alliances, and in the best of her tradition, she is actively involved in the strife for progress and peace.

I trust, Mr. President, that the results of our meeting will also contribute to the strengthening of international détente. This latter process, in particular, fortified by the improvement of Soviet-American relations which are of exceptional significance to world peace, has already brought about many favorable changes in the international situation; it has reduced dangerous tensions and provided new vistas for constructive cooperation.

We can particularly sense this in Europe, where the process has been advanced most. Yet, even there, a great deal still remains to be done in order to ensure peace for the entire future to come. May we all move further along that road to free mankind completely from the nuclear threat, to give the world of today and all its nations a feeling of lasting security, and to resolve successfully the great socio-economic and civilization problems which confront us now and are likely to emerge in near future.

I am happy, Mr. President, that, as has been reflected in our joint statement, we are in agreement as to the need for further action at making irreversible the progress achieved in peaceful relations among states with different socio-economic systems.

Mr. President, ladies and gentlemen, tomorrow I shall be leaving Washington to visit other centers of your great and beautiful country. On behalf of Mrs. Gierek and persons accompanying me, as well as in my own name, I wish to thank you, Mr. President, for the friendly reception and hospitality accorded to us. Permit me at the same time to reiterate my very cordial invitation for you and Mrs. Ford, whom we wish a very speedy recovery, to pay a visit to Poland. With the fresh memories of our Washington encounter, I shall be looking forward to meeting you again, this time in our capital, the city of Warsaw.

I would also like to say once more how happy I was to have met the prominent Representatives of the U.S. Congress. My meeting with them has reaffirmed me of the Congressional favorable attitude towards matters concerning further development of Polish-American cooperation.

I take this opportunity to thank the Secretary of State, as well as your other collaborators, for their contribution to the fruitful results of my visit to Washington. I thank all who helped make this visit a success.

Through you, Mr. President, I wish to convey to the American nation my heartfelt greetings and best wishes which I am bringing from the people of Poland.

THE PRESIDENT. Thank you very, very much, Mr. First Secretary. I have enjoyed meeting you, becoming well-acquainted with you, and I look forward to the opportunity of visiting Poland.

I told Mrs. Ford on the telephone today of your kind invitation, and she remembers vividly our visit to Poland some years ago. She, as well as I, are looking forward to a return to your nation and to meet again the wonderful Polish people.

I can assure you, Mr. First Secretary, that as you travel around the rest of the United States—and I wish you could stay longer and visit more places—that you will find a great warmth on the part of the American people for the people of Poland, and you will be welcome wherever you go. I know the warmth of the welcome here will be equal wherever you visit in our country.

We hope you will come back. I look forward to seeing you in the future.

THE FIRST SECRETARY. I wish to thank you most heartily, Mr. President, and we are expecting you in Warsaw, and Mrs. Ford. We shall be trying to greet you, Mr. President and Mrs. Ford, according to the Polish tradition and our saying, "My home is your home."

THE PRESIDENT. Thank you, sir.

NOTE: The President spoke at 3:31 p.m. in the Cabinet Room at the White House.

129

Text of the "Joint Statement on Principles of United States-Polish Relations." *October 9, 1974*

THE PRESIDENT of the United States of America, Gerald R. Ford, and the First Secretary of the Central Committee of the Polish United Workers' Party, Edward Gierek,

—having met in a cordial, businesslike and constructive atmosphere, which provided the opportunity for a useful and comprehensive exchange of views,

—mindful of the long-standing and rich traditions of relations between their two peoples and the feelings of friendship and respect toward each other,

—being convinced that further development of American-Polish relations and the expansion of mutual cooperation serves the interests of both nations and contributes to peace and security in the world,

agreed on a statement of principles of friendly relations and cooperation between the United States of America and the Polish People's Republic.

I

The President and the First Secretary reaffirmed that bilateral relations between the United States of America and the Polish People's Republic are founded on the purposes and principles of the United Nations Charter and international law, and in particular the following interrelated principles:

—sovereign equality;
—refraining from the threat or use of force;
—inviolability of frontiers;
—territorial integrity of states;
—peaceful settlement of disputes;
—non-intervention in internal affairs;
—respect for human rights and fundamental freedoms;
—equal rights and self-determination of peoples;
—cooperation among states;
—fulfillment in good faith of obligations under international law.

II

The President and the First Secretary expressed their determination to develop relations of the two countries in a spirit of cooperation and mutual respect.

They resolved to expand and encourage as appropriate the long range development of commercial, economic, cultural, scientific and technical cooperation of the two countries under conditions of reciprocity of advantages and obligations, in particular in agriculture, industry, transportation, health and environment.

They also resolved to continue to support the development of cooperation through the Joint American-Polish Trade Commission, between organizations, institutions and firms, as set forth in the "Joint Statement on the Expansion of Economic, Industrial and Technological Cooperation between the United States of America and the Polish People's Republic,, signed on October 9, 1974. They affirmed that mutually beneficial economic relations are conducive to good political relations.

They will facilitate and support, through all appropriate means, agreements concerning exchange of experts, students, and other persons as well as exchanges in the fields of science, culture, the arts, education, and other fields, between their two governments or directly between research organizations, institutions and firms as well as people.

Being aware of the importance of cultural and scientific cooperation as a means of promoting mutual understanding and trust, they resolve to promote the development of cultural relations providing opportunities for the citizens of both nations to learn the language of each other and to acquire a better knowledge of their respective achievements and values.

They will support the expansion of contacts between citizens of the two countries, including tourism, as well as contacts between representatives of federal and local authorities and youth and vocational organizations.

They reaffirmed their commitment to develop further relations between the two countries through frequent consultations at various levels, on matters pertaining to their mutual relations, including implementation of the principles contained herein, as well as important international issues of mutual interest.

III

The President and the First Secretary welcomed the progress in recent years toward the general relaxation of tension and the development of peaceful relations between countries of different socio-economic systems. In this connection they stressed the importance of making that progress irreversible. They are determined to continue efforts aimed at strengthening these positive changes to which all countries, irrespective of their size and potential, can and should contribute in the interest of peace and security of all nations.

They will continue to work toward strengthening European security, in particular by contributing to the success of the Conference on Security and Co-operation in Europe and the negotiations on Mutual Reduction of Forces and Armaments and Associated Measures in Central Europe.

They stressed the importance of achieving effective measures of disarmament conducive to strengthening peace and security in the world.

They expressed their willingness to cooperate on various international matters concerning the consolidation of peace, international security and economic, social and cultural progress, with a view to making their own contribution to the settlement of important international problems in the spirit of good will and mutual trust.

They recognized the necessity of strengthening the effectiveness of the United Nations in the maintenance and consolidation of international peace, and in developing cooperation among all nations on the basis of the United Nations Charter.

They acknowledged that this Joint Statement does not infringe upon the obligations of the United States of America and the Polish People's Republic with respect to other states.

Washington, October 9, 1974

For the United States of America:

Gerald R. Ford
President of the United States of America

For the Polish People's Republic:

Edward Gierek
First Secretary of the Central Committee of the Polish United Workers' Party

130

Text of the Joint Statement on United States-Polish Economic, Industrial, and Technological Cooperation. *October 9, 1974*

THE PRESIDENT of the United States of America, Gerald R. Ford, and the First Secretary of the Central Committee of the Polish United Workers' Party, Edward Gierek,

—having held talks on the present state and further development of economic, industrial and technological cooperation between the United States of America and the Polish People's Republic,

agreed on the following statement:

I

The President and the First Secretary expressed gratification with the results achieved in their mutual economic and trade relations in recent years. They endorsed the guidelines for their further development that are set forth in this Joint Statement, and affirmed the positive role of these guidelines for the further development of mutual economic, industrial, and technological cooperation between the United States of America and the Polish People's Republic.

Recognizing further growth of international trade as fundamental to economic development and improved standards of living, and guided by the provisions contained in the Joint Statement on Principles of United States-Polish Relations, they reaffirmed their determination to seek continued expansion of economic and trade relations pursuant to a liberal export and import policy consistent with the legal requirements of each country and with the principles of the General Agreement on Tariffs and Trade, including most-favored-nation treatment. They also expressed confidence that their two countries' bilateral trade relations would be strengthened by the participation of their countries in the multilateral trade negotiations.

They recognize the existence of favorable prospects for further rapid development of bilateral trade in the coming years. They anticipate that their trade may reach $1 billion in 1976 and grow to $2 billion by 1980. They will seek to ensure the existence of proper conditions for economic relations in order that these goals may be achieved. Fields offering particular opportunities for the development of their economic relations include various light industries, food-processing, chemical and petrochemical industry, construction and transportation equipment, machinery, electronic and electrical equipment industries, coal mining and utilization and nonferrous metallurgy.

II

Considering industrial cooperation as a particularly important factor in the development of trade and the diversification of its structure, the President and the First Secretary will facilitate cooperation between American firms and Polish enterprises and economic organizations consistent with applicable laws and regulations of each of the two countries, including long-term understandings in production; construction of new industrial facilities, as well as expansion and modernization of existing facilities; technological cooperation and research including exchanges of know-how, licenses and patents; training and exchange of technicians and specialists; organization of exhibits and conferences; and market and management research; in both countries and in third countries.

They affirmed that favorable consideration should also be given to new forms and methods of industrial cooperation suggested by interested firms and organizations. With a view to the development of economic cooperation, they will examine ways and means for the application of customs and fiscal facilitation for goods assigned to, and resulting from, cooperation projects within the provisions of customs legislation in force in the two countries.

III

Positively evaluating the development to date of scientific and technological cooperation between the United States and Poland, including cooperative projects undertaken in accordance with the United States-Polish Agreement on Science and Technology, the President and the First Secretary expressed the view that further cooperation of this kind in fields of interest to both countries should be pursued.

With a view toward the facilitation of projects for industrial and agricultural development, they, by mutual agreement, will exchange information concerning various fields in which the expansion of industrial and technological cooperation is desirable, and, on the basis of such exchange, will examine areas appropriate for consideration.

They positively evaluated the development to date of mutual financial and credit relations, especially the cooperation between the Export-Import Bank of the United States and the Bank Handlowy in Warsaw, which contributed to the rapid rise of trade and economic cooperation, and pledged continued cooperation in the development of these relations.

Attaching great meaning to the progress achieved in creating reciprocal trade facilities, they will examine ways of resolving administrative, tax, visa, and customs problems which may arise, and will facilitate as appropriate access to information concerning actual and potential markets, operation of business offices, trade promotion and other endeavors which contribute to the development of trade and economic cooperation.

Evaluating positively the work to date of the Joint American-Polish Trade Commission in developing and coordinating action in the area of mutual economic and trade relations, they will continue to work through the Commission to promote economic cooperation and resolve problems arising in the course of their economic, industrial and technological cooperation.

In issuing this Joint Statement, they express the hope that it will become an important practical contribution to utilization of the potential for development of economic, industrial, and scientific and technological cooperation between the United States of America and the Polish People's Republic.

Washington, October 9, 1974

FOR THE UNITED STATES OF AMERICA:

GERALD R. FORD
President of the United States of America

FOR THE POLISH PEOPLE'S REPUBLIC:

EDWARD GIEREK
First Secretary of the Central Committee of the Polish United Workers' Party

131

Remarks at a Dinner Honoring William W. Scranton in Philadelphia, Pennsylvania. *October 9, 1974*

THANK YOU very much, Hugh, and knowing of our long and warm friendship and our wonderful working relationship for so many years, I cannot express deeply enough my heartfelt thanks and wonderful appreciation for those kind words, and I thank you very, very much.

Bill and Mary, Dick Schweiker and Claire, Drew and Marilyn, my former colleagues in the House—and I know there are some here—would I be inappropriate if I asked all those former House members just to stand up, because they are pretty important guys, too.

I saw Pete and Joe and John Ware and Larry Williams,[1] and with these lights I cannot quite see them all, but let me express to them as well as to Dick and Hugh, my deep appreciation for their superb assistance and cooperation in some of the tough times we have had in recent weeks.

Let me add, if I might, my appreciation for the most kind communications

[1] Representatives Edward (Pete) Biester, Joseph M. McDade, John H. Ware, and Lawrence G. Williams.

and good thoughts and prayers from so many all over the country, as Hugh said, some 40,000 cards, telegrams, telephone calls, et cetera on behalf of Betty. She is doing great, and what you all have done has been material in making her get well much quicker. Thank you very, very much.

As some of you might have seen in the last few days, either through the newspapers or television, the White House has a new addition. My daughter, Susan, and Dave Kennerly, our new White House photographer, got together a few days ago and surprised Betty and me with an 8-month-old golden retriever.

This puppy has really taken over the White House. In fact, you may have seen some of us laughing up here during dinner. As I reached in my pocket to get a match to light my pipe, look what I pulled out of the pocket—some dog biscuits! [*Laughter*]

Let me tell you the story about Susan and Dave and how they bought this dog. I first should preface that the Fords had had two previous golden retrievers. One lived 13 years and unfortunately died, and then another one died a year ago in August after 9 years. So we are fairly partial, I would say, to golden retrievers.

Well, Dave and Susan called up a very highly recommended individual who had contacts with the people who raise golden retrievers all over the country. And Dave, as I understand it—who is communicating with the individual up in Minneapolis who happened to have a golden retriever about this age—Dave asked the individual if they had a dog and was it available, and the owner said that they had this 8-month-old golden retriever, but the proprietor or the owner was a little cautious—they're very possessive about these dogs— and he asked in a very nice way who the dog's owner would be.

And they said, Dave and Susan, that they had to keep it a secret. Well, the kennel owner said that they don't sell dogs that way. He would have to know who the dog's owner would be, and he wanted to know would the dog have a good home.

So, Dave and Susan very specifically assured the dog owner that it would have a good home. They explained that the parents were friendly and middle-aged and they had four children. The kennel owner said, "That sounds fine. What kind of a house do they live in?"

Susan and Dave said, "Well, it is a big white house with a fence around it." The kennel owner said, "This is a big dog. Will it have enough to eat? Does the father have a steady job?" Well, on that question, they were stuck a bit. [*Laughter*]

Needless to say they got the dog and, in the appropriate spirit of the city of Philadelphia, we have named her "Liberty." One of those inquisitive reporters that we have in Washington asked Susan who is going to take care of Liberty; who is going to feed her and groom her and take her out each night or every morning? And Susan did not hesitate one minute. She said, "Of course, it will be Dad." So, I have this feeling—this is one Liberty that is going to cost me some of mine. [*Laughter*]

But in a very broader sense, that is the true nature of liberty. It comes with both privileges and obligations. Freedom, we all know, is seldom free.

And it is a pleasure for me to be in Philadelphia again—the second time in less than a month—and for such a great purpose here tonight.

And I must say, having been in many political rallies in 25 or 26 years, the spirit, the participation, the look in your eye, and the feeling in the air gives me great hope for the things that we believe are good for the Commonwealth of Pennsylvania and the great United States. And I thank you very much.

I think we all recognize that the strength of the Republican Party in this State is a tribute to Dick Frame, Tom McCabe, who has always been here and doing things when the going was the toughest—and I can tell you some stories about that, back in 1965—Sally Stauffer,[2] and all of you who are here because you have conviction and dedication.

I am here because I want to thank so many of you for what you have done, and quite frankly, I am here to call upon you for a very great effort in the weeks ahead, because, in my judgment, so very much hangs in the balance, dependent on what you do—you have done it tonight—but the other things that you can do between now and November 5.

I am, however, here because I wish to express my deep personal appreciation for an old and dear friend of mine, Bill Scranton. I think I have known Bill longer than I have known almost anybody here in this room tonight. He and I were in law school together, and that is a long time ago. He does not show it as much as I.

But we all know that a political party is not just a set of principles; it is also a group of people, and it will be judged, as we know, by the kind and the quality of the people that seek the recognition in the ballot box. And I can assure you that is why Bill Scranton is such an asset to our party. He brings out nothing but the best in public service, and you in the Commonwealth of Pennsylvania recognized it. And, Bill and Mary, we from outside the State are just as grateful for what you have done as all of you in the State of Pennsylvania. I thank you and congratulate you.

---

[2] Richard C. Frame was chairman of the Pennsylvania State Republican Committee, and Thomas B. McCabe and Sarah Ann Stauffer were Republican National Committeemen for Pennsylvania.

As I was sitting here, I looked around at the head table and there were three people on the podium, or at the head table, that I had the privilege of serving with in the House of Representatives—Bill Scranton, Hugh Scott, Dick Schweiker.

Let me first speak about Hugh, if I might. He was a more senior Member of the House of Representatives when I came to Washington in January of 1949. He was friendly, courteous, helpful. And then you sent him to the United States Senate. We had many opportunities to work together during the early days of his Senate service, and then he and I became the minority leaders in the Senate and in the House.

I can say without any hesitation or qualification that I've had nothing but the finest opportunities to work with Hugh, to do things on the plus side, to work together in total unison, and to fight for those things that are important to your State and to our country and to peace throughout the world.

And this working relationship, Hugh—then, when we were together in the Congress, and now—I cherish. And I am deeply grateful and thank you very, very much.

Then back in 1960 you all sent from his particular Congressional district, Dick Schweiker, and then subsequently you sent him to the United States Senate. I remember when Dick and Bill Scranton came to the House. I thought I was a pretty senior person and knew a lot and so forth. I did know one thing. I could tell that in Bill Scranton and Dick Schweiker, the Commonwealth of Pennsylvania had sent two first-class Members of the House.

And when I ran for the minority leadership in 1965 and won by the landslide margin of 73 to 67, those two fellows were very, very helpful in my behalf.

So, I express to Dick my appreciation, and I wish him the very best, because in the limited time that I served as the presiding officer, as a first instant Vice President, I noticed that Dick Schweiker did a great job for you in Pennsylvania, for the country, and Dick, I know you will when all of these good people with thousands of others in Pennsylvania send you back for another 6 years.

If I might, I would like to make one observation. In the 8 or 9 years that I was the minority leader, I traveled an awful lot. You have no idea how many airports I have slept in and aircraft I have dozed in because I wanted to help the party and good candidates the length and the breadth of the country.

Most years during that period of time I traveled some 200,000 miles each year. And during the period of this experience, I met many outstanding candidates for public office—Governors, et cetera. And I learned a bit about judging who was good and who was bad, and you sort of develop a capability of saying, "Gee, that fellow has got it," or "This fellow does not have it."

I have known Drew Lewis over the last 4 or 5 years, and let me say to each and every one of you in this State: If you elect Drew Lewis to be your next Governor—and I think you will—you will elect one of the finest Governors I have had an opportunity to see, and I hope you do.

When I was privileged to come to the great city of Philadelphia in September, I pledged then that with the help of the American people we would win the battle against inflation. Yesterday, before the joint session of the House and Senate, in trying to speak to the American people I outlined what I think was a fair and equitable plan to win this battle, and I asked the Congress and the American people to join me in this struggle. It has been a great experience that in the last 24 hours, the American people have responded tremendously.

And the response of the Congress, basically, has been good. We have had some who have been critical, but I think they, in their own heart, know—as Hugh Scott said—they either buy this total plan or concept or design, or they have to come up with something else, because America cannot afford to lose this struggle.

As I said yesterday, I fully understand the reaction to some extent, or the criticism that a portion of the voters of this country might rise up in righteous wrath and turn them out of office if they would not face up to the tough decisions.

I tried to express yesterday, and I reiterate it tonight: I have an infinitely greater faith in the American people than those that want us to play politics with the economy and the strength of the political fabric of our country.

The American people want us to do what is right, not what is politically expedient. Some of you may have heard or watched—I had a press conference today, and one of my friends in the press made some comment or asked a question, well, wasn't this tax proposal that I suggested unfair and inequitable?

I am not sure this is the best audience for me to make the argument, but let me just take one or two examples, and I think you will agree with me when you see the facts. For a family with a gross income of wages of $20,000 per year, the 5 percent surtax that I think is essential to provide the revenue that we can do other things that will indicate compassion for those that are less fortunate—for that family of four and gross income of $20,000 a year, under this proposal they will pay $42 more a year in Federal income taxes, which is about 12 cents a day.

This new tax will affect some 28 percent of the total Federal personal income tax payers in this country. And I happen to think that those 28 percent—good Americans, dedicated to the preservation of those things that are so essential for our children and our grandchildren—they won't fall back and criticize, they will step up and do what is right. And the politicians ought to do the same thing.

In the remarks I made about a month ago here in Philadelphia, saluting the convening of the First Continental Congress about 200 years ago, I cited—it was interesting, some of the parallels that Congress, *that* Congress and the 93d Congress today face.

One of the basic issues at that time, two centuries ago in this great city, was inflation. By taking tough positions then, the inflation fighters of 1774 whipped that problem, just as the inflation fighters and energy savers in 1974 will whip this one.

But as I tried to express, and reiterated today, this is not something Hugh or Dick or Drew or Bill Scranton or my former colleagues in the House can do alone. The 1,500, or whatever the number here is tonight, can be massively helpful. And the millions of people throughout this country can do exactly the same. And if the mail I've received or the communications that we have gotten are indicative of the feeling of the American people, they want to participate. They want to do something, and they will, because they know there is a challenge here at home and a challenge throughout the world to win this battle, and we will.

I don't have to portray to this group—you are very sophisticated and knowledgeable—but the problem is if we don't, we lessen our economic security here in America, we weaken our capability to govern ourselves, we threaten our domestic stability, and we lose our leadership throughout the world. We don't want that.

What I ask you to do tonight is to help us in every Congressional district in every State. Support those candidates that want to charge ahead, to whip—to whip inflation and to save energy. You can do it. You can send to the Congress those individuals whose record justifies it. And I am confident that those here tonight warrant and justify your support.

But let me take a minute, if I might, to talk about a particular subject that is related to inflation. The facts show that our energy problem is a major difficulty in the battle against inflation. We know that the cost of energy has gone up very substantially, primarily because of the fact that we import some 6 million barrels of oil from outside the continental limits every 24 hours, and the cost of that oil has gone up unbelievably.

If we are to get a hold, if we are to grasp successfully the problems of energy, we have to do something affirmatively to find other sources. We have to develop and produce those resources at home—whether it is oil or coal or geothermal or solar or any one of the other alternatives, nuclear included, that will be a substitute—so we cannot be held up by others who come from lands across the oceans.

There are some 17—or were, I should say—some 17 bills before the Congress that would have helped significantly in this battle to provide alternative means of energy or to expedite the utilization of energy, the energy that we have. Thus far, two out of those 17 have been approved by the Congress. One more is probably going to come to my desk in the next several days. But that leaves some 14 major proposals that the Congress must act upon, if we are to get the kind of energy sources and supplies that are needed to give us alternative opportunities to those that we've relied on for so long, if we are to use those resources at home in a proper and effective way.

And let me say that here in Pennsylvania you have had a great experience. I talked to Hugh and Dick on the way up from Washington today. One of those bills is a proposal to provide reasonable environmental safeguards while permitting vitally needed increases in coal production through surface mining in Pennsylvania and other States.

Each, if I might point out, each ton of unmined Pennsylvania coal makes it necessary for us to import four barrels of expensive foreign oil. You know better than I that Pennsylvania has a totally adequate and effective State law governing surface mining which has achieved a reasonable balance between productivity and environmental concerns. What we need at the Federal level is a piece of legislation comparable to that which you have in the Commonwealth of Pennsylvania, and I hope the Congress will see the wisdom of putting the final touches on such legislation.

But in addition, we need some changes in what is called the Clean Air Act to remove unrealistic deadlines and to permit the use of available domestic coal supplies. I think this can be done—the record is clear—without endangering the health of any of our citizens.

The Administration, for example, has proposed 13 amendments to the existing Clean Air Act. Unfortunately, neither the House nor Senate has held any meaningful hearings in this regard. I can assure you that if the Congress were to pass this legislation, it would help materially in us meeting the challenge of domestic energy and would help us immeasurably in cutting down 1 million barrels per day of foreign oil imports.

Let me make one observation concerning the elections in 1974—and I happen to think that we should concentrate on '74, not on '76, because we cannot afford in this country to have the wrong kind of a Congress for the next 2 years.

Some of our friendly adversaries on the other side of the aisle early this year were tremendously optimistic about the possibility that they were going to pick up a net gain of 50 House seats and maybe 4 or 5 U.S. Senate seats, and they were anticipating that they would have what they designated as a veto-proof Congress.

I said then, and I reiterate now, I do not think the American people want a veto-proof Congress. One of the basic, important, crucial aspects of our society is that our Government works on a system of checks and balances—executive, legislative, judicial. Fortunately, we are blessed with a two-party system in America that permits us to have two strong major political parties. And the fact that one checks the other and the pendulum swings back and forth has given us probably more liberty, more benefits than any other political system in the history of the United States. And if you ended up with a veto-proof Congress, that balance will be gone.

And so, the American people, as I have traveled and listened, are saying, "We want to retain a balance," and so some of our good friends on the other side of the aisle, recognizing that the American people do not want a dictatorial political system, are backing off.

But it does depend on November 5 on what you do. In order to preclude a veto-proof Congress and to elect an inflation-proof Congress, you have to elect or reelect Dick Schweiker and the Republican nominees for the House of Representatives on November 5, and I urge you to do so.

Let me simply close by thanking you again and saying a special kind word about a dear, close, old friend of mine, Bill Scranton. I have known Bill, as I indicated earlier, probably as long as anybody I have known in this room, and I have gotten to know his lovely wife, Mary.

I saw Bill as a law student, as a Member of the House, as a Governor. And when the Office of the Presidency was precipitated so quickly and I needed help, I asked Bill Scranton to come down and help me. He was a major factor in this difficult transition process from August 9, and for the month or two after that. He epitomizes the highest qualities of character and service in government.

And so I am especially honored, Bill, to join with the many, many people here tonight, to join them in honoring you and to, of course, honor Mary. You represent what many of us appreciate as the very, very best. We wish you the finest, and before you say "no," sometime I am going to call on you to come down and help us some more.

Bill, from a Michigander to a great citizen of the Commonwealth of Pennsylvania, it is a privilege for me to give you this Distinguished Republican Award: to William W. Scranton, citizen and patriot extraordinary, by me, President of the United States.

Thank you, Bill.

NOTE: The President spoke at 9:35 p.m. at the Philadelphia Sheraton Hotel. Prior to the dinner, the President attended a reception for Republican contributors.

132

Memorandum on Fiscal Year 1975 Budget Cuts. *October 10, 1974*

MEMORANDUM FOR

THE SECRETARY OF STATE
THE SECRETARY OF THE TREASURY
THE SECRETARY OF DEFENSE
THE ATTORNEY GENERAL
THE SECRETARY OF THE INTERIOR
THE SECRETARY OF AGRICULTURE
THE SECRETARY OF COMMERCE
THE SECRETARY OF LABOR
THE SECRETARY OF HEALTH, EDUCATION, AND WELFARE
THE SECRETARY OF HOUSING AND URBAN DEVELOPMENT
THE SECRETARY OF TRANSPORTATION

SUBJECT: *Fiscal Year 1975 Budget Cuts*

As I noted at the last Cabinet meeting, the suggestions which you and others have made for reducing 1975 spending are insufficient if we are to hold spending to $300 billion or below. I have asked Roy Ash and his staff to work with you and your staff in finding further reductions.

I recognize that this will be a very difficult task. There are few programs in which large cuts are desirable from the point of view of achieving agency missions. Nevertheless, under current economic conditions, it is essential that we present the Congress with a significant package of legislative and budgetary proposals that would allow us to reach our 1975 goal.

Time is short. We are well into the fiscal year. It is essential, therefore, that we complete work on our proposals so that I can send them to the Congress at an early date. I attach special urgency to this effort and look forward to your support and cooperation.

GERALD R. FORD

NOTE: The text of the memorandum, dated October 8, 1974, was released October 10.

133

Message to the Congress Transmitting Annual Report of the National Advisory Council on Extension and Continuing Education. *October 10, 1974*

To the Congress of the United States:

I herewith transmit the Eighth Annual Report of the National Advisory Council on Extension and Continuing Education. The Council is authorized by Public Law 89–329.

The Council again this year points to the problems caused by the multiplicity of legislative authorities, funding mechanisms, and responsible departments and agencies involved in the programs it has studied. While I cannot agree with all of the specific program recommendations contained in the Council's eighth report, I would call your attention to the members' support for the objectives and purposes of revenue sharing.

I share the Council's concern on the mechanics of decisionmaking under special revenue sharing. It is of vital importance that legislation be enacted which permits State and local determinations to prevail.

Policymakers at the State and local level are most capable of making decisions which respond to the needs of the people. At the same time, organizations with broad mandates such as the National Foundation on the Arts and the Humanities and the Fund for the Improvement of Postsecondary Education will continue their support of diverse projects in many areas of social, cultural, and educational concern.

GERALD R. FORD

The White House,
October 10, 1974.

NOTE: The 53-page report is entitled "The Importance of Service: Federal Support for Continuing Education."

134

Remarks to the Seventh General Convention of the American Lutheran Church, Detroit, Michigan. *October 10, 1974*

Dr. Preus, delegates to the Seventh General Convention of the American Lutheran Church, and friends:

I am deeply indebted to and most grateful for the extremely warm welcome and the wonderful opportunity to meet with all of you just for a few minutes here this evening.

I would like to address my remarks, if I might, not only to those who are here but also to the more than 2,500,000 Lutherans each of you represent in this gathering here tonight, and the more than 9 million Lutherans in the United States, our homeland.

Very honestly and frankly, I am very moved by the theme of the American Lutheran Church—this convention—both as a President and as a Christian.

"Ministering to a hungry world" would serve, in my judgment, as a very stimulating, a very enthusiastic call to any assembly of committed people.

I think all of us recognize that the world hungers not only today but yesterday and tomorrow for food. And as I look at the facts and the figures in the office I presently hold, I think even more will be needed in the future.

Equally, perhaps more importantly, is the need, as I see it, for spiritual sustenance. Your president, Dr. David Preus, said it so well in his report to the convention, and let me quote, if I might: Bread is no little word designed only to describe the loaves we place in our mouth. It signifies the answer to all our deep human needs. It points beyond the loaf and the kernel of wheat to the Almighty, ministering in love to a hungry world.

As I entered this room, I was taken by the simple but very dramatic backdrop that has been provided by the Seventh American Lutheran Church General Convention—a child, a mother, a native mother with child, a couple, all looking hopefully toward the light that flows from the bread and the cup, the wheat and the grape.

I think the facts are that we all yearn to feed the starving, and when I say that, I mean all Americans. We all thirst for those who are living out their lives in desperation. We all want to win the fight against inflation, maintain peace, and assure justice for all people.

The lesson, I think, is that of every Sabbath, for everyone to hear in our churches and our synagogues, as Americans we must live it.

I am hopeful that we will be able to continue America's humane tradition, your theme of administering to the hungry, to the hungry in all 130 or more nations throughout the world. And as I have told the American people, sacrifices will be required.

Our lifestyles to some extent must be adjusted if we are to remain a source of strength for all peoples in all nations throughout the world. And if I could make one plea here tonight, I would like it to be in this context. I ask for your help in making that possible for all peoples throughout all the world.

Each and every one of us yearn to feed the starving. We all thirst for those living out their lives in some desperation, and there are literally thousands and millions that are doing it. We all want to do these things that are good for everybody.

But may I say just one word in a somewhat or slightly different tack. I note that the convention will be talking about the Bicentennial—and aren't we proud that our Nation is about to celebrate its 200th anniversary, two centuries of freedom and liberty for all people? And I must say that I have been greatly impressed with the originality reflected in the title that you at this convention have used, "The Commission on the Third Century of the American Life," and I commend you, Dr. Preus, and all of you here at this convention for that.

The understandable emphasis, I think, in the past has been what we recognize has been good for America. But it is my judgment, if I could offer just a bit of advice, that instead of looking at the past in toto, we should connect our great traditions and achievements of the past with what we can do in the future.

We must, as a nation, build from the past and move forward to the future.

I thank you. I congratulate you. I am deeply grateful for the warm reception and the opportunity to just say hello, to commend you, and to encourage you for a most successful convention, and all the wonderful things that—I know from the friends that I have, my former colleague in the Congress, Congressman Al Quie, and others—to do what is good for America, what is wonderful for the world.

I thank you and I urge—because I know it is true—you will have God's blessings.

Thank you very much.

NOTE: The President spoke at 7:17 p.m. at Cobo Hall.

135

Remarks at a Republican Fundraising Dinner in Detroit. *October 10, 1974*

Max Fisher, Governor Bill Milliken, Senator Bob Griffin, distinguished members of the executive branch in Lansing, members of the State legislature, public officials, ladies and gentlemen:

It is just wonderfully warming and refreshing to be here, and I thank you from the bottom of my heart.

Before I begin, I really should tell you what a great day it has been today. In a State where automobiles are so much a part of our everyday life, you don't know how much fun it was driving in from the airport and seeing so many wonderfully nice people just come out and watch this Ford go by. [*Laughter*]

I have been asked by a good many friends of mine whether I will be able to stay for the next day or two and see that tremendously important, that great traditional football game between Michigan and Michigan State this Saturday. Unfortunately, I won't be able to do so, but I do have to be honest. When the Wolverines are playing, asking me who I am rooting for is about as necessary as asking Bill Milliken and Bob Griffin how to get to Traverse City.

It is great to be here, as I indicated at the outset, among so many old friends and so many outstanding leaders who are here to pay tribute to Bill Milliken and the ticket.

If I might, I would like to relax a minute, and if I might, I would like to tell the latest shaggy dog story from Washington, and the truth is, it is accurate.

As a matter of fact, I was sitting up here talking to Max Fisher and Helen Milliken, and I was trying to light my pipe. And I reached into my pocket, and I picked out of the pocket a big dog bone, which I carry now because for the last 3 or 4 days we have had a new tenant at the White House.

Actually, it is a story of how my daughter, Susan, and Dave Kennerly, the new White House photographer, surprised me and Betty with an 8-month-old golden retriever last Saturday. In the process of trying to get this dog, because we had had a great affection for golden retrievers—we had two, one 13 years old and one 9; both have died—so they called up a very highly recommended kennel and said they wanted to buy a golden retriever.

The owner of the kennel said that was fine, who will the dog's owner be? They said it is a surprise, and they would like to keep it secret. Well, the kennel owner said he did not sell dogs that way. He would have to know who the dog was going to and whether it would have a good home or not.

So, Susan and Dave assured the kennel owner that the dog would have a good home. They explained that the parents are friendly, middle-aged, and have four children. The kennel owner said, "Good. What kind of a house do they live in?"

Susan and Dave said, "Well, it is a big white house with a fence around it." Then the kennel owner went on to say—he was very inquisitive, protecting the dogs that he was trying to sell—the kennel owner said, "This is a big dog who will eat a lot. Does the father have a steady job?" Well, both Dave and Susan were stuck for an answer to that one. [*Laughter*]

Well, needless to say, they got the dog, and with it a very appropriate spirit of the Bicentennial. And in that spirit we have named her "Liberty."

A reporter asked Susan and Dave, "Who is going to take care of Liberty? Who is going to feed her and groom her and take her out each night or every morning?" And Susan did not hesitate one minute. She said, "Daddy," which is typical. [*Laughter*]

So, I have this feeling that this is one Liberty that is going to cost me some of my own. [*Laughter*]

But let me reiterate and reemphasize: It is wonderful to be back with all of you good Michiganders. And as I sat here talking with Max and Helen and others and looked out at this tremendous audience, I could not help but have the feeling that the enthusiasm, the numbers, the people—were a reflection of the support that the people in Michigan will give to a great Governor, Bill Milliken, on November 5.

Bill, as you know probably better than I, has done a superb job. The thing that I like about Bill is that he is a problemsolver. Now, I may not agree with everything Bill has done, and I am sure it is reciprocated, but I do look at a person in the executive branch who has the conflicting advice and counsel of many people, who has the obligation to represent the cross-section of a great State, totaling 9 million people—he has to take into consideration the plusses and the minuses of a total population, and Bill Milliken has proved to me that he is a problemsolver, and those are the kind of people I like.

And quite frankly, that is why I am here tonight, to do what I can in a small way to help the cause of a person who has done much for Michigan and can do infinitely more.

Bill, good luck.

If I might add parenthetically, his problemsolving has not been in a small part of the spectrum. His problemsolving has covered the waterfront, so to speak, with the environment, education, taxation, transportation.

What he has done in the field of education is really landmark. And all of us who feel that we must upgrade education for the future generations and for the benefit of our country, this should be a particular selling point for all of you as you go the length and the breadth of our great State.

Bill and I have discussed on a number of occasions since August 9, the problems of inflation and employment. Frankly, I took Bill's personal recommendations when I had to make some of those decisions in the last week concerning our program to win the battle against inflation, and one of them that can be very helpful here in our State is the question of public service employment. I thank Bill for his specific understanding and recommendations in this regard.

And about a month ago, in accord with what Bill had proposed, I made available on a national basis a substantial amount of money, but for Michigan alone it was approximately $35 million, which will be highly beneficial and very effective for some 300,000 unemployed in our State. And Bill, I thank you for the advice and good counsel on this program.

Let me say to the people of the city of Detroit, I had their problems in mind when I made some decisions in the last few days concerning the economy and energy. I think we all recognize that inflation strikes citizens most unevenly. There are those for one reason or another, because they are awfully young or they are rather old, who suffer in a discriminatory way inflation's evils.

Some of them do not have jobs or some of them are living on fixed incomes which are, unfortunately, too low under our current circumstances. But let me say that in our total package of programs—some 31 specific recommendations that I made last Tuesday—we had some ideas in there which we will implement with the help of the Congress and the American people.

To help the young and to protect the old, we have a Community Improvement Corps program which will give to the young people, particularly, but as well to the old, an opportunity to work with their hands and their minds to improve our environment, our communities.

It is aimed at the short-range problem that we have of getting us over the hump of a threatened recession and too-high inflation. In this area, Bill Milliken was particularly beneficial because he knows that there are places in our State—that with the helping hand of the Federal Government, we can do things to improve the environment, to better our communities. And of course, in speaking of Bill, I am delighted to recommend to you someone that I have gotten to know who will be a great partner with Bill as Lieutenant Governor, Lieutenant Governor Jim Damman.[1]

Jim, good luck to you.

As Bob Griffin was speaking tonight, I reminisced a good bit in my own mind because in January of 1965, Bob Griffin did more to help me become minority leader than anybody else in the House of Representatives. And for all the trouble I have gotten in in the meantime, you can blame Bob Griffin. He was the campaign manager of the campaign where I challenged an older man, and we won by the landslide margin of 73 to 67.

But it was Bob's skill, his support, that made it possible, and it has been a great privilege and pleasure for me to watch Bob's progress as he went from the House to the Senate, and from the Senate to the second leadership post on our side of the aisle.

Now, Bob and I have done a lot of things together. But he is a good bit younger, so we never played football together. But Bob is the kind of an individual that I respect in politics. He is a teamplayer, and I just hope and trust, as Bob moves along in the political ladder and up the priority list, that we in Michigan can see in Bob Griffin a higher and higher and more and more responsible role in our Federal Government. He deserves it, and he will make it.

Bob, it is nice to be here with you.

You have been introduced to the wives of the Members of the House. They are the ones that really are helpful in the tough times that a Member of the House has to make decisions. They look after the families, they are nice to their husbands, and I just think we owe a special round of applause to the wives of Marv Esch, Ed Hutchinson, Chuck Chamberlain, Al Cederberg, Phil Ruppe, and Bill Broomfield. They are wonderful, and let's give them a big hand.

We had anticipated that their husbands would be traveling with me coming out here. We have a few more accommodations now than we had a couple of months ago. But unfortunately, all of them are in Washington staying on the job, and that is what you elected them to do.

So, I think we should applaud them for being there rather than here with us tonight. And even though we've missed all of the Republican Members of the delegation who could not be here, and that is sad, I would like to share some good news with you tonight.

It is often said that being President of the United States is the loneliest job in the

[1] State Representative James J. Damman was the Republican candidate for Lieutenant Governor of Michigan.

world. To me, personally, that becomes a lot less lonely tomorrow. I am glad to report to all of you that Betty is coming home tomorrow.

And may I express to all of you her appreciation and mine, too, for the wonderful cards and letters and telegrams and telephone calls of good wishes and welcome. I can assure you that the some 20,000 or more that have come to the White House and to the hospital—it has been tremendously helpful. And she is coming home with a great spirit and a complete recovery, and I thank you for your help and assistance.

I should reemphasize that I have learned in the last 2 months that the Presidency is a lonely job because the toughest decisions, the toughest decisions in the Federal Government come to the President's desk. And these are the kind of decisions that only the President can make under our system.

I always had doubts about it before, but I have found it is true. And one of the toughest decisions that I had to make as President was whether or not to ask the Congress, 4 weeks before an election, to raise taxes on some individuals and on all corporate income.

I am sure you know what my decision was, but before giving you an illustration or two, let me say a choice I disregarded was the proposal by some to put a 10 or 15 or 20 cent-per-gallon tax on gasoline. I discarded it because it was wrong under the circumstances.

Now, there have been some small tremors on Capitol Hill, and I am not blaming anybody for not immediately understanding how the proposed Federal surtax works. But let me illustrate how this tax actually is applicable to a good many taxpayers—a 5 percent surcharge on personal income.

Number one, it will affect only 28 percent of all individual tax returns. Seventy-two percent of the individual tax returns will have no additional income tax applied.

Number two, a 5 percent surcharge is not a repressive tax which will drive families to the wall to pay their taxes, nor will it significantly cut back their buying power.

Let me assure you, if we do not do something about double-digit inflation, that will be infinitely more harmful, it will be far more injurious than a 5 percent surtax on the taxes that you are paying at the present time.

Let me illustrate quite categorically what it means. For a person with a $15,000 income—wages—with a family of four, there won't be any extra tax. A family of four earning $20,000 a year will have to pay an additional tax in a 12-month period of $42, about 12 cents a day.

Isn't that a good investment to stop double-digit inflation? I think it is.

Let me ask you this: Wasn't it worthwhile to get this additional tax revenue, if the Congress responds, so that we can help to pay for some of the programs that are needed on a short-term basis, to help the people who are far worse off than we?

The program has to be fair; it has to be compassionate on one hand and calling for equity and sacrifice on the other. And that is what we have tried to do—to balance. We have also had to make sure that we tighten the screws enough to do something about inflation, but not to do too much so that we would continue down the road of some economic difficulty.

It was a finely tuned, combined package of 31 proposals—enough pressure but enough flexibility; enough sacrifice but enough equity. And as we looked at it honestly and conscientiously, we tried to do something that would make it a program for success without severe penalty. And I urge you from the very bottom of my heart to come out and be a zealot, a salesman for a program that is good for America and fair to everybody. And I hope you will.

Now, speaking of responsibility—and this is a responsibility that we all have to take care of, public enemy number one—let me speak about another responsibility if I might. And here it is: a question, basically, of how the United States can continue its leadership role in building peace, a peace that was established following World War II, so that we, in the last 25 or 30 years, could enjoy the benefits in Western Europe of no conflict between the East and the West.

That building block of peace between the Soviet Union and its bloc allies and ourselves and our allies has been a cornerstone of nonaggression and understanding.

But we are at a very critical moment right now. I think many of you are aware of the Congressional action to cut off all military assistance to one of our NATO allies, Turkey. This Congress, I think, has made a serious mistake in this regard. The Congress has arbitrarily made a decision, despite the opposition of the Democratic as well as Republican leadership in the House and the Senate, and it is my unalterable conviction that such a drastic action under these circumstances will severely damage the interests of the United States and the free world.

And let me tell you why, if I could express my deep, personal conviction. If this action of arbitrarily cutting off an ally is not reversed, history could well record that this Congress has embarked on a dangerous and misguided course of action which regrettably, tragically, catastrophically, could damage Greece—another ally—and undermine the North Atlantic Treaty Organization.

It is unbelievable to me that the Congress would act in such a way. As I have told you, the Democratic and Republican leadership of the House and Senate fought the action that was taken in both bodies, but unfortunately, the majority in the House and Senate at this moment have prevailed. And what they have done—they have not helped Greece, they have not helped NATO, they have not helped settle the problem in Cyprus one bit. They've probably hurt all three.

Now the United States, because of the skillful diplomatic leadership of Dr. Henry Kissinger, is in a position to be helpful in the solution of this problem. And if we get some flexibility from the Congress—and the chips are down tomorrow—with 60 days of flexibility, we can make some progress. We can do something to help Greece and at the same time keep Turkey within the NATO organization and, simultaneously, help to negotiate a meaningful, constructive solution to the problems in Cyprus.

What I am trying to say to you is, if you have any influence on any of your Members of Congress, Democratic or Republican, urge them in the House of Representatives tomorrow to give us just 60 days to use our influence in trying to bring about a solution that will help Greece and keep Turkey within the Alliance and find a key to the problems of Cyprus. Just urge your friends in the House, both Democratic and Republican, to vote for the Mansfield amendment [2] which passed the Senate yesterday.

I say this as strongly as I possibly can. And I say it because just a quarter of a century ago, when I first went to the House of Representatives, the Congress was under the control of the Republicans, and there was a Democratic President by the name of Harry Truman. And at that stage, just after World War II, there was a massive bipartisan effort to rebuild Western Europe and to lay the foundation of our alliance in Europe today.

A Democratic President from Independence, Missouri, was helped tremendously by a Republican Senator from Grand Rapids, Arthur Vandenberg. And those two people were the architects of a bipartisan foreign policy that gave us a foundation for peace and strength in Western Europe.

Now, what I am saying to you and to my friends in the Congress—wouldn't it be tragic if there was a division between a Democratic Congress and a Republican President a quarter of a century later?

They and I have the obligation to work together, to build on this quarter of a century of progress, and we can and we will. The leadership on both sides of the aisle and both ends of the Capitol are working with me, but we need the

[2] Senator Mike Mansfield of Montana sponsored S.J. Res. 247, which proposed that the amendment to the continuing appropriations resolution, suspending American military assistance to Turkey, be deferred for 60 days, should the President determine that it would serve prospects for a negotiated settlement of the Cyprus conflict.

S.J. Res. 247 (H. Res. 1438) failed to pass the House of Representatives on October 11, 1974.

help of a lot of others in the House as well as in the Senate if we want to help Greece, if we want to keep the NATO organization strong, if we want to solve the humanitarian problems in Cyprus.

Let me conclude with these final observations and comments. We have got not only problems at home in the economic field and problems in foreign policy around the world, but we have the basic problem of trying to maintain the political structure of our country.

I know that some people fear the demise of some of our basic political institutions, one of them being the two-party system. And if you look at the Gallup or Roper polls, you can see that the Republican Party has suffered greatly according to their calculations. The Democratic Party has not picked up, in fact they have lost a few, too, and there is a great mass in the middle who call themselves Independents.

I respect and admire Independents, but as I look back over the history of this country, I find that the periods of greatest political stability and progress and movement have come when we had two strong political parties. It seems to me that our history has been greater and more glorious when we have had no splinter parties, that we have been unified in one of two major political parties.

Now, independence is good, but if we are to make our system work in the traditional way where you have competition from the Democrats on one hand and the Republicans on the other, we have got to maintain these organizations which give to every American an opportunity to be a participant.

Now, I have some prejudice as to which party I think people ought to belong, but the main problem we have is to make sure that these two political parties survive, grow, and participate in a more meaningful way. This is the way that our party can nominate people like Bill Milliken, John Damman, Bob Griffin, the members of the Michigan Congressional delegation, the members of the State legislature. And so I plead with you to support a strong two-party system.

History throughout the world tells us that if you have a multitude of political parties, you have chaos and you end up in that nation suffering with no progress. On the other hand, if you have one political party, we have the evils of dictation and all that goes with it.

So, let's make the choice of a two-party system. And this election has something to do with that. A catastrophic defeat, as some forecasters are predicting for the Republican Party, could have a terribly depressing effect on the Republican Party and could—could, I say—write the obituary.

I don't think it will happen to the Republican Party and all for which we stand. So as I close, let me say I am confident of our faith in the Republican

Party. I am confident that our candidates will do well at the State level, the Federal level.

Why? Because they have good principles, they have done a good job. They deserve the support of the people of Michigan, but more importantly, it is important to preserve the strength, the fiber of a political system that has done more for more people in freedom, material things, and God's blessings—the political system of the United States.

Thank you very much.

[The President spoke at 8:55 p.m. at Cobo Hall. In his opening remarks, the President referred to Max M. Fisher, chairman of the dinner.

Following the President's remarks, Lt. Gov. James H. Brickley of Michigan presented the President with the Michigan American Revolution Bicentennial Medallion. Their exchange of remarks, beginning at 9:31 p.m., follows.]

LIEUTENANT GOVERNOR BRICKLEY. Mr. President, on behalf of the Michigan Bicentennial Commission, I am very proud to present to you, the 38th President of the United States, Michigan's Bicentennial Medallion, the 38th one to be struck, containing a caricature on the back that was designed for the President by a Michigan high school student who won a statewide high school contest for that purpose.

We are going to be doing many things, hopefully, in Michigan to celebrate that birthday, but I think we of the Bicentennial Commission, and all of us here, and certainly all of Michigan's citizens, will be most proud that of all the things, that you will be the President of this Republic on its 200th birthday in July of 1976.

Mr. President.

THE PRESIDENT. Thank you very much, Lieutenant Governor Brickley—Jim, as I know him. It is a wonderful, wonderful little object that I will have on my desk in the Oval Office. It will remind me of the great State that means so much to me and the people who mean so much to me.

Thank you very much.

136

Statement Following a Meeting With the President's Committee on Mental Retardation. *October 11, 1974*

THREE years ago, America committed itself to cutting the rate of mental retardation in half by the end of the century. That is a notable goal, worthy of a great nation, and today in meeting with the President's Committee on Mental Retardation, I have renewed our commitment to that goal.

The problem of mental retardation deserves our attention, not only for the sake of the more than 6 million afflicted Americans and their families but for all of us. The majority of retarded citizens can become productive members of society.

There are three important points about mental retardation that must be understood:

One, with appropriate training, retarded people are capable of continuing development in normal community settings. Primarily through its housing agencies, the Federal Government will help retarded adults obtain suitable homes. But the real help must come from the local level.

Two, corrective measures in early childhood can reduce the severity of a handicap. Young children should be screened for handicaps, and when found, they should be corrected.

Three, since we know some of the causes of mental retardation, we know some ways to prevent it. Biomedical research may be helpful in extending this knowledge.

At present rates, some 4 million of our children expected to be born by the year 2000 will be retarded or become retarded. The members of the Committee have advised me that it is realistic to believe that the number can be reduced by half, and I urge all segments of our society to do their part in achieving this objective.

To attain this goal, every prospective mother should have available to her good prenatal care, including the most current techniques of fetal diagnosis and genetic counseling where necessary. She should know the kind of diet which will promote proper growth of the fetus. Good care for mother and child should continue postnatally, with special attention for premature infants. Infants and young children should be screened at appropriate intervals for hearing, visual, and other defects which could impede their learning ability, so that defects may be corrected before the child falls far behind.

A healthy environment and an adequate, balanced diet are especially important throughout the younger years, as is vaccination against rubella and other diseases.

Our school systems must be strengthened, so that they can provide the appropriate education which both the law and our conscience say may not be denied to retarded or otherwise handicapped children. By appropriate education, I mean training in academic, vocational, and social skills which will enable these children to live up to their highest potential. And let us never underestimate how high that potential is.

In the last few years, great progress has been made in winning legal recognition for the rights of retarded citizens—not only the right to education but the right not to be confined in an institution without habilitative treatment, the right to be paid for work done, and other rights that belong to all citizens.

I urge employers to consider the very real job capabilities of retarded persons and to use the U.S. Employment Service to the fullest possible extent in hiring retarded persons. If we forget stereotypes and look at retarded people as people, we will recognize what so many of them have already proved—that they can do hundreds of different jobs reliably and well.

There is urgent need to chart a concerted effort to minimize the occurrence of retardation and to assure humane services and full citizenship for those who are retarded. I encourage this Committee to pursue to completion its report on the directions that effort should take over the next quarter century.

Finally, I call upon all Americans to become more familiar with the problems of retardation and the potentials of retarded people. With our understanding. they will thrive. With our love, they will flower.

137

Remarks on Signing the Energy Reorganization Act of 1974. *October 11, 1974*

BEFORE signing, I just want to thank all the Members of Congress who are here. I can recall rather vividly when this recommendation came to the Congress, and I am especially pleased that I have an opportunity to sign the legislation which establishes ERDA.

I think it is a tremendous step forward. It is really the result of hard work by the Congress and, I think, good recommendations by the Administration.

Now we are going to turn over to Rog—Rog Morton here—the overall responsibility to make sure that this, as well as the other parts of the energy program for this Government, proceeds as fast, and as effectively, and as efficiently as possible.

So, it is a particular pleasure for me to sign a rather short name with 11 pens, but I will do my best. [*Laughter*] I found that there was another left-handed President, President Garfield.

We will get a couple more and see that those are properly passed out.

Thanks for coming down. I apologize for being late, but we had the President of Somalia on his first visit in the Oval Office, and we had a very interesting conversation. I just could not break away.

So, thank you for waiting, and good luck to you, and I hope you all have a good vacation between now and November 11.

NOTE: The President spoke at 3:50 p.m. in the Cabinet Room at the White House.

As enacted, the bill (H.R. 11510) is Public Law 93–438 (88 Stat. 1233).

138

Statement on the Energy Reorganization Act of 1974. *October 11, 1974*

IT IS my privilege today to sign into law a bill which takes a big step forward in this Nation's program to face up to and solve its crucial energy needs for the future.

H.R. 11510 abolishes the present Atomic Energy Commission and establishes three new Federal entities:

1. The *Energy Research and Development Administration* (*ERDA*) which, for the first time, will bring together into one agency major Federal programs of research and development for all forms of energy and will organize these programs for cooperation with industry, academic institutions, and other organizations in the Nation's rapidly expanding energy research and development effort.

2. The *Energy Resources Council* composed of the Secretaries of State and Interior, the Administrators of ERDA and the Federal Energy Administration, the Director of the Office of Management and Budget, and other members as I may designate. I am pleased that the Congress acted consistent with my suggestion for an interagency council, which I had announced in my economic message October 8. It is, therefore, my pleasure to name the Secretary of the Interior to chair this Council and I am today issuing an Executive order [11814] to assure prompt action.

3. The *Nuclear Regulatory Commission* (*NRC*) which will take over the licensing and regulation responsibilities previously performed by the Atomic Energy Commission.

My Administration is already committed to a greatly accelerated 5-year program of over $10 billion for energy research and development. ERDA gives us the unified, high quality scientific, technical, and management organization to achieve the greatest benefit from this investment of public funds. By combining the research and development capabilities of AEC with the fossil fuels research capability of the Interior Department, and with energy research skills from EPA and the National Science Foundation, we are bringing together in ERDA the best of our government skills in energy research and development.

From these agencies, we will be drawing upon a highly respected team of scientists, engineers, and program managers, capable of making immediate contributions to research on all forms of energy. Bringing together these skills, using AEC as its base, represents the quickest way in which the Federal Government can work with industry and others in mobilizing the talents, facilities, and skills needed to undertake the major expansion and extension of the Nation's energy research and development programs.

The Energy Research and Development Administration is being given a broad range of challenging and important research missions:

1. It will continue the research of the present Atomic Energy Commission in nuclear fusion and fission, working with the American industry to design, develop, and demonstrate increasingly more effective nuclear power systems to meet our growing electric power needs, and to see to it that these systems are completely safe in operation, economically feasible, and environmentally clean.

2. It will continue to expand fossil fuels research programs which the Department of the Interior initiated to capitalize on our immense national reserves of coal and oil shale, with emphasis on advancing the technology for the clean use of coal, including gasification and liquefaction.

3. It will continue to serve our national security needs by carrying on AEC's responsibility for the design, development, and fabrication of weapons systems for the Department of Defense.

4. It will maintain our nuclear materials production capability which serves both military and civilian needs, including international commitments for supplying nuclear reactor fuel.

5. It will give us greatly strengthened Government scientific and engineering capability to expand and upgrade our research into making use of new and potentially important forms of energy such as solar and geothermal sources.

6. It will move immediately into a substantial new effort in energy conservation research and development, including the utilization of the best scientific and engineering talent to find new ways to make our factories, our automobiles, our buildings, and our appliances more energy efficient and economical.

7. It will additionally continue and expand a program of environmental con-

trol technology and assessment of environmental and health effects of energy technologies.

8. It will continue strong basic research programs in such areas as physics, environmental and biological sciences and extend these scientific capabilities to support *all* energy areas— not just nuclear energy.

ERDA must and will become a lot more than the sum of its present parts. What is envisioned is nothing less than a *complete* energy research and development organization. It will be one which will fill in the gaps in our present research efforts and provide a balanced national research program. It will give proper emphasis to each energy source according to its potential and its readiness for practical use. It will closely integrate our energy research and development efforts with overall national energy policy.

In addition to creating ERDA, H.R. 11510 also creates a new Nuclear Regulatory Commission (NRC) which will assume the licensing and regulatory responsibilities previously carried out under the Director of Regulation within the Atomic Energy Commission. The highly technical nature of our nuclear facilities and the special potential hazards which are involved in the use of nuclear fuels fully warrant the creation of an independent and technically competent regulatory agency to assure adequate protection of public health and safety.

NRC will be responsible for the licensing and regulation of the nuclear industry under the provisions of the Atomic Energy Act. This means that NRC will be fully empowered to see to it that reactors using nuclear materials will be properly and safely designed, constructed, and operated to guarantee against hazards to the public from leakage or accident. NRC will also exercise strengthened authority to assure that the public is fully safeguarded from hazards arising from the storage, handling, and transportation of nuclear materials being used in power reactors, hospitals, research laboratories, or for any other purpose.

With the creation of ERDA and NRC, the Federal Government has acted in a timely way to participate in the national effort to meet our future energy research and development needs. This action has been feasible through the very best kind of cooperation between the Congress and the executive branch. I want especially to express my appreciation and gratitude to those Members of both Houses who, by their leadership, brought this legislation to reality.

139

Remarks at the Swearing In of Richard L. Roudebush as Administrator of Veterans Affairs. *October 12, 1974*

Roudy and Karen, and my former colleagues in the Congress, and Government officials, and friends:

This is a landmark day in that a man who served in the Congress and helped to write some of the laws, a man who fought in the service of his country and who also participated very, very actively in veterans organizations, is going to be the Administrator of the Veterans Administration.

All of you know here, probably better than I, the magnitude of the responsibilities of the Veterans Administration, the magnitude not only in the facilities and the employees and the responsibilities but the great and important work that the VA does for people.

The number of veterans in this country is almost beyond comprehension when you go back through the war in Vietnam, Korea, and World War II. When you take into consideration World War I, the number of veterans that are in our population of 213 million is a very substantial portion.

So, Roudy, you have an obligation to do a first-class job on behalf of a good share of the population of this country, the people who have given dedicated service on behalf of freedom, on behalf of our national security.

All of us here and your fellow citizens expect that the Veterans Administration is going to have an outlook that is dedicated to the best in service.

I said at the VFW speech in Chicago [on August 19] that we were not going to treat veterans as a number in a computer. We were going to treat veterans as persons, individuals who had made sacrifices, sacrifices for our freedom and our way of life.

So, as you handle the problems of pensions and compensation, the problems of health service with our hospitals and out-patient treatment, as you handle the problems that cover the life of the thousands and thousands of veterans, I am convinced that you will do a first-class job.

The obligation is great, but the person who has been selected and confirmed I know will do the job. And so, I congratulate you and the Members of the Congress with whom you served, the members of the various veterans organizations of which you were a part, and the individuals in the service with whom you participated. I congratulate you on behalf of all of them.

Good luck. We are counting on you.

Mr. Roudebush. Thank you very much, Mr. President.

Certainly, I want to first say how very deeply grateful I am to you, sir, for your confidence. I am also deeply grateful that you take the time from a schedule that must be backbreaking to have this public ceremony here today in the beautiful Rose Garden of the White House.

I am deeply grateful that my daughter could come out from Indiana—Karen—and be with me today. I am sure the President is aware of the fact that my father is in very bad condition, and my wife had to remain in Indiana and could not be present with us today. So, Karen appeared in her behalf.

I want to acknowledge the presence of my former colleagues in the Congress, in both bodies, and may I say to them I appreciate them coming. My comrades of the veterans organizations, I am very deeply grateful to you.

Mr. President, the charge you have given me is a tremendous one. I am aware of this. The task before the Veterans Administration, administering benefits for more than 29 million of our citizens—and when you take into account the families of those 29 million veterans, a total, an aggregate you might say, of over 100 million of our citizens, nearly half of our population—it is a tremendous undertaking.

But, Mr. President, I am happy to report to you today, although I have actually been aboard as the acting Administrator only a very short period of time, I think we have a new feeling at the Veterans Administration.

I think we have a great increase in our morale down there, and we appreciate your support, sir, and the support of our great veterans organizations, and I know that we are going to solve all the problems that do lie in front of us.

I am so happy that my colleagues from the VA, men like Odell Vaughn, could be here today, our Chief Benefits Director; Rufus Wilson, who runs our cemetery system, Mr. President; and Dr. Jack Chase, who, of course, heads up the greatest hospital system in the world, all 171 of our hospitals, and I am just so happy that they could come down today.

So, Mr. President, I believe that is all I have to say at this time, but thank you all for coming. And to you, sir, I offer again my sincere thanks, my appreciation, and I assure you, sir, I will never let you down.

Thank you so much.

The President. Well, thank you all for coming. It is wonderful to have you here on this beautiful day. We are proud of Roudy, and we know he will do a first-class job.

Thank you.

NOTE: The President spoke at 10:51 a.m. in the Rose Garden at the White House.

140

Veto of Railroad Retirement Benefits Legislation. *October 12, 1974*

To the House of Representatives:

I am returning today without my approval, H.R. 15301, a bill which would finance a long-standing deficit in the Railroad Retirement System at the expense of the general taxpayer.

The Railroad Retirement System, under current law, is headed toward bankruptcy by the mid-1980s. This condition arises largely because benefits have been increased 68 percent since 1970 without requiring the beneficiaries of the system, railroad employees and employers, to pay the added costs.

This bill proposes to solve the financial problems of the Railroad Retirement System by placing a seven billion dollar burden on the general taxpayer, requiring him to contribute $285 million to the Railroad Retirement Trust Fund each year for the next twenty-five years. In return for his seven billion dollar contribution, the general taxpayer would earn no entitlement to benefits and would receive no return on his investment.

At a time when the taxpayer is already carrying the double burden of taxes and inflation, legislation such as this is most inappropriate.

Recognizing the financial straits of the Railroad Retirement System, the Executive Branch in 1970 proposed and the Congress authorized an independent study of the System. After eighteen months of careful work, the study group recommended that the benefits be financed ". . . on an assured, fully self-supporting basis by contributions from the railroad community through the crisis period of the next 20 to 30 years and then beyond."

Following receipt of the report, the Congress directed representatives of railroad employees and management to submit their combined recommendations for restoring financial soundness to the System, taking into account the report and the specific recommendations of the Commission.

The bill which is now before me is true neither to the recommendation of the Commission nor to the charge placed on the industry by the Congress.

Forcing the general taxpayer to carry an unfair burden is not the only defect in this bill. It would also establish a special investment procedure for the Railroad Retirement Trust Fund.

Under the bill, the interest paid by the Treasury on Railroad Retirement investments and Federal securities would rise when interest rates increase but would not fall when they decrease. This "heads I win; tails you lose" arrangement, with the taxpayer being the loser, has been suggested before, but never adopted. It should not be a part of the solution to the Railroad Retirement System's financial problem.

Furthermore, the provisions of the benefit formula are so complex that they would be extremely difficult to administer and virtually impossible to explain to the persons who are supposed to benefit from it. Now is the time to simplify the benefit structure of the Railroad Retirement System, not make it more complex. Splitting administrative responsibility between the Railroad Retirement System and the Social Security System over benefits that depend on entitlement under the Social Security Act is bad law. Full responsibility for administering Social Security benefits should be vested in the Social Security Administration, not divided among agencies with resultant uncertainty as to who should be held accountable.

I believe it is our obligation to the general taxpayer to see that the problems of this system are overcome by the industry and people it serves—those who have benefited from it in the past and will continue to receive its benefits in the future. Other industries—other parts of the transportation industry—pay for their own pension systems. There is no justification for singling out the railroads for special treatment.

There are only two ways this obligation can be met—by increasing revenues or by limiting benefits or by a combination of both. Administration spokesmen have proposed constructive ways to achieve this goal, but our proposals have not received serious consideration by the Congress.

We are in need of a better railroad retirement system and a financially sound one. This bill does not meet that need. I urge the Congress to reconsider that need and to develop a new bill which is fair to the taxpayers as well as to the beneficiaries of the Railroad Retirement System. This Administration stands ready to help in any way it can.

GERALD R. FORD

The White House,
October 12, 1974.

NOTE: H.R. 15301 was enacted over the President's veto on October 16, 1974, as Public Law 93–445 (88 Stat. 1305).

141

Veto of Atomic Energy Act Amendments. *October 12, 1974*

To the House of Representatives:

I am returning without my approval H.R. 15323, "To amend the Atomic Energy Act, as amended, to revise the method of providing public remuneration in the event of a nuclear incident, and for other purposes."

The first eleven sections of the bill basically carry out recommendations of the Atomic Energy Commission, and I would be glad to approve them if they stood alone.

Section 12, however, would provide that "the provisions of this Act shall become effective thirty (30) days after the date on which the Joint Committee on Atomic Energy submits to the Congress an evaluation of the Reactor Study, entitled 'An Assessment of Accident Risks in the U.S. Commercial Nuclear Power Plants,' AEC Report Number WASH–1400, except that it shall not become effective if within the thirty (30) day period after the Joint Committee submits its evaluation, the Congress adopts a concurrent resolution disapproving the extension of the Price-Anderson Act." The import of this section is that after I have approved the bill, the Joint Committee and the Congress would further consider whether it should ever become effective.

I cannot approve legislation under these circumstances—if, indeed, the bill can properly be called legislation rather than merely the expression of an intent to legislate. The presentation of a bill to me pursuant to Article I, section 7 of the Constitution amounts to a representation by Congress that, as far as it is concerned, the legislation is ready to become effective, subject perhaps to some extrinsic condition precedent, but not to further congressional deliberation. Here, however, Congress in effect requests my approval before it has given its own.

In this instance, the clear constitutional infirmity of the bill not only affects my powers and duties but directly endangers substantial and important private rights. If the bill is unconstitutional, it will remain unconstitutional despite my signing it. As a result, a sure source of funds for prompt payment of public liability claims, a primary objective of the Price-Anderson Act, would be in doubt. The uncertainty over nuclear liability protection would also adversely affect that private investment which will be necessary as nuclear power assumes its vital role in meeting the nation's energy requirements. The public interest would not be served by approving legislation which creates these uncertainties.

I urge the Congress to reenact the bill promptly so as to remove the problems which Section 12 now raises.

GERALD R. FORD

The White House,
October 12, 1974.

142

Remarks on Boston School Desegregation Violence. *October 12, 1974*

BOSTON is a fine, proud city, the cradle of liberty, where many of the freedoms that we all so cherish today in this country, were born, 200 years ago. The people of Boston share a tradition for reason, fairness, and respect for the rights of others. Now, in a difficult period for all of you, it is a time to reflect on all that your city means to you, to react in the finest tradition of your city's people. It is up to you, every one of you, every parent, child, to reject violence of any kind in your city, to reject hatred and the shrill voices of the violent few.

I know that nothing is more important to you than the safety of the children in Boston. And only your calm and thoughtful action now can guarantee that safety. I know that you will all work together for that goal, and have one more thing to be proud of in the cradle of liberty.

NOTE: The President's remarks were recorded for use on Boston radio stations, at the request of Boston media representatives.

143

Joint Communique Following Discussions With First Secretary Gierek of Poland. *October 13, 1974*

AT THE invitation of the President of the United States of America, Gerald R. Ford, and Mrs. Ford, the First Secretary of the Central Committee of the Polish United Workers' Party, Edward Gierek, and Mrs. Gierek, paid an official visit to the United States October 8 through 13, 1974.

The First Secretary was accompanied by: Mieczyslaw Jagielski, Deputy Chairman of the Council of Ministers, and Mrs. Jagielski; Stefan Olszowski, Foreign Minister, and Mrs. Olszowski; Ryszard Frelek, Member of the Secretariat of the Central Committee of the Polish United Workers' Party; Witold Trampczynski, Polish Ambassador to the United States of America.

The First Secretary was also accompanied by a group of advisers and experts

The official party also visited New York, Pittsburgh, and Houston.

During his stay in Washington, First Secretary Gierek held talks with President Ford on the development of relations between Poland and the United States as well as on international issues.

He also met with Secretary of State and Assistant to the President for National Security Affairs Henry A. Kissinger, Secretary of Agriculture Earl Butz, Secretary of Commerce Frederick Dent, Secretary of Health, Education, and Welfare Caspar Weinberger, and Chairman of the Export-Import Bank William Casey.

The First Secretary paid a visit to Congress and met with members of the Senate and the House of Representatives. He also had talks with leading American businessmen and bankers.

Talks were also held between Foreign Minister Olszowski and Secretary of State Kissinger.

The talks and meetings were held in a friendly and businesslike atmosphere and were characterized by a mutual desire to expand and strengthen the relations between Poland and the United States.

In the course of the talks, the President and the First Secretary noted with satisfaction the significant progress which has recently been made in Polish-American relations. Both leaders expressed their desire to further develop these relations, which are based on the long-standing traditions of friendship and sympathy existing between the Polish and American peoples.

They agreed that the "Joint Statement on Principles of U.S.-Polish Relations" signed during the visit provides a firm basis for broad cooperation between the two countries and contributes to the process of strengthening world peace. security, and international cooperation.

The President and the First Secretary also attached importance to the "Joint Statement on the Development of Economic, Industrial and Technological Cooperation between the United States of America and the Polish People's Republic," which they signed. They agreed that the main directions and scope of cooperation stipulated in the field of trade, industrial and technological cooperation should contribute to the further advancement of bilateral economic relations.

The President and the First Secretary noted with satisfaction the rapid growth of trade between the United States and Poland in the past two years, accompanied by a substantial intensification of general economic relations between the two countries. They considered a mutual trade turnover of one billion dollars by 1976 and two billion dollars by 1980 to be a realistic and desirable goal.

They also agreed that the provisions contained in the "Joint Statement on the Development of Agricultural Trade between the United States of America and the Polish People's Republic" create possibilities for a further expansion of trade in food and agricultural products as well as for cooperation in various sectors of the agricultural economy.

They noted that the Joint American-Polish Trade Commission plays an important role in the development of trade and economic cooperation.

President Ford and First Secretary Gierek expressed their deep satisfaction at the conclusion during the visit of agreements in the fields of: Coal research; Health; Environmental Protection; Cooperation in Science and Technology; and Avoidance of Double Taxation.

They also welcome the conclusion of an agreement on the establishment of working relationships between the U.S. and Polish Chambers of Commerce.

Both leaders stressed the significance of the broad development of cultural and scientific cooperation between the United States and Poland and expressed their conviction that this cooperation should be further developed.

The President and the First Secretary emphasized the importance of historical traditions in strengthening the bonds of sympathy and friendship between the United States and Poland. A positive role in this strengthening of mutual relations has been played by American citizens of Polish descent. Both leaders undertook to encourage and support further development of those and other contacts between the American and Polish people.

The President and the First Secretary conducted a broad and useful exchange of views on the most important international issues with special emphasis on European questions. They agreed that there exist a number of spheres in which both countries can contribute to the strengthening of peace and international security.

Both leaders expressed satisfaction with the results of the talks they held and agreed that consultations will continue between the two countries at various levels on matters concerning their mutual relations, including the assessment of the implementation of the agreements that were concluded as well as on important international issues of mutual interest.

The First Secretary and Mrs. Gierek expressed their warm gratitude for the hospitality and friendliness accorded to them in the United States.

The First Secretary extended an invitation to the President of the United States and Mrs. Ford to pay an official visit to the Polish People's Republic at a time convenient to them. The invitation was accepted with pleasure.

144

Remarks on Signing Veto of Continuing Appropriations Resolution Containing an Amendment Suspending Military Aid to Turkey. *October 14, 1974*

TODAY, in the interest of preserving the ability of the United States to assist the Governments of Greece, Turkey, and Cyprus to negotiate a peaceful settlement of the Cyprus dispute, I am returning to the Congress without my approval the continuing resolution which the Congress has amended to cut off military aid to Turkey.

In so doing, I want to clear the air of a number of misunderstandings concerning the U.S. position toward the Cyprus crisis.

Since the outbreak of the crisis, our objectives have been to establish a cease-fire, to provide humanitarian aid to the refugees, to assist the parties toward a negotiation and a settlement, and to strengthen and to improve our historically friendly ties with Greece, Turkey, and Cyprus.

I have discussed these goals with the bipartisan leadership of the Congress and have received their unanimous and vigorous support. Our ability to pursue these goals depends, however, on being able to maintain a constructive relationship with the parties involved. The cutoff of assistance to Turkey is destructive of that relationship.

Further, it in no way helps the Greek people or the people of Cyprus who have suffered so much in the past months. In fact, by dashing hopes for negotiations, it prolongs their suffering.

We recognize clearly the need to ensure that the honor and the integrity of the Greek people be maintained. We seek a settlement which ensures that fundamental requirement. United States friendship with Greece has been established through generations of cooperation and mutual respect, based on shared values and common goals. I intend firmly to carry on and strengthen that relationship.

I cannot, however, carry out this pledge if my ability to act in the current crisis is undercut by restrictions imposed by the Congress. We all seek a peaceful resolution of this problem; we all seek justice for the people of Cyprus; we all seek to maintain the strength and cooperation in our relationship that is a cornerstone to Western security in the Mediterranean.

It is for these reasons that I return this resolution to the Congress and ask that it thoughtfully reconsider its position.

I pledge to continue working closely in partnership with the Congress to enable the United States to play a useful role in helping the parties toward a peaceful resolution of the Cyprus dispute.

I am now signing my veto message, which will be delivered today to the Congress.

Thank you very much.

NOTE: The President spoke at 2:23 p.m. in the Oval Office at the White House.

145

Veto of Continuing Appropriations Resolution. *October 14, 1974*

To the House of Representatives:

At the beginning of my Administration I pledged to work closely and cooperatively with the Congress. I believe I have kept that promise. I have appeared before two joint sessions of the Congress, I have met frequently with the leadership of both Houses, and I have agreed to appear personally before a subcommittee of the House of Representatives—a step no other President has undertaken in more than a century.

These actions are an earnest of my commitment to a new partnership between the legislative and executive branches of our government. They reflect my deep belief that the antagonisms that have too long divided our Nation must be resolved, that hopes for partisan advantage must be put aside, and that we must get on with the business of doing the best we can for our country.

The cooperation I have received from the leadership of the Congress—Democratic and Republican alike—has been truly remarkable. The leaders have advised me and I have listened; I have explained my problems to them and they have responded with understanding and support. For this I am deeply grateful.

It is, therefore, with deep regret that I am returning today without my approval the recently passed Continuing Resolution, H.J. Res. 1131, granting funds for the operation of several departments and agencies and for the temporary continuation of our foreign aid programs. I take this step with great reluctance, but in the belief that I have no other choice.

The Continuing Resolution the Congress has passed and sent to me for signature contains an amendment requiring an immediate cut-off of all military assistance to Turkey. That amendment was passed despite my own public objection to it, and in the face of the unanimous opposition of the bipartisan leadership of both Houses of Congress. It is an act which is harmful even to those it purports to help.

The United States is making every effort to play a useful role in assisting the parties to a resolution of the Cyprus dispute. The Continuing Resolution as amended is entirely destructive of those efforts. Instead of encouraging the parties involved in the Cyprus dispute to return to the negotiating table, an arms cut-off to Turkey could mean the indefinite postponement of meaningful negotiations. Instead of strengthening America's ability to persuade the parties to resolve the dispute, it would lessen our influence on all the parties concerned. It would as well imperil our relationships with our Turkish ally and weaken us in the crucial Eastern Mediterranean. It directly jeopardizes the NATO alliance.

Most tragic of all, an arms cut-off would not help Greece or the Greek Cypriot people who have suffered so tragically over the past several months. We recognize that we are still far from a settlement consistent with the honor and dignity of Greece, and are prepared to exert our influence to that end. But reckless acts that prevent progress toward a Cyprus settlement harm Greece, for it is the Greek government and the Greek Cypriots who have the most to gain from a compromise settlement. And it is they who have the most to lose from continued deadlock.

It is for these reasons that I am vetoing the bill sent to me. I do so because, should this measure become law, it would be impossible for the United States to continue to play any meaningful role in assisting the parties to resolve the Cyprus dispute. We would inevitably be forced to withdraw from the negotiations because the Congress would have taken from us the tools we need to affect the outcome.

My choice, then, is unavoidable; my responsibility clear. I ask that the Congress reconsider its action and send to me a bill that we can all support; a bill that provides the flexibility needed to carry forward the foreign policy of the United States.

GERALD R. FORD

The White House,
October 14, 1974.

NOTE: The House of Representatives sustained the President's veto on October 15, 1974.

146

Telegram on State and Local Efforts To Fight Inflation. *October 14, 1974*

THE NONPARTISAN voluntary Citizens' Action Committee to Fight Inflation has recommended a 10-point program which I plan to pass on to the Nation in a speech in Kansas City Tuesday evening. Two of their recommendations also can be implemented by State and local authorities: (1) conserve energy by enforcing the 55-mile per hour speed limit, and (2) eliminate outmoded regulations that keep costs of goods and services high and enforce regulations that advance efficiency, health, and safety.

The Committee also asked me to call upon all Governors, mayors, and other local officials to set up similar voluntary citizens' action committees to fight inflation in the States and communities. I urge you to assist by prompt action on the Committee's recommendations. Thanks for your cooperation.

Warm regards,

GERALD R. FORD

NOTE: This is the text of identical telegrams sent to 54 Governors, 150 mayors, and 30 county executives.

147

Statement on House Action Sustaining Veto of the Continuing Appropriations Resolution. *October 15, 1974*

I AM deeply gratified by the House vote sustaining my veto of the continuing resolution. This wise and responsive action will serve the cause of peace on Cyprus while maintaining the strength of our vital security relationships in the Eastern Mediterranean.

I want to thank the Congressional leadership for its understanding and support. I look forward to working in partnership with the Congress to enhance the ability of the United States to assist the parties in negotiating a peaceful and lasting resolution of the Cyprus dispute and in responding generously to the humanitarian relief needs of the Cypriot people. At the same time, I ask Congress for prompt action to provide continued funding without encumbering restrictions for the operation of several departments and agencies.

148

Remarks on Signing the Federal Election Campaign Act Amendments of 1974. *October 15, 1974*

Distinguished Members of the Congress, and guests:

It is really a great privilege for me to have a part in what I think is historic legislation. As all of my good friends from the Congress know, a tremendous amount of work, a lot of extra labor, went into the putting together of this legislation.

Quite frankly, I had some strong reservations about one version or one provision or another of the legislation, and I suspect some of the people here on both sides of the aisle have the same.

But we got together in a spirit of cooperation, a willingness to work together, to give a little and take a little, and the net result is legislation that I think the American people want. It is legislation for the times.

I am not telling you any secrets. I have some reservations about the final version. But, in the spirit of cooperation and compromise, I think it ought to be signed and become a part of our statutory law.

I can assure you from what I have heard, from the American people in writing and other communications, they want this legislation. So, it will soon be law. I think we do recognize that this legislation seeks to eliminate to a maximum degree some of the influences that have created some of the problems in recent years. And if that is the end result, certainly it is worth all the labor and all the compromises that were necessary in the process.

Now, this is a major step in one direction. To a substantial degree, there will be a degree of public financing. As long as it stays within the checkoff system, I am willing to go along with it. And I hope that the American taxpayers, as they make out their returns in the years ahead, will be generous so that those campaigns can and will be adequately financed.

Well, what it all comes down to, in my judgment, is that between a Congress controlled by one party, a White House in the hands of another, and a working cooperation between the Senate and the House, and the hard working members of that conference—I guess you were part of that, weren't you, Wayne—[*laughter*]—we ended up with some legislation that I think deserves the support of the American people, and I think they will support it.

I congratulate the conferees, the House and the Senate, and the people from the outside who had a significant impact in urging the Congress and the White House to be forthcoming.

So, I think this is a good day for 213 million Americans.

Thank you very, very much.

NOTE: The President spoke at 4:20 p.m. in the East Room at the White House. In his remarks, the President referred to Representative Wayne L. Hays, chairman of the Committee on House Administration and member of the Committee of Conference on the legislation.

As enacted, the bill (S. 3044) is Public Law 93–443 (88 Stat. 1263).

149

Statement on the Federal Election Campaign Act Amendments of 1974. *October 15, 1974*

TODAY I am signing into law the Federal [Election] Campaign Act Amendments of 1974.

By removing whatever influence big money and special interests may have on our Federal electoral process, this bill should stand as a landmark of campaign reform legislation.

In brief, the bill provides for reforms in five areas:

—It limits the amounts that can be contributed to any candidate in any Federal election, and it limits the amounts that those candidates can expend in their campaigns.

—It provides for matching funds for Presidential primaries and public financing for Presidential nominating conventions and Presidential elections through use of the $1 voluntary tax checkoff.

—It tightens the rules on any use of cash, it limits the amount of speaking honorariums, and it outlaws campaign dirty tricks.

—It requires strict campaign financial reporting and disclosure.

—It establishes a bipartisan six-member Federal Election Commission to see that the provisions of the act are followed.

Although I support the aim of this legislation, I still have some reservations about it—especially about the use of Federal funds to finance elections. I am pleased that the money used for Federal financing will come from the $1 checkoff, however, thus allowing each taxpayer to make his own decision as to whether he wants his money spent this way. I maintain my strong hope that the voluntary contribution will not become mandatory and that it will not in the future be extended to Congressional races. And although I do have reservations about the first amendment implications inherent in the limits on individual contributions and candidate expenditures, I am sure that such issues can be resolved in the courts.

I am pleased with the bipartisan spirit that has led to this legislation. Both the Republican National Committee and the Democratic National Committee have expressed their pleasure with this bill, noting that it allows them to compete fairly.

The times demand this legislation.

There are certain periods in our Nation's history when it becomes necessary to face up to certain unpleasant truths.

We have passed through one of those periods. The unpleasant truth is that
It is a great privilege and a very high honor to have an opportunity of partic-
ess. This bill will help to right that wrong.

I commend the extensive work done by my colleagues in both houses of Congress on this bill, and I am pleased to sign it today.

150

Remarks to the Annual Convention of the Future Farmers of America, Kansas City, Missouri. *October 15, 1974*

Thank you very, very much, President Mark Mayfield, the 13,000 Future Farmers of America registered for this wonderful 47th Convention, the 500,000 Future Farmers of America in every State of the Union, and your guests:

It is a great privilege and a very high honor to have an opportunity of participating in this wonderful convention, and I thank you. And I thank you on behalf of Betty, because she wanted me to come, too.

One week ago I asked the Congress and the American people to help me revitalize the economy, slow inflation, and save energy. At that time I proposed specific and urgent actions.

The American people, I can report tonight, have responded magnificently. A great citizens' mobilization has begun and is beginning to roll. It is already evident here in this eager, up-beat convention of Future Farmers of America, and I thank you from the bottom of my heart.

In this last week, I have received inflation-fighter enlistments from Americans of every conceivable occupation, economic circumstances, and political persuasion. Support has been freely offered by organizations and groups representing all ages, races, religions, and reaching into every corner of our great land.

America is arousing itself, as it always does in time of great challenge, to prove that we are a people who can do anything we want to do when we really want to do it. We are going to win in America.

Now some have said that instead of asking Congress and the Nation to bite the bullet, I offered only a marshmallow. Well, I had already asked the Congress to postpone for 3 months a 5.5 percent pay increase for Federal Government employees which would have saved $700 million. Congress wouldn't even chew that marshmallow. They haven't, as yet, shown much appetite for some of the other "marshmallows" in my latest message.

But if they don't like the menu, I may be back with some tough turkey.

It is my observation and view that the American people are hungry for some tough stuff to chew on in this crisis. I don't know of any better place to look to the future of America than right here in the 13,000 faces of the Future Farmers of America.

I don't see anyone in this auditorium, not one, wearing a button that says "lose." You want to win, and we are going to win.

When your State presidents came to Washington last July during a time of tension in our national affairs, I pointed out to them that people around the world have great faith in America. I asked Future Farmers to have confidence in themselves, in our system of Government, and in our free competitive society.

I appreciated their response and your response. I think it is well expressed in the creed of the Future Farmers. I believe with you, for example, "in the future of farming, with a faith born not of words but of deeds . . . in the promise of better days through better ways, even as the better things we now enjoy have come to us from the struggles of former years." It couldn't be expressed better.

Number one of the major points in my address to the Congress last week was food. In a war against inflation, farmers are the frontline soldiers. They have done a great job in America, making our country the breadbasket of the world.

To halt higher food prices, obviously we must produce more food. I called upon, in that message, every farmer to grow to full capacity. In return—and properly so—I promised every farmer the fuel and the fertilizer that he needs to do the job, plus a fair return for the crops that he produces.

It is not only the young people in this auditorium who must lend their hands and their hearts to this task. I need help from young Americans all over this great land. The creative energy and the enthusiasm of youth in my judgment is our sure guarantee of winning.

But in all honesty, youth has the most to gain. Restoring stability and strength to our economy doesn't call for sacrifices so much as for contributions to one's own future well-being.

Last Saturday, 22 members of the Citizens' Action Committee to Fight Inflation met with me at the White House. It was a beautiful fall afternoon, and I am sure many would have preferred on that committee to watch their favorite football game or play some golf or be with their family.

But I am deeply grateful that this fine committee took the time and made the effort to join with me on a Saturday to work on our national enemy number one.

Let me stress this point, if I could: This is a volunteer working committee, a completely nonpartisan group dealing with a nonpartisan problem. It will seek to mobilize America against inflation and for energy conservation.

I told the committee that if there was a scintilla of partisanship or if the group seemed to be merely a front for the White House, its efforts would be doomed to failure.

Columnist Sylvia Porter, who has agreed to serve as national chairperson of this committee, responded that if I tried to manipulate the committee or seek to influence its actions, she and the other members would not participate. We understand each other.

And I say with all the conviction that I have that I was greatly impressed with the membership of this committee and the cross section of America which it represents.

Let me illustrate, if I might. In addition to Sylvia Porter, the committee elected four co-chairmen. They are: Carol T. Foreman, executive director of the Consumer Federation of America; William J. Meyer, president of a small business company in Lansdale, Pennsylvania; Leo Perlis, director of community service of the AFL–CIO; and Frank Stanton, president of the National Red Cross.

A task force headed by Ralph Nader, one of the committee's members, came up with suggestions which coincide to a large extent with the views emanating from the Conference on Inflation which the Future Farmers of America and many other groups attended, and your fine president, Mark Mayfield, was one of the participants and made a substantial contribution on behalf of all of you.

I had touched upon some of the proposals in my message to Congress a week ago—grow more, waste less, drive less, and heat less. But the committee, last Saturday, added a few suggestions of their own. And I promised to pass the committee's recommendations along to all of you here tonight.

I will add some of the comments I have received, for example, in the mail at the White House from thousands upon thousands of individuals who responded enthusiastically to my request at the summit Conference on Inflation.

Committee recommendation number one: Bring budgeting back in style.

Balance your family budget and expect your Government officials to do exactly the same thing.

I have already asked the Congress to work with me on this, the handling appropriately of the Federal budget. As to your family budget, I know how hard it is to balance, but many of your letters prove that it can be done. For example, Mr. and Mrs. Roland Spaek live in Holland, Michigan. He is a locomotive engineer working on a freight run between Grand Rapids and Chicago. Mr. and Mrs. Spaek describe in their letter to me how they are cutting their household budget, but they urge, and I quote: Our Federal budget should be pared to the bone.

Don't we all agree?

Robert Stewart writes from Waverly, Tennessee, that he has a heart condition, unfortunately, and draws a pension of only $251.28 a month. This allows him just two meals a day. "But thank God, we are not on welfare," says Mr. Stewart. He asks me, and again I quote: Cut our Government spending except for national defense.

Again, I think his example is a good one for all of us to observe.

Committee recommendation number two was stated to me this way by Sylvia Porter: Learn how to use credit wisely. Postpone unnecessary borrowing. Wait for interest rates to come down, as they will, and pay down as much as you can, and pay off as quickly as you can. The cheapest way to buy anything, we all know, is to pay cash. But credit wisely used is essential to our way of life in America.

Committee recommendation number three is to save as much as you can and watch your money grow, which it will. Mrs. Frank Tennant writes from Climax, Michigan, that her husband works hard and she helps stretch the paycheck through systematic savings. Mr. Tennant is a self-taught machinist and a veteran who lost his leg in Korea. But it is his ability rather than his disability that comes through in his dear wife's letter. The Tennants report they do not use credit cards. They put something in their credit union each week and buy a Government bond every month. They should be applauded.

James Kincaid of Belleville, Illinois, suggests a new type of Government anti-inflation bond, purchased through payroll deduction in which the interest rate is more competitive. Because I received many communications in this area, I have asked the Treasury Department to look into the possibility of issuing a new series of WIN bonds and report to me the feasibility of Mr. Kincaid's idea.

Meanwhile, if you can save more, the hard-pressed homebuilding mortgage market, homebuilders and home purchasers need your dollars. For those who can't save much, or anything, under the present circumstances, here is a very simple formula—every time the cost of living drops 1 percent in the [Consumer Price] Index, put just 1 percent of your spendable income into savings.

Committee recommendation number four: Conserve energy, save on fuel, and take the pressure off scarce supplies. The committee advocates observance of the 55-mile speed limit. It urges that we use public transit and carpools. And they respectfully suggest that all of us walk a bit more.

Enforcement of the 55-mile speed limit is largely a State and local responsibility with voluntary cooperation from all of you, which is an essential ingredient. Here, we can save both gasoline and lives. Yesterday, I wired every Governor and many local officials urging them to follow through on this recommendation.

At the same time, I directed the strict enforcement of the 55-mile speed limit, except in emergencies, on all Federal property and by drivers of all Federal Government cars, including my own. And I say this now, with some firmness, but some trepidation: I will ask for voluntary cooperation and compliance from the four younger Fords in our family.

From Hillsboro, Oregon, the Stevens family writes they are fixing up their bikes to do the family errands. They are also using fewer electrical appliances, turning the thermostat down, and the lights off.

Bob Cantrell, a 14-year-old in Pasadena, California, gave up his stereo to save energy. Bob urges the initiation of high school courses that teach students how to conserve energy. He adds, and I quote: If a kid nags his parents to conserve energy long enough, it will help.

And I might add from my own experiences, believe me, it will.

Committee recommendation number five is directed at business and labor. It calls upon them not to raise prices or wages more than costs or services absolutely require.

Admittedly, this is a very complex subject, and it cannot be handled on a nationwide basis. I believe that local citizen action committees, including labor and management representation, should be set up in every community to interpret this recommendation, set realistic goals for themselves, and to report by Thanksgiving—just 6 weeks away—which plants, which stores, or other enterprises are doing the best job of holding the line in their community on costs and on prices.

If they do a good job, and we find the winners around the country in every community, in every State, I will then award WIN flags to the most outstanding as public recognition of their contribution to the fight on inflation.

Similar recognition will be given to outstanding energy savers, both individuals and groups. Saving energy is, of course, a major way to save costs.

The national committee will help local groups to organize.

Committee recommendation number six: To help offset pay increases, insist on productivity improvements where you work from the boss on down the line. In short, work better, waste less, both of time and materials.

And there is not a place where business is done or activity is undertaken where the boss and everyone else can't work better and save more. And we should urge them to do it as soon as possible.

Now, Mr. and Mrs. Ed Monson write from San Antonio to urge support of companies showing a higher degree of concern for energy solutions and the unemployment problems.

Mrs. Hannah Folsom of Ojai, California, offers an additional suggestion. She urges that steps be taken to cut down on the proportion of administrative personnel to productive workers in plants and stores and the like. I think this is a great idea.

And let me say to Mrs. Folsom, I will apply this good idea to the Federal bureaucracy.

Committee recommendation number seven proposes we make economizing fashionable. Let me repeat that—economizing fashionable. Shop wisely, look for bargains, go for the lowest-cost item, and most importantly, brag about the fact that you are a bargain hunter. You should be proud of it.

The committee certainly is not suggesting Americans should buy less. We should all buy smarter, stick to a shopping list. The experts tell us that is the best way to get a real bargain.

Kathy Daly, a student at Sacred Heart High School in Weymouth, Massachusetts, has one formula for shopping wisely and saving energy. Kathy suggests buying warmer clothes this winter.

G. M. Knapp of Tucson, Arizona, puts it this way: "Only you can stop inflation. Buy only if you need it."

Committee recommendation number eight asks Americans to work with others to eliminate outmoded regulations that keep the cost of goods and services high and to enforce regulations that advance efficiency, health, and safety.

W. A. Taylor of Cambridge, Massachusetts, points out that because of Interstate Commerce Commission regulations, many, many trucks return empty—"deadheading," so to speak. I have already asked the Congress to undertake a joint review of restrictive and outdated rules by the Federal Government and its independent regulatory agencies.

Yesterday, I called upon Governors and mayors and others to do the same thing.

Committee recommendation number nine is do it yourself. Plant WIN gardens for yourself or within your community. Pool other do-it-yourself skills, and you can.

Sylvia Porter tells me that $10 worth of seeds on a 25′-by-30′ plot will grow $290 worth of vegetables. And she contends that community gardens can grow even in the inner cities of our major metropolitan areas. Many letters to the White House propose WIN gardens.

Rick Jacobsen of the fifth grade at Sault Ste. Marie, Michigan, writes the White House that "we planted our own garden so we could save on vegetables." In southern areas of our country, there is still plenty of time to plant WIN gardens. The rest of us who come from the northern States can plan for the next spring.

Committee recommendation number ten asks Americans to assist in recycling programs and the reuse of scrap metals.

Margaret and Bill Dalton of High Falls, New York, write me on recycled paper that 1 ton of recycled fibers saves 17 live trees and a ton of waste.

Talbert and Elaine Stein of Detroit ask for more recycling centers at local sites so you don't have to travel so far to deposit a few cans or bottles.

Mrs. Laird Barber of Morris, Minnesota, wants to know if a national program can be organized to collect cans, glass, newspapers. The Citizens' Committee is going to stimulate local organizations throughout our country in this regard.

I cite these because they are typical of thousands and thousands of creative suggestions from Americans in all 50 States.

I would like to add, if I might, just two points on my own to round out the committee's ten to make it a daily dozen.

Number eleven, waste less in every way. Unfortunately, Americans have an international reputation as the world's worst wasters. We waste food, gasoline, paper, electricity, natural resources. As a matter of fact, we waste most everything. We litter our streets and countryside with waste.

One friend told me we could probably whip—just understand this—whip inflation with the contents of our trash cans. In your own home, let me make a simple suggestion. Just take one hour to make a trash inventory.

In the letters that I have received at the White House are thousands of good suggestions; for instance, take all you want, but eat all you take. The first words I can remember in my dad's house were very simple but very direct: Clean up your plate before you get up from the table. And that is still pretty good advice.

When you aren't using them, turn off the lights, turn off the television, turn off the radio, turn off the water, use less hot water, insulate attics and windows, shut doors, keep rooms at 68 degrees in wintertime when you are awake, and lower temperatures when you sleep.

Reducing waste, we know, can save money and energy at the very same time. It is a double duty for inflation fighters.

My twelfth and final point is an important one to every one of us: Guard your health. One of the worst wastes we have in America is days lost through sickness. Statistically, we are one of the healthiest nations in the world, and your governments and the medical profession are constantly trying to improve public health and disease prevention.

But the facts are we can do much better. This will materially strengthen our attack on inflation by increasing individual productivity, by reducing demand for health care and the checking of its soaring costs, by helping balance the family budget in this essential but unpredictable cost item.

The success of cooperative voluntary action will depend on a mutuality of effort, a sense of fairness, and a widespread support of goals. The benefits of such action will lead to greater civic efforts by millions of Americans and a focused awareness of what directions public policy should take toward economic justice for all.

I have requested the Governors of every State and the governing authorities of our territories and the District of Columbia to form WIN committees on the State and local levels. It is my observation that a chain reaction has started. Our Government will not dictate this drive but will use its existing mechanisms to assure the cumulative effort.

I have asked the Federal Energy Administration to continue and make public, to exhibit for all of us to look at, monthly reports on gasoline consumption so we can make sure that we save that 1 million barrels per day from foreign imports.

Earlier, I asked every American to drive or to cut his car mileage by 5 percent. That is not very hard. That would save one-fourth of the 1975 goal for petroleum savings.

Tonight, I ask those who can to make it 10 percent, and I am ordering an even larger reduction for all Federal vehicles.

A national reporting system will be instituted before this year ends to assure a new year of less inflation and greater self-confidence for all Americans. We will know exactly where we are going and how fast we are getting there.

As I listen and travel, I hear each day of new and exciting efforts by individuals and volunteer groups in our great country. This is the real WIN spirit of America. I am greatly encouraged. I think we are on our way.

With your help, each new day will bring more good news than bad news for our economy. Yes, there will be some setbacks. We will not be out of the economic trenches by Christmas. But I remind you, if I might, of just one fact: Every battle in history has been won by the side that held on for just 5 minutes longer. Our enemy in this battle has been called inflation. But perhaps Pogo was wiser when he said, "I have met the enemy, and he is us."

If we, the people, can overcome ourselves as we have other enemies in our history, we will surely overcome our economic difficulties and come out a happier and a better people.

Let me close by reading you an energy-saving suggestion of an 8-year-old girl in Bristol, Virginia. Her name is Luette Drumheller, and here is what she wrote: "Turn off lights when not needed, and if you are scared when you go to bed without the light on, tell your mother or father, and they will do something about it."

Luette, we are not going to be scared of the dark, any of us, because we are all in this together—mothers and fathers, grandparents and great, great grandparents, sisters and brothers—until together, we turn back on the lights of a brighter tomorrow in America.

Thank you very, very much.

NOTE: The President spoke at 7:05 p.m. at the Municipal Auditorium. His remarks were broadcast live on radio and television.

151

Remarks at a Breakfast for Republican Candidates in Kansas City, Missouri. *October 16, 1974*

Thank you very, very much, Tom.[1] *Governor Bond, your associates of State government, public officials, wonderful people from Missouri and elsewhere:*

It is a great privilege and pleasure to be here for this occasion.

I had a great meeting last night with some 13,000 or 14,000 Future Farmers of America. I looked outside this morning and the weather is super. I have met some grand people here today, and I ate a breakfast I didn't have to make myself. [*Laughter*]

Let me just summarize by saying everything is up-to-date in Kansas City.

I might tell one story about the White House of the last few weeks. We have a new addition—you might have seen it on television or on the media. My daughter Susan and our new White House photographer, Dave Kennerly, got together and surprised me with a beautiful 8-month-old golden retriever.

The Fords had had two over the last 20-some years, the last one dying a year ago in August.

Let me tell you the story of how Susan and Dave acquired this beautiful new dog for the White House. They called up a very highly recommended kennel and said that they wanted to buy a golden retriever puppy. The owner said that was fine, but who will the owner be.

And they said it is a surprise, they wanted to keep it secret. Well, the owner said he didn't sell dogs that way. He would have to know whether the dog was going to have a good home.

So Susan and Dave said to him, said to the kennel owner, that the parents were friendly, they were middle-aged, and they lived in a big, white house with a fence around it.

The kennel owner said that was good, do they own or rent?

Well, Dave and Susan were a little perplexed with that question, and they thought for a moment and said, "Well, I guess you might call it public housing."

The kennel owner said, well, that was all right—the way they explained it. They said the dog was healthy and was going to eat a lot. Does the father have a steady job?

Well, they were stuck for an answer with that one. [*Laughter*]

[1] Thomas B. Curtis, United States Representative from Missouri 1951–69, was the Republican candidate for United States Senator.

Well, we got the dog and in the true Bicentennial spirit, we named the dog Liberty. And one of the inquisitive reporters asked Susan, "Who is going to take care of Liberty? Who is going to feed her? Who is going to groom her? Who is going to take her out at night and bring her in in the morning?"

And of course, Susan, in a typical 17-year-old daughter fashion, said, "Daddy." [*Laughter*]

Well, I have a little feeling that this Liberty is going to restrict just a bit of mine, but with a great dog like that, we are very fortunate.

Let me make about four points this morning. I can recall very vividly quite a few years ago, when I first started campaigning for Republican candidates, coming to the great State of Missouri. And at that time, if my memory is accurate, there wasn't a single statewide public office held by a Republican.

There was just one Republican Member of the House, Tom Curtis. A few years later, I had the privilege of coming back to campaign on behalf of our candidates. At that time, we had two Republican Members of the House of Representatives—Tom Curtis and that venerable Doc Hall.[2]

And at that time, you had just elected a fine, outstanding Attorney General, Jack Danforth. And then, in 1972, I came back and you had a superb ticket headed by Kit Bond. And on that occasion, you elected Kit, his running mate, Bill Phelps, and you also elected Gene Taylor to replace Doc Hall.

It just seems to me that what the Republican Party has presented to the State of Missouri at the State level is a ticket that believes in reform and who does something about it—a ticket that gives honesty and integrity and vision to the State of Missouri.

And I can say to you it is a privilege and pleasure for me to be here in the company of this group of State officeholders represented at the top by Kit Bond. And I congratulate you in this State for what you have done.

But the problem we face in 1974, particularly as I see it from Washington, is how we can strengthen the Congress, strengthen the Congress in the United States Senate and the House of Representatives.

Now, you have in Gene Taylor, of the Seventh District, a strong, strong Member of the House, a small businessman who knows not only his own business but the needs and the requirements of the people of that Congressional district. And during the time that I was the minority leader of the House of Representatives early in this present Congress, Gene Taylor was a big help to me in fighting the problems that we face—inflation, inadequate national defense pro-

[2] Durward G. "Doc" Hall, United States Representative from Missouri 1961–73.

grams, the problems that come up every day—to make sure that our Government at the Federal level is run properly.

Gene Taylor, in my humble opinion, meets all of the criteria for a great Member of the House of Representatives, and I hope the people in the Seventh District send him back to Washington with a resounding margin.

But at the national level in the two big areas of how we keep our economy strong and how we maintain the peace, I need a stronger Congress.

Let's take the first issue, the issue of how to put a lid on inflation on the one hand and keep our economy strong on the other. This is a very difficult line to draw. It requires leadership in the White House; it requires cooperation in the Congress; it requires the total cooperation of Governors and local officials throughout all 50 States.

Let me speak for a moment, if I might, about Kit Bond. When I arrived yesterday at the airport, Kit handed me his response to the telegram that I sent every Governor the day before asking for their help, their cooperation. And here is the letter that Kit sent me. It indicates that he and the people of Missouri have cooperated. And he indicates that he and his administration will continue that cooperation.

It means we have to save energy by driving less—the enforcement of the 55-mile speed limit, the conservation in your State government and its affairs. By driving less you save money and you save lives—and, as I recall the letter, Kit, a 31-percent reduction in lives saved on the highways of Missouri.

I congratulate you and the people of Missouri for this great achievement.

But what I am saying is that if we got from every Governor of every State the cooperation we have gotten from Kit and his associates, we would be well ahead of the program and the schedule that I have outlined.

But a moment ago I said we had to have the help and assistance of the Congress, and this brings up my comments concerning an old and dear friend of mine, Tom Curtis. We served together in the House of Representatives for about 20 years.

Tom Curtis is one of the most expert individuals I have ever known in the Congress on the problems of taxation. He served on the Committee on Ways and Means with skill and dedication, total integrity, also served for a number of years on the Joint Economic Committee—the House and Senate, the experts that are drawn from both the House and the Senate to take a look not just at taxation but the total economic problems.

And from that experience, he can contribute significantly to not only Missouri but to the country as a whole when he is elected on November 5.

But I can speak from very personal relations with Tom Curtis. We were friends. Our families were good friends. I watched him day after day after day on the floor of the House, and he was the kind of a Congressman and he is the kind of a Senator that I would want to vote for if I lived in the State of Missouri.

I often say that one of the things our big spenders don't understand and don't realize is that as they try to allegedly help some beneficiaries and promise them this and promise them that—and I think Tom would agree with me 100 percent in this very simple statement—some of the big spenders don't understand that a government big enough to give us everything we want is a government big enough to take from us everything we have.

And in the economic message that I sent to the Congress a week ago Tuesday, I asked the Congress to set a spending limit of $300 billion, which is $5.4 billion less than the proposed expenditures submitted to the Congress last January.

We can meet that target and it would be a lot more attainable if we had some of those "show me" Congressmen from Missouri like Gene Taylor and Tom Curtis.

They would ask those tough questions: What is the money for? What are you going to do with it? Why can't you trim it? Why can't we cut back in a reasonable, responsible way in this tough struggle that we have to get away from double-digit inflation, to give our country the leadership throughout the world in trying to set an example for other nations, to tighten our belts and bolster the free world as it meets in many ways the challenges of those who have a different philosophical view, a different ideology?

Well, the other question I would like to speak about this morning was brought home to me very vividly last night and again this morning. One of our major objectives, in this case it is Democratic and Republican, is the maintenance of peace throughout the world—peace through negotiation, not through confrontation.

Last night, as I was having a cup of coffee working with some of my staff, I was sitting in a room in the Muehlebach Hotel, and I looked up and there were two pictures of Harry Truman. One of those pictures showed Harry Truman, a great Democratic President, signing in May of 1947 the Greek-Turkish aid program. And history has a strange way of repeating itself. The cooperation between a great Democratic President from the State of Missouri and the cooperation of a great United States Senator from my home State, the State of Michigan, Arthur Vandenberg, brought together the United States in a program aimed at saving the Mediterranean—helping Greece and Turkey and laying the foundation for NATO, an alliance with our friends in Europe that has maintained the peace in that continent for better than a quarter of a century.

And right now, a Republican President is having some trouble with a Democratic Congress in almost the same way. I want to say here and now that the Democratic leadership in both the House and the Senate agree with me, but unfortunately, a majority of the Congress do not understand that some of the efforts that are being made are hurting Greece, precluding the possibility of a legitimate settlement of the problem of Cyprus, and undermining NATO which has given us peace in Western Europe for better than a quarter of a century.

And what we need in the Congress right now is Members who understand that the United States, if it has flexibility, if it has leadership, if it has unity between the Executive and the Congress, can continue to give the guiding hand for the maintenance of peace not only in Western Europe but in the Mediterranean and in other parts of the world.

And I know that I can count on people like Tom Curtis when he is there to help and assist in this great struggle for peace, not only on a temporary basis but on a permanent basis.

And one final comment: I have been reading the polls lately. If you read them, I guess, in my position—and some others who feel so strongly about our party—they are a little discouraging. Well, the polls have been wrong in the past. But let me point out that if the polls are right—and I don't assume they are—you could have what some of the most partisan members of the opposition say, a veto-proof Congress.

Now, what does that mean? It means that you will have a concentration of power in one of the three branches of the Federal Government. In effect, you will have a legislative dictatorship. One of the basic strengths of America for the last 200 years has been balance—checks and balances.

Our forefathers put together in that Constitution a system predicated on a strong President in the White House, a strong Congress in the legislative branch, a strong judicial system in the Supreme Court, one checking on the other, and that finely tuned balance has given us the great blessings that we have had for almost 200 years.

Now if you have a veto-proof Congress, you in effect have one branch of the Government dictating to at least one of the others.

Americans don't like dictatorships. They like a system of checks and balances. And so in order to maintain that balance, I think we have got to go out and make a massive effort aimed at a Congress that will cooperate to beat inflation, to strengthen our economy; a Congress that will give us the tools to maintain the peace and not handicap and hamstring us with restrictions that interfere with our capability to do the job; a Congress that will be cooperative, not a Congress that will be subservient; not a Congress that will be a dictator, but a Congress that is a part of a team with some give-and-take.

And so I say to you, the odds are tough, but I think those odds were pretty tough last Saturday when Missouri played Nebraska.

And those tough ballplayers from Missouri did a job, and if you do your job, if you enlist in this great struggle for the kind of representation Tom Curtis can give you, the kind of representation other candidates on the ticket can give you, you can win just as they did.

Thank you very much.

NOTE: The President spoke at 9:36 a.m. at the Muehlebach Hotel.

152

Remarks in Sioux Falls, South Dakota. *October 16, 1974*

THANK YOU very, very much, my good friend and former colleague in the House of Representatives, Jim Abdnor. And may I express from the bottom of my heart the tremendous welcome, the enthusiasm and the warmth of this reception. I cannot in any words in my vocabulary express my deep gratitude and appreciation. Thank you very, very much.

And if I might on a very personal note: A good many years ago I matriculated to the University of Michigan. This was back in 1931, and I didn't have much money, but a woman here today and her husband made it possible for me to rent a room on the third floor—the cheapest part of their roominghouse—at the cost of $4 a week to go to the University. And I want to thank Elizabeth Van Wye, the widow of John Van Wye, who was connected with your university for a long, long time. Elizabeth, it is nice to see you.

It is good to be back in South Dakota. I have been here a good many times. And I especially enjoy it here in the Mount Rushmore area. There are four faces on that great, great national monument. One is a Federalist, one is a Democrat, and two are historical pillars of the Republican Party. This is the kind of political scorecard that I like in South Dakota.

Naturally, I am delighted to be on the same platform with some truly fine, outstanding people who fit the tradition of Abraham Lincoln, Teddy Roosevelt, and other greats in our political system—people like Jim Abdnor, Leo Thorsness, John Olson, Larry Pressler.

Leo, as you know better than I—well, he mentioned as we were coming in that the hunting season opened in South Dakota last Saturday, and by coincidence, you might have seen in the newspapers or on TV in the last week or so that the White House has a new addition.

My daughter Susan and Dave Kennerly, the new White House photographer, got together and surprised me and my wife Betty with a new, 8-month-old golden retriever. The Fords had had two golden retrievers in the last 20 years. Unfortunately, both had passed away. So, I would like to tell you a story about how Dave and Susan acquired this new White House tenant.

They called up a very highly recommended kennel and said they wanted to buy a golden retriever puppy. The owner of the kennel said, "Fine. Who will the owner be?" And they said, "It is a surprise." They would like to keep it a secret.

Well, the kennel owner said he didn't sell his fine dogs under those circumstances. He would have to know if the puppy was going to have a good owner, a nice home.

So, Susan and Dave assured the kennel owner that it would be and that the parents were friendly, middle-aged, and lived in a big white house with a fence around it.

The kennel owner said, well, that sounded all right. Do they own it or do they rent it?

Well, Susan and Dave thought a minute and said, "Well, I guess you might call it public housing."

Well, the kennel owner said that was all right. Now, he also added, "This is a big dog. It likes to eat. It will need a lot of food. Does the father have a steady job?"

Well, Susan and David were stuck with an answer to that question. [*Laughter*]

All I can say is I've heard a lot about your great hunting out here. I sometime hope that I can come out and enjoy the great outdoor facilities and the great outdoor opportunities you have in South Dakota which I don't think are matched by any State in the Union.

Your fine Congressman, Jim Abdnor, flew with me from Washington, and I can assure you from the time that I had a close opportunity to work with him in the House of Representatives—he was sworn in in January of 1973—that you in South Dakota are fortunate to have someone who understands the problems of the farmers, the problems of balancing a budget, the problems of handling taxes in the right and the best way. I just think you in South Dakota have a great, great Congressman in Jim Abdnor.

And having looked at a lot of Congressmen over 25 years—some of them kind of coming and going like Greyhound buses—Jim Abdnor is the kind of a person I would vote to keep in Congress, because he does a good job for his people at home.

Leo Thorsness—I heard about Leo before he got into the political arena, and his reputation then was one that I envied, a reputation of total dedication to his country, a dedication to principles under the most adverse circumstances, a man with a strong background, a strong background based on real, deep conviction about the principles that are so essential to make our country an even better land in the future.

I know that Leo will be a full-time fighter against inflation on a year-in and year-out basis instead of once every 6 years at election time.

And I happen to think that Larry Pressler can do a great job for you in the Congress.

Leo and Larry will bring you, when elected November 5, a full strength of sound people handling your money and your problems in the House as well as the Senate.

And of course, under the theory that I believe in, that we don't have to make all the decisions and all the judgments in Washington, that we need sound, responsible, thoughtful people at the State and local level, we need John Olson to be the next Governor of the State of South Dakota.

And if I might, in a very personal way, explain to you why I am here in South Dakota. There has been some criticism that maybe the President ought to stay in the White House, and work in the Oval Office, and never leave the banks of the Potomac.

I don't agree with that. I happen to believe that the American people have a right to see their President and to hear him defend the kind of programs that he believes are in the best interest of our country, both at home and abroad.

I think I get a better understanding of what people in South Dakota want and believe by being right here in this great auditorium rather than peering out of some window in the White House.

You can tell me with criticism, with comments, with endorsements of what we are doing right or what we are doing wrong, and I can get it better at the grassroots than I can from some ivory tower on the banks of the Potomac.

And I thank you for coming here just to give me that advice. I appreciate it.

As I see it, we have got two or three major problems in this country. One, we have got to lick the battle of inflation and keep our economy strong at the same time.

And I submitted to the Congress a week ago, on Tuesday, a 31-proposition package that, if enacted, if supported, will give us a better handle and success against inflation and, if enacted and supported by the American people, will keep us going on a steady, steady course upward to provide a better and better living for all our people.

And I happen to think guys like Jim Abdnor, Leo Thorsness are the kind of people than can work at helping in the problems not only at home but abroad.

What we need in this country is not a partisan foreign policy. Some 26 years ago it was my privilege to go as a brand new freshman Congressman to the Nation's Capital, and I was engulfed by a bipartisan foreign policy with a Democratic President, Harry Truman, working with a Republican Congress in the 80th Congress. And those two people representing the executive branch, on the one hand, and the Congress, on the other, gave us peace in Western Europe, helped us to build the kind of policy that has been good for us in Western Europe for almost 30 years.

What we need is a bipartisan foreign policy, and that can be supplied by Jim Abdnor, by Leo, by Larry Pressler. We need that kind of support if we are going to keep the peace and build the peace in the future. And I hope you support them for those two very, very good reasons.

I know the State of South Dakota is one of the greatest States in the Union for many reasons. But you have a particular pride, a special feeling about the contributions that this great State of South Dakota does in being a significant part of the breadbasket of not only the United States but the world.

Now let me talk, if I might, about the part that farmers and those associated with them can do in this great struggle to win the battle against inflation.

I have assured the farmers of this and every State that they will have all the fuel, all the fertilizer that they need to harvest their bountiful crops this year and next year. They will be in your hands.

And let me add one other thing while I am talking about fuel. Prior to my speech a week ago, everybody else but myself was telling the American people what I was going to say about gasoline taxes. Well, I have now said or given my own views, but I want to reiterate it right here to you in South Dakota: I am vigorously opposed to any additional Federal tax on gasoline, and I will fight it as hard as I possibly can.

We want to keep this country rolling, not parked on a dead-end street.

Let me add one special concern that I had for the people of South Dakota when this issue was presented to me and I rejected it. I thought of the people of South Dakota and other States who have to travel not a couple of miles but many miles to go to the doctor or to the hospital. I thought about the people in South Dakota who have to go from their farms or their ranch to the implement dealer or to the community where they trade.

A gasoline tax would unfairly, in my judgment, penalize those people. And for that reason, among many others, I rejected it. And we are not going to have it as long as I am in the White House.

There are some other things that have to be done, not just in agriculture, but they have to be done in agriculture. We have got to increase productivity. But I always like to add, when talking about productivity, that the statistics show that in the last 20 or more years, the farmers of America have increased their productivity more than any other segment of our economy in the whole United States, and I applaud you for it.

But just because you are the champs doesn't mean you can't do better. And so I am urging every one of you to make that little extra effort to make sure that we get the maximum from our soil and from the toil of all of you.

Now there is one question that is always raised that if the farmer produces more, responds to the demands of people in this country and around the world, what kind of protection, what kind of guarantee does the farmer who has made this special effort get?

Let me add this: I promise a fair return, a fully fair and adequate return to the farmers of America, a fair profit on what you put in on your time, your labor, your investment, and your facilities. This is what you deserve, and this is what we have to guarantee.

And let me add, if I might, the problems and the concerns of the people of rural America will not be buried under the concrete of big city interests.

There is one comment I would like to make, and it is somewhat a sad one. I am particularly disturbed by the wasteful protest, the protest resulting in the slaughtering of calves in Wisconsin just yesterday, at a time when we are trying to increase the supply of food.

I fully recognize the frustration that prompted this shocking demonstration, but their actions, I think, even if they reflect on it themselves, will contribute nothing, nothing toward a solution to the problem that they face or the problems that our country faces.

I am aware of the cost-price squeeze in which livestock producers and feeders find themselves. I have requested from the Department of Agriculture and every other department in the Federal Government the reports that I can look at and analyze, and I will meet very shortly at the White House with fair representation of the farmers and ranchers to get their solutions from them directly.

I am disturbed by the disparity between the reduced earnings of the cattle-growers and the higher prices charged to consumers throughout the Nation on the shelves of the supermarkets. And I am asking the new Council on Wage and Price Stability to examine the reasons behind this gap which is paid to the farmer and what must be paid on the other end of the line by the individual consumer.

Something is obviously wrong, and I intend to do what I can to find out the cause and do something about it.

Our livestock producers here in South Dakota obviously cannot tolerate a situation in which calves cost more to raise than they bring at the marketplace, but there certainly is a better way of redressing these legitimate grievances than by the drastic and wasteful destruction of our food supply.

Now there is another problem which equally concerns me—the tremendous cost-price squeeze in which America's dairymen find themselves. I met last Friday in Washington in the Cabinet Room with a representative group of dairy farmers on the one hand and a group of Democratic and Republican Congressmen and Senators on the other. And they outlined to me the practical problems that the dairy producers in their respective States are faced with.

I am very sympathetic to the problem. I understand the concern of those dairy producers that the United States dairy price system should not be allowed—and this is very important—that this price system should not be allowed to be undermined by efforts of foreign dairy producers.

Now some of these foreign dairy producers, as we know from the sampling that we have taken, are seeking to shift the burden of their own cost-price problems to the United States market, aided by artificial incentives from their own government.

And because of my own concern about the economic problems dairymen are facing, I intend today announcing that no action will be taken to change the present system of dairy import quotas without a thorough review of market conditions and full opportunity for our dairy producers to be heard at that time.

I think the record proves that our farmers can compete with any group of farmers or the farmers from any nation throughout the world. And I am looking forward to those negotiations where we can equalize our opportunities to compete with foreign markets around the world.

Now, these are some of the reasons I am here, to listen to what you have to say, to get your reactions to what I say. I have a button up here that says "WIN." WIN *now*. And I see some signs and I see some buttons in the crowd here.

People of the United States have always been strong. We have met adversity when we were challenged from abroad. We have met adversity when we were faced with internal difficulties—the Depression and the conflicts of one kind or another—that have plagued us over some 200 years.

But we found one answer in the political arena that gives us the opportunity to present alternative solutions, to permit candidates who have one philosophy and candidates who have another to meet in the political arena. And we have developed over a period of some 200 years in this great country a two-party system that is wholesome and healthy and gives us in all 50 States the opportunity to participate.

Now, this system of a two-party arrangement protects us because it is an integral part of a system of checks and balances, a system that is not in the Constitution but it is one that has been developed as our political challenges have gone from almost 200 years ago to today.

But if we ever lose the two-party system, if we ever go to a one-party system, we will have the same problems that they have behind the Iron Curtain. If we ever go to a multi-party system with five or ten parties, we will lose that strength that comes from what we have today.

And so, as you proceed with this great election in the State of South Dakota on November 5, what you are really doing is participating in the continuation of a system that has given us so much materially and ideologically, that has made America a blessed nation of some 213 million people; a country that has representative government; a country that gives you the freedom of choice in many, many ways as well as politically.

And this election that comes up gives you an opportunity in the solemnity of the ballot box, a chance to make a choice, where you are the only judge, where you can decide what is best for your country.

Oh, I know there is no gun so mighty, no force so powerful as the quiet symbol of what you do and what others do throughout our country on November 5. It is the opportunity; it is the responsibility; actually, it is part of your contribution to a greater America. You can balance the ledger sheets of good government.

I have just an unbelievable faith in the people of South Dakota, as I do the people all over America. We can strengthen the two-party system. You can pick the best candidates, and we in America will be blessed by the good judgment of what you do in South Dakota and what your fellow Americans do in every State on November 5.

I thank you. It is a pleasure and a privilege to be here.

[The President spoke at 1:27 p.m. at the Sioux Falls Arena. In his remarks, the President referred to Leo J. Thorsness, Republican candidate for United States Senator from South Dakota, and Larry Pressler, Republican candidate in the First Congressional District.

On departing from the arena at 2 p.m., the President spoke to a crowd that had gathered outside, as follows:]

Let me thank all of you—the young ones, the old ones, the middle-aged ones, the boys and girls, mothers and dads, grandmas and grandpas.

Well, it is just nice to be out here in this typical South Dakota weather in October, on October 15 [16]. Don't you always have it this way by this time of the year?

Well, I am out here with some very good friends of mine—Jim Abdnor, who is your darned good Congressman, Leo Thorsness, Larry Pressler, and your candidate for Governor. And I appreciate your thoughtfulness concerning them.

But the main thing, I want to say a word or two to all of you. You have got the greatest, greatest country in the world, and all of you know it here in South Dakota just like we do in Michigan and people do in 48 other States. But if we are going to keep this kind of country, if we are going to maintain everything it stands for and do justice to the sacrifices that were made by your forefathers and mine, then we have to tighten our belts and sacrifice a little for another few months ahead of us.

Now the fact that you are all here gives me hope that in South Dakota you are going to do better than any other of the 50 States in the Union. I know that. Do I have your assurance?

You know, I have a little button here that says "WIN." I don't see any buttons on anybody in South Dakota that says "lose." All you want is to win, not for yourselves but for your country, and that is what I want, you want, and people in other States want.

So thank you for being here. It has been a tremendous, tremendous experience. I am deeply grateful. Good luck and God bless every one of you. Thank you very, very much.

153

Remarks at Lincoln, Nebraska. *October 16, 1974*

Thank you very, very much, Charley Thone. Distinguished public officials, candidates, all of you wonderful, wonderful people from Lincoln, the State of Nebraska, and elsewhere:

I am just tremendously impressed with the size of the crowd, the enthusiasm, and naturally, I am deeply appreciative of the kind, kind comments made concerning my wife Betty. She is doing great, and it is the prayers and the good wishes of literally thousands and thousands of people, not only in America but elsewhere, that have made her recovery faster and better. And I thank you on behalf of her.

This has been a wonderful day, and we are three-quarters of the way through it. I started in Kansas City this morning with a breakfast. We had a wonderful meeting in South Dakota. We are here in Lincoln. We are going to Indianapolis for a dinner and a meeting tonight, and back to Washington and the White House this evening.

Now, I don't know what my scheduler wants for Christmas, but let me tell you I am going to give him a map, so that he understands what travel means.

I am delighted to see Bob Devaney [1] here. You know we Michiganders think we had some impact on the great success that Bob has brought to the State of Nebraska, the success that the Cornhuskers have had. And I watched, as a has-been athlete and a onetime football player, some of the great games that Nebraska has played under his leadership.

Let me just say this—and I pass no judgment, because there is nothing I dislike more than grandstand quarterbacks or Monday-morning experts, and I don't know what happened over there the other day in the last few minutes of that ballgame—but I have learned, as an ex-football player and as an ex-football coach a long time back when the ball was round, that there is a great relationship between football or athletic competition and coaching and politics.

And if I might just say a word to Bob in that regard, I found that both as far as coaches and athletic directors are concerned—and politicians—that one day they will name a street after you, and the next day they will chase you down it. [*Laughter*]

As Charley Thone said in the introduction, I was born in Nebraska, in

---

[1] Head coach of the University of Nebraska football team.

Omaha, just a few miles down the pike here. And I am proud of it, and I am delighted to be back here.

Now, I left when I was about 18 months old, and depending on how you put it, I was either exported or deported. But I am glad to be back under any circumstances.

It is wonderful to see Charley Thone here. I understand Charley's campaign theme is "Thone works." Well, I can attest to that. For quite a few years I was the minority leader in the House of Representatives while Charley was in the House, and I can say without any hesitation, qualification, or reservation that Charley Thone was one of the hardest, most conscientious, most dedicated workers in the House of Representatives. And if I was in this district, Democrat or Republican, I would vote for Charley Thone.

And he had two other fine, fine Nebraskans alongside of him in the House of Representatives—John McCollister, an outstanding Member of the House, the Committee on Interstate and Foreign Commerce, a committee that has tremendous responsibilities that relate directly to the problems you have here in the State of Nebraska. And I am sure in this great crowd there are some people that can help John McCollister, and because I think so highly of him, I hope and trust that they will do everything they possibly can to see that Charley does come back to continue his fine work in the House of Representatives.

You do have in the State of Nebraska one of our senior statesmen leaving, leaving of his own free will. We have Dave Martin who served so ably and so well. Dave is [not] coming back, but I hope and trust that the people of that Congressional district send to replace Dave Martin, Mrs. Helen Smith, who I am sure will carry on the fine tradition that Dave Martin established in the representation of that Congressional district.

And if Helen has friends here, go out and do the same thing for her that you have done for Dave Martin, and I would thank you for it.

It is Mrs. Haven Martin, Virginia Martin, and I apologize.[2]

But let me at this point make one or two observations and comments concerning some of the problems we have in America. I know that this great State—because I have visited many places in it. I've traveled across a good portion of the State—north, south, east, and west. I know that Nebraska is one of the most vitally important producers of food in all 50 States.

And I know, from talking with some of the members of the Congressional delegation, that farmers have had some difficult times for a wide variety of rea-

[2] Virginia (Mrs. Haven) Smith was the Republican candidate in the Third Congressional District of Nebraska.

sons—the elements; a lack of, maybe, fertilizer; and some other problems that I won't enumerate. But I want to compliment the farmers of the State of Nebraska for the job they have done. They deserve your applause and your support, because they are real inflation fighters that have and can contribute.

In return for the request that I have made to each and every one of them that they produce to full capacity, I think we ought to make some commitments to them. And let me enumerate some commitments that I will make, representing the executive branch of the Government.

Number one, I am committed to give them the fuel and the fertilizer for them to do the job. Even though we are going to cut back 1 million barrels of imported fuel oil every day, the farmers will get fuel and fertilizer if we have to allocate it arbitrarily.

Prior to my speech to the Congress a week or so ago, I was quoted extensively by a lot of people who thought they were reading my mind. And they were reading it on the belief that I was going to ask the Congress to pass an increase in the Federal gasoline tax. Well, some of these oracle readers or people who thought they could read my mind were 100 percent wrong. I did not ask for a gas tax; I am opposed to a gas tax; and, I know the Congress won't pass one.

About a week ago Saturday, I was faced with a real tough decision. There had been some very substantial orders placed for wheat and corn for shipment overseas.

Now, I am against the export controls for our farm commodities, and I do not intend to impose them. But at the same time, because I do feel I have an obligation to protect adequate reserves, we are going to monitor those sales. We will permit the sales of reasonable amounts phased over a reasonable period of time so our farmers will be able to sell their commodities, because those commodities are important as we, a great country, sell those things abroad that are necessary for our balance of payments. So the farmers can have full assurance from me: There will be no blanket embargo on the products they produce on the land with their own toil.

One day last week, Charley Thone and a number of other Congressmen, Democrats as well as Republicans, along with some dairy farmers, came to the White House to talk to me about the problems of the dairy farmer. I know the dairy farmer in America has been hit by rising costs. I know the dairy farmer has been hit with some of the problems of getting an adequate price in the marketplace. The cost-price squeeze to the dairy farmer is a serious one. But I make a pledge here today as I did in Sioux Falls earlier: We are not going to let subsidized foreign dairy imports destroy the American dairy farmers' domestic market.

Now, having made these pledges to the farmers who have done so much over the years and who will do so much in the future, I feel obligated to make a comment on a sad and tragic incident that happened in Wisconsin yesterday.

Although I understand the frustrations of the farmers in Wisconsin who slaughtered their cattle yesterday, I am deeply concerned at this wasteful protest when we as Americans are trying to increase the supply of food for 213 million Americans and millions all over the world. Unfortunately, these actions contributed nothing to the solution of the problem or to the problem of inflation which concerns all of us.

I am aware, as I said earlier, of the cost-price squeeze in which livestock producers and feeders and dairymen find themselves. And to do whatever I can, I am meeting with representatives from those groups in Washington within a relatively short period of time to find out what they recommend that their Government do in this very serious problem, in this dilemma that they face.

I can only say that I hope and trust that what transpired in Wisconsin yesterday will not be duplicated. It didn't help them. It won't help solve the problem that they face, and it won't help the problem that we face as Americans, which is more food for all of us. And so I urge, to the extent that you can, that you counsel with them or with those who have any similar ideas. We are going to work with them. We are going to solve their problem, and they should not do in the future what a few did yesterday.

In conclusion, let me discuss very quickly these problems that I think we face here in Nebraska and others face around our 50 States. We have a problem concerning our economy.

About a week or 10 days ago, I submitted to the Congress, to the American people, a 31-provision program that is aimed at tightening up the screws on inflation and, at the same time, giving us the strength to improve our economy. This program requires certain actions by the Congress. This program requires certain individual efforts by volunteers throughout the country. I have faith in the Congress and faith in the American people. We are going to win the battle against inflation, and we are going to have a strong, burgeoning economy so all of us will be better off.

The role of the United States on a global basis is aimed at building peace not only for ourselves but for the world as a whole. I was in Kansas City this morning, and I stayed last night in a hotel where a great Democratic President,

20-some years ago, signed a bill which was called the Greek-Turkish aid bill. And that legislation was sponsored and promoted and guided through the Congress by a great Republican statesman from Michigan, Senator Arthur Vandenburg.

And as a result of bipartisan leadership in the field of foreign policy between a Democratic President and a Republican Congress, we laid the foundation for the North Atlantic Treaty Organization which has kept the peace in Western Europe for almost 30 years.

And this kind of bipartisanship is essential today as it was during the days of Harry Truman and Arthur Vandenburg. And I can assure you that as a Republican President, I will work with a Democratic Congress to continue a bipartisan foreign policy that is good for America and good for the rest of the world.

Now, one final comment: I was reading the polls the other day, and the polls seem to indicate that the Republican Party is going to take some kind of a shellacking on November 5. I don't happen to agree with that, but that is what some of the experts were speculating or forecasting.

But let me tell you what could happen if they are right. They could end up with a veto-proof Congress, and what does that mean? It means that the important balance between the executive branch, the Congress, and the judicial branches of our Government will be upset. And if we look back over the history of this country, we know that balance in government has contributed significantly to the progress we have made, to the freedom that we have.

A veto-proof Congress will upset that balance. The American people don't want a dictatorship in the White House or in the Congress or in the Court. They want a system of checks and balances that protect their freedom and give to each and every one of us a better life. And so I say, instead of a veto-proof Congress, I hope and trust that every one of you will work for an inflation-proof Congress on November 5.

And now, let me just conclude by thanking every one of you for being here. It is a thrill. It is a wonderful afternoon.

Charley, I thank you for the kind words in the introduction. I wish you well so you will be back to help us. I hope and trust that John McCollister is back, that Mrs. Smith is with us so that they can join your two great Senators, Roman Hruska and Carl Curtis, with a good, strong Congress in 1975.

Thank you very, very much.

NOTE: The President spoke at 3:18 p.m. at Lincoln Municipal Airport.

154

Remarks in Indianapolis, Indiana. *October 16, 1974*

I MUST SAY it is an unbelievable audience, tremendous in size and overwhelming in enthusiasm. And I thank you not for whatever impact I might have had; I thank you because you are here to elect Dick Lugar to the United States Senate, and to pay tribute to an outstanding Governor of the State of Indiana, [Otis R.] Doc Bowen, and to elect, reelect those fine members of the Republican delegation in the House of Representatives in Washington like Bill Hudnut and the rest on November 5.

And may I say to the wonderful people who are blocked out by the news media—and they are all my friends—I am for an open Administration. And I apologize that the good friends—and the news media inadvertently, unavoidably are precluding me from looking at you—but I will be talking to you as much as I am to the others.

Governor Bowen, members of your administration, my former colleagues in the House of Representatives, Dick Lugar, of course, who I can't wait to be in the United States Senate, and all of you who have participated in this great affair, I thank you from the very bottom of my heart. But let me say, I particularly appreciated the invitation to be here tonight because I had a suspicion that I wouldn't be among enemies, I would be among friendly Americans.

Frankly, I wanted to be visible, and I want to be an accessible President. And obviously I need it.

Let me tell you why. As I was walking through the lobby, a very friendly lady came up to me, shook my hand and said, "I know you from somewhere, but I just can't remember your name." So in a friendly way, I tried to help her out, I said, "I am Jerry Ford." She said, "No, but you are close." [*Laughter*]

It is a pleasure to be with you all here tonight—with so many enthusiastic Indiana Republicans, discerning Independents, and wise Democrats. It has been my privilege to visit Indianapolis many times, and I have loved every visit. But I still come away, and particularly on this occasion, more impressed, more enthusiastic about the great future of this city and this great State, and I compliment you.

Obviously, one of the reasons why I feel so optimistic about Indianapolis is here with us tonight, Dick Lugar.

As I traveled around the country for 7 or 8 years, maybe a bit longer—I traveled some 200,000 miles a year and I had many, many opportunities to meet mayors, other public officials—and I can say without any hesitation or qualification that you in Indianapolis, as many of you claim, a vast majority, you have got the best darned mayor in the United States.

But, you know, the good thing about it is that Dick Lugar will do as much for Indianapolis and the State of Indiana and the country as he has done for this city, and that is a darned good recommendation why he ought to be the next United States Senator.

Dick has got a tough fight on his hands. I don't think we ought to gloss it over. I think we ought to be pragmatic and realistic about it. There is a lot of hard political muscle out to beat him. There is a lot of out-of-State money involved in trying to defeat Dick. But with your help, Dick Lugar can make it, and he deserves it.

And if I might add just a little personal note, I think we—and when I say "we," I mean us Michiganders and all of the rest of us around the country—need a person like Dick representing Indiana and the country in the United States Senate, a man who will support economy in Government and fight inflation year around, not just in election time. He will vote in Washington as he talks in Indiana.

Let me just conclude this comment or two that I have made about Dick, but I think this represents my firm conviction, and I would be remiss if I didn't say it. Dick is young, dynamic, honest, smart. He does his homework, he will be a full-time Senator for Indiana who will represent the responsible, the commonsense approach to the issues that Hoosiers believe are important for your State and for our country.

And Dick, I am looking forward to seeing you be sworn in on January 3, 1977 (1975).

I want to add one point that I have indicated at the outset. I have great respect and admiration for Doc Bowen. Again, I have met many mayors and Governors and other public officials, and as I travel around the country, I see the good ones and the bad ones.

It seems to me that you have got one of the best. But you know, I had planned to meet with Doc at the White House a few weeks or a month or so ago, but I found out that like so many doctors these days, he doesn't make house calls any more. [*Laughter*] So, I have come to see Doc in Indiana.

Well, he is popular. He is hard-working, a great inspiration to the Republican Party, and I know I speak for everyone here when I say how grateful Republicans and all other Hoosiers are for his tireless campaigning for a great candidate, Dick Lugar, in this election in 1974.

Thank you very much, Doc.

If I can take just a minute or two and speak from personal experience, from the bottom of my heart, and the appreciation that I really feel. I served 25 years plus in the House of Representatives in Washington. It was the greatest experience of my life for many reasons.

But one of the reasons that it meant so much to me was the opportunity to be associated with, to depend on, to rely on the Indiana delegation. And I want to express my utmost gratitude and appreciation to people like Bill Bray, Earl Landgrebe, John Myers, Roger Zion, Dave Dennis—men I can count on as President to win the battle against inflation. They are good fighters for good programs, and they deserve your support down the line.

But there are some that are right in this area—I have spoken about those that are a little farther away from Indianapolis—right in the Marion County area, you have a special obligation, you who come from this particular part of this great State.

Bill Bray—gosh, he is a great guy and a first-class Congressman. Bud Hillis, a relative newcomer, but a darned fine Member of the House and one you should send back. And then we are right in the heartland of Bill Hudnut's district, and believe me, he deserves to be reelected, and I mean it.

Whether it is Bill Bray, Bud Hillis, or Bill Hudnut, they are real inflation fighters and they deserve your entire, your total dedication if we are going to win this battle against inflation in the years ahead.

You know, speaking of Bill Hudnut, Bill is a great friend of mine, but you also know he is an ordained minister, which isn't a bad thing in politics today. [*Laughter*]

Frankly, I never knew Bill Hudnut was a minister until one day I saw him pick up a phone and call "Dial-A-Prayer," collect. [*Laughter*]

Well, in Bill's first term in the House of Representatives, he and I developed a very special relationship because our oldest son is going to theological school, and I was trying to get some advice and counsel. Yes, in the time that I served with Bill as a Member of the House when he was, I learned to have that sort of inward rapport, that close feeling that here was a person who had all the qualifications to be a first-class Member of the Congress.

And so I am particularly pleased to be in Indianapolis, which is the heartland of his district, and to add my voice—and if I could vote here—my vote for Bill Hudnut to be reelected to the Congress of the United States.

And Bill, I understand this is your 42d birthday. Congratulations.

Now, speaking of birthdays, I can't help thinking back to my 42d. Some of us, including myself, hate to think back that long. It was 19 years ago, in 1955. There is an old saying that many of us recollect, from time to time—the more things change, the more they stay the same.

Looking back for a moment to 1955, there seems something to it. In 1955, if you will refresh your memories, violence in Cyprus was making headlines; people were worried about peace in the Middle East; and threats of inflation and recession weighed heavily on the minds of a lot of worried Americans.

Here we are 19 years later—strife in Cyprus, the Middle East is on a very difficult balance right at the moment. On the front page, of course, the economy in America is again a worry.

Americans have been rediscovering a lot of other things, too. In the wake of Vietnam, Watergate, the energy crisis, and the economic challenge, we are learning some of the very basic things that help to build America into the great country it is.

I have in mind, for example, things like the need for integrity in government, a need for fiscal responsibility to fight inflation, the timeless balance created by Founders—those great Founders of our country almost 200 years ago—between the three branches of Government, and the need for a balance in Congress through a viable two-party system.

I think it is the need for this balance and the challenge it faces in this election that I would like to say a few words about tonight.

A great English statesman of a few decades ago, Lord Acton, once said—it is a frequently but, I think, appropriately quoted comment from him—it goes like this: "Power tends to corrupt, and absolute power corrupts absolutely."

Again and again the truth of those words has been well proven. Whenever any one branch of Government, any one person, or any class or faction in a country enjoys monopoly of power, corruption and extremism are the inevitable result.

Only checks and balances, the free play of different ideas, and the vital competitive two-party system, in my judgment, can preserve a nation's freedom and deal adequately with corruption and wrongdoing in any part of our Government.

We need the built-in protection now and in the future of a strong, two-party political system in the United States, and the public must stand for it and fight for it and defend it.

Oh, I have listened to the forecasts and the speculation of people who look at the polls and say our party is going to take a shellacking, a licking, on November 5. Well, I don't happen to agree with that. But I do add this, and I say it to every one of you in this tremendous audience—one of the most impressive audiences I have seen in my many travels and many gatherings: Make no mistake; that is exactly what you are not going to get if you and other responsible citizens stay home on November 5.

You won't have that balance, you won't have that check and balance. If you stay home and do nothing—which I can't imagine you all doing here—you will only blindly penalize good Republican candidates for the unfortunate misdeeds of others.

And so, such a development, as I see it, would be dangerous at any time, but today perhaps more than perhaps any other time in my political career. We need the maximum effort by all of you and all the people you can enlist and all of the people that you can persuade.

I think if you do that, we will have people in Congress willing to work with us, people who will have a vision, people who will have determination, people who will have the vigor to do the right thing on the problems that we face at home and abroad.

Frankly, speaking of inflation, we need people on the Hill who won't go over the hill on the battle against inflation.

If we end up with a lopsided veto-proof Congress, as some people are saying they are going to get or they demand or they insist will be the result of the voters on November 5, let me say this: You will end up with a legislative dictatorship, which is totally contrary to the concept of a free government.

Our forefathers so wisely decided almost 200 years ago that we needed a strong President in the White House, we needed a strong Congress in the legislative branch, we needed a strong judicial system headed by the Supreme Court. But they were all co-equal, coordinate, and they were to be a check and a balance, one against the other. Because we had that balance, we have had freedom and the greatest material benefits and blessings of any nation in the world.

But, if because of negligence, if because of a lack of enthusiasm or participation we end up with a veto-proof Congress, that delicate balance, that finely tuned relationship between the three branches of our Government will be destroyed, and we will have a legislative dictatorship. And believe me, if we have a legislative dictatorship, tighten your seatbelts, folks, the spending will go right out of the top of the dome of the Capitol.

So, what I am saying: Don't elect the spendthrift Congress; don't elect a veto-proof Congress. Fight inflation, and send back to the House as well as the Senate those individuals who will be in favor of an inflation-proof Congress. That is what will save America.

You know, I arrived in town, and as we flew in, I couldn't help but see the Indianapolis Speedway, and gee, that is a great thrill. Somebody said to me, a veto-proof Congress to fight inflation makes about as much sense as going into the Indianapolis Speedway—or the 500, I should say—on a skateboard.

In the economic program that I submitted to the Congress, we have 31 different provisions and proposals. It was a package finally put together with the best brains, the best talents, the greatest cooperation and participation by people all over the country.

We had some 12 or 15 minisummits, and we had two or three summits in Washington. And then after all of these ideas came from so many, many people, we tried to discard the ones that wouldn't work, and we decided to incorporate those that we thought would.

It was done for this particular purpose. We are faced with high inflation. We had to tighten the screws. On the other hand, in some areas of our country, we have got economic problems. Some people call them a recession, some people describe them otherwise, but the problem is, we do in some areas of this country face difficulties. So, we had to devise a plan or a program that meant a dual challenge, a challenge that could be met if we had the right approach. One of those approaches was to hold down Federal spending. And believe me, that is an awfully important part of our program.

I said to the Congress, "You agree with me that we won't spend more than $300 billion in this fiscal year, and I will find a way to do it." And we can.

And the kind of people that we have here in the Congress on our side of the aisle and the kind you are going to send to Congress with Dick Lugar will help us find those ways.

But there also is another part of that program, and I would like to talk about it. I suggested that the Congress ought to bite the bullet. Some people said that I only suggested they take a marshmallow bite. Well, if the Congress doesn't like what I suggested, we will give them some real tough turkey talk very soon.

Now, let me speak, if I might, about one aspect—the tax suggestions that I made. Let me, at the outset, say I am against, I won't recommend, I will oppose any addition to the gasoline tax as far as the Federal Government is concerned.

Now, let me just speak quite frankly. I think if we are going to be compassionate, we are going to balance the budget, we have to find some new areas of revenue. And there are, I am sure, some people who say I was not the wisest person to recommend some increases on certain elements of our population and taxes.

Well, I wonder if all of you know the real impact of that proposal—5 percent on personal income for everybody who files an income tax with taxable income of over $15,000. And if it is that, you don't pay any additional tax. If you have a family of four and a $20,000 income, you pay $42 more a year or 12 cents every day. Aren't you willing to make that sacrifice to win the battle against inflation?

I just happen to think that the American people at this critical time, at this serious period in our American history, are willing to do battle today if we are going to preserve our form of government, if we are going to win the battle against inflation and keep a healthy economy. Hoosiers have never backed away from anything, and they are not going to back away from this struggle.

And you have the opportunity in this great State—as I look at the eyes of the people out here—to be the leaders, to be the leaders in meeting this challenge. Yes, I think this inspirational group here tonight can be what all of us hope for and seek for, a group of 5,500 people who have got the courage and the wisdom, the vision, the imagination to meet the challenges, the challenges that are important to the preservation of those things that we think so dear, that have been given to us by the sacrifices of so many before us.

And let me conclude, if I might, by reminding Democrats, Independents, and Republicans, and the like, November 5 is just a few days away. It is closer than you think. And Congressional elections for the Senate and for the House are really what it is all about in 1974.

I think you have to sit back and take a close look at the stewardship of people who are candidates for reelection and candidates who seek election. I have no doubt that you can support the people that have served you on our side of the aisle, because they are first-class. I have no doubt that as you reflect in your home or in that voting booth, that you can support a person like Dick Lugar.

And if I were a Hoosier, believe me, I could support him with vigor and vehemence and with a good, clear conscience.

There is nothing in America really like the sanctity of the voting booth. That is where you have an opportunity to reflect on what is best for America. And as I talk to Dick, and as I have worked with our candidates and our incumbents from Indiana, my reflection in that voting booth would give me a clear message: They are the kind of people that will lick inflation. They are the kind of people that will give America the leadership in trying to preserve the peace. They are the kind of people that will fight for and preserve the two-party system. They are the kind of people that you will be proud of on the basis of personal integrity and Government service dedication. And they are the kind of people that will be a part of this great bipartisan effort that we have to have if we are going to solve our problems, either at home or abroad.

Yes, your support for them—not just for you individually, not just because of what they can do for your Congressional district or your city or your State, but more importantly, what they can do for what is good for America and what is good for people around the world.

They will be a part of a strong and responsive Congress. And as one commentator put it on television last week, and let me quote: I am looking for a Congress that will praise the Lord and pass the legislation.

Thank you very, very much.

NOTE: The President spoke at 9:05 p.m. at a dinner for Republican candidates at the Indiana Convention-Exposition Center. Prior to the dinner, the President attended a reception for Republican candidates at the center.

155

Statement and Responses to Questions From Members of the House Judiciary Committee Concerning the Pardon of Richard Nixon. *October 17, 1974*

WE MEET here today to review the facts and circumstances that were the basis for my pardon of former President Nixon on September 8, 1974.

I want very much to have those facts and circumstances known. The American people want to know them. And Members of the Congress want to know them. The two Congressional resolutions of inquiry now before this committee serve those purposes. That is why I have volunteered to appear before you this morning, and I welcome and thank you for this opportunity to speak to the questions raised by the resolutions.

My appearance at this hearing of your distinguished subcommittee of the House Committee on the Judiciary has been looked upon as an unusual historic event—one that has no firm precedent in the whole history of Presidential relations with the Congress. Yet, I am here not to make history, but to report on history.

The history you are interested in covers so recent a period that it is still not well understood. If, with your assistance, I can make for better understanding of the pardon of our former President, then we can help to achieve the purpose I had for granting the pardon when I did.

That purpose was to change our national focus. I wanted to do all I could to shift our attentions from the pursuit of a fallen President to the pursuit of the urgent needs of a rising nation. Our Nation is under the severest of challenges now to employ its full energies and efforts in the pursuit of a sound and growing economy at home and a stable and peaceful world around us.

We would needlessly be diverted from meeting those challenges if we as a people were to remain sharply divided over whether to indict, bring to trial, and punish a former President, who already is condemned to suffer long and deeply in the shame and disgrace brought upon the office he held. Surely, we are not a revengeful people. We have often demonstrated a readiness to feel compassion and to act out of mercy. As a people, we have a long record of forgiving even those who have been our country's most destructive foes.

Yet, to forgive is not to forget the lessons of evil in whatever ways evil has operated against us. And certainly the pardon granted the former President will not cause us to forget the evils of Watergate-type offenses or to forget the lessons we have learned that a government which deceives its supporters and treats its opponents as enemies must never, never be tolerated.

The pardon power entrusted to the President under the Constitution of the United States has a long history and rests on precedents going back centuries before our Constitution was drafted and adopted. The power has been used sometimes as Alexander Hamilton saw its purpose: "In seasons of insurrection . . . when a well-timed offer of pardon to the insurgents or rebels may restore the tranquillity of the commonwealth; and which, if suffered to pass unimproved, it may never be possible afterwards to recall." [1] Other times it has been applied to one person as "an act of grace . . . which exempts the individual, on whom it is bestowed, from the punishment the law inflicts for a crime he has committed." [2] When a pardon is granted, it also represents "the determination of the ultimate authority that the public welfare will be better served by inflicting less than what the judgment fixed." [3] However, the Constitution does not limit the pardon power to cases of convicted offenders or even indicted offenders.[4] Thus, I am firm in my conviction that as President I did have the authority to proclaim a pardon for the former President when I did.

---

[1] *The F d ralist* No. 74, at 79 (Central Law Journal ed. 1914) (A. Hamilton).
[2] Marshall, C. J., in *United States* v. *Wilson*, 32 U.S. (7 Pet.) 150, 160 (1833).
[3] *Biddle* v. *Perovich*, 247 U.S. 480, 486 (1927).
[4] *Ex Parte Garland*, 4 Wall. 333, 380 (1867); *Burdick* v. *United States*, 236 U.S. 79 (1915).

Yet, I can also understand why people are moved to question my action. Some may still question my authority, but I find much of the disagreement turns on whether I should have acted when I did. Even then many people have concluded as I did that the pardon was in the best interests of the country because it came at a time when it would best serve the purpose I have stated.

I come to this hearing in a spirit of cooperation to respond to your inquiries. I do so with the understanding that the subjects to be covered are defined and limited by the questions as they appear in the resolutions before you. But even then we may not mutually agree on what information falls within the proper scope of inquiry by the Congress.

I feel a responsibility as you do that each separate branch of our government must preserve a degree of confidentiality for its internal communications. Congress, for its part, has seen the wisdom of assuring that members be permitted to work under conditions of confidentiality. Indeed, earlier this year the United States Senate passed a resolution which reads in part as follows:

> ". . . no evidence under the control and in the possession of the Senate of the United States can, by the mandate of process of the ordinary courts of justice, be taken from such control or possession, but by its permission." (S. Res. 338, passed June 12, 1974)

In *United States* v. *Nixon,* 42 U.S.L.W. 5237, 5244 (U.S. July 24, 1974), the Supreme Court unanimously recognized a rightful sphere of confidentiality within the executive branch, which the Court determined could only be invaded for overriding reasons of the fifth and sixth amendments to the Constitution.

As I have stated before, my own view is that the right of executive privilege is to be exercised with caution and restraint. When I was a Member of Congress, I did not hesitate to question the right of the executive branch to claim a privilege against supplying information to the Congress if I thought the claim of privilege was being abused. Yet, I did then, and I do now, respect the right of executive privilege when it protects advice given to a President in the expectation that it will not be disclosed. Otherwise, no President could any longer count on receiving free and frank views from people designated to help him reach his official decisions.

Also, it is certainly not my intention or even within my authority to detract on this occasion or in any other instance from the generally recognized rights of the President to preserve the confidentiality of internal discussions or communications whenever it is properly within his constitutional responsibility to do so. These rights are within the authority of any President while he is in office, and I believe may be exercised as well by a past President if the information sought pertains to his official functions when he was serving in office.

I bring up these important points before going into the balance of my statement, so there can be no doubt that I remain mindful of the rights of confidentiality which a President may and ought to exercise in appropriate situations. However, I do not regard my answers as I have prepared them for purposes of this inquiry to be prejudicial to those rights in the present circumstances or to constitute a precedent for responding to Congressional inquiries different in nature or scope or under different circumstances.

Accordingly, I shall proceed to explain as fully as I can in my present answers the facts and circumstances covered by the present resolutions of inquiry. I shall start with an explanation of these events which were the first to occur in the period covered by the inquiry, before I became President. Then I will respond to the separate questions as they are numbered in H. Res. 1367 and as they specifically relate to the period after I became President.

H. Res. 1367 [5] before this subcommittee asks for information about certain conversations that may have occurred over a period that includes when I was a Member of Congress or the Vice President. In that entire period, no references or discussions on a possible pardon for then President Nixon occurred until August 1 and 2, 1974.

You will recall that since the beginning of the Watergate investigations, I had consistently made statements and speeches about President Nixon's innocence of either planning the break-in or of participating in the coverup. I sincerely believed he was innocent.

Even in the closing months before the President resigned, I made public statements that in my opinion the adverse revelations so far did not constitute an impeachable offense. I was coming under increasing criticism for such public statements, but I still believed them to be true based on the facts as I knew them.

In the early morning of Thursday, August 1, 1974, I had a meeting in my Vice Presidential office, with Alexander M. Haig, Jr., chief of staff for President Nixon. At this meeting, I was told in a general way about fears arising because of additional tape evidence scheduled for delivery to Judge Sirica on Monday, August 5, 1974. I was told that there could be evidence which, when disclosed to the House of Representatives, would likely tip the vote in favor of impeachment. However, I was given no indication that this development would lead to any change in President Nixon's plans to oppose the impeachment vote.

[5] Tab A attached [page 350].

Then shortly after noon, General Haig requested another appointment as promptly as possible. He came to my office about 3:30 p.m. for a meeting that was to last for approximately three-quarters of an hour. Only then did I learn of the damaging nature of a conversation on June 23, 1972, in one of the tapes which was due to go to Judge Sirica the following Monday.

I describe this meeting because at one point it did include references to a possible pardon for Mr. Nixon, to which the third and fourth questions in H. Res. 1367 are directed. However, nearly the entire meeting covered other subjects, all dealing with the totally new situation resulting from the critical evidence on the tape of June 23, 1972. General Haig told me he had been told of the new and damaging evidence by lawyers on the White House Staff who had first-hand knowledge of what was on the tape. The substance of his conversation was that the new disclosure would be devastating, even catastrophic, insofar as President Nixon was concerned. Based on what he had learned of the conversation on the tape, he wanted to know whether I was prepared to assume the Presidency within a very short time and whether I would be willing to make recommendations to the President as to what course he should now follow.

I cannot really express adequately in words how shocked and stunned I was by this unbelievable revelation. First, was the sudden awareness I was likely to become President under these most troubled circumstances; and secondly, the realization these new disclosures ran completely counter to the position I had taken for months, in that I believed the President was not guilty of any impeachable offense.

General Haig in his conversation at my office went on to tell me of discussions in the White House among those who knew of this new evidence.

General Haig asked for my assessment of the whole situation. He wanted my thoughts about the timing of a resignation, if that decision were to be made, and about how to do it and accomplish an orderly change of Administration. We discussed what scheduling problems there might be and what the early organizational problems would be.

General Haig outlined for me President Nixon's situation as he saw it and the different views in the White House as to the courses of action that might be available, and which were being advanced by various people around him on the White House Staff. As I recall there were different major courses being considered:

(1) Some suggested "riding it out" by letting the impeachment take its course through the House and the Senate trial, fighting all the way against conviction.

(2) Others were urging resignation sooner or later. I was told some people backed the first course and other people a resignation but not with the same views as to how and when it should take place.

On the resignation issue, there were put forth a number of options which General Haig reviewed with me. As I recall his conversation, various possible options being considered included:

(1) the President temporarily step aside under the 25th amendment;

(2) delaying resignation until further along the impeachment process;

(3) trying first to settle for a censure vote as a means of avoiding either impeachment or a need to resign;

(4) the question of whether the President could pardon himself;

(5) pardoning various Watergate defendants, then himself, followed by resignation;

(6) a pardon to the President, should he resign;

The rush of events placed an urgency on what was to be done. It became even more critical in view of a prolonged impeachment trial which was expected to last possibly 4 months or longer.

The impact of the Senate trial on the country, the handling of possible international crises, the economic situation here at home, and the marked slowdown in the decisionmaking process within the Federal Government were all factors to be considered and were discussed.

General Haig wanted my views on the various courses of action as well as my attitude on the options of resignation. However, he indicated he was not advocating any of the options. I inquired as to what was the President's pardon power, and he answered that it was his understanding from a White House lawyer that a President did have the authority to grant a pardon even before any criminal action had been taken against an individual, but, obviously, he was in no position to have any opinion on a matter of law.

As I saw it, at this point the question clearly before me was, under the circumstances, what course of action should I recommend that would be in the best interest of the country.

I told General Haig I had to have time to think; further, that I wanted to talk to James St. Clair. I also said I wanted to talk to my wife before giving any response. I had consistently and firmly held the view previously that in no way whatsoever could I recommend either publicly or privately any step by the President that might cause a change in my status as Vice President. As the person who would become President if a vacancy occurred for any reason in that office, a Vice President, I believed, should endeavor not to do or say anything which might affect his President's tenure in office. Therefore, I certainly was not ready even under these new circumstances to make any recommendations about resignation without having adequate time to consider further what I should properly do.

Shortly after 8 o'clock the next morning, James St. Clair came to my office. Although he did not spell out in detail the new evidence, there was no question in my mind that he considered these revelations to be so damaging that impeachment in the House was a certainty and conviction in the Senate a high probability. When I asked Mr. St. Clair if he knew of any other new and damaging evidence besides that on the June 23, 1972, tape, he said "no." When I pointed out to him the various options mentioned to me by General Haig, he told me he had not been the source of any opinion about Presidential pardon power.

After further thought on the matter, I was determined not to make any recommendations to President Nixon on his resignation. I had not given any advice or recommendations in my conversations with his aides, but I also did not want anyone who might talk to the President to suggest that I had some intention to do so.

For that reason I decided I should call General Haig the afternoon of August 2. I did make the call late that afternoon and told him I wanted him to understand that I had no intention of recommending what President Nixon should do about resigning or not resigning, and that nothing we had talked about the previous afternoon should be given any consideration in whatever decision the President might make. General Haig told me he was in full agreement with this position.

My travel schedule called for me to make appearances in Mississippi and Louisiana over Saturday, Sunday, and part of Monday, August 3, 4, and 5. In the previous 8 months, I had repeatedly stated my opinion that the President would not be found guilty of an impeachable offense. Any change from my stated views, or even refusal to comment further, I feared, would lead in the press to conclusions that I now wanted to see the President resign to avoid an impeachment vote in the House and probable conviction vote in the Senate. For that reason I remained firm in my answers to press questions during my trip and repeated my belief in the President's innocence of an impeachable offense. Not until I returned to Washington did I learn that President Nixon was to release the new evidence late on Monday, August 5, 1974.

At about the same time I was notified that the President had called a Cabinet meeting for Tuesday morning, August 6, 1974. At that meeting in the Cabinet Room, I announced that I was making no recommendations to the President as to what he should do in the light of the new evidence. And I made no recommendations to him either at the meeting or at any time after that.

In summary, I assure you that there never was at any time any agreement whatsoever concerning a pardon to Mr. Nixon if he were to resign and I were to become President.

The first question of H. Res. 1367 asks whether I or my representative had "specific knowledge of any formal criminal charges pending against Richard M. Nixon." The answer is "no."

I had known, of course, that the grand jury investigating the Watergate break-in and coverup had wanted to name President Nixon as an unindicted co-conspirator in the coverup. Also, I knew that an extensive report had been prepared by the Watergate Special Prosecution Force for the grand jury and had been sent to the House Committee on the Judiciary, where, I believe, it served the staff and members of the committee in the development of its report on the proposed articles of impeachment. Beyond what was disclosed in the publications of the Judiciary Committee on the subject and additional evidence released by President Nixon on August 5, 1974, I saw on or shortly after September 4 a copy of a memorandum prepared for Special Prosecutor Jaworski by the Deputy Special Prosecutor, Henry Ruth.[6] Copy of this memorandum had been furnished by Mr. Jaworski to my Counsel and was later made public during a press briefing at the White House on September 10, 1974.

I have supplied the subcommittee with a copy of this memorandum. The memorandum lists matters still under investigation which "may prove to have some direct connection to activities in which Mr. Nixon is personally involved." The Watergate coverup is not included in this list, and the alleged coverup is mentioned only as being the subject of a separate memorandum not furnished to me. Of those matters which are listed in the memorandum, it is stated that none of them "at the moment rises to the level of our ability to prove even a probable criminal violation by Mr. Nixon."

This is all the information I had which related even to the possibility of "formal criminal charges" involving the former President while he had been in office.

The second question in the resolution asks whether Alexander Haig referred to or discussed a pardon with Richard M. Nixon or his representatives at any time during the week of August 4, 1974, or any subsequent time. My answer to that question is: "not to my knowledge." If any such discussions did occur, they could not have been a factor in my decision to grant the pardon when I did because I was not aware of them.

[6] Tab B attached [page 351].

Questions three and four of H. Res. 1367 deal with the first and all subsequent references to, or discussions of, a pardon for Richard M. Nixon, with him or any of his representatives or aides. I have already described at length what discussions took place on August 1 and 2, 1974, and how these discussions brought no recommendations or commitments whatsoever on my part. These were the only discussions related to questions three and four before I became President, but question four relates also to subsequent discussions.

At no time after I became President on August 9, 1974, was the subject of a pardon for Richard M. Nixon raised by the former President or by anyone representing him. Also, no one on my staff brought up the subject until the day before my first press conference on August 28, 1974. At that time, I was advised that questions on the subject might be raised by media reporters at the press conference.

As the press conference proceeded, the first question asked involved the subject, as did other later questions. In my answers to these questions, I took a position that, while I was the final authority on this matter, I expected to make no commitment one way or the other depending on what the Special Prosecutor and courts would do. However, I also stated that I believed the general view of the American people was to spare the former President from a criminal trial.

Shortly afterwards I became greatly concerned that if Mr. Nixon's prosecution and trial were prolonged, the passions generated over a long period of time would seriously disrupt the healing of our country from the wounds of the past. I could see that the new Administration could not be effective if it had to operate in the atmosphere of having a former President under prosecution and criminal trial. Each step along the way, I was deeply concerned, would become a public spectacle and the topic of wide public debate and controversy.

As I have before stated publicly, these concerns led me to ask from my own legal counsel what my full right of pardon was under the Constitution in this situation and from the Special Prosecutor what criminal actions, if any, were likely to be brought against the former President, and how long his prosecution and trial would take.

As soon as I had been given this information, I authorized my Counsel, Philip Buchen, to tell Herbert J. Miller, as attorney for Richard M. Nixon, of my pending decision to grant a pardon for the former President. I was advised that the disclosure was made on September 4, 1974, when Mr. Buchen, accompanied by Benton Becker, met with Mr. Miller. Mr. Becker had been asked, with my concurrence, to take on a temporary special assignment to assist Mr. Buchen, at a time when no one else of my selection had yet been appointed to the legal staff of the White House.

The fourth question in the resolution also asks about "negotiations" with Mr. Nixon or his representatives on the subject of a pardon for the former President. The pardon under consideration was not, so far as I was concerned, a matter of negotiation. I realized that unless Mr. Nixon actually accepted the pardon I was preparing to grant, it probably would not be effective. So I certainly had no intention to proceed without knowing if it would be accepted. Otherwise, I put no conditions on my granting of a pardon which required any negotiations.

Although negotiations had been started earlier and were conducted through September 6 concerning White House records of the prior administration, I did not make any agreement on that subject a condition of the pardon. The circumstances leading to an initial agreement on Presidential records are not covered by the resolutions before this subcommittee. Therefore, I have mentioned discussions on that subject with Mr. Nixon's attorney only to show they were related in time to the pardon discussions but were not a basis for my decision to grant a pardon to the former President.

The fifth, sixth, and seventh questions of H. Res. 1367 ask whether I consulted with certain persons before making my pardon decision.

I did not consult at all with Attorney General Saxbe on the subject of a pardon for Mr. Nixon. My only conversation on the subject with Vice Presidential nominee Nelson Rockefeller was to report to him on September 6, 1974, that I was planning to grant the pardon.

Special Prosecutor Jaworski was contacted on my instructions by my Counsel, Philip Buchen. One purpose of their discussions was to seek the information I wanted on what possible criminal charges might be brought against Mr. Nixon. The result of that inquiry was a copy of the memorandum I have already referred to and have furnished to this subcommittee. The only other purpose was to find out the opinion of the Special Prosecutor as to how long a delay would follow, in the event of Mr. Nixon's indictment, before a trial could be started and concluded.

At a White House press briefing on September 8, 1974, the principal portions of Mr. Jaworski's opinion were made public. In this opinion, Mr. Jaworski wrote that selection of a jury for the trial of the former President, if he were indicted, would require a delay "of a period from nine months to a year, and perhaps even longer." On the question of how long it would take to conduct such a trial, he noted that the complexities of the jury selection made it difficult to estimate the time. Copy of the full text of his opinion, dated September 4, 1974, I have now furnished to this subcommittee.[7]

I did consult with my Counsel, Philip Buchen, with Benton Becker, and with my Counsellor, John Marsh, who is also an attorney. Outside of these men, serving at the time on my immediate staff, I consulted with no other attorneys or professors of law for facts or legal authorities bearing on my decision to grant a pardon to the former President.

Questions eight and nine of H. Res. 1367 deal with the circumstances of any statement requested or received from Mr. Nixon. I asked for no confession or statement of guilt, only a statement in acceptance of the pardon when it was granted. No language was suggested or requested by anyone acting for me to my knowledge. My Counsel advised me that he had told the attorney for Mr. Nixon that he believed the statement should be one expressing contrition, and in this respect, I was told Mr. Miller concurred. Before I announced the pardon, I saw a preliminary draft of a proposed statement from Mr. Nixon, but I did not regard the language of the statement, as subsequently issued, to be subject to approval by me or my representatives.

The tenth question covers any report to me on Mr. Nixon's health by a physician or psychiatrist, which led to my pardon decision. I received no such report. Whatever information was generally known to me at the time of my pardon decision was based on my own observations of his condition at the time he resigned as President and observations reported to me after that from others who had later seen or talked with him. No such reports were by people qualified to evaluate medically the condition of Mr. Nixon's health, and so they were not a controlling factor in my decision. However, I believed and still do, that prosecution and trial of the former President would have proved a serious threat to his health, as I stated in my message on September 8, 1974.

[7] Tab C attached [page 351].

H. Res. 1370[8] is the other resolution of inquiry before this subcommittee. It presents no questions but asks for the full and complete facts upon which was based my decision to grant a pardon to Richard M. Nixon.

I know of no such facts that are not covered by my answers to the questions in H. Res. 1367. Also:

Subparagraphs (1) and (4): There were no representations made by me or for me and none by Mr. Nixon or for him on which my pardon decision was based.

Subparagraph (2): The health issue is dealt with by me in answer to question 10 of the previous resolution.

Subparagraph (3): Information available to me about possible offenses in which Mr. Nixon might have been involved is covered in my answer to the first question of the earlier resolution.

In addition, in an unnumbered paragraph at the end, H. Res. 1370 seeks information on possible pardons for Watergate-related offenses which others may have committed. I have decided that all persons requesting consideration of pardon requests should submit them through the Department of Justice.

Only when I receive information on any request duly filed and considered first by the Pardon Attorney at the Department of Justice would I consider the matter. As yet no such information has been received, and if it does I will act or decline to act according to the particular circumstances presented, and not on the basis of the unique circumstances, as I saw them, of former President Nixon.

By these responses to the resolutions of inquiry, I believe I have fully and fairly presented the facts and circumstances preceding my pardon of former President Nixon. In this way, I hope I have contributed to a much better understanding by the American people of the action I took to grant the pardon when I did. For having afforded me this opportunity, I do express my appreciation to you, Mr. Chairman, and to Mr. Smith, the ranking minority member, and to all the other distinguished members of this subcommittee; also to Chairman Rodino of the Committee on the Judiciary, to Mr. Hutchinson, the ranking minority member of the full committee, and to other distinguished members of the full committee who are present.

In closing, I would like to reemphasize that I acted solely for the reasons I stated in my proclamation of September 8, 1974, and my accompanying message and that I acted out of my concern to serve the best interests of my country.

---

[8] Tab D attached [page 352].

As I stated then: "My concern is the immediate future of this great country . . . My conscience tells me it is my duty, not merely to proclaim domestic tranquility, but to use every means that I have to insure it."

TAB A

H. RES. 1367

93d Congress

2d Session

IN THE HOUSE OF REPRESENTATIVES

SEPTEMBER 16, 1974

Ms. ABZUG (for herself, Mr. BADILLO, Mr. JOHN L. BURTON, Mr. DELLUMS, Mr. EILBERG, Mr. HECHLER of West Virginia, Mr. HELSTOSKI, Ms. HOLTZMAN, Mr. KOCH, Mr. ROSENTHAL, Mr. STARK, Mr. STOKES, Mr. SYMINGTON, and Mr. CHARLES H. WILSON of California) submitted the following resolution; which was referred to the Committee on the Judiciary

---

RESOLUTION

Resolved, That the President of the United States is hereby requested to furnish the House, within ten days, with the following information:

1. Did you or your representatives have specific knowledge of any formal criminal charges pending against Richard M. Nixon prior to issuance of the pardon? If so, what were these charges?

2. Did Alexander Haig refer to or discuss a pardon for Richard M. Nixon with Richard M. Nixon or representatives of Mr. Nixon at any time during the week of August 4, 1974, or at any subsequent time? If so, what promises were made or conditions set for a pardon, if any? If so, were tapes or transcriptions of any kind made of these conversations or were any notes taken? If so, please provide such tapes, transcriptions or notes.

3. When was a pardon for Richard M. Nixon first referred to or discussed with Richard M. Nixon, or representatives of Mr. Nixon, by you or your representatives or aides, including the period when you were a Member of Congress or Vice President?

4. Who participated in these and subsequent discussions or negotiations with Richard M. Nixon or his representatives regarding a pardon, and at what specific times and locations?

5. Did you consult with Attorney General William Saxbe or Special Prosecutor Leon Jaworski before making the decision to pardon Richard M. Nixon and, if so, what facts and legal authorities did they give to you?

6. Did you consult with the Vice Presidential nominee, Nelson Rockefeller, before making the decision to pardon Richard M. Nixon and, if so, what facts and legal authorities did he give to you?

7. Did you consult with any other attorneys or professors of law before making the decision to pardon Richard M. Nixon and, if so, what facts or legal authorities did they give to you?

8. Did you or your representatives ask Richard M. Nixon to make a confession or statement of criminal guilt, and, if so, what language was suggested or requested by you, your representatives, Mr. Nixon, or his representatives? Was any statement of any kind requested from Mr. Nixon in exchange for the pardon, and, if so, please provide the suggested or requested language.

9. Was the statement issued by Richard M. Nixon immediately subsequent to announcement of the pardon made known to you or your representatives prior to its announcement, and was it approved by you or your representatives?

10. Did you receive any report fom a psychiatrist or other physician stating that Richard M. Nixon was in other than good health? If so, please provide such reports.

TAB B

Memorandum to: Leon Jaworski
From: Henry Ruth
Subject: Mr. Nixon

The following matters are still under investigation in this Office and may prove to have some direct connection to activities in which Mr. Nixon is personally involved:

1. Tax deductions relating to the gift of pre-Presidential papers.
2. The Colson obstruction of justice plea in the Ellsberg matter.
3. The transfer of the national security wire tap records from the FBI to the White House.
4. The initiating of wire tapping of John Sears.
5. Misuse of IRS information.
6. Misuse of IRS through attempted initiation of audits as to "enemies."
7. The dairy industry pledge and its relationship to the price support change.
8. Filing of a challenge to the Washington Post ownership of two Florida television stations.
9. False and evasive testimony at the Kleindienst confirmation hearings as to White House participation in Department of Justice decisions about ITT.
10. The handling of campaign contribution by Mr. Rebozo for the personal benefit of Mr. Nixon.

None of these matters at the moment rises to the level of our ability to prove even a probable criminal violation by Mr. Nixon, but I thought you ought to know which of the pending investigations were even remotely connected to Mr. Nixon. Of course, the Watergate cover-up is the subject of a separate memorandum.

cc: Mr. Lacovara

TAB C

September 4, 1974

Dear Mr. Buchen:

You have inquired as to my opinion regarding the length of delay that would follow, in the event of an indictment of former President Richard M. Nixon, before a trial could reasonably be had by a fair and impartial jury as guaranteed by the Constitution.

The factual situation regarding a trial of Richard M. Nixon within constitutional bounds, is unprecedented. It is especially unique in view of the recent House Judiciary Committee inquiry on impeachment, resulting in a unanimous adverse finding to Richard M. Nixon on the Article involving obstruction of justice. The massive publicity given the hearings and the findings that ensued, the reversal of judgment of a number of the members of the Republican Party following release of the June 23 tape recording, and their statements carried nationwide, and finally, the resignation of Richard M. Nixon, require a delay, before selection of a jury is begun, of a period from nine months to a year, and perhaps even longer. This judgment is predicated on a review of the decisions of United States Courts involving prejudicial pre-trial publicity. The Government's decision to pursue impeachment proceedings and the tremendous volume of television, radio and newspaper coverage given thereto, are factors emphasized by the Courts in weighing the time a trial can be had. The complexities involved in the process of selecting a jury and the time it will take to complete the process, I find difficult to estimate at this time.

The situation involving Richard M. Nixon is readily distinguishable from the facts involved in the case of *United States* v. *Mitchell, et al.*, set for trial on September 30th. The defendants in the Mitchell case were indicted by a grand jury operating in secret session. They will be called to trial, unlike Richard M. Nixon, if indicted, without any previous adverse finding by an investigatory body holding public hearings on its conclusions. It is precisely the condemnation of Richard M. Nixon already made in the impeachment process, that would make it unfair to the defendants in the case of *United States* v. *Mitchell, et al.*, for Richard M. Nixon now to be joined as a coconspirator, should it be concluded that an indictment of him was proper.

The *United States* v. *Mitchell, et al.*, trial will within itself generate new publicity, some undoubtedly prejudicial to Richard M. Nixon. I bear this in mind when I estimate the earliest time of trial of Richard M. Nixon under his constitutional guarantees, in the event of indictment, to be as indicated above.

If further information is desired, please advise me.

Sincerely,

LEON JAWORSKI
Special Prosecutor

[Philip W. Buchen, Esq., Counsel to the President, The White House, Washington, D.C.]

TAB D

H. RES. 1370

93d Congress

2d Session

IN THE HOUSE OF REPRESENTATIVES

SEPTEMBER 17, 1974

Mr. CONYERS submitted the following resolution; which was referred to the Committee on the Judiciary

---

RESOLUTION

Resolved, That the President is directed to furnish to the House of Representatives the full and complete information and facts upon which was based the decision to grant a pardon to Richard M. Nixon, including—

(1) any representations made by or on behalf of Richard M. Nixon to the President;

(2) any information or facts presented to the President with respect to the mental or physical health of Richard M. Nixon;

(3) any information in possession or control of the President with respect to the offenses which were allegedly committed by Richard M. Nixon and for which a pardon was granted;

(4) any representations made by or on behalf of the President to Richard M. Nixon in connection with a pardon for alleged offenses against the United States.

The President is further directed to furnish to the House of Repesentatives the full and complete information and facts in his possession or control and relating to any pardon which may be granted to any person who is or may be charged or convicted of any offense against the United States within the prosecutorial jurisdiction of the Office of Watergate Special Prosecution Force.

[The statement as printed above was not read literally by the President at the hearing, which began at 10 a.m. in the Rayburn House Office Building. The hearing was broadcast live on radio and television.

All footnotes appeared in the statement.

Following his opening statement, the President responded to questions from members of the Subcommittee on Criminal Justice of the House Committee on the Judiciary, as follows:]

THE PRESIDENT. Mr. Chairman, I thank you and the committee members of the subcommittee for this opportunity to make these views known.

CONGRESSMAN WILLIAM L. HUNGATE. Mr. President, on behalf of the subcommittee, we express our appreciation for your appearance here, bringing facts that will be helpful to the American people and the Congress.

There will be some who will find the answers fully satisfactory and forthright. There will be others who will not. But I would hope that all would appreciate your openness and willingness to come before the American public and the Congress to discuss this important matter.

The gentleman from Wisconsin, Mr. Kastenmeier.

CONGRESSMAN ROBERT W. KASTENMEIER. Thank you, Mr. Chairman.

I, too, would like to join my colleagues in welcoming the President. I don't believe any of us could have anticipated a year ago, when the President then appeared as a nominee under the 25th amendment for Vice President, that you would once again appear before this committee as President of the United States.

I would only comment, no matter how well-motivated the desire to put Watergate behind us, I can only acknowledge today that several key issues in the news this morning—the President's appearance before this committee, the trial downtown, the Watergate trial itself, and even the nomination of Mr. Rockefeller to be the Vice President, occasioned by a vacancy due to Watergate—all of these still command the attention of the American people, and I guess we will just have to be patient.

Mr. President, you indicated that you wanted to spare Mr. Nixon a criminal trial. Did you specifically have any other end in view in terms of protecting Mr. Nixon in terms of a pardon; that is to say, whatever a pardon would spare the President other than a criminal trial, were there any other adversities which a pardon would help Mr. Nixon with, as you saw it?

THE PRESIDENT. As I indicated in the proclamation that I issued, and as I indicated in the statement I made at the time on September 8, my prime reason was for the benefit of the country, not for any benefits that might be for Mr. Nixon.

I exercised my pardon authority under the Constitution, which relates only to those criminal matters during the period from January 20, 1969, until August 9, 1974.

CONGRESSMAN KASTENMEIER. I appreciate that, Mr. President, but it must have been something you foresaw which could happen to Mr. Nixon which justified a pardon, if in fact you were advised, and perhaps you were not, that there was no proceeding going to be commenced against Mr. Nixon, that nothing would happen to him, really a pardon may have been an empty gesture in that event?

THE PRESIDENT. As I indicated, Mr. Kastenmeier, after the press conference on August 28 where three questions were raised about the pardon or the possibility of a pardon, I asked my Counsel to find out from the Special Prosecutor what, if any, charges were being considered by the Special Prosecutor's office.

As I indicated in my prepared statement, I received from Mr. Jaworski certain information indicating that there were possible or potential criminal proceedings against Mr. Nixon.

CONGRESSMAN KASTENMEIER. But you did not determine, as a matter of fact, that there was any intention to proceed to indictment with any of those matters, is that not correct?

THE PRESIDENT. In the memorandum, I believe of September 4, from Mr.

Jaworski, prepared by Mr. Ruth, there were 10 possibilities listed. On the other hand, there was, I think, well-known information that there was a distinct possibility of Mr. Nixon being indicted on the grounds of obstructing justice.

CONGRESSMAN KASTENMEIER. The effect of the pardon in terms of the 10 possible areas of investigation as you saw it at the time was to terminate those investigations, as well as end any possibility of indictment on those grounds.

THE PRESIDENT. Well, the power of pardon does cover any criminal actions during a stipulated period, and as the pardon itself indicated, it went from the day that Mr. Nixon first took the oath of office until he actually resigned on August 9.

CONGRESSMAN KASTENMEIER. My question is, did you have reason to believe that other than the 10 areas of investigation and the coverup, that the former President might need to be protected in any other area where possibility of criminal prosecution existed?

THE PRESIDENT. I knew of no other potential or possible criminal charges, no.

CONGRESSMAN KASTENMEIER. My time has expired, Mr. Chairman.

CONGRESSMAN HUNGATE. The gentleman from New York, Mr. Smith.

CONGRESSMAN HENRY P. SMITH III. Mr. President, in regard to your answer on page 18 [page 347] of your statement of whether you consulted with certain persons and in that connection and in connection with question number six of H.R. 1367, you stated in regard to the Vice Presidential nominee, Nelson Rockefeller, that your only conversation on the subject with him was to report to him on September 6, 1974, that "I was planning to grant the pardon."

Now, the question asks whether he gave you any facts or legal authorities and my question is, did he do so?

THE PRESIDENT. Nelson Rockefeller did not give me any facts or legal authorities. He was in my office to discuss with me the proceedings concerning his nomination, and at the conclusion of a discussion on that matter, I felt that I should inform him of the possible or prospective action that I would be taking, but he gave me no facts, he gave me no legal advice concerning the pardon.

CONGRESSMAN SMITH. Mr. President, as you were minority leader of the Congress before you became Vice President of the United States, did you at any time discuss the wisdom or advisability of a possible Presidential pardon for President Nixon with President Nixon or any of his representatives or any member of the White House Staff?

This was in the period before you became Vice President.

THE PRESIDENT. The answer is categorically no. Before I became Vice President, Mr. Smith, I, on several occasions—I can't recall how many—indicated to President Nixon himself that I thought he should not resign.

If my memory is accurate, Mr. Smith, before I became Vice President, there were individuals both in the Congress and otherwise who were advocating that Mr. Nixon resign.

I do recall on one or more occasions telling Mr. Nixon in my judgment he should not, because I thought that would be an admission of guilt, and on the information I had at that time, I did not believe Mr. Nixon was guilty of any impeachable offense.

CONGRESSMAN SMITH. Thank you, Mr. President. You touched upon your observations of President Nixon's health, and I wonder whether at any time before you became Vice President of the United States did you learn any facts about his physical or mental health which later became relevant to your decision to pardon Mr. Nixon?

THE PRESIDENT. Before I was Vice President I saw Mr. Nixon periodically, coming to the White House for leadership meetings or for other reasons, and during that period, I had the distinct impression that his health was good.

I didn't see any discernible change, in my own opinion, until the last day or two of his Presidency. I did notice the last time I saw him in the Oval Office on August 9—thought he was drawn and possibly a little thinner, but that is the only observation I made.

CONGRESSMAN HUNGATE. The gentleman from California, Mr. Edwards.

CONGRESSMAN DON EDWARDS. Thank you, Mr. Chairman.

Mr. President, on pages 10 and 11 [pages 343 and 344] of your statement, you indicate that there were some general discussions with General Haig and Mr. St. Clair, before the resignation, about the pardon power in general.

Did they have any reason to carry a message to then President Nixon that this pardon power could possibly be used on his behalf if he resigned?

THE PRESIDENT. None whatsoever. Categorically no.

CONGRESSMAN EDWARDS. Then why, Mr. President, those general discussions about pardon?

THE PRESIDENT. Well, as I indicated in my prepared statement, General Haig came to me first to apprise me of the dramatic change in the situation, and as I indicated in the prepared statement, told me that I should be prepared to assume the Presidency very quickly, and wanted to know whether I was ready to do that.

Secondly, he did indicate that in the White House among the President's advisers there were many options being discussed as to what course of action the President should take, and in the course of my discussion on August 1 with General Haig, he outlined, as I did in the prepared text, the many options that were being discussed.

He asked for any recommendations I would make, and as I indicated in the prepared text, I made none.

CONGRESSMAN EDWARDS. Thank you.

Mr. President, Mr. Buchen said several times, and I believe you mentioned, that the pardon did involve a certain aspect of mercy. Would not the same considerations of mercy apply to the Watergate defendants downtown who now are putting forth as their chief defense their allegation that they were merely acting under orders of Mr. Nixon, then President and their boss?

THE PRESIDENT. Mr. Edwards, in light of the fact that these trials are being carried out at the present time, I think it is inadvisable for me to comment on any of the proceedings in those trials.

CONGRESSMAN EDWARDS. Mr. President, put yourself in the position of the high school teacher, shall we say, in Watts or the barrios of San Jose or Harlem, and if you were such a teacher, how would you explain to the young people of America the American concept of equal justice under law?

THE PRESIDENT. Mr. Edwards, Mr. Nixon was the 37th President of the United States. He had been preceded by 36 others. He is the only President in the history of this country who has resigned under shame and disgrace.

I think that that, in and of itself, can be understood, can be explained to students or to others. That was a major, major step, and a matter of, I am sure, grave, grave deliberations by the former President, and it certainly, as I have said several times, constituted shame and disgrace.

CONGRESSMAN EDWARDS. Thank you, Mr. President.

Mr. President, do you think that it is wise to pardon a man before indictment or trial for offenses that are completely unknown to you and which might possibly be terribly serious?

THE PRESIDENT. Well, as I indicated, Mr. Edwards, I did to the best of my ability check with probably the best authority in the country on what, if any, charges would be made against Mr. Nixon. Those were, or potentially were, serious charges.

I think that in taking the action I did concerning those charges, I was exercising in a proper way the pardon authority given a President under the Constitution.

Congressman Edwards. Thank you, Mr. President.

Congressman Hungate. The gentleman from Indiana, Mr. Dennis.

Congressman David W. Dennis. Thank you, Mr. Chairman.

Mr. President, I would like to state that I, too, share with my colleagues, deep appreciation for your appearance here before our subcommittee this morning.

Mr. President, on page 7 [page 342] of your statement where you were talking about your second interview with General Haig in the afternoon of August 1, you state that, "I describe this meeting because at one point it did include references to a possible pardon for Mr. Nixon."

I take it that you have spelled out what those references were over on page 9 [pages 342 and 343], where the options are spelled out, and page 10 [page 343], where you state that you inquired as to what was the President's pardon power.

The President. Yes, it is spelled out in the item instances 1 through 6, the various options involving a pardon.

Congressman Dennis. And does that include everything that was said at that time on the subject of pardon, substantially?

The President. Yes, sir.

Congressman Dennis. Mr. President, I note that on page 10 [page 343] you state that you asked the General as to what the President's pardon power was, and he very properly replied that he had certain information but couldn't give legal opinion.

When, where, and from whom did you ultimately obtain the opinion that you were entitled under the doctrine of *Ex Parte Garland* and so on, to issue a pardon when there has been no charge or no conviction?

The President. When I came back to the Oval Office, Mr. Dennis, following the press conference on August 28, where three questions were raised by the news media involving a pardon, I instructed my Counsel, Mr. Buchen, to check in an authoritative way what pardon power a President had. And he, several days later—I don't recall precisely—came back and briefed me on my pardon power as President of the United States.

Congressman Dennis. Mr. President, the exercise of executive clemency is, of course, a well-recognized part of the legal system in this country, exercised by you and all your predecessors, is that not the fact?

The President. That is correct, sir.

Congressman Dennis. And you have given this committee, as I understand your testimony this morning, your complete statement as to your reasons for exercising that power in this particular case?

The President. I have, sir.

CONGRESSMAN DENNIS. And in answer to my friend, Mr. Edwards, you have stated the fact that you felt that for an ex-President of the United States to resign under these circumstances was sufficient, strong punishment, and that that should answer the problems of those who have raised the question of equal justice under law?

THE PRESIDENT. That is correct, sir.

CONGRESSMAN DENNIS. And that you would consider other possible pardons on the facts of those particular cases when and if they were presented to you?

THE PRESIDENT. That is correct.

CONGRESSMAN DENNIS. And that there was no condition attached to this pardon and no sort of agreement made in respect thereto before it was granted?

THE PRESIDENT. None whatsoever, sir.

CONGRESSMAN DENNIS. Thank you, Mr. President. I have no further questions, Mr. Chairman.

CONGRESSMAN HUNGATE. The gentleman from South Carolina, Mr. Mann.

CONGRESSMAN JAMES R. MANN. Thank you, Mr. Chairman.

Mr. President, Mr. Kastenmeier asked you about the termination of the investigation by the Special Prosecutor's office. Was it your intention, by the pardon, to terminate the investigation by the Special Prosecutor's office in the 10 areas that you received the report from that office upon?

THE PRESIDENT. I think the net result of the pardon was, in effect, just that; yes, sir.

CONGRESSMAN MANN. And is that part of the reason that you didn't consult with Mr. Jaworski with reference to the tape agreements as to how that might affect his further investigations?

THE PRESIDENT. Well, as I pointed out, the tape agreement was initiated between my legal counsel and Mr. Nixon sometime before the question of a pardon ever arose.

The reason for that, Mr. Mann, is that I came into office, and almost immediately there were demands and requests, not only from the Special Prosecutor, as I recall, but from other sources as to those tapes and other documents. And one of the first things I did when these problems came to my desk was to ask the Attorney General for his opinion as to the ownership of those tapes or any other documents.

And once we got that information, then we felt that there ought to be some discussion as to where the tapes and other documents would be held and under what circumstances.

CONGRESSMAN MANN. Of course, the mandate of the Special Prosecutor's office was not directed solely at President Nixon.

But is it not so that the pardon in effect terminated that investigation insofar as other parties, other possible defendants, in getting to the true facts of the matters that have disturbed our national political life during these past 2 years?

THE PRESIDENT. I do not believe that the action I took in pardoning President Nixon had any impact on any other mandate that that Special Prosecutor's office had.

CONGRESSMAN MANN. What response would you have if the Special Prosecutor's office now requested access to certain of the tapes now in the custody of the Government?

THE PRESIDENT. The material that is still held by the Government, in my understanding of the Supreme Court decision, permits the Special Prosecutor to obtain any of that material for its responsibility, and I, of course not in a personal way, would make certain that that information was made available to the Special Prosecutor's office.

CONGRESSMAN MANN. According to press reports, Mr. Clement Stone visited Mr. Nixon on September 2 and thereafter met with you in Washington. Are you at liberty to tell us the gist of the communication involving President Nixon from Mr. Stone to you?

THE PRESIDENT. Mr. Stone came to see me about a program that he has used very successfully in his business, a program which he is very proud of, and he was urging me to institute it in the various bureaus and departments of the Federal Government.

There was no other message conveyed by him from Mr. Nixon to me.

CONGRESSMAN MANN. Did you ever discuss the pardon with former President Nixon after his resignation and prior to the granting of the pardon?

THE PRESIDENT. Will you repeat that again, please?

CONGRESSMAN MANN. Did you have any personal conversation with former President Nixon concerning the pardon, between his resignation and September 8?

THE PRESIDENT. Absolutely not.

CONGRESSMAN MANN. Now, in response to Mr. Edwards' question about equal justice under the law, I know that you make a distinction that here we are talking about the Office of President of the United States.

But let's assume that we are talking about the president of a bank or Governor of a State or Chief Justice of the United States Supreme Court, and in our minds those are very high political offices. Do you think any of those persons who are allegedly criminally culpable through resignation should be entitled to any treatment different from any other citizen?

The President. Mr. Mann, I don't think I should answer a hypothetical question of that kind. I was dealing with reality, and I have given, in my best judgment, the reasons for the action that I took. And to pass judgment on any other person or individual holding any other office in public or private, I think it would be inappropriate for me.

Congressman Dennis. You have heard the maxim that the law is no respecter of persons. Do you agree with that?

The President. Certainly it should be.

Congressman Dennis. Thank you, Mr. President.

Congressman Hungate. The gentleman from Iowa, Mr. Mayne.

Congressman Wiley Mayne. Thank you, Mr. Chairman.

Mr. President, I believe that the chairman and others in their questioning have established very clearly that your appearance here today is an entirely voluntary one on your part, that it was your idea, that you had not been requested by the committee to come in person, that we had indicated that it would be entirely satisfactory as far as we were concerned if some assistant appeared instead.

The President. That is correct, sir.

Congressman Mayne. I do not think, however, that it has yet been made clear in the record, and I think this should be, that it is also true that you were willing to come and to tell this full story, as you have done, before the committee and on television before the American people, much earlier than today. Is that not true?

The President. Yes. I think the original schedule was set for about a week ago. I have forgotten the exact date.

Congressman Mayne. My recollection, and you can correct me if I am wrong, is that as early as September 30, you offered and volunteered to appear before the subcommittee at our next regular meeting, which would have been on October 1, but it was indicated to you that that would be too early for the committee to be able to accommodate such an appearance.

The President. I don't recall that detail, but when I indicated that I would voluntarily appear, a member of my staff met with, I think, Chairman Hungate, and between them they tried to work out what was an acceptable, agreeable time as to when I should appear.

Congressman Mayne. There was, of course, the concern which developed in the subcommittee as to whether there would be any possible jeopardy to the impaneling of the jury in the Watergate cases, but I think this timetable should be established, and I would ask the chairman if that is not his recollection, that originally, the President did say that he would be glad to appear on October 1.

CONGRESSMAN HUNGATE. Not being under oath, the Chair is glad to reply. The gentleman's recollection is the same as mine.

CONGRESSMAN MAYNE. Thank you, Mr. Chairman. I just think the point should be made that there has been no stalling at all or delay on the part of the President in making this appearance, but that he was not only willing to make the statement but to do it much earlier.

CONGRESSMAN EDWARDS. If the gentleman would yield briefly—that is precisely the fact, and it was consideration on behalf of many of us concerning the proper effect on any trials that held us till this day.

CONGRESSMAN MAYNE. Now, Mr. President, I think there was perhaps one part of Mr. Kastenmeier's questioning of you that was left unanswered, and I am going to try to go into that again.

Did you, by granting this pardon, have any intention of stopping the investigations of any other defendants or potential defendants?

THE PRESIDENT. None whatsoever.

CONGRESSMAN MAYNE. Mr. President, ever since I first heard of the Watergate break-in, I have felt that this was a matter which should be fully investigated and prosecuted, and that anyone found to be criminally involved should be punished as provided by the law, and I have repeatedly stated I thought our American system of justice, as administered in the courts, was fully capable of handling the situation if permitted to proceed without interference.

I have been apprehensive that the activities of some of the legislative committees and the large amount of publicity attending upon those activities might make it impossible for our court system to function as it should, and I have also been fearful that the executive branch would intervene to limit or handicap the normal functioning of the courts.

Now, Mr. President, I must say to you I am deeply concerned that both the legislative and executive branches have indeed interfered with our courts making it extremely difficult for the traditional American system of justice to proceed in the regular manner in this case, and I was very disturbed by the granting of this pardon, particularly at such an early stage, even though, certainly, there is no question that under the law, you had the right to act as you did.

Now, I realize that hindsight is always better than foresight, but I am wondering if after all that has happened and with further opportunity for reflection, if you do not now feel that you perhaps acted too hastily in this case.

THE PRESIDENT. Mr. Mayne, I have thought about that a great deal because there has been criticism of the timing. But as I reviewed my thoughts prior to the granting of the pardon, I had to look at this factual situation: If I granted the pardon when I did, it would, as quickly as possible, achieve the results that I wanted, which was to permit our Government, both the Congress and the President, to proceed to the solution of the problems.

Now, some people say in their criticism—and I understand it and I am not critical of the points they raise—I should have waited until Mr. Nixon was indicted, inferring that I should have then pardoned him, if I was going to do so. Well, other people say that I should have waited until he was convicted, if he was convicted, and at that time, I should have pardoned him.

Others have indicated that I should have waited for a conviction and a jail sentence, if that were the result. Now, all of that process, whether it is the indictment, the possible conviction, a conviction plus a jail sentence, would have taken, as I have tried to explain, at least a year and probably much longer.

And during that whole period of time, Mr. Mayne, all of the things that I wanted to avoid, namely the opportunity for our Government, the President and the Congress, and others, to get to the problems we have, would have been, I think, deeply upset and roadblocked.

So, I am convinced, after reflection, as I was previously, that the timing of the pardon was done at the right time.

CONGRESSMAN MAYNE. Thank you, Mr. President.

CONGRESSMAN HUNGATE. The Representative from New York, Ms. Holtzman.

CONGRESSWOMAN ELIZABETH HOLTZMAN. Thank you, Mr. Chairman, and Mr. Ford, I too, wish to applaud your historical appearance here today. At the same time, however, I wish to express my dismay that the format of this hearing will not be able to provide to the American public the full truth and all of the facts respecting your assurance of a pardon to Richard Nixon.

Unfortunately, each member of this committee will have only 5 minutes in which to ask questions about this most serious matter, and unfortunately, despite my urging, the committee declined to provide sufficient time for each committee member to ask the questions that were appropriate.

The committee declined to prepare fully for your coming by calling other witnesses, such as Alexander Haig, Mr. Buchen, Mr. Becker, and has failed to insist also on full production of documents by you respecting the issuance of this pardon.

I must confess my own lack of easiness at participating in a proceeding that has raised such high expectations and, unfortunately, will not be able to respond to them.

I would like to point out, Mr. President, that the resolutions of inquiry which have prompted your appearance here today have resulted from very dark suspicions that have been created in the public's mind.

Perhaps these suspicions are totally unfounded, and I sincerely hope that they are. But nonetheless, we must all confront the reality of these suspicions and the suspicions that were created by the circumstances of the pardon which you issued, the secrecy with which it was issued, and the reasons for which it was issued which made people question whether or not, in fact, it was a deal.

THE PRESIDENT. May I comment there? I want to assure you, the members of this subcommittee, the Members of the Congress, and the American people, there was no deal, period, under no circumstances.

CONGRESSWOMAN HOLTZMAN. Mr. President, I appreciate that statement, and I am sure many of the American people do, as well. But they also are asking questions about the pardon, and I would like to specify a few of them for you so that perhaps we can have some of these answered.

I think, from the mail I have received from all over the country, as well as my own district, I know that the people want to understand how you can explain having pardoned Richard Nixon without specifying any of the crimes for which he was pardoned. And how can you explain pardoning Richard Nixon without obtaining any acknowledgement of guilt from him? How do you explain the failure to consult the Attorney General of the United States with respect to the issuance of the pardon, even though in your confirmation hearings you had indicated the Attorney General's opinion would be critical in any decision to pardon the former President?

How can this extraordinary haste in which the pardon was decided on and the secrecy with which it was carried out be explained, and how can you explain the pardon of Richard Nixon, accompanied by an agreement with respect to the tapes which, in essence, in the public's mind, hampered the Special Prosecutor's access to these materials, and this was done, also, in the public's mind, in disregard of the public's right to know the full story about Richard Nixon's misconduct in office?

And in addition, the public, I think, wants an explanation of how Benton Becker was used to represent the interests of the United States in negotiating a tapes agreement when at that very time, he was under investigation by the United States for possible criminal charges?

And how, also, can you explain not having consulted Leon Jaworski, the Special Prosecutor, before approving of the tapes agreement? And I think, Mr. President, that these are only a few of the questions that have existed in the public's mind before and, unfortunately, still remain not resolved. And since I have very brief time, I would like to ask you, in addition to these questions, one further one, and that is that suspicions have been raised that the reason for the pardon and the simultaneous tapes agreement was to insure that the tape recordings between yourself and Richard Nixon never came out in public. To alleviate this suspicion once and for all, would you be willing to turn over to this subcommittee all tape recordings of conversations between yourself and Richard Nixon?

THE PRESIDENT. Those tapes, under an opinion of the Attorney General which I sought, according to the Attorney General—and, I might add, according to past precedent—belong to President Nixon. Those tapes are in our control. They are under an agreement which protects them, totally, fully, for the Special Prosecutor's office or for any other criminal proceedings.

Those tapes will not be delivered to anybody until a satisfactory agreement is reached with the Special Prosecutor's office. We have held them because his office did request that, and as long as we have them held in our possession for the Special Prosecutor's benefit, I see no way whatsoever that they can be destroyed, that they can be kept from proper utilization in criminal proceedings.

Now, those tapes belong to Mr. Nixon according to the Attorney General, but they are being held for the benefit of the Special Prosecutor, and I think that is the proper place for them to be kept.

CONGRESSMAN HUNGATE. The gentleman from Maryland, Mr. Hogan.

CONGRESSMAN LAWRENCE J. HOGAN. Thank you, Mr. Chairman. I am frankly amazed at my good friend, the gentlelady from New York, and her accusatory opening speech, because certainly, the gentlelady knows it is the usual and ordinary and routine procedure of this subcommittee and this committee, to operate under the 5-minute rule.

There is nothing extraordinary about us today allocating 5 minutes of time for questioning to each member of the committee. We always operate this way.

Her other observation about not doing any preparatory work by calling other witnesses was rejected as far as I recall by all other members of the subcommittee on the basis that this resolution of inquiry is directed to the President of the United States and properly so.

So, it would be totally inappropriate for the resolution of inquiry to address itself to individuals other than the subject of that resolution of inquiry.

Mr. President, I would like to join, too, in commending you for your statement and your openness and candor in coming in this very historic event.

Frankly, I am concerned at some of the questioning by my colleagues, asking questions, if all men are not equal under the law, because certainly, being the outstanding lawyers that they are, they know that the pardoning power itself is inherently inequitable, but for a larger purpose, it grants to the Chief Executive of the Federal Government or the State, in the case of State crimes, to pardon individuals who may or have been indicted or convicted of crimes.

So, we should not expect this to apply as if there were a trial of these criminal offenses. And furthermore, we also know that in our system of criminal justice, even the prosecutors themselves exercise prosecutive discretion. There is no question whatsoever that the Constitution gives to the President of the United States broad and absolute power to pardon individuals of criminal offenses.

We also know, from the debates of the framers of the Constitution, that they specifically rejected including in the Constitution the words "after conviction."

They also, in the debate at that time, indicated situations where it might be necessary or desirable to grant a pardon even before indictment, as was the case in this instance.

Mr. President, I know that you followed very carefully the deliberations of this committee during the impeachment inquiry, and I know you are also aware that this committee unanimously concluded that the President was guilty of an impeachable offense growing out of obstruction of justice.

So, in a sense, couldn't we not say that this was at least the basis for a possible criminal charge which was already spread on the record with ample evidence to justify it? So, those who say you should have waited until there were formalized charges really are overlooking the fact that there was a very formalized charge and indictment, if you will, by this committee.

The President. Well, the unanimous vote of the House Committee on the Judiciary, all 35 members, certainly is very, very substantial evidence that the former President was guilty of an impeachable offense.

There is no doubt in my mind that that recommendation of this full committee would have carried in the House, which would have been even more formal as an indication of criminal activity, or certainly to be more specific, an impeachable offense. And, of course, the prospects in the Senate with such a formidable vote in the committee and in the House would have been even more persuasive.

Congressman Hogan. Mr. President, referring to the memorandum from Mr. Ruth to Mr. Jaworski enumerating the 10 possible criminal offenses, it is true that this committee addressed itself, if I am not mistaken, to every single one of these charges and assessed evidence as to each one of them, and we found them wanting, that they were not sufficient justification for an impeachable offense.

The last paragraph of that memorandum says, and I quote: None of these matters at the moment rises to the level of our ability to prove even a probable criminal violation by Mr. Nixon.

Now, this memorandum does not include the obstruction of justice which I addressed myself to earlier, so I think we can logically assume that there would not have been any indictments resulting from Mr. Jaworski's activities other than in the area of obstruction of justice, and with further corroboration of that point, I allude to a story in the Wall Street Journal yesterday where Mr. Jaworski—who, incidentally, not only agrees with your pardon but also the legality and timeliness of it—and he says very specifically that there was going to be no additional disclosures resulting from his activities that the public was not already aware of relating to Mr. Nixon.

So, those who are saying we should wait until there is a formal charge I think are missing the point that there already has been a formal charge approved by this committee.

Mr. President, don't you feel that the very acceptance of the pardon by the former President is tantamount to an admission of guilt on his part?

THE PRESIDENT. I do, sir.

CONGRESSMAN HOGAN. So, those who say again that they would have preferred that the President admit his culpability before a pardon being issued again are overlooking that fact?

THE PRESIDENT. The acceptance of a pardon, according to the legal authorities—and we have checked them out very carefully—does indicate that by the acceptance, the person who has accepted it does, in effect, admit guilt.

CONGRESSMAN HOGAN. Thank you, Mr. President, and again I would like to express my personal appreciation for your candor and your openness and your cooperation with the coequal branch.

THE PRESIDENT. Thank you very much.

CONGRESSMAN HUNGATE. Mr. President, as you can see, the peculiar strength of this subcommittee lies in the fact that the subcommittee members bring so much knowledge to it and the subcommittee chairman takes so little away.

And I noticed in page 10 [page 343] of your statement that when you were first hit with the possibility of this responsibility, you indicated you wanted to talk to your wife before making a decision.

Mr. President, did you do that?

THE PRESIDENT. I certainly did, Mr. Chairman, because the probability or possibility of my becoming President obviously would have had a significant impact on her life as well as our lives.

CONGRESSMAN HUNGATE. That destroys my theory that, if you had talked to her, you would have waited until indictment or Christmas Eve, one or the other.

Let me ask if any attempt was made by you or your representative to contact the Federal Pardon Attorney as to his opinion as to customary procedures followed in issuing a pardon?

THE PRESIDENT. I did not, sir.

CONGRESSMAN HUNGATE. Mr. President, I go to page 20 [page 348] of the statement, and I am addressing myself to the health question. In the first responses provided, the press releases, in one of these, page 3, it refers to September 16 now as the date of this press conference after the pardon decision in which you were quoted, "I asked Dr. Lukash, who is the head physician in the White House, to keep me posted in proper channels as to the former President's health. I have been informed on a routine day-to-day basis, but I don't think I am at liberty to give information."

My question is, Mr. President, had he reported prior to the pardon date or only after?

THE PRESIDENT. Dr. Lukash gave me no information concerning President Nixon's health prior to the time that I issued the pardon. He did, at my request, when I heard rumors about the former President's health, keep me posted in proper channels, but that all occurred after the pardon took place.

CONGRESSMAN HUNGATE. The gentleman from Indiana is seeking recognition.

CONGRESSMAN DENNIS. Thank you, Mr. Chairman.

I would just like to request that we make a part of the record the text of the opinion of the United States Supreme Court in *Ex Parte Garland* 4 Wall. 333 and also the opinion of the United States Supreme Court in *Burdick* against *the United States,* 236 U.S. 79, which deals with the point that a pardon must be accepted.

CONGRESSMAN HUNGATE. Without objection, it will be made part of the record.

CONGRESSMAN DENNIS. Mr. Chairman, I would also like to make a part of the record, if I may, the article referred to by my colleague Mr. Hogan, which appeared in the Wall Street Journal of October 16, 1974, and is headed "The Pardon of Nixon Was Timely, Legal, Jaworski Believes."

CONGRESSMAN HUNGATE. Without objection, it is so ordered, and now briefly——

THE PRESIDENT. Mr. Chairman, may I add to something I said just to make it correct?

CONGRESSMAN HUNGATE. Yes, sir.

THE PRESIDENT. Somebody asked about when I last saw the President. I said that I had seen him on the 9th. I did as he departed, but I had also seen the President the morning of the 8th at the time I was asked to come and see him, and at that time we spent an hour and 20 minutes together, or thereabouts, when he told me that he was going to resign.

So, I saw him both the 8th and the 9th, just to make the record accurate.

CONGRESSMAN HUNGATE. All of us are aware of our time constraints. I yield to the gentleman from Wisconsin for a question.

CONGRESSMAN KASTENMEIER. Thank you, Mr. Chairman.

I would like to, for the record, indicate that the statement of the gentleman from Maryland, Mr. Hogan, the effect that the proposal that this subcommittee try to contact certain staff members, such as General Haig and others, was supported by me.

I think it would have been excellent. We have in the past done very well in terms of staff work preliminary to hearings that might have helped put some of the questions Ms. Holtzman had to rest.

Mr. President, you indicated that as far as Mr. Haig was concerned, that he had suggested certain options to you, but did not in fact make a recommendation to you with respect to the pardon, is that correct?

THE PRESIDENT. That is correct. I answered that, I think, as fully as I can in my prepared statement. He discussed the options. He made no recommendation.

CONGRESSMAN KASTENMEIER. Which other persons to you personally made recommendations that the former President be pardoned from that time in early August to the day of September 6 when you made your decision?

THE PRESIDENT. No other person, to my knowledge, made any recommendation to me from that time until the time that I made a decision about September 6; nobody made any recommendation to me for the pardon of the former President.

CONGRESSMAN KASTENMEIER. With respect to discussions between General Haig and Mr. Nixon, or other matters in question, too, you indicated you had no personal knowledge, both in writing and, I think, in your statement today.

I take it you would have no objection if the subcommittee sought to question Mr. Haig or others on the subject before us this morning to supplement this hearing and this inquiry?

THE PRESIDENT. I don't think that is within my prerogative. I have come here to testify as to the specific facts, as I know them, but what the subcommittee does is a judgment for the subcommittee and not me.

CONGRESSMAN KASTENMEIER. The Chair has advised that the House is in recess waiting for the conclusion of this hearing before reconvening, so if I might, I will yield to Mr. Hogan for a question at this point, and then to Ms. Holtzman for a question, and we will then conclude.

Mr. Hogan.

CONGRESSMAN HOGAN. Thank you, Mr. Chairman.

Mr. President, on page 20 [page 348] of your statement you talk about the health issue and that you had not gotten any official reports from physicians that were controlling in your decision. You state that observations were reported to you from others.

Now, there have been press reports that Dr. Kissinger is alleged to have said to you that he feared that former President Nixon would commit suicide. That's appeared in several news accounts. Is there any truth to that?

THE PRESIDENT. There is no truth to it whatsoever as far as I know.

CONGRESSMAN HOGAN. It appeared in the New York Times, the Washington Post on two occasions, and is alluded to in a research paper prepared for the subcommittee.

THE PRESIDENT. There was no discussion between Dr. Kissinger and myself that included any such comment.

CONGRESSMAN HOGAN. I think if I might add a gratuitous comment, Mr. Chairman, that much of the controversy has been generated by the press, by just such erroneous statements that have been given wide circulation.

Thank you, Mr. President.

CONGRESSMAN HUNGATE. I will ask for one concise question because we want to respect the time.

CONGRESSMAN EDWARDS. Thank you, Mr. Chairman. Mr. President, what were the precise instructions given to Benton Becker by you when he went to San Clemente to negotiate Mr. Nixon's acceptance of the pardon?

THE PRESIDENT. The precise instructions given to Mr. Becker were actually given by my Counsel, Mr. Buchen. In general I knew what they were. They were instructions to negotiate the protection of those documents, including the tapes, for the benefit of the Special Prosecutor in whatever use he felt was essential, and at the same time to keep them inviolate during a period of time which we felt was a proper one.

CONGRESSMAN EDWARDS. But not to offer the pardon unless that agreement had been negotiated?

THE PRESIDENT. Mr. Edwards, those negotiations as to the custody or ownership of the documents, including tapes, were undertaken prior to August 27, because we were more or less besieged—when I say "we," the White House—as to what to do with those documents, including tapes.

That negotiation had no relevance whatsoever to the decision on my part to pardon the President.

CONGRESSMAN HUNGATE. The Chair would remind all of the constraints of time, and call on Ms. Holtzman for one final question.

CONGRESSWOMAN HOLTZMAN. Thank you, Mr. Chairman.

Mr. Ford, you've stated that the theory on which you pardoned Richard Nixon was that he had suffered enough, and I am interested in that theory because the logical consequence of that is that somebody who resigns in the face of virtually certain impeachment or somebody who is impeached should not be punished because the impeachment or the resignation in face of impeachment is punishment enough.

And I wondered whether anybody had brought to your attention the fact the Constitution specifically states that even though somebody is impeached, that person shall nonetheless be liable to punishment according to law.

THE PRESIDENT. Ms. Holtzman, I was fully cognizant of the fact that the President on resignation was accountable for any criminal charges. But I would like to say that the reason I gave the pardon was not as to Mr. Nixon himself. I repeat, and I repeat with emphasis, the purpose of the pardon was to try and get the United States, the Congress, the President, and the American people focusing on the serious problems we have both at home and abroad, and I was absolutely convinced then, as I am now, that if we had this series—an indictment, a trial, a conviction, and anything else that transpired after that—that the attention of the President, the Congress, and the American people would have been diverted from the problems that we have to solve.

That was the principal reason for my granting of the pardon.

CONGRESSMAN HUNGATE. Mr. Smith.

CONGRESSMAN SMITH. Mr. Chairman, just before we adjourn this hearing, I again would like to commend the President and thank him for coming.

I think, Mr. President, that you have probably opened a new era between the executive and the legislative departments, and I am very happy for it.

THE PRESIDENT. Mr. Chairman, I want to express to you and to the other members of the committee or subcommittee my appreciation for the fine manner and, I think, the fair way in which this meeting was held this morning.

I felt that it was absolutely essential, because I am the only one who could explain the background and the decisionmaking process. And I hope, as I said in my opening statement, Mr. Chairman, that I have at least cleared the air so that most Americans will understand what was done and why it was done.

And again I trust that all of us can get back to the job of trying to solve our problems, both at home and abroad.

I thank you very, very much.

CONGRESSMAN HUNGATE. Mr. President, on behalf of the subcommittee, we express our appreciation to you for your appearance here today and recognition of the responsibility we all have to complete this work and get on with the business.

The transcripts will be furnished as quickly as possible to members of the subcommittee.

The subcommittee will adjourn subject to call of the Chair.

156

Veto of Second Continuing Appropriations Resolution Providing for Suspension of Military Aid to Turkey. *October 17, 1974*

To the House of Representatives:

I greatly regret that for the second time I must return without my approval the Continuing Resolution granting funds for the operation of several departments and agencies and for the temporary continuation of our foreign aid programs, H.J. Res. 1163.

My previous veto message and my public statements on this matter have clearly expressed our objectives with respect to the resolution of the Cyprus dispute as well as the dangers posed by legislative restrictions destroying our ability to assist the parties involved. The Congress, despite the best efforts of the bipartisan leaders of both Houses, has for the second time refused to recognize the realities of the situation.

While the language of this new bill is different, its effect is similar to the earlier Continuing Resolution which required my veto on October 14. I need not reiterate the extensive comments which I made at that time and which again compel a veto. The provisions of this bill as they would apply to Turkey would do nothing to bring an end to the suffering of the Cypriot people, would do nothing to encourage the two sides to resolve the dispute peacefully, and would bring a further deterioration of the posture of the NATO alliance in the crucial Eastern

Mediterranean. It is for these reasons and those previously stated that I must reluctantly veto the bill before me.

In addition, I am compelled to point out again that should this measure become law, the United States would have lost the ability to play a useful role in this dispute and would in effect have to withdraw from the negotiations. Should the Congress force such an action, it must do so in the clear knowledge that it assumes full responsibility for the situation which would then prevail.

I ask that the Congress not choose that path but that it reconsider its action and provide a bill which will permit the continued execution of United States foreign policy in a constructive and responsible manner.

GERALD R. FORD

The White House,
October 17, 1974.

NOTE: The House of Representatives sustained the President's veto on October 17, 1974.

157

Message to the Senate Transmitting Amendments to the International Convention for the Safety of Life at Sea. *October 17, 1974*

To the Senate of the United States:

I transmit herewith, for the advice and consent of the Senate, amendments to seven regulations contained in Chapters II, III, IV and V of the International Convention for the Safety of Life at Sea, 1960, and an amendment replacing and superseding the regulations in Chapter VI of that Convention, all of which were adopted on November 20, 1973, by the Assembly of the Inter-Governmental Maritime Consultative Organization (IMCO) at its eighth session.

The amendments to Chapters II, III, IV and V are directed toward the improvement of safety of navigation and were recommended by the Maritime Safety Committee of IMCO at its 24th through 27th sessions. The amendment to Chapter VI, Carriage of Grain, will replace and supersede the existing Chapter VI in its entirety. It is directed toward the improvement of safety requirements for the carriage of grain in bulk, and was recommended by the Maritime Safety Committee at its 27th session.

The United States Delegation to the IMCO Assembly actively supported the amendments, some of which had been formulated at United States initiative. The enclosed report of the Department of State provides additional information concerning the amendments.

The amendments represent significant improvements in the standards for ship safety. I recommend that the Senate give its advice and consent to acceptance of the amendments by the United States.

GERALD R. FORD

The White House,
October 17, 1974.

NOTE: The text of the amendments to the convention and accompanying papers are printed in Senate Executive K (93d Cong., 2d sess.).

158

Message to the Senate Transmitting the International Telecommunication Convention. *October 17, 1974*

To the Senate of the United States:

For advice and consent to ratification, I herewith transmit to the Senate the International Telecommunication Convention reached at Malaga-Torremolinos on October 25, 1973. This transmittal also includes the Annexes and Final Protocol to the Convention, as well as a report by the Department of State.

This new Convention will abrogate and replace the International Telecommunication Convention of 1965. It generally follows the provisions of the 1965 Convention with a considerable number of minor improvements and a few major modifications to take account of technical developments in the field and developments in international organizations.

One notable change from the 1965 Convention is the deletion of the separate membership of the territories of the several member States, including the United States. Although this change will deprive the United States of its vote on behalf of the territories, the redistribution of financial obligations which accompany this change will result in a relatively lower financial contribution from this country.

The International Telecommunication Convention constitutes the procedural and organizational framework for the orderly conduct of international telecommunications, and it is in the public and commercial interest of the United States to continue to play an active role within this framework. I recommend that the Senate give early and favorable consideration to this new Convention, and subject to a reservation noted in the State Department report, give its advice and consent to ratification.

GERALD R. FORD

The White House,
October 17, 1974.

NOTE: The text of the convention and accompanying papers are printed in Senate Executive J (93d Cong., 2d sess.).

159

Ramadan Message. *October 17, 1974*

ON THE occasion of the special feast days concluding Ramadan, Mrs. Ford and I wish to extend our warmest greetings to all Americans of the Islamic Faith.

For nearly two hundred years, our nation has derived its strength from the diversity of its people and of their beliefs. That strength has been greatly enhanced by your own religious heritage.

I am sure that the completion of your month of fasting will bring home to you more than ever the importance of religious responsibilities in daily life. Fellow citizens of all faiths join you in this sentiment. We will be with you in spirit as you reaffirm your commitment to principles which exalt man's existence.

May your celebration and the special message of these holy days fortify and uplift each of you and add to our vitality as a nation.

GERALD R. FORD

NOTE: The text of the message was issued by the White House.

160

Veto of Freedom of Information Act Amendments. *October 17, 1974*

To the House of Representatives:

I am returning herewith without my approval H.R. 12471, a bill to amend the public access to documents provisions of the Administrative Procedures Act. In August, I transmitted a letter to the conferees expressing my support for the direction of this legislation and presenting my concern with some of its provisions. Although I am gratified by the Congressional response in amending several of these provisions, significant problems have not been resolved.

First, I remain concerned that our military or intelligence secrets and diplomatic relations could be adversely affected by this bill. This provision remains unaltered following my earlier letter.

I am prepared to accept those aspects of the provision which would enable courts to inspect classified documents and review the justification for their classification. However, the courts should not be forced to make what amounts to the initial classification decision in sensitive and complex areas where they have no particular expertise. As the legislation now stands, a determination by the Secretary of Defense that disclosure of a document would endanger our national security would, even though reasonable, have to be overturned by a district judge who thought the plaintiff's position just as reasonable. Such a provision would violate constitutional principles, and give less weight before the courts to an executive determination involving the protection of our most vital national defense interests than is accorded determinations involving routine regulatory matters.

I propose, therefore, that where classified documents are requested the courts could review the classification, but would have to uphold the classification if there is a reasonable basis to support it. In determining the reasonableness of the classification, the courts would consider all attendant evidence prior to resorting to an *in camera* examination of the document.

Second, I believe that confidentiality would not be maintained if many millions of pages of FBI and other investigatory law enforcement files would be subject to compulsory disclosure at the behest of any person unless the Government could prove to a court—separately for each paragraph of each document—that disclosure "would" cause a type of harm specified in the amendment. Our law enforcement agencies do not have, and could not obtain, the large number of trained and knowledgeable personnel that would be needed to make such a line-by-line examination of information requests that sometimes involve hundreds of thousands of documents, within the time constraints added to current law by this bill.

Therefore, I propose that more flexible criteria govern the responses to requests for particularly lengthy investigatory records to mitigate the burden which these amendments would otherwise impose, in order not to dilute the primary responsibilities of these law enforcement activities.

Finally, the ten days afforded an agency to determine whether to furnish a requested document and the twenty days afforded for determinations on appeal are, despite the provision concerning unusual circumstances, simply unrealistic in some cases. It is essential that additional latitude be provided.

I shall submit shortly language which would dispel my concerns regarding the manner of judicial review of classified material and for mitigating the administrative burden placed on the agencies, especially our law enforcement agencies, by the bill as presently enrolled. It is only my conviction that the bill as enrolled is unconstitutional and unworkable that would cause me to return the bill without my approval. I sincerely hope that this legislation, which has come so far toward realizing its laudable goals, will be reenacted with the changes I propose and returned to me for signature during this session of Congress.

GERALD R. FORD

The White House,
October 17, 1974.

NOTE: H.R. 12471 was enacted over the President's veto on November 21, 1974, as Public Law 93–502 (88 Stat. 1561).

161

Remarks on Signing the Emergency Home Purchase Assistance Act of 1974. *October 18, 1974*

LET ME at the outset express my appreciation to the Congress for responding so quickly and, I think, basically so well, in passing this housing legislation, which is needed for an industry that is in serious trouble.

We cannot tolerate a building program at the present rate for homebuilding. And this legislation which the Congress has passed will materially help, in my judgment, in turning the corner as far as the housing industry is concerned.

It is not enough, and other things have to be done, but it will provide a shot in the arm for the housing industry. I regret, of course, that it didn't include condominiums and apartments, but be that as it may, it is good legislation. We will make it work.

I wish there was a little more flexibility in one or two of the provisions, but nevertheless, considering the time factor, I compliment the Congress for moving so quickly and, particularly, Senator Cranston and Senator Brooke, who were instrumental in the first instance. But I think the credit goes to the Congress as a whole in moving ahead so rapidly at a time when the housing industry needed help.

So, it is a privilege and a pleasure for me to sign this bill in the presence of a number of Members who had a very major factor in making this possible.

I do thank you all very, very much. As I said, we are going to move ahead, I hope, in some other areas, and we will get a lot more homes built.

Thank you all for being here.

I should have said the Secretary is going to start implementing, I think, this next Tuesday. I do want to compliment the Secretary, who I think worked with the Congress and did a fine job in moving with the Congress and getting it through, and now he is going to make it work.

Thank you.

NOTE: The President spoke at 10:36 a.m. in the Cabinet Room at the White House. In his remarks, the President referred to Secretary of Housing and Urban Development James T. Lynn.

As enacted, the bill (S. 3979) is Public Law 93–449 (88 Stat. 1364).

162

Statement on the Emergency Home Purchase Assistance Act of 1974. *October 18, 1974*

IT IS with great pleasure today that I am signing into law S. 3979, the Emergency Home Purchase Assistance Act of 1974.

In my remarks to the joint session of the Congress on October 8, I urged the Congress to enact, before recess, additional legislation to make most home mortgages eligible for purchase by an agency of the Federal Government. I also remarked that I remembered how much Congress can get done when it wants to.

I am most pleased that exactly one week after my remarks, the Congress responded with passage of the Emergency Home Purchase Assistance Act of 1974.

This bill authorizes the Government National Mortgage Association in the Department of Housing and Urban Development to make commitments at predetermined interest rates to purchase mortgages, both on new and existing homes, which are not Federal Housing Administration insured or Veterans Administration guaranteed—the so-called "conventional" mortgages which comprise about 80 percent of all mortgages. The advantage of the plan is that with the GNMA commitment, the home buyer, builder, and lender have an assured source of financing at a known, favorable interest rate. The cost to the Government is limited to the loss which GNMA realizes if its selling price for a mortgage is less than its original purchase price.

Like most emergency measures, this bill has some minuses. Notwithstanding the increasing proportion of American families that choose each year to live in apartments or condominiums, the bill unfortunately does not cover conventional mortgages for apartment or condominium projects. Moreover, I had hoped that this help for the housing industry could be delivered with a minimum inflationary impact, and I know that the Congress intended the program to be self-supporting. However, the bill establishes a rigid, illogical interest ceiling formula that fails to relate interest income to actual borrowing costs and to cover adequately administrative costs.

163

Remarks at the Dedication of the New Department of Labor Building. *October 18, 1974*

Secretary Brennan, Secretary Weinberger, Administrator Sampson, former Secretaries of Labor, distinguished leaders of organized labor, reverend clergy:

It is really a great privilege and pleasure for me to have the opportunity of saying a few words this morning and to subsequently participate in the cornerstone laying.

Now, let me at the outset say that at the White House this morning I received an honorary membership in the Bricklayers, Masons and Plasterers, from Tom Murphy.[1] This was the shortest apprenticeship that any bricklayer, mason, or plasterer ever went through. But I thank them, nevertheless.

And may I add to what the Secretary of Labor said a moment ago. He gave me, as I came to the podium, this wonderful resolution signed by those who were here, and some are here this morning—the vocational industrial youth organization. I thank them and express my deep gratitude for their resolution.[2]

Well, Mr. Secretary and distinguished guests, this building will house the administration of programs that vividly demonstrate America's sense of concern, compassion, and equity.

Enormous progress, as you have mentioned, Mr. Secretary, has been made since 1913 when the Department of Labor started its work. Its most urgent concern then, as we look back on history, was child labor. Unemployment insurance and workmen's compensation did not exist at that time. Neither did the dozens

[1] Thomas F. Murphy, president of the Bricklayers, Masons and Plasterers International Union of America.

[2] The Vocational Industrial Clubs of America, Inc., during their national leadership conference, held October 12–18, 1974, in Washington, D.C., passed a resolution of support for the President's WIN (Whip Inflation Now) program.

and dozens of other programs of assistance to America's working men and women.

Since 1913, which, incidentally, was the year that I was born, the United States has protected workers with a very broad network of legislation and administrative safeguards.

In recent years, we have sought to attack the problems of hard-core unemployment. We have sought to assist the chronically unemployed who lack the skills required for today's job market.

Over the past 10 years, the manpower training programs of the Department helped provide over 9½ million workers with the skills needed to move up that important job ladder. Working standards have been upgraded as they should have been, and job discrimination has been curbed, although, I think we have to recognize, not totally ended. We will work on that; we will continue to make a maximum effort in that regard.

I am very, very proud, Mr. Secretary, of the 13,000 people who work in this Department, and I am told some 5,000 will work in this new building.

In demonstrating the competence and the creativity of their work, they help State and local governments cut through Federal redtape and afford these units maximum latitude in adapting programs to local needs.

The 13,000 people that work for the Department, not only here but all over the world—primarily, of course, in our country—they help to build a constructive State-Federal relationship.

In short, they help the working people of this country who we all recognize are the indispensable ingredient of America's greatness.

During the economic summit meeting last month, I got some good advice from Secretary Brennan and from our national labor leaders on how to cope with our number one problem, a problem which affects every citizen, every worker, every one of us. And of course, I refer to public enemy number one—inflation.

What is needed to whip inflation, it was suggested, are compassionate, sensible, equitable policies presented to the American people with honesty and with candor.

In outlining my programs to Congress to overcome this threat, I tried my very best to meet this standard, to offer policies that are compassionate, that are sensible, and of course, are equitable.

In calling on the American people to join in this effort, I used the very same yardstick. And let me, if I might, emphasize this particular point. Whatever they deal with, whether the economy at home or our foreign relations abroad, the programs and policies of this Administration will continue to be predicated on the same basic principles.

Now, Mr. Secretary and distinguished guests, the building we dedicate today demonstrates that Labor Day is not confined to a single day in September. Every day is Labor Day in the view of this Administration toward America's working men and women.

I thank you very, very much.

NOTE: The President spoke at 11:28 a.m. In his opening remarks, the President referred to Arthur F. Sampson, Administrator of General Services; Arthur J. Goldberg, Secretary of Labor 1961–62; and W. Willard Wirtz, Secretary of Labor 1962–69.

164

Statement on Signing the Continuing Appropriations Resolution. *October 18, 1974*

I HAVE signed, with serious reservations, the continuing resolution (H. J. Res. 1167) providing necessary funds after a 3-week delay for the operation of several departments and agencies and for the temporary continuation of our foreign aid programs.

Despite two vetoes of similar versions of this bill and my public statements concerning the damage to our diplomacy that would result from its restrictions on military aid to Turkey, Congress has nevertheless persisted by clear majorities in a course which I consider ill-advised and dangerous.

The restrictions imposed in this bill on our military assistance to Turkey create serious problems. Without substantial benefit to any other country, these restrictions threaten our relations with a country which is a close ally, which is the eastern anchor of an alliance vital to the security of the United States, and which plays a fundamental role in the strategic interests of the United States in the Eastern Mediterranean area. It is for these reasons—the national security interests of the United States—that we have been providing military assistance to Turkey.

The problem created by these legislative restrictions with respect to our relations with Turkey are not compensated for in any way by benefits to Greece or the Greek Cypriots. Contrary to the intentions of the supporters of these restrictions, this bill can only hinder progress toward a settlement of the Cypriot dispute which is so much in the interest of both Greece and the people of Cyprus.

As a result of my vetoes of two earlier versions of this continuing resolution, the Congress has eased the most troublesome of the earlier restrictions. Nevertheless, the risks created by the remaining ones fail to provide compensating benefits. I will, of course, do my best to accomplish the goals which we had set before the Congress took this action. Whatever we can still do to assist in resolving the Cyprus dispute will be done. But if we fail despite our best efforts, those in the Congress who overrode the Congressional leadership must bear the full responsibility for that failure.

NOTE: As enacted, H.J. Res. 1167, approved October 17, 1974, is Public Law 93–448 (88 Stat. 1363).

165

Memorandum on Federal Energy Conservation. *October 18, 1974*

MEMORANDUM FOR HEADS OF DEPARTMENTS AND AGENCIES
SUBJECT: Energy Conservation by the Federal Government

Last year, Federal agencies were directed to reduce anticipated energy use during fiscal year 1974 by seven percent. I have now been advised that actual results for the year will show a reduction of about 24% from anticipated energy demand—more than tripling the original objective. This savings is equivalent to about 90 million barrels of oil and $725 million in energy costs to the Federal taxpayer. Part of this savings was due to the severe petroleum shortages we experienced during the embargo and to the mild winter, but the total savings reflects serious and dedicated efforts to conserve energy.

I congratulate you and your employees for this fine achievement. The success of the Federal Energy Management Program provides an excellent example for all Americans, both of what can be accomplished in efforts to conserve energy and of the dedication and sacrifice which employees of the Federal Government are bringing to this important task.

I hereby direct that the Federal Energy Management Program be continued through fiscal year 1975. I am today establishing a new energy conservation goal for the Federal agencies for fiscal year 1975 of 15 percent savings below energy consumed in fiscal year 1973. This will result in energy savings equivalent to approximately 55 million barrels of oil during the year.

To achieve this new savings goal, it is imperative that all Federal agencies examine facilities and operations, including Government owned–contractor operated activities, for energy conservation potential during the remainder of this year. In addition, I am asking the Administrators of the Federal Energy

Administration and General Services Administration to recommend to Secretary Morton, Chairman of the Energy Resources Council, a multi-year program to increase energy efficiency of all Federal facilities and operations. These two officials will also provide instructions and guidelines to assist you in evaluating the economic efficiency of energy conservation improvements.

I look forward to your continued cooperation and assistance in this energy conservation effort.

GERALD R. FORD

166

Statement on Federal Energy Conservation. *October 18, 1974*

DURING the past month, I have made clear that the United States must and will act to increase its energy independence. One effective way—which can have immediate payoff—is to reduce unnecessary energy demands.

Today, I have ordered that the Federal Government continue during the current fiscal year its energy savings program. I have directed that agencies hold energy consumption to levels 15 percent below the amount consumed in fiscal year 1973. In addition, I have instructed the Administrators of the Federal Energy Administration and General Services Administration to recommend to Secretary Morton, Chairman of the Energy Resources Council, a multi-year program to assure that energy efficiency is considered in all decisions involving Federal facilities and operations.

Last year, actions by Federal agencies saved the equivalent of 90 million barrels of oil. Both these accomplishments and these new goals can serve as examples for all sectors—for business and industry, State and local governments, and for all our citizens in their daily activities.

The new objective for Federal energy conservation is one step. We are now working with industry to find ways to reduce energy requirements for its activities and products. We will continue working with all sectors to find other steps that can be taken to conserve energy.

I again urge all Americans to join in this effort with serious voluntary actions to conserve energy. All of us contribute daily to the demand for energy. We can all act to reduce that demand.

167

Remarks on Signing a Drug Abuse Prevention Week Proclamation. *October 18, 1974*

I AM ABOUT to sign the Drug Abuse Prevention Week proclamation [4328], and I will sign it in the presence of these three very important members of the team that gives leadership to our effort in trying to handle the entry of drugs from outside of the country, the handling of those who abuse our laws as far as drugs are concerned, and the problem of trying to, through research, find answers to the drug problem in advance.

So, on this occasion, it is a privilege for me to sign this proclamation, which I hope will have an impact on our very sizable effort of about $750 million a year in meeting the challenge of the drug problem in the United States.

Thank you very much, gentlemen.

NOTE: The President spoke at 2:45 p.m. in the Cabinet Room at the White House. Present at the signing ceremony were Ambassador Sheldon B. Vance, Senior Adviser to the Secretary of State and Coordinator for International Narcotics Matters; Dr. Robert L. DuPont, Director of the Special Action Office for Drug Abuse Prevention; and John R. Bartels, Administrator of the Drug Enforcement Administration, Department of Justice.

Following the signing ceremony, the participants met with the President to discuss current Government efforts to control drug abuse through treatment, law enforcement, and international incentives.

168

Joint Communique Following Discussions With President Francisco da Costa Gomes of Portugal. *October 18, 1974*

AT THE INVITATION of President Ford, His Excellency Francisco da Costa Gomes, President of the Republic of Portugal, visited Washington on October 18. President Costa Gomes, who was accompanied by the Foreign Minister, Dr. Mario Soares, had meetings with President Ford and with Secretary of State Kissinger and was the guest of honor at a luncheon given by Secretary Kissinger.

President Costa Gomes outlined the achievements of the Portuguese Government in light of recent events in restoring civil and political liberties to Portugal and in creating the basis for a return to democracy. He reported on the negotiations which had led to the independence of Guinea-Bissau and explained his government's plans for the granting of self-determination and independence to the remaining overseas territories. He reaffirmed his government's commitment to the North Atlantic Treaty and its desire to develop even closer ties to the United States.

President Ford expressed his admiration for the statesmanship shown by Portuguese leaders in undertaking to restore democracy to Portugal by holding free elections soon and in making possible the enjoyment of the right of self-determination and independence by the peoples of Portugal's overseas territories. He noted with pleasure President Costa Gomes' reaffirmation of Portugal's commitment to NATO and expressed his confidence that ties between the United States and Portugal will become ever closer.

The two Presidents agreed that, as these developments proceed, it would be in our mutual interest to intensify the cooperation between the two countries to embrace new activities in a broad range of areas, such as education, health, energy, agriculture, transportation and communications, among others. They agreed that this expansion of their cooperation could begin with technical talks in the fields of agriculture, public health, education and financial and economic matters, as requested by the Portuguese authorities.

They also agreed that the two countries should continue and intensify negotiations relating to cooperation in the Azores.

169

Letter to the Chairman of the National Cancer Advisory Board About Regulation of Cigarette Tar and Nicotine Content. *October 18, 1974*

Dear Dr. Rhoads:

I have received and reviewed a preliminary copy of the 1974 annual report of the National Cancer Advisory Board.

In several places, the Board's report recommends Federal regulation of the tar and nicotine content of cigarettes. The report does not, however, provide an assessment of the scientific evidence at hand which should provide the basis for such regulation.

In order that all concerned may be fully informed, I would like to request that the National Cancer Advisory Board review the existing scientific evidence on an urgent basis and provide me with an assessment of the extent to which there exists a scientific basis for responsible regulation of cigarettes.

I recognize that all questions of regulation necessarily involve a certain amount of reasonable disagreement as well as the exercise of sound judgment. Nevertheless, it is critically important that our judgments be soundly based so that we may proceed with the greatest amount of wisdom.

I know I can count on the National Cancer Advisory Board to provide me with scientific advice on this important matter of public concern. I would greatly appreciate the Board's assessment by December 1, 1974.

Sincerely,

GERALD R. FORD

[The Honorable Jonathan E. Rhoads, Department of Surgery, School of Medicine, University of Pennsylvania, 36th and Hamilton Walk, Philadelphia, Pa. 19104]

170

Remarks at Spartanburg, South Carolina. *October 19, 1974*

Strom Thurmond, Jesse Helms over here, and Secretary Dent, my old friend General Westmoreland, and Mayor Baehr, and all of you from South Carolina:

As I said a moment ago, it is a great privilege and pleasure to be back in South Carolina. I have had this opportunity on a number of occasions in the past over the years, and I thank you now for the warm hospitality extended me then. And I deeply appreciate this tremendous crowd, the wonderful enthusiasm here on this occasion at this airport, and I can't express deeply enough my gratitude, my appreciation. Just thank you very, very much.

But let me say I am here primarily for three, maybe four reasons. Number one, I am here to enlist every one of you as well as all of your friends throughout the State of South Carolina in our WIN effort, which is to "Whip Inflation Now."

And I am here—and I am proud to be—to indicate my pride in the Republican candidates for State and Federal offices in the great State of South Carolina.

I am also here to extend my acquaintanceship, my friendship with people in the State of South Carolina. The ones that I have known and gotten acquainted with over the years are the kind of people we Michiganders like, and I hope I can find many, many more like you in the travels through the State of South Carolina today.

Within the last 10 days or 2 weeks, on two occasions I addressed myself to the basic problems we face in the Nation—number one, to whip inflation; number two, to keep our economy strong and growing; and number three, to enlist every one of you as well as 213 million other Americans in this effort which involves saving not only our economy through prudent use of our funds, through the prudent use of our energy but through the efforts of every one of you in wasting less and saving more.

Now let me speak, if I might, as to how you can participate and cooperate. You see on my lapel here a button that says W-I-N, WIN. It means "Whip Inflation Now."

So far, in the White House we have received over 100,000 communications from citizens all over this great country—rich, poor, old, young—individuals who understand that it is essential, it is vital, that if we are to preserve our way of life, our economy, our Government, that we have to enlist in this battle, a battle to save America.

And so I urge every one of you here to write the White House, and we will send you a WIN button which indicates that you have pledged yourself and that you will get others to join in this struggle which is crucial to the future of our great country.

Now in this program that I submitted to the Congress about 10 days ago, there were 31 different proposals. It was a comprehensive program aimed at winning the battle against inflation, keeping our economy strong and constructive and moving forward. It was a plan and a program to conserve energy and to develop our natural resources so we would have more supplies and not be in a practical problem of allocating shortages.

Now the Congress has a responsibility to move on that program, and one of the ingredients of that program was to ask the Congress to set a ceiling of $300 billion on Federal spending which would amount to about a $5.4 billion saving.

I regret to tell you that the Congress has not sent to my desk this spending limitation.

Now what we need in Congress are candidates who will cut redtape, who will cut the budget, and, in effect, cut the mustard. And I urge you to make sure that the ones you elect this fall meet those criteria.

Now, let me say a word or two, if I might, about some of the gentlemen that have appeared here, others you will see between now and November 5. I indicated at the outset that I am proud of the candidates that the Republican Party have fielded in the State of South Carolina. They are good people. They are seeking to give to you and South Carolina competition.

A long time ago I competed in college athletics, and I found there that competition was good for everybody. Later, I practiced law, and I found that competition in the legal field was good. I have been in the Congress, or I was in the Congress, for almost 26 years. I found that competition in Congress was good for America. Competition is one of the basic ingredients of the American system.

Competition is good for everybody. And so I am proud to be here and to say that in Jim Edwards, Carroll Campbell,[2] you have good candidates for the two highest State offices in South Carolina.

They are the kind that believe in reform. They have experience in State government. And I think all of you would be proud to support their candidacy.

But I am also delighted to be in South Carolina to speak up with pride for Gwen Bush, Marshall Parker, Len Phillips, Bob Watkins.[3] These are candidates who come from you, the people of South Carolina, who want to represent you.

And it seems to me that it is important in South Carolina, as it is in every one of the other 49 States, that we develop this competition, a strong two-party system, that will give to all of you in this great State an opportunity to make a choice.

And as I said a moment ago, I am proud of the people that my party has fielded to give you that choice.

I happen to know Floyd Spence and Ed Young from your State who served with me in the House of Representatives—fine, fine Members of Congress. They represent your State with the kind of forward-looking attitude, the kind of voting record, that is good for your State and good for our Nation.

And of course, it has been my privilege over a long period of time to know your great Senator, Strom Thurmond, who has the same point of view, the same strength.

So, let me just say that in Strom Thurmond, Ed Young, Floyd Spence, we have given you the kind of people that I think are good for your State, are good for our country. And I hope and trust, as you meditate and contemplate between now and November 5, you will feel, as I do, the pride in the kind of candidates that are represented by the party that is headed by Strom Thurmond in the great State of South Carolina.

Thank you very, very much.

NOTE: The President spoke at 9:22 a.m. at the Greenville-Spartanburg Jet Airport. In his opening remarks, the President referred to Gen. William C. Westmoreland, USA (Ret.), United States Army Chief of Staff 1968–72, and John Baehr, mayor of Spartanburg, S.C.

---

[2] State Senator James B. Edwards was the Republican candidate for Governor of South Carolina, and State Representative Carroll A. Campbell, Jr., was the Republican candidate for Lieutenant Governor.

[3] Republican candidates for United States Senator and for Congress from the Third, Fifth, and Fourth Districts of South Carolina, respectively.

171

Remarks at the Dedication of the Anderson Independent and Anderson Daily Mail Building in Anderson, South Carolina. *October 19, 1974*

Governor West, Senator Thurmond, Senator Hollings, John Ginn—distinguished president and chairman of the board—the owners of these two fine newspapers, the wonderful citizens of the Third Congressional District in the State of South Carolina:

It is a very high privilege and a great honor for me to have the opportunity of being in Anderson on this occasion, and I thank you for your warm and very friendly welcome. It is just nice to be here.

I am here for four reasons, and let me indicate them at the outset.

I am here because I like the people of South Carolina. I am here because I like the philosophy, the political philosophy of the people of South Carolina. I am also here to do a little selling on a program that I think will strengthen America and make us stronger and better and make us even more proud of a great country, the United States of America. And I am here to participate in an auspicious occasion, the dedication of this fine facility for these two outstanding newspapers.

As I said at the outset, I am here because I like the people of South Carolina. And I think, since I have been in South Carolina four times in the last 12 or 13 months, I have some individuals on the platform who can attest—Governor West, Senator Thurmond, Senator Hollings, they have been with me on several or all of these occasions—and they know from firsthand experience that the people of South Carolina have a deep affection in my heart. I like what they believe, and I like how they react, and you are just darned nice people. I thank you for your hospitality.

I also indicated that I have a great sympathy for and adherence to the philosophy of the people of South Carolina. I know that you in South Carolina believe that it is important to have strong local government and to have strong State government, and you also believe in the freedom and independence of the individual.

You also recognize that the Federal Government is important, but you want your Federal Government to be a partner and not the dominating force as the problems arise and the solutions are sought.

You believe in a partnership between State, local, and Federal government. And that is the kind of philosophy in which I believe.

There is another little observation I would like to make—and I don't mean to be critical of those who differ with me—but oftentimes in the 25-plus years that I served in the Congress of the United States, I saw well-intentioned individuals in the House as well as in the Senate who believed that if they gave and gave and gave to individuals that in the long run perhaps that was helpful and beneficial.

But oftentimes, as I sat in the Chamber of the House of Representatives and watched this effort being made, I frequently wondered whether those who pushed and worked for those programs of piling one Federal program on top of another day after day after day, whether they ever realized and recognized that a government big enough to give you everything you want is a government big enough to take from you everything you have.

We want a government that does what we as individuals can't do, but we don't want a government in Washington so big that at some time or some point down the road, it can take from us everything we have.

One of the things that I liked about Marshall Parker is that I feel that his philosophy and mine coincide almost identically. And Marshall, it is nice to see you, and I thank you for your very kind and friendly words.

As I said, I am here to do a little propagandizing and selling for a program that I think is good for America. We, as a nation, I found in the 60 or 70 days that I have been President, we have some problems. We have the problem of inflation. We have the problem of trying to keep the economy strong and get it stronger so that we have jobs, that we have profits, that we have a better, better life for all our people.

And so, about 10 days or 2 weeks ago, I submitted to the Congress and to the American people a 31-point program. I think it is well thought out, I think it is well-constructed, so it would follow that important path of whipping inflation on the one hand and providing a strong economy on the other.

I am confident that the Congress will support it. They did some things before their recess that began yesterday or the day before. There is more on the matter to be done when they return after November 5.

But also, it is important that 213 million Americans, individually as well as collectively, join in this struggle to keep America strong.

We have these WIN buttons—W-I-N—"Whip Inflation Now." We have had already over 100,000 people write the White House enlisting in this crusade. And I urge that every one of you here do exactly the same—waste less, save more, and build a better America, conserve our energy, and tackle the problems of inflation, and strengthen the longrun economy of the greatest country in the history of mankind.

The fourth reason I am here is to speak about the importance of the news media and to congratulate the owners, publishers of these two fine newspapers.

Now I have been warned on occasion that it is sometimes risky to expose myself to the press. I don't happen to necessarily agree with that philosophy, although I did have a press conference in the Rose Garden the other day at the White House, and I must confess that not everything turned out or turned up roses.

But those are the problems you face in meeting the good friends of the news media. But, as it should be and in keeping with my own personal philosophy of being as accessible as possible to the press, I intend to continue frequent, open, friendly meetings with the news media. I think that is good for the country, for the press, and I hope for myself.

And although I wouldn't call this gathering here today a press conference, I am delighted to participate in the dedication of the new Anderson Independent and the Anderson Daily Mail building. I congratulate the owners, the publishers, the employees, and also the subscribers, because you are all an integral part of the dissemination of the news thoroughly, accurately, and without fear of reprisal. And I know that what comes from these two newspapers will be in the highest traditions of the news media.

I hope to continue the traditions that I established as a Member of Congress and as Vice President of meeting with the press, and I hope and trust that the relationship that I have had with the press will continue.

I don't think I do things any differently today than I did when I was a Member of the Congress or even as Vice President. The only difference seems to be that they pay more attention to what I say. [*Laughter*]

There have been a lot of changes in America in all of our lifetimes, but there is one thing that must be preserved above all others. And I refer here very specifically to the first amendment and all of the rest of the Constitution that Senator Thurmond, Senator Hollings, myself, at the Federal level, and Governor West have sworn to uphold, and that is the Constitution of the United States—the greatest document ever written in the history of mankind—that gives more freedom and more opportunity to more people than any other document drafted by man.

Now we must have a climate of trust and understanding between the Government and the people. This is essential if our system is to work. The Anderson newspapers and the rest of America's press have much to do with that climate, and of course, so do those of us who hold high office.

Now I don't put as much emphasis on public relations as I do on human relations. As John Ginn said—I will say it a little differently—we can all disagree without being disagreeable. That is an important ingredient in maintaining progress in America.

I don't think it is the function of the press to propagandize for any party, any President, or any section of the public. They, as well as the rest of us, should call them as we see them. And I say to every journalist on the occasion of this dedication that I am particularly pleased to see a new building housing two fine newspapers at a time in our Nation's history when too many newspapers have been folding throughout the Nation.

We need more, not fewer, news media and including newspapers. Every reporter, as I see it, is now under an even greater responsibility to report without fear and without favor, and every newspaper has the responsibility to keep alive the tradition of a free press.

Now I happen to differ with those who categorize the journalists I know, and others, as a different kind of American. I prefer to consider everyone on his or her merits and to treat each one of them as I would expect to be treated if our jobs were reversed. I think this is the way we have to deal with one another, whether it is a politician and the news media, or a politician and a constituent, or a competitor in one business or another.

And although I have had a lot of adversaries in my lifetime in the political arena, to my knowledge I have no enemies, nor will I ever have a list of enemies in this White House that I now occupy.

Now there are four of us on the platform who have had a few years, if you total them all up, in political life. And Marshall Parker, of course, was in your State legislature and is seeking election to the Congress of the United States. And if I might just say one nice thing in addition about Marshall, he is the kind of guy I would like to have in the House of Representatives.

But the point I was trying to make is that between the Governor and Strom and Fritz [1] and Marshall and myself, we have been exposed to the press, and I suspect all of us in one way or another have been criticized by the press. I am not sure any one of us like it particularly.

But what is more important, I would be more concerned if the press of this country were not free to criticize me or the others that I have mentioned.

But let me say that the ceremony we have undertaken is a dedication to the perpetuation of a free press and the great role that the press plays in our society. And any time I can participate in an occasion that pays tribute to one part or all of our Constitution, I am honored and pleased.

[1] Senator Ernest F. Hollings of South Carolina.

And so, I congratulate John Ginn and his associates. I congratulate all of you. I thank you again.

And join me in that campaign to WIN. We don't want to be a loser. We will be a winner for America.

Thank you very, very much.

NOTE: The President spoke at 10:40 a.m. Prior to his remarks, the President participated in the unveiling of the dedicatory plaque for the building.

172

Remarks in Rock Hill, South Carolina. *October 19, 1974*

Len Phillips, Strom Thurmond, Mayor Lyle, distinguished guests, ladies and gentlemen:

It is a real thrill to be here in Rock Hill, to see this tremendous gathering, and to see the enthusiasm that you have and the warm welcome that you are giving me. I thank you from the bottom of my heart.

Now, some of you may not have noticed when this fine young lady came up to give the Pledge of Allegiance. I shook hands with her and thanked her, Len Phillips shook hands and thanked her, but you know what Strom Thurmond did? He kissed her. [*Laughter*]

Well, you know we have had a wonderful day so far. We were in Spartanburg, we were in Anderson, and now we are here in Rock Hill. It is obvious to me that when you get a little tired, the days get a little long. It is great to come to South Carolina and get revitalized.

I found that it gives you new life. Don't take my word for it. Ask Strom Thurmond. [*Laughter*]

You know, the motto of the sovereign State of South Carolina is "Prepared in Spirit and Resources." Strom Thurmond certainly has that. In fact, there are 2 days in particular when Strom really proves that he is prepared in spirit and in resources. One is election day, the other is Father's Day. [*Laughter*]

I do, of course, want to add something that I say from the bottom of my heart. I have known Strom Thurmond all the time that I have been in Congress, the Vice Presidency, and the Presidency, and I can say nothing but the very finest about your senior Senator.

He is strong, he is courageous, he is intelligent, he is dedicated, he is a great Senator, and I admire him, as I am sure all of you do.

But Strom and I need some help. Strom needs a good, strong Congressman from the Fifth Congressional District in the great State of South Carolina, and Len Phillips will be that on November 5.

During the day, I have had an opportunity to talk to Len. I know that Len Phillips has worked to develop his own business, and in the process of making that business successful, he has learned that you have to pay your bills. He has learned that you have to run a business effectively, that you have to take in more than you spend. And Len Phillips also knows that that is the way you ought to run the Federal Government.

Strom Thurmond was telling me on the way over here today that in the last 23 years, the Federal Government has balanced its budget, I think, 5 out of the 23. That is not a very good record. You couldn't run your household, your church, your business, your Boy Scout organization, your schools with that kind of record.

Now what we need in Washington to win the battle against inflation, among other things, is Members of the House as well as Members of the Senate who will stand up and be counted and spend less, so we can win the battle against inflation.

And Len Phillips will help Strom Thurmond and me in that most important, vital, essential responsibility.

I came down here for the purpose of renewing my acquaintanceship with many people of South Carolina. I came down to make some new friends. I came down here also for the purpose of enlisting all of you in the battle against inflation.

Now Strom and Len Phillips and I, we can do part of the job, but if we are going to win this battle against inflation, with those words up there—WIN—and with that button that I have—and I see many on others, "Whip Inflation"—we have to have your help.

About 10 days ago, I gave a speech to the Congress of the United States, and I laid out in cold turkey 31 proposals whereby we could have a plan and a program to WIN. The Congress has a part of it, the President has a part of it, and all of you have a part of it with 213 million other Americans.

One hundred thousand-plus have written to the White House in the last week or so and enlisted. I urge you, every one of you, to join with Strom and Len Phillips and myself, enlist in the battle against inflation so that we can win for America.

I have said, and I think we all must concede, that inflation is public enemy number one. The plan and the program that I have suggested, that I have proposed, recommended, will put the lid on inflation. At the same time, it will do those things that are needed and necessary to provide us an expanding economy, a strong economy, a good economy.

But if we don't win this battle by conserving energy, by doing the other things that are an integral and important part of it, the great blessings of this country will not be for our younger generation.

I admire the sacrifices that have been made by the senior citizens who are here. I admire and respect you, and we thank you. You have done much to give us all what we have today.

But we have an obligation to these young people in the bands, in the Boy Scouts, the Camp Fire Girls, the Girl Scouts. We have an obligation to them, as this group had to us.

And so what we have to do is join the ranks, arm-in-arm, shoulder-to-shoulder, to spend less, and that means spend less of your taxpayer dollars so that we will have more for you to spend for yourself, for your city, for your State, for your country.

One of the important things to me and something that I like and enjoy about people from South Carolina is the political philosophy that you have—a philosophy that says yes. The government at the local, State, and Federal level, they are important, but the philosophy that you have—that you can stand and will stand on your own two feet—is what I believe in, and I respect you, I admire you for it.

Now we recognize that there are circumstances and problems that are beyond the scope and beyond the capability of individuals. But there are, unfortunately, people in the Congress and elsewhere in our society who think every problem has to be solved by some Government program or excessive Federal spending.

I don't agree with that. But what worries me, what worries me is that the people who have this philosophy are too strong, are getting too much of a stranglehold on some of our areas in our Federal Government and elsewhere. What they don't tell us when they propose all these benefits that they are going to give you from our Government, they don't tell you the end result, the final conclusion. They don't inform you that a government big enough to give us everything we want is a government big enough to take from us everything we have.

Now, South Carolina is one of the great States of this Union. South Carolina has had a long history and tradition of being strong in a crisis, whether it was from outside our continental limits, or whether it was from within. You have measured up to the challenges abroad and at home.

And you in South Carolina know that the strength of our form of government is one of balance. You had people that represented your great State when our Founding Fathers drafted the Constitution and when they went to the city of Philadelphia and put together that Constitution. They wove into it the concept of balance: a strong President in the White House, a strong Congress in the legislative branch, a strong judicial system, headed by the Supreme Court, a system of checks and balances to protect freedom and give opportunity to everybody to move ahead and live their own private lives.

But at some moments in our history there has been a shift of that balance. Now there are people who want to impose on this system a veto-proof Congress.

What does that mean? It means that they want to remove the checks and balances. They want all power in the Congress. The American people want balance for the protection of themselves, their families, their local, their State government.

We don't want a veto-proof Congress. We want a Congress that will reflect your views in Rock Hill, your views in South Carolina, working in a partnership with the President. And so, instead of a veto-proof Congress, I urge you to give me an inflation-proof Congress in November.

And I say from the bottom of my heart—because I know what he stands for, I know what his philosophy is, I know he has courage, I know he has character, I know he has background and experience—you can help Strom Thurmond in his struggles to do a good job in the United States Senate, you can help me, you can help yourself, you can help the State of South Carolina, you can help America by electing Len Phillips to the United States Congress.

Thank you very, very much.

NOTE: The President spoke at 12:27 p.m. at the Rock Hill Mall. In his opening remarks, the President referred to David Lyle, mayor of Rock Hill, S.C.

173

Remarks in Greenville, South Carolina. *October 19, 1974*

Distinguished guests at the head table, all of you wonderful South Carolinians:

It is just a wonderful experience for me to be here in South Carolina. We arrived early, had a fine airport reception at Spartanburg. We had a delightful meeting down in Anderson. And we had a fantastic meeting in Rock Hill.

It is just wonderful to be here in Greenville, and I thank you all for your hospitality, your enthusiasm, and I like all of you wonderful people from South Carolina. Thank you very much.

I wish Betty were with me. She had planned to come, but we had a little problem develop. But let me say, as I left this morning, she said to say hello to everybody from South Carolina. She is feeling great. Thank you very, very much.

We had an interesting experience over at Rock Hill. They had a little 7- or 8-year-old girl come up and give the Pledge of Allegiance. I was sitting next to Len Phillips, and on Len's right was Senator Thurmond.

This young lady, after leading the Pledge of Allegiance, came by, and I thanked her, and Len Phillips thanked her, and then Strom Thurmond, he kissed her. [*Laughter*]

Well, this sort of makes me think of the motto of the great sovereign State of South Carolina: "Prepared in Spirit and Resources." You know, Strom Thurmond certainly exemplifies that.

I think there are 2 days in particular every year which prove that Strom has really been prepared in spirit and in resources. One is election day, and the other is Father's Day. [*Laughter*]

But all kidding aside, one of the great experiences that I have enjoyed in the 26 years that I have been in Washington, almost all of it in the Congress, was getting to know an outstanding Senator like Strom Thurmond—courageous, a man of character, dedication, devotion. You are just lucky to have him in the State of South Carolina.

Well, it is great, especially to be here in Greenville. They tell me it is the textile capital of the world. On the other hand, I would have been not at all surprised if I had found nobody here today. I thought everybody would be at the Clemson homecoming, and I apologize if I have kept you from it.

I am grateful for the sacrifice that you have made, and I am also indebted to you for being here to join with me in paying tribute to one of your fellow South Carolinians, the Secretary of Commerce, Fred Dent, who has done a superb job as the head of the Department of Commerce.

Fred, we are grateful.

Next Monday, I understand, the Southern Textile Exposition opens here in Greenville, which will be another reminder of the great contribution that this area, this State, makes to a healthy American economy.

The textile industry, the apparel industries, are important to this State, but they are equally important to our country as a whole. And I am fully aware of the competitive situation that is facing the textile industry and the apparel industry. But let me say that if we win the battle against inflation, if we get through the Congress, with the help of the American people, the economic program that I submitted to the Congress and to the American people about 10 days ago, the textile and the apparel industry in this State will thrive even better than it ever has in the past and will make an equally great, if not greater, contribution to the industrial well-being of our great country.

I am confident that that program is good. I believe the Congress will recognize it, and I trust when they get back from this next election, they will adopt it. It will be good for all of us.

I have already said to you what a friend and what a great Congressman I think Strom Thurmond is. He sort of bridges that generation gap, and he gets the support, as he deserves it, from young and old, from all segments of our society, or your society, in South Carolina. And I congratulate you for having the wisdom of having Strom represent you for so long and so well.

But to go along with Strom, I think that you need a strong State government, because Strom and Floyd Spence and Ed Young and your new Republican Congressman you are going to elect are going to continue to transfer the power from Washington back to the States and back to local units of government, which is where we can have the best government, because it is closer to the people.

If you are going to implement that program of seeking to get government at the local and State level, you need a person like Jim Edwards as the next Governor of the great State of South Carolina.

Jim has had the experience in the State legislature. He is a mover. He is a reform-oriented individual in politics. And this is what you need and what South Carolina needs if we are going to achieve a concept to implement the program of New Federalism.

There is always better government at the local and State level, particularly if you have people like Jim Edwards and his running mate, Carroll Campbell, as Governor and Lieutenant Governor of the State of South Carolina.

It has been my observation in some 26 years in politics that a political monopoly, one party in absolute power too long, is never a good thing, statewide or nationally. Jim Edwards can clear away the cobwebs and bring some new life, new dedication to State government here in South Carolina.

Obviously, he has Strom's and my full support, and I hope and trust that you will give it from yourself to him. And I can't help but be impressed by the fact that in Gwen Bush you have a mighty fine candidate for the United States Senate.

And as I have traveled around the State today and as I have been here before, I am proud to have on our ticket the quality candidates that I have seen and talked with. Of course, you are familiar with Floyd Spence up here, one of those real fine, strong, dedicated Members of the House of Representatives.

Then Ed Young, he joined us at the time of the 1972 election—strong, tough, able, dedicated. When I was the minority leader of the House, he was great, he was wonderful, he helped me tremendously, and I hope that you send Ed back, along with Floyd.

Marshall Parker was with me up in Anderson. Fantastic. We dedicated a new building for the two newspapers up there. I expected maybe a couple—300 or 500 people. How many were there, Strom? Ten thousand, ten thousand people. I think Marshall Parker is going to win, and he will be a great Member of the House of Representatives.

Then we just came from Rock Hill. How many people were there, Strom? Ten or twelve thousand in Rock Hill, a tremendous crowd. The enthusiasm convinces me that Len Phillips is going to win that election in that Fifth Congressional District.

Bob Watkins, who I met for the first time today in the Fourth District—Bob is a good candidate. I certainly wish him the very, very, very best.

A few moments ago, I mentioned the need and the necessity for the two-party system, how it has grown and thrived under the leadership and the guidance, the inspiration of Strom Thurmond. I happen to think that a two-party system brings competition to the political arena.

I know from my own experience that competition in athletics is good for the players, the spectators. I know that competition in business is good for the businessman, for the consumer. I know in education or law or any other field of endeavor, competition is a necessary ingredient if we want the best produced for those who will be the beneficiaries.

And it is exactly true in politics. A two-party system generates that kind of competition. It gives individuals who go into that sacred voting booth a choice. And gee, we want a choice.

And that brings up something that I would like to speak on, if I might. A choice today, as far as the battle against inflation is concerned, is a choice on the one hand between the big spenders or the savers. And I happen to believe from personal observation—and I watched it for 25 years in the House of Representatives—the Republican Members of the House and the Senate are primarily the savers, and their opposition are the spenders.

And if we are going to win the battle against inflation, we have to have more savers than spenders. That is why you ought to have Republicans.

I know that some of the people who want a different kind of a Congress are saying, because they have read some of the polls, they have listened to some of the political seers, they are just wringing their hands for the opportunity of getting in their grasp what they call a veto-proof Congress.

A veto-proof Congress—what does that mean? It means that it will totally upset the basic concept that has been so good for America—balance. Our forefathers, particularly yours from South Carolina, when they joined with others and met in the city of Philadelphia to draft our Constitution, wove into our constitutional balance, checks and balances.

They didn't want a dictator in either the Congress or the White House or the courts. And they had this system of checks and balances, and because of it, we have ended up with freedom and opportunity and material blessings beyond any expectation.

But if they get in their grasp a veto-proof Congress, they will upset that balance. I don't think we want a veto-proof Congress which would be a legislative dictatorship. You want balance so the President has an input, the Congress has an input, the Supreme Court has an input.

So, we have a mission, in my humble judgment, between now and November 5, to maximize our efforts to make sure, to make positive that they don't get this legislative dictatorship which some of them want.

If I have my choice—let's forget the veto-proof Congress, let's get an inflation-proof Congress. Doesn't that make a lot more sense?

I can't help but say a word or two at this point about a conversation I had, not too many months before he died, with the late, great President and General, Dwight D. Eisenhower. Obviously, he was a hero to literally millions of Americans, beloved by all. He came into the Presidency with the massive support of people from all over the country, both political parties.

I don't think Ike really considered himself a politician. No one, on the other hand, knew better than General Eisenhower how vital a two-party system is to the future of this country.

Just a few months before his death at his farm in Gettysburg, I had an opportunity to talk to Ike. He shared with me his own personal views and convictions on the two-party system. And what he told me is even more timely today than it was then.

And if I can paraphrase his words, this is roughly what he said: We are tending too much in the direction of a one-party system in the United States. We are awfully close to a political monopoly of power in America.

Ike went on to explain, as only he could say it—he said the stakes were very high; he said that if we have an approximately equal balance, an approximate equality in the Congress in both political parties, it will keep one political party from running away with things. It will keep one political party from bowing to the extremists. But if we lack this balance in the Congress, if one party stays in power far too long, it will become increasingly difficult to stop its successes.

And this is what has been happening for far too long on Capitol Hill, in the House as well as in the Senate. We have a party controlling the Congress today that has controlled the national legislative process for 38 out of the last 42 years and for the past 20 straight years.

It is a Congress, in my judgment, that is stacked against fiscal responsibility. And if they increase their power instead of lose, if they multiply their strength, let me just make one observation: With a veto-proof Congress of the kind of membership they will get, tighten your seatbelts, folks. They will spend the dome of the Capitol right off Capitol Hill.

So, what I am urging you to do here in a great State like South Carolina, to make sure that you contribute—Floyd Spence, Ed Young—reelect them. Make sure that you add to the South Carolina delegation—and you have got some outstanding candidates that can serve, that will avoid, will roadblock, will hamstring that kind of a veto-proof Congress.

That kind of representation in the House of Representatives will fight a legislative dictatorship, will preclude it. And so what I am saying to you is, do your best to send us some more troops. If you do, we can save the two-party system. And if you send us those new Congressmen, then I think the chances are very good that you will have Jim Edwards and Carroll Campbell running your State here in South Carolina.

What we want are people who are strong, effective, dedicated, honest men of experience, men who will truly represent the kind of philosophy in which all of you believe.

And now let me simply conclude with this observation. You know, I think it is more than just whatever material interest you might have. I think you have a far broader reason to make a maximum effort. And the fact that you are here at a fundraising lunch is indicative of your concern.

But you have roughly a few more days than 2 weeks to do more. And it is not just a personal satisfaction. You have almost an honor and a duty to do something about it. I happen to think the chips are down. It really results in a sacred duty.

Robert E. Lee once said, and I quote: Duty is the sublimest word in our language. Do your duty in all things. You cannot do more. You should never wish to do less.

That admonition from a great American ought to be your motto between now and November 5. That is what I ask of each and every one of you. Do your best, yes, your best for your party, your State, and your Nation. And if we all do it, we can transform these difficult days, the problems at home, and our challenges abroad. And instead of looking at America from the dim eyes of the prophets of doom and gloom, we can look at the future of America that will be the America of our fondest visions.

And we have that obligation—an obligation to ourselves, yes, but more importantly, to those generations to come. That is what you want. That is what I want. That is what we must do.

Thank you very, very much.

NOTE: The President spoke at 2:01 p.m. at a Republican fundraising luncheon in the Greenville Memorial Auditorium.

174

Remarks at Greensboro, North Carolina. *October 19, 1974*

Bill [Stevens], my former colleagues in the House of Representatives, Governor Jim Holshouser, our other candidates for the Congress, Jim Carson, the candidate for the Attorney General's office, and all of you who are here:

It is just great to be in Greensboro, and you are wonderful. I love it, and I appreciate it. Thank you very, very much.

Let me start out by saying I am no stranger to North Carolina. I was down here a couple of months ago and played golf. For your safety's sake, I want you to know I didn't bring my golf clubs. [*Laughter*]

But anyhow, I have been here a good many times. I served here for 9 months in the Navy. I went to law school here one summer. I have been down here to make a good many political campaign speeches. I had one son that went to Wake Forest University. I had another one that was entered in Duke this year, but decided he wanted to go out and be a ranch hand for 12 months, so he may come back.

But anyhow, I like North Carolina, and I am proud of my association with it.

This is a great crowd, but I want to warn you, this morning we started bright and early from Washington, D.C. We flew to Spartanburg, and then to Anderson, South Carolina, Rock Hill, and then to Greenville. They had anywhere from 7,000 to 12,000 people down there to see a Republican President, and believe me, they are on the move, and so are you in North Carolina.

Why do I say that? You have a great crowd here, and most of you, I am sure, would rather be out watching a good football game or doing something else.

But here is what you have done in the short span of time that I was in the Congress about 25 years. You have now a Republican Governor in Jim Holshouser, and he is a first-class chief executive.

And you have in Jesse Helms an outstanding Member of the United States Senate. You should be proud of him.

And I can speak with some considerable authority about the great people you have in the House of Representatives—Jim Broyhill, Earl Ruth, "Vinegar Bend" Mizell, Jim Martin, and pretty soon, about November 5, you are going to have Steve Ritchie and Ward Purrington.[1] And if you don't, gee, I will be disappointed.

With all this power you have got here, you ought to make certain and positive that somebody as able as Steve and somebody as able as Ward takes the oath of office on January 3 in the House of Representatives. They will save you money, they will win the battle against inflation, they will give you good representation, and you will be darned proud of both of them. Do your best.

Now let's talk about the United States Senate. In Bill Stevens you have got an opportunity to put a fellow in that high office to stand shoulder-to-shoulder with Jesse Helms. Isn't that what you want? Somebody who is going to be strong, determined, dedicated? And I will be so pleased if the great State of North Carolina sends that kind of Member to the United States Senate.

Now let me make two or three points. I know it is a little chilly, but nevertheless I want to talk heart-to-heart, straight-to-straight to you. I have gotten a lot of advice in recent weeks that I ought to sit in Washington, D.C., as President of the United States, read the polls and get discouraged and wring my hands and, you know, look out the window of the Oval Office and say, "Gee, things are terrible."

I think that is a lousy approach to the responsibilities of the President of the United States. I know all these experts are saying these things, that you can't change the results, and if I tried and I lost, then my Presidency for the next 2 years will go down the drain. I don't believe that. It is a lot better for me to be out talking to you in Greensboro than sitting around the Oval Office and wringing my hands.

I don't understand people who want to admit defeat. I have got a WIN button on, not a loser's button.

---

[1] Richard Steven (Steve) Ritchie was the Republican candidate in the Sixth Congressional District of North Carolina, and J. Ward Purrington was the Republican candidate in the Fourth Congressional District.

You know, the first election I ever participated in, boy, it taught me a good lesson, and it wasn't a lesson taught me by a Republican. It was a lesson that I learned from a good Democrat, Harry Truman. He was man enough, strong enough, convinced enough to come out here and fight for what he believed was right, and we are.

Harry Truman didn't win in 1948 by sitting in the Oval Office looking at all the polls. He came out here and fought and won. And America, under his leadership, had a great, great next 4 years.

I want your help right here in Greensboro, and I want your help in Charlotte, in Raleigh, and I want it everyplace else, in Winston-Salem. You have got an obligation, and so do I, and we don't achieve it by sitting on our hands and wringing our hands and saying, "Gentlemen, the polls look terrible." What is the matter with us? Have we lost that old fighting spirit? Have you?

All right, now let's talk about the issues. The issue is very clear. We have got a problem in the economy. We have got inflation that is too high, resulting from spending too much money for the last 20 years.

Look, the sun is even coming out!

We spent too much money for the last 20 years, and if my figures are right, you know who controlled the Congress for 19 out of the last 25 years? Our Democratic friends. They are the ones that made all the money available to be spent, and if we spent too much money, it is on their shoulders, not on ours.

But let's be reasonable and responsible about what we ought to do about it. I presented to the Congress about 10 days ago a good economic package that will whip inflation and keep our economy growing and constructive so young people will have jobs and older people will be taken care of. Now, how can you beat that?

Now the problem is on the shoulders and on the backs of Congress. I have heard some criticism of my plan, but I haven't heard any solution. You know, a lot of talk is cheap, but a program presented for action will save America, and a lot of talk won't do much good.

And so, I urge you to put pressure on the Congress—Democrats and a few Republicans, too. They have to step up and bite the bullet, because the chips are too high. The chips are so high for the future and the preservation of this country.

We have got to lick inflation. If we don't, it will tear our Government asunder. It will destroy all the principles we believe in. It will weaken us in our resolution to keep peace abroad.

We have a great, great responsibility, individually and collectively. We can't just brush it off. We can't back away and say it is somebody else's responsibility. We, individually and collectively, have to stand up and fight for what we know is right.

Now, I am confident, I am optimistic, I believe in Bill Stevens, Ward Purrington, Steve Ritchie, Jim Broyhill, Jim Martin, Earl Ruth, "Vinegar Bend" Mizell—those are strong, fine people. They are good and they will do what is right for North Carolina.

They will do what is right for the country, and therefore, I leave this great State with a conviction that instead of a veto-proof Congress, that some of the power-hungry people want, a veto-proof Congress, we are going to end up with an inflation-proof Congress, and that is pretty darned good for America

One final point, if I might. About 200 years ago our forefathers put together the greatest document for the governing of people in the history of mankind. How well it has done for us. We have got freedom, we have opportunity, we have done pretty well materialistically. We are blessed, we are so blessed. And a basic ingredient of that is balance—balance, a system of checks and balances that doesn't let any one political party, any one President, any one Congress be the dictator. Americans don't like dictators.

But the people who want a veto-proof Congress in effect want a legislative dictatorship. They want one branch of the Federal Government to dominate and control all other branches of the Federal Government, and that is completely opposite of the fundamental concept of our Constitution.

And so, the best way I think you can avoid that legislative dictatorship is to make sure that you keep our Members of the House that I have mentioned—Jim Broyhill, "Vinegar Bend," Jim Martin, and Earl Ruth—and add to them so that we avoid the veto-proof Congress, that is, a legislative dictatorship, and that we give to America a balance which is the basic ingredient that has contributed to our progress and our growth and our freedom and our liberties and opportunities.

Really, I look in your eyes and I plead with your hearts and I beg with your mind that you maximize your efforts in the next 10 days, 2 weeks, or 2 weeks and a half, because the stakes are very, very high.

And what you do, each one of you, can make a difference—your own vote and the votes that you can convince—that America doesn't want a legislative dictatorship; America wants a sound economic program, America wants good candidates like the ones we have serving them in the Congress.

Yes, I plead with you, I beg of you, not for yourselves, not for me, but for our country: Do your best.

Thank you very much.

NOTE: The President spoke at 3:54 p.m. at the Greensboro–High Point–Winston-Salem Regional Airport.

175

Remarks in Louisville, Kentucky. *October 19, 1974*

John Sherman Cooper, Thruston, Gene Snyder, Tim Lee Carter, Governor Nunn:

You know, all of them have been so nice and so great. They have said some awfully nice things. They all call me Mr. President now. If you only knew what they used to call me. But it is nice to have them a bit circumscribed—at least publicly. [*Laughter*]

But it is wonderful to be here, and the truth is, I have had a super day. I went to the great State of South Carolina, and we had four unbelievable, stupendous meetings. There were 5,000, 10,000, 12,000. They had a wonderful fundraising gathering—can you imagine—in the State of South Carolina. Then we went to the State of North Carolina, and they had an unbelievable airport gathering. And here tonight you have so many great people. I think it is indicative of the reaction of the American people to some things I will try to discuss later on.

Now it would be terribly remiss for me not to express my appreciation to Marlow Cook. I got into this situation where I find myself—not by any choosing of my own—but when I was nominated, it was Marlow Cook who said, "I want everything on the record. I want everything you have done, everything you have said laid out." And that is typical of Marlow. He wants it on the record.

And I expressed to him and expressed to the Senate committee and subsequently to the House committee the record as it was. This Administration is open, candid, forthright. It may not be popular in some respects because we have to call them as we see them.

But the thing that I admire most about Marlow Cook is that he is straightforward, he is honest, he is strong, he is dedicated, and he is a darned good Member of the United States Senate. He sort of follows in the pattern of John Sherman Cooper and Thruston Morton. We are a little different, you know. We all have a different style. I am not sure I could do as well as John or as well as Thruston.

But the truth is that the great State of Kentucky has a tradition of fine, fine Members of the United States Senate, and Marlow Cook follows in that pattern.

It was my good fortune to serve in the House of Representatives for almost 26 years, and during the time that you spend in a legislative body, you see Members of the House come and go. And you learn to pick out the ones that have class, that have capability, that have all of the attributes that are essential to make the right decision. Not that they always agree with me, but they have the capabilities of doing a superb job for the people that they represent, and every district is a shade different from other districts throughout the country.

And I can assure you from my almost—well, more than a quarter of a century of service in the House of Representatives—the State of Kentucky couldn't be better represented in their respective districts than by Tim Lee Carter and Gene Snyder. And I mean it from the bottom of my heart.

As I was saying, we had a wonderful reception all day long, and I am just as enthusiastic tonight as I was at the first meeting at Spartanburg airport this morning, because of the response and the reaction that I find among the American people.

There has been a little criticism by some of the members of the news media that maybe I was getting out—to Kentucky and to South Carolina and to South Dakota and to Kansas and to Nebraska—they know where I am going for the next couple of weeks. They have by innuendo said, well, maybe I should sit and think in the Oval Office. Well, let me just put it this way: I think there are an awful lot of fine brains and good ideas out in Kentucky that might be more helpful than if I sat there and listened to a bunch of bureaucrats in Washington, D.C.

The first time I ran for Congress was back in 1948, and I remember a great Democrat, and I mean a great Democrat. All of the polls said he was going to lose. They predicted that he was not only going to lose but lose badly. As I recollect, one of our great newspapers in this country, early in the evening of that election, printed a headline that his opponent won.

Well, let me just say this: We have got the same kinds of polls that I am sure that he saw, and I don't believe those polls any more than he did. I happen to think that the American people want somebody from the White House to come out and fight for what they believe is right, regardless of what the polls say, and I intend to do what Harry Truman did.

Harry Truman had the strength and the will and the desire, and he thought he was right, and he went out and sold himself and his policies and his programs to the American people. He didn't sit around the Oval Office cogitating this and that. He wanted to find out what was in the minds of the American people, and those suggestions are pretty darned important.

And I intend to do the same thing, because I happen to think the policies we are pursuing abroad and the policies we are pursuing at home are right, and I intend to try and sell them to the American people. The last thing I am going to do is be barricaded in Washington, D.C., by people who don't want our point of view sold to the American people.

I may have a little trouble at home. I might say I got special dispensation from Betty to come here for Marlow Cook. She was here a few weeks ago, and she loved it. And you were all great to her, and she said give all of you her very, very best. She is doing great.

Now, what are the fundamental issues we face here, we face as a nation? I could go on in the foreign policy area, but the facts of life are we are moving ahead, we are making headway in foreign policy. This Administration is going to continue the policy of strength and peace, of negotiation rather than confrontation.

But let's talk about what the real facts of life are here at home. It has been alluded to by others before me. Some of our opponents are alleging, in fact are almost believing themselves, that they are going to end up with significant gains in the House and the Senate, and the net result is they will have a veto-proof Congress.

If I could take just a minute, let me illustrate what that means. But I have to go back just a little bit and point out, if I might, what your forefathers and what mine did.

When they sat down in the city of Philadelphia to draft a Constitution for the benefit of a new nation, a new nation which is now almost 200 years old, most of them had come from areas in Western Europe where they had been dominated and dictated to by a king or some other kind of dictatorial authority.

And they, after having fought for freedom, decided that they wanted a system of checks and balances. They wanted a strong President in the White House; they wanted a strong Congress heading the legislative branch; they wanted a strong judicial system headed by the Supreme Court.

But in the process of weaving that Constitution together, they determined that they wanted a system of checks and balances. They wanted a tripartite form of government with three coequal branches, one looking after the other two and vice versa.

And how blessed we have been, how fortunate this country has been because of that finely tuned system. No one person, no one part of our Government, no segment of our society has dominated. And the net result is that we have made progress maintaining our freedom, giving opportunity to people, and giving us material blessings beyond anything that has happened to any nation or to any people in the history of mankind.

But this system of checks and balances requires that everybody in each of the three branches has a part. But some of our opponents are looking at the prospects, they have looked at the polls—I don't agree with the polls, but that is immaterial—they look at the polls and they say, "Oh, boy, we have got a legislative dictatorship with a veto-proof Congress."

What does that mean to you and to your friends, your neighbors, your associates? A veto-proof Congress means a legislative dictatorship. Do you want a dictatorship in any one of the three branches of our form of government? Of course you don't. You want that same finely tuned balance that has made so much for all of us and those that are to follow.

A legislative dictatorship in this country is not good for America. And what does that mean that you have to do on November 5, or I should say between now and November 5? It means that you show your support financially, your support at the polls, your support by convincing others that a person like Marlow Cook is going to be reelected to the United States Senate because he is for you and he won't be a part of any legislative dictatorship.

He may listen to me; he doesn't always agree with me. He is going to be a representative of the great Commonwealth of Kentucky, and that is what you want, and that is why I am here to make sure that he is going to be reelected.

And the same holds true in the House of Representatives with Tim Lee Carter and Gene Snyder. I used to have to talk to both Gene and Tim Lee. Occasionally, I had a little difficulty with them. They didn't always do as I said or as I wanted, but they were independent; they were strong. They represented you, and I admired them for it, and I respected them.

But they are the kind of people that I think you in the great Commonwealth of Kentucky should have representing you, and they are the opposite of those that will bend with the individuals who talk about a veto-proof Congress and a legislative dictatorship.

But let me present the alternative. I can assure you, as I think Marlow said, that if you get a veto-proof Congress and the kind of people that will be elected on the other side of the aisle, I can tell you what will happen in the way of spending. Let me put it just as bluntly as I can. If you get a veto-proof Congress, boy, tighten your seatbelts. You are going right through the roof of the United States Capitol as far as the Federal Treasury is concerned.

They have spent too much already, and if they get another 40 or 50 or 75 in the House of Representatives and another 7 or 8 in the United States Senate like they are talking about, the key to the Treasury will be thrown away and the money will pour out unbelievably. That is the record. I mean, we can lay it out.

And speaking of excessive Federal spending, let me talk about the second point. Ten days, eleven days ago, I submitted to the Congress and to the American people a 31-point program aimed with three basic objectives: one, to save energy; number two, to tighten the screws on inflation; and number three, to keep our economy moving in a healthy, constructive way, so that in the years ahead we would be able to compete overseas, we would be able to provide jobs at home, and that we would be strong and capable of meeting any competition anyplace else in the world.

I happen to think this was a sound, finely tuned program that calls upon the Congress to react favorably in a number of areas, and the American people to react.

I followed it up with a speech in Kansas City last Monday or Tuesday night, asking the American people to respond, to respond to what I call WIN—"Whip Inflation Now."

You can do something about it; the Congress can do something about it. One of the basic ingredients of that program is to hold the lid on Federal spending, and it has been said here tonight that the Congress in the last 25 years has had some 19 years of deficit spending. You couldn't run your family, your church, your business, your schools, with that kind of a record. And we can't win the battle against inflation with that kind of a record.

We have in the months ahead, between now and next June 30, to save about $5.4 billion. I can count on Marlow Cook; I can count on Tim Lee Carter; I can count on Gene Snyder. They will hold the lid, but if you elect their opponents, there is no hope, there is no prospect, there is no possibility. Their opponents will do just the opposite.

So, if you want your Government to set an example so that when I or others ask you to sacrifice just a bit, you ought to have people like Marlow and Gene and Tim Lee Carter in the Congress. I can't ask you in good conscience, I can't ask you with any degree of conscientiousness to help if Uncle Sam is going to just spend money, you know, like it was out of style.

So, I need some help in the Congress, because no money is spent by the Federal Government unless the Congress appropriates it—which brings up an interesting fact.

We think the Congress—the Government, I should say—has done a bad job in handling your tax money. Do you realize that 38 of the last 42 years, the opposition has controlled the Congress? So, if they have spent too much money, I think you can honestly say it is the opposition's responsibility, and they have controlled the Congress the last 20 years.

So, I would really think if the national debt is too high—$485 billion—if they spent much too much money, we can legitimately look at the opposition and say, "You control the Congress, you control expenditures, you are responsible."

What we need is not only Marlow and Gene and Tim Lee Carter but we need these other good candidates who are just as dedicated to fight for fiscal responsibility, not only because it is sound economically but because it is right in this battle that we face in trying to whip public enemy number one—inflation.

You know, I submitted, as I said a moment ago, 31 plans or programs or particulars for a winning battle against inflation. And I have heard some criticism about it. They have nitpicked here and they have nitpicked there, and so forth. Well, some of the critics remind me a little bit of Secretariat—they are running very fast, but not producing very much. [*Laughter*]

So, when we come right down to it, we have got some problems that have to be solved, and I happen to think the reelection of Marlow or reelection of Gene and Tim Lee—that is highly essential. But if we are going to win the battle against inflation, we have to accept and fight for and be dedicated to this kind of sound economics. It calls for a little sacrifice upon the part of every one of us. It calls upon us to be compassionate, because we are going through a traumatic experience that I suspect few of you had anything to do in creating. But the fact is that the United States can't afford to have double-digit inflation as we try to meet the challenges from abroad.

I am encouraged with what I hear and what I see, and I happen to think that the Congress, after it gets through this next election, will respond. If we don't, if we just abandon our responsibility, this kind of inflation will tear the fabric of our political society asunder. It will destroy what we have inherited from those that preceded us. It will completely knock out the capabilities of the United States to be the leader in the world in trying to solve the problems of

President Gerald R. Ford

Above: After taking the oath of office in the East Room at the White House, August 9, 1974.

A Collection of Photographs: 1974

Above: Signing the Employee Retirement Income Security Act of 1974 in the White House Rose Garden, September 2, 1974.

Above: At a campaign rally at Calvin College in Grand Rapids, Michigan, October 29, 1974.

Above: Addressing a Joint Session of the Congress, August 12, 1974.

Right: News conference in the White House Rose Garden, October 9, 1974.

Left: At the opening session of the Conference on Inflation in the East Room at the White House, September 5, 1974.

Above: With Vice President-designate Nelson A. Rockefeller in the Oval Office, November 12, 1974.

Above: Awaiting the arrival of King Hussein of Jordan for a State Dinner at the White House, August 16, 1974.

Left: With troops of the U.S. Army 2d Infantry Division at Camp Casey, Republic of Korea, November 22, 1974.

Below: With Secretary of State Henry A. Kissinger outside the Imperial Palace in Kyoto, Japan, November 21, 1974.

Wally McNamee—Newsweek

Left: General Secretary Brezhnev welcomes the President at Vozdvizhenka Airport near Vladivostok, November 23, 1974.

Except as indicated, photography was under the direction of David Hume Kennerly, Personal Photographer to the President.

Above: On the grounds of the Imperial Palace in Tokyo, November 19, 1974.

peace, whether it is in the Mediterranean, the Middle East, Greece and Turkey, whether it is in Western Europe, or Southeast Asia. If we don't have a strong economy at home, we can't go to the other countries with the firm hand and the respect that is so essential to get them to solve their problems wherever they might be in the world as a whole.

And I happen to have great faith in the kind of people that you have elected to statesmanship. I say John Sherman Cooper, who is going to be our Ambassador to East Germany, Thruston Morton, who was an Assistant Secretary of State as well as a Member of the Senate and Member of the House—they come from the Bluegrass, but they had a vision infinitely beyond that. And they know, as well as I do, that America at this moment has a responsibility as well as an opportunity to do things that no other nation in the free world side can do to help solve those problems in the Middle East, to negotiate the differences between two good allies—Greece and Turkey—to keep NATO together, to work in the vineyard in trying to achieve a responsible policy of détente with the Soviet Union, to open up new vistas in the Pacific with the People's Republic.

This country, if we are strong at home, can do these things. But we can't be strong at home if we don't have a Congress that is responsive, a Congress that will fight in the battle against inflation, a Congress that will give us the tools to keep our economy moving ahead as we travel that very narrow path between too much inflation and not enough stimulation to provide the jobs for those who are coming into the working market.

We need individuals who have the strength at home and the vision abroad. And I hope and trust, as I close a long but wonderful day, that I can see in this audience tonight in Louisville—I don't know how many are here, but it is a great audience—people who will not only do what you have done by being here but, between now and November 5, will maximize your effort, yes, to a degree for yourself; but I think everybody I see in this audience has a broader objective, to do what you can to help Kentucky and America.

We are the last and strongest fortress for the free world, and if we fail—and I happen to think that 1974 is sort of a testing ground—if we fail, all that we have inherited and all we stand for and all we hope to pass on to others could go down the drain.

So, you can do something. You have done it already, but you can do more. It is sort of a 24-hour-a-day job between now and November 5. I am confident as I have met many of you, as I have heard others, as I know this great Commonwealth that you and your associates will do what is needed and necessary for

Marlow, because the Congress needs him, I need him, you need him. I hope you will do the same for Tim Lee and Gene and the others. That is good for America.

Thank you very, very much.

NOTE: The President spoke at 8:28 p.m. at a Republican fundraising dinner in Freedom Hall.

176

Statement on Signing the Federal Columbia River Transmission System Act. *October 19, 1974*

I AM pleased to sign into law S. 3362, the Federal Columbia River Transmission System Act. In an era of deepening concern over the Nation's energy well-being, this bill is a solid step forward in meeting our energy requirements on an orderly, planned basis.

The Congress is to be congratulated for enacting this important legislation. Its passage is also a tribute to the broad-based support this measure received from the region's electric utilities, business and labor organizations, and State and local governments.

This partnership has also produced the Pacific Northwest-Pacific Southwest intertie and the Columbia River Basin treaty with Canada. These agreements are vital to a sound interregional power system and serve the overriding need for conserving our energy resources. Transfers of surplus hydropower from the Pacific Northwest to California have already conserved over 16 million barrels of vital oil this year. This is an outstanding example of partnership planning and demonstrates once again that the Federal establishment can work in close concert with State and local government and industry to solve problems at the regional level.

This bill authorizes the Bonneville Power Administration to issue revenue bonds and to use the proceeds in carrying out its mission. Such bonding authority, together with provisions enabling BPA to utilize its revenues, should eliminate the need for Congressional appropriations. The legislation does provide for continuing Congressional review of the BPA program.

In sum, this new law will assist in the efforts outlined in my speech to the Congress last week to assure efficient use of America's precious energy resources.

NOTE: As enacted, S. 3362, approved October 18, 1974, is Public Law 93–454 (88 Stat. 1376).

177

Exchange of Remarks With President Luis Echeverría Alvarez of Mexico at Nogales, Mexico. *October 21, 1974*

Mr. President, amigos:

I am delighted to be here this morning to meet with you on our border at Nogales. I am delighted and highly honored to participate in these meetings today, which will be partly held in Mexico and partly held in the United States, which symbolize, Mr. President, the relationship between our two countries.

It is a working partnership of mutual cooperation which exemplifies the spirit behind the new dialog into which we have entered with all nations of Latin America and which we will not forget, Mr. President, which started last year at Tlatelolco in Mexico City.

In our meetings today, Mr. President, let us give new meaning to the special relationship of us as two good neighbors—Mexico and the United States—through frank and friendly consultations.

It is very significant, Mr. President, that my first trip outside of the United States as President of our country is to Mexico—our longtime friend and very good neighbor. It provides a living demonstration of how we are inextricably linked by historical ties, by geographical position, by our mutual desire to be good neighbors.

It is my fervent wish that this meeting will mark the beginning of a very close personal relationship between us and contribute to the close cooperation and the very friendly relation of our peoples and our Governments.

Our relationship is of very great mutual benefit. Each of our countries, Mr. President, receives much from the other—material goods of all kinds, increased understanding through tourism and cultural exchanges, and the enrichment of human life and consciousness through expanded knowledge and warm, warm friendship.

This exchange is especially evident in the border area. I thank all of you who have come here to welcome me and to see this spirit of friendship which exists between President Echeverría and myself, representing our two countries.

Actually, we witness today the flow of people, goods, food, music, art, and language. We note the existence of a binational commission—not one, but several—and binational groups of many kinds. We see the efforts by people on both sides of the border to work together in a joint effort to solve the everyday problems of their respective lives.

There are countless other instances demonstrating the strong, the vital, the flourishing and friendly relations that exist between us. And in this border area, Mr. President, we also see living examples of how two governments disposed to work together in good will can meet and solve problems.

Along our common border, we have jointly faced and together resolved problems of flood control, sanitation, minor border adjustments necessitated by the vagaries of the Rio Grande.

We are extremely proud, Mr. President, of our recent resolution of long-standing and complex issues involving the salinity of the water of the Colorado River delivered to your country. Our successful efforts in these areas over the past few years are precedents for the solution of problems that may arise in the future. We must continue to draw upon the spirit of mutual respect, good will which made this cooperation possible in the past.

Mr. President, let us today consider how we can cooperate in solving common problems which will result in a better and better life for the people of our two countries and for all the people everywhere.

Muchas gracias.

NOTE: The President spoke at 9:45 a.m. in response to President Echeverría's remarks of welcome.

Following a wreath-laying ceremony at the monument to Benito Juarez, the two Presidents flew to Magdelena de Kino, Mexico, where they laid a wreath at the tomb of Padre Eusebio Francisco Kino and held the first of two meetings. They then flew to Tubac, Ariz., for a luncheon and the conclusion of their meetings.

President Echeverría spoke in Spanish. His remarks were translated by an interpreter as follows:

Your Excellency, Mr. Gerald Ford, President of the United States of America:

We bid you welcome to Mexico. The people of Mexico receive you with the expression of their friendship for the American people. Through me, our people wish to offer you the most cordial welcome, to convey a cordial greeting which we would ask you to take back with you for all the American people.

Coexistence between Mexico and the United States of America has been a long one. We have an extensive borderline between us. And all along this border for a long time now, the sometimes dramatic and even tragic problems have been left behind.

During the last decades, it has been possible to solve the problems that affect us both through civilized practices by applying norms of law and of reciprocal respect. And now during the very difficult period that the entire world is living through, we both, the United States, in these difficult times, and Mexico, are making efforts so that our coexistence will be a harmonious one, an understanding one, and a respectful one.

In our country, within our country domestically, we are struggling to foster social justice in accordance with old moral guidelines and with a spirit of cooperation which we believe would benefit all the countries of the world.

Internationally, we struggle to achieve norms of cooperation, balance, understanding on the part of each nation for all other countries. In Mexico, we believe that inflation is only one of the manifestations of lack of balance between the interests of the one and the other—between the rich and the poor, between the people that are just developing and the industrialized countries. We feel that we have to reach an equilibrium in order to fight against these problems. And we believe that it is possible that we can trust international relations and that we can find a system of cooperation that would lead to international balance, that would lead to peace and not to war.

We should understand that whatever problem comes up in any corner of the world—in Asia, Africa, Oceania, Latin America—are problems that affect all of us, even the richest and most industrialized countries, because we must understand that the destiny of mankind is one and indivisible.

President Ford, this is the doctrine of Mexico, sir, with which we receive you with great cordiality. We want you to feel at home among us.

178

Toasts of the President and President Echeverría of Mexico at a Luncheon in Tubac, Arizona. *October 21, 1974*

Mr. President, distinguished guests, friends:

I am very pleased to have the opportunity to have our distinguished guest here in Tubac, Arizona, and to reciprocate on this occasion for the warm welcome that he and the people of Mexico gave to me and to the American people during the day, which was an unbelievably pleasant, warm, and just a wonderful opportunity to be together.

I am most grateful to you, Mr. President, for having suggested that we meet in Magdalena de Kino for the meetings that we had during the day. Your sense of history, your understanding of the great role that Father Kino played in the history of this part of the world, made it an ideal setting for the discussions that we had on very important matters.

Mr. President, the Jesuit priest whose statue is in the United States Capitol and whose statue is in the state capitol of Sonora and the capitol of Arizona, lived and worked here almost three centuries ago. His efforts gave the first great stimulant to progress among the people of this part of the North American Continent, and we are all proud of his contribution to this flourishing part of our Nation as well as yours.

Mr. President, with the horse, the cross, and the plow, he explored this area of your country as well as ours. He not only served his faith, Mr. President, but he also introduced agriculture, livestock to the inhabitants of this area. And all of these ingredients, Mr. President, are vital to the progress of your country as well as ours.

Father Kino lives in the memories of those in the town that we visited this morning. On both sides of the border we owe him a very great debt of gratitude. The heritage of Father Kino is an inspiration for all of us to continue the work that he started three centuries ago.

Mr. President, as I am sure you realize, I am a great believer in personal dialog. I believe that the straight talk that you and I had today contributed significantly to a better understanding, greater cooperation, and greater potentialities for your country as well as ours.

Mr. President, we had straight talk today with openness and candor, and as a result, it seems to me that the relationship between your country and mine has increased very significantly.

Your great patriot, Benito Juarez, said over 100 years ago, and I quote: Respect for the rights of others is peace.

And this relationship that has been built between Mexico and the United States is built on that foundation which is solid rock.

Mr. President, we have discussed a number of very important issues and we have done it with openness and candor, and the spirit that we discussed these matters, I think, will be the foundation upon which we can continue the dialog—a dialog that will be beneficial to Mexico as well as to the United States, to Latin America, and to the world as a whole.

Mr. President, we are greatly honored to have on the soil of the United States the President of Mexico and his official party. We believe that the relationship between us will grow from this beginning under my Administration and during your time as President, and we will work together to build a better and better world in this hemisphere as well as throughout the globe.

May I offer a toast to the President of Mexico and to the people of the great country of Mexico and to the growing and improved relationships between our people, our country, and you and myself.

NOTE: The President spoke at 4:20 p.m. at the Tubac Country Club.

President Echeverría spoke in Spanish. His remarks were translated by an interpreter as follows:

Mr. President of the United States of America:

I believe, Mr. President, that among the many important points of agreement that we have reached during this very brief visit, but a very intensive one, we can mention the enormous success of this visit.

The cordiality, the expressions of welcome and affection with which you have been received in Magdalena and in Nogales, we all know would have been the same whatever part of the country you would have visited.

It is not only the fact of the coexistence between Mexicans and North Americans and United States citizens that intensifies the bonds that bring our two countries together. It is not only the relationship that exists on the two sides of the border. It is the fact that throughout all our history, the American history and the Mexican history, we have been able to bring up our problems very openly, we have been able to foster and foment our friendship.

When you and I, Mr. President, explored the different possibilities of meeting along the border area, we decided to meet in this vast region which was at that time a desert and which Father Kino discovered and civilized.

Father Kino's untiring work, Father Kino's great foresight and vision and all his dedication are examples that are to be followed in the work that needs to be done in this very vast desert area in which we are at present.

In researching the work that was done by Father Kino, many students of the United States and many students of history of Mexico participated, and similarly, to the way in which they joined forces and participated, we can join forces in order to solve the problems of the United States and of Mexico.

May I say out loud, Mr. President, that to deal with you personally is very gratifying; that, very simply and very directly and fully informed, you take up the most complex matters; that you do not elude the problems with a great many high sounding phrases:

and that it is easy to perceive that you are embued with good faith in our bilateral relations, and that this will be beneficial for an international life which every day becomes more complex throughout the world and which makes it necessary for political leaders to contribute with the greatest intelligence and experience and all of their good will.

We know that the world is living through very difficult times and that it is only through the spirit of understanding, of frankness that we can transcend these difficult times so that they will not become too long.

And Mr. President, I do believe that if in the future the problems and all other matters that should come up are to be dealt with as we have dealt with our problems today in this border area, we will have done a great deal to lighten our burden and to solve these problems.

Mr. President, it has been a great pleasure for me to meet you personally, to dialog with you, Mr. President, in the direct and clear manner in which you speak, not only from conviction but also because this is your way. And in Mexico, we have no doubt that this is a very, very favorable sign so that the friendship between the two countries will become deeper and will continue into the future, strengthened, vigorous, and without ever being blemished.

Gentlemen, I offer a toast to the health of the President of the United States and of the friendship of the two countries.

179

News Conference of the President and President Echeverría of Mexico in Tubac, Arizona. *October 21, 1974*

PRESIDENT FORD. [1.] It has been a very great privilege and pleasure, Mr. President, to have the opportunity of visiting your country today and to discuss with you a number of very important issues. And let me just emphasize one.

You, of course, are the author and promoter of some very far-reaching action in the United Nations which we believe, as a charter for economic development throughout the world, has very great merit and very great support, and I compliment you for it. And I can assure you that I and Secretary Kissinger will work with you and others in your Government in trying to find the key and the answer to the economic development of all parts of our great globe.

It is nice to have you in the United States, and I thank you for the warm welcome given to me by you as well as all the people of Mexico.

QUESTIONS

ACCESS TO MEXICAN OIL

[2.] Q. I would like to address a question to both Presidents. Among the issues you discussed today, was there a discussion of American access to the recently discovered oil deposits in southern Mexico, and could you give us an estimate of the size of those deposits?

PRESIDENT ECHEVERRÍA.[1] Yes. Mexico is selling to whoever wants to buy the oil

[1] President Echeverría spoke in Spanish and his remarks were translated by an interpreter.

at the market price in the world market. We sell our surplus oil. I hope that we can drill for more oil in Mexico in order to be able to export a greater amount.

We have sold to the United States, to Uruguay, to Brazil, and to Israel, and we hope to continue to sell without making any differences among the buyers in order to contribute to satisfy the demand.

TRADE REFORM LEGISLATION

[3.] Q. I would like to know, President Ford, if, during your talks, there was any mention made of the trade reform act, and if so, what are the repercussions that this will have for Mexico?

PRESIDENT FORD. I am very happy and very pleased that you raised the question. The new trade legislation, which I hope will pass the Congress this year, will significantly increase the trade relations between Mexico and the United States, helping to balance the trade between Mexico and the United States.

This trade legislation which I have worked very hard to promote, which I believe will pass the United States Senate and I believe the Congress, will be very helpful in making good trade relations between the United States and Mexico.

MIGRANT FARMWORKERS

[4.] Q. Can you tell us whether any progress has been made on a new approach resolving the question of migrant farmworkers from Mexico and the related questions involved in that?

PRESIDENT ECHEVERRÍA. Yes. Yes, we did discuss this point and I brought up in the name of Mexico, I told the President of the United States that we have definitely desisted from our intention of signing an agreement, and this is due to the fact that we made a revision of the previous agreement, and we saw that in practice, in the way it works, it is not good. It gives opposite results from the ones we want.

What happened at that time was that, attracted by this agreement that we had with the United States, the migrant workers, or the would-be migrant workers, would come to the border cities of the United States. And then it happened that they did not receive a contract, and then they stayed at the border city and increased the number of the population or else they went illegally into the United States.

Now, with the policy of self-criticism that at present prevails in Mexico, we have reviewed this matter, and we have come to realize and accept that the responsibility belongs to Mexico.

In Mexico, we need to increase the sources of employment. We need to send more resources out into the countryside. We need to organize the farmers in a better way. We need to keep them within the land. I do not know if President Ford has anything to add, because we analyzed this point jointly.

President Ford. As you can see, we discussed this matter in great depth. It has a long history. It has current problems. In fact, we have some new problems. And in order to get an up-to-date reading on what should be done, how we can best help, we have decided to reanalyze—through a commission that will bring up the data that involves those going from Mexico to the United States and will update data that will involve individuals who are in the United States seeking employment, trying to find the right answer. And this revitalized commission, I think, will give both of us, and our countries, better answers to solve the problem.

President Echeverría. Now, however, there is a point that Mexico insists upon in reference to the migrant workers—whether they are legally in the country or illegally in the country. That is, Mexico insists that they enjoy the rights and prerogatives that is granted by the law to any person.

When a person is contracted legally and comes to work in the United States, this person under contract has certain rights—the right to a decent salary, the right to social security, and that is to say all the rights that are granted by the law. This is when the person comes to work legally.

Now, if the migrant worker comes in illegally, he still has some rights that must be observed—this is basic.

CUBA

[5.] Q. I have a question for President Ford. I would like to ask President Ford whether the hemispheric problems were taken up, and if they did take up the hemispheric problems, what is the attitude of the United States with reference to Cuba and if this attitude is to be maintained at the next Conference of Foreign Ministers.

President Ford. We did take up the question of the United States' attitude toward Cuba. I indicated that we had not seen any change in the attitude of Mr. Castro or any of the other individuals in the Cuban Government, and inasmuch as there had been no change, no attitude that was different regarding the United States, it was not expected that our attitude would change toward Cuba.

We did discuss the meeting that is to be held in Quito, I think, on November 7 or 8, where the matter will be brought before the OAS. But our attitude as of the present time is, since no change in the attitude of Cuba, we certainly have to retain our point of view concerning them.

EXTENT OF MEXICAN OIL DEPOSITS

[6.] Q. President Echeverría, I wonder if you could answer one part of Mr. Shaw's [Gaylord Shaw, Associated Press] question which was not answered, and that is, can you give us some estimate of the size of the new oil discovery in Mexico?

PRESIDENT ECHEVERRÍA. Yes, the discoveries are very important and significant, and the significance we can find in the following figures. Of the 640,000 barrels a day that are obtained throughout all of Mexico, 37 percent—that is 241,000 barrels—come from only a few wells. This has made it possible for us now to begin to export, after having transcended the stage where it was necessary for us to import in order to satisfy our own consumption.

Therefore, this is very important for the Mexican economy, first and foremost, if we take into account the prices that prevail for oil in the world market, prices which we respect.

RESULTS OF MEETING

[7.] Q. This is a question for both Presidents. Can you give us a list of the specific agreements that you reached today?

PRESIDENT ECHEVERRÍA. Actually, no, we did not come to international agreements. It was the first meeting between the President of the United States and the President of Mexico in order to get together to discuss, to analyze very frankly, very openly, very clearly, very directly, some of the problems that have already been dealt with in this room.

For me, the most important part of our meeting is the way in which President Ford underlined to me personally, and later on here during our meeting in this place, the importance that he gives the Charter of Economic Rights and Duties of States.

And I thank President Ford and the people of the United States for this opinion that has been expressed to me, because actually, this is a complete change from what it was before, and this is very valuable support for this charter that is gaining ground within the United Nations, and for the already 100 and some odd countries that are supporting the charter.

The United States had never before expressed as much interest as it has now in the approval of the Charter of Economic Rights and Duties of States. Of course, it rather matters that we still have to elucidate, that we have to define, but I feel very optimistic that we shall.

REPORTER. *Muchas gracias.*

NOTE: The news conference began at 5:10 p.m. at the Tubac Country Club.

180

Remarks on Departure of President Echeverría of Mexico From Tucson, Arizona. *October 21, 1974*

MR. PRESIDENT, it has been a very great privilege and an extremely high honor for me to have had this opportunity early in my Administration to meet with you and your very distinguished delegation, to have visited Nogales and Magdalena de Kino in your very great nation, and to have had the honor of your hospitality in Tubac. Let me say that the reception received in Magdalena, in Nogales, was unbelievable, and I can say to all of my friends here in Arizona we could not have had a warmer greeting and a friendlier reception.

Now, Mr. President, the time has been all too short, but what we have shared together has been most valuable to me in the handling of the problems that we see down the road. It provided a very opportune moment for a warm welcome, to know you personally, to be able to establish a close personal friendship—the friendship between the Presidents of two great countries—a neighbor to the north for Mexico and a good neighbor to the south from the United States. This opportunity provided us the establishment of a first-hand dialog which is so important in the understanding and cooperation of our peoples and our Governments. It provided a chance, Mr. President, to hear your points of view representing your great country and your great people on matters of mutual concern to our countries and to give me an opportunity to express to you the views of our people and our Government.

To me, Mr. President, the personal relationship we have initiated today is equal to the substantive discussions we have held. I am confident that the meeting beginning early today and ending shortly will be only the beginning of a close, personal relationship, an important link in the special relationship which unites our countries.

Mr. President, during my short visit to your side of the border this morning, you and the people made me feel very much at home, and I assure you that the warmth of this friendship by our people to you I hope equals that of your people to me.

As I say goodby and take leave, let me wish you a safe and pleasant return journey, Mr. President. I will not say goodby but rather, following the tradition of your country, I will say *hasta luego*.

I know there will be other opportunities in the future to meet, to discuss the vital questions, but more importantly, to get better acquainted.

It is a privilege and a pleasure to have had this opportunity on your border and ours.

Mr. President, I thank you.

NOTE: The President spoke at 5:35 p.m. at Davis-Monthan Air Force Base.

President Echeverría spoke in Spanish. His remarks were translated by an interpreter as follows:

President Ford, it is only due to the great spirit of friendship which unites our two countries that it has been possible in a few hours, and without any personal contact between the two of us previously—it has been possible, I repeat, to revise the enormous amount of matters that we have between our two countries.

We are practicing—and this is well for the people of the United States and for the people of Mexico to know—we are practicing a simple type of democracy, a democracy in which there is no secrets, a democracy in which there is nothing hidden, a democracy that is characterized by frankness.

I believe that this conference between the United States and Mexico can set an example, can set an example that should be followed by all—by the great and the small countries, by the industrialized nations and the developing nations.

I see that from here on in, with good will, with the study of our common problems, with mutual understanding, the relationship between our two governments will improve.

Mr. President, in expressing my gratitude for your personal acquaintance, Mr. President, and for the hospitality that has been shown to us by the United States and also this expression of good will on the part of the people of the United States, I, too, wish to say *hasta luego,* until we meet again, because we hope that we will have you in Mexico City so that the Mexican people will get to know you as I do.

Mr. President, in taking my leave, I do so with a warm handshake, with an *abrazzo*—Mexican style—with an embrace that we hope will travel to all the homes of the United States and convey the great affection of Mexico.

181

Remarks to a Meeting of the National Council on Crime and Delinquency. *October 21, 1974*

IT IS a pleasure for me to address this gathering of the National Council on Crime and Delinquency. I only regret that a tight schedule has forced me to appear on film instead of in person.

In a year when we as a nation have begun to pay long overdue attention to conserving our energy and natural resources, it is only fitting that we have also taken a major stride forward in preserving our greatest resource of all—our Nation's youth.

It was in this spirit that on September 7, I signed S. 821, the Juvenile Justice and Delinquency Prevention Act of 1974, into law.

While not agreeing with all the provisions of the act, I strongly believe in its overall purpose. We must save as many of our young people as we can before they become trapped in a life of crime. And we owe every juvenile the full protection of his or her constitutional rights.

In signing this bill, I said that it represents a constructive effort to consolidate and make more efficient the various Federal programs to assist States and localities in dealing with juvenile delinquency. The direction of our Federal programs has been fragmented for too long.

This restructuring will better assist State and local governments to carry out the responsibilities in this field—a responsibility which should remain at the local level. I also expressed the hope that the result will be greater security for all citizens and more purpose, sense, and happiness in the lives of young Americans.

No group worked longer or harder for the passage of this milestone legislation than you have. No group deserves greater credit for transforming it from a goal to a reality.

I am proud that the signing of this measure was one of my earliest official acts as President of the United States, and I salute you for your magnificent work in making it possible.

Again, I only regret that I cannot be with you in person this afternoon, speaking from the same rostrum as Francis Dale and Elliot Richardson.

The more all of us do to prevent juvenile crime, the more we protect its potential victims—before, rather than after the damage has been done.

You have my personal assurance that I am fully committed to meeting the Federal Government's fair and attainable share of this responsibility. Working together with the general public and State and local governments, we can make the year ahead another year of progress—of making America a better, safer country for young and old alike.

NOTE: The President's remarks were filmed for use at the council's meeting in New York City on October 21, 1974. In his remarks, the President referred to Francis L. Dale, chairman of the council's board of directors, and Elliot L. Richardson, Attorney General of the United States from May to October 1973, and member of the board of directors.

182

Remarks at a Republican Fundraising Breakfast for Senator Henry Bellmon in Oklahoma City, Oklahoma. *October 22, 1974*

Dewey Bartlett, Happy Camp, distinguished guests, ladies and gentlemen:

It is a very great privilege and a very high honor for me to have the opportunity of joining with you this morning for a cause that I think is of great, great national significance.

It has been a good morning. I don't know what I have enjoyed more—seeing so many good, loyal Sooners on the one hand, or sitting down to a breakfast that I didn't have to make myself. [*Laughter*]

It is a particular pleasure, as I indicated at the outset, to participate in something that pays honor to Henry Bellmon. You know, Henry is known as a very tightfisted Member of the Congress. He really looks after your tax dollars.

To be perfectly honest, however, I didn't know how tightfisted Henry was until the waiter came up and gave me the check a few minutes ago. [*Laughter*]

But it is significant for me to come to the great State of Oklahoma and to see what has happened and transpired in the years that I have been in politics in Washington, to see the Republican Party in this State grow from a political party that had literally no organization, very few winnable candidates, to a party that has an organization, that has won with good candidates. And the net result is that you have in the United States Senate, in Henry Bellmon and Dewey Bartlett, two of the very, very best Members of the Senate that I have been able to observe.

And of course, both Henry and Dewey served as superb Governors of your State, and it is a pleasure and a privilege to me to meet Jim Inhofe [1] and to see the quality of the candidate that you are offering to the citizens of Oklahoma in Jim, and I congratulate you.

If I might, I would like to say a word or two about a two-party system. In January of 1949 when I came to the United States Congress, there were a good many States in this Union that had no two-party system, and Oklahoma was one of them.

Because you developed people as fine, fine candidates, and because you have developed an organization, you have now made Oklahoma a two-party sys-

[1] State Senator James M. Inhofe was the Republican candidate for Governor of Oklahoma.

tem—a State that has a viable two-party contest and competition. As a consequence, you have put Oklahoma on the map as a State that offers the kind of competition in the political arena that is good, healthy, and beneficial to your State.

I think most of you would agree that competition in business results in a better product and a better price as far as the consumer is concerned. I happen to think competition in professions—the law and medicine—competition in politics is likewise good, and Oklahoma has been the beneficiary of people like Henry and Dewey and Happy Camp. These are the kind of candidates that, in my opinion, make Oklahoma better represented in the Congress of the United States.

Now, let me say just a word or two about the slate that I think you have presented to the State of Oklahoma in 1974. In the travels that I have made around the country, both as a minority leader, as Vice President, and for the last 2½ months as President of the United States, I have an opportunity to see firsthand the candidates that the Republican Party submits to the voters in various States of the Union.

In the course of serving in the Congress for 25-plus years, you see Members of Congress—both in the Senate as well as in the House of Representatives. When I look at what Oklahoma has contributed in Henry and Dewey in the United States Senate, and Happy Camp in the House of Representatives, I think that every one of you could be very, very proud. They do a first-class job not only in what they do, but in how they perform in every way, and I hope and trust that you will return Henry to stand alongside with Dewey and that you will reelect Happy and give him some help in the Oklahoma delegation.

I have known Henry more particularly in the last several years, because I presided over the United States Senate for about 9 months. And sitting there looking, watching, observing, I came to the conclusion that Henry was a thoughtful, hard-working, activist type who took the practical experience that he had learned in his long years as a citizen of Oklahoma and put those practical experiences, that exposure to the problems to use in the legislative actions that he took.

Now, some point, I am told, has been made of how Henry has differed with White House views. The truth is, I respect Henry for his forthrightness, for his independence, for his willingness to put the cards on the table.

I was reading the paper last night, one of the Oklahoma papers, and I noticed a comment to the effect—by one of your fellow Oklahomans—that I was coming to Oklahoma for the purpose of pardoning Henry Bellmon. Let me tell you, I am here to praise him, not to pardon him. [*Laughter*]

On the question of whether Henry and I agree on everything, the question as to whether Henry has agreed with the White House on every issue—naturally, we try to go down the same path. Philosophically, our interests, our views are identical. Sometimes we, of necessity, for one reason or another, have to differ—not in the objective but in trying to come to the ultimate answer. There are honest differences as to the method by which you can achieve a certain aim, a certain objective.

Now, Henry and I share—we have talked about it before, we talked about it last night—we share in the desire to achieve quality education for every child in every State. That is our aim, that is our objective. Now, there may be some differences as to how that is achieved and accomplished, but let me say that in this very difficult area, I am impressed with Henry's recommendation that a commission be established for the purpose of trying to get some uniformity, some sensible answers out of the United States courts as far as quality education is concerned, and I commend you for that recommendation, Henry.

The Congress has been under some challenge, and I think some of our institutions in Government have been challenged as to integrity, as to forthrightness. In Henry Bellmon, I know of no person in the United States Senate or in the Congress who is more forthright, who has more integrity. It is a quiet sort of deep-seated belief that you have to be honest, you have to have maximum candor. I respect you for that, Henry. We have had too little of that in recent years, and frankly, that was one of the prime reasons that I thought it was vitally important last week for me to appear before a Congressional committee.

There have been some challenges to the wisdom or the method as to why I had taken the action I did concerning my predecessor. But it seemed to me that in this day and age, when our system of government is under such challenge from many, many sources, that the best way to lay aside, hopefully once and for all, any challenge as to why and under what circumstances I should, as the first President of the United States, appear voluntarily before a Congressional committee—they had their chance; I appeared, and I hope and trust the answers satisfied this committee of the Congress.

What I am trying to say is that today there is no higher ingredient essential to the future of this country than openness, candor; and I say this in Oklahoma because I know from firsthand experience, in Henry you have a person whose life is an open book, whose attitude is one of candor, forthrightness, and total integrity. I can't think of a higher ingredient essential in the election of 1974. Congratulations, Henry.

I can recall vividly the first time I met Happy Camp. Where was it, Happy, that I came—Enid? Six years ago, I visited Enid, Oklahoma, and had an opportunity to see that great part of your superb State, and believe me, it was a great experience for two reasons: One, I met an outstanding candidate for the Congress of the United States who had experience in the State legislature, and everything they told me about Happy at that time has come true—that he was able, he was knowledgeable, he was experienced, and he had that kind of strong, tough character that was needed. Happy, I sure hope that you come back to continue your outstanding work.

I have had an opportunity to look over the slate that the Republican Party has presented. I only know the incumbents, and I have had the privilege of meeting Jim, but if you want a two-party system to grow and thrive, I think you have to give maximum consideration to the rest of the candidates if we are to have this essential competition which is good for the voters and, I think, good for the country.

Let me make one or two observations concerning some substantive matters. When I became President on August 9, that is about 2½ months ago, we were faced at that time with a very serious economic situation. We were faced with what is commonly called today double-digit inflation—inflation of 10 percent per year, inflation that we were not accustomed to in this country.

At the same time, we were faced with—in some areas of our economy, it is almost paradoxical—some softness. There was concern in some areas that there was a loss of vigor in the economy, and we had the alternative, which was also very difficult, of increasing inflation.

Now, as a result of these almost paradoxical circumstances, we started what was called a summit meeting, a program of getting the views of people from all over the country, from all segments of our society, with their specific recommendations as to what ought to be done.

We covered the country literally in, as I recall, about 10 different mini-summits. We invited people in to give their views, their recommendations, and we concluded it with a rather historic economic summit in Washington, D.C. After accumulating all of this evidence, all of these proposals, we sat down and filtered them out and came up with a 31-point program which is a program very, I think, wisely devised to meet the challenge of inflation on the one hand, and the problems of a softening economy in some areas of America on the other.

I hope and trust that the Congress will respond. I trust that the American people will respond, because it called upon them to volunteer to do certain things in the area of energy conservation, to do certain things in the area of wasting less and saving more.

So far, the response from the American people has been excellent. So far, the Congress has done a part-time job. I ask particularly for a proposal in the Congress to set a spending ceiling of $300 billion, which is about $5,400 million less than the budget that was submitted in January of this year. If we are to call upon the American people, whether it is individual or otherwise, to sacrifice, it seems to me that the Federal Government itself—the White House, the Congress, the executive branch—must do the same. We cannot expect people, 213 million Americans, to sacrifice as we get over this economic hump unless the Government does it.

So, the Congress, unfortunately, did not respond. But I can tell you that in Henry and in Dewey and in Happy Camp, you have the kind of people that do respond to a requirement to hold down Federal spending, and I compliment you for it.

Something that has, I think, attracted a great deal of attention that ought to be discussed quite frankly is the demand on the part of some of our opponents—opponents, philosophically, who are saying this election on November 5, which is 15 days away—for what is commonly called a veto-proof Congress.

A veto-proof Congress, in my judgment, would have two serious end results. Number one, undoubtedly, it would result in the election of candidates who would be bigger spenders, not bigger savers. So, if we cannot hold down Federal spending with this Congress, I can assure you a veto-proof Congress will be a Congress that will spend more and more and more, and they will do it over Presidential veto.

So, if you want a Congress that is fiscally responsible, I think you have to defeat what is broadly called a veto-proof Congress. I think we ought to have an inflation-proof Congress, not a veto-proof Congress.

But there is a broader problem that I see if a veto-proof Congress is elected. And what would that mean in numbers? For example, to get a veto-proof Congress, they need on the other side of the aisle roughly 50 more Members, so they would have not what the margin is today—roughly 3-to-2—but a margin that is far better than 2-to-1. And in the United States Senate, it would undoubtedly call for the defeat of Henry and Pete Dominick and some of the other stalwarts.

Now, if a veto-proof Congress is elected, it will destroy, to a substantial degree, the necessary balance that we have in the Federal Government. Let's go back historically just a minute. Our forefathers put together probably the greatest document for the governing of people when they wrote the Constitution of the United States.

They didn't want an all-powerful President. They didn't want an all-powerful

Congress. They didn't want a judicial system that would dominate all branches of the Government. They wanted a system of checks and balances. And the net result is we have had for almost 200 years this finely tuned form of government which is a system of checks and balances. And the consequence is we have ended up with more freedom, more opportunity, and more material blessings than any people in the history of the world.

But if a veto-proof Congress is elected, that finely tuned balance will not exist, because one branch of the Federal Government, one of the three, will totally dominate at least one of the others, and possibly the third. And that system of checks and balances will be gone. Much of the freedom, much of the opportunity, much of the material blessings that all of us and our predecessors have enjoyed will be in jeopardy.

So, in a broad, philosophical sense as well as the fiscal aspect that I discussed, the challenge is in the next 15 days for all of us to maximize our efforts.

Let me close with one comment, if I might. Some of those on the other side of the political aisle, some of the news media, have suggested that I, as President, ought to stay in Washington and worry about the polls and do nothing about the situation.

I respectfully disagree with those who make that recommendation. I happen to think by coming to Oklahoma City, by going to Cleveland on the way back to Washington tonight, and by other trips throughout our country, I am going to be the beneficiary of some valid recommendations, observations, and proposals.

It seems to me it is wholesome and very healthy for a President to listen to people other than those you see on the banks of the Potomac, and I am here in Oklahoma City for that purpose. I am going to be in Cleveland tonight for that purpose, and I am going to be elsewhere between now and November 5.

I am the beneficiary of what I can learn in all 50 States, and I hope and trust, as I speak to people such as you here this morning, I can stimulate you individually and collectively to broaden your effort, to influence your friends, to protect that very important ingredient in our Government of checks and balances, and also to the maximum degree do what you can to make sure we have an inflation-proof Congress, not a veto-proof Congress.

Thank you very much.

NOTE: The President spoke at 9:35 a.m. in the Crystal Ballroom at the Skirvin Plaza Hotel.

183

Remarks at a Rally in Oklahoma City. *October 22, 1974*

Thank you very, very much, Senator Henry Bellmon. Thank you, Dewey Bartlett, Happy Camp. Thank all of you for being here.

It is a great, great opportunity for me to meet many, many of you again and to see so many enthusiastic, vigorous individuals—Republicans, Democrats, and Independents—who want to make sure that Henry Bellmon is reelected.

It should be obvious to you that it is a great pleasure for me to be back in Oklahoma again, the home of Will Rogers, who never met a man he didn't like, and the home of the Oklahoma Sooners, a team who never met a team they couldn't lick.

Yes, it is great to be here in "Switzer Land" [1] again.

As an old football player, and I mean old—when I played it was back when the ball was round—it is nice to see Ron Shotts here and Rod Shoate.[2] It is wonderful to see one of those great all-American running backs. As a former lineman myself, I have always envied—as I am sure Rod does over here—those men in the backfield who seem to get a little more publicity than some of us linemen.

I never regretted their achievements. We always thought we helped a bit. But let me say this. I was once introduced at a dinner given at the University of Michigan. I was introduced by an old teammate from the University, and I will never forget his introduction.

He happened to say in the course of that introduction, "It might interest you to know that I played football with Jerry Ford for 2 years, and it made a lasting impression on me. I was a quarterback, Jerry Ford was the center. And you might say it gave me a completely different view of the President." [*Laughter*]

Let me comment, if I might, on some views and perceptions of the coming election. I am convinced that a campaign can come from behind and win, and you are going to do it in Oklahoma.

I am totally convinced that this State has energy, not only in its oil fields, on its football fields, but also in the open-minded spirit of its population, including Democrats and Independents as well as Republicans.

Oklahoma, as a State, has produced a great winning football team, and it is going to produce a great winning Republican team this fall.

---

[1] The President was referring to Barry L. Switzer, head coach of the University of Oklahoma football team.

[2] Ron Shotts was three-time all-Big Eight Conference tailback for the University of Oklahoma 1965–67, and Rod Shoate was three-time all-American linebacker for the University of Oklahoma 1972–74.

I am deeply honored to be introduced by one of the most independent men in the United States Senate, and I refer to your distinguished Senator, Henry Bellmon, who is so highly regarded in Washington—and I say this with some authority and great respect. He is respected by both Democrats as well as Republicans. I have heard that Henry Bellmon is the only honest-to-goodness dirt farmer in the United States Senate. He calls the shots as he sees them.

And a person with that strength of independence obviously, on some occasions, will differ with me, but I respect that independence of thought, that independence of action, as well as his total dedication to honesty and candor and forthrightness serving in the United States Senate. You must reelect Henry Bellmon.

In the 25-plus years that I served in the House of Representatives I found that it takes some courage to make unpopular decisions. It takes some courage to be your own man. And I say with the depth of my conviction that I respect individuals who have those qualities.

Henry, because of his background, is a top authority on agriculture and the expansion of food production. He is, therefore, a person of utmost importance in our battle against inflation.

In addition, Henry is sought on both sides of the political aisle for his knowledge about oil and energy. And I am glad to know that Henry Bellmon is energetically seeking a vast new nuclear development park through the Atomic Energy Commission near Muskogee, and I commend and congratulate you, Henry, for that effort.

A man who served 4 years in the statehouse as Governor, a man who has served almost 6 years as the United States Senator does not have to prove his devotion to the people of Oklahoma. It is obvious that he has their best interests at heart, and as a team, he and Senator Dewey Bartlett represent, in my judgment, Oklahoma's finest, especially in the areas of food and energy, the State's leading industries. And both of them are vitally important to us in the other 49 States.

Since all but one of Oklahoma's delegation, Happy Camp, are Democrats, a balance is provided by keeping these two Republican Senators in the Senate delegation. But Happy needs some help in the House, and we have some good Republican candidates on the ticket in other districts.

In the First District, George Mizer, Jr., of Oklahoma Cherokee heritage, is a forthright, courageous man. A former U.S. Navy pilot, he has shown brilliance in management as well as in business. He has acquired a reputation of integrity, and he has accumulated considerable political experience. I think you and Oklahoma need George in Washington.

In the Second District, Ralph Keen is an excellent candidate. Ralph is a distinguished attorney. He has served as general business manager of the Cherokee Nation of Oklahoma. He is the kind of a man who will represent all the people of this great State, regardless of political labels or background. You need Ralph in Washington.

In the Fifth District, Marvin "Mickey" Edwards, an outstanding newspaperman, is your candidate. He served in the national leadership of the Young Republicans, as a member of the State Republican executive committee, and as a delegate to the 1972 GOP National Convention. Mickey needs your help.

And now, if I might say just a word about my former colleague and dear friend, Happy Camp. Six years ago I visited Enid, Oklahoma, to campaign for Happy as a new candidate for the House of Representatives. All the promises that were made to me that Happy would be an excellent Member of the House, all those promises were kept by his performance. It would certainly make me happy to see Happy back in the House of Representatives, and I think it would make you happy, too.

Traveling around the country, as I am pleased and honored to do—as a matter of fact, for several years I traveled about 200,000 miles a year—I had the opportunity of meeting many Governors of various States, Democrats and Republicans, and you learn after a period of time to look at their records to see them. I can say, after having met Jim Inhofe, that your candidate for Governor is a first-class candidate. I hope he is elected.

But now, let's talk about 1974, not 1976. This is the year of decision, as I see it, for the survival of the two-party system in our great country. It is a year when we seek to enlist a new Congress in the war against inflation. It is a year in which I strongly appeal to all voters—Democratic, Republican, and Independent—to elect candidates who will fight against inflation.

Henry Bellmon has a reputation not only in Oklahoma but in Washington as a tightfisted man with your tax dollars. He has been a general in the war against wasteful Federal spending. He has been against topheavy bureaucratic dictatorship in Washington. He has been against legislative dictatorship by those who would wreck the budget and waste our dollars on far-out schemes and programs. I think you need—we do, I do—Henry Bellmon to continue as the man in his command post in the coming attack against the Federal Treasury.

You need the other Republican candidates who are here today to help Henry and Dewey Bartlett and Happy Camp. You can expand your Oklahoma delegation of inflation fighters.

Now, let me ask you this very simple question: Why do I, as your President, call for the election of more fighters in the war against inflation? If the Democrats, for example, gain 7 Senate seats on November 5, and 25 or more House seats on that day, they will make, in effect, the Congress veto-proof.

Such a Congress, unrestrained by any veto powers of the President, could resurrect those wild spending programs of the years of 1965 and 1966. Refresh your memory, if you will. The election of these additional extremists in the Democratic Party—and they would come from that element—could threaten the internal balance of our legislative process.

In my judgment, this would endanger our basic concept of government in America, the system of checks and balances. I have found in my time in the Congress of the United States that one of the greatest protections we all have—it is not a part of the Constitution as such, but it has grown up with our political history—I have found that a two-party system is good for America in every State, in all 50 States. And I am deeply concerned that this system of checks and balances, through a two-party system, faces its greatest threat in our lifetime on November 5.

I ask all voters across the political spectrum—Democrat, Independent, and Republican—to think as inflation fighters and not along strictly partisan political lines.

The record ought to be reviewed, and let me take just a minute, if I might. The Democrats have controlled the national legislature, our Congress in Washington, for 38 out of the last 42 years. The last 20 years they have controlled it consecutively. Fiscal responsibility has not been in this instance, for this span of time, honored except in words—they certainly have not honored it in votes.

During this period of time, unfortunately, Pandora's box of inflation has been opened. Today's Congress is stacked, in my judgment, against fiscal responsibility.

Let me cite another thing here that ought to awaken our concern, our interest. For 19 out of the 25-plus years that I served in the House, we ended up with deficits in the Federal Treasury. Nineteen out of 25 years, your Federal Government spent more money than it took in. Twenty-three of the 25-plus years that I served in the House, the Democrats controlled the Congress. I think these statistics, these facts illustrate who has been responsible for the irresponsible spending of your tax dollars.

Now, if this heavy spending majority in the Congress of the United States is substantially increased in the next Congress, the two-party system will be in jeopardy. We must not permit a legislative dictatorship. We must elect an inflation-proof Congress and not a veto-proof Congress.

It is essential to every working man, every housewife, every citizen that we have a Congress in the great tradition of our political history, a Congress that respects the common sense of checks and balances, the common sense of protecting your pocketbook and your job. From my experience, a veto-proof Congress for 1975 and 1976 could literally run the country through a lopsided power over legislation and spending. It could mean a Congress so deficient, so lacking in internal balance through a huge influx of a group of freshmen Democrats—unfortunately, the probability is they would be the most liberal spenders, more liberal in spending your tax dollars than even those who have been there—that a mandate for more spending will be what many will read on November 5.

Let me refresh your memory just a moment, if I might. Think back to what happened in 1964. The Democrats gained 38 House seats giving them a total of 295 to 140 on our side of the aisle. For 2 years, unsound legislation was pushed through the Congress by a vigorous President and a rubber-stamp House and Senate. Interest rates climbed; the value of the dollar began to decline.

We have been trying ever since to repair that damage. We have recovered some ground in 1966. The American people saw the mistake they made in 1964. There was a net gain of 47 Republicans in the House. To this extent, this righted that imbalance. We prevented, as a consequence, the unsound legislation being further pushed, and we, to some extent, recaptured and held the lid.

But let me say this as I look at the past: The Republican Party is resilient, it is strong—because of the sound principles that I have learned in my time in political life—it is in the great tradition of our great country. We have good people, good candidates. And we as a party have the capability and the ability to come back to start from your own 2-yard line and score on November 5.

The man- and womanpower in this audience here today, if you will rally around the great candidates that you have, if you explain the true legislative issues and the differences between one candidate and another, the difference between an inflation fighter and an inflationary spender, I am sure that your friends and your fellow Oklahomans will understand and make the right decision November 5.

I must repeat a point with great emphasis: A veto-proof Congress could roadblock vital legislation, including measures that I have recommended to increase energy on the one hand and stifle and handicap the anti-inflation proposals that I have made on the other. A veto-proof Congress would undermine the philosophy of revenue sharing which gives to local people far more control in the use of their tax dollars. A veto-proof Congress would mean a flow of power away from the local communities. A veto-proof Congress would mean the concentration of power again in Washington, D.C.

I think most of us in this audience agree that you get wiser spending, better spending, if your locally elected officials, if your State officials have the power. We can do infinitely better in solving the problems if you can keep your eye on those people right here locally. You can do it far better, and your money will be infinitely better spent than if you have to go 1,200, 1,500 miles to Washington to see what is being done.

I think, with the efforts that you can make, you can retain that power at home and keep it from the bureaucrats in Washington.

I am not a peddler of despair. I happen to believe that games can be won, political elections can be won with a massive effort and determination. We must correct what is wrong, strengthen what is right, and move forward rather than backward.

I think this will help to solve the problems at the local, the State, and the national level.

I don't know of a State in the Union that I have found that has more belief in and dedication to the free enterprise system, to individual initiative, and Oklahoma is the leader in making certain and positive that our country continues to have the adherence and the belief in, the conviction in free enterprise and individual freedom. And I think the people in this audience, whether they are Democratic or Republican or Independent, share that view.

As a result, if we do what we should between now and November 5, we can continue to move forward as a great nation. We can reduce Federal spending. We can whip inflation. We will open a new era of achievement in State and local governments. The body politic and the economic condition and resources of America can be strengthened.

We have in our heart and our minds in some 213 million Americans the capability of continuing to be a leader in the world. We are entering the final stretch. It is like the last few minutes of a ballgame. We are in the final days of a great political campaign, convinced that we have the right philosophy, the best candidates, and a good organization.

I am not downhearted about the fate of the Republican Party in Oklahoma or elsewhere, and I am far from downhearted about the prospects for our great country. As I travel around—and I am delighted that I am here because of the enthusiasm—I see nothing but strength and optimism and dedication and conviction on the part of our Americans everywhere I go.

Now if I might, let me conclude with one final observation. We have to whip inflation now, we have to strengthen our economy, and we must have peace abroad.

When I came to the Congress on January 3, 1949, we had a Democratic President—I think a good one—Harry Truman. We had a Republican Congress for the 2 previous years. Recall, if you will, that this was right after World War II, a war that involved some 16 million Americans on a global basis, and there was the feeling in our country and a bipartisan attitude that if Democrats and Republicans joined together, we could lay the foundation for peace on a global basis.

This bipartisanship—a Democratic President and a Republican Congress—did lay the foundation. We helped to rebuild; we strengthened our relations on a global basis. And as a result, I think there has been great progress in meeting the challenges from enemies as well as friends.

I am concerned about the breach of this bipartisanship between a Republican President and a Democratic Congress. But I hasten to add, a very good friend of mine, a good and fine Oklahoman—the Speaker of the House, Carl Albert of Bug Tussle, Oklahoma—understands that there has to be a working relationship, a unity, a bipartisanship in foreign policy. But unfortunately, this Congress, dominated by the opposition, does not seem to understand it.

I am concerned that if we get a Congress that is veto-proof, a Congress that has the wrong philosophy—both domestically and internationally—the possibility for the next 2 years when our country faces the challenges in the Middle East, the challenges in the Mediterranean, the challenges in the Caribbean and Latin America, the challenges in the Pacific—as we try to work to broaden détente, as we try to continue the normalization of relations with the People's Republic of China, as we in the White House and those in the Congress who understand bipartisanship and who believe that partisanship should end at the water's edge—if we get the wrong kind of Congress, peace could be in jeopardy.

So, I end my remarks here today by pleading with you to give to America—not to me—a Congress that will be farsighted, visionary, imaginative, cooperative, so that we can have peace abroad, so we can work on our problems at home.

I thank you for the welcome. I urge you to send back Henry Bellmon, Happy Camp, and a good slate of Republicans.

Thank you very much.

NOTE: The President spoke at 1:05 p.m. in the Main Arena at the Myriad Center.

184

Remarks in Cleveland, Ohio. *October 22, 1974*

Bob Taft, Ralph Perk, distinguished members of the official family in the great State of Ohio, and candidates, and ladies and gentlemen:

It is a great privilege and a very high honor for me to have an opportunity to be back in Cleveland.

In talking to Bud, it brought back some very great memories. A good many years ago, longer than I would like to remember, I had my first opportunity of meeting Bud Humphrey.[1] He was an aspiring football player at Yale University, and I was a young and not very competent football coach. But Bud made it then, and he has made it since.

I also had the privilege in those days, a good many years ago, of coaching Bob Taft and Bud Brown and working with Del Latta. It is just nice to be here with old friends that have done so well and contributed so much. And I thank you very, very much, Bud and Bob, Bill [Bud] and Del.

You know, when I was down at Ohio State about a month ago—and they were so kind to ask a Michigander to make a commencement address and were so kind to make available two tickets to the Michigan-Ohio State game—I thought it was wonderful. And I went back to Washington, and I had my daily meeting the next morning with Henry Kissinger—we usually discuss things for about an hour every morning—and I found that Henry is a great football enthusiast. And I said to Henry, the people at Ohio State had been generous and invited me and given me two tickets to come out to that classic game between the Buckeyes and the Wolverines, and I said, "Henry, would you not like to join me?"

And he said, "Well, what time is it, or what is the date?"

And I gave him the date. He looked sorely disappointed. He said, "The Japanese have invited you to a Presidential visit to Japan during that period of time."

And I looked at Henry, and I said, "That is the first mistake you have ever made." [*Laughter*]

Let me thank Jack Dwyer and Tim Timkins [2] and all of you for participating in this affair and the many others that you have on behalf of the Republican Party and its candidates. Those who head these meetings and work to make them successful seldom get the recognition that they deserve.

---

[1] Gilbert W. (Bud) Humphrey was chairman of the dinner.

[2] John J. Dwyer was chairman of the Cuyahoga/Lake Counties Republican Finance Committee, and Tim Timkins was chairman of the Ohio Republican Finance Committee.

Let me say from the bottom of my heart, I am deeply grateful, as all the rest of us are, for what you have done, Jack. Thank you, and you, too, Tim.

Before I get into some substance, I would like to thank Virginia Coy [3] for creating this wonderful button. It says, as I am sure all of you know, "President Gerald Ford, Model A–1 Ford."

Thank you, Virginia. That is very kind.

Some of us here are old enough to remember what a Model A Ford was. As I recall, it was brand new. It was economical. It was dependable. It was uncomplicated. And it got us where we wanted to go. And that is exactly the kind of Ford I would like to be.

And to you, Virginia and Frank, I express my deep appreciation and gratitude.

As I intimated, I am no stranger to Ohio. I think the first two times I came to Ohio was down in Columbus. We were lucky once and were badly beaten the second time, but the people were friendly and very kind.

I have been to Cleveland several times in recent years. In fact, I was here in this very hotel—and perhaps in this same room—just a few months ago.

Now, all of you in Ohio have a great reputation for being honest and very frank—direct is another way of saying it—but I never knew how honest and direct Ohioans were until that last visit. After making my remarks that night, I was invited to a reception in another part of town. And at the reception a very sweet, wonderfully thoughtful grandmother came up to me, put her gloved hand in mine and said, "I heard you gave a speech here in Cleveland tonight."

And trying to be a little modest, I said, "Oh, it was nothing." And she said, "That is exactly what I heard." [*Laughter*]

Well, such a warm and personal touch is, of course, what we all like to hear, but I am deeply grateful on this occasion for Bud's introduction. As I said, our friendship goes back a long, long time, and I appreciate, Bud, your very kind and your very thoughtful remarks here tonight.

From my experiences going back to the 1930's when I first got interested in collegiate athletics, but also interested in politics, I found that people from Ohio had a very emphatic way, a reputation for carrying the ball and winning. I think that is indicative of the kind of Congressional team you have in Washington.

You cannot argue with the scoreboard. Your Congressional delegation on the Republican side of the aisle is outstanding, and I hope and trust that you in Ohio

---

[3] Wife of Francis A. Coy, chairman and chief executive officer of the May Department Stores Co.

will keep that strong, affirmative, dedicated team in Washington representing all of you on November 5.

I am told that the prospects in the political arena, as Kent McGough [4] has said, are good for the retention of your circumstances in the State legislature, that you have a good chance to win the statehouse, and of course, Kent's report concerning the Governorship is very encouraging.

Oh, I know that some of the pollsters and the speculators in the political arena are saying that Jim Rhodes does not have a chance. Well, I have known Jim Rhodes a long, long time. I count on him. I count on him as a winner, not as a loser. And that is important from the point of view of the State of Ohio, and I trust that every one of you will make a maximum effort between now and November 5 to make sure that Jim is a winner.

You know, it is pretty hard to get candidates of proven experience in conducting the high office of Governor. It is very difficult to find individuals who have experience and capability who will carry on.

Now, you know I am a sports fan—a has-been, but a sports fan. At the same time, I like politics. As I read the sports page and look at what is possibly the result here in the State of Ohio, I can't help but think that Jim Rhodes is the Cornelius Greene [5] of politics. Jim also knows how to carry the ball and score. So, let's have Jim as your next Governor in January 1975.

It has been my experience over a period of time when I was in Congress, when I was Vice President, and more recently as President, to get to know Ralph Perk. As one travels as I do from one city to another, as I sit in meetings with mayors from all over the country, it is my honest observation that Ralph Perk has done a superb job as the mayor of this great community. He ranks at the very top as a mayor of a big city, and it is my judgment that that is the kind of a person you want in the United States Senate to represent you for the next 6 years. Ralph, I hope you win.

I said a few moments ago that your Congressional delegation was outstanding on our side of the aisle. Let me repeat it. They are the kind of people that I have worked with as minority leader, as Vice President, and more recently, as President.

I think your delegation's quality, your delegation's capability is exemplified by the high standards that Bob Taft himself represents. Bob Taft, first in the House, more recently in the Senate, has done the kind of a job that is in the great tradi-

[4] Chairman of the Ohio State Republican Committee.
[5] Quarterback of the Ohio State University football team.

tion of the Taft family. And Bob, I know you are not a candidate, but you certainly are the kind of a person that I would want representing me in the United States Senate, and I congratulate you.

Of course, Chuck Mosher, over here, I have known all the time he was in the House, does a superb job; Bill Stanton, sitting next to him; two of the fine, fine, outstanding Members of the House of Representatives. I know because I worked with them on a day-to-day basis. I have to concede they did not always agree with me, but I will also confess I am not always right. And I can assure you that when they take a position, whether it is with me or against me, I respect their judgment. And you—and I say this from the very bottom of my heart—Chuck Mosher and Bill Stanton are the kind of Representatives that I know do a first-class job for their constituency, and believe me, you need them back in the House of Representatives.

Then, in the great delegation that you have in the House there is Del Latta, Sam Devine, Don Clancy, John Ashbrook, Bill Harsha, Bud Brown, Chuck Whalen, Chalmers Wylie, Clarence Miller, Ralph Regula, and Tenny Guyer. It is an outstanding group. It is big in numbers but strong in character and responsibility. The State of Ohio should be proud of every one of them.

But I think it is important if you make your effort to increase the numbers, and in the Cleveland area you do have some excellent candidates. Kent has introduced them. There is George Mastics, Bill Franz, Bill Mack, Bob Franz.[6] I am convinced with a little extra effort you can help add to the quality as well as the quantity in the Ohio delegation in the House of Representatives.

I am pleased to have a telegram that was delivered to me out in Oklahoma City this morning. I was out there making a plea to reelect a great United States Senator, George [Henry] Bellmon. But on the way I got a telegram from my very dear friend, Bill Minshall. I will paraphrase it, and I will paraphrase it with some interpolation on my own.

What Bill says is he endorses, supports every Republican candidate on the ticket and he specifically speaks of those candidates for the House of Representatives. I hope Bill's good, sound advice will be supported as the voters go to the polls this coming November 5. Bill—I am sorry he is leaving—he was a dear friend and a darned good Member of the House. But it is my judgment that George Mastics will be an outstanding successor to Bill Minshall.

I never had the privilege of serving in the State legislature. Whether it was right or wrong, I ran for Congress in the first instance. But I have learned, over

[6] Republican candidates for Congress from the 23d, 22d, 21st, and 20th Districts of Ohio, respectively.

a period of time, to have nothing but respect and admiration for those who make the laws in a great State like Ohio or Michigan.

Of course, here in this area, you have some fine members of the State legislature, or candidates for those positions of responsibility—Tom Corts, Paul Matia, Charlie Bolton. And every time I hear that name or read it, my mind goes back to the great experiences I had in the House of serving with Frances Bolton, Ollie Bolton.[7] It would be great to have another Bolton starting up the political ladder. And I certainly hope that Charlie is successful on November 5.

Of course, it is an observation that I can make as an outsider coming in, even though I have been here many times for a good many reasons over a long period of time, that the people in Ohio are responsive to the needs—the needs of the hour, the day, the time, the year. The people that you have sent to Congress that I have known are problemsolvers, and you ought to be proud of the job they have done and what they can do for you in the future.

I have been told by some of my friends in the press that lately my speeches have gotten a little partisan—well, that I am using the word "Republican" too frequently. The truth is they are right. I intend to do more of it, because I happen to think our party has the best candidates, and I am proud of the party and its candidates.

As a matter of fact, I think I am a little restrained, at least relatively so. They may not have seen anything yet as we go in the next 2 weeks, because the issues are very, very important and the quality of the candidates are vital.

Speaking of being restrained, there is a great quotation from an English parliamentarian by the name of Edmund Burke. And let me use it if I might. "There is, however, a limit at which forebearance ceases to be a virtue." We are close to that point. [*Laughter*]

I think it is important that the public know precisely what I am saying so there is no danger whatsoever of any misunderstanding. The message is simply this—it is very concise, I think it is very proper, and that message is this: Inflation is the chief problem we face in this country and throughout the free world. Rising prices in America cannot and will not be stopped by a free-spending Congress.

It is just that simple. This Congress that we have had for the last 2 years has been controlled by the Democratic Party just as it has been for 38 out of the last 42 years and for the last 20 years consecutively.

---

[7] Frances P. Bolton was United States Representative from Ohio 1940–69, and her son, Oliver P. Bolton, was United States Representative from Ohio 1953–57 and 1963–65.

Now, some elements of the Democratic Party are not satisfied with the domination and the control they have had 38 out of 42 years, the last 20 years consecutively. They want complete and total domination. They want—and they have said so openly—they want to elect what they call a veto-proof Congress, one where the numbers are so overwhelming that they can override any Presidential veto.

It is my honest judgment that that kind of numerical control would be tantamount to a legislative dictatorship, and I don't think a legislative dictatorship coincides with our great history, our great traditions, our Constitution.

If that happens, ladies and gentlemen, let me put it this way: Buckle your seatbelts. It is going to make the inflation rate look like it is tied to a Moon shot, because Federal spending will go out of sight. It will be far beyond anything that has happened in the past.

Those of us like Chuck Mosher and Bill Stanton and Bob Taft, who have served in the House as well as in the Senate, know that the inevitable tendency, the almost irreversible direction of a Congress dominated by the free spenders on the Democratic side, will mean more and more and more spending. And that is not the way to control inflation.

I think it is interesting to note that a recent Gallup poll indicates that a majority of the American people blame big government, big government spending, for the rampant inflation, the double-digit inflation we have had in recent months. And I happen to agree that big government, big government spending is a basic cause of the inflation spiral that is plaguing us at this moment.

Inflation, as I see it, is public enemy number one. But one point of view that I think is often overlooked, every penny, every dollar that is spent by the Federal Government, is appropriated by the Congress.

A President can't spend a nickel that Congress has not appropriated, and so, as we look at the control of the Congress for the last 42 years—38 out of the last 42 controlled by the opposition—if we have spent too much, the blame has to inevitably rest with those who had the control.

Now if that is true, and I think it is, I would like to challenge the American people tonight to follow through with their belief that Government spending is a basic cause of inflation. And I would like to urge those who feel that way to make their votes consistent with their views—to elect a Congress, men and women, who are committed to curbing Federal spending and thereby checking inflation.

To quote Edmund Burke once again, and I quote as follows: The only thing necessary for the triumph of evil is for good men to do nothing.

And I think that forewarning is most applicable today, because every poll you read and every political pundit who writes is saying there is a great apathy throughout the country, that people are disgusted and discouraged about politics, and therefore they are not going to vote.

Yes, I have been told from various sources that this apathy even extends in the great State of Ohio. People are not going to vote. They are disgusted; they are discouraged; they are turned off by politics; they are going to sit this one out.

Frankly, I don't believe it. That kind of attitude—it is akin to setting fire to your house to keep warm. That is not the way to change things. That is not the way to reverse the situation.

And so I, with as much sincerity as I can, urge Republicans in Ohio, and actually in the rest of the country, to vote November 5 like you have never voted before. I don't mean more than once. [*Laughter*] But at least once, and to get many others to do the same.

Confound the doomsayers. Fool the pessimists, the pollsters who are putting out this propaganda. And I respectfully urge you to work as you have never worked before for the candidates that deserve your support. Work on those thoughtful Independents and some of the wise Democrats who believe as you do. At least they are open-minded enough to be convinced by the views and the recommendations that you personally hold.

Work, if you might, at preserving the two-party system, this system which has provided so much in the way of freedom and opportunity and material blessings for all of those that preceded us and 213 million people today—no other nation has been so blessed as we.

I think it is perfectly obvious, as we look at the voting patterns in the last few months, that apathy is a chief villain. Some people think it has just happened this year, but as you look back—and my good friend Ray Bliss knows it probably better than I—some of these statistics show that this apathy has been much, much too evident, even since 1960. And let me quote a statistic or two that shows how bad it has been and how evil it might be in 1974.

Take the national percentages of votes cast in Congressional off-year elections like the one coming up. Based on the total number of eligible voters, only 46.3 percent turned out to cast ballots in 1962. Unbelievable! Only 45.6 percent took the time to do so in 1966. And the percentage of eligibles who voted in the last off-year election, 1970, was even lower—43.8 percent.

On the basis of these figures, one computer program suggests that only 42.7 percent of eligible voters will cast ballots for Congressional races and candidates 2 weeks from today. I think we ought to be ashamed. Think of those who have given so much over the recent two or three decades to save the opportunity for us to vote, to participate in free elections—and to find that some 42 percent are going to participate 2 weeks from today!

If that happens—and I trust it won't—it means that the composition of the next Congress that will be sworn in January 3, 1975, will be decided by slightly more than 4 out of every 10 voters. In short, the majority would let the minority decide.

What really concerns me even to a greater degree is the inclination of the American people to consider politics something they would rather not be involved in. Obviously, I think that is wrong. Let's not make politics a spectator sport. If you can get 85,000 people to come out on a Saturday to watch Ohio State win—and they always do—why can't we get 5 million voters to the polls in the State of Ohio on November 5? I think you can.

The sad fact is that in America, one of our fellow citizens in thirty has anything to do with politics. Now, that obviously does not include all of you, because you are interested, you participate in one way or another. You contribute, you work, you help in every way you can with the party. But one person out of every thirty in this great country has anything to do with the political system, and yet it is that part of our system—politics—which makes our government good or bad.

The selection of candidates, working in a campaign, researching the issues, raising or helping to contribute for the election of good candidates or even running for office—those should be honorable things. Those should be something that people want to do that feel an obligation to do.

I think what this Nation needs, less than 2 years from now, before the celebration of our 200th anniversary, is not less, but more citizen participation in politics.

Oh, I know, it is frequently written and more often said that politics is a dirty word which should be eliminated from government. Let me remind you, from the viewpoint of one who has been in it 26 years, that politics *is* government—government in action. And there is nothing wrong with this political system of ours that a massive injection of citizen involvement will not cure.

Having spent almost a quarter of a century on Capitol Hill as a Member of the House—and I am proud of it—I am convinced of the importance of getting out and away from Washington to find what the people of this great country beyond the Potomac are thinking and are concerned about. And that is why I am here tonight.

Now, I have had a lot of advice from people who say I should sit in the Oval Office and contemplate and listen to advisers who, in the main, send things into the office, and to a substantial degree they are pretty much permanent residents of Washington, D.C.

I don't think that is the role of a President. In the first place, as I travel, I find that I get a tremendous amount of beneficial input from people, whether it is in Oklahoma City, whether it is in Sioux Falls, South Dakota, or whether it is in Cleveland, Ohio.

Your views are important to me—as vital, as critical as the views I get from those who are in Government in Washington. And to sit there and be shielded, to be barricaded, in my judgment is not what a President ought to do. And in addition, a President ought to be out trying to sell what he, at least, believes is the right course of action for our policies, whether they are those policies involving our problems at home or our problems abroad.

We have just 14 days, and we have got some very critical decisions to make. You can have an impact, not just on a 1-day basis but for another 24 months, on the kind of Government you are going to have.

You want Senators and Representatives who won't go over the hill in the battle against inflation. You want Members in the United States Senate and in the House of Representatives who will cut redtape, who will cut the budget, and more importantly, cut the mustard.

Yes, Congressional elections are what our elections are all about in America—certainly this year. Every 2 years in the House and every 6 years in the United States Senate, these Members go before you to have their record looked at, analyzed, compared to the promises made by those who are challenging them.

I happen to think, after knowing intimately the records of our candidates, that ours deserve your full, unequivocal, unhesitating support. And it would please me tremendously to see a tremendous Republican victory in the great State of Ohio.

There is one thing we cannot forget. There is no weapon so mighty, no force so powerful as the quiet, symbolic voice of the American citizen spoken in the privacy of the voting booth on election day. And that voice is not only heeded but heard, heard by your elected officials, and they won't forget it in the next few years.

I hope that you will send a message to the Congress. You represent the consumer, the working man and woman, the housewife, the plain citizen. Tell them that you are sick and tired of rising prices, that you want something done about it.

Let the Congress know that you want some affirmative action on what I think was a sound, constructive, 31-point program for the controlling of inflation on the one hand and a stimulant in a constructive way for our economy on the other.

Yes, we can whip inflation. We can keep the economy moving. We can save energy. But Congress has to act. And so far, their performance, controlled by the opposition, has been minimal.

I happen to think what this country needs is a responsive and responsible House as well as Senate. We need men and women who will, in the words of one television commentator, praise the Lord and pass the legislation.

Let me conclude with one final plea. I came to Washington in January of 1949—young, enthusiastic, stimulated by what had transpired in the previous 2 years. We had a Democratic President, Harry Truman, and the previous 2 years, we had had a Republican Congress, the so-called 80th Congress.

And that Democratic President and that Republican Congress, seeing the evils and failures of the twenties and thirties in the handling of foreign policy in this country, decided that on a bipartisan basis we ought to forget partisanship and move in foreign policy for the country, regardless of your party affiliation.

We had the Marshall Plan. We had foreign aid. We had decisions made by President Truman supported by a Republican Congress. And we laid the foundation, the groundwork for a quarter of a century or more of, I think, constructive foreign policy.

This last Congress, despite the leadership of the Democrats as well as the Republicans, started to tear apart this bipartisanship. We have a Republican President and a Democratic Congress, and I fear that if this destruction of a bipartisan foreign policy goes on, our leadership in this country—as a country at the head of the free world, trying to avoid and avert a catastrophic situation—if this bipartisanship is destroyed by one roadblock, one hindrance, one limitation after another, no President, me or anyone that follows me, can do a job for peace—a job for peace.

We need a Congress that will stand up and go shoulder-to-shoulder with the President who wants to find and keep peace in the Middle East, who wants to find the key to the problems between the Greeks and the Turks over Cyprus, a President who wants to see that the Mediterranean is free of Soviet domination.

Teamwork between the Congress and the President can insure this kind of success whether it is making NATO stronger, making Western Europe a bastion of strength economically, diplomatically.

Yes, we need the kind of cooperation in the Congress to make sure that we do what is right in Latin America, that we try to help Africa to become an emerging continent, raising the levels that are so essential for them as well as for others.

We need the kind of cooperation between the Congress and the President to see that the Pacific does not have another kind of conflagration that lasted for 10 years in Vietnam.

I am worried. This last Congress, in my judgment, despite the leadership on both sides of the aisle, began to tear apart that cooperation between a President and the Congress. I happen to think if you work, if you do what you can, we can have a Congress in the next 2 years that will stand with the President who wants the peace, who believes we have a unique opportunity in this time in history to build for peace, not for a year but for longer.

Now, I ask for your help. I ask for your support—not just for me, not for the Republican Party, but for the country and millions and millions of people all over the world.

Thank you very much.

NOTE: The President spoke at 8:40 p.m. at a dinner for Republican candidates in the Gold Room at the Sheraton-Cleveland Hotel.

185

Veto of National Wildlife Refuge System Legislation. *October 22, 1974*

To the House of Representatives:

I am withholding my approval from H.R. 11541, a bill which would amend the National Wildlife Refuge System Administration Act of 1966. I am advised by the Attorney General and I have determined that the absence of my signature from this bill prevents it from becoming law. Without in any way qualifying this determination, I am also returning it without my approval to those designated by Congress to receive messages at this time.

This bill would amend section 4(d) of the Act of October 15, 1966, by adding a new standard in determining the authority of the Secretary of the Interior to allow certain rights-of-way across lands of the National Wildlife Refuge System. This new standard would require the Secretary to review all reasonable alternatives to the use of such area, and then make a determination that the proposed right-of-way use is the most feasible and prudent alternative for such purpose.

If we are to have adequate energy-transmission and communication facilities, we must have rights-of-way on which to locate them. Of course, when such lands have a special status as wildlife refuges or national parks, we must fully protect this status when portions of these areas are sought for use as rights-of-way.

However, I believe that such protection is properly provided under existing law which requires environmental impact review and further requires the Secretary of the Interior to determine that granting a right-of-way across a national wildlife refuge or national park must be compatible with the purposes for which the park or refuge had been established. Only last year, Congress enacted legislation which had the effect of reiterating this protection in the case of refuges.

In short, our wildlife refuges are properly protected by existing law. We should avoid changes in the law that could create further obstacles and delays in the construction of vitally needed facilities, particularly those facilities designed to help meet urgent energy needs.

Accordingly, I am withholding my approval from H.R. 11541.

GERALD R. FORD

The White House,
October 22, 1974.

NOTE: The text of the message was released at Cleveland, Ohio.

186

Message to the Congress Transmitting Annual Report of the National Cancer Advisory Board. *October 23, 1974*

To the Congress of the United States:

In accord with section 410B(g) of the "National Cancer Act of 1971" (P.L. 92–218), I am transmitting the second annual report of the National Cancer Advisory Board on the progress of the National Cancer Institute.

As the Board's report indicates, the activities of the National Cancer Institute are progressing smoothly. The report highlights several areas in which significant scientific advances are being made.

In several instances, the Board raises major policy issues and makes recommendations to the Congress. For example, the Board's report urges Federal regulation of cigarettes. It should be pointed out that there is considerable dispute as to whether there exists adequate scientific evidence on which to base safe levels of tar and nicotine under responsible regulatory action. In response to the Board's concern, I have asked the National Cancer Advisory Board to provide me with an assessment of the scientific evidence that would provide a basis for responsible Federal regulation of cigarettes.

While I think it is important for the Congress to have the benefit of the Board's views, those views must necessarily be considered along with other diverse and responsible points of view.

GERALD R. FORD

The White House,
October 23, 1974.

NOTE: The 11-page report is entitled "National Cancer Program, 1974, Report of the National Cancer Advisory Board."

187

Remarks at the Iowa State House, Des Moines, Iowa. *October 24, 1974*

Governor Bob Ray, Lieutenant Governor Neu, my former colleagues in the House, Bill Scherle, Wiley Mayne, and I guess H. R. Gross is here someplace:

Let me say it has been a wonderful visit to Des Moines already—the crowds on the highway, the tremendous group here, the enthusiasm, the warm welcome. I can only say, from a Michigander to a Hawkeye, thank you very, very much.

On some occasions, Governor Ray, I have thought that having Iowa still a part of Michigan would be extremely helpful to us in Michigan, but I would be in a real tough spot now if Michigan and Iowa were somehow joined. We have got a great, good Governor in Bill Milliken, and you have a great, good Governor in Bob Ray. It would be real tough to decide.

I know one contribution that was made by Michigan to Iowa a few years ago. As you know, I played football at the University of Michigan a long time ago, back when the ball was round. But in later years, one of our great Michigan stars came to the University of Iowa—Forrest Evashevski—who did a great job out here. And I have often wondered why we didn't keep him at Michigan, because he was such a great competitor, a great football coach, and a great contribution to our State.

Let me just say from my observations that the weather, the people, the candidates, the Governor—you have a great State, and I think all of you should be very proud of it.

During the 25 years that I was in the Congress, I will say without any hesitation or qualification that I have always been impressed with the men, frankly, from both parties that were sent to the Congress of the United States.

They have been strong men, independent individuals, men of integrity, men of action—like your Governor, Bob Ray. I happen to believe that he has provided the sort of independence and the leadership that we have come to expect from Hawkeyes in whatever office they serve, and I congratulate you for the three terms that Governor Ray has already had, and I urge you from the bottom of my heart to make sure that he is your first Governor elected for a 4-year term.

I think that you have in this great State something that the rest of us could well use. Iowa is solvent. You have a long history of stable government, particularly under Bob Ray. You even have a balanced budget, which is progress by any standard. I have to admit that I was bit startled when the Governor told me that the budget was not only balanced but had substantial surplus of something like $200 million. I was startled because it has been years and years and years since I have heard of a surplus back in Washington in the Federal Treasury.

Yes, these are open spaces out here in Iowa, which give all of you room to move, to bring up your children. I think you have achieved in this great State that urban-rural balance that is the envy of every State in the Union.

I was most impressed with the figures that your Governor cited on stemming migration out of Iowa for the first time since the 1890's. I am told people are no longer pouring out of Iowa. They are no longer pouring off the farms, leaving the State, and this is a pattern that I hope we can develop—that we can develop not only in a few States but all States; a pattern that we can develop across the Nation.

The problems that we have been experiencing with our economy since the end of the involvement in Vietnam—including shortages, including scarcities—have brought home, it is my judgment, some of the basic lessons that our people have to remember, have to recall, and have to build on. It is my judgment that we have to simplify our lifestyles. We must return to some of the basics. We must make the best use of what we have. We must cut out the waste. We must strip away the nonessentials. In short, we have to return to the state of mind and the way of life that made us the greatest nation in the history of mankind.

If we will sit back and look, reflect just a bit, we can see ourselves as part of a community with people directly influencing things that shape their individual lives. If you take this time to reflect, I think you will find that people—yourself and others—can determine their own priorities, and that sense of community has not been lost here in Iowa.

In the coming years, we will continue to see Iowa, under the leadership of Bob Ray, serving as a model for the rest of the Nation. You have in this great State what so many people all over the United States are seeking. You have the basic values upon which America was built over a period of some 200 years. I personally think of Iowa when I think of stability, of progress, and just as importantly, balance. I like the balance that you are achieving in Iowa between industry and agriculture.

Some of my advisers in Washington have suggested that I should avoid the subject of agriculture here today. They said our Iowa farmers and farmers throughout the Midwest are especially frustrated this year. I certainly and very deeply share the concern of farmers whose corn and soybean crops were stunted by drought and destroyed by early frosts.

The trend, however, for urbanization during the past few decades resulted in the downplaying of the farmer's central role in America's society. But recent problems have refocused our national attention on the farmer as one of our greatest national assets—an asset we should be proud of. It is my judgment that this is the time that we should be expanding farming in America. Let us encourage our young people to remain on the farms and others to return to them.

Iowa, your great State, for obvious reasons, is aware of the importance of agriculture, not only to your State but to our Nation and to the world. It is absolutely essential to the well-being of our total society here as well as around the world.

America can no longer expect the farmer to sacrifice so that others can live well. All Americans now realize that we are all in this problem together, and the farmer should not be called upon to make an extra sacrifice. It must be shared by all.

We rely upon the farmer for the strength of the community. The American farmer can outplant, outgrow, and outmarket any farmer—I don't care what nation in the world. However, if the farmer gets a fair shake, the American farmer can not only feed the people of the United States but human beings all over the world. And this in itself is something that we should appreciate and be grateful for.

In the immediate years ahead, American agriculture will be our greatest asset in the world trade market. In the last 2 or 3 years, the availability of the production of the American farmer has been extremely helpful as we try to help those who are less well-off than ourselves, for good humanitarian reasons.

As we try to use our food that is produced on the farms in America for reasons to benefit the United States, we should be so thankful that we are blessed with the land and the farms of America.

Food is, as we know, a basic key to world peace, and we in America hold that key. As I said in my speech last month to the United Nations General Assembly, the United States recognizes the special responsibility that we bear as the world's largest producer of food. We recognize that responsibility and I think we will accept it. I know it as a matter of fact, because of the people I see here in Iowa today, especially these attractive, enthusiastic, young people in the front of the audience—the cream of Iowa's bountiful crop.

This group of some 600—as I said, the cream of Iowa's bountiful crop—are delegates to the United Nations Youth Conference Day. I commend Icwa for its emphasis on the United Nations Day, and I thank all of you young people for participating.

Yes, the decisions they make as citizens of this great food-producing State will directly affect the well-being of the citizens of the world—I know that everybody in Iowa is very proud of each and every one of you—and the understanding that they are individually developing of the world situation will serve us all well in the future.

I am convinced that the future is now, right here in Iowa, and I pledge to you today—and especially to all of you young people, whether you are in this group or any other group—that I will do everything in my power to make sure that the American farmer is fully rewarded for his services rendered. America owes that to the American farmer, and so does the world.

If I might, let me stress this point, and I speak to you on this point not as a political partisan but as a partisan of the American system of government. Our system rests not only on the balance of urban and rural America but also on the balance within our Federal Government.

The basic principle underlying our system is balance, a finely tuned balance, the timely balance conceived by the Founding Fathers some 200 years ago among three branches of Government—the delicate balance within the Congress and the country through the two-party system.

This year the polls are telling us that our delicately balanced, two-party system is in some trouble, some jeopardy. If one party upsets that balance because members of the other party are apathetic, not concerned, and as a consequence, won't get out and vote, then we stand guilty, as I see it, of abusing the American electoral process and forfeiting our hope for an effective Government. Therefore, with deep conviction I urge you to keep this very great, balanced system intact. Let's not lose an integral, important, essential part of our Government by default.

What concerns me very greatly is the inclination of the American people to consider politics something they would rather not become involved in, which is something in the minds of too many. As a matter of fact, the sad fact is that less than one American out of 30 has anything to do with politics, with the selection of candidates, the working in a campaign, researching issues, with raising contributions for the election of a candidate, or even running for office. It is almost unbelievable that only one American out of 30 has any connection, direct or indirect, with politics.

It is my considered judgment that what this Nation needs less than 2 years from the 200th year of our founding, on the 200th birthday of this Nation, is more, not less participation by the citizenry in politics.

To those who say that politics is a dirty word which should be eliminated from government, let me respectfully remind each and every one of you that politics *is* government. Politics *is* government—government in action.

There is nothing wrong with the political system of ours that a massive injection of citizen involvement will not cure. You never win a football game by sitting on the sidelines. You never do well in your business, your profession, on your farm, by doing nothing, and it is precisely the same thing in politics at the local, the State, or the Federal level. If you want to make a contribution, if you wish to be a participant, get off the sidelines and into the ballgame.

I have spent a quarter of a century on Capitol Hill as a Member of the House of Representatives, and I happen to believe that it is important to get out and away from Washington on occasions such as this. I know there are some so-called experts who suggest that your President ought to sit in the Oval Office and listen to nothing but bureaucrats telling him what to do, yes or no, or sitting in the Oval Office reading documents that are prepared by people in Washington. I reject that advice. It is more important that I come to Des Moines.

This can be a two-way street. I want to discuss with you my policies and my programs, and in turn, I beg for a reaction and recommendations from all of you as to whether we are doing things right or wrong. And if we are doing them wrong, tell us how we can do them better. We solicit your participation. That is one reason I am here in Des Moines. I believe that it is vital that this two-way communication exists.

May I conclude with one other observation. I am told by the political forecasters that in this election year, 1974, there will be less people, a lesser number of eligible voters throughout the country voting on November 5 than at any time in any off-year election for the last 20 or more years. I don't believe that is going to happen. You won't, through apathy, let a minority make a decision for the majority. I only hope that instead of the 42 percent that they are forecasting who will actually vote, that it will be 50 or 60 percent—so that we get a true reflection of what people want done; so the majority makes a decision, not the minority making a determination.

Yes, Congressional, State, and local elections are what it is all about. I say as strongly and as sincerely as I can, there is no weapon so mighty, no force so powerful as the silent vote in the privacy of the voting booth.

It is the duty as well as the opportunity of every eligible voter in Iowa and the other 49 States to balance the ledger sheet on good government.

So, I say to all this wonderful group of Iowa friends, get out this time, vote as you have never voted before. The future of our American political system depends on your participation. It does in 1974, and it will in the years to come.

Thank you very, very much.

NOTE: The President spoke at 11:50 a.m. on the east steps of the Iowa State House.

188

Remarks at a Luncheon for Republican Candidates in Des Moines. *October 24, 1974*

Governor Bob Ray, Lieutenant Governor Neu, Dave Stanley,[1] *my former colleagues in the House, Wiley Mayne, Bill Scherle, all of the other fine Republican candidates, and all of you wonderful citizens of the great State of Iowa, thank you very, very much:*

You know, when I saw this grand old ballroom, it brought back to my mind, anyhow, so many happy memories of Tommy Dorsey, Woody Herman, Benny Goodman—some of you can remember it.

As a matter of fact, when my wife Betty and I used to go courting, we would go dancing to the music of those old big bands, as we called them. We had a problem, though. Betty had studied modern dance, and I was a former football player. [*Laughter*]

She was very polite, never really came right out and said I was a lousy dancer—she was much too kind for that—but she did have a rather interesting theory as

[1] David M. Stanley was the Republican candidate for United States Senator from Iowa.

to why I played center rather than quarterback. She said a center is one of the few positions on a football team where you don't have to move your feet. [*Laughter*]

Somehow, it seems very appropriate to me that we are holding this political gathering in this fine ballroom. You might, I guess, call this a Congressional square dance. Every 2 years we change partners. [*Laughter*]

And if you stop to think about it, really good dancers do have one thing in common with good Congressmen and good Senators—they have to know how to take the right steps. And when it comes to facing the very hard issues and the very difficult problems that we face at home and abroad today, there is only one step our good Republican candidates at this table don't know, and that is the sidestep.

It is my observation in watching your Republican delegation in Congress that they face the problems and they make an honest, conscientious, intelligent effort to solve them. I congratulate Bill Scherle, Wiley Mayne, H. R. Gross, and I congratulate some of those good candidates that you are going to elect on the Republican ticket to send a bigger Republican delegation to Congress next November 5.

You know, I have had this new office a relatively short period of time, something like 2½ months. I have found it somewhat difficult to shed some old habits. One of those habits over the last 26 years has been campaigning for fellow Republicans.

I don't know how many times I have been in various Congressional districts in Iowa, but I have always enjoyed it, and I have always been proud of it. I think it is the part of people when called upon to go out and stand up for, campaign for candidates that deserve support.

Now, while my job is different at the present time from what it has been in the past, the call to me is the exact same one. There is just a little major difference in the last 10 years. No one this year can accuse me of campaigning to become Speaker of the House of Representatives. [*Laughter*]

To be very honest, very frank about it, I believe in this country. I believe in the American people. In the last year, I have traveled all over our country, some 42 out of the 50 States, over 128,000 miles, and here is what I have found:

There is work to be done in America. That is why I am here, to seek your support for programs, for policies that I have proposed to the Congress, programs and policies which, in my judgment, will meet our country's pressing needs.

These are programs I have submitted to the Congress that would tackle affirmatively and effectively the problems of inflation, energy overuse, and peace abroad. I am here because I think the elections coming up in a relatively short period of time—12 days to be exact—that is what America's democracy is all about.

It is time for you and your fellow Iowans to speak up for those that you want in Washington to speak up for you, and you have an opportunity in this relatively short period of time to make a difference. You are here because you can make a contribution, but you have got 12 short days to spread your influence, your enthusiasm, your dedication, your conviction.

I think we all recognize there is no force so powerful as that very quiet decision that you and other Iowans and millions of other Americans make in the privacy of the voting booth. I think you here understand the power, and you in the past, because of your dedication and support, have used it wisely, and obviously, because you are here, you will use it wisely November 5.

But let me make a few observations, if I can, to maybe reach, invigorate some of the enthusiasm you have, the conviction that you really have.

Your Governor, Bob Ray, is the living proof of your wise decision in three previous gubernatorial elections. As I travel around the country, I have an opportunity to see Governors—Democrats as well as Republicans—and I can say without any hestitation, reservation, or qualification, that you in Iowa have in Bob Ray one of the very, very best, and I congratulate you. He is a problem-solver, a man of action. He is the kind of Republican leader that I like. And he is the kind you need as your Governor for the next 4 years.

But, if I might, let's move from Des Moines to Washington. Dave Stanley is campaigning vigorously. He has crossed the State and recrossed it, and he is campaigning for one of the highest offices in our land. He is tireless, imaginative, experienced—a man committed to squeezing the last bit, the last bit of spending out of the taxpayer's dollar, so that you get a good return for the dollars you send to Washington, D.C. And I urge you as strongly as I can to send Dave Stanley to Washington.

On January 3, 1949, I had the privilege of being sworn in alongside of H. R. Gross. Let me make this prediction: The House of Representatives will never be the same without him. H. R. Gross has been the conscience of the House of Representatives for more than 25 years, and he has been a tremendous saver of the taxpayer's dollars. Believe me, he set a high standard. We need more people like H. R. Gross in the Washington scene in the House as well as in the Senate.

Bill Scherle and Wiley Mayne I served with, and I can give a personal testimonial about both of them. They worked with me, they were helpful, yet they could be independent. When they had deep convictions, they differed with me, and I respect them for it.

They are not rubber stamps for the Republican Party. They were not rubber stamps for me. But they make a tremendous, conscientious, effective—I think—intelligent effort to represent their respective districts. And I hope and trust that both Wiley Mayne and Bill Scherle are sent back with a sound, strong vote from their districts.

I have had the privilege of looking into the backgrounds and qualifications of your other Congressional candidates. I know one or two of them, but Jim Leach, Charley Grassley, Tom Riley, Charles Dick [2]—they are out campaigning, and they need your help. And we need their kind of representation in the House of Representatives. I urge you, I implore you to give them the hand that will get you and, I think, us a victory on November 5.

Let me be quite categorical and explain, as I see it, why we need tightfisted Members of the House and Senate to help us in this battle against inflation.

In every poll that I see, whether it is national or in Iowa, there is a clear indication that inflation is the one problem that transcends all others, and it is the one problem where the American people want some action by their Government—and for good reason.

Inflation means money stolen out of your pocketbook by a thief as real as a pickpocket. The rising cost of living is a problem which is not matched in magnitude nor equaled in its impact on our Nation's future.

I didn't come all this way out to Iowa to talk to you or tell you about a problem that you know as much about as I do or as any other politician does. I came out here to tell you that, in my judgment, we have got a program that will be an answer, and we want Members of the Congress sent down who are going to help us find those answers.

We searched very hard for the right answers. I think we have now a better understanding as a result of our various mini-summit and summit economic meetings. It is now time, as I look at it, not to point the finger of blame at just a few people or a few institutions. Most institutions—and, I think, most people—are involved in the inflationary process. But just as much responsibility, if not more so, for inflation today rests squarely on the Federal Government, the Congress in Washington, D.C. And that is where we better do something about it.

[2] Republican candidates for Congress from the First, Third, Second, and Fourth Districts of Iowa, respectively.

We came to some other conclusions in these various meetings that we had where business, labor, education, housing, economists contributed very significantly to the thoughts and the recommendations that we finally put together in a 31-point program package. But we came to some other conclusions.

There is no quick fix. There is no easy cure for the inflationary illness that we face. It is going to take some time, some patience, and just as importantly, some work.

You know, some of my political opposition have said that the plan I submitted was a marshmallow; it didn't ask for anybody to bite the bullet very hard. Well then, just a couple of days ago, I saw and then I read the anti-inflation program put forth by the opposition.

Well, if mine was a marshmallow, theirs was a lemon.

The second observation that we came to is that victory over inflation is going to require some short-term sacrifices to serve our long-term well-being in America. As I said, in the 31-point program to Congress and my daily dozen suggestions to the American people, the burden will have to be evenly distributed. It will not be borne if we implement the recommendations that I have proposed—the burden will not be borne by those least able to afford it.

The third point there must be—and this is where my former colleagues in the Congress and the prospective ones come into play—there must be a substantial cut in the amount of Federal spending this year as well as next year.

For the remainder of this year, I have urged the Congress to make a cut of about $5.5 billion, and next year we are going to hold the lid on unless the next Congress blows it off.

Now finally, we are in a very serious battle where national unity is every bit as important as it has been for the past national crises, whether they were from outside or from within.

If we do not march shoulder-to-shoulder together, we will fall by the wayside one-by-one.

I am determined to win this fight. I know that there have been some unhappy people with some of the suggestions I have made. Yes, I have made some power interests somewhat unhappy, but these are tough decisions I have to make and the Congress has to make and all of you have to make.

If we don't, nobody will. Unfortunately, the problem has waited too long to be tackled. Unfortunately, it will not go away.

Now, the first shot being fired in the war against inflation will come out of the ballot box November 5. And I implore you to have that a shot heard round the world, or at least around the country. And if it is, the country will be far better off.

You might ask yourself what can your vote accomplish? The answer is very simple: It can send to the Congress men and women who are not big spenders.

Look at the record. Look at the promises. We need men and women in Congress who can say no to programs and to policies and projects which are completely unnecessary at the present time—programs that we can get along without for the time being.

We don't need men and women in Congress who talk about halting inflation or cutting spending in their home States, their home Congressional district, and vote the opposite way in the Congress.

Let me add a personal postscript, if I might. Wiley Mayne, Bill Scherle, H. R. Gross—they talk like they vote. They are against big spending, and I can show you the record to prove it. That is why you ought to send them back there.

But I have a second postscript, if I might. Dave Stanley is a man who has the same dedication to saving, who has the same opposition to spending, and although I know his opponent and his record, I can assure you that Dave Stanley is a saver, and his opponent is a big, big spender.

Now, the next Congress needs Members who will, in my judgment, rise above short-term thinking Representatives who recognize that the red ink route that we have traveled for 19 out of the last 25 years is a losing game, losing from the point of view of our Nation's future.

Nobody benefits from inflation—not business, not labor, not the rich, not the poor, not the farmer, not anybody. It is the losing proposition across the board. Everybody gets hurt. Oh, I know it is easy to yield to that temptation to give people what some politicians think they want. But I remind you, a government big enough to give us everything we want is a government big enough to take from us everything we have.

Despite some of the skeptics, the foundation of our economy in all 50 States is strong. It has been the most productive economy in the history of civilization. We have an abundance beyond the wildest imagination of our parents or our grandparents.

We are able to share, fortunately, our wealth with the poor of our own Nation as well as the poor of the world, but we must defend this economy from the attacks which would erode it.

Now, some of my friends in the opposition seem to think that what is needed to solve the problem is a veto-proof Congress. The fact of the matter is, it was a heavy Democratic majority over the years which helped to create most of the problems we face domestically.

Therefore, I think it is fair to say we do not need a Congress or we don't need to make a Congress immune from veto. We do need to make our Nation safe from inflation. What we need is not a veto-proof Congress. But let's take the affirmative: What we need is an inflation-proof Congress.

That is why you need—frankly, why I need—in Washington, Members of Congress who will join me in making some of these very hard decisions—decisions to cut spending, to cut the budget, to cut the redtape, and as I said before, to cut the mustard.

With that kind of teamwork, we can get the job done. With that kind of support, we will do what we promised—we will whip inflation, we will effect savings in energy, we will save our natural resources, we will be on our way to our 200th birthday in 1976 strong, stable, prosperous in a world at peace.

Some of my dear friends on the other side of the political aisle make promises at election time to be fiscal watchdogs and keepers of the Treasury, but we can see by the way they spend your money they have failed year after year after year.

Let me cite a statistic that proves it—the facts are there: The problems we face today were spawned over the last 42 years by programs and policies of the opposition party which has controlled the Congress of the United States, both the House and the Senate, 38 out of the last 42 years.

To make the point even more emphatic, they have controlled the House and the Senate in the national Congress the last 20 years consecutively.

Let me add this as a postscript: There is not a dime of money spent by a President that is not appropriated by the Congress. So, they are responsible for the excessive spending that has caused most of our inflation.

The question that I want you to ponder today is, are you, are we going to continue down that same path, that same road which produced the problems in the first place—problems of ever-rising prices, of piling more centralization of power in Washington, of undermining our foreign relations with handcuff restrictions on the policies of the President and the Secretary of State?

We have got to do better than that today. What happened in the past was largely the failure of a legislative dictatorship by a party so smug in its seniority and its power that it no longer responded to the true needs of the people.

I except the members of the leadership in the House and Senate of the Democratic Party. They have tried, they have sought to be helpful, at least to me as the President, and I can testify as to that, but their troops run wild.

Therefore, I urge you today, I urge all Americans to vote with your heads as well as your hearts, but most important, vote. Don't let that most precious liberty ever devised by man disappear because it was ignored. Pull the lever and cast your vote a week from Tuesday for candidates of the political party that brought peace to this country and stability to the world.

Cast your vote for the party that will, with a cooperative Congress, restore stability to America's economy and inject some commonsense into its Government.

With God's help and your hand we will go down that path together with confidence, understanding of the greatness that still lies before us. We can say honestly with conviction that we are proud to be Americans, proud of America.

Thank you very much.

NOTE: The President spoke at 12:55 p.m. at the Val Air Ballroom.

189

Statement on Signing the Commodity Futures Trading Commission Act of 1974. *October 24, 1974*

I AM pleased to announce that I have signed into law H.R. 13113, the Commodity Futures Trading Commission Act of 1974.

This act will provide the first major overhaul of the existing Commodity Exchange Act since its inception by establishing a new regulatory structure to apply to all commodity futures trading. This is an objective which I fully support.

This legislation was prompted by increasing concern that Federal regulation of commodity futures trading is too narrow in scope and that the present regulatory system is inadequate. In the past few years, the Federal Government has disposed of large accumulations of minerals and agricultural commodities. But present stocks are not large enough to stabilize prices. The recent market situation has been characterized by widely swinging prices. The futures markets have become increasingly important to our marketing system—with the value of futures trading now totaling $500 billion annually.

The increased trading has attracted more speculators and vastly increased the potential for unethical and illegal practices. This has resulted in failures of financial firms and losses by innocent investors.

Consumers also have suffered, since the gyrations of the futures markets have, in some cases, driven up prices to consumers.

It is important that futures trading take place under conditions in which traders and the public have full confidence in the system. This new law is an important step in this direction.

Unfortunately, in passing an otherwise desirable bill, the Congress has incorporated three objectionable provisions which would enable the new Commodity Futures Trading Commission to compromise traditional executive branch functions. I find these provisions unacceptable as well as being unnecessary for the effective operation of the Commission.

The first one would require the concurrent submission of Commission budget requests to Congress and to the President or to the Office of Management and Budget. This would in effect undercut the provisions of the Budget and Accounting Act of 1921, which requires the President to submit to Congress a single, coordinated budget. It also represents a retreat from my goal of reduced Federal spending, since it will make it more difficult for me to review all requests for Federal spending in advance of submission to Congress.

Second, as with the budget requests, it would require concurrent submission of the Commission's legislative proposals. If extended to other agencies, such a requirement would make it difficult for me to develop and present to the Congress a coherent, coordinated legislative program.

Third, the Commission is empowered to appoint an Executive Director, by and with the advice and consent of the Senate. This raises serious constitutional questions, by providing for an executive branch appointment in a manner not contemplated by the Constitution. This encroachment on the separation of powers can easily be corrected by deletion of the request for Senate confirmation of the Executive Director.

Nevertheless, because of the need for better regulation of commodity futures trading, I have signed H.R. 13113, notwithstanding my strong objections to these three provisions which erode necessary executive control. I will submit to the Congress legislation which would correct these three provisions, and I will strongly urge its passage during this session of the 93d Congress.

NOTE: As enacted, H.R. 13113, approved October 23, 1974, is Public Law 93–463 (88 Stat. 1389). The statement was released at Des Moines, Iowa.

190

Remarks at Ceremonies Honoring Representative Leslie C. Arends in Melvin, Illinois. *October 24, 1974*

Betty Arends, Louella Dirksen, my dear friend Charlie Halleck, Bill Springer:

We are kind of old-timers, but then there are some new ones—Cliff Carlson, George O'Brien, Ed Madigan, George Burditt, your candidate for the Senate, Bill Scott [1]—well, a number of outstanding, wonderful servants of the people of the great State of Illinois.

It is almost unbelievable for me to be in Melvin and see this magnificent crowd. You would not think it could happen anyplace in the country, except you know and I know and Charlie Halleck knows and Louella Dirksen knows what a great, great guy Les Arends is. And that is why all of us are here.

I am sure that many of you made a much bigger effort than I, but we are here because you know and I know and literally thousands of other people know that Les Arends gave 110 percent in anything he ever did. He did it for you all in this Congressional district. He did it for the State, and he did it for the country. He did it for his family, his friends. Les Arends, on each and every occasion that he ever undertook to do anything, made the most maximum effort, and that is why you love him—we do; why you respect him, and why we do.

Les, I can't thank you enough for those years that we worked in tandem trying to lead the minority to do a responsible and constructive job with the help of many, many others. But, I think we developed a close, warm, deep, personal relationship that has not been matched by any that I have ever had in the Congress, or almost anyplace. And for that experience, Les—a very personal one—I thank you very much.

It has already been alluded to, but aside from the reasons I have just given for being here on behalf of Les, there are not many Ford Counties in the whole United States. We don't have one in Michigan, so I am here just to get acquainted with a lot of people from Ford County. I don't know whether any of my ancestors ever settled here, but if not, obviously they should have, with one exception: If they ever had, and Les Arends had been in Congress, I would never have made it to Washington, D.C.

---

[1] Cliffard D. Carlson was the Republican candidate in the 15th Congressional District of Illinois; Representative George M. O'Brien was the Republican candidate in the 17th Congressional District; Representative Edward R. Madigan was the Republican candidate in the 21st Congressional District; and William J. Scott was attorney general of Illinois.

The weather, the location, the people just make this an ideal setting for this testimonial to Les. I am told Melvin has a population of roughly 500, and Les' comment as he was speaking indicated that, well, maybe you might lose an inch or two with all the people.

Let me add this postscript, if I can. All of you—the 500 of you from Melvin—are so darned proud of Les, you will just stand up and take charge, and you are not going to sink one inch or one one-eighth of an inch because you have something that will never be forgotten in the history of Melvin, and that is Les Arends.

I have been told that three Presidents have visited Melvin and they all appeared for the same, the precise, the identical reason—to tell all of you in Melvin and all of you who have come from many other places, the high regard that all of us have for Les Arends.

I looked at the history. I thought I knew it about Les—20 terms, 40 years. It will be a sad day in Washington, D.C., when Les Arends takes the final step out of Room 2306 in the Rayburn Building. Sometime in January, that will be the last time Les Arends will leave an office building where he had the honor to serve all of you in the House of Representatives.

The history books record that out of the 9,442 elected Members of the House of Representatives, from the very beginning until the last election, only 10 of them—10 out of 9,442—have spent a longer time in the House of Representatives than Les Arends. So, his name and his service will go down in the history books of our country.

Now I know, as I look across this tremendous crowd that is paying tribute to Les Arends, that your grandparents and your great-grandparents, in some instances, and your parents and literally hundreds of you have participated in sending Les Arends to Congress for these 20 elections.

It is a lot easier, Les, as you know, to get to Washington today than it was that first trip. When you first left in 1934, it was either a long, bumpy drive—probably took 3 to 4 days—or maybe it was a pretty rough railroad trip. But you made it every year. You served conscientiously, constructively, with compassion, with firmness. All the accolades that have come Les Arends' way, he richly deserved.

I am told that back in the 1934 election, Les was campaigning to unseat an incumbent Democrat. And that was not a very good year for Republicans, as many of you may remember, but Les won. And his opponent, who he defeated, the incumbent, was pretty upset. After the election he was quoted as saying he didn't mind getting beat, but he didn't like the idea of being licked by a pair of long legs.

Well, I think all of you know that it was not Les' legs that endeared him to you; it was his door-to-door, his barnyard-to-barnyard campaigning. He started it in 1934, and for the next 19 elections he did the same thing. In his own inimitable way, Les Arends got to know people, he got to know their problems, and he indicated a desire to work to solve those problems. He didn't ask whether a person was a Democrat, an Independent, or a Republican. He did it the way Abe Lincoln did.

Les Arends wanted to solve problems of people and do what was right for the district and the State and the country, and for those reasons Les never had much trouble. He was respected, admired, and loved.

On the issues—and I know intimately because we had some tough ones in recent years—Les never looked at the problem from a political sense. He looked at those problems from the point of view of what was right, and he voted the way he thought it was right for people in the country. And that basic ingredient, which is so necessary in this day and age, made it possible for Les to serve this district for so long. I don't have to embellish his record; it speaks for itself. He did a great job in a period of time which was unique in our country's history.

Let me cite a few figures, a fact or two, to indicate the change that went on in this country from 1934 until today—this span of time, four decades, when Les Arends did a job for all of you.

When Les entered the Congress in 1935, the Federal budget for everything was $6 billion. Isn't that right, Charlie? Les? Six billion dollars to run everything for the Federal Government. Now it is $305 billion. We are trying to cut it about $5.4 billion.

Back in 1934, Les Arends entered Congress, and at that time the Federal payroll for everybody was $780,582. Today it is over $2 billion, something around $2.1 billion.

Back in 1935, the budget for the Army, the Navy—there was not an Air Force; it was the Air Corps in those days—the total budget for the Department of Defense—they didn't actually have that in those days—but for whatever we bought for guns and aircraft was under $1 billion. Today it is $88 billion.

Back in those days, the national debt was $29 billion, and it was forecast as a catastrophe for America. I hate to admit it now, but today the national debt is $507 billion.

I don't bring these facts and figures up to indicate in any way whatsoever that

Les Arends had anything to do with what took place or the things that happened—just the opposite. Les fought against deficit financing; he did his utmost to hold down the growth in the Federal deficits and national debt. But I can't help but indicate that in these four decades, this 40 years, Les Arends was in the majority only four out of the 40 years, so whatever happened that made these things go wrong, it was not Les' fault. He didn't control, or he was not in the majority.

One thing that always impressed me about Les—he was a member of the Committee on Armed Services—he had a substantial part in helping us catch up to get prepared to eventually win against the dictators, Hitler, Mussolini. He helped us gear up to take care of the problems that resulted from an invasion of an ally, South Korea. It was Les Arends who made sure from the very beginning that the only way to make sure that we would win the peace and keep the peace was through strength.

I am proud of that record of Les Arends, and all of you are proud of the record. You know as well as I do that peace comes from strength, and war comes from weakness.

There is one other fact that I think is a tribute to Les. Charlie Halleck and I and others who have served in the Congress know of the vital role that a whip plays. I didn't know it until I came to the Congress, but I have learned of the importance of that key responsibility in any legislative body, but particularly in the House of Representatives where you have 435 Members.

Les Arends served as whip of the House—of the Republicans in the House of Representatives—from 1943 until now, the longest service of a whip in either Democratic or Republican Party in the history of the House of Representatives. That is a tribute to him beyond almost anything.

But let me just conclude with one final observation and comment. Just before the House recessed, I was up on Capitol Hill, and I saw a good many of the Republican as well as Democratic leaders. We were chatting about what they were going to do and what I was going to do after the recess began and before the election on November 5, and I indicated to the Democratic as well as Republican leaders that I was coming out to Melvin to pay tribute to one of the great Members of the Congress in the history of that legislative body.

Les, everybody on both sides of the aisle in the leadership and many, many others with whom you have served, whether they are Democratic or Republican, asked me to say to you that they are proud of their personal relationship, they are indebted to you for their friendship with you, and they asked me to say to the people who are gathered here today, and I will add as a personal remark:

We are all deeply indebted to you for your service, your friendship, and your example as a great, great American.

Thank you for the opportunity of being here in Melvin on this occasion.

NOTE: The President spoke at 4:20 p.m. at the "Les Arends Day" celebration at the Melvin Fairgrounds. In his opening remarks, the President referred to Charles A. Halleck, United States Representative from Indiana 1935–69, and William L. Springer, United States Representative from Illinois 1951–73.

191

Remarks at the United Republican Fund Dinner in Chicago, Illinois. *October 24, 1974*

Chuck Percy, Bill Scott, Les Arends, my former colleagues in the House, your two former great Governors—Ogilvie and Stratton—and your outstanding candidate for the United States Senate, George Burditt, Harry Page, and all the rest of the candidates for reelection or candidates against incumbents:

It is a great privilege and a very high honor to be here at this 40th anniversary of the United Republican Fund of Illinois.

And Dan, I thank you and Bill Croft [1] for the super participation that you give to what I think is a most worthwhile organization.

It is always wonderful to be in Chicago, the home of the Bears—and I understand my old friend George Halas is out here—the home of the Bulls,[2] and the kangaroo.

You know, that is what I like about Chicago. You could always count on exciting things happening in the Windy City.

Dan Terra tells me the way that kangaroo has been dodging tacklers lately, there is a big controversy in the city of Chicago over what to do with him when they do catch him. The Chicago police want to put him in the zoo; the Chicago Bears want to put him in the backfield; and of course, the Democrats in Chicago want to register him—at least once! [*Laughter*]

I was talking to my old friend George "Papa Bear" Halas before the dinner, and I was telling him how, since I became President, I am usually introduced as Dan did, in a very stately and dignified manner.

This particular occasion that I will mention—the format was a little different—I was introduced by a former teammate of mine at the University of Mich-

[1] Daniel J. Terra, president of the United Republican Fund, and William C. Croft, dinner chairman.

[2] The President was referring to George S. Halas, president and general manager of the Chicago Bears professional football team, and to the Chicago Bulls professional basketball team.

igan, and I will never forget that introduction. He said, and I quote: Ladies and gentlemen, it might interest you to know that I played football with Jerry Ford for 2 years, and it made a lasting impression on me. I was a quarterback, Jerry Ford was the center. And you might say it gave me a completely different view of the President. [*Laughter*]

Chicago is getting to be quite a habit with me, as well as my bride Betty, and both of us love the place. I was here in June for a Congressional booster's fund-raiser and again at a July dinner for the State Senate incumbents and their candidates. And Betty was here in September for a luncheon honoring Republican women candidates.

I might say, incidentally, Betty, who is a native of Chicago, sends her love. She is doing excellently, and she hopes to be back here again in Chicago real soon to see her old friends.

I happen to think as a Michigander it is true what they say about the big dynamic city of Chicago. It looks tough on the outside, but at heart, as all of you know, it is a real softy, a warm and very friendly place, and I thank you for your warm and enthusiastic welcome here tonight.

That is why I am glad to be back, and that is why I am so proud—and I say this with conviction and enthusiasm—of the outstanding, the fine slate of candidates of the Republican Party which you are fielding here for this great election on November 5.

Chicago is one of the biggest, the best, one of the outstanding communities in our whole United States. It deserves the best, and your blue-ribbon slate, in my judgment, is an outstanding group that every one of you should support from top to bottom.

I sat and listened to the people that preceded me—George Burditt, Harry Page, Chuck Percy, Bill Croft, Dan Terra—every one of them super guys dedicated to the same basic principles that each and every one of us espouses, principles that are sound, constructive, good for America. And I hope and trust that George and Harry and the rest, including Pete Bensinger,[3] are elected on November 5. They have my full, unequivocal support.

I have known Chuck Percy a long, long time. As a matter of fact, back in 1949—wasn't it, Chuck?—he and I, along with 8 others, were selected by the Jaycees as one of the 10 outstanding young men in America. That was my first exposure to Chuck, and I was impressed then.

---

[3] Peter B. Bensinger was the Republican candidate for sheriff of Cook County, Ill.

I know of his quality and his caliber now. Chuck, you need to go with you the kind of a Senator that George Burditt can give in the United States Senate.

I have listened to a lot of 5-minute speeches, and those of us who served in the House of Representatives know that we have a 5-minute limitation, but George Burditt gave one of the finest, I think, soundest speeches on the fundamental issue that faces us in this country that I have ever heard, and I congratulate you, George.

Needless to say, I thank Dan and Bill Croft. They work in the trenches every day and get little or no recognition, and a word from me, I hope, will be some benefit to the hours and hours of sacrifice that you have made. We are all very, very grateful.

Since this campaign began and since I became President roughly 2½ months ago, I have traveled a good bit in America—according to my staff about 128,000 miles—and I am going to travel some more, primarily because I happen to believe that a President of the United States, if he has conviction and dedication, if he believes in the principles and the policies, ought to get out and try to sell them.

He should not sit in the Oval Office barricaded from the reaction of people, citizens—Republicans, Democrats, or Independents. A President of the United States who has some belief and real down-to-earth feeling about what ought to be done for America ought to come out and say something, speak up for what he believes, and in reciprocity, listen to the people of this great country.

So, I have traveled, and I am going to travel. I think people are concerned about the quality of our government. People are worried about where we are heading as a nation and what is being done about the problems that we face, both home and abroad. And people are fed up about corruption in government, whether it is graft at the local level or abuse of power at the top.

I think it is up to those of us in political life to give the kind of leadership, the kind of example that Americans can honestly and truly believe in, and that is what the Illinois GOP has done here in Cook County, as well as throughout the State.

Now, I know there are some political prophets throughout the United States, a good many of them in Washington, who think the game is up, that we ought to quit, that people are going to stampede blindly into the Democratic column for no good reason, but just for some inward reaction that they have.

When the chips are down, I don't think that is going to happen, and that is why I am here tonight. I have been in political life in the Congress and in the office of Vice President, and now as President, for almost 26 years. I have seen a lot of elections. I have heard a lot of wise predictions. They were almost always wrong.

Frankly, it is about the only thing that you could count on—that they could be inaccurate—because no one really knows what the individual voter is going to do in the sanctity of that voting booth. They will tell you one thing when they are being polled. But they might very well do something different as they sit and contemplate in that voting booth.

The only rule of thumb I know—and it is one that has never failed me—was taught to me by one of my very dearest friends. He was a great Congressman, a super Senator, and probably the greatest orator of this era. And because of a warm and personal relationship that I had with him, I will never forget him.

His wife Louella Dirksen is here. He came from Illinois. His name was Ev. We used to have what was called "The Ev and Jerry Show" when we were in the minority and the opposition held the White House.

I vividly recall one afternoon when Ev and I were talking, just chatting before one of these press conferences—television programs—in Ev's office. Ev was a giant among giants. I have always wished that I had some of the qualities and capabilities that Ev had.

But anyhow, at that time the war in Vietnam was going full blast, inflation was then a problem, the Democrats had swamped us in 1964, and a lot of people were saying that the Republican Party was finished.

Well, frankly, I was feeling a little blue, let down, and quite frankly, very discouraged. And I told Ev of my reaction. Ev, in his inimitable way, paused for a moment, looked at me and said, "Jerry, don't let it get you down. You just keep in there doing your best for the people, and the people will do their best for you."

I think that was the best advice I ever got in a political sense. Ev was right then as he was right for many, many years.

Well, in my lifetime in the political arena, that advice worked for me in Congress, and I think it will work for me in the White House. But to do my best for the people and for America, I am going to need the help, the assistance, the support of good people, men and women, in the Congress of the United States—men and women who will forthrightly fight excessive Government spending and will make an honest and conscientious effort to do something in the battle against inflation, which I think is public enemy number one. And all the polls that are taken indicate that that is the feeling of the American people.

What we need, what we must have if we are to see America through this very difficult economic period is not a veto-proof Congress but, in my judgment, an inflation-proof Congress. And that is the issue on November 5.

All of you are a very sophisticated group. You have learned that in life problems that plague you at home or the office or elsewhere—the really big problems that you have—just don't spring up overnight, and they don't get solved overnight either. And of course, inflation is precisely that kind of a problem.

It has been building up over a long period of years like a disease in our economy. Curing it, unfortunately, will take a little time, but it can be done with the right kind of a program, patience, work, dedication.

Let's take a minute to analyze why it happened, how it happened. There is no single answer, I concede, but there is an answer that ought to be reflected here. One big reason is excessive Federal spending over a long, long period of time.

This excessive spending that has gone on and on seems to go hand in glove with the problems of an increase in the cost of living. Each unbalanced budget, each wasteful spending bill rammed through the Congress has added to your cost of living and fed inflation.

It is legitimate to ask—and I concede this—who is to blame? I recognize there are many villains, but the biggest burden of guilt lies specifically on the shoulders of the big spenders in the Congress of the United States.

The fact of life is that one political party has run the Congress, as Les Arends knows and others here in this head table complex likewise know. One political party has run the Congress, opened up the Nation's purse strings—your tax dollars—for 38 out of the last 42 years and, incidentally, unfortunately, for the last 20 years consecutively.

So, I think it is pretty simple that if excessive Federal spending is the principal villain, those in control of the Congress have to bear the responsibility. That party is the Democratic Party, and we cannot, as I look at it anyhow, allow it to drive the budget deeper and deeper and deeper into the red and the rate of inflation higher and higher in the blue sky.

That is why each of you is more important than ever this year when so much, such a crucial part of our society actually hangs in the balance. Your enthusiasm tonight is tremendous, your support I am deeply grateful for, your volunteer work which I have heard about is unbelievable, your vote November 5—these are the keys that we can use in whipping inflation and preserving a two-party system in the United States.

Here in Illinois you are lucky. George Burditt referred to it and very eloquently. You have 12 great Republican Members of the House of Representatives running for reelection—Bob Michel, Ed Derwinski, John Anderson, Paul Findley, Bob McClory, John Erlenborn, Tom Railsback, Phil Crane, George O'Brien, Ed Madigan, Bob Hanrahan, Sam Young. I can tell you from personal experience, and I have seen a lot of Members of the House come and go—sort of like Greyhound buses. But the truth is that your delegation—and I have mentioned them—is outstanding. You should be proud of them, and you should support them wholeheartedly. They will do a first-class job on your behalf.

Each of these individuals, great and good friends of mine—and believe me, they basically were invaluable when I was the minority leader in the House—are hard-hitting inflation fighters, and I am sure that the candidates you fielded to challenge the incumbent Democrats deserve your full support.

I could say easily, because I feel it, that I want them there for good and sufficient reasons—that, for example, I can depend on them—but that is really only one of the keys in the formula. You need them, Illinois needs them, and the country needs them.

So, I urge you from the bottom of my heart that you maximize your effort, make that last-minute contribution, that last-minute effort to make sure that they come back to serve you and to serve our country. But you just don't fight inflation in Washington. The battlefield, as I see it, is the whole country—every State, every county, every city.

So, I hope that you will equally support your Republican candidates for the State legislature. They can give you responsible, economical action down in your State capital, and a State capital today under our system of trying to transfer power from Washington to your capital and ours in Michigan is an important citadel of strength, good judgment.

The Republican Party has a major purpose. It has had from Lincoln's day to the present: to be just, to be fair, to be responsible, to stand up for what is right for America, and to give America the kind of government that is good for us individually, for our people collectively, for the world at large.

If I might just say that some of the big spenders who have ideas about programs for one individual or one segment of our society, their motives may be good, but the money they spend and the direction they take their Government, in my judgment, is bad. And, as I used to sit in the House with Les and John Anderson, Bob Michel, and the rest, I often used to think as these programs sort of flowed out of one committee after another, didn't those proponents ever understand that a government big enough to give you everything you want is a government big enough to take from you everything you have?

As I have looked through the pages of history, trying to analyze what one political party or another has done for our people and to see if we were wrong and the opposition was right, it is my thoughtful, honest judgment that the Republican Party historically has stood the test.

It ended, in our recent memory, the longest and the bloodiest war in America's history. It has begun the long, hard process of returning the power from Washington back to our local and State units of government—government back to the people from those that wanted to control everything in the Nation's Capital, returning authority and discretion to locally elected officials who are under your more careful scrutiny.

The Republican Party, as I have seen it, has made an honest, determined effort to give you a program that will fight inflation, conserve our energy, and keep our economy strong.

Now, I was criticized for submitting a 31-point program to the Congress a couple of weeks ago. Some of my Democratic critics called it a marshmallow approach. Well, then I had the opportunity just the other night to listen to one of the leading spokesmen for the Democrats coming up with their program.

Well, if mine was a marshmallow, theirs was a lemon.

Let me conclude with this: We can make headway both at home and abroad. We have got a good program. We just need a few more troops. We can't afford to lose some of the outstanding people that have been with us—some much longer than others, some newcomers. They are all good. But we have got some great problems here at home, and we have got some serious ones abroad.

I can recall vividly coming to the Congress on January 3, 1949. At that time, we had just ended World War II, and our country was embarked on a great bipartisan effort to have a foreign policy in America that would keep the peace won so wonderfully in Europe and the Pacific.

There was a Democratic President by the name of Harry Truman who worked very successfully with a Republican Congress, the 80th Congress, and this bipartisan effort was successful in laying the foundation for peace, a foundation that developed the North Atlantic Treaty.

It laid the foundation for strength in doing what was right from a humanitarian point of view in Latin America or in Africa or Southeast Asia. It was a bipartisanship that was predicated on politics stopping at the water's edge. And as we look back over the last 25 or 30 years, that kind of approach has been highly successful in meeting the challenge of those who have a different political philosophy or a governmental point of view.

We have some terribly serious problems facing us, yes, at home, but equally abroad. The Middle East is still a tinderbox. Unfortunately, two good allies—Greece and Turkey—are at swords' points over Cyprus. We have problems in the Pacific. We are trying to build a new relationship with the People's Republic of China, which needs a very, very careful maneuvering to be sure that it is right and strong and sound.

We are trying to broaden a détente with Moscow. What we need today is a strong continuation of that bipartisanship that was so successful in the post-World War II era. If that bipartisanship is ruptured, if that bipartisanship is torn asunder, our problems worldwide can be complicated.

Let me say so that it is not construed to be partisan, in recent weeks I, as a Republican President, had the full support of the Democratic leadership in the House and Senate, but their troops were all over the lot, and the net result is we may have some difficulties.

So, as I conclude, let me just add this final comment: You elect the right kind of a Congress, and we will solve our problems at home and will meet those challenges abroad for the benefit of all of us—Democrats, Republicans, and Independents.

Thank you very much.

NOTE: The President spoke at 9:25 p.m. in the International Ballroom at the Conrad Hilton Hotel. In his opening remarks, the President referred to Richard B. Ogilvie, Governor of Illinois 1969–73; William G. Stratton, Governor of Illinois 1953–61; and Ray H. (Harry) Page, Republican candidate for State treasurer of Illinois.

192

Remarks at Veterans Day Ceremonies at Arlington National Cemetery. *October 28, 1974*

Mr. Smith, Mr. Roudebush, Mr. Holt, Sergeant Littrell, distinguished representatives of America's veterans organizations and their auxiliaries, my fellow Americans:

Today, as we all know, is a very special day for all Americans. But to those of us who are veterans ourselves, it has a very special and added meaning. Memories come back of families and old comrades—of distant days and places from the past. Some of those friends are still with us, sharing in the challenges of peace, just as they did their duty in wartime. Others we shall never see again. But they, especially, are here with us in spirit in the shadow of the Tomb of the Unknowns.

We are all here today and we are all free today because for nearly 200 years, whenever freedom has been threatened, gallant men and women have answered the call of their country. From all branches of the services they risked and sometimes gave their lives for this Nation.

We owe more than we can ever repay to the veterans of all wars in which this Nation has been involved. But today, if I might, I would like to emphasize our debt to the Vietnam veterans.

They served in spite of the most difficult psychological pressures. They served at a time when many of their peers and their elders were denouncing service to one's country as immoral. They served while some avoided service. And they served without the full moral support that this Nation has usually given to its fighting forces.

Nevertheless, the veterans of the Vietnam generation served with high professional competence, with courage, and with honor. America has a deep moral obligation to these fine men and fine women. As they served us in war, so must we serve them in peace. As they protected our freedom and prosperity, so must we see to it that they participate fully in the benefits that our system offers.

It has been said that the forgotten men of the Vietnam conflict are those who served. They are the silent heroes of their generation. Too often those who failed in their duty have monopolized the headlines and distorted the image of their generation. I intend to see to it that the silent heroes—the more than 6½ million Americans who served their country in the Vietnam era with quiet courage—are not forgotten. And I intend to make it certain, just as certain as well, that the men missing in action are not forgotten. And to their families and their friends I make this pledge: I will do everything possible to resolve the uncertainty of their status.

It should be a source of great pride to all of us that this country is now providing higher education and training to 1¼ million veterans of the Vietnam era. But like all of us, they are feeling the pinch of inflation and feeling it badly. With this in mind, we have proposed that their wide range of benefits be increased to keep up with the cost of living.

I am particularly concerned, however, with the plight of the young veteran without a job, especially if he is a disabled member or one of a minority group. For several months now a special interagency task force has been at work developing a program to meet his needs. My assistants have met with representatives of a number of Vietnam veterans organizations at the White House and elsewhere to get their views and to get their opinions.

This task force has submitted a jobs-for-veterans plan of action with the objective of recruiting and hiring into the Government at least 70,000 Vietnam-era veterans during fiscal year 1975. I am ordering Federal departments and agencies to move—and to move now—on this action plan, to make sure these veterans are hired as quickly as possible.

I am glad to report that important progress is already being made. Unemployment among veterans has dropped, fortunately, since its peak in 1971, but we are not satisfied.

The National Alliance of Businessmen deserves a great deal of credit for this progress. They have mounted an effective private sector job program for veterans. They have set high goals, and they have met them. This coming year they hope to provide 200,000 jobs for veterans, including the placement of some 7,500 disabled veterans. I commend them. They are doing a magnificent job. They deserve the admiration, respect, and cooperation of all Americans.

However, we have another major moral commitment to the American veteran. It is, as Lincoln put it, "to care for him who shall have borne the battle." To do so, America has created one of the largest, most comprehensive government health systems in the world—our Veterans Administration hospitals and clinics throughout our 50 States.

On the whole, the Veterans Administration has done a very fine job under very, very difficult circumstances. Despite repeated and often complicated changes in the laws governing veterans health benefits, despite the many complex new developments in medicine itself, and despite nearly 1,800,000 applications for care in fiscal year 1974 alone, the VA is providing the latest and the very best possible treatment to veterans, ranging all the way from major surgery to dental care.

In a special survey completed July 31, which I have personally carefully studied, the whole range of VA assets and liabilities was reviewed. And I am frank to admit, as I think we should, that real problems do exist. Overcrowding is one problem in some facilities. At some hospitals patients have to wait longer than they should to receive proper treatment. Attracting and holding top quality medical professionals and support personnel is another problem.

But the study also discovered through polling that 80 percent of the VA patients felt that their doctors were giving them the very best possible care and that the hospital employees were dedicated people who treated them with respect and with understanding. Eighty percent also said that if they needed hospital care again, they would want to come back to the very same hospital. That is, in my judgment, a pretty impressive vote of confidence from the veterans themselves.

By and large, the report concludes that, in general, VA medicine is first-rate. Where problems still exist, I have asked the VA Administrator, Dick Roudebush, to let me know what is needed to eliminate those problems. I am determined to do everything I can to make a good system even better—and it will be—to make sure that the veterans receive the best possible treatment. Dick Roudebush understands veterans' problems and has the legislative experience it will take to work with the Congress as well as with the Administration and veterans organizations in meeting this very great challenge.

In difficult times, our veterans of all ages agreed with and kept faith with us. They kept America free and enabled us to keep faith with the free world. On this historic day, let us resolve anew to keep faith with them.

One of the first and the greatest men to serve the American flag was George Washington, and he left behind an eloquent warning, and I quote: "To be prepared for war," George Washington said, "is one of the most effectual means of preserving peace."

More than once in our history we have forgotten that warning. Each time we have paid a very, very heavy toll in human suffering.

As a young man myself in the 1930's, I remember the isolationism that blinded so many Americans to the menace of Hitler's Germany and its totalitarianism. Most of us regrettably thought that the vast oceans, the Atlantic and the Pacific, would somehow insulate our country from any foreign danger. We thought, mistakenly, that we could go it alone, but we had a very rude awakening December 7, 1941.

Then a young generation of Americans witnessed firsthand the devastation of World War II and vowed never again to repeat the mistakes of the twenties and the thirties. We vowed to keep America strong. Never again would our weakness invite attack. We built an international network of mutual security so that the strength and the solidarity of the free world would deter any adversaries from aggression.

During the past decade, our whole fundamental policy of mutual security and strength has come under sharp attack. I do not intend on this occasion to go into any detailed justification of our entire post-World War II national security policy.

I do point out that, in terms of its original fundamental objectives, it has been successful, and we have succeeded in something more. We have managed to build a better world. The economic aid that went into our mutual security program built strong allies and strong, prosperous trading partners.

Encouraging new developments in our relations with both allies and potential adversaries have raised the hopes that finally, after so many unwanted wars and so much tragic suffering, mankind may finally be on the path to a lasting peace.

If this is so—and I believe it is—no one deserves more credit than our veterans, and nothing will do more to insure peace than a continued policy of national strength.

The markers over the graves of the known and the unknown whom we salute here today stand as silent sentinels to nearly 200 years of sacrifice and freedom. The men and women with us here today, whom we honor for the uniforms they once wore, stand as attentive guardians of this Nation which Lincoln once aptly described as "The last, best hope of earth."

Let us make sure, on this beautiful day, the debt we owe to so many is properly honored. Let this Veterans Day strengthen our resolve to always walk the extra mile for peace, but always walk it strong and unafraid—for without a mighty America no peace can long survive.

Thank you very, very much.

NOTE: The President spoke at 11:18 a.m. in the Amphitheater at Arlington National Cemetery, Arlington, Va., after laying a wreath at the Tomb of the Unknowns.

In his opening remarks, the President referred to R. D. Smith, junior vice commander, and Cooper T. Holt, Washington office executive director, Veterans of Foreign Wars; and Sfc. Gary L. Littrell, USA, who had received the Medal of Honor on October 15, 1973.

On October 7, 1974, the President signed Proclamation 4323, Veterans Day, 1974.

193

Statement on Signing the Foreign Investment Study Act of 1974. *October 28, 1974*

IT GIVES me great pleasure to have signed S. 2840, the Foreign Investment Study Act of 1974.

A recent study by the executive branch concluded that the available information on the activities of foreign investors in the United States is inadequate. The bill I sign into law today will go a long way toward remedying that deficiency.

This bill provides for the Departments of Commerce and the Treasury to undertake comprehensive studies of foreign direct and portfolio investment in the United States. Under the authority provided by the bill they will (1) conduct "benchmark" surveys of all existing foreign direct and portfolio investment in the United States; (2) analyze the effects of foreign investment on the U.S. economy; (3) review our existing reporting requirements that apply to foreign investors; and (4) make recommendations on means for us to keep our information and statistics on foreign investment current. These surveys will be conducted early next year and cover data for 1974; an interim report of the results will be submitted to the Congress 12 months after the date of enactment of this act and a full and complete report, together with appropriate recommendations, within 18 months of the date of enactment.

When this study is completed, we will be in a position to know better how to conduct ongoing monitoring of foreign investment activity in the United States. Earlier, this Administration had opposed new reporting systems which would have lacked the benefits of the information which will be generated by the actions under S. 2840. We are not opposed to keeping a watch on foreign investment, but we do want to do it in the most efficient and helpful way, with the aid of the greatest possible amount of data.

As I sign this act, I reaffirm that it is intended to gather information only. It is not in any sense a sign of a change in America's traditional open door policy towards foreign investment. We continue to believe that the operation of free market forces will direct worldwide investment flows in the most productive way. Therefore, my Administration will oppose any new restriction on foreign investment in the United States except where absolutely necessary on national security grounds or to protect an essential national interest.

NOTE: As enacted, S. 2840, approved October 26, 1974, is Public Law 93–479 (88 Stat. 1450).

194

Statement on Signing the Motor Vehicle and Schoolbus Safety Amendments of 1974. *October 28, 1974*

I HAVE signed S. 355, the Motor Vehicle and Schoolbus Safety Amendments of 1974.

This act renews our national commitment to the promotion of highway safety, a goal shared not only by the Congress and my Administration but by every American. Last year, more than 56,000 people lost their lives on America's highways. Although the accident and death rates on our highways are declining, we can never be satisfied with the level of tragic loss and injury on our roads.

By signing S. 355, I believe we will accelerate our commitment to reduce deaths and injuries on the highway. It authorizes $55 million for the current fiscal year and $60 million for fiscal year 1976 to carry out the important mandate contained in the National Traffic and Motor Vehicle Safety Act of 1966.

In addition, this act establishes procedures for the remedy and recall of certain defective motor vehicles without any charge to the owner. As for the very important matter of schoolbus safety, this act requires the Department of Transportation to establish minimum schoolbus safety standards within 15 months. I think we can do the job faster, and I have asked Secretary of Transportation Claude Brinegar to try to have the standards out before the end of next summer.

Finally, this act also does away with the so-called seatbelt interlock systems. This system had the laudable goal of encouraging motorists to wear their safety belts. In practice, however, it has proved to be intensely unpopular with the American motorist. I can fully understand why drivers might object to being forced by the Federal Government, in effect, to buckle up. This constitutes an unacceptable governmental intrusion into the life of the individual.

However, in signing this removal of the interlock system, I am in no way encouraging drivers to desist from using their seatbelts. To the contrary, safety restraints save lives and prevent injuries. I give my strongest recommendation that all Americans follow the sound advice which tells us to "buckle up for safety."

To emphasize my concern for highway safety, I want also to remind every American to observe sensible driving speeds and especially not to exceed 55 miles per hour. As we all know, the lowering of the highway speed limit has saved lives and conserved energy. Saving lives, saving fuel, and saving the motorist money in the operation of his vehicle are goals we can all find worthy in the months ahead.

NOTE: As enacted, S. 355, approved October 27, 1974, is Public Law 93–492 (88 Stat. 1470).

195

The President's News Conference of *October 29, 1974*

Appointments in the Energy Program

The President. [1.] This morning, before the press conference, I would like to announce several appointments, and then we will have the press conference subsequently.

At the outset, let me remind you that on October 8, I announced that Rog Morton would be the head of the Energy [Resources] Council and that subsequently I would make several other appointments predicated on legislation enacted by the Congress and some reorganization in the [Federal] Energy Administration [FEA].

Rog Morton is here. Rog—I think most of you know him; he is pretty hard to miss. [*Laughter*] But the new appointments are as follows:

Dr. Robert Seamans, former Secretary of the Air Force and formerly a very high-ranking official in NASA, had a great deal to do with the manned space program, will be the new Administrator of the ERDA, the Energy Research and Development Agency [Administration].

Bob, we are glad to have you on board.

Then to head FEA, John Sawhill is resigning, and we will give him a good appointment in the Government, but the new head of FEA will be Andy Gibson, who was an Assistant Secretary of Commerce and was in charge of the Maritime Administration, will be the new head of FEA.

Andy, glad to have you on board.

Then, for the new nuclear regulatory agency, I am nominating Bill Anders, who is currently a member of the AEC, but who will be the Chairman, once confirmed, of the new regulatory agency.

You are all familiar with Bill Anders' record as an astronaut and his service as a member of the Atomic Energy Commission.

And then, Dixy Lee Ray will be the new Assistant Secretary of State for Oceans and International Environmental and Scientific Matters.

Dixy Lee.

This is the new team that will be in charge of the energy program, which we will see moving ahead, I think, under Rog Morton's stewardship with the new faces and the experience of Bob Seamans, Andy Gibson, Bill Anders, and Dixy Lee Ray.

And I thank all of them for taking on these new responsibilities. I think they are an outstanding group of administrators with experience both outside of Government and within the Government.

So, Rog, you have got a good group, and I am proud of them, and I think they will do a first-class job. Thank you very, very much.

Well, with those preliminary announcements, I will be glad now to respond to any questions.

Mr. Cormier [Frank Cormier, Associated Press].

QUESTIONS

THE ECONOMY

[2.] Q. Mr. President, the Government's leading economic indicators announced today show that last month they experienced the sharpest drop in 23 years. Might this sort of thing prompt you to amend your economic program to put more emphasis on fighting recession rather that fighting inflation? And if so, what steps might you take?

THE PRESIDENT. The 31-point program that I submitted to the Congress and the American people did take into recognition the problems of some deterioration in some parts of the economy and at the same time recognized the need to do something about inflation.

It was a finely tuned, I think, constructive program to meet both of these problems.

Now, the program is before the Congress and the Congress must act on certain aspects of it. This, perhaps, will take some time, and in the interim, if there are any economic factors which justify a change, I will be open to suggestions.

But at this point, I still believe the plan or program, as I submitted it, is sound, both to meet the challenge of inflation and any deterioration in the economy.

VOTER INTEREST IN THE ELECTION

[3.] Q. Mr. President, in view of the Watergate and inflation and other urgent problems facing the Nation, how do you account for the voter apathy in this country? And I have a followup.

THE PRESIDENT. I wish I knew the answer to that, Mr. Sperling [Godfrey Sperling, Christian Science Monitor]. It would seem to me that with the problems we have, particularly at home—both Watergate and others—that the voters should be extremely interested in the kind of Members of the House and Senate that are elected or defeated.

One of the reasons that I am campaigning is to try and get the voters off of apathy and on to interest. I happen to believe that a big public showing of voter participation would be very helpful, and I am disturbed that these forecasters say that only 42 percent of the eligible voters are going to vote on November 5.

So, if I can in any way stimulate voter interest, I intend to do so.

Q. That leads to my second question. Do you think you are breaking through this apathy, are you shaking up this interest? What is your finding?

THE PRESIDENT. From my contacts with Members of Congress or candidates who are in the various places where I have stopped, they tell me that voter interest has been stimulated by my appearance. I suspect we will get a few who don't approve of my appearance in a certain community, but I believe overall there has been an increase in voter interest as a result of my visits. And as I said, that is one reason why I intend to continue them.

Miss Thomas [Helen Thomas, United Press International].

VICE PRESIDENT-DESIGNATE ROCKEFELLER

[4.] Q. Mr. President, do you think that Nelson Rockefeller will be confirmed as Vice President, and when?

THE PRESIDENT. I believe that Nelson Rockefeller will be confirmed. I strongly support him today as I did when I nominated him in August. I hope and trust that the Senate and House committees, as well as the two bodies themselves, will act promptly on the nomination. I think he would make a very good Vice President.

Q. Then you don't think the financial problems that have suddenly cropped up will affect the outcome? [1]

THE PRESIDENT. I do not.

THE PRESIDENT'S CONGRESSIONAL VOTING RECORD

[5.] Q. Mr. President, the Democratic Study Group, in an analysis they made of your voting record over the last 3 years you were in the House, showed you voted 86 percent of the time in support of spending proposals beyond the Nixon budget, and it amounted to some $16.9 billion. How do you square that with your campaign argument that the Democrats are the big spenders?

THE PRESIDENT. I think their own survey, Mr. Lisagor [Peter Lisagor, Chicago

---

[1] See Item 127 [16].

Daily News], showed that I had a much better record of saving than the Democrats did in the House of Representatives.

In other words, their own document showed that the Democrats were much bigger spenders than I was and that I was a much better saver than they were. So, I will rely on their document to prove that I am a saver and they are spenders.

Q. Mr. President, do you know how you came out net?

THE PRESIDENT. It is my recollection that I was about 8 percentage points better than the Democrats as a whole, so even using their figures or their document, I am a saver and the Democrats are spenders.

VETERANS EDUCATION BILL

[6.] Q. Mr. President, sir, I want to know if you are going to sign the veterans G.I. education bill that has been left at the Senate so you would not pocket veto it, but they are ready to send it down if you are ready to say today you will sign it.

THE PRESIDENT. Well, I worked very closely, Sarah [Sarah McClendon, McClendon News Service], with the members of that conference committee in trying to find a solution to a bill that I want to sign. The bill has not come down. It has not been staffed out by my staff. Until it arrives at the White House, I am not going to prejudge what I am going to do. I hope that we can find a way for me to sign it, because I want to help the Vietnam veterans, particularly, but until it comes down to the White House, I think it is premature for me to make any decision.

Q. Sir, it calls for an 18 percent cost-of-living increase, plus up to 23 percent, and that additional would pay for the cost of going to college. Would that be agreeable to you?

THE PRESIDENT. Well, as I recall, that compromise is 20 percent.

Q. Twenty-three percent.

THE PRESIDENT. But in addition, they did add a $600 loan provision to the veteran. They did add 9 more months of eligibility beyond what either World War II or Korean veterans got in the way of educational benefits.

So when they, the Congress, send the conference report down to me, we will staff it out. I will make an honest judgment. I hope it is a piece of legislation that I can sign.

BUDGET REDUCTIONS

[7.] Q. Mr. President, in your speech before Congress on the economy, you said you would do the hard work of making decisions where to cut. Could you give us some specific examples, maybe half a dozen, of the programs you would like to cut?

THE PRESIDENT. I have had one meeting with the OMB [Office of Management and Budget] and others on that very subject, and later today, before I go to Grand Rapids, I am spending another hour with the same group. We have a long list of items where they give me certain options.

We have not made any final determination. If all of them were put into effect—and some of them would require legislative action by the Congress—I think the anticipated saving in fiscal year 1975 would be around $7.5 billion.

We are going to make a maximum effort to cut at least $5.4 billion, so there is some flexibility between the 5.4 and the 7.5, and I am going to continue to work on it. And when Congress comes back, we will have some recommendations.

Q. Mr. President, as to specifics now of some of those programs that you would put priorities to cut——

THE PRESIDENT. I would rather not give any specifics, because it is a long shopping list, and I think it is unwise for me to be categorical as long as I try to make an honest judgment on which of maybe a hundred or more proposals they have submitted to me for consideration.

THE MIDDLE EAST; PLANS FOR TRIP TO JAPAN

[8.] Q. Mr. President, I have a two-part question on foreign affairs.

Number one, the emergence of the PLO [Palestine Liberation Organization] in the Middle East, how does this affect our position regarding the Middle East?

And the second part, also on foreign affairs, negative reports out of Japan, anti-American feelings and items like that, whether you are reconsidering going to Japan.

THE PRESIDENT. Let me answer the second question first.

No developments in Japan have changed my attitude. I intend to go to Japan, as has been planned for some time.

The decision by the Arab nations to turn over the negotiating for the west bank to the PLO may or may not—at this stage we aren't certain what impact it will have on our role in the Middle East.

We, of course, feel that there must be movement toward settlement of the problems between Israel and Egypt on the one hand, between Israel and Jordan or the PLO on the other, and the problems between Israel and Syria in the other category.

We have not had an opportunity yet to make any firm decision on what impact there will be from this Arab decision. I can only say that we think it is of maximum importance that continued movement toward peace on a justifiable basis in the Middle East is vital to that area of the world, and probably to the world as a whole.

OUTLOOK FOR CONGRESSIONAL ELECTIONS

[9.] Q. Mr. President—you, as one who knows the House better than we do—what is your best estimate of Republican losses or gains in the House, and what would be the level which would make your efforts seem all worthwhile?

THE PRESIDENT. I don't like to get into a numbers game. I did on one occasion back in 1966, but I had somewhat different responsibilities then. I can only say that it is important to have a competitive relationship or ratio in the House as well as in the Senate.

It seems to me that if you have a reasonably close ratio of Democrats to Republicans, the public is better off. They get better legislation. They get better handling of appropriations. They get, I think, a better tax bill, whenever the relationship between the two major political parties is reasonably similar.

At the present time in the House, I think it is 243 [247] to 187. I would hope that that ratio would not be seriously changed.

RESIGNATION OF JOHN SAWHILL

[10.] Q. Mr. President, I would like to ask you about your energy program. Why have you dumped John Sawhill? Was his advice too blunt and politically unattractive at this time?

THE PRESIDENT. Not at all. I put a new man in charge—Secretary Morton. He replaced the Secretary of State (the Treasury), Bill Simon, who went over to the economic council [Economic Policy Board].

Rogers Morton and I discussed the kind of a team that he wanted and that I thought would do a good job. And the people that I have nominated fit that pattern.

THE VICE PRESIDENT-DESIGNATE

[11.] Q. Mr. President, I wonder if we could return to the Rockefeller affair. If you had known then, before the nomination, all that is public knowledge now about Mr. Rockefeller's financial dealings, would you still have named him to be your Vice President?

THE PRESIDENT. I think I would. Nelson Rockefeller has been a superb Governor of the State of New York. He served both Democratic and Republican Presidents in the past in the executive branch of the Government. It is my judgment that he would be a very good Vice President. And therefore, these disclosures indicate that he does believe in helping his friends. And a man of that wealth certainly, in my judgment, has that right to give as long as the law is obeyed, and as I understand it, he has.

It seems to me that his qualifications from previous public service fully qualify him to be Vice President. And therefore, I fully support his nomination.

THE 25TH AMENDMENT

[12.] Q. Mr. President, as the only living veteran of the 25th amendment, how say you as to its continuance?

THE PRESIDENT. I believe that the 25th amendment has served a good purpose despite my own involvement in it. But leave that aside. It was, of course, if you go back and study the history of it, actually proposed and approved for quite different reasons.

On the other hand, in the last year, certain circumstances have arisen which, in my judgment, may prompt the need for some changes.

I think, for example, the Congress ought to study the desirability of putting a time limitation on the time that the Congress should have for the consideration—approval or rejection. But these are matters that Congress can, in the remaining days of this session or in the next session, investigate, because of the experiences of the last year or so.

CONDITION OF THE ECONOMY

[13.] Q. Mr. President, your friend, Paul McCracken, has said that we are entering a V-shaped recession and that we ought to call a spade a spade. Yet Administration officials have been avoiding the word "recession." Would you apply that term to our economic condition now?

THE PRESIDENT. Recession has been defined. I think the national bureau of economic research [Bureau of Economic Analysis] actually is the authority on this matter. It is my understanding they are going to come up with some answer on this question in the very near future.

But let me make an observation of my own, if I might. We are facing some difficult economic circumstances. We have too many people unemployed, and we want to do something about it. And my economic package that I submitted to the Congress and the American people will do something about it.

The American people are concerned about inflation, and my economic program would do something about inflation. So, what we have tried to do, instead of getting into semantics, is to offer constructive proposals to meet the problem. Whether it is a recession or not a recession is immaterial. We have problems. The plan I submitted is aimed at solving these problems. And therefore, I really do not care what the name is. We want solutions. And my proposal, I think, will offer that opportunity.

STRATEGIC ARMS LIMITATION TALKS

[14.] Q. Mr. President, since Secretary Kissinger has been to Moscow, do you have any optimistic outlook now on the SALT agreement?

THE PRESIDENT. I believe that the Secretary's discussions with the General Secretary, Mr. Brezhnev, were very constructive. Some of the differences, as I understand it, between their view and ours, have been narrowed. And as a result of the progress that was made in Moscow, the announcement was made [on October 26, 1974] that I would meet with Mr. Brezhnev in Vladivostok the latter part of November. We hope that each step will mean more progress and that we will end up with a SALT Two agreement.

OIL IMPORTS

[15.] Q. Mr. President, your Press Secretary, Mr. Nessen, has hinted or implied that you may be considering limiting oil imports; that is, limiting imports of Arab oil, if necessary, to make your goal of cutting oil imports by 1 million [barrels] a day, perhaps in the form of a dollar figure, a dollar limit on imports. Are you considering it? Is this a live possibility?

THE PRESIDENT. Our first objective is to cut the 6 million barrels per day imports of crude oil by 1 million barrels. We believe that, with the energy conservation recommendations we have made, that objective can be accomplished.

However, if there isn't the saving of 1 million barrels per day of oil imports by voluntary action, we will, of course, move to any other alternative, including the possibility of mandatory limitations, to achieve that result.

That is essential from the point of view of our economy, our balance of payments, et cetera.

THE VICE PRESIDENT-DESIGNATE

[16.] Q. Mr. President, if Rockefeller is confirmed, would you ask him to refrain from giving gifts as he has given in the past to public officials and other politicians?

THE PRESIDENT. My judgment would be that Mr. Rockefeller would use excellent judgment in the future in however he wishes to dispense the funds that he has available. I think that his approach in the future would certainly be related to the experiences he has had in the past.

CONGRESSIONAL PAY INCREASE

[17.] Q. Mr. President, there is a lot of talk on the Hill that Congress might come back after the election and vote themselves a pay increase. There is also talk if they don't do it this fall, it certainly will be voted early next year. Would you sign a bill that would provide Congress with a pay increase at this time?

THE PRESIDENT. I think it is premature for me to make any judgment. I have not talked to the Democratic or Republican leadership about the matter. I know of no specific proposal by the Congress nor by this Administration, so I don't feel that it is appropriate for me to make any judgment at this point.

PLANS FOR CABINET CHANGES

[18.] Q. Are you planning any other Cabinet changes, particularly in the Agriculture Department?

THE PRESIDENT. I think Secretary Butz, over a period of 3 or 4 years, has done a good job. He has been very outspoken. He is a good, hard worker, and I have no plans to remove the Secretary of Agriculture or no specific plans to call for the resignation of any other Cabinet officer.

FORMER PRESIDENT'S TAPES AND DOCUMENTS

[19.] Q. Mr. President, could you tell us the status of negotiations on the Nixon administration's tapes and documents? Are they still in the White House or——

THE PRESIDENT. They are being held—I can't give you the precise location—but they are being held under an agreement with the Special Prosecutor's office, and of course, now there are two other elements that have developed. One, Judge Richey has issued an injunction concerning all or some of the documents.[2] A third involvement is a law suit by former President Nixon against the head of GSA, Mr. Sampson. So we think, under the circumstances, and particularly under our agreement with the Special Prosecutor's office, they should remain intact until legal matters and any other commitments have been handled.

---

[2] On October 21, 1974, Judge Charles R. Richey of the United States District Court for the District of Columbia issued a temporary restraining order preventing former President Nixon from obtaining control of his Presidential tape recordings and documents in the custody of the United States.

RESIGNATION OF MR. SAWHILL

[20.] Q. To follow that up, the Mr. Sawhill matter for a minute——

THE PRESIDENT. I can't see who asked that. I can't see with the lights and without my glasses.

Q. Kraslow [David Kraslow, Cox Newspapers]. What policy differences, sir, did you have, you and Mr. Morton have with Mr. Sawhill which precipitated his resignation?

THE PRESIDENT. As I said a moment ago, I appointed a new man to head up the Energy Council, and that requires, I think, when you give a man a new assignment, the opportunity to make recommendations for those that will work with him on the Council. It seems to me that with Rog Morton being given that job, he ought to have the right, with my approval, to make changes, and that is why we made the changes. I think they are good people. Mr. Sawhill, who I admire, will be offered a first-class assignment in this Administration.

Q. Are you saying, Mr. President, that there were no policy disagreements?

THE PRESIDENT. I don't think there were any major policy differences. I think there may have been some differences in approach or technique, but if you give a man a job, you have to give him the people he wants to carry out that responsibility.

CAMPAIGN STATEMENTS CONCERNING THE CONGRESS AND FOREIGN POLICY

[21.] Q. Mr. President, in Oklahoma City, you said that overwhelming victories in Congress this fall by the opposition party, being the Democrats, would seriously jeopardize world peace. This is our first chance to question you on that. I was wondering if you would elaborate on that. Did you mean it in the sense that some Democrats accused you of, demagoguery, or is this consistent with your original announced policy that you were going to try to unify the country after Watergate?

THE PRESIDENT. Well, I think the facts that I referred to involved the conflict we had with a majority of the Members of the House and Senate over the limitations and restrictions they put on the continuing resolution. Those limitations and restrictions on that particular piece of legislation, in my judgment and in the judgment of the Secretary of State, will make it more difficult for the United States to help the Greeks. It will make it more difficult for us to work to bring about a negotiated settlement in the Cyprus matter.

That Congressional limitation will not help our relations with Turkey.

I point out that both the United States and Turkey are members of NATO, and if our relationship with Turkey is destroyed or harmed, it will hurt our interest as well as NATO's.

Secondly, we do have an agreement with Turkey as to some military installations, and those installations are important for both Turkey and ourselves. And if, through Congressional action, we undercut our relationship with Turkey, hurt our relations with NATO, hurt the Greeks, because it will make it more difficult for a settlement of the Cyprus matter, then I think the Congress has made a mistake. And if a Congress that is more prone to do that is elected on November 5, it will make our efforts much harder to execute and implement foreign policy to build for peace and maintain the peace.

As Mr. Nessen explained in a subsequent press conference, I was referring as much to Republicans as I was to Democrats who don't cooperate in giving a President of the United States an opportunity to meet the day-to-day problems that are involved in foreign policy.

A President has to be able to act. He has to be able to work with allies and with some potential adversaries. And if the Congress is going to so limit a President, whether he is a Democrat or Republican, that he has no flexibility, in my opinion, the opportunity for a successful foreign policy is harmed considerably.

Q. A followup question, please, Mr. President.

How would overwhelming Democratic majorities in Congress undermine your policy and Secretary Kissinger's policy of détente and relations with China?

THE PRESIDENT. Let me say at the outset the Democratic leadership—both Senator Mansfield and the Speaker of the House and other leading Democrats—were very helpful to me in that struggle that I just described.

If you will carefully read, which I have, reread my statements both in Oklahoma City and Cleveland, I was very careful not to be critical of the Democratic leadership, because they did try very hard.

The problem was the troops did not believe either their own leadership or the President of the United States.

If we have a runaway Congress that does not understand the need and necessity for the broadening of détente, that does not understand the need and necessity for a continuation of our policy vis-a-vis the People's Republic of China, then it is going to make it much harder for a President to carry out a policy of peace abroad.

Now, a runaway Congress is one that does not, at least, pay some attention to their own leadership on both sides of the aisle and to the President of the United States.

PARDON FOR FORMER PRESIDENT NIXON

[22.] Q. Mr. President, can I get back to the conversation with General Haig in early August. I know you said there was no deal or no commitment, but sometimes things are done more subtly. When he brought up as a sixth option the possibility of a pardon, did you point out to him that in your testimony on confirmation you had indicated opposition to such a move, or did you in some way indicate to him that you might be inclined, without exactly saying so, that you might be inclined to go along with an early pardon?

THE PRESIDENT. I think the testimony I gave before the House Committee on the Judiciary or subcommittee of that committee speaks for itself, and I will stand by that testimony.

I would like to point out, in addition, in the testimony before the Senate Committee on Rules and Administration, I answered it as follows:

One, I did not think the American people would stand for a pardon, in answer to the hypothetical question that was asked me.

Secondly, because I was not familiar with the precise authority and power of a President to grant a pardon, I did not want to get into any of the technicalities involving that issue, but the testimony I gave before the House committee will speak for itself, and I will let it stand at that.

FISCAL YEAR 1976 BUDGET

[23.] Q. Mr. President, looking a bit further down the road on your anti-inflation program, sir, do you have any particular figures or program in mind for your 1976 budget, which is now in the process of being prepared?

THE PRESIDENT. Well, that is another matter that I will be working with Roy Ash and his people on after we get through the long shopping list of proposed rescissions, deferrals, and cutbacks for fiscal year 1975.

I can assure you it will be a tight budget, very tight budget, because we do have to hold the lid on spending, not only in the remaining months of fiscal year 1975 but we have to reassure the American people that in the next fiscal year we will be just as firm in controlling and holding down expenditures.

Q. Mr. President, when you say a tight budget, do you mean a budget surplus or balanced or possible deficit?

THE PRESIDENT. Our objective will be a balanced budget. We will do the very best we can.

REPORTER. Thank you.

THE PRESIDENT. Thank you very much, ladies and gentlemen.

NOTE: President Ford's fourth news conference began at 10:56 a.m. in the Briefing Room at the White House.

196

Letter Accepting the Resignation of John C. Sawhill as Administrator of the Federal Energy Administration. *October 29, 1974*

Dear John:

Thank you for your October 25, 1974 letter of resignation as Administrator of the Federal Energy Administration. In accepting your resignation, I want to express to you my deep personal thanks for your dedicated and capable service to the Nation, first as Deputy and then as Administrator of the Federal Energy Administration. You have performed with distinction in a difficult job during a period when, for the first time, America has confronted a major energy shortage. In particular, along with millions of other Americans, I have admired your candor and directness in addressing the difficult choices which face the Nation as we confront the energy problem.

As I indicated during our conversation together, it is my strong desire that you continue to serve in government so that the American people and my Administration may continue to benefit from your very great talents and your broad experience.

Finally, I am grateful for your agreement to stay at the Federal Energy Administration until the first of the year to bring the Project Independence Blueprint to a conclusion and to insure a smooth transition in the leadership of that very important agency.

With warm personal regards.

Sincerely,

JERRY FORD

[The Honorable John C. Sawhill, Administrator, Federal Energy Administration, Washington, D.C. 20461]

NOTE: Mr. Sawhill's letter of resignation, dated October 25, 1974, and released with the President's letter, read as follows:

Dear Mr. President:

I am today submitting my resignation as Administrator of the Federal Energy Administration.

When I began my present assignment several months ago, I set three major goals for myself and the organization. The first was to establish the new Administration, the second was to prepare a Blueprint for Project Independence which could serve as the basis for developing a national energy policy, and the third was to set in motion an orderly process for decontrolling the oil industry. The FEA is now established and fully staffed; the Project Independence Blueprint is nearing completion; and—with the implementation of an entitlements program—the groundwork has been laid for beginning to remove controls from the oil industry. Thus, the tasks that I set out to accomplish are complete, and I feel that the time has come for me to move on to new responsibilities.

We must now begin a new phase in the government's energy program by moving quickly to implement a set of energy resource development and energy conservation actions which can bring this Nation's energy budget into better balance. However, because of the time delays involved in expanding energy supplies, I feel it is particularly important to focus on energy conservation. By doing so, we will improve our balance of payments position, reduce inflationary pressures and aid in cleaning up the environment. In addition to these actions, we must resolve a number of critical international issues affecting energy including recycling surplus oil funds, compensating for the impact of high oil prices on a number of industrialized and developing countries, and defining the role of our government vis-a-vis the international oil companies.

FEA has important responsibilities in each of these areas. I will be glad to remain with the organization during the transition period to assist in preparing for the tasks ahead and to support the activities of Secretary Morton and the Energy Resources Council. I have enjoyed working as a member of your team and would be delighted to serve you again should the opportunity present itself.

Sincerely,

JOHN C. SAWHILL

[The President, The White House]

197

Statement on Signing the Federal Fire Prevention and Control Act of 1974. *October 29, 1974*

I AM today signing into law S. 1769, the Federal Fire Prevention and Control Act of 1974.

While fire prevention and control is and will remain a State and local responsibility, I believe the Federal Government can make useful contributions. I endorse the intention of this act to supplement rather than supplant existing State and local government activities.

The program established by this act, which will be implemented by an agency within the Department of Commerce, will contribute to our knowledge of fire and our ability to prevent it.

Federal assistance for research and development on fire problems will be consolidated and expanded to provide the scientific and technological base for the development of materials, equipment, and systems to reduce the number and severity of fires.

The Fire Academy system will supplement existing education and training for fire prevention personnel across the Nation.

The research and development program will be closely tied to the education and training program, thereby insuring that research and development results are disseminated quickly to communities.

The data base of the National Fire Data Center will assist States and communities in setting priorities and in identifying possible solutions to problems. It will monitor the progress of the Nation in reducing fire losses.

The bill contains a provision that requires the Secretary of Health, Education, and Welfare to establish 25 burn treatment centers, 90 burn programs, and 25 centers for expanded research on burns. Since these centers would duplicate the burn research carried on through the trauma program of the National Institute of General Medical Sciences and would add $5 million to the FY 75 budget, I will not seek appropriations to implement this particular provision of the bill.

NOTE: As enacted, S. 1767, approved October 29, 1974, is Public Law 93–498 (88 Stat. 1535).

198

Statement on Signing Indian Claims Commission Appropriations Legislation. *October 29, 1974*

I HAVE signed S. 3007, an act to authorize appropriations for the Indian Claims Commission for 1975.

It is a particular pleasure for me to be able to sign this bill because there are not many opportunities in life to take clear and decisive action designed to right a past wrong.

The background is this:

In 1877, the United States Government took over lands from the Sioux Indians in the Black Hills of South Dakota. At the same time, to prevent widespread starvation of these Indians deprived of their hunting grounds, the Government supplied them with food and other provisions for a number of years.

Earlier this year, the Indian Claims Commission ruled that the United States took the Black Hills lands illegally in violation of the fifth amendment. The 1877 value of the land and gold was estimated at $17.5 million which, together with interest from that point, boosts the value today to nearly $103 million.

However, the Indian Claims Commission Act of 1946 contains a provision requiring that the Government-supplied food and other provisions, valued at approximately $57 million, be used to offset the Indians' claims against the Government. If this offsetting provision stayed in effect, it would totally wipe out the $17.5 million original evaluation and leave the Sioux Indians with nothing.

The basic legal question of whether or not the Sioux have a legitimate claim against the United States over the Black Hills land is still being litigated in the courts. However, in passing this act Congress has determined—and I agree—that if such a claim is held to be valid, it would be unfair and unjust to try to avoid paying it by deducting the cost of previously supplied food and provisions.

Although we cannot undo the injustices from our history, we can insure that the actions we take today are just and fair and designed to heal such wounds from the past.

NOTE: As enacted, S. 3007, approved October 27, 1974, is Public Law 93–494 (88 Stat. 1499).

199

Statement on Signing Legislation Concerning the Regulation of Interest Rates. *October 29, 1974*

I AM signing into law today S. 3838, "To authorize the regulation of interest rates payable on obligations issued by affiliates of certain depository institutions. and for other purposes".

Titles II and III of the bill would remove burdensome inequities by authorizing exemptions from State usury laws of large business and agricultural loans and of large borrowings of bank holding companies and bank deposits. Such usury laws as this bill addresses are well-meaning but futile attempts to keep interest rates at "reasonable" levels. In fact, their net effect is that the same borrowers who are supposedly protected from "unreasonable" interest rates are, instead, unable to obtain funds at the levels set by law.

S. 3838 seems to me a clearly second-best remedy to this problem, and the States which have these usury laws may wish to reconsider their applicability under today's conditions.

On the other hand, I am deeply concerned about title I of the bill which enables the Federal financial regulatory agencies to place interest rate ceilings on securities issued by holding companies which at present are not subject to such regulations. I believe this provision goes in the same direction as the State usury laws from which the other titles of this bill authorize exemptions. I hope that the regulatory agencies will not see fit to exercise the discretionary authority granted by this provision.

The Administration has introduced a bill, the financial institutions act (S. 2591), containing a set of reforms that would gradually free the credit market from harmful regulations of the sort imposed by title I of S. 3838. I strongly urge the Congress to pass S. 2591.

NOTE: As enacted, S. 3838, approved October 29, 1974, is Public Law 93–501 (88 Stat. 1557).

200

Statement on Signing Legislation Increasing Federal Deposit Insurance. *October 29, 1974*

I HAVE signed H.R. 11221, which provides important new consumer protection in the area of credit and finance.

This legislation would double the basic Federal insurance limits for deposits and savings accounts in insured banks, savings and loan associations, and credit unions from $20,000 to $40,000. This increase will help these financial institutions to attract larger deposits. It will also encourage savers to build up funds for retirement or other purposes in institutions with which they are familiar and which are insured by Federal agencies that have earned their confidence over the years.

H.R. 11221 also contains fair credit billing provisions which will protect consumers against the repeated incorrect billings of computers that sometimes fail to respond to consumer's inquiries. Now creditors must acknowledge customer inquiries within 30 days. Moreover, the creditor must resolve and dispute within 90 days either by correcting the customer's bill or explaining why the original bill is correct. Until these requirements have been met, there can be no dunning letters sent or other action taken to collect amounts in dispute.

Another extremely important provision in this legislation prohibits discrimination on the basis of sex or marital status in the granting or denying of credit. While there has been a voluntary improvement in credit procedures in recent years, women are still too often treated as second-class citizens in the credit world. This legislation officially recognizes the basic principle that women should have access to credit on the same terms as men.

This bill should also have a beneficial impact on the availability of mortgage credit, since it returns to institutions insured by the Federal Savings and Loan Insurance Corporation well over a billion dollars in insurance premiums not now required by the corporation.

One provision of H.R. 11221 is particularly unfortunate, however, in that it will severely undermine the present method of gathering legitimate views of other executive branch agencies and identifying potential conflicts with other existing legislation in this field. Thus, it could seriously hamper efforts to achieve a coherent Administration legislative program. Therefore, I am asking the Congress to amend the law by deleting section 111. This would preserve the executive branch's ability to develop a coordinated and coherent legislative program.

This bill includes a number of provisions which could more appropriately be considered in the framework of a larger, more comprehensive approach to strengthening this country's financial system. As a result, I will continue to press hard for Congressional passage of S. 2591, the financial institutions act, which seeks to accomplish such a strengthening through reducing, rather than increasing or perpetuating, the extent of Government control over financial institutions.

NOTE: As enacted, H.R. 11221, approved October 28, 1974, is Public Law 93–495 (88 Stat. 1500).

201

Statement on Signing the Amtrak Improvement Act of 1974. *October 29, 1974*

I HAVE signed H.R. 15427, the Amtrak Improvement Act of 1974. However, I believe that one provision of this act is undesirable. I refer to the section which requires mandatory customs inspection aboard trains operated in the international intercity rail passenger service.

This provision would adversely affect the interdiction of the flow of narcotics and other contraband at ports of entry. Onboard customs inspection is inconsistent with effective enforcement of customs laws and not always practical. There must be flexibility in determining when and where onboard inspection is to be conducted. Moreover, the requirement for onboard inspection on trains could result in requests for similar treatment aboard airlines and ocean vessels.

I request that the Congress take action to revise the provision to provide for customs inspection consistent with the effective enforcement of the customs and related laws.

NOTE: As enacted, H.R. 15427, approved October 28, 1974, is Public Law 93–496 (88 Stat. 1526).

202

Statement on Signing the Reclamation Development Act of 1974. *October 29, 1974*

I HAVE approved H.R. 15736, the Reclamation Development Act of 1974.

This bill contains many desirable and needed reclamation program authorizations. For example, it will transfer the town of Page, Arizona—currently owned by the Federal Government—to non-Federal interests, thereby permitting it to function as a viable community with most residential and commercial property in private ownership. The bill will also provide for inclusion of additional hydroelectric power facilities in an existing major Colorado project.

On the other hand, H.R. 15736 contains some features which represent undesirable departures from established Federal water resource policies. In particular, several authorizations would impose on the Federal Government costs that properly should be borne by State and local interests. In addition, there are unresolved questions regarding the environmental impacts of several projects.

On balance, I have concluded that the desirable features of H.R. 15736 outweigh the undesirable ones. However, I have directed the executive agencies concerned, as part of the post-authorization review process, to carefully examine those program authorizations which depart from established policies or involve unresolved environmental problems.

On the basis of this review, I will determine whether corrective legislation is necessary or whether funding for questionable projects should be requested.

At the same time, in order to achieve a reduction in Federal spending, I urge the Congress to approve my request for rescission and deferral of funds already approved by Congress for certain reclamation projects to make certain we stay within the $300 billion budget for fiscal 1975.

NOTE: As enacted, H.R. 15736, approved October 27, 1974, is Public Law 93–493 (88 Stat. 1486).

203

Veto of Legislation for the Relief of Alvin V. Burt, Jr., and the Survivors of Douglas E. Kennedy. *October 29, 1974*

To the House of Representatives:

I am today withholding my approval from H.R. 6624, a bill "For the relief of Alvin V. Burt, Junior, Eileen Wallace Kennedy Pope, and David Douglas

Kennedy, a minor." I am advised by the Attorney General and I have determined that the absence of my signature from this bill prevents it from becoming law. Without in any way qualifying this determination, I am also returning it without my approval to those designated by Congress to receive messages at this time.

This bill would provide for payment, "as a gratuity," of $45,482 to Mr. Burt and for similar payments of $36,750 each to the widow and son of Douglas E. Kennedy for injuries and other damages Mr. Burt and Mr. Kennedy sustained as a result of gunshot wounds inflicted by U.S. military personnel in the Dominican Republic in 1965. The amounts in the bill were recommended in a congressional reference case opinion by a review panel of the Court of Claims.

The claims presented in this bill arise from an admittedly tragic and unfortunate incident. On May 6, 1965, Mr. Burt and Mr. Kennedy, two newspapermen who were covering the civil upheaval in the Dominican Republic and the peacekeeping operation in that country of U.S. military forces, attempted to drive through a U.S. checkpoint in Santo Domingo en route from rebel-held territory in the city. The Marines manning the checkpoint opened fire on their car when the men failed to get out as ordered and when it accelerated violently in reverse at the same time that the Marines were fired upon by snipers from an area behind the car. Both Mr. Burt and Mr. Kennedy were seriously injured as a result of the Marines' actions.

After the incident, both men received, without charge, extensive medical care and treatment from U.S. personnel in the field and later in U.S. military facilities. Their employer, the *Miami Herald,* paid their salaries while they were hospitalized, and guaranteed them continued employment. They also received workmen's compensation benefits during hospitalization, including prescribed lump-sum payments.

A majority of the members on a Court of Claims' review panel, which considered the present claims, held that the claimants had not established a "legal" or "equitable" claim within the meaning of the congressional reference statute. In fact, their opinion strongly suggests that the claimants' own negligence contributed to the injuries they received and further suggests that in pursuing their professions in the face of known hazards, the claimants assumed the risk of personal injury.

Notwithstanding these findings, however, the majority concluded that payment of reasonable compensation in this case was justified on "broad moral considerations" as a matter of "good conscience." Accordingly, they recommended awards in the amounts contained in the current bill.

I have considered carefully the merits of this case, and can find no reason to approve H.R. 6624. Equitable considerations growing out of Governmental actions have traditionally been the basis for private relief awards where no legal remedy is available. But the record clearly establishes that no such considerations are present in this case.

Approval of H.R. 6624 cannot, in my view, be justified by invoking terms such as "gratuity," as the awards are characterized in the bill, or "broad moral considerations," the basis used by the Court of Claims panel. To adopt such an approach could easily set a precedent for the payment of a myriad of claims involving financial hardship to selected individuals simply on the grounds that they lack legal redress. Once we start down this road, it will be difficult, if not impossible, to turn back.

I urge that in the future Congress adhere to the traditional equity basis for awards, whether or not they have been recommended by the Court of Claims under congressional reference procedures.

GERALD R. FORD

The White House,
October 29, 1974.

NOTE: The House of Representatives sustained the President's veto on November 20, 1974.

204

Veto of Legislation for the Relief of Nolan Sharp. *October 29, 1974*

To the House of Representatives:

I am withholding my approval of H.R. 7768, a bill for the relief of Mr. Nolan Sharp. I am advised by the Attorney General and I have determined that the absence of my signature from this bill prevents it becoming law. Without in any way qualifying this determination, I am also returning it without my approval to those designated by the Congress to receive messages at this time.

H.R. 7768 would authorize retroactive service-connected disability payments to Mr. Sharp, because of multiple sclerosis, for the period from January 16, 1956, to October 1, 1962. Under the bill, these payments would have to be offset against certain non-service-connected benefits Mr. Sharp received during the same period.

Mr. Sharp had honorable Army service from December 1, 1942, to June 5,

1943, when he was discharged because of severe hypochondriasis and anxiety state. The first confirmed medical diagnosis of an organic neurological disease identifiable as multiple sclerosis was made in 1949, six years after his discharge. At that time, the law allowed payment of service-connected disability benefits for multiple sclerosis manifesting itself within three years after separation from wartime service.

Mr. Sharp's claim for service-connected benefits based on multiple sclerosis received several adjudicative reviews and was the subject of appellate consideration on four occasions. On the basis of available evidence, the Veterans Administration was unable to determine direct connection of multiple sclerosis with the veteran's military service as required by law. He was, however, granted non-service-connected disability pension, effective January 16, 1956.

Effective October 1, 1962, the Congress extended the presumption of service connection for multiple sclerosis from three to seven years. The liberalizing statute, however, prohibited any retroactive payments based on the new presumption. Since Mr. Sharp qualified for service-connected benefits under the new statutory presumption, he has been receiving such payments since October 1, 1962.

Having carefully considered the circumstances of this case, I am unable to find sufficient reasons for approving this legislation to pay. Mr. Sharp's benefits from an earlier date than the law permits. To make such a special award would seriously discriminate against similarly situated veterans.

Moreover, once the precedent for such special awards is established, it would be difficult to deny awards to other veterans who have been prohibited from receiving retroactive benefits under the 1962 law or similar statutes. The inevitable result would be to undermine the integrity and impartiality essential to the administration of such veterans' benefits.

For these reasons, I am constrained to withhold my approval from H.R. 7768.

GERALD R. FORD

The White House,
October 29, 1974.

205

Veto of Farm Labor Contractor Registration Legislation Containing Personnel Reclassification Rider. *October 29, 1974*

To the House of Representatives:

I am returning today, without my approval, H.R. 13342, The Farm Labor Contractor Registration Act Amendments of 1974. I am advised by the Attorney General and I have determined that the absence of my signature from this bill prevents it from becoming law. Without in any way qualifying this determination, I am also returning it without my approval to those designated by Congress to receive messages at this time.

This bill contains provisions designed to strengthen the protection of migrant farm workers under that Act, which I support. I cannot approve the bill, however, because it contains an unrelated rider which creates serious inequities and distortions in the Federal personnel system.

In the decade since the enactment of the Farm Labor Contractor Registration Act of 1963, it has become apparent that the provisions of that law have not been adequate to accomplish its purpose of protecting migrant farm workers from abuses by farm labor contractors. For nearly a year, the Administration has been working with the Congress to develop legislation which would improve the Act, and there has been give and take on all sides. I am pleased with this spirit of cooperation, and endorse those provisions of H.R. 13342 which apply to migrant farm workers.

Unfortunately, the Congress has seen fit to add a rider to this bill which is totally unrelated to the needs of migrant farm workers.

Section 17 of the bill would arbitrarily reclassify hearing officer positions in the Department of Labor, and make existing hearing officers Administrative Law Judges regardless of their qualifications.

I am gravely disturbed by that part of Section 17 relating to the hearing officers now employed by the Labor Department to hear and decide "black lung" claims. These employees would by fiat be declared to be Administrative Law Judges without regard to their capacity to fill such positions. Since Administrative Law Judges hired in the usual manner must demonstrate such capacity, this feature would be contrary to all principles of a civil service system based upon merit and competition among candidates.

I also cannot accept the feature of Section 17 which would legislatively classify and pay at the GS–16 level these newly designated Administrative Law Judges for the "black lung" program, as well as those who currently hear claims under the Longshoremen's and Harbor Workers' Compensation Act and the members of the Benefits Review Board established by the Longshore Amendments of 1972. Such a provision would arbitrarily impose a grade level without due regard for the relative complexity and difficulty of the work involved. By over-classifying certain positions, it would be disruptive of the principle of equal pay for equal work. This would create inequities within the Labor Department, and between positions of that agency and those in a number of other agencies, including approximately 400 GS–15 Administrative Law Judges in the Social Security Administration.

My concern about legislating classifications and pay of special groups of employees was the basis for my disapproving H.R. 5094, which provided for an arbitrary and inequitable reclassification of deputy U.S. marshals. In my first veto upon assuming the Presidency, I expressed my strong concern about granting preferential pay treatment by statute, and indicated that our policy must be to provide equal salaries for equal work. The rider to H.R. 13342 contains deficiencies similar to those in H.R. 5094.

In summary, I cannot accept a legislative provision which would disrupt sound principles of personnel administration, would create serious pay inequities by providing overly liberal salaries to employees in one agency leading to demands for similar treatment by large numbers of employees in other agencies, and would not effectively serve the public interest.

I urge the Congress, upon its return next month, to send me a bill—which I will promptly approve—without the unacceptable personnel provision I have described, a bill which is directed only toward strengthening the Farm Labor Contractor Registration Act.

GERALD R. FORD

The White House,
October 29, 1974.

206

Veto of Vocational Rehabilitation Act Amendments. *October 29, 1974*

To the House of Representatives:

I am today returning, without my approval, H.R. 14225, the Rehabilitation

Act and Randolph-Sheppard Act Amendments of 1974, and the White House Conference on Handicapped Individuals Act. I am advised by the Attorney General and I have determined that the absence of my signature from this bill prevents it from becoming law. Without in any way qualifying this determination, I am also returning it without my approval to those designated by Congress to receive messages at this time.

The Vocational Rehabilitation Amendments of 1974 pose some fundamental issues which far transcend this particular bill. No group in our country is more in need of supportive services than the Handicapped. Our handicapped citizens have demonstrated time and again that, given a fair break, they can lead as full and productive lives as other citizens.

Throughout my years in Congress I consistently supported good Federal programs designed to assist the handicapped.

During the last two years spending on the basic grant programs for Vocational Rehabilitation has grown from $589 million to $680 million. The key issue posed by this bill is not how much money will be spent. The issue posed is how well the programs will be run.

This bill passed the House of Representatives without any hearings. Had hearings been held we would have explained the disruption that would result from such a massive legislative incursion into the administration of a program.

The Congress has the responsibility to legislate, but I have the responsibility for the successful administration of the programs they enact. This bill is an attempt to administer through legislation. It transfers a program from one part of HEW to another for no good reason—indeed for very bad reasons. It dictates where in HEW minute decisions must be made, it creates independent organizational units at subordinate levels that are wasteful and duplicative and it sets up a monitoring process for the construction and modernization of Federal facilities that would force me to create a new 250-man bureaucracy in HEW to duplicate functions carried out elsewhere in the Executive Branch. Most importantly, the bill blurs accountability. I cannot be responsible for the good management of all Federal programs if I cannot hold my Cabinet Secretaries accountable. Under this legislation accountability would be diffused. I find myself obliged to return to the Congress unsigned a bill that would disrupt existing Federal programs and ill serve the needs of our Nation's handicapped citizens. The present Vocational Rehabilitation legislation does not expire until mid 1975. Plenty of time remains for us to work out a bill which will improve Federal programs for the handicapped rather than create the disruptions that will inevitably result from this hastily drawn piece of legislation. I have requested

HEW Secretary Weinberger to meet with congressional leaders immediately upon their return to initiate this process.

GERALD R. FORD

The White House,
October 29, 1974.

NOTE: On November 21, 1974, the Senate voted to override the President's veto of H.R. 14225. The bill, however, did not become law due to a question of whether or not it had been pocket vetoed by the President (see first paragraph, above).

The legislation was subsequently reintroduced as H.R. 17503, which was passed by the Congress on November 26 and signed by the President on December 7 as Public Law 93–516 (88 Stat. 1617).

207

Remarks at a Rally in Grand Rapids, Michigan. *October 29, 1974*

Well, thank you very, very much, Governor Milliken, Mayor Parks, Jack Root, every one of you for being here:

Nobody, nobody can accuse any of you of being fair weather friends. Thank you very much.

But let me say somewhat inadequately, there is no way in which I can personally express my gratitude, my appreciation, my indebtedness to all of you who are here in this difficult weather to say hello, to warmly welcome me. I am just overwhelmed, and words are inadequate to express everything that I feel deep down in my heart. Thank you very, very much.

There was a wonderful crowd at the airport, and we stopped at one of the crowds on the way in. I just cannot believe so many are here in these circumstances, and as I shook hands, either at the airport or on the way in or with those that I have had the privilege of saying hello to here tonight, I saw friends that I went to Madison School with, friends that I went to South High with, friends that I worked with in many, many civic projects—Democrats, Independents, Republicans, young and old. There is nothing I can say except thank you, every one of you, for being here.

And may I thank Althea Bennett here for the box of cookies which she has given me. As was indicated, I used to stop in at Petersen's Drug Store for an early breakfast, and she was there to help prepare it, and I used to enjoy those cookies very much then, and I am sure I will now.

But I must tell Althea I have a big appetite. It is a long trip back to Washington. They may all be gone before Betty sees a single one.

Now, let me talk about why I am here. I came back to Grand Rapids because on 13 different occasions in the past, over a period of 26 years, I campaigned in the Fifth Congressional District—which originally was Ottawa and Kent Counties and is now Kent and Ionia and four other counties—because I love people, because I love the communities. And whether it was Ottawa, Kent, Ionia, Clinton, Montcalm, et cetera, I love the communities and the people.

And as many of you know, I have taken "Jerry Ford's Main Street" office to Byron Center, Standale, Caledonia, Alto, Rockford, Kent City, Sand Lake, Ionia, Belding, Wells, Portland, and everyplace else, and it was a great privilege for me to talk with you in the trailer.

It was a great privilege to go to your service club, to your farm bureau community meetings, to go to your churches, to your city hall, to meet you on the street, to go to the Lowell Showboat, the Sparta rodeo, the red flannel celebration—well, you name it, wherever you had five people I went there, because I like you. And I am back here today because I just could not stay away from this area one more time. I thank you again for the opportunities of the past.

As I have seen so many of you here today, and as I said a moment ago, Grand Rapids, Kent County, Ionia, Ottawa County, and the others—you are a good cross-section of America. You represent all segments of our society. We have some wonderful farms, we have some excellent businesses, we have some tremendously productive working people in this community. We have—I am prejudiced—but I think we have the best here, and all of you who are here represent the best in America.

As I have said to our good friend, Mayor Lyman Parks, Grand Rapids is big enough to have many of the problems of some of the major metropolitan areas. We have enough diversification in agriculture, so that I learned from firsthand experience the problems of the dairymen, the cattlemen, the applegrower, the other people that produce so that all of us can eat.

But the main thing that I loved about this area was we had some big city problems, but we were small enough so that you got to know people. You have got to love them. You have got to enjoy working for whatever the problem was. I do not know how many times I have walked down Cedar Springs behind about five bands in that Cedar Springs Red Flannel Parade, or how many times I have had the privilege of visiting one community or another.

It is a warmth, it is a friendliness, it is a look in the eye of people that makes you welcome. And the most important thing is that people in this area seem to want to work out the problems that they have, whether they are labor and management on the one hand or consumer and producer on the other.

I cannot help but make a comment, Lyman, about that Calder that you gave me. I was in Chicago a couple of days ago, and some of my friends over there were kidding me about Grand Rapids being a small town. And some of the commentators and writers were kidding me about, perhaps, the lack of culture in Grand Rapids. Well, I happen to think—if my memory is correct—we had a Calder in Grand Rapids before Chicago thought of it.

And then I have had some friends from various parts of the country tell me that, well, Grand Rapids was a little on the conservative side. Well, I cannot help but ask them in good conscience what they mean. Do they mean the people here have a healthy skepticism of quick and easy solutions? If that is a definition of conservatism, yes, we are skeptical. We are a little conservative about some of these superficial answers that some people try to sell us.

But if they mean that Grand Rapids and its environs are skeptical about new ideas, the answer is no. We are broadminded; we have a good outlook. And when a new idea comes along that is constructive, that is fair to everybody, we in Grand Rapids embrace it and make it work. And that is what we have done all my lifetime.

Let me reminisce a moment, if I might. Some of us in the audience here can remember when the old B. F. Keith Theater was down here on Lyon Street, and some of us can remember when the Regent Theater was right over there, just where the Federal Building was, I guess, and some of the other old broken-down business places that needed to be removed and this wonderful Vandenberg Center constructed.

And in honor of one of Grand Rapids' outstanding citizens, in my judgment, probably the outstanding Senator that I have known in Washington, we built this Vandenberg Center in honor and in tribute to Senator Arthur H. Vandenberg.

And you know that Federal Building—I used to have an office right up there in the corner. I used to look down here, and I could see at various times of the day there would be periodic meetings and wonderful luncheon gatherings. Occasionally we had a demonstration or two, and sometimes in the moonlight I could look down and see a few friendly people holding hands. And what is wrong with that?

But the point is that this great Vandenberg Center with the Calder stabile is, in my opinion, a tribute to a great Senator. It is a tribute to a great people. It is the product of a community that had the vision and the foresight to do something for themselves in conjunction or in partnership with the Federal Government.

And that is the way Arthur Vandenberg believed; he was receptive to new ideas. He was a senior Senator in Washington when Betty and I first went to the Nation's Capital. He and his wonderful wife Hazel could not have been kinder, could not have been more receptive to two newcomers to the Nation's Capital. He gave me, in all honesty, the inspiration to take a look at the world as a whole. Arthur Vandenberg, some of you may recall—with former President Harry Truman—was the architect of a bipartisan foreign policy following World War II.

The two of them—a great Democratic President, Harry Truman, and a great Republican Senator, Senator Arthur Vandenberg—worked together hand-in-glove following World War II when the world was in devastation, when a good share of the world was on its back, and other nations—like our own—had serious problems.

But from those ashes, Harry Truman and Arthur Vandenberg put together a foreign policy that brought allies together, presented a common front against potential adversaries, helped underdeveloped nations grow and become a vital part of our world society. And that bipartisan foreign policy which I learned—and, fortunately, learned from one of the masters—I think, is the future of the world.

And we in Washington today, representing all of you—Democrats, Republicans, Independents—should march shoulder-to-shoulder to make sure that our country, our great United States of America, gives the leadership in consolidating friends and gives leadership in trying to make new contacts, broader contacts with potential adversaries. What we want to build is a world of peace so that your children and my children and their children can live in safety and security and a better world wherever they might live—Grand Rapids or elsewhere.

And I pledge to you, as President of the United States—and believe me, folks, my friends at home, I never thought for one minute when Betty and I left here in December of 1949, that I would be coming home to all of you as your President—but as President, I will pledge to you, as I have pledged to you in 13 previous elections, that I will do my best; I will be fair; I will be open; I will work; and I will continue the love and affection and the dedication that I have, that all of you have, for your community, for your friends, for your State, and for your Nation. This is what you can give and what I can give, and on behalf of Betty and myself, I pledge you nothing but all I can do for all of you and many like you.

Thank you very, very much.

NOTE: The President spoke at 5:35 p.m. at Calder Plaza. In his opening remarks, the President referred to Jackson Root, chairman of the Kent County Board of Commissioners.

208

Remarks at a Reception for Republican Candidates in Grand Rapids. *October 29, 1974*

MAY I say just a word, and it will be very, very short, because it has been a long day, but a wonderful day, and there is no way that I can express in words or sentences or in paragraphs or a speech the appreciation that I have for all of the wonderful people who are here.

I look at so many of you, and I cannot help but be appreciative of what you have done for Betty and for me over the 13 past elections where, you know, without your support, I could not have been in the Congress and therefore could not have been in a position where I finally got where I am today.

But without all that you have done—and I don't mean financially, because I know how hard most of you have worked in the vineyards as precinct people, as party workers, as well as donors, and this kind of just deep feeling, whether you agreed with me on every issue—and as I look around the room, I see some people who have written some critical letters from time to time, but at least you had an open door then, and the truth is you will have an open door now.

So, on behalf of Betty—and I will say to you that she is deeply apologetic; that is not quite the right word—that she is not out here, but she is doing great, she is just coming along fine. She is giving me a few harsh words, and I know that is the fact that she is getting better and better. And I am being silenced more and more, and that is a sign that I am noticing that she is better and better.

So, on behalf of Betty and myself, I thank you all for coming.

Now, let me make one quick observation. I used to be, as an outside observer, as minority leader in the House of Representatives, going down to talk with Democratic Presidents and Republican Presidents. And I wondered how the office operated. Well, I am learning.

And as Harry Truman once said, "The buck stops here." And the trouble is that you have to say yes or no, you cannot say maybe. And the net result is that you have to disappoint some and, hopefully, please a few others. But what I am pledged to do—to you and to millions of others—I am going to do it as I see best from the point of view of anybody and everybody.

I think most of you knew my working schedule when I was around Grand Rapids and the surrounding area. It started very early and ended very late. Well, it has not changed, and it is not going to change. I love it. I thrive on it. And the net result is that you can get a lot more work done in 12 and 14 hours than you can in 8, and we are going to keep working at it, and we are going to do the very best we know how. And we are going to call them as we see them.

There are some tough decisions, but I happen to believe, despite some of the comments, that we are making headway overseas. I have gotten not one but several reports from Henry Kissinger every day he has been gone. We are encouraged, whether it is in Moscow, whether it is in India. And I am confident that we are going to continue to make progress in the solution of the difficult problems in the Middle East, between Greece and Cyprus and Turkey.

I am confident we are going to strengthen and solidify the Western alliance. We are looking forward to the trip to Vladivostok to meet Mr. Brezhnev. We hope to have a successful—and I believe we will—meeting in Japan as well as South Korea.

All of this is aimed at peace, not only for this year but for a long, long time. And that is what our objective is.

Now, I am not going to stand here in front of so many of you and deny that we are having some troubles, economically, at home. I never tried to kid anybody when I was campaigning on 13 different occasions. I am going to tell you the truth. We have some problems at home, economically, both because the economy is a little soft on the one hand and inflation is a little high on the other.

But the program that I submitted to the Congress—if it is enacted, if it is implemented in its entirety—will get over both problems, will strengthen the economy, and will whip inflation. So, let's work for that kind of a program.

Now, if I could conclude with one political observation. I have known the Goebel family a long time. I first knew that family when Paul Goebel, Sr., was officiating high school games around Grand Rapids and I was a beginner in the football arena in this area.

I have to tell you a personal story. Paul, one time when he was officiating a game—this is Paul, Sr., who is about 5 inches taller than I—I must have made some infraction of the rules, and he grabbed me and said, "Ford, you did this." I did not argue with him.

But Paul Goebel, Sr., set a great example for his son, as my father did for me. As you know, my father, I think, was one of the great citizens of this community, our State, and the Nation.

And I think Paul Goebel, Sr., fits the same pattern and the same category, but he has got a great son in Paul, Jr. I hope and trust that Paul, Jr., will be elected to the Congress.

I know Paul. I have known him from his early youth. I have watched his political progress. I have seen what he can do and how he has made honest, conscientious, tough decisions.

I cannot imagine someone doing a finer job in this Congressional district than Paul Goebel, Jr., and I strongly urge you, from the depth of my conviction and dedication, urge you to maximize your efforts on behalf of Paul. He is the kind of guy I would like in Washington.

Thank you very much.

NOTE: The President spoke at 6:40 p.m. in the ballroom at the Hospitality Inn.

209

Remarks at Calvin College in Grand Rapids. *October 29, 1974*

Thanks, Bill Farr, Bob VanderLaan, Milt Zaagman, Pete, Marty, all of the other candidates at the State and local level, all of you who in all honesty overwhelm me as they did down at the Vandenberg plaza:

I have been in a good many States in recent weeks, and I am going to a couple more the latter part of this week and the first of next. And let me say that this is beyond—above and beyond the call of duty. I thank you. It is just wonderful to be here. I am deeply indebted to each and every one of you.

You know Bill Spoelhof, the great president of Calvin College. Bill and I started out as precinct workers together a long time ago. I was always scared to death that he would be a candidate for Congress. [*Applause*] Thank goodness he did not, after that reaction.

But Bill, I want to thank you for always making the Calvin facilities available. I have been here a number of times. As you know, I have always had a warm welcome, and this crowd tonight reminds me of a good Calvin-Hope basketball contest. Since I did not go to either one, I could be completely objective, pulling for both.

But I did see something that was on the chair as I sat down. It has been sort of a tradition of my campaign to put out these hot pads, or whatever they call them.

And they were always gobbled up by thoughtful women who wanted to be reminded what a good Congressman would do. And we always used to put on those hot pads, "Vote for some Congressman by the name of Ford who works for you in Congress." That is what we emphasized—work for you in Congress. And that is what Paul Goebel will do for you. He will work for you in Congress.

Well, I can see, as I look around this great crowd, some wonderful people from Ionia, from Montcalm, from Barry, from Eaton, from Clinton, as well as from Kent County. I love you, and it is just great to see you all.

Naturally, I am delighted to be back home. I just wish Betty were here. But she did ask me to extend to you, one and all, her gratitude for the many prayers, many thoughtful messages—all of which have been extremely helpful to her and to us during this difficult period.

I thank you very much on her behalf.

I think all these wonderful balloons—she is the best part of the family; I have always said that—but I got a big kick out of watching all these balloons come down from the ceiling at the start of the program. You might say this is the big difference between our position on our side of the aisle and their position on the other side of the aisle. We put hot air in the balloons, and they put it in their speeches. [*Laughter*]

You know, a few weeks ago the Ohio State University was thoughtful enough to ask me to—I said they were thoughtful enough to invite me to come and give a commencement address. And gee, they could not have been nicer. But it does create a bit of a problem, with this contest coming up in a couple of weeks between the Buckeyes and the Wolverines. I try to be nonpartisan as I go from one State to another, but it is particularly difficult to be nonpartisan when it comes to such basic matters as football.

Now, take this game between Ohio and Michigan in a couple of weeks. People keep asking me who I will be rooting for. Well, I think the late President Kennedy had a real good answer. He handled the problem extremely well. He was in Iowa, just before their big game with Notre Dame. And someone asked him the very same question, "Who will you be rooting for, Mr. President?"

And Jack Kennedy said, "I will be rooting for Iowa."

And then he added, after a tremendous cheer went up, "But I will be praying for Notre Dame." [*Laughter*]

So, come the Michigan-Ohio game, I will let you figure out who I will be rooting for and who I will be praying for.

Now, every 2 years for the last 25, for 13 campaigns, I have come back to our

Congressional district seeking your support and gratefully receiving it. I have never been disappointed. I have always been most appreciative.

I guess it is kind of a habit to come back, and on the 14th it just seemed to me, even if I could come back for just one day, it would be like coming home. Now, it does not mean I can go from Kent to Ionia to Montcalm to Eaton to Clinton to Barry Counties.

That would be quite a bit in the limited time available, but whether I am in all six counties or not, my heart, my soul, my conviction, my dedication is there for the purpose of electing Paul Goebel to Congress from the Fifth Congressional District.

I thought it was very wonderful for the Governor to come to Grand Rapids today to participate in our ceremonies down at Vandenberg Center and to thoughtfully introduce me.

I have known Bill Milliken for a long time. I knew him when he was a State senator. I knew him in his other responsibilities, and I watched him very carefully and extremely closely as Governor of our great State. And in the process, over the last month, I have had the opportunity of looking—and I say this to anybody who has any doubt whatsoever—I have had the privilege of looking at Governors from many States—Democrats, Republicans—and Bill Milliken by any standard—and I say this as strongly, as vigorously as I can—Bill Milliken by any standard is at the very top, and I hope he is reelected.

I guess I am prejudiced, but for good reasons. If Bill Milliken is going to do the job that he is expected to do as Governor of our great State, then Bill needs support in the State legislature.

You know the ones that have served you well, the ones who are seeking to serve you well. And I just hope that Bill gets the team that he deserves to do the best job for the great Wolverine State. Do your best, if you possibly can, for this great group of State legislative candidates.

You know, I have gotten a lot of advice lately from friends and foes and neutral observers. They said, "Mr. President, you ought to stay in Washington, surround yourself with that beautiful atmosphere at the White House, spend some time with your new dog, Liberty, and cogitate over these great decisions that are presented to you, and then let the voters out in the respective areas of this country make up their own minds."

Well, I respectfully disagree with that view. I happen to believe that a President of the United States who has conviction and dedication ought to go out and talk to the people and listen to them instead of sitting in the Oval Office at the time of a great campaign.

It is my deep belief, it is my honest conviction that we are doing right, both at home and abroad. We have some tough hurdles to cover, but as you look across the spectrum internationally or domestically and compare the role of our country with other countries, the problems of our country with other countries, the United States is doing well, and we should be darned proud to be Americans and to participate in our society.

In the last 3 months since I became President, I have traveled almost 17,000 miles, met literally hundreds and thousands of citizens in many, many States, and I think it is the most refreshing, the most helpful experience, because there are, literally, unbelievably great numbers of wonderful people who have some thoughts and ideas and suggestions and contributions to make.

I think their help and assistance is just as vital as what I can get sitting in the White House looking at a lot of memorandums and papers that come from a fine staff or come from others.

This group here has got the power, the genius, the drive, the help, and I am darned fortunate to be here and to see you all and to get the message that you are giving me, which is the message that you gave me in 13 previous elections—integrity, dedication, work, objectivity, and a love for America as much as you have it, and I hope I do, and I believe I do.

I am here tonight for a particular purpose, but I must express my gratitude to the local officials, Jack Root of the county, Lyman Parks of the city, and their respective associates for the unbelievable reception down at the Vandenberg Center and in the Calder [Plaza] area.

You know, the weather was a little bad, but I think it is fair to say that they were not good weather friends. They were there because we had a rapport. And I did not ask that group because it is a nonpartisan group, but I am here to ask every one of you to help in any way you can—and this is a message from Betty as well as from me—to elect Paul Goebel on November 5 so I can have the good help that I need from the Fifth District in Washington, D.C.

I said a moment ago I have traveled almost 17,000 miles, 16 States. My hope is that to some extent I can be beneficial, helpful in electing a Congress that will help me in the battle we are undertaking to lick inflation and to strengthen our economy.

What I want is a Congress that will help me make sure—and let me emphasize this very specifically, very categorically—I want a Congress that will help me make certain and positive that your paycheck buys as much on the day you cash it as on the day that you earned it. That is our program.

If I know anything about the people of this district, whether you are in business or on the production line or on a farm or in the service or in a service organization, the people of this district understand the sound fundamentals of how to run a business, a church, a school, a PTA, or the Government.

I want to, if I might, address a few observations and comments to what I believe, and I hope you believe, is public enemy number one—inflation. With your help and with the election of a cooperative Congress, I am confident that we can whip inflation, and this button, WIN, means Whip Inflation Now. And we can with a good program, which I have submitted to the Congress, and with the cooperation of 213 million Americans, we can do it, but we need the Congress, and we need the help of all of you.

And as I look around here, I see a great many people who have the WIN button on them, and if you don't have one, write us, and the White House will see that you get it as long as you enlist in that army to Whip Inflation Now.

But let me make this observation: When I talk about a cooperative Congress, I am talking about a Congress that will be conscientious about how they handle your tax dollars.

In the Congress, from 25 years experience, I could pick out the big spenders and the savers, and the record clearly shows that in the Congress of the United States, the majority of the big spenders are on the Democratic side of the aisle.

The majority of the savers are on our side of the aisle. It is just that simple.

Now, I admit there are a few crossovers on one issue, or perhaps on the overall. But I am talking to you very pragmatically, that this district has consistently had a Congressman who is in the category of a saver, not a spender. And if you want to restore that reputation, you darn well better vote for Paul Goebel in the next election.

Now, I have been reading newspapers and listening to some of the commentators recently, and I have noticed that everybody is predicting the worst possible results from the Republican point of view. They say we are going to be clobbered, we are going to be wiped out, there is going to be a catastrophic defeat for the Republican Party, we are going to have a terrible time in this election.

Well, I respect those who want to vote for a legislative dictatorship. I don't agree with it, because the balance in our Government is predicated on what our forefathers wrote in the Constitution and what we have adopted by practice over the last 200 years, of a balance between the executive, the legislative, and the judicial branches, so that no part of our Government, no individual could control the destinies, the fate of people in this great land.

And this system of checks and balances, this finely tuned system of balance between our three coordinate branches of Government has given us more freedom, more opportunity, and more blessings than any people in the history of mankind. And we have got to keep that balance.

But you can destroy that balance. You can destroy that balance if the opposition were to gain a net of 50 in the House or 7 or 8 in the Senate. It would put a stranglehold on the legislative process, because it would mean the inevitable election of those of the most liberal persuasion in the Democratic Party.

I am not condemning all Democrats, because some of them have been extremely helpful, and particularly the Democratic leadership in the House and the Senate. But their troops run wild. They are like a commander who tells them to do what is right, and then they scatter all over the ballpark.

And so, what I am saying to you is what we really need is competition in the Congress, not an overwhelming majority in the ranks of one political party, because if you get that kind of 2-to-1, 3-to-1, 4-to-1 strength in one political party, inevitably you have this legislative dictatorship which destroys that very fundamental concept that has made it so great for all of us in America, a balance.

So, a veto-proof Congress is not what we want. I have got a better idea, this forecast: We want an inflation-proof Congress, not a veto-proof Congress. And Paul Goebel will give us that result.

Now, if you get a veto-proof Congress, if you get a legislative dictatorship, as I have indicated, the whole system of checks and balances go out the window.

Now, some of my good Democratic friends have a different idea of checks and balances—a little different from mine. They write the checks even though there are never any balances.

And from your own personal experience, you know where that could lead. But let me make this observation, if I can. I am told that there is a great degree of apathy in America, and yet when I go to Sioux Falls, South Dakota, they had 10,000 in an auditorium like this and 5,000 people who could not get in. When I went to Lincoln, Nebraska, they had 5,000 or 6,000 at an airport rally. We have been to other communities where the crowds have been good. We have had a few disappointments, but we have had good reception.

Tonight is the best, and I thank you for it.

But do you realize that all of you here tonight can directly affect this election come November 5? You have it within your own grasp. You have it by your own vote and how you can persuade, how you can help, by just what this group does here tonight.

On the other hand, if some of you sit it out, this election can be lost. I do not think you are going to be the kind of a villain who won't participate.

I don't think you are going to be apathetic or you would not be here tonight, but there are many of your neighbors and your friends who, according to the statisticians, are not going to participate.

Let me give you something that is terribly disturbing—it ought to scare you as it does me. Take the national percentage of votes cast in the Congressional off-year elections, like the one that is coming up next week: Based on a total number of eligible voters, only 46.3 percent cast their ballots in 1962, only 45.6 percent took the time to do so in 1966, and the percentage of eligibles who voted in the last off-year election, 1970, was even lower—43.8.

Now, in this last special election that was held in February, about 35 percent in this district went to the polls. According to the statisticians, the computer projection, only 42 percent of your fellow Americans are going to vote in this election in all 50 States on November 5.

I made a speech earlier this week at the Arlington Cemetery. I made a speech there because it was Veterans Day. We were paying tribute to and memorializing the hundreds and hundreds who have been buried in that wonderful cemetery. It gave me an inspiration to say to you that if they could give their lives to give you the right to vote, you ought to exercise that right to vote.

I cannot imagine an election that is more important to this district, to this State, than what will take place and transpire right here in the Fifth District next week.

Paul Goebel I have known since he was just a lad. His dad knew me when I was back at South High—an inspired if not very competent football player. But I have known the Goebel family a long time, and they are strong and they are tall, and they are the kind of people who are dedicated to public service. Paul, Jr.'s, father was; Paul, Jr., himself is.

And I have seen nothing but the finest in that family, and young Paul, he epitomizes all the great characteristics of that family.

And therefore, on the basis of quality as a person and experience in business and government, you have a great candidate. You have the kind of candidate that will do a job for all of you and for our State and for our country.

I know that he will stand up when the going is tough in the House of Representatives. And I know the trials and the tribulations that a Member of Congress goes through when he has to decide what is good and what is bad—and it is not always black or white; it is a little gray here and there.

But Paul has the brains and the conscience and the understanding to sift out the good from the bad and to give you a right answer. And therefore, without hesitation, reservation, or qualification, I can tell you I have already voted for Paul by absentee voter's ballot.

I am not going to try and vote again. Once is enough to show my support for a darned good Congressional candidate.

Now, let me add one final word, if I may. There are some people on the dais here who, to some extent, began politics about the same time I did or had an interest in it.

We are sort of—that generation that came along after World War II—most of us came back from some military service. Most of us saw the mistakes that our country made in the twenties and the thirties when we thought, mistakenly, that the Atlantic Ocean on one side and the Pacific on the other would be an adequate protection, and that we as a nation could close our eyes, close our ears, and not pay attention to the problems in the rest of the world and let them fight it out, whatever they wanted to do.

That was the mistake of the twenties and the thirties, and the consequence was, between Hitler and Mussolini and others, we got involved in a contest between freedom on the one hand and the effort on the part of some to subjugate people on the other.

Whether it was in Hitler's Germany or Mussolini's Italy or elsewhere, the issue was clear-cut, and 16 million Americans went to war in the Pacific or in the Atlantic. And you know, most of us came back convinced that this was a globe and we had to live together and work together, to find peace together, to build together, to help one another in one way or another.

As I said down at Calder, the one that convinced me that this approach was right—the approach of cooperation—was Arthur Vandenberg, a great Senator from our city and from our State.

And Arthur Vandenberg convinced me that if we were going to solve the problems of the Mediterranean, we had to support Harry Truman's program of Greek-Turkey aid; that we had to help a Democratic President even though both Senator Vandenberg and I were Republicans, by helping the rehabilitation, the reconstruction of Western Europe, including the Netherlands.

And he convinced me that we on the other side of the political aisle had to help a Democratic President build a sufficiently strong defense program, not for aggression, but for the maintenance of peace. So, Arthur Vandenberg was a great, great leader for our country and a great inspiration to me.

He taught me how to work with Democrats. He taught me the right approach as far as foreign policy was concerned. And the net result was we have had, relatively speaking, in Western Europe and many other parts of the world, a policy that was basically bipartisan—some variations, some deviations—and all of us, in my judgment, have been better off. It has led to peace in Europe. It has led to the détente that was initiated in the last 5 years. It has led to the achievements of a new approach to our relations with the People's Republic of China.

This bipartisanship under the leadership of our party has given to us, I think, the most solid foundation for peace over a long period of time.

Now, this last session of the Congress was very difficult. The Democratic leadership and the Republican leadership have worked with me, a Republican President. But unfortunately, too many of the troops have gone off in a hundred different directions.

And the consequence is, we have not had the support to find the proper answer to help the Greeks and Turks resolve their problems in Cyprus. There has not been the kind of support which we need to keep a sound policy in Southeast Asia. There has not been the kind of support that I think is needed to help us find the difficult key to the problems of the Middle East. And they are tough, and they are treacherous, and they are explosive.

Now, what I am saying is we have got some tough problems overseas, and Paul Goebel—because I know him, I have talked to him, and because I have looked at the record of his opponent—in my judgment is the best man to help me keep the peace and strengthen the peace in the months ahead. And I hope you will support him.

Well, it has just been wonderful to be here. I love every one of you. You have put up with me in the past. You have been kind to me when you thought I was wrong. You supported me much too often, for which I am grateful. But I hope and trust that in the months ahead, whatever I do will justify your faith, because I promise you, as I did the day I was sworn in, that I will do everything I can to make America strong and good, and do everything I can to make America for the best of all.

Thank you very, very much.

NOTE: The President spoke at 9:02 p.m. at Knollcrest Fieldhouse. In his opening remarks, the President referred to William S. Farr, Jr., chairman of the Fifth District Republican Committee; Robert VanderLaan, Republican candidate for State senator; and State Senator Milton Zaagman, who was running for reelection.

210

Remarks at Sioux City, Iowa. *October 31, 1974*

Wiley Mayne, Dave Stanley, Mayor Cole, my very good and old friend, former colleague in the House, Charlie Hoeven, all of the wonderful people from the Sixth Congressional District:

It is just great to be here a third time, and I thank you so much for the warm and tremendous welcome. I am deeply indebted and very, very grateful. Thank you very much.

A few days ago, I went to my hometown. We had a wonderful reception, but I can say without any reservation or qualification the reception here is just as enthusiastic, just as warm. And I wish to pay a special tribute to all of you who have come out on this occasion to meet me and to pay tribute to your Congressman, Wiley Mayne, and your next Senator, Dave Stanley.

I think it is very appropriate that we are having this rally at the airport. I have flown in today on a wing and a prayer. I ask you to send me some good men to Congress who will praise the Lord and pass the legislation.

It is particularly nice to be here in Sioux City, the largest community in the Sixth Congressional District in Iowa, and particularly, to pay tribute on this occasion to Wiley Mayne. You know, I have always been taught this from my early childhood—when you have a good thing going for you, you ought to keep it. And in Wiley Mayne you have that kind of a Congressman, so you darn well better keep him in the House of Representatives.

I served with Wiley almost 8 years in the House of Representatives. I have seen him on a day-to-day basis, working. I have seen him work in those two great committees—the House Committee on Agriculture and the House Committee on the Judiciary. And I can assure you from this very personal experience that he is a man of skill, a man of stature, a man who understands your problems, my problems, and is in a position because of his seniority to do something about it. So, I come here and speak with conviction when I urge you to see that Wiley is reelected.

Since we are in the heartland of American agriculture, there is no better place to commend the production, actually the production genius of the American farmer, and to say thanks to so many of you who are here and thousands upon thousands of others who are not here who have labored long and effectively in the fields of America. We thank you for a job well done.

At times over the past few years, farmers, in my judgment, have been unfairly criticized as the cause of high food prices. Now, as you well know, farmers are more likely—as a matter of fact, they are probably, without any doubt, the victims of inflation more than its cause. By farmer efficiency and by American agriculture's ever-increasing productivity, farmers are actually in the frontline troops, who are staving off what might well have been an even more serious round of inflation if it had not been for their efforts.

I am acutely aware of the problems that have beset agriculture in America and the very challenging problems that you face in the growing of your crops and the marketing of your efforts.

Now, some of these have been aggravated by unwise decisions by your Government. Others are the result of absolutely unusual weather problems. It was too wet in the spring, you had a drought in the summer, and you have had unseasonably early frost in the fall. And all of this, of course, complicated by the great need of additional food throughout the world.

Now, because of the price incentive and provisions in our agricultural legislation and because of the encouragement by Government to expand planted acreage, farmers throughout the States of this great Union have responded magnificently, superbly, to boost the supply of feed grains and soybeans.

Thanks to the flexibility written into the 1973 Agriculture and Consumer Protection Act, farmers were able to move relatively smoothly from a limited to a full production program. And incidentally, great credit for the major provisions of the 1973 act can and must be given to Wiley Mayne, the top ranking Republican of the important House Committee on Agriculture, Subcommittee on Livestock and Grain.

Let me give you a little inside or cloakroom story. While the 1973 agricultural act was being considered in committee, Wiley was being considered on the floor of the House of Representatives. I conferred very frequently with your Congressman, Wiley Mayne. I know from firsthand experience how hard he worked to help effect its enactment and to liberate farmers from the discredited, income-restrictive programs of the past 40 years.

So I, as a former colleague of Wiley's and one who worked with him as the Republican leader in the House, wish to express my deep gratitude and appreciation, Wiley, for the fine job that you did on this vitally important legislation.

I think there is another area of concern—corn and soybean production is falling short of our worldwide needs. Even so, the corn crop is, I think, the fifth largest in the history of the United States, the soybean crop is the third largest, and wheat and rice the largest ever in America.

We cannot, however, in fairness, ask our farmers to produce, produce more from their soil and from their labor, unless all of us are willing to share at least a part of the production risk.

And furthermore, there are certain things that we must do and, I will promise you, that we will do. Fuel and fertilizer, especially fertilizer, adequate to supply farm needs, continue to be a very serious problem. And as I have stated before, I will ask authorities from the Congress to assure farmers all of the fertilizer that you need for your farms. And I will make certain and positive that you will have all of the fuel that you need to do the job for all of us and consumers throughout the world.

And may I repeat for emphasis, I will not ask Congress to increase gasoline taxes. That is one tax that is high enough, believe me.

I could not come to Sioux City, the heart of the slaughter and livestock industry, particularly the cattle-feeding business, and not say a word about the production of meat. Livestock producers, particularly cattle feeders, have called to the attention of responsible officials in the Federal Government many, many times in the past year the financial wringer that they have been put through. Adjusting to higher feed costs and the increased supply of beef animals is a very painful process.

And so, today, despite a headline that I read in the newspaper here in Des Moines—not the one in Sioux City, but Des Moines—I will make an announcement—not one, but two, and reaffirm a third, and perhaps give you some other information concerning farming in 1974.

I think these announcements will relieve some of the anxiety and possibly restore some of the confidence among producers so that this great part of agriculture, which is centered in Sioux City, can become again profitable.

First, this Administration intends to carry out precisely the intent of the meat import law.

And let me be quite specific. If imports of meat, subject to the meat import law, threaten to pick up markedly during the next year, and the Agriculture Department's estimate of 1975 imports exceeds the trigger level under the meat import law, I will impose meat quotas or negotiate volunteer agreements with foreign suppliers.

Second, no action will be taken to change the present system of dairy import quotas, which means that dairy quotas for imports will not be increased unless and until there has been a thorough review of the overall problem and full opportunity for our dairy producers to be heard at that time.

There is no intention on my part to increase dairy imports into the United States.

Third, this Administration is not going to permit foreign dairy producers to compete against the American dairymen in the U.S. market with subsidized products. If the Europeans reinstitute their export subsidies on dairy products directed at this market, I will impose countervailing duties on their products.

And one final announcement, which I think rounds out a pattern of strong, effective action to help the cattle and dairy business—and let me be quite specific. In addition, I have asked the Secretary of Agriculture to investigate USDA purchases of ground beef for use in the National School Lunch Program. These purchases would provide a highly nutritious food to schools for, I think, proper use in the school lunch program.

Let me add this, because it is not too well understood by many. These purchases will not be an additional cost to the Government, as the USDA is obligated by law to finance each school lunch program by 10 cents, either in cash or in commodities.

So, this report by the Secretary of Agriculture on prospective purchases should be in my hands in a relatively short period of time, and I hope his recommendation is favorable for these purchases.

Now, as I have in the past—as Republican leader in the House, and as Vice President, and now as President—as I look at the problems of agriculture, I will consult with Wiley Mayne for guidance, for help in the solving of agriculture's problems.

I hope that I do not duplicate some of what Wiley has been telling you as he has campaigned all over the Sixth District in the northwest corner of Iowa, but I want to remind you, if I might, about the kind of service I know he has rendered to this district.

In a period when big corporate farms are taking over some of agriculture's production, Wiley has been in there fighting for the family farm and the family farmer.

Let me just quote, if I might, one precise example. Wiley has helped lead the fight in the House during the last 3 or 4 years to limit Government payments to the total of $20,000 per farm. He did so because he was in contact on a person-to-person basis with the farmers in this district who advised him that these massive payments to big farms were discrediting your total farm program.

That is the kind of a Congressman, in my judgment, that this district deserves; one who can listen to people, the 460-some thousand who reside in this district;

one who can listen and respond to the legitimate problems, complaints, criticisms, suggestions.

And I might add a postscript. Dave Stanley, when he is elected to the United States Senate, will be the same kind of United States Senator that Wiley Mayne is as a Member of the House of Representatives.

Speaking of Dave Stanley, I was in Des Moines a week or so ago. I saw Dave, talked to him. He has been carrying on one of the most vigorous campaigns for the United States Senate. I applaud him for his efforts to meet you, talk to you, listen to you.

His experience in the State legislature, his experience as a campaigner, his fine background as a good Iowan, a good Hawkeye, in my opinion will help you and help me and help your State in the United States Senate.

Wiley said that I have been in this district three times. I have enjoyed every visit. And as Wiley said, the crowds are a little bigger this time, and maybe you are listening a little more. But let me say this and say it with emphasis: When you have someone like Wiley Mayne representing you in the Sixth District, when you have somebody like him that stands up for you in the highest councils of the Federal Government, then I hope you feel that it is time for you to stand up for him in return.

I left Washington a little after noon. I am on the way to California, going to Oregon, to Utah, to Kansas, to—well, a couple of other places in the next 3 days. But I stopped here because I wanted to convey a specific message.

I wanted to convey my deep conviction of how I feel about Wiley. I think you need him. I need him. The country needs him. And on a very personal and intimate basis, I respect his judgment and his integrity.

If Wiley is not returned to the Congress from this Congressional district, this important agricultural district will not only lose one of the finest men in the Congress but it will lose a seniority on a committee that affects very vitally agriculture.

If Wiley is not in the next Congress, the potency of your representation on this great Committee on Agriculture will nosedive.

Now, one of my old and very good friends, Charlie Hoeven, knows that better than anybody. Charlie Hoeven, who represented this district for many, many years, was the senior Republican on the House Committee on Agriculture and knows very well the impact of a high-ranking position on that committee, the potency of that representation as it affects all of you who are interested in agriculture—whether it is on the farm or in the implement business or in the banking business or otherwise.

So, I strongly urge just on this very, almost selfish ground, that you make certain that Wiley continues this representation.

I do not mean to infer that Wiley Mayne rubberstamps everything I suggest, either as President or as I did as Vice President or even as Republican leader in the House. He does not. He is an independent guy who gets your ideas and translates them into legislative action.

But even in those areas where we disagree, one thing that I particularly like about Wiley is the fact that we can disagree without being disagreeable, and that is a pretty darn good trait in any American.

And let me give you one illustration. Just recently, Wiley let me know very candidly, very forcefully, that he protested the action that I took on a certain Saturday to suspend—and I say suspend—certain sales of corn and wheat to the Soviet Union.

It did not take Wiley Mayne very long to get from Capitol Hill down to the White House to let me explain to him the justification for the action and to inform him that what I did was not a permanent one, involving this sale to the Soviet Union.

I assured Wiley at that time that my action on that particular occasion was not to limit exports on a permanent basis but to make certain that no single nation cornered either the corn or wheat market.

Forty million bushels of corn, 40 million bushels of wheat, have already been released since that time to the Soviet Union.

But the point I wanted to make, and make most emphatically, was that Wiley Mayne was on the firing line protecting your interest and your concern, and I congratulate you for it, Wiley.

One other area of great concern to you as citizens—and here is an area where both Wiley and Dave, I think, agree with me without any question—and this is the determination by them and by me to stop the rising cost of living, to do something effectively, as far as our Government is concerned, about inflation.

The principal cause of rising prices is the fact that our Government has been spending more than it takes in. Wiley Mayne has voted to cut spending and to balance the Federal budget in the past, and I can assure you he can be counted upon to do so in the future.

That is why I am here personally asking each of you, the people of the Sixth District, to send Wiley Mayne back to Congress on election day next Tuesday.

I can reemphasize, it really matters. America needs his very strong and his very reliable vote in the House of Representatives to help us keep back rising prices and the problems of inflation.

I want to also use this occasion, with your indulgence, to put some myths to rest here in Sioux City. I have seen some very interesting reports in this campaign here, and I consider it a very superb coincidence that we can bury these political hobgoblins on Halloween eve.

I have seen some reports around the country that some candidates of the other party are laying claim to being fiscal watchdogs. I have seen some reports that they are even accusing the Republican Party of being for high spending.

Now, you and I know what causes inflation. It is not the Republican Party. The facts are that it is largely due to the Government spending more money than it should. And I will tell you flatly and categorically the votes to break the budget did not come from Wiley Mayne or from those on his side of the political aisle.

Let's take a look at the record. Some great politicians in the past have said, "Let's look at what the record shows." And this is something I would like to call to your particular attention, to many people in this audience today. As I look around, I see there are a number between the ages of 20 and 42. This is an interesting fact often forgotten or not known: If you are in this age group, from 20 to 42, the Congress of the United States has been in control of one political party 85 percent of the time in your lifetime.

That means that 85 percent of your life has been lived under the legislative control of a single political party, and this is the party which has to be held accountable for so many of the problems that we face in this country today, including inflation—especially inflation, which is the biggest legacy of this period of monolithic Federal control.

Now, next Tuesday—it is a day that we cannot forget. I cannot believe there is voter apathy in the great State of Iowa. I do not believe there is voter apathy in the other 49 States. The issues are critical. The problems are serious. So, let's all make up our minds that we do not go down the same road again that has given us control by one party in 38 out of the last 42 years.

They have done a bad job, and they ought to be replaced.

Now, if you send Wiley Mayne—you send him back to the House of Representatives, and you send Dave Stanley to the United States Senate, and if you reelect Bob Ray, your great Governor, then the ticket, the Republican ticket, will be of great help in meeting the problems here in Iowa and helping to meet the challenges of those problems we face both at home and abroad and in the Nation's Capital.

I repeat, I need Wiley and Dave—you need them in Washington, you need Bob Ray in Des Moines. And if you go out and do the job that you can do with your friends, your neighbors, your relatives—Independents, Democrats, and others—then I am confident that you will achieve something good for yourself, your community, your State, and our great Nation.

Thank you very, very much.

NOTE: The President spoke at 3:25 p.m. at the Sioux City Municipal Airport. In his opening remarks, the President referred to George A. Cole, mayor of Sioux City, Iowa, and Charles B. Hoeven, United States Representative from Iowa 1943–65.

211

Remarks in Los Angeles, California. *October 31, 1974*

IT IS really a great privilege and pleasure for me to be introduced on this occasion by the next Governor of the great State of California, Hugh Flournoy.

Hugh, Governor Reagan, Bob Hope, my former colleagues in the Congress, distinguished guests, ladies and gentlemen:

It is really wonderful to be here, and I do want to thank Hugh for his very fine introduction. Since I became President, I am usually introduced in a very stately and a very dignified manner, such as Hugh did tonight in a very appropriate way. But I would like to tell you about one dinner that happened quite recently when I was introduced by a former teammate of mine at the University of Michigan when I was playing football back there when the ball was round.

I will never forget that introduction. He said something like this: "Ladies and gentlemen, it might interest you to know that I played football with Jerry Ford for 2 years, and it made a lasting impression on me. I was a quarterback, and Jerry was the center. And you might say it gave me a completely different view of the President of the United States." [*Laughter*]

But it is a particular pleasure to be in California again, and I have been here a number of times over the last 25 years in political life. California—the State that puts together such great football teams as the UCLA Bruins and the USC Trojans.

As a former football player for the Big Ten, I have always been very, very grateful for those practice teams that you have given us to play against. Well, we call it practice—I think you call it the Rose Bowl.

The last time—this is the last time I am going to buy a joke from Woody Hayes at Ohio State. [*Laughter*]

It is pretty obvious I enjoy being here in California, the State that is governed by Ronnie Reagan, served by Hugh Flournoy, and owned by Bob Hope. [*Laughter*]

It was very kind of Bob to mention my golf game, but as he well knows, it is not worth mentioning. Bob vows he will never carry me again as a partner on the golf course, and it is reciprocal, Bob. [*Laughter*]

Frankly, I have the same problem with golf that George Foreman had with Muhammad Ali. My swing is very good; I just did not or don't connect often enough.[1] [*Laughter*]

I appreciate, as Bob knows, his being here tonight, because at 10:00 tonight, the Dean Martin roast of Bob Hope will be shown on television. Dean and Bob had invited me to be on the show, but unfortunately, at almost the last minute some special problems arose in the Oval Office that precluded my participation. I think it is a shame, Bob, because lately, if there is anybody who knows about roasts, it is me. [*Laughter*]

As a matter of fact, Bob and I have a great deal in common. For the last 24 years Bob has been seen on television, and for the last 25 years I have been in politics. So, we both know how to live quite dangerously. At least by the ratings. [*Laughter*]

I will only conclude by saying that Bob has done very well.

But I do wish to express to Governor Reagan and to Hugh and to all of the others my appreciation for being invited to visit all of you in California. I think you have achieved something quite unique in politics in America. You elected a great Governor who was an actor-turned-politician. Back in Washington, we have the reverse problem—too many politicians who have turned actor. [*Laughter*]

Quite frankly, I am talking about some Congressmen and Senators who play the role of fiscal conservatives at home, and Diamond Jim Brady in Washington.

I think you might call them "method politicians." They will try any method to get elected, and if indeed you do elect them to the House or to the Senate, they are like the child you sent at one time to the grocery store—one of your own—sometimes they don't remember what you sent them for. [*Laughter*]

Today is Halloween, a warm, affectionate holiday, close to the hearts of all of us in America. But my message for tonight is this: Let's keep Halloween for the children. The last thing we need in Washington is a trick and treat Congress.

To be very blunt, I am talking about a Congress that hands out multi-billion

---

[1] George Foreman lost the world heavyweight boxing championship to Muhammad Ali on October 30, 1974.

dollar treats, and then the trick is how to pay for them without higher taxation or more inflation.

And it is my observation that one Halloween a year is enough. What we need the rest of the time in Washington, in Sacramento, in State capitals across the country, and in our county and local governments, are serious-minded, dedicated individuals, inflation fighters and energy savers.

I am told that Hugh Flournoy's opponent in the California gubernatorial race claims that one State alone cannot do much about inflation, that it is mainly a Federal problem.

Well, I for one consider California part of the Union and a very important part of our Union. One out of every ten Americans lives in this great State. You have the largest of all delegations in the Congress and the largest number of eligible voters of any State in the Union. You excel in so many, many fields—in industry, agriculture, automobiles, advanced technologies, education, effective State and local government, the arts, recreation, conservation, natural resources.

You have all of these great attributes and resources. You even, in my conversations with many from California, run out of superlatives when you talk about the State. And I think for good reason. So I ask, in all sincerity, this problem: California not involved in the inflation problem?

My answer is categorical: nonsense. You are not only one-tenth of the problem, you are also one-tenth of the solution.

This State has shown the rest of the country and the world there is nothing Californians can't do when they really put their shoulder to the wheel. California outstrips all but a handful of nations in wealth and productivity. Nothing California can do about inflation? I repeat, nonsense.

If inflation were only a problem for Washington, I would be staying in Washington trying to solve it. But the state of our economy is a national problem, and to the extent that it is a problem of the Federal Government, it is a political problem.

Frankly, that is why I am traveling here in California this evening and Fresno tomorrow and five or six other States this last weekend of this great campaign—to share at least my views on the 1974 political campaign and the issues that are involved.

And I am asking—as I and Hugh and the rest of the State ticket, including your Congressional candidates, campaign day and night, literally—I am asking all Californians to do their full share.

You have 10 percent of the political clout in the Congress and, I am quite frank to say, one of the ablest, as well as one of the largest Republican delegations in the House of Representatives, and I see two or three of my former colleagues in that delegation here in this room.

You have had a great Republican Governor and a Republican administration in Sacramento which has practiced as well as preached a progressive but fiscally sound policy of good government, in political terms.

There used to be a saying that "As Maine goes, so goes the Nation." The fact is, during my lifetime, it is the polls in California that the Nation has turned to every election night, and it is becoming more so as you grow in population and power. This is the way it will be next Tuesday, because what happens in this great State next Tuesday will be a bellwether as to what might happen in 1976.

If it is true that there is great voter apathy across the Nation—and the polls seem to indicate—then, in my judgment, there is time to change it, and we had better do it.

If only 42 percent of the eligible voters are going to turn out next Tuesday on the tremendous issues and the candidates that are involved—and this is what the experts are predicting or forecasting—that means that a slight fraction of over 21 percent of the eligible voters in this country can determine how this Nation will operate for the next 2 years in Washington, D.C.

Let me, in all sincerity, ask this question: Do you want that kind of minority rule in the United States of America? I do not think you do.

So, I say to my friends in California—to Republicans, Independents, and what President Eisenhower used to call "discerning Democrats," and you have plenty of them here in California—let's prove that the pessimistic pollsters are totally wrong. Let's prove that you care what kind of government you have in Sacramento and in Washington, that you appreciate the kind of leadership that you have had with Ron Reagan, John Harmer, Hugh Flournoy, Ev Younger, what they have given to you in California for the past 8 years, and that you want an even stronger Congressional delegation to represent you in the Nation's Capital and to protect your paycheck and your savings in the Congress of the United States.

Very frankly, if you do just that, California will have won one-tenth of the battle against inflation and will once again set an example for the rest of the Nation.

As I indicated in the economic message that I submitted to the Congress and to the American people about a month or so ago, if we are to win against inflation, we must enlist the efforts of every individual American and every unit of government across this great country.

We need teamwork. We need cooperation between the Federal Government and the States like California; cooperation between individuals, between individual States and their counties and their communities. If we are going to win the struggle against inflation, we must exercise some rigid fiscal control and responsibility and prudence at every level, from the housewife making better use of her budget to the Congress in Washington curbing its appetite for uncontrollable spending.

I think you are fortunate here in California in that you have already established a tradition of fiscal prudence in your State government. When my good friend Ron Reagan replaced the Democrat in Sacramento nearly 8 years ago, California was suffering from a deficit of about $325 million. During the last Brown administration, I understand you could do real well in Sacramento selling red ink to the statehouse. It was not much, but it was very steady.

Fortunately, your great Governor cleaned up the mess that he inherited, using modern management techniques that are now being copied by Governors from many, many States, both Democratic as well as Republican.

As a result of this technique or technology, he was able to get your State out of the financial grief that he inherited. When Ron leaves office, I am told California will be enjoying a surplus of around $400 million.

That kind of fiscal prudence can make a big dent in inflation. California, as I see it, cannot afford the risk of losing what he has done by electing a big round of new spenders, statewide or nationwide. Hugh Flournoy understands this; John Harmer, your outstanding Lieutenant Governor candidate knows this. So does Bill Richardson, who will make a great Senator for your State. So does Evelle Younger, Brian [Van] Camp, Bill Bagley, John Kehoe.[2] I have had the privilege in several visits to California to meet them, to compare them with the kind of people that I see on the other side of the political aisle and in other States throughout the Union.

So, I think in California you are fortunate, lucky to have this talent available to elect, to run your State for the next 4 years. And unlike Hugh's opponent, they also understand the concept of teamwork; teamwork in the fight against inflation and the benefits that can be derived from cooperation between the State and the Federal Government, and between the State and local units of government.

From Hugh Flournoy on down on the ballot, California has a Republican slate

---

[2] Evelle J. Younger was the Republican candidate for reelection as State attorney general; Brian R. Van Camp was the Republican candidate for secretary of state; State Assemblyman William T. Bagley was the Republican candidate for State comptroller; and John T. Kehoe was the Republican candidate for State treasurer.

of experienced public servants—men of proven competence, integrity; men who have demonstrated that they know how to do the job and how to get it done.

It is my observation we need more teamwork in Washington as well.

I first learned this concept, how important it was, some 25 years ago when I first took the oath of office in Washington, D.C. Earlier, a Republican Congress had worked very, very closely with a Democratic President, Harry Truman, to build a strong, bipartisan foreign policy, one that was good for America and, fortunately, good for the rest of the free world.

And because the Congress, which was then Republican, and the Democratic President did work together, we succeeded in mounting the Marshall Plan, the Greek-Turkish aid program, and the programs that followed, that rebuilt Europe, NATO, and produced an alliance which protected the free world from the threat of aggression from those early post-war days.

Today, that bipartisanship in foreign policy which has carried this Nation through some of its very roughest times, some of its greatest challenges, is being eroded by the irresponsible actions of some Members of the Congress.

What really concerns me is this: If the ranks of the shortsighted are swelled by elections next Tuesday, not only that delicate bipartisanship which served this country so well for over a quarter of a century could be destroyed and our total foreign policy, which is one of maintaining and building the peace, could be undermined.

Now, at home, we have another threat, certainly the greatest we face domestically in this country—inflation. In its own way, this deadly domestic enemy is every bit as serious as the threat that we face from abroad.

Again, what concerns me, if the ranks of the big spenders in the Congress, House and Senate, are increased next Tuesday the inflation-fighting program that I have asked the Congress to approve will be swamped—overloaded with massive deficit spending.

What we need is not a veto-proof Congress, as some have proposed, but what we actually need is an inflation-proof Congress, and we can get it next Tuesday.

If I might, let me be quite precise about what I mean. I do not want anyone to misunderstand. I do not believe that either of our great major political parties has a total monopoly on wisdom or on the solutions to the Nation's economic problems. We have Members on both sides of the aisle, and some of my former colleagues know who they are, who are indispensable to an inflation-proof Congress.

Unfortunately and very regrettably, some of the staunchest Democrats who stood up and fought to be cooperative and to be helpful are regrettably retiring voluntarily this year. And so, who they are replaced by is critical and crucial.

Now, I am sure that virtually every Member of the Congress has only the very best interests of our Nation at heart, and it depends on how he or she sees it.

Generally, when we differ, it is not so much as to the goals but the road by which you achieve it. The question we face right today—it will be reemphasized and reiterated when Congress comes back on November 18—what is the best way to beat inflation? I have labeled it public enemy number one. A lot of different people have a lot of different views, and as I think most of you know, we had this summit meeting on the economy that was the result of 12 mini-summits that were held all over the United States where we had labor, management, economists, bankers, housewives, and others participating.

I, at least, had an open mind and was the beneficiary of the suggestions that were made by this broad-based cross section of America. There was one point, however, on which there was substantial, almost unanimous agreement on which a majority of Americans seemed to agree: that excess Government spending has been, and will continue to be, a root cause of inflation.

No government, no government that I have read about, studied about, participated in, can keep on spending more than it takes in without driving down the buying power of its currency and driving up the cost of living for its people.

In the short haul, it is very easy for government to yield to the temptation to give people what they want or what the politicians tell them that they ought to have, but keep this in mind: In the long haul, a government big enough to give us everything we want is a government big enough to take from us everything we have.

So, when you come right down to a very basic subject, we must curb Federal spending as far as the Federal Government, the Congress, the President are concerned. In the economic message that I submitted to the Congress just before the recess, I proposed that we establish a spending ceiling this year of some $300 billion, or some $5.5 billion less than the budget as it was submitted last January. But the current Congress has not yet approved that spending ceiling. The House of Representatives did act, but the Senate did not.

There are some other proposals in that economic package which is aimed at tightening the screws on inflation and yet giving some help and assistance as far as the economy is concerned to strengthen it.

I hope when Congress reconvenes in the month or the weeks between November 18 and January 3, we will meet the challenge and act effectively on this, I think, finely tuned proposal.

Now, I am not going to be so brash as to stand here and tell you that all of the big spenders belong to the opposition party, although the percentages tilt pretty far that way. But I would like to note—I would like you to note, and Governor Reagan mentioned it, others have said it, but I think it is good to reemphasize it—that the Democratic Party has controlled the United States Congress for 38 out of the last 42 years, and for the last 20 years consecutively.

During this period of time, Federal spending has shot up from roughly $4.5 billion on an annual basis in 1934 to $300-plus billion in the current fiscal year. It is a simple fact that no President and no Administration can spend a single dollar—and to be more precise, a single penny—that Congress has first not appropriated.

I cannot emphasize that enough. Congress appropriates every penny that is spent by any President or by any Administration. So, when you look at it, if you are unhappy about the handling of our Nation's finances in the Capital over the past 20 years, if you think it is time for a change, remember next Tuesday who the big spenders are and throw the big spenders out. And if some of them are Republicans, so be it.

I think it is time for responsible men and women of all political persuasions—Republicans, Democrats, Independents—to come together, not in an effort for a political advantage, but in a spirit of true American patriotism, to whip problems like inflation, energy, the environment, to strengthen our successful foreign policy by the restoration of bipartisanship. And it is also time for the American voter, whatever his views, to demonstrate by the ballot that he supports a responsible and responsive anti-inflation policy; that he opposes wasteful Government spending; that he demands a strong, secure national defense program; and most important, that he wants elected representatives who feel the same way.

And in Congress, that does not mean a one-party monopoly. It does mean a Congress in which reasonable men of both parties can work together with an administration in a spirit of cooperation for the good of all of us.

I think this is the kind of Congress I have tried to campaign for in some 14 or 15 States in the last month, and with your help, it is the kind of a Congress that we can elect.

If we are successful next Tuesday, the average hard-working American citizen will be the beneficiary.

Just a few weeks ago, while I was out on the campaign trail, I met a lovely lady whose husband is now retired. After working very, very hard all their lives, they are living on social security and a small pension. They were beautiful people.

After I shook hands with her, she reached in her purse and handed me a little slip of paper. It was a supermarket register receipt like the one I am holding in my hand.

She told me that she appreciated many of the suggestions I had made on television on what an individual citizen or family might do to help in the battle against inflation. But she said both of them—she and her husband—already were doing most of those things and were trying to do more. Yet the total each week of this little grocery slip kept going up and up and up.

She said, "Mr. President, can't you do something about this?"

I looked her in the eye. I said, "Yes, but I cannot do it all alone. I need a lot of help. I need the help of responsible people, like-minded individuals in the Senate, in the House of Representatives."

And she looked at me with a kindly smile and said she understood and would do her part on election day.

In the final analysis, let me say to each and every one of you, that is what this great national election is all about—to make sure we have a responsible and responsive Congress for the next 2 years, responsible to the people and responsive to their needs.

As I close, let me make this suggestion to each of you. When you go into the voting booth next Tuesday, take with you your latest grocery slip, your check-out receipt, and before you vote, take a good hard look at the bottom line. Then vote for the candidates who will really make sure and certain that your paycheck buys as much on the day that you spend it as on the day that you earned it.

Thank you very much.

NOTE: The President spoke at 10:14 p.m. at a dinner for Republican candidates at the Century Plaza Hotel.

212

Remarks to Reporters Following a Visit With Former President Nixon at Long Beach, California. *November 1, 1974*

I SPENT approximately 8 minutes with the President. Obviously he is a very, very sick man, but I think he is coming along very, very well.

He was very interested in some discussions that I had with him concerning my prospective trip to Japan and to South Korea and to the Soviet Union. I gave him a quick rundown on Dr. Kissinger's trips to the Soviet Union, to India, to Pakistan, and the last message I had was to Afghanistan, as he continues this trip.

The President was very alert. He was very interested, but it was very obvious to me that he had been very, very ill. But he showed a great deal of strength mentally and, I think, physically in meeting this very serious challenge.

I told him that I had talked this morning to my wife before I came here and indicated to him that she had asked me, as I told him, that all of our family were praying for his full and complete recovery.

Thank you very much.

NOTE: The President spoke at 10:33 a.m. outside Long Beach Memorial Hospital.

On October 29, 1974, Mr. Nixon had undergone surgery to remove blood clots from his abdomen and left leg. Following the operation, he went into shock after hemorrhaging was caused by anti-clotting medication.

213

Remarks at Fresno, California. *November 1, 1974*

BOB MATHIAS, Congressman Chuck Wiggins, Carol Harner, distinguished mayors, members of the State legislature, members of the Board of County Commissioners, the wonderful bands from—I still get a great thrill out of hearing the National Anthem played, as I am sure Bob Mathias did, both at London and Helsinki when he won, representing all of us in the decathlon. It is a great, great thrill.

It is nice to see all these wonderful young people and all of you from Fresno, Kings, and Tulare Counties. I thank you for a super-enthusiastic, warm welcome. I am very, very, very grateful. Thank you very much.

I think you can tell from the reaction that it is a great experience for me to be in the central valley of California. And as I look around this big valley to fine people, I noticed that as I flew in this morning it is a big valley, and the big crops that it produces, the big yields that come from the soil, and the labor, the big livestock, to serve its people in Congress it produces big men, mentally and otherwise, in Bob Mathias. And frankly, that is why I am here.

It is really no secret—I need Bob Mathias. I think you need Bob Mathias. I think the country needs Bob Mathias back in Washington to represent these three great counties of Fresno, Kings, and Tulare. And I am counting on your doing it.

I have been asked many times why have I traveled extensively in the last few weeks, candidly asking American voters to return men like Bob Mathias back to Congress. People have asked why, and let me give you the answer. It is very simple. I am here because the issues are far, far too important. It is far, far too vital for me to sit on the sidelines. I never have, and I don't intend to, when I feel strongly about people and about issues. The stakes are far too high to be a sideline sitter when we have got people like Bob Mathias out in the hustings.

And there is another answer, too. I do it because the people of Fresno, the 340,000 or 350,000 people in this 17th Congressional District, in my judgment, deserve to see their President and deserve to see a President who believes with conviction and dedication in the issues and in the solutions that I think can make America a bigger, better, stronger, finer country for all of us—particularly these fine young people down here in the front rows.

Public service, public responsibility are far too important for me to sit in that beautiful Oval Office in a mystic seance in Washington, D.C., when I can come out here to Fresno in the 17th Congressional District and have an opportunity to see the wonderful faces, the enthusiasm.

I enjoy being on the banks of the Potomac, but I get a big thrill and a big shot in the arm coming to Fresno on an occasion like this.

I am out here—I am particularly here because there are some issues that, in my judgment, deserve to be talked about, to be discussed, so that the problems we have can be communicated to you with the solutions and the answers that we have.

We do have a serious problem of inflation. We have some other economic problems, but the answers can be gotten by all of you and by all of us in the executive as well as in the legislative branch.

To solve those problems, I need people like Bob Mathias who, in my opinion, from his past record, can be extremely helpful. He is a big man, but he is a big man in action. He is not a big man of talk. He is a big man as a problemsolver, and that is what you want in the 17th District representing you.

And let me give you if I can, very seriously, an extremely practical reason why I think Bob ought to be sent back next Tuesday, for you, for me, for the country. I could not help but notice as we flew in and saw the beautiful fields and the people working in them—Bob Mathias, when he is returned to Congress will be the second man on our side of the aisle on the great Committee on Agriculture, and agriculture is important to all of you.

That is the committee that drafts the legislation. That is the committee that guides it through the House of Representatives. That is the committee that has a direct connection with the Department of Agriculture, and with Bob Mathias in that high-ranking, number two position on the Committee on Agriculture, you will have a voice at the top, a voice of experience instead of a person at the bottom with a big voice but no communication.

Let me tell you something else about Bob. When I was the minority leader in the House of Representatives, I had the opportunity of working intimately, very closely with Bob Mathias on a number of legislative matters. But what was important in that relationship to all of you was that when I wanted some straight answers, some sound suggestions about agriculture, one of the finest, most helpful voices, to me, was the observations, the recommendations, the advice from Bob Mathias.

He advised me then and he advises me on agriculture as the occupant of the White House, and I thank you, Bob, for your help then and your assistance now.

I have heard, Bob, about the hard campaign that you are running, working literally night and day to communicate your positions, your achievements to the 400,000-plus people that live in the 17th Congressional District. And I won't try to repeat all the things that you can speak up about, what you have done, how you voted.

I do know—and let me mention very quickly—some areas that ought to be re-emphasized. For example, you have introduced a number of important, very vital pieces of legislation that affect all the young people, as well as the old; legislation to protect our natural resources and our environment, preserving the beauty of our national parks—and I saw some of them as I flew from the Los Angeles area here this morning.

I think it is vitally important for everybody, the young as well as the others, to know that you have introduced and pushed legislation to provide new jobs for all of the people in the central valley.

I think people ought to know what you have done in the way of legislation to open the flow of energy resources to our people, and if we are going to grow and prosper and to provide jobs and homes and opportunities for these young people, particularly—and I am looking right at them and talking to them directly—we need energy. We need energy to make a better America.

And I know, Bob, of your personal interest in education. You are interested in health legislation. So you have had not only great experience in the field of agriculture but you have had an interest in environment, our ecology. You have had an interest in energy, you have had an interest in jobs and health and education. Yes, your experience in these areas has been invaluable to the people in this Congressional district.

But let me mention one other area that I hope and trust does have an impact on all of you, and I speak now of the field of foreign policy. Bob Mathias has another great committee responsibility, as a member of the Committee on Foreign Affairs. That is the committee that puts together that legislation that helped to achieve the peace. It is the committee that puts together the legislation that will maintain the peace. It is the committee that will build a better America here so we can have peace abroad.

But let me speak, if I might, about the subject that I consider public enemy number one, domestically—inflation. Inflation, according to all polls, is the matter of primary interest, the highest-ranking matter of concern to the American people, some 83 percent. There is one way that all of us, and particularly those in the Congress, can do something about it, and that is to cut, to slice the fat off the Federal budget.

This can help us curb rampant inflation. Bob Mathias has a reputation in the Congress for being an inflation fighter. I understand that his opponent is pretty well beholden to the people that want a veto-proof Congress.

Well, a veto-proof Congress, in my judgment, will do more to increase inflation than anything I can imagine. What we want is not a veto-proof Congress, but we want an inflation-proof Congress, and Bob Mathias can give us that.

As I heard the Star-Spangled Banner, or National Anthem, being played, I thought back—in 1948 when I first ran for the Congress of the United States as an ex-athlete, and it goes back a long time. I was proud of the representation that Bob Mathias at the ripe old age of 17 was giving our country in the Olympics, a gold medal winner both in London as well as Helsinki. And I was proud of him then, and I am very proud of him and the contributions that he has made to our country today.

This kind of representation, as a young man and as a legislator, is good for our country.

I am informed that in this area, perhaps—maybe around the Nation—there is an apathy about this election. I hope and trust this is not true in Kings and Fresno and Tulare Counties. I hope it is not true in the great State of California. And I am going to do the maximum that I can to prevent it from being true in the rest of the country.

I don't believe people are discouraged, disillusioned, turned off. I don't believe we are going to have only 42 percent of the eligible voters in America participate in that great election in all 50 States next Tuesday.

Let me tell you why I think it would be tragic, why it would be catastrophic. If only 42 percent of the American people vote next Tuesday, it means that 21 percent of the eligible voters in America will make the decision for 100 percent.

Now, we want not 21 percent of the people telling us how to run the Government. I think we want 100 percent of the people. And I say to all of you young people, those right in front of me and those in the bands: I think you have a very special mission. You have more impact, you have more influence, you can do more to get your parents to go and cast that ballot than anybody else in the whole area of Fresno and the surrounding environs.

I hope you will make that a special mission, to grab Mom and Dad by the hand and ask them on Tuesday morning, "Are you going to vote?" You can, and you will.

And this is important for Democrats, Independents, and Republicans alike. If they do, I am confident that you will send people like Bob Mathias back to Congress. You will send people like Hugh Flournoy to the statehouse in Sacramento. I think you will send a good team to help Hugh Flournoy in your great State capital of Sacramento.

Now, it is just as important to attack the problems in Sacramento as it is in Washington. We want a creative Congress. We want a forward-looking occupant of your statehouse, your State capital in Sacramento. We want responsive, responsible government in all parts of our government at the local, State, and national level.

The urgency of the problem to be responsible and responsive in the handling of your tax dollars is not just at the national, it is at the State or the local level.

I am told that Hugh Flournoy's opponent for the office of Governor in the State of California says inflation is not the problem of California.

I respectfully disagree with that very limited observation. California is one-tenth of the American people. It is the biggest State. It has got the biggest vision. It is a rapidly growing State, and I am amazed that a candidate for the Governorship of California would have such a limited perspective of the problem.

It seems to me that a prospective, or a candidate for Governor of California ought to recognize that with a State as big, as wealthy, as powerful—can have an impact on inflation. One out of every ten people in the United States lives in California. And what you do and what your delegation does in the Congress of the United States will have an impact.

I respectfully say that California must be involved, and for any candidate for Governor to say that it is not, is pure nonsense.

We cannot fight inflation without the help of California, and a Governor like Hugh Flournoy will help us fight inflation. And with that kind of help, we can do something about it.

Let me just make this final observation. My message to you here today is a very simple one, and I hope you will pass it on to your friends between now and Tuesday. If the big spenders get control of Congress, if the big spenders control your statehouse and your State capital, we cannot, in all honesty, do much about inflation, because excessive spending at the State level or at the Federal level is a major cause, a principal reason for inflation.

And so I ask you very strongly, but very simply, to send the kind of people back to Washington who you can trust, who will watch your tax dollars. I urge you to send people to Sacramento who will do a first-class job in watching the money that you send to your State capital.

Actually, the key to the battle against inflation is within our honest, personal reach. All you have to do on November 5 is to go into the sanctity of that voting booth and pull the right lever. Good leadership is the answer. I am trying to do it in the White House. Bob Mathias has sought to do it in the Congress of the United States. Hugh Flournoy will do it for you in the State capital.

Leadership, whether it is in Washington or Sacramento, is vital. And what you do in the quiet, personal relationship that you have in that voting booth is of great importance—yes, to you and to me, but more importantly to all of us.

And I urge you, not for the sake of one political party but for the sake of America, be a leader next Tuesday; be a leader in making the right decision. Let your vote and your voice reelect and elect the kind of men and women to public office who will bring out the best in our great country.

I am confident that you will, and that is why I am here to see all of you.

Good luck, Bob. Good luck to all of you who support him.

Let me express my very deep appreciation and gratitude. I am not going to get into a discussion whether your band or your football team is the best, but let me say this: I like a mayor who thinks they have the best band and the best football team.

And may I add that I have got a 16-year-old son who is working as a ranch hand out in Lolo, Montana. He decided that he wanted to learn to be a rancher, so he is out there, and I am going to see him tomorrow. And I am not going to tell him I have this great, great cowboy hat. I will tell him, maybe I cannot ride as well as he can, but I might look like a cowboy if I cannot perform the function.

Thank you very, very much.

NOTE: The President spoke at 12:10 p.m. at the Fresno Air Terminal. In his opening remarks, the President referred to Carol O. Harner, Republican candidate in the 15th Congressional District of California.

214

Remarks to the White House Conference on Domestic and Economic Affairs in Portland, Oregon. *November 1, 1974*

Governor McCall, Mr. Johnson, Mr. Killion, Secretary of the Treasury Simon, Secretary of HUD Jim Lynn, distinguished guests, ladies and gentlemen:

Let me express my deep gratitude for the very warm welcome that Tom McCall has extended on this occasion. If my memory is correct, Governor, you were the first Governor that I saw in the first State that I visited back about a year ago when I was nominated Vice President of the United States. The warmth of the reception then is only duplicated by the kindness that you have shown me on this occasion.

I am deeply grateful, I am especially pleased to be here to participate in one of Bill Baroody's [1] programs, the White House Conference on Domestic and Economic Affairs, where business, labor, consumer, environmental organizations have joined in sponsoring this meeting to improve the lines of communication between nongovernmental organizations and the White House itself.

You can generate a new climate of confidence and understanding on national issues of greatest concern to us individually as well as collectively.

This is my first participation in this nationwide series of meetings that can have, as I see it, a very vital impact on America's response to the state of our economy, housing, environment, and general domestic affairs. And the fact that the Secretary of the Treasury and the Secretary of HUD are here, I think, portrays vividly the importance that we consider meetings of this sort.

In this context, I would like to discuss the question of confidence in our political system and our ability as a nation to cope with this very serious issue.

The question of credibility is often raised. A mood of some cynicism exists in certain quarters. There are even those who say that my Administration's open-

[1] William J. Baroody, Jr., Assistant to the President.

ness is just another coverup. The question is asked: Is everything phony? Is everything cynical in government today?

I categorically reject any such conclusion. But I would like to offer some thoughts on why there is some doubt and, perhaps, some division.

Confidence in America's institutions has been deteriorating since the early 1960's. There were, unfortunately, assassinations, upheavals in great cities and in school systems throughout our country, riots and terrorism, crime, drug abuse, pollution, the Vietnam war, the Watergate affair with the first Presidential resignation in America's history, the energy shortage, rising inflation, and other almost unbelievable blows to America's self-image.

This chain of tragic events affected our institutions and actually our way of life. It did not start with the present inflationary problem nor with Watergate nor even the tragic murder of President Kennedy. America and the world are going through a hurricane of very rapid change—technological, economical, social, and political.

Americans put men on the Moon, but have yet to cope with the rapidly changing life on this globe. Other industrial nations are also, in varying degrees—often without our resilience and our resources—going through precisely the same experience.

That explains my participation in this meeting today. I came to talk with you about how Americans can mobilize to regenerate our institutions, beginning with the economy.

I am speaking now to Republicans, Democrats, Independents, to labor, to management, and to every segment of our great society. We are all in this problem together, and that is why I consider it so very vital, so very important to be in Portland on this occasion.

I offered, approximately a month ago, a comprehensive program to mobilize America against inflation. I concede and admit that we are not in what one would call a traditional problem of inflation with an accelerating rate of cost-of-living problems.

We are faced with inflation on the one hand and some softness in our economy on the other, and this rather finely tuned program that I submitted was aimed at meeting this problem, the dual difficulties—one of a softening of the economy and the devastation of inflation itself.

This conference, however, as I understand it, was generated to take an honest look at the problems of inflation. A 31-point program that I submitted to the Congress and to the American people, as I indicated a moment ago, was finely tuned, a comprehensive plan aimed at the dual difficulties we face.

I am pleased to report to you that a massive voluntary citizens' mobilization is gearing up. We in the White House have received roughly 150,000 requests for these WIN buttons and any other information and helpful hints that we can give to people all throughout the United States.

New steps, I think you recognize, have been taken to cope with the energy situation, and all of our actions seek to avoid an unfair burden on those who can least afford the tragedy of inflation or the tragedy of a softening economy.

It is my judgment that Americans are rallying to whip inflation. They can help—and have been helping—by demanding action on legislative proposals pending before the Congress. They can press for State and local initiatives. They can innovate voluntary programs at the local level.

America, if we look back over the history, does not require dogmatic laws to control every action that we take, whether it is action at home, in our schools, in our businesses, in our labor organizations, in our churches.

My policies, as I have presented them, I think are firm and good and sound. But any President has to be cognizant of the need, if circumstances change, to take a new look.

I am committed to no rigid economic formula, but the basic American philosophy that made our economy great, I am totally committed to.

As I look back over the history during my lifetime, America is built primarily on mutual trust. It is governed by popular consent and consensus. Federal, State, and local units of government responding to the will of the people will whip inflation. I am perfectly confident that industries, businesses, and great trade unions will whip inflation. I also have an abiding faith that consumer and environmental groups will whip inflation.

Let us begin the dialog that was referred to by Governor McCall. Let's build that dialog that can establish this confidence between environmentalists and energy and industry, between consumers and between business, between labor and management, and between 213 million Americans and their government, at the Federal, State, or local level.

Let's give dialog a chance for a change. Let's continue to challenge, but also continue in the sincere good will on both sides of every issue.

Institutions, as I have looked at it, are nothing more than people. Let us never lose faith in humanity, the individuals that we meet, regardless of the circumstances. Let us never lose faith in that one-to-one confrontation, and of course, let's not lose faith in ourselves.

Meetings of this sort are excellent forums to generate confidence. Yet, the time has come for action as well as for talk. Accordingly, the function of leadership belongs to those placed in responsibility.

As President, I accept my obligation, and I call upon every Member of the Congress, Governors, mayors, and all others concerned with government, and the leaders of every private sector in America, including all of you represented here. We, individually and collectively, must provide that leadership. A free government, if we look over history, cannot cope with inflation or energy shortages or any other problem without the consent and the total cooperation of those governed.

Too many people have been saying what the other guy should do to whip inflation. We hear that all the time. We hear business complaining about labor and labor complaining about business. We hear about other segments complaining about their adversaries, never reflecting as to what their own responsibility might be. Some tell us what the oil companies should do. Others would instruct labor on its responsibilities. Yet others have all kinds of sacrifices to suggest. Almost inevitably, it is not how *they* can sacrifice.

Our great Northwest—and I am pleased to be here again—is aware that inflation has dried up the supply of mortgage credit and sent housing into a tailspin. Now, Jim Lynn over here is going to solve all of those problems for you, along with the money provided by Bill Simon, but it is a lot broader and a lot deeper subject than what those two fine Secretaries in the Cabinet can do. And it has been inflation that hit consumer confidence and put the brakes on consumer spending harder than at any time since World War II.

I assure the people of the great Northwest that I do not accept the dismal projection that pollution is the inevitable price of prosperity, nor that we must compromise the environment to gain economic growth in the future.

We cannot enrich our lives by impoverishing our land. We can raise both the standard of living on the one hand and the quality of life on the other. The worst inflationary toll of all is the most subtle—the erosion of confidence in the future, the loss of faith in the American society and our government.

Indeed, this disenchantment seems to grow at the same pace that prices increase. That is why fighting inflation is my priority as President of this great country.

Americans do have the will to preserve our economy and our institutions. The central, absolutely crucial need my program underscores is to control government spending on the one hand and to finance any new outlays with new taxes. Government simply can no longer go on spending beyond its means.

Inflation, as I have said so many times—and the more I say it, the more I believe it—is public enemy number one. And all the polls seems to conclude that. The latest I saw indicated on a nationwide basis that among all of the problems, all of the issues, regardless of your position in life, 83 percent of the Americans selected inflation as that which was of most concern to them.

Obviously, under those circumstances, the fight against inflation is a nonpartisan challenge. It is everyone's fight.

If I were to take the easy route of additional pump priming and deficit spending as the economy cools off this winter, it would really cause trouble. We could see the current inflation rate—and I speak very categorically—the current inflation rate, if we don't do a little sacrificing and belt tightening, that rate could double by 1976.

That is not a very happy prospect. So, it ought to encourage us to make the big battle now in order not to have that problem then.

America, as I have seen it, remains a model for the rest of the world. Later this month, I am visiting the Far East, going first to Japan, then to South Korea, and then finally to Vladivostok in the U.S.S.R.—the latter, of course, to move forward, laying additional steppingstones for the culmination of what I hope and I believe is an agreement in strategic arms limitations beyond the present.

But as I visit these three vital areas of the world, I will seek to cement relationships essential for world economic stability as well as SALT Two.

It is obvious as we read—and both Secretary Simon and Secretary Lynn have been abroad—we know that inflation crosses borders and somehow leapfrogs oceans. And if I can be helpful by going to the other side of the world on this dual mission—and I think I can be helpful—that is part of my obligation.

As President, I am convinced that this Nation—yours and mine—can show the world that Americans do retain confidence in our system. We can conserve, we can stop wasting, we can expand our production base while preserving our national heritage. We can become more efficient, more productive, and pay for what we spend in our government as we go.

Now, some cynics and skeptics freely predict the end of America—that great country that we know and we love. I feel just the opposite. I think they are very wrong. I intend to prove they are wrong, because I am totally confident in the dedication of this group and so many others throughout America.

As Abraham Lincoln once put it, this Nation is still "the last, best hope of earth." And a new and stronger United States will grow from the disillusion of the past. Indeed, the ordeal that we have gone through since the early sixties may serve, as I see it, like a national purge, clearing our system, renewing our energies, and creating a new and more realistic American ethic and, perhaps, an American lifestyle.

The bountiful resources of this blessed land are available, and you in Oregon are about as blessed as any of the 50 States, and you should be happy and proud that you are so blessed.

Let us, on the overall, however, devise a future based on conservation as well as consumption. The truth is, if you look at the statistics, and I get them weekly—I used to from Bill Simon, now from Rog Morton—we have run short of energy. But we are going to do something about it as we conserve on the one hand and build a productive base on the other.

We have run short of mortgage credit—and don't blame Jim Lynn altogether—and we have run short of a lot of other things. But we have not, as I see it, run short of American know-how or the American spirit of fairplay or of American forgiveness or American self-respect or American pride, nor will we ever.

A great national test will be imposed in the days and the months ahead. But that ought to be a challenge. That ought to appeal to us. We ought to respond to it. If we do, we will meet the test. And I pledge all of my energies to a free society with a strong economy, a sound environment, sufficient energy, and a secure and inspiring future.

And I ask each and every one of you here, and those that follow in other meetings, to join with me in that wonderful quest.

Thank you very much.

NOTE: The President spoke at 5:10 p.m. at the Memorial Coliseum. In his opening remarks, the President referred to Leland H. Johnson, president of the Portland Chamber of Commerce, and Dean Killion, president of the Oregon AFL–CIO.

The White House Conference on Domestic and Economic Affairs held in Portland was the third in a series of conferences co-sponsored by nongovernmental organizations in various cities throughout the Nation.

215

Remarks at a Reception for Republican Candidates in Portland. *November 1, 1974*

IT IS just wonderful to be here in a gathering of this magnitude and friendliness. Every time I come to Oregon, I seem to find more friendly people, more diversification in all the things you do.

Last year, I think 48 hours after I was nominated as Vice President, I came out for a longstanding speaking commitment that I had made. And your great Governor, Tom McCall, met me and was so hospitable and helpful.

I come back today and I have been busy thus far with some wonderful crowds on the street, a warm welcome—[*laughter*]—there are a couple of dissident voices; I have heard those chants before, and I don't think they influence many people. But anyhow, it is—I went over to the meeting at the OMSI [Oregon Museum of Science and Industry] this afternoon—a great crowd of wonderful people. I am here right now and have been to a reception before, and I am going to the Coliseum a little later. And because the day was not long enough, I thought I might sneak out and see the last quarter of the Trail Blazers and the Braves.[1] And then, Vernon Jordan of the Urban League sent me a telegram and said there was some fundraiser for the Urban League going on. And I thought, gee, we might as well go there after—because I believe that Vernon Jordan, and the Urban League, does a first-class job, I am sure, here as well as elsewhere.

All I am saying is, you have lots of activity in Oregon, and I enjoy everything I have been invited to and participated in, and particularly for the fine, fine turnout here on this occasion.

Tom McCall—I have observed and I have watched him for 8 years—has done a superb job. You are lucky. He is a top quality Governor, and you, I am sure, know better than I that the State of Oregon is infinitely better off because of his stewardship.

Tom, you have done a great job.

And in the process of traveling around and meeting many people in high office in various States, you develop a knack of picking out those that really have quality, of those that are coming up, who have achieved something in the process of public service in experience and courage and wisdom. And you say, "There is somebody that really will do a job."

And so I speak on this occasion on behalf of your candidate for Governor, Vic Atiyeh. He was in Washington a couple of weeks ago—I have forgotten what group, because I meet with a good many, as you might suspect—but I do remember him.

He handed me something, and he said, "I am a man with a plan." And that is kind of good advice. That is the way I would like a Governor to operate before he gets in office and after he is in office.

So, Vic, good luck to you.

---

[1] The Portland Trail Blazers and Buffalo Braves professional basketball teams.

If I might now, I would like to say a word or two about some people that I know very intimately, that I have known through my contacts both in the Congress and as Vice President and now as President—and I say this, not because of what somebody wrote for me but because I know, know from working in the relationship between a House leader and a Senator, or a House leader and the people with whom he works on a day-to-day basis.

I presided over the United States Senate roughly 6, 7 months, and I used to sit there and watch the 100 Members of the Senate—and there are some fine, outstanding Members. In Mark Hatfield, you have a fine Senator.

But let me just say now that in Bob Packwood, you have in your junior Senator the kind of a person that I admire and respect, the type of an individual who seems to pick the right issues, the right side of issues. He works at the job, he is highly respected on this side or that side of the aisle. So I am delighted to be here in Oregon to urge you to maximize your effort on behalf of Bob Packwood.

I served 25-plus years in the House of Representatives, and I was told the first year that I was sworn in—I sat down next to an old-timer, and he said, "Jerry, do you know the definition of a Member of the House?"

And I said, "No." I was 35, and this man was 70. I looked at him with awe. He had been there 30 years, and I had just been sworn in.

He said, "Jerry, do you know the definition of a Congressman?"

I said, "No, I don't, Earl."

He said, "It is the shortest distance between 2 years." [*Laughter*]

Well, I survived that, but you have sent, in my lifetime, some great Members of the House. One is leaving—a dear friend of mine—Wendell Wyatt. We will miss him.

But in Diarmuid O'Scanlain you have a person who is starting out at a young age, who can build a great career and ably represent the First Congressional District in the State of Oregon. I hope you work to make sure that he is down there to do the job for you.

You have an incumbent that many of you know is extremely able, just a tremendous campaigner. His name has been mentioned here. He also is a very close and very dear friend of mine—John Dellenback. You need him back there representing Oregon.

And then, of course, you have got a vacancy here, a vacancy that ought to be filled by the kind of a person that John Piacentini [2] is. John, we sure hope you will make it. Good luck. We will see you down there January 3.

---

[2] Republican candidate in the Third Congressional District of Oregon.

Now, let me take just a minute to make two very simple points. I know it is crowded, it is hot—or at least I am hot up here—and the night is young, and we have to, you know, get organized here.

I looked at some figures the other day of some of these experts, and they say there is great public apathy. There is a great lack of public interest in voting on November 5.

And the pollsters say that there will be the lowest percentage participation in this Congressional election on a national basis in the history of the United States. That is unbelievable.

With the problems we have, both at home and abroad, it is hard to comprehend that people won't go to the polls to exercise their sacred privilege of voting yes or no, or for or against somebody. They say that approximately 42 percent of the eligible voters in America will make the effort, sometime between 7:00 in the morning and 8:00 at night, to just say yes or no, or I am for or I am against.

Gee, that is hard to believe. And you know what that means if that happens or transpires? Supposing 42 percent vote, out of all of the people that are eligible to pull that lever. It means that a little more than 21 percent of the American people will decide your fate for Governor, for Senator, for Members of the House, for members of your State legislature or local office.

That means a little more than 21 percent of the American people will decide what will be done locally, statewide, or nationally.

That is a real small minority deciding what is right or wrong. I just cannot believe the American people will tolerate that.

I don't know how many are here—about 300, 500—but you can multiply your activity and influence by getting many, many, many people all over this great State of Oregon to go to the polls, so that your State will not be one that lets 21.1 percent of the people decide your fate for the next 2 years, whether it is taxes or spending, this legislation or that legislation.

You know, an awful lot of our fellow citizens over the years, almost 200 years, have given a great deal to keep that right to vote; some of them made the maximum sacrifice. And for us now to abuse it or to leave it unused is beyond my comprehension.

Now, I know, because you are here, you are going to vote. You are going to get a lot of people to vote. But the message I want to go out, here in this State and elsewhere, is that we all have to vote, and then we can say the public made a decision, right or wrong.

Let me talk about two of my favorite subjects; I think they are crucial. Public enemy number one in this country is inflation. About a month ago, I submitted to the Congress and to the American people a well-balanced, finely tuned program. I concede it is controversial, but at least I bit the bullet.

Oh, I know some people have said to me that it was kind of "marshmallowy." Some of the opposition made that allegation. Then, I listened to what they submitted, and I said, "Boy, that is a lemon, not a marshmallow."

All I am trying to say is, it was a plan aimed at tightening the screws on inflation on the one hand and recognizing that we have some soft spots in our economy on the other.

We made some recommendations that will help the housing industry, and I asked the Congress to do something, and they did it. And Jim Lynn has already initiated the action that I recommended following enactment by the Congress. It is not enough, but I think it is a start, and if we do the other things, the housing industry will again have a great upsurge. So, instead of 1.2 million housing units per year, it will go up to what it ought to be, of 2.2 million housing units per year, and then the people out in the industries here in Oregon will be producing, for housing, for people that need it.

You will have the kinds of burgeoning, booming economy that we want in this State, as well as in others. But at the same time, we are tightening the screws on those areas where inflation is serious, and we are going to win it.

We want strong, stalwart people in Congress who will bite the bullet and not fade away when they ought to be strong, when they ought to be facing up to the issues and not play politics with something that is involved in the national security.

Speaking of national security, let me just make one observation. I get twice-a-day messages from Henry Kissinger. He just spent about 4 days in Moscow, and he spent a couple of days in India. He spent a couple of days in Pakistan. I got messages from him today in Afghanistan, and he is going two or three or four places after that. But here is a man who is carrying the torch of peace for America. Here is a man that worked night and day to achieve a peace and who is laying the groundwork for a broadening of that peace, whether it is in the Middle East, whether it is in the case of Cyprus or Greece, or whether it is in the case of Western Europe, or whether it is in Latin America, Africa, or Southeast Asia.

Here is a man that is on our side, leading the way with a torch of peace. And what we need in the Congress is Members of the Congress who will back up that kind of leadership, people who won't play politics with national security, who won't play politics with what is good in the furtherance of peace throughout the world.

Now, I am sure that the people here who are seeking office, or seeking reelection, are the kind that won't play politics with peace, who will give to a President the kind of flexibility he needs to negotiate with the Russians, or to broaden our relationships with China, or strengthen our allies in Europe, or negotiate between Israel and Arab nations on a fair and equitable basis in the Middle East, or to bring together our two allies, Greece and Turkey.

These are the kind of people we want in the Congress, who will trust the President as a Republican Congress did in 1947 and 1948 when they trusted a Democratic President to give us the leadership to build NATO, to strengthen Western Europe. And it has been the bulwark of strength as we meet the challenges, or have met them, for the last 25 years.

I am confident that the kind of Members of the House and Senate that you will send to Washington next Tuesday will win the battle against inflation, stabilize and build up our economy, and lead the charge for the extension of peace throughout the world. And in the process, you are going to give us a Governor in the great State of Oregon to follow the pattern, the practices, the leadership of Tom McCall. I cannot imagine a better man than Vic Atiyeh.

Thank you very much.

NOTE: The President spoke at 8:02 p.m. at the Benson Hotel.

216

Remarks at the Oregon Museum of Science and Industry's Annual Auction in Portland. *November 1, 1974*

THANK YOU very, very much, Bob, for the more than generous introduction, and I think for any of us in political life, that is the one thing that we want and cherish. And you have it, and I am proud to be here in Oregon with you on that basis.

You know, I feel very much at home here in Oregon. Our new White House photographer, Dave Kennerly, he comes from Portland, and he keeps me up to date on everything that happens out here. Dave, stand up and give us a bow. Oh, there he is. Right over there.

As you all know by now, I am sure—if you don't know in Portland, there are some down here in the Washington photographic corps who know it—that Dave is Washington's number one bachelor.

So after this talk, for the men, we are going to auction off a special set of

Presidential cufflinks. For the kids, we are going to auction off two autographed footballs. And for the girls, we are going to auction off Kennerly. [*Laughter*]

Really, I am terribly pleased to be here. I have heard so much about your science and industry museum. These are certainly two areas where our Nation excels, and I think it is only fitting that OMSI should be recognized worldwide as one of the finest museums of science and industry in the whole world.

We Americans have always been a very stubborn lot, so it is, I think, relatively characteristic that in America this fine institution was created by people, and it never asked for any tax subsidies, and I congratulate you.

I am delighted and honored to participate on an occasion like this where you raise your money, and you do not come down and see all of us in Washington, asking for a little help. I would do this 24 hours a day for all organizations if we could avoid that, believe me.

But any institution that is organized, run, and paid for by people in sort of the good, old-fashioned way, the barnraising method, I think it is great. And to do this here in Oregon, in Portland, I think is sort of characteristic of the wonderful people and the concepts and the principles that you have.

And although I would not suggest seriously that we move this project to Washington—[*laughter*]—I think Members of Congress could benefit by a visit here, not only by people in government but a lot of people outside, in many other parts of our country.

You know, they tell me the day we landed a man on the Moon, you were already teaching a course here at OMSI about Moon topography, and I congratulate you. And I made a speech a few weeks ago about exploring new sources of energy, and I find here at OMSI, you already have an exhibit—actually working models of just about all these new sources of energy, whether it is solar, geothermal, or what have you.

This is the kind of vision, the kind of imagination that I think is what we need, not only in Portland but elsewhere. And I am also greatly interested in your latest development here, with the cooperation of the Bureau of Standards, of an exhibit on how the metric system works.

I am not sure I understand it, but I am glad you are teaching the younger generation, because I think it is important as we become more and more integrated in a global sense.

I understand this exhibit is scheduled to travel all over the United States, and that, in and of itself, is a tribute to Portland, and I congratulate you.

Sometimes, we think of museums as old, musty, out-of-the-way places, remnants of the dead past. But OMSI, as I understand it, is an example of how alive, how useful, how exciting a great museum can be, and I congratulate you for it.

As I look around this room and see some of the younger generation, those in the middle group—[*laughter*]—and some of us, some of you my age, I cannot help but think that the people make a State and the people make a country. And actually, Oregon is a symbol with this project and what you do in many other fields: a great State with a proud history, but even more importantly, a promising future.

I am grateful for your invitation, I am deeply indebted to you for the opportunity to be here. And I especially am grateful for Bob Packwood's very kind introduction. Thank you very much.

NOTE: The President spoke at 8:55 p.m. at the Memorial Coliseum.

217

Remarks at an Urban League Dance in Portland. *November 1, 1974*

I AM HERE with Bob Packwood to participate in a very small way in a great cause, which is the Urban League. I belong to it. We have a great Urban League in my hometown, and the head of that in Grand Rapids is Paul Phillips. Some of you may know him—a very dear friend of mine.

It is just wonderful to be here with Hazel and all of you. I did not come to make a speech. I came to say hello and meet some of you and enjoy myself.

We have had a great, great day in Portland. It has been long but wonderful, and this is sort of a climax. And I thank you for your warm, warm welcome.

You might be interested—I saw the last half of the Trail Blazers and the Braves. The Trail Blazers won 109 to 102 (113 to 106).

NOTE: The President spoke at 10:30 p.m. at the Masonic Temple. The Urban League sponsored the dance for the benefit of the Albina Human Resources Center in Portland.

218

Remarks in Salt Lake City, Utah. *November 2, 1974*

Jake Garn, Senator Wallace Bennett, my good friend, Steve Harmsen, Ron Inkley:

It is wonderful to be here in this wonderful, just tremendous basketball arena and to be on the campus of the University of Utah, and to you, President David Gardner, I thank you very, very much.

I am delighted that Jake Garn did not mention too much about my career as a football player. I played at the University of Michigan so far back—it was back when the ball was round—and after winning the national championship for my first 2 years, my senior year we won one and lost seven. And at the end of the season, my teammates voted me the most valuable player. I don't know what they were trying to tell me. [*Laughter*]

But I am particularly pleased to be in Utah, because I have been here many, many times. I have skied at Alta, Park City, Snow Basin. I hope to come out again and ski at Snow Bird.

I like people from Utah. Some of our closest and best friends come from your great State.

Let me express my deep appreciation to the Kearns High School band as well as to the Davis High School band. The music that was played by both was wonderful, stirring, the kind of music that I like.

You know, music usually provides us with great beauty, but sometimes it provides us with the truth as well.

Last week, I went back to my hometown of Grand Rapids, Michigan, and we had a big night rally in an arena at Calvin College, much like this one. As I came into the building, I heard the master of ceremonies ask the band for just one more selection, something that would be appropriate for the President of the United States.

So, they played "Nobody Knows the Trouble I've Seen." [*Laughter*]

But I do express my gratitude for the warm and very friendly welcome, and I cannot think of one trouble I could ever have in the State of Utah. You are the kind of people I like and enjoy.

It convinces me that when I agreed to come to visit Utah today, this is one Ford who really did have a better idea.

And let me congratulate you—because I know them, I have met them, I have worked with them—on the exceptional slate of Republican candidates that you have here in Utah. I have seen a lot, and they are among the very best. And I look forward to working with them next year in Washington, D.C.

I have seen a lot of mayors. I worked with a great many Senators. And it is my honest judgment and recommendation that the country, the State, all of you as well as myself, need Jake Garn in the United States Senate.

I never got that kind of an accolade when I was running for the House of Representatives in my own district. So, Jake, you are doing very well, and for good and sufficient reasons.

But I am a product, as all of you know, of the House of Representatives, and I am proud of the 25-plus years that I served with 435 other Members on both sides of the aisle. So, I know a little bit about the kind of Members of the House that will do a good job, and I can recommend to you Steve Harmsen for his youth, his vigor, his organized approach to the problems that he will face on your behalf.

I strongly recommend Steve to be returned and sent to Washington on your behalf.

And although my contact with Ron has not been as extensive, I am impressed with a fine, strong, able young man. Good luck to you, Ron.

There is one particular area where Jake Garn and I wholeheartedly agree—and this really ought not to be a partisan issue, because there are as many Democratic mayors in this country as there are Republican mayors who have the same thoughts, the same beliefs—that decentralization of the Federal Government would make our system work far, far better. And therefore, in my opinion, there is no more urgent need or item, if I might say, of long-range, national business before us to day. We must cut the power. We must trim the size of the bureaucracy in Washington. It would be good for the country.

I should add that I have ordered a cut of 40,000 in the bureaucracy, in the Federal bureaucracy, and we are going to achieve that end. It will save us about $300 million in 1 year, but it will make the system work better just as well.

There is only one real way that we are going to solve some of these difficult problems that we face as fellow citizens in this country. We must communicate more effectively with one another. And frankly, that is why I am here in Utah. I can learn much more about the needs and the desires of the citizens of Utah in 1 hour's worth of conversation with men like Jake Garn, your great senior Senator, Wallace Bennett, than I could learn in 8 months back in the Oval Office talking to Potomac bureaucrats about the problems of Utah.

Frankly, that is precisely the problem with an overgrown, all-political bureaucracy. There is no two-way communication. Each State and locality in this

Nation has its own needs, its own priorities, and the priorities of Salt Lake are different than those of Miami, and the ones of Seattle are quite different from those of Baltimore.

So, these unique, these unusual needs and priorities cannot be understood and dealt with from a very, very remote vantage point in the Nation's Capital.

The day is past, in my honest judgment, when an octopus-like Government in the Nation's Capital can stretch its tentacles across the Nation and literally squeeze into itself more and more power.

In my judgment, we have to chop off those tentacles, and as each of those tentacles wither, we have to return the power and the revenue that they have grasped back to the States and to the local communities where they honestly belong—back to the taxpayers, the local taxpayers who made the funds available in the first place.

As we carry out this decentralization process, it is absolutely essential that we have men in Washington who can tell us precisely what their constituents want and how they want it done.

And that is why, without any hesitation, reservation, or qualification, I urge you to send Jake Garn to the United States Senate.

As a local official, Jake has a unique and firsthand knowledge of what the people of Utah really want. As a Senator, he will be able to put that knowledge to use, firsthand.

Now, one of my primary goals as President is to return governmental control to the American people, and I need Jake in Washington to help me achieve and realize that very important goal.

It will not be an easy job. I am not standing here trying to kid you. It is never easy to dismantle a rickety structure that has been reinforced in a patchwork way for decades. If you knock out the wrong section, the whole thing could or is liable to fall and hurt a lot of innocent people.

We do not want that. But the job has to be done. For too long, politicians have operated on the principle that you can bring heaven to Earth by piling Federal programs like layer cake and frosting them with Federal money. It won't and it has not worked.

The result or the consequence has been a huge, cumbersome, totally unresponsive central government that increasingly threatens to assert control over nearly every aspect of our personal lives.

The intentions of the people who have helped build the Federal layer cake are noble ones. I do not challenge their motives or their intentions. They actually, sincerely believe that if the Government ministers to every need and to every concern that it has among all the 213 million citizens, those citizens will be happier and will be better off. But let me make a critical, crucial point. What they really forget, and what millions of Americans are now remembering, is that a government big enough to give us everything we want is a government big enough to take from us everything we have.

But what they forget, and what millions of Americans are now remembering, is that in the end, no government can make us better and happier people if it takes from us that one essential ingredient for happiness, our individual freedom.

The lesson of the past few decades has been a basic one. We cannot spend our way into happiness. But we can spend ourselves into debt, and we can spend our Nation's strength straight into raging inflation.

That is why, in these past few weeks, I have been speaking out for realistic, fiscally responsible Congressional candidates.

Inflation is our Nation's public enemy number one, and one way to beat inflation most effectively is to keep the lid on Federal spending. That is why I urge you to send to the Congress an inflation-proof Congress next Tuesday.

If the people who wish to spend and spend—and they can be called big spenders—win heavily on November 5, we are in danger of electing a veto-proof Congress, rather than an inflation-proof Congress. I think you want an inflation-proof Congress, not a veto-proof Congress.

Such a Congress threatened, or unrestrained by a threat of a Presidential veto, would spend the dome right off our Nation's Capitol. Our Nation, in this very challenging world, simply cannot afford a veto-proof Congress controlled by those that want to spend all of your money and much more, too.

Big spending got our economy into the trouble it is experiencing today, and now we are threatened with a Congress whose prescription is more spending.

I do not think it makes much sense. It is my judgment that the immediate medicine our economy needs is a good strong dose of fiscal discipline. And frankly, that is why I am asking voters all across this Nation, all across the political spectrum—Democrats, Independents, and Republicans—to vote as inflation fighters rather than as political partisans.

I pledge to do everything possible in my power to hold down excessive spending from the Federal Treasury, and I ask you to send men and women to Washington, men like Jake Garn, who—I know from his record, his experience, his knowledge—will help me in this vitally important task.

I don't stand here and kid you that it is an easy task. There is no easy cure for the inflationary illness that infects our economy, and I do not think it makes you any happier for me to be able to say that our inflationary rates, our increases in the cost of living are less than those in Japan or Great Britain or any one of a number of other countries; that does not help us do something about the problem.

But we have to understand that it takes patience, it takes hard work, it takes strength of character, and it takes a little time, unfortunately.

It will also require some short-term sacrifices to serve our long-term national interest. As I said in my 31-point program to Congress, which is aimed at controlling inflation and stabilizing and strengthening our economy and also calling upon people to help us in the conservation of energy, in the building of greater energy potential—in the 31-point program that I submitted to the Congress were suggestions by individual citizens who might participate in the battle against inflation so that we as a country, 213 million of us, can share that burden equally.

Each of us must make a little sacrifice so that none will suffer. And as you know, the sacrifice that all of us make, I think, will make it better for everybody.

Now, one important recommendation in my inflation-fighting and energy-saving program, one of the 31 proposals that I made was to tighten up and to increase the penalties for antitrust and price-fixing action.

That legislation has been lying dormant in the House Committee on the Judiciary. I think it is legitimate to ask every member of that committee why haven't they acted.

If we can do something about price fixing, if we can do something about the antitrust action—and let me illustrate what I recommended: that we increase the penalties for violations from $50,000 to $1 million—and nothing has happened in the Congress or in the Committee on the Judiciary.

You may remember that I recently made a speech to the Future Farmers of America in which I attempted to outline some specific ways in which all Americans could pitch into the fight against inflation.

But as I prepared these remarks for this wonderful audience in Utah and as I thought about your wonderful way of life in this tremendous State, it occurred to me that perhaps what I was suggesting in the speech to the Future Farmers of America was not really sacrifice at all. Perhaps I was just suggesting that my fellow Americans return to those good, sound, basic values of self-sufficiency, thrift, and self-reliance.

Those are the values, combined with a belief in God and a love of family, that built this great State of Utah.

Fortunately, those are the same fundamental values that made America great.

Yes, I have asked Americans to save. I have asked them to budget. I have asked them to economize. I have asked them to guard their health. And I have asked them to cut out waste—and that includes the Ford family as well.

As I prepared these remarks, I realized that what I have been suggesting to millions and millions of Americans was simply accepted practice in the State of Utah. So, there is really no need for me to preach about those old basic values to all of you, for your daily lives in Utah are shaped by those wonderful values that I respect and admire.

But I do want you to know that by living those values, you are a source of inspiration to all Americans, including myself. And I want to thank you from the bottom of my heart for proving to all of us that old values are alive and well and working.

And I can also tell you that Wallace Bennett has done an inspiring job. And when Wallace leaves, we will miss Frances just as well. She has been great in every, every way possible.

I just told Wallace that he may leave the Senate, but we are going to make use of him someplace. Anybody that is as strong and as good and dedicated as Wallace—America needs him, and we are going to take advantage of him.

I know, because our careers started relatively the same time. Here was a man, a giant of the Senate: strong, a stainless moral leader, and a tireless champion of fiscal responsibility.

We all hate to see him go, but our prayers and our very, very best wishes will be with him and Frances as they come home again to their beloved Utah. And with people like Wallace Bennett and Jake Garn and people like all of you to serve as examples. I am more and more confident than ever that we can bring our economy back to full and lasting health.

And perhaps in the process of doing so, perhaps as we do cut away frills and nonessentials, we will rediscover something valuable about ourselves that some of us may, unfortunately, have forgotten.

You understand very precisely here in Utah what those basic values are. Now it is time to get out and to preach them to our fellow Americans in the other 49 States. Now is the time to apply them to the war against inflation.

Let us let the first shot in that war come out of the ballot box next Tuesday, and let it be a shot heard around the country and around the world.

Cast your vote for the party that will, with a cooperative Congress, reestablish stability in our economy and common sense and good direction to our government. Cast your vote for the men who will be a part of a strong, responsive, responsible, inflation-proof Congress.

We need them now, much more than ever. As one TV commentator put it recently, and let me quote him: I am looking for a Congress that will praise the Lord and pass the legislation.

Thank you very much.

NOTE: The President spoke at 12:05 p.m. at the University of Utah Special Events Center. In his opening remarks, the President referred to Stephen Harmsen, Republican candidate in the Second Congressional District of Utah, and Ronald W. Inkley, Republican candidate in the First Congressional District.

219

Remarks in Grand Junction, Colorado. *November 2, 1974*

Pete, Governor Vanderhoof, Lieutenant Governor Strickland, my former colleagues in the House of Representatives, Jim Johnson, who represents an area of this great country that I love and adore:

It gives me a lot of trouble—Vail, Colorado—but let me also say it is wonderful to be here with my old and very, very dear friend, Wayne Aspinall, who took the same oath of office that I did on January 3, 1949. I am proud—you know, I just feel emotional about our relationship over a long period of time.

I can tell you that his office was opposite mine on the corridor—as a matter of fact, Jack Kennedy's was just a couple of offices down—and all I am saying is that in Wayne Aspinall, I developed a close, personal rapport that transcends partisan politics. He and I disagreed, but friendship you don't sell out. You keep it. You love it. And that is my relationship with Wayne Aspinall.

You know, it is great to be in Colorado—West—again. It has often been said that Colorado is a land of breathtaking beauty, and after crowning your homecoming queen and her lovely court—I would have a tough time picking who was going to win, I might add—a breathtaking beauty as well, and I congratulate you for everything. A college homecoming is a happy time and I wish Mesa College Mavericks—*Mesa*—but we have some community names out in Michigan all of you could not pronounce, either. I love you, anyhow.

But I understand this has been one of your better years, and as a former football player at the University of Michigan, I know what a 1–5–1 season is. You know, my senior year at Michigan, after being national champions with undefeated teams for 2 years, the year that I was supposed to be constructive we ended up with a one win and seven lost—and we lost to Ohio State 34 to 0. We are going to do better this fall.

Well, anyhow, I was elected the most valuable player by my teammates after losing seven out of the eight games, and I did not know whether to sue or smile. [*Laughter*]

Well, as some of you already know, the Ford family has a very special place in our heart for Colorado. It is our second home. We are not voting taxpayers, but we don't mind because we think we get our money's worth under your good Governor and under Pete Dominick and the others, so we just love being here in Colorado. We wish we could be here more often, and we might surprise you.

I just hope you get a little more snow earlier than you did last year. Have you got some?

That is Vail over there, I guess, isn't it? All right. We love it. We will be here if we get a cooperative Congress. I wish you could promise me that; it would be good for the country.

Well, anyhow, Betty and the Ford children and I have had great times here. We have been to Aspen. We have been to Vail. We have been many other places in Colorado and we love the people. We love the country. We love the total atmosphere, and it is so nice to be here on a Saturday afternoon. We are looking forward to coming back, and thank you very, very much.

Let me just say that when I come to a place like this with a ballpark and so many people and so many fine public servants and your Governor and Pete and Jim Johnson and my former colleague, Wayne Aspinall, it just convinces me that this country is predicated on the strength and the diversity of people—Democrats, Republicans, Independents—you know, people who were born here, people who came here, people who migrate to Colorado. Aren't we lucky to have a country where all of these assets and attributes just come out in a place like Grand Junction? I think it is wonderful.

You know, you are a long way from Florida, you are a long way from Alaska, you are far, far away from New York and California, but you have something special. The Continental Divide does not divide our country. As long as we remain one people in spirit, as long as we continue to share the ideals of freedom, dignity, opportunity that brought us together in the first place, we will remain united.

And it is because of this "grand junction" of interest in ideals that I am optimistic when it comes to America. There are plenty of big problems that are waiting to be solved—inflation, energy, pollution, crime—to name only a few. But there is not one of them that we as Americans can't lick if we pull together and act responsibly. There is, however, one thing our elected officials must remember. No government can expect the people to act responsibly when it fails to do so itself.

If your government does not act to give you an example, if it does not tighten its belt, if it does not give you vision, imagination, strength, courage, dedication, how can government ask you to respond accordingly?

You cannot, from a governmental point of view, ask people to do something about whipping inflation if the Congress is dominated by the people that want to spend and spend and spend, keep on stoking the fires of inflation with excessive spending. If they are going to spend more than they take in, year after year after year, how can we ask honest, decent, responsible citizens to act a little differently if you cannot do it? There is not a double standard.

Well, we cannot expect people to set aside their differences and pull together as long as a spirit of irresponsibility—irresponsible partisanship, if I can define it a bit—and rankling prevails in government.

And this is one of the reasons, quite frankly, that I am here today. I want to ask for your help, your help in giving the American people the kind of problem-solving government all of us want and every one of us deserves. And believe me, as Coloradans there is plenty of that that all of you and I, as a taxpaying but nonvoting Coloradan, can do, too.

Again and again, as I have traveled around this country in recent weeks—and I have traveled around 18,000 miles—I have tried to stimulate people in our country. Yes, I have a little partisan interest, but I have a greater interest—and I think Wayne Aspinall would agree with me—I have got an interest that involves you, whether you are Democrats, Republicans, Independents, or otherwise.

Gosh, what a stake we have in a country like this. If you have ever traveled abroad you have understood the comparison between what we have and what others might have.

It is almost unbelievable, but I am told that the speculators and forecasters are saying that 42 percent of the people eligible to vote on next Tuesday will cast their ballots. Forty-two percent; which means that if 21 percent of the people eligible to vote, or slightly over 50 percent of those 42 percent, decide something, you are going to be in the minority; you will have decisions made by people that are in the minority. I will abide by what the majority of our people say, whether they are Democrat, Independent, or Republican. But I cannot accept the fact that Americans—bearing in mind what so many have given in the way of their life, their sacrifices overseas and otherwise—that only 42 percent are going to let 21 percent of the people make their decisions. Is that

American? Is that what our country was founded on, what is the concept of our whole system?

We want people to get out and vote and to express themselves, to make a determination. And if we do, we will accept it, and it will be better for all of us. And you in Colorado know that if that is done you will reelect your fine Governor, who has done much to make your State healthy economically, burgeoning in activity, and yet who has done a great job in keeping the right balance in-between growth and our environment. And I am glad to be here, John, to participate in something that is a tribute to you and your leadership in the statehouse.

Something I have been interested in for a long time is reorganization of the executive branch. We are going to do something about it in the Federal Government, but your fine Governor has already done something about it in the State government. And I congratulate you and compliment you for this achievement.

Now, let me say something about your Congressional delegation. You have got, in Jim Johnson, you have got a person who represents this district with great capability, character, and dedication. Now, Jim—when I was minority leader in the House—did not always agree with me. We always disagreed without being disagreeable. But I respected his independence; but I also appreciated his willingness to be a teamplayer when he could move and be strong and helpful. So, I express to you, Jim, my deep gratitude not only for your teamwork but your independence. It is good for our country.

Bill Armstrong, another one of your fine Members of the House of Representatives—I think he is great. He came when Jim did. He represents a little different part of your great State, but it is an important, an integral part of our great State of Colorado. And I congratulate him, and I hope you will support him in this reelection campaign.

I had the opportunity of knowing Don Brotzman for a number of years, and Don—I have skied with him and I also served with him—he is a little better in both respects, and I therefore recommend him to be reelected by the people of Colorado.

Well, you have got some challengers, some candidates, that I hope you will support. Keith Records [1]—I hope you will give him the best support, and the biggest help that you possibly can. He has got a good, sound approach to the problems that I think are important to our country.

Then you have Frank Southworth.[2] I know Frank. I know the problems, some

---

[1] Republican candidate in the Third Congressional District of Colorado.

[2] Republican candidate in the First Congressional District of Colorado.

of the difficult areas of the city of Denver. He has got range and depth and experience. He served on the school board and has been a leader in trying to give quality education to the people and to the students of Denver. I congratulate him and urge his full and total support.

But now I come to something that really—if I could just make a special contribution here, it is to Pete Dominick. You know, Pete and I have known one another for 30 years, so it is not one of these political convenience acquaintanceships. I have known Pete when he was a law school student and I was. I have known Pete in subsequent years. I knew him as a Member of the House of Representatives. I watched him when he was a Member of the Senate and I was the presiding officer as Vice President. I have watched him intimately as I have been President and he has been a Senator. I think he has done a great job. And if I were in Colorado with the right to vote, I would vote for Pete Dominick as strongly and as effectively as I possibly could.

Well, Pete gives me the kind of representation that I would like, and therefore, I am delighted to be in Grand Junction. He has all the attributes, the wisdom, the experience, and the kind of knowledge that makes the difference between doing what is right and what is wrong.

Well, let me turn very quickly, if I might—I am going to throw away this part of my prepared text and talk to you frankly. I come from an area in Michigan that probably has more people with the name of "Van" of any area in the whole United States. I had Holland, Michigan; Zeeland, Michigan; Great London, Michigan, et cetera. Gee, they had good judgment. They voted 76 percent Republican. And I was not a Hollander, but I had, I think, a sound philosophy, or at least they think I did.

And so, when I come out and see a Vanderhoof, that is like talking to my old friends that I tried hard to represent in Holland and Zeeland and Great London and all the other places for 26 years. So, I understand a good public servant in John Vanderhoof. You better reelect him. He is good for Colorado.

Now, certainly, after I meet this great gang here today on this platform, I am going to meet with the Colorado cattlemen. This is not the first group of cattlemen that I have met with in the last week. I have met with a group in Oklahoma City. I met with a group in Washington. I met with a group in Portland, Oregon, yesterday, and I am looking forward to meeting this group in Colorado this afternoon.

I know that they have got particular problems, and you have similar problems here in this area of this great State. But let me make an observation or two.

I intend to carry out the meat import law, which means there will be no meat imports in violation of that legislation. We will not grant any exceptions or waivers thereto. And I suspect there are a few dairy farmers in this group. How many are here? Aren't we lucky? They are all out working, and we are having a good time.

But let me say this: I intend to not change the present dairy import quotas, because I do not think we can, under the present circumstances, justify any increase in the quotas. And therefore, I think the dairy people will support the fine, firm, discerning action that Secretary Butz has recommended to me.

But let me add one other thing. You know, we as Americans like competition. I don't mind a German or a Dutchman or a Frenchman competing with me on an equal basis, but I will be doggone if I want the Government to subsidize the product he is trying to sell to the American people.

We will challenge him on the open fields, head-to-head, and we will do all right. Some of the foreign governments in Western Europe have been doing—by what they call countervailing duties—subsidizing dairy products in their countries. We won't stand for it, and if they are going to do that, we will challenge them, head-to-head.

Now, one final observation in the great field of agriculture: You produce tremendous cattle in this country, either cattle feeders or out on the range. I like it either way, but let me say this: We know that in some of the countries such as Australia, Argentina, and elsewhere, they have got tremendous numbers that are about to be exported, some perhaps to us.

In the meantime, Japan, Western Europe, Canada has imposed arbitrary limitations on the export of American products to those countries. I will say to you: They are not going to limit our imports, and we are going to hold the line on exports to the United States.

Let me make one final observation and comment. Inflation, according to all the scorecards, is the biggest problem that faces most Americans. Eighty-three percent of the American people think this is the hardest, the toughest, the strongest issue in this great campaign, and I think I agree. As I travel around the country, I have listened to a lot of people; I talked with many. And it does bother people.

One of the root causes of inflation in America is the irresponsible fiscal policy of your Federal Government. We have to change it. Now, I don't believe that in good conscience I could stand here and say that every Republican is an inflation fighter and every Democrat is a spender. I could not honestly say that, and if I have any conscience, I want to be honest with you. But I will say that the tilt of spenders is in the opposition party, and the tilt of savers is in our party. So, as I travel around the country, I want savers not spenders elected to the Congress, so we can whip inflation.

Well, there is one other thing that I would like to mention before closing. You know, we have three great branches of this Government of ours. I fervently respect it as a lawyer, as a public servant, as a citizen. We have a strong President, supposedly, in the White House. We have a strong Congress, supposedly, in the legislative branch. We have a strong Supreme Court, supposedly, heading the judiciary system. They are equal, coequal branches of our Government. Our forefathers, some 200 years ago, put together this system that was to be so finely tuned that it would protect our freedom, give us the opportunity for participation, and also make it right for us as we moved on to pass through the years ahead.

How lucky we were they were right, they did it correctly. But now we face a challenge, and I do say it right to all of you. There is the possibility that through apathy, you could end up in this next Congress with what I very pragmatically call a veto-proof Congress.

What does that mean? It totally disrupts and tears apart that finely tuned balance so that you no longer have a system of checks and balances. It means that one branch of our Federal Government will have a totally dominating, controlling impact on how your Government is run.

Wayne knows that. He and I have not always agreed on whether a veto ought to be sustained or not, or whether it ought to be done on a Democratic or Republican basis. But if you so distort the ratio in the Congress so that the Congress can totally override by a veto-proof Congress whatever a President decides, you have destroyed, you have upset, you have literally torn asunder a basic concept of what is good for America.

I don't want to come back here 2 years from now and say, "I told you so," because I think you have more judgment. You are going to send Jim Johnson, Pete Dominick, and your good Governor, not only to Washington but to your State capital, to give you the kind of government that will be balanced, that will be right, that will have vision, that will have responsibility. It is the kind of government that is good for all of us, and I pray you will do your very best on November 5.

NOTE: The President spoke at 2:57 p.m. at Lincoln Park Baseball Field.

220

Remarks in Wichita, Kansas. *November 2, 1974*

Bob, Larry Winn, Garner Shriver, Keith Sebelius, Bob Bennett, other distinguished officeholders and candidates, wonderful Kansans:

It is great to be here, despite the weather. I love you. Thank you.

You know, it just came to my attention as I was sitting here that I have been at a good many cities, communities in the last several months as I have tried to get out and meet people and talk to the American people. And we have had abnormally wonderful weather, until tonight. There were only two places where we had any rain—one in Tucson, Arizona, where they are never supposed to have any, and the other in my home of Grand Rapids, Michigan, when I went back for a homecoming last week.

Well, they were great in both Tucson and Grand Rapids, and you are superb here in Wichita. And I thank you for your warm, friendly, enthusiastic welcome.

As Bob was going through the process of making the introduction, I tried to think of how many times, how many places I have been in Kansas in the last 25-plus years as a Member of the House, as minority leader, as Vice President, and President.

And I wrote down, I think, most of them—I am sure I have missed some—but we went out to Great Bend. Wasn't that wonderful out there last year? It rained there, too, but that was all right. But I have been in Dodge City, and you know what they do to you in Dodge City. And I have been in Kansas City, Kansas, just recently, and I have been in Wichita here several times.

Well, I like Kansas. I like Kansas because of the people, but I have another good reason. It has been the home of one of the finest Presidents this Nation has ever known, the great statesman from Abilene, Dwight D. Eisenhower.

As you look at the history of Ike Eisenhower, you know that he set a standard of integrity, achievement that is everlasting, both to his country and to his State. Ike's record was unblemished. And I pledge to you that I will do, to the very best of my ability, to follow the path and the footsteps of that great American. If I can achieve just a bit of what he did, it will be worth every hour, every day of anything I can do in the years ahead.

I have another reason to enjoy coming to Kansas. The campaigns here always seem to have a little more fun than other States. You know, take the race for Governor. Somebody just told me the latest Republican slogan. It goes something like this: "Let's put Bob Bennett in the driver's seat and keep Vern Miller in the trunk." [*Laughter and applause*]

It is obvious from the reaction that you have a great candidate in Bob Bennett. His honesty, reliability, complete and total integrity—the only thing that Bob has ever covered up is his chin. [*Laughter*]

But speaking of things that, you know, get at a little different perspective once in a while, a long time ago when I was at the University of Michigan, I played center on the football team. And normally, of late at least, I have been getting some very stately and dignified introductions. But I can remember quite vividly an introduction I got about a month ago from an old teammate of mine. He was a quarterback. And in the process of the introduction he said, "I played center on the same football team with Jerry Ford. I was a quarterback, but I want you to know I got a little different perspective of the President than most of you." [*Laughter*]

Well, as I have looked at the great Republican slate that the party has put up here for the Senate, State offices, Congress, I must say that I am proud to be a Republican, and I hope you will all support it.

Having said that, let me add this as a postscript: I am not here just because of party labels. And as Bob said, I suspect there are many in this audience who are here who are Democrats, Independents, Republicans, but I am here to say a word of personal support for those individuals that I know and who I know, over the past years, have done a super job in working in the Congress for Kansas, for you, and for our country.

I come because of a personal affection that I have for everyone whose name I mentioned and a respect for a group of people that I have known since all of them came to the Congress, because I came before any one of them.

And I have seen them come. I have seen them grow. I have seen them assume great responsibilities far beyond that of others in comparable seniority.

Bob Dole, for example. I got to know Bob when he came and spent 8 years in the House of Representatives—all of it I was not the minority leader, but a part of it was, and the rest of the time I was a senior member of the House Committee on Appropriations. And I learned then, in that capacity, in these responsibilities, that Bob was smart, hard working, independent, and I can assure you that when he disagrees with you, it is firm; it is a little friendly, but it is firm.

He can disagree without being disagreeable. But what I want you to know is that his independence is predicated on conscience, and his support, when he can and does, is based on teamwork. You just could not get a better combination. So, if I were in Kansas, I know who I would vote for.

Now, I have talked about a personal relationship. Let me talk to you about a very pragmatic reason why you in Kansas should support Bob. Next year, with a new Congress, Bob will be the senior Republican member of the Senate Committee on Agriculture.

You in Kansas have a great State. I won't get into the argument of whether seniority is right or wrong. The fact of life is that in the Senate of the United States, they will keep that system, and Bob will be in that very influential position which has a great impact as far as your State is concerned.

But the combination of that responsibility on the one hand and a member of the Senate Finance Committee on the other, plus the added duty under a new setup of being on the Senate Budget Committee—I don't know how Bob is going to handle all these great responsibilities, except I know him, and I know he will do all three in a first-class way for Kansas and the country. So, as a pragmatic reason, you darned well ought to vote for Bob for the United States Senate.

I am told Bob is in for the political fight of his life. I suspect that is true. But Bob has been through those fights before. He did it in the service of his country. He has done it in one political campaign after another. And I say the test of the man is the achievement that he has accomplished.

And when I look at his record, believe me, you just could not do better.

So, I am here to help in any way I can to say to Kansans, whether they are Democrats, Republicans, or Independents: You ought to keep something that is as good as Bob is. And he is great.

I have also gotten to know all of your House Members extremely well. After all, it was part of my duty as the Republican minority leader for almost 10 years to try and corral votes to organize the minority, to do the best job we could despite the fact that we were outnumbered 240-something to 180-something.

The Kansas delegation always seems to have quality, and in Garner Shriver you have got one who has nothing but quality, and he comes from this great community, Wichita, in this great Congressional district. Garner deserves your support.

And let me say—again, going from what I would say would be maybe ideological reasons to pragmatic reasons—a little over a year ago, we had a fuel oil shortage. I can recall vividly in the process of allocating a shortage, the initial decision was to cut back the portion or the allocation for general aviation.

I was Vice President then. Larry Winn, Garner Shriver, Bob Dole, Joe Skubitz, Keith Sebelius—all of them came and knocked on my door. But the ones who came first, for good and sufficient reason, were Bob Dole and Garner Shriver.

And the result was that you got a better break, and therefore, you ought to support them just on that ground, if not for any other reason.

Well, I don't have to say a lot about Larry Winn, Joe Skubitz, Keith Sebelius. They all have tremendous records. They have done a great job. We are not in their respective districts. You just ought to be darned proud of the Kansas delegation. They are responsible, and they are responsive. And how much better could you ask a delegation than to have that kind of a reputation?

Now, let me speak, if I might, about some issues. Our biggest problem is twofold. Our biggest problem is to keep a strong economy, to whip the problems of inflation, to save the energy that we have, and develop plans and programs to produce more. That is our domestic issue.

On the other hand we have a major responsibility of maintaining the peace and building and broadening and expanding it, working with our allies, trying to expand our relationship with any potential adversaries.

Yes, those are serious problems, and I know some have predicted that the United States is in worse shape than some of our partners in Europe. Others say that they are far worse off than we. And then they make allegations that the free world as a whole—economically, militarily, diplomatically—is in serious trouble and that we should be cowed by and we should be fearful of those who have a different ideology or political philosophy.

Let me start out by making this one strong, categorical, firm statement: I have faith in America. We are going to make it, and our allies and our philosophy will prevail, both at home and abroad.

Now, we have to do this with the help and assistance of Republicans, Democrats, Independents. I know in some instances partisanship has interjected itself, become a principal element in some of the Congressional or senatorial or gubernatorial races.

Well, in the case of Bob Bennett, I don't know why it should, because you have a great candidate and he is going to win. I don't know why it should in the case of Bob Dole, because he has a proven record, both at home and abroad.

I don't know why it should in the case of Larry or Garner or Joe Skubitz or Keith or your fine new candidate, John Peterson.[1] These are people who ought to be supported just on the basis of their background and experience and their dedication.

And I am not going to condemn a Democrat—because there are some good

[1] State Representative John C. Peterson was the Republican candidate in the Second Congressional District of Kansas.

ones--but what I am concerned about is the kind of strength in programs and policies.

Let me take the problem of inflation and strengthening our economy, saving energy, 31-point program.

I think it is good. I believe it will meet the challenges that we face. One of the important ingredients is to hold down Federal spending. There are other parts of it, but I know that Bob Dole, Larry, Joe, Garner, and the others are the kind of people who will be most effective in holding down unnecessary spending, and you and I know that Federal spending of the magnitude that we have had over the last 10 or 15 years has been a significant cause of the inflation that we have today.

So, when you go into that voting booth next Tuesday, take a look at the voting record of those individuals on this issue. It is important to you if we are going to win this battle to save our economic system from the disasters of others historically and to give us the strength to meet the challenges of some of the weaknesses in our economy.

But let us turn, if I might, to the problem of building, strengthening, expanding peace. When I went to the Congress 26 years ago, or almost that, a great, great Democratic President working with a fine Republican Congress—the 80th—laid the foundation for the rehabilitation of Europe and the broadening of our free world throughout the total globe. It was started with the Greek-Turkish aid and the Marshall Plan and some of the other programs implemented by a military capability and strength that is aimed at deterrence, not at aggression.

And you in Wichita have a significant part of it with the Boeing operation here. Strength means peace, and weakness means war.

Well, anyhow, this combination of strength in the diplomatic field and the military has given to us in this great country, and to our allies, this kind of opportunity worldwide. And it has given us the opportunity to open the doors of greater and broader relationships with some of our potential adversaries, whether it is the Soviet Union or the People's Republic of China.

We, at this moment, have a unique opportunity, both at home and abroad, to do something to give us for the next decades—not one; two or maybe three—a brighter America and a better world. And when you look at this next election—and I don't mean in a partisan sense—what you have to decide is who, what Members of the Congress, what candidates are best qualified to give us strength here and vision and strength abroad.

I think you have got them in the kind of people I have mentioned, and I know you have because I have worked with them. I have seen them under pressure. I have seen them do things that might not have been popular at the moment because they were right. I have seen them just perform as wonderful representatives of the people of Kansas and the people of the United States.

One of the great men of this and any century, of course, was Winston Churchill. He led, as we all know, Great Britain through a period of far, far greater danger than anything we face today. But he, too, like myself, was an optimist. When many, many in Great Britain, and some of the free world back in those dark days in the late thirties had given up, Winston Churchill would not succumb to tyranny or the dark era or age of defeat.

Churchill still—and I can recall vividly because I was driving a car in, I think it was 1939, and I heard that wonderful blood, sweat, and tears speech. It was a great speech in an era, in a period, in a day of challenge to Britain.

Sometimes, maybe we ought to go back and listen to what Winston Churchill said in that hour of darkness for Britain and the free world. He said then, and not that precise day but on another occasion, and I quote: Do not let us speak of darker days. Let us speak of sterner days. There are not dark days. These are just great days.

I say to you in all sincerity, we are living in great days. We are going to have to work maybe a little harder and sacrifice just a bit more. But if we do our best and keep faith in ourselves and our values, America and all the other great things that we as a country stand for, our Nation will emerge stronger and better than ever.

I know there are some who wish to have the Government do something for everybody in massive amounts, but as they seek to promote these kinds of efforts in the short haul, I do not think they really forecast what the long pull means.

Let me put it this way: I think it is fair to say a government big enough to give us everything we want is a government big enough to take from us everything we have.

So, as I close my participation in this great campaign—and I have no apologies for traveling some 20,000 or more miles, being away from the Oval Office, seeing people as I did in Los Angeles, in Fresno, in Portland, Salt Lake, and here in Wichita, being in many other places for the last month or 6 weeks—I think the American people have the right to see their President and to have him discuss face-to-face with them his views and to get from them, by one means or another, their reactions, their views, their expressions. This is what I think America was built on.

The town hall concept may be a little out of date, but the town hall concept was good enough to take America through the Revolution and all the other trials and tribulations that followed. And if it was good enough in those days, I think it is good enough for a President to participate in 1974.

And so, as we move to that fateful day next Tuesday, not in a partisan sense but in an objective sense, I think we should all say a little prayer before we go into the sanctity of that voting booth where you and your neighbors will make some decisions that will have a great impact on you individually and your community, on your State, on your Nation, and some 4 billion people all over this great globe.

So, do the best yourself and find literally hundreds of others to get them to do their best under these circumstances.

I ask you to pray, for the benefit of our country and all mankind, and to do your duty.

Thank you very much.

NOTE: The President spoke at 8:37 p.m. at the Century II Convention Center.

221

Remarks on Election Eve. *November 4, 1974*

AS YOU KNOW, tomorrow is election day all over America. Every eligible voter will be sending a message to Washington and to the world. Those who vote, whether they vote for the Republican or Democratic candidates or for others, will be voting yes for our system of government, our tradition of American government of the people and by the people.

Everyone who can get to the polls and who doesn't go to the polls and who refuses to exercise the precious right of a free citizen to vote his or her honest conviction is actually voting no under our system of government.

Now, some surveys indicate a turnout tomorrow of only 40 percent of the voting population. If this is true, the Congress with which I must work in Washington, the Congress that will be working with me on controlling inflation, strengthening our economy, and preserving world peace could be elected by only 21 percent of the voters. I don't think anyone wants that kind of minority decision.

So, I ask you, my fellow citizens, to take the time tomorrow to go to the polls and vote for the candidates of your choice. You will be voting for your own future and exercising the power vested in free people which has carried this country forward for almost 200 years. You will not just be voting for Democrats or for Republicans, you will be casting your vote, a vote of confidence in the United States of America.

Thank you very much.

NOTE: The President's remarks were recorded at 11:29 a.m. in the Rose Garden at the White House.

222

Message to the Congress Transmitting Annual Report on the National Cancer Program. *November 4, 1974*

To the Congress of the United States:

I am pleased to submit to you the annual report on the National Cancer Program's activities, progress and accomplishments during calendar year 1973, as well as the plan for the program for the next five years. Both the report and the plan are required by section 410A(b) of the Public Health Service Act as amended by The National Cancer Act of 1971.

The plan is provided in two documents. The first, called "National Cancer Program Operational Plan," covers the five-year plan for the program and delineates the major policies and procedures used to operate the program. The second document, called "Appendices to the National Cancer Program Operational Plan," includes separate brief descriptions of the individual research, control and support programs of the National Cancer Institute. The funding levels contained in the plan do not constitute a specific commitment or recommendation by the Administration. Among other things, those levels do not adequately take into account overall budgetary constraints and the competing demands of other biomedical research programs.

The Administration is also deeply committed to an effective cancer research program. The progress and accomplishments made in 1973 are gratifying. The National Cancer Program is beginning to have an impact on Americans who have cancer or are at risk to it. Today, more Americans than ever before have access to the most advanced methods of cancer diagnosis, treatment and rehabilitation. This human endeavor and its successes are the result of the National Cancer Institute's expanding research programs, and its efforts to apply for the benefit of the people, as quickly as possible, the knowledge emerging from the clinical bedside and research laboratory.

Our national research program to conquer cancer will take years before achieving ultimate success. The recent enactment of the National Cancer Act Amendments of 1974, which continue the National Cancer Program, demonstrates the abiding commitment of the Congress and the executive branch to solve this major health problem.

Success in this endeavor will ultimately come, however, only with the sustained dedication and hard work of the physicians, scientists, health professionals, voluntary agencies, and the volunteers who support this program.

GERALD R. FORD

The White House,
November 4, 1974.

223

Statement on Receiving a Crystal Grown Aboard the Skylab Space Station. *November 4, 1974*

MOST OF US become so involved in trying to find solutions to the serious problems that we face today that we sometimes lose sight of the developments that hold promise for a better tomorrow.

The small segment of a crystal grown in space aboard the Skylab Space Station last January, which was presented to me today, is a reminder that we should raise our sights to the broadening horizon available to us through our national investment in science and technology.

The experiment aboard Skylab demonstrates that it is possible to grow crystals in space in the absence of gravity—crystals that are more perfect than the Earth-grown variety. It was one of several experiments to determine whether superior materials can be produced in space.

But beyond its scientific value and the potential applications for this new knowledge, this successful demonstration serves as a useful reminder of the contributions that science and technology make toward improving and enriching our daily lives and building a broader foundation for an even better tomorrow.

NOTE: The President received the crystal from James C. Fletcher, Administrator of the National Aeronautics and Space Administration, and Howard Johnson, chairman of the board of the Massachusetts Institute of Technology, in a ceremony in the Cabinet Room at the White House.

224

Letter Accepting the Resignation of Henry E. Petersen as Assistant Attorney General, Criminal Division. *November 5, 1974*

Dear Mr. Petersen:

It is with deep regret and even deeper appreciation of your contributions to government that I accept your resignation as Assistant Attorney General, effective December 31, 1974. Your three decades at the Department of Justice represent the highest standards of both the Federal career service and appointive office. The record of those years is one in which you can take great pride—it is a record of unique achievement. Your ability, integrity, candor and good humor will be sorely missed but fondly remembered by those with whom you served. More importantly, you leave with the respect and admiration of all who were privileged to be your colleagues.

As you move on to private life, you have my best wishes for continued success and satisfaction.

Sincerely,

JERRY FORD

[The Honorable Henry E. Petersen, Assistant Attorney General, Criminal Division, Department of Justice, Washington, D.C. 20530]

NOTE: The President's letter, dated November 4, 1974, was released November 5. Mr. Petersen's letter of resignation, dated November 1, and released with the President's letter, read as follows:

Dear Mr. President:

After 27 years in the service of the Department of Justice I have decided to submit my resignation as Assistant Attorney General to take effect at the close of business on December 31, 1974.

Needless to say I reach this decision after considerable thought and not without some sense of regret. I am keenly aware that I have been most fortunate in having the opportunity to serve the Government of the United States. I recognize too that my duties with the Department of Justice have given me an excellent opportunity to observe at first hand the concern for fairness and due process of law which is the hallmark of the Government's pursuit of litigation. Clearly, it has been a privilege to practice law as an attorney for the Government.

To you Mr. President I want to express my gratitude for the honor which has been accorded to me and to extend my very best wishes for the success of your efforts in behalf of our country.

Sincerely,

HENRY E. PETERSEN

[Honorable Gerald R. Ford, President, The White House, Washington, D.C.]

225

Statement on the Results of the 1974 Elections. *November 5, 1974*

THE PEOPLE have spoken, and for 26 years I have accepted the verdict of the people, which is the essence of our system of free government.

First, may I congratulate every citizen who did his duty by voting today. I have not seen the total turnout, but I am sure it was greater than anticipated in many places.

I also congratulate the winners of both parties and extend my sympathy to those who lost. The willingness of candidates to fight for their convictions and their party is an important ingredient of representative democracy. And those who lose often come back to win another day.

There was no argument about the number one issue in this campaign: inflation and its crippling effect on our economy and on the lives of all Americans. The mandate of the electorate places upon the next Congress a full measure of responsibility for resolving this problem. I will work with them wholeheartedly in this urgent task which is certainly beyond partisanship.

Also beyond partisanship, I am confident, is the necessity of keeping America strong both economically and militarily as the leader of the free world, of moving forward toward a safer and saner international order, of strengthening our cooperation with old allies and old adversaries alike. I am confident that the new Congress will work wholeheartedly with me in this urgent task.

226

Remarks Following a Meeting With Secretary of State Kissinger. *November 10, 1974*

I JUST want to announce that I had a very, very interesting, helpful, and in-depth 3-hour meeting with the Secretary of State. He reviewed the 17 countries on a backbreaking 17-day trip, and I can say on the basis of his analysis that it was basically very encouraging; the meeting with Mr. Brezhnev was very helpful.

The various capitals that the Secretary stopped in in the Middle East I think also brought back some encouraging news. The trips that he made to the subcontinent were very helpful in redirecting our policies in that vitally important area of the world.

So I, for one, am very grateful and most appreciative of the almost superhuman efforts that the Secretary has made on this trip as well as in the past, and we are looking forward to a constructive trip to Japan and South Korea and to the Soviet Union.

So, let me just thank you very, very much, Henry, for a great job for us as Americans and for me personally.

Thank you very, very much.

NOTE: The President spoke at 7:11 p.m. at the South Portico of the White House following his return from Camp David, Md., where his meeting with Secretary Kissinger was held.

227

Remarks of Welcome to Chancellor Bruno Kreisky of Austria. *November 12, 1974*

MR. CHANCELLOR, it is a great privilege and a very high honor to welcome you to the United States. I might apologize for the weather. We could not do much about that.

But speaking on behalf of the American people, let me say how very happy we are for this further opportunity to strengthen the ties of affection and the ties of respect that bind our two nations and our two peoples together.

Like all of the world, America has profited very greatly, Mr. Chancellor, from Austria's great contributions to the arts, to the law, education, medicine, and psychology; and of course, there is the great legacy of music, the legacy of Vienna that the whole world treasures, the music of Mozart, the Strausses, and so many others; additionally, the great importance that Austria has served as a continuing force for peace and stability throughout the world.

Mr. Chancellor, modern Austria has proven beyond any doubt again and again in recent years that a small country can make big contributions to world peace and world understanding. Your positive involvement in world affairs, your generous support of the United Nations, including an important role in the peace-keeping forces in the Middle East and Cyprus, your gracious hosting of important international conferences, such as the initial phase of the Soviet-American strategic arms negotiations and the force reduction talks now in process—all of these Austrian contributions are helping to build a better and more peaceful world.

We Americans, of course, are very, very proud of our long and sincere friendship with Austria. We cherish our many, many American citizens of

Austrian ancestry. And we look with satisfaction and admiration at Austria's impressive economic achievements over the past 10 years.

Mr. Chancellor, we also look forward to our discussions and to the future good relations of Austria and the United States. The nations of the world face many, many challenges today—challenges in the field of finance, food, and energy, to name only a few.

Meeting them will require our best common efforts and the counsel and understanding of many of our friends.

So, Mr. Chancellor, in anticipation of our session together and with our traditional Austro-American friendship in mind, America, one and all, bids you welcome and wishes you an enjoyable and most productive visit.

NOTE: The President spoke at 10:50 a.m. in the East Room at the White House. The Chancellor was given a formal welcome with full military honors at the North Portico. The President and the Chancellor then proceeded to the East Room, where the welcoming ceremony was held because of inclement weather.

Chancellor Kreisky spoke in German. His remarks were translated by an interpreter as follows:

Mr. President, first of all, let me thank you for having invited me to come to Washington on an official visit at a time when you are extremely busy. We in Austria greatly appreciate this high privilege, and we take it as proof of the strong and unimpaired friendship which has existed for decades between the American people and the Austrian people.

Mr. President, I come from a country which greatly appreciates the great contribution made by the United States—and we know this from experience—for the liberation of Europe and for the economic reconstruction of our continent.

We remember with great gratitude the sacrifices which the American people in so many ways have made for the restoration of peaceful conditions in Europe.

Today, Austria is an economically prosperous country, enjoying the blessings of freedom and democracy. We have not forgotten the significant contributions made by your country for this development.

Austria belongs among the smaller nations of Europe, and I regard it as an expression of international democracy that in its dealings with Austria, the United States has never disregarded the principles of equality and of respect for the sovereignty and freedom of our country. The friendship between our two countries and between our two peoples rests on the solid foundation of mutual trust and mutual respect.

Let me assure you, Mr. President and Mrs. Ford, that Mrs. Kreisky deeply regretted to have been unable to join me in this trip and to see her fervent wish to be here unfulfilled.

Mr. President, I want to again thank you sincerely for this invitation, and I am looking forward to our discussions, with my Minister, also with the greatest of interest.

Thank you.

228

Letter Accepting Withdrawal of the Candidacy of Andrew E. Gibson To Be Administrator of the Federal Energy Administration. *November 12, 1974*

Dear Andy:

I have your letter asking that your name be withdrawn as a candidate for Administrator of the Federal Energy Administration, and I accept it with the deepest regret. As you recognize in your letter, the national interest requires that the Federal Energy Administration have new leadership as swiftly as possible. The energy problems we confront are of such a magnitude as to render unacceptable any undue delays in the nomination and confirmation process. It is therefore my intention to announce a new nominee for this important post very soon.

I want you to know of my continuing high regard for your abilities. You did not seek the post of the Federal Energy Administration Administrator; we sought you out because of your proven record as a superior government manager during your tenure at the Commerce Department. You agreed to serve, if nominated and confirmed, out of a spirit of patriotism and a desire to serve the public interest.

It would be unfair to you to leave unanswered the charges made against you. I, therefore, intend to have the FBI investigation, which was routinely begun on the date that you were announced, run to its completion and, when appropriate, to appoint you to another responsible position in government. We need people in public service of your ability and your experience.

With warm regards,

Sincerely,

GERALD R. FORD

NOTE: Mr. Gibson's letter, released with the President's letter, read as follows:

Dear President Ford:

The existence of the agreement between myself and Interstate Oil Transport Company under which I resigned as President in April of this year has raised the question of whether this contract would impair my ability to discharge impartially my responsibilities as Federal Energy Administrator. A review of this contract will show that the obligations of the company to me are specific and unconditional and I therefore believe that this contract would not inhibit the discharge of my official responsibilities as Federal Energy Administrator. Nevertheless, because of its existence it seems apparent that any hearing on my confirmation will be a lengthy matter. Believing as I do that the energy problems facing our nation are critical and require prompt and effective leadership, I am reluctantly compelled to conclude that a lengthy confirmation hearing would not be in the best interests of the nation. Accordingly, I request that my name not be transmitted to the Senate for the position of Federal Energy Administrator.

Other questions have been raised with respect to the propriety of my conduct during the course of my tenure as Assistant Secretary of Commerce for Maritime Affairs. I have every confidence that the FBI investigation now underway will demonstrate the complete absence of any substance to such allegations. Indeed, were such allegations the only obstacle to my confirmation, I should feel quite differently about the withdrawal of my name. Therefore, I respectfully request that the FBI investigation continue and be completed promptly.

I greatly appreciate the confidence you have shown in selecting me for the position as Administrator of the Federal Energy Administration. It would be an honor to have the opportunity of serving the nation in some other position.

Sincerely,

ANDREW E. GIBSON

[The Honorable Gerald R. Ford, President of the United States, The White House]

229

Toasts of the President and Chancellor Kreisky of Austria. *November 12, 1974*

Mr. Chancellor and distinguished guests:

It is a great privilege to honor you in the White House on this occasion. As I look around the room, I see many, many people that I know from personal experience, including Mrs. Ford and myself, who have visited Austria and been the beneficiaries of the wonderful hospitality, the warmth, the friendship of the many, many fine Austrians who have bent over backwards to make us from America warmly welcome.

I must say to you, Mr. Chancellor, that sometime—I can't give you the date—but I am going to wander into Austria and take advantage of those wonderful Tyrolean Alps, because I do like to ski. And hopefully I will have an opportunity to do so just to not only enjoy the benefits of the mountains, but the benefit of the wonderful people from your country.

There are many, Mr. Chancellor, who pass judgment on a country by its size in geography and its size in population. I don't think those are the most significant ways on which you really can judge a people or a country. And we recognize, of course, that Austria is relatively small in population and relatively small in geography. But as we look at the great history and the present in Austria, we find that, looking from the outside to the country, that you have a great humanitarian spirit, you have a great belief in friendship, but more importantly than almost anything, the people of Austria have a character.

And that is how we judge, in my opinion, the strength of a nation, despite its size either geographically or population-wise.

We know over the years since the end of the decade of the forties that Austria has contributed very significantly, despite many problems. You have contributed in the Middle East and Cyprus, and we commend you and we thank you for these efforts that have helped to preserve the peace and to build for it in the future.

I would simply like to express on behalf of all of us in the United States our gratitude for the friendship that we have with the people of Austria, the gratitude that we have for the actions of your Government. And we look forward, I can say, Mr. Chancellor, without any reservation or qualification, to the opportunity to work with you and the people of your country in the years ahead.

It is an enduring friendship predicated on a firm foundation of people to people and Government to Government. And may I ask all of our distinguished guests here tonight to join me in a toast to Dr. Bruno Kreisky, the Chancellor of the Republic of Austria.

NOTE: The President spoke at 10:02 p.m. in the State Dining Room at the White House. Chancellor Kreisky responded as follows:

Mr. President, Mrs. Ford, ladies and gentlemen:

In your warm words of welcome, Mr. President, for which I sincerely thank you, you have mentioned the longstanding and proven ties between the United States and Austria. Certainly, the peoples of the former Austro-Hungarian monarchy always harbored feelings of genuine friendship and admiration for the American people.

To the best of my recollection, however, the relations between the two Governments were not always quite that cordial. [*Laughter*] It appears that His Imperial and Royal Apostolic Majesty Franz Joseph could not bring himself for a long time to receive the American envoy to Vienna.

Early in this century, the developing official relations between Austria-Hungary and the United States of America—at least until the outbreak of World War I and the ensuing disintegration of the Hapsburg monarchy—were really never more than correct relations and, therefore, completely different from those we are fortunate to enjoy today.

Why do I choose to point this out? Because the development of our relations serves as a most convincing example which shows that a very special and close relationship between two nations can be developed in quite a few decades.

I see three reasons for this. In 1945, the United States became one of the four occupation powers in Austria and helped us from the very first day to lay all those foundations needed for the restoration of democracy. Nothing has made a greater contribution to the history of our democracy than the presence of the United States in Austria. You virtually were the guardian of our freedom, Mr. President.

Secondly, Austria was in ruins, and it was hard to imagine at that time how our State could ever again become the home and heaven of our people. You gave to those of us who set out to clear the ruins not only a healthy dose of American optimism but also the most generous material assistance. Mr. President, I hope you will have the opportunity to see with your own eyes the fruits which have sprung from your country's contributions to the economic revival of Austria.

Aid under the Marshall Plan was the foundation of our economic prosperity, and its effects are still being felt today. This aid constituted one of the chief reasons why twice as many people than in 1937 earn a good living in Austria today. During the period from 1937 to 1970, our gross national product, given constant prices, quadrupled and has shown a marked increase since.

Let me add that your material assistance of that time still keeps giving today, as many Austrian firms receive lower interest, long-term investment loans from the ERP [European Recovery Program] counterpart fund, which is sustained through repayment of earlier loans.

The fact that this aid by the United States for the restoration of our economy was given to us free of any contingencies of political dogma enabled us to utilize those sums, which appeared gigantic to us in the light of our circumstances, in complete independence.

And finally, the third reason. Through generous grants, Austrian scientists, engineers, and experts of every specialty have been afforded the opportunity to explore new dimensions in the advanced areas of your cultural and scientific life.

A further example is the considerable contribution made by the Ford Foundation to the Institute for Advanced Studies in Vienna from which a great number of eminent social scientists have emerged in recent years. This constitutes ample reward for the contributions made by Austria to the cultural life of the United States.

Before raising my glass to the continued prospering of these relations, I would like to again voice my regret that Mrs. Kreisky was unable, for reasons of health, to participate in this beautiful and impressive visit. She regretted this all the more because it robbed her of the opportunity to meet Mrs. Ford, whose restoration to health has made us all very happy and to whom I wish to extend warm personal wishes.

And now, ladies and gentlemen, I ask you to raise your glasses and join me in a toast to the health of the President of the United States and his charming wife and to the continued development of the excellent relations between our two countries.

230

Message to the Senate Transmitting Convention on the Prevention and Punishment of Crimes Against Diplomats. *November 13, 1974*

To the Senate of the United States:

With a view to receiving the advice and consent of the Senate to ratification, I transmit herewith a copy of the Convention on the Prevention and Punishment of Crimes against Internationally Protected Persons, including Diplomatic Agents, adopted by the United Nations General Assembly on December 14, 1973 and signed in behalf of the United States of America on December 28, 1973. The report of the Department of State with respect to the Convention is also transmitted for the information of the Senate.

The effective conduct of international relations depends in large part on the ability of diplomatic agents to travel and live freely and securely while representing the interests of their respective countries. We have witnessed in recent years an unprecedented increase in acts of violence directed against diplomatic agents and other internationally protected persons. This development has demonstrated the urgent need to take affirmative action to minimize the threats which can be directed against diplomatic agents. Although the legal obligation to protect these persons was never questioned, the mechanism for international cooperation to ensure that perpetrators of serious attacks against them are brought to justice, no matter where they may flee, was lacking.

The Convention is designed to rectify this serious situation by creating a legal mechanism whereby persons alleged to have committed serious crimes against diplomats will be prosecuted or extradited. It also sets out a framework for international cooperation in the prevention and punishment of such crimes.

This Convention is vitally important to assure continued safe and orderly conduct of the diplomatic process. I hope that all States will become Parties to this Convention. I recommend, therefore, that the Senate give early and favorable consideration to this Convention.

GERALD R. FORD

The White House,
November 13, 1974.

NOTE: The text of the convention and accompanying papers are printed in Senate Executive L (93d Cong., 2d sess.).

231

Message to the Congress Transmitting Annual Report of the National Capital Housing Authority. *November 13, 1974*

To the Congress of the United States:

I am herewith transmitting the National Capital Housing Authority's annual report for the fiscal year ending June 30, 1973. The report sets forth the efforts of the Authority to improve and expand the housing opportunities in the District of Columbia.

In light of the recent transfer of the National Capital Housing Authority to the District of Columbia Government, I hope that even greater efforts will be made to improve housing conditions in the Nation's Capital.

GERALD R. FORD

The White House,
November 13, 1974.

NOTE: The report is entitled "Public Housing in Transition, National Capital Housing Authority Annual Report—1973" (Government Printing Office, 36 pp.).

232

Remarks on Signing the WIN Consumer Pledge. *November 13, 1974*

BEFORE SIGNING, I would like to read a statement that has been prepared:

Mrs. Ford and I are signing today the first consumer pledge prepared for Americans by the nonpartisan Citizens' [Action] Committee to Fight Inflation.

The WIN committee is asking mayors and principal county officials across this country to set up local action committees for distribution in the near future of similar pledges for citizens to sign in a concerted mass effort to stop inflation. The committee has also prepared a businessman and businesswoman's pledge and a worker's pledge for local distribution. Each Governor is being asked to establish one statewide committee to determine ways and means to slow inflation and to save energy in each State.

If all Americans will pull together to hold down prices, to buy wisely, to increase productivity, and to save energy, this citizens' mobilization to slow inflation can and will work. Inflation is sapping the economic strength of this country, and it must be brought under control.

So, at this point Betty will sign the first pledge, and I will join her.

REPORTER. Mr. President, what are you going to do to carry out this plan?

THE PRESIDENT. Well, the things that I buy, I will be very careful in purchasing. I think we have got to increase our productivity—that includes me. We have to be Yankee traders when we buy, and we have to cooperate individually and collectively. And Mrs. Ford has pledged to me, as well as here, she will do the same.

NOTE: The President spoke at 1:13 p.m. in the Cabinet Room at the White House. The texts of the WIN pledges follow:

Consumers:

I pledge to my fellow citizens that I will buy, when possible, only those products and services priced at or below present levels. I also promise to conserve energy and I urge others to sign this pledge.

Businessmen and Businesswomen:

I pledge to my customers that to the very best of my ability I will hold or reduce prices and will buy whenever possible from those who have pledged to do the same. I also pledge to be an energy saver. This signed pledge is evidence of my participation in, and support of, the WIN Program.

Workers:

I pledge that I—through my union—will join with my fellow workers and my employer in seeking ways to conserve energy and eliminate waste on the job. I also promise to urge others to sign this pledge.

233

Remarks at a Meeting With Coastal State Governors on Outer Continental Shelf Oil and Gas Development. *November 13, 1974*

THE IMBALANCE between our Nation's demand for oil and gas and our domestic production of these resources is one of the most serious problems we face. The rapid increase in energy costs in the past years has been a major driving force behind today's inflation.

The essence of this problem is that while we produce about 11 million barrels per day, we consume about 17 million. Domestic demand is increasing, but domestic production is dropping because most of our onshore oil fields are being depleted.

We must adopt rigorous conservation measures, but it is clear that regardless of what conservation steps we take and what eventual long-range energy policy we adopt, in the near term we must increase our domestic production of oil and gas.

I believe that the Outer Continental Shelf [O.C.S.] oil and gas deposits can provide the largest single source of increased domestic energy during the years when we need it most. The O.C.S. can supply this energy with less damage to the environment and at a lower cost to the U.S. economy than any other alternative. We must proceed with a program that is designed to develop these resources.

Legitimate concerns have been expressed about O.C.S. leasing and development. Let me briefly address myself to these concerns.

First, concern has been expressed that industry does not have the manpower and equipment necessary for exploration and development of 10 million acres of O.C.S. lands and that this could lead to the sale of leases at bargain prices.

We believe that industry can make the manpower and equipment available. And I might note that although the 10 million acres has been a useful planning objective, we are not wedded to this particular goal. Our primary objective is to produce oil and gas where we can do so safely. But in any case, we will insure that leases are not sold below fair market values. I have directed Secretary Morton to insure that these objectives are attained.

Second, concern has been expressed that we should not lease any new areas of the U.S. continental shelf until the coastal States have completed detailed plans to accommodate the onshore impact of offshore production.

Coastal States have only begun to establish the mechanisms for coastal zone planning, and that activity must proceed rapidly. But the steps needed now to prepare for a leasing program need not await completion of these detailed plans by the States. The prolonged delay would only postpone the date when we will learn whether substantial reserves can, in fact, be produced from our O.C.S. and would lengthen the time that we will have to rely on costly imported oil.

Furthermore, the shoreside impact will not occur for several years following institution of a leasing program. That period will enable State and local governments to prepare for the shoreside impact. To help insure effective, cooperative action, State and local officials will be asked to participate in the process of selecting tracts to be considered for detailed environmental and resource study.

In order to facilitate coastal State participation in this effort, I plan to request an additional $3 million in the current fiscal year for the coastal zone management program to accelerate State planning efforts. I have also directed Secretary Morton and Secretary Dent to consult with coastal Governors regarding any additional steps that might be required to plan adequately for onshore development associated with offshore leases that are actually issued.

Third, concern has also been expressed that our proposed leasing program cannot be conducted without unacceptable risks to the environment. We are taking the steps necessary to reallocate additional funds during the current fiscal year to strengthen our preleasing environmental assessment and monitoring activities. If our studies show that development cannot occur in a particular area without unacceptable risk, then we will not hold a lease sale. The step that must now be taken is to begin the detailed studies to identify risks in specific areas to be considered for leasing.

We have made great strides in our O.C.S. safety program thus far, and we will work closely with the coastal States so that they understand and have a part in the further development of regulations that govern these operations off their coast.

I also recognize the concern about oil spills. Our energy and environmental experts have concluded that the greatest danger to our coasts from oil spills is not from offshore production but, instead, from the greatly expanded tanker traffic that would result from increasing imports.

To assure that any spills that might occur do not cause uncompensated harm, however, I have also asked Secretary Morton and Chairman Peterson to prepare a proposed comprehensive liability statute governing oil spills. This bill will be ready for introduction in the next Congress.

In summary, the resources of the Outer Continental Shelf represent a potential contribution of major proportions to the solution of our energy problem. I am confident that concerns about leasing exploration and development of the Outer Continental Shelf can be addressed openly and fairly, that planning can proceed in an orderly, cooperative way, and the problems confronting us in opening new areas can be resolved.

I pledge the cooperation of my Administration in this task.

NOTE: The President met with the officials at 5 p.m. in the Cabinet Room at the White House. Attending the meeting were the Governors of Connecticut, Delaware, Louisiana, Maine, Massachusetts, Mississippi, New Hampshire, and New Jersey; the Governors-elect of Maine, Georgia, and New York; the Lieutenant Governors of Maryland and Rhode Island; and the Lieutenant Governors-elect of Alaska, Connecticut, Massachusetts, and South Carolina.

In his remarks, the President referred to Russell W. Peterson, Chairman of the Council on Environmental Quality.

234

Remarks to the Annual Convention of the National Association of Realtors, Las Vegas, Nevada. *November 14, 1974*

President Doherty, President-elect Leitch, ladies and gentlemen:

It is truly a great privilege and a very high honor to have the opportunity of appearing before this convention of the National Association of Realtors, and I thank you from the bottom of my heart for your warm and friendly welcome. It is nice to be here.

At the outset, I wish to pay a very special tribute to the members of the National Association of Realtors for all that you have achieved in the face of a very, very serious and difficult economic environment.

You know, I always think it is a help, as a matter of fact, when the complex problems we all deal with are at least recognized in part by others, and sometimes this happens in very strange ways.

Two weeks ago, I went back to my hometown of Grand Rapids, Michigan, for a rally in a tremendous college fieldhouse. And just as I was coming into the building, I heard the master of ceremonies ask the marching band to play one more selection, something that would be appropriate for the President of the United States. So, they played "Nobody Knows the Trouble I've Seen." [*Laughter*]

But one of the things I have always admired about the members of the National Association of Realtors is that you are always optimists, and I am, too. Believe me, anyone who wears a WIN button in Las Vegas has to be an optimist. [*Laughter*]

Well, in the area of real estate, I am something of an optimist, too. The Ford family owns a condominium in Colorado, a house in Virginia, an apartment in Grand Rapids, and for the last 3 months, we have been living in a one-family dwelling at 1600 Pennsylvania Avenue. We call it home. I believe some of you might call it public housing. [*Laughter*]

But the White House is just one of some 70 million housing units in America today, and that figure is nearly double the number of 1940. The National Association of Realtors has played a very major role in bringing about this phenomenal growth, and I am delighted to be able to join in this well-deserved tribute and salute, I should say, to you and your association.

John Ruskin, the English author, wrote a book called "The Seven Lamps of Architecture." In this book he told us a very great truth: It is more important to build a life than to build a cathedral.

Your association is fortunate, however, to combine both—to be involved in building good lives as well as good cathedrals. The cathedrals of this land are its homes. It is the family home which is the foundation of what we call the American dream. Your industry and the housing industry are closely related. One hardly need look beyond this community to recognize that the housing industry is suffering the ill-effects of inflation more intensely than most other industries in our great Nation.

Primarily because of a sharp spurt in the cost of money—although fortunately it has now started back down—and shortages of mortgage money, housing sales are off substantially in many, many parts of America.

Unemployment in the construction industry is more than double the national average. It has always been higher, unfortunately, because of the nature of the industry. But we must reduce that figure.

Public officials would rather swallow this grim statistic than speak about it, but it is my duty to face unpleasant facts, unpleasant circumstances, and it is my responsibility to do something about them—mine and the Congress'. I assure you that I will do more than my part in this situation.

In recent weeks, as you know, this Administration has authorized $3 billion under the Home Purchase Assistance Act for the purchase of mortgages on new single family homes. This program aims to not only help ease the high jobless rate in the construction trades but to add to our housing inventory.

This $3 billion could mean up to 100,000 new homes for Americans with mortgage payments that they can afford. I know this action, as first announced, would not have helped you realtors directly. Your commodity is primarily in existing homes, not new homes under this program. But you understand, and you went along with us, because your commitment was to the industry across the board, and I salute all of you, and I thank you on this occasion today.

I think you provide a good example for the rest of us. You did not say, "Me first." You said, "We first." We—*all* Americans. Let's do what is best for America.

Now, as we face the Nation's major problems in the weeks and months ahead, it will be well to remember this: It is not I alone, the President, who faces these enormous tasks and problems; it is not you who must battle them individually and collectively; it is *we* who must win, or *we* will lose—the President and the Congress together, Republicans and Democrats alike, Nevadans and Michiganders and New Yorkers, rich and poor, black and white, young and old.

I am no arm twister—never have been. And I see no reason to become a prophet of gloom. But in the weeks and the months ahead, I will call upon the American people—and I underline "people"—to sacrifice for the national good. And I happen to think that the American people will respond.

We, the Congress and I, must reduce Federal spending. At the same time, we, the Congress and I, must increase Federal tax revenues. And we, all of us, must save energy so that we will import less high-priced foreign oil.

Although you will be called upon to make additional sacrifices, so will your Government. I will send to the Congress shortly after it reconvenes, my recommendations for the reduction of Federal spending in 1975. These have been hard decisions for me. They will be equally hard decisions for the Congress.

But it is my strong and firm conviction that Uncle Sam must slim down to what I consider fighting trim for the battle ahead of us, all 213 million.

But even though Uncle Sam tightens his own belt, he should not tighten the noose on vital industry such as yours.

Earlier, I mentioned that the Administration has made $3 billion available for commitments to purchase mortgages on new single family homes. As you know, I have sought to curtail and cut additional Federal financial outlays as inflationary. At the same time, we have targeted expenditures under this new program to counteract the declines in production and employment in new home construction.

However, there is authority under this new act to purchase mortgages on existing homes as well.

As you know better than I, because purchase of a new home often depends on the sale of an existing home, and for other reasons, we have concluded that provision should also be made for existing homes under this program.

Therefore, I have an announcement for you this morning. Effective today, up to 10 percent of each of the $3 billion in commitments under this program can be used for mortgages on existing homes—[*applause*]—thank you very much. That is, the Federal Government under this plan or program will strengthen the existing home mortgage market by about $300 million, assisting both the buyer and the seller. This will ease the burden somewhat, but I emphasize that the real solutions, the ultimate solutions will not be provided by the Government. The victories must and will be won in the free marketplace, and you know it better than I.

Without question, mortgage credit is the lifeblood of the real estate industry. Today, after a long drought that began in the spring of this year, we are seeing a reversal in the outflows from the savings institutions. If money is available to the savings and loan associations, there will be more money available for mortgages. If money is available for mortgages, home sales will rise. It is just that simple.

There are, however, other hopeful signs of a greater availability of credit. Interest rates have started downward. Even more significantly, rates on forward commitments have begun to decline.

For instance, the average yield of a 4-month commitment to purchase FHA–VA mortgages was 9.9 percent in Fannie Mae's [Federal National Mortgage Association] auction of November 4, compared to 10.6 in September of this year.

This indicates that mortgages on both new and existing homes will be available on somewhat easier terms in the future.

The dramatic decline in short-term interest rates over the last 3 months is particularly encouraging. And please take note, if you will, that this was not produced by any undue inflationary expansion of the money supply. Rather, this decline stemmed from a return to a more normal market in business loan demand. As the yield on instruments that compete with savings deposits decline, the supply of funds to and from the thrift institutions will continue to grow.

In short, the signs are becoming quite clear that the real estate picture will brighten. And as inflation recedes, which it will, we expect that the forces suppressing new construction, not only new construction but sales as well on new and existing homes, will ease.

The $300 million funding which will be made available to strengthen the existing home market is only part of the $7,750 million Home Purchase Assistance Act approved by the Congress. In signing the bill into law, I referred to some shortcomings in that act. If Congress really wants to help when it reconvenes next Monday, why not include in that new legislation privately financed, multi-family projects and individual condominium units?

Rising land costs, rising material costs underline the importance of utilizing all of our housing resources. Condominiums and rental housing are a very vital part of our national housing program, and I hope and trust that Congress will respond.

Our inner cities must not be denied assistance because the high cost of land could be, and in many instances is, a barrier to a housing assistance program. The public knows all too well that the housing needs of our major metropolitan areas, the inner cities, must be met in significant part through the construction of rental housing.

Further, I believe that more fundamental reforms are necessary to put a clamp on the up-and-down cycles in the housing industry. The current downturn should be clear indication that the stopgap and patchwork solutions in the past are not adequate for the future.

In my judgment, we must make basic changes in the way in which we supply capital, in the way in which we supply credit for the housing industry. The cyclical variations in the industry that you represent may thus be brought within more reasonable limits.

Therefore, let me mention another piece of legislation that is currently before the Congress. There is a bill called the "Financial Institutions Act," which is one of 31 economic proposals that I recommended to the Congress on October 8.

Enactment of this bill would do a great deal to moderate these cyclical swings in housing credit. For one thing, it would reduce the structural differences between commercial banks and thrift institutions and help them to compete more effectively during periods of high interest rates, and it would provide, also, a broader range of financial services for consumers.

In addition, it would offer a higher rate of return for savers. But even more importantly to the real estate business in particular, it would attract greater investor interest in the mortgage market through the mortgage interest tax credit. This would offer investors a tax credit of 1½ to 3⅓ percent, depending, of course, on the percentage of their portfolio in mortgages.

Significantly—and this is quite important—unlike other tax proposals, the benefit under the mortgage interest tax credit must go to the mortgagee. In short, I believe that the passage of the financial institutions act would provide very, very significant benefits for the housing industry. In particular, it would moderate the traditional boom-and-bust cycles in your great industry, and I will press for enactment when Congress returns next week.

Let me leave you with this final thought. You come from all parts of this vast, vast Nation. You represent its length and breadth, its diverse people, and its differing viewpoints. And indeed, you individually and collectively reflect the aspirations and the inspirations of all Americans. You, as salesmen and saleswomen, see daily the workings of this great, free society that we have. You see it in your communities every day of every year. And all of this activity can be summed up in one word in your business—sales. And sales are the result of both aspiration and inspiration, not to mention just a little perspiration.

Somehow the word has gone out that the best way to defeat inflation and to revitalize the economy is to curtail buying. Nothing could be further from the truth, and I strongly oppose that point of view.

I believe a free society means precisely that—a free market—and sales are the heartbeat of a free market. Instead of curtailing purchases, I say to consumers quite simply: Buy wisely, shop smarter. To you in sales, I say: Sell harder, sell more aggressively.

What we need at this time in this country are more tough Yankee traders and more supersalesmen, and I am sure you are in the latter category.

Even while dealing with these very practical matters, a nation must never lose its vision. I remember a story about Michelangelo. The sculptor was chiseling a block of marble. Every day a very small boy came and shyly watched his labors. He never said a word to Michelangelo.

Then one day, the magnificent figure of David appeared. The astonished boy finally broke his silence and asked Michelangelo, "But how did you know he was there?"

Vision, imagination—these are the qualities that make a people great. Americans have these qualities, they always have. And we as a nation will respond to the challenges that we face.

Inflation will be cooled. Despite some economic weakness—recession, business fallback, call it what you will—there will be an upturn in the Nation's economic patterns. In fact, here in Las Vegas, where it is legal, I will even bet on it.

Thank you very much.

NOTE: The President spoke at 9:57 a.m. at the Las Vegas Hilton Hotel. In his opening remarks, the President referred to Joseph B. Doherty, president, and Arthur S. Leitch, first vice president and president-elect, National Association of Realtors.

235

Remarks on Accepting the F–15 Aircraft for the United States Air Force at Luke Air Force Base, Arizona. *November 14, 1974*

Governor Williams, Senator Fannin, Congressman John Rhodes, General Jones, General Dixon, General Haeffner, Mr. McDonnell, Mr. Graff, distinguished guests, ladies and gentlemen:

This is the month of the pioneer in America. It is the month of the Mayflower and of our earliest settlers. And this is the day of a new pioneer, a pioneer of the skies, a pioneer of peace: the F–15 fighter.

According to history, there were 102 passengers on the Mayflower when it crossed the Atlantic. The crossing from England to the new world took more than 2 months, and the end of the journey was freedom. The F–15 can fly across the same Atlantic in a matter of hours. The end of its journey is still the one of the Mayflower more than 350 years ago—freedom.

That is what really matters, the purpose of a journey, and I am here today to underscore to you and to the world that this great aircraft was constructed by the American people in the pursuit of peace. Our only aim with all of this aircraft's new maneuverability, speed, and power is the defense of freedom.

I would rather walk a thousand miles for peace than to have to take a single step for war.

I am here to congratulate you: the United States Air Force, McDonnell Douglas, Pratt and Whitney, all of the many contractors and workers who participated in this very, very successful effort, as well as the pilots who have so diligently flight-tested the F-15 Eagle. All of you can underline my feeling that we are still pilgrims on this Earth, and there still is a place for pioneers in America today.

The challenges involving our country here at home and abroad, we all recognize, are enormous. But I am confident that the F-15 and your example here today is that this Nation is a nation of limitless horizons. There is no boundary to the energy, the ingenuity of the American people. Frankly, that is why we will whip inflation, conquer our energy problems, and win the battle to make a stable economy.

It is the job of all of us, it is our job, in this last quarter century of the 20th century, to prepare our country for leadership in the 21st century. And we can do this by economic strength at home and by peaceful partners abroad. These are my aims, my goals, and the goals of America now and in the future.

As I said in a Thanksgiving message [Proclamation 4333] which I made just a few days ago, and I quote: Let us pray for the courage, resourcefulness, and sense of purpose we will need to continue America's saga of progress and to be worthy of the Pilgrim spirit. May we, too, find the strength and the vision to leave behind us a better world and an example that will inspire future generations to new accomplishments.

So I say to you, congratulations, best wishes to all who had any part whatsoever in this great accomplishment. It will serve the purpose of freedom and peace for a generation and more.

Thank you very, very much.

NOTE: The President spoke at 12 noon. In his opening remarks, the President referred to Gen. David C. Jones, USAF, United States Air Force Chief of Staff; Gen. Robert J. Dixon, USAF, Commander, Tactical Air Command; Brig. Gen. Fred A. Haeffner, USAF, Commander, 58th Tactical Fighter Training Wing; James S. McDonnell, chairman and chief executive officer, and George S. Graff, president, McDonnell Douglas Corporation.

236

Remarks and a Question-and-Answer Session at the Annual Convention of the Society of Professional Journalists, Sigma Delta Chi, Phoenix, Arizona. *November 14, 1974*

President Otwell, Gene Pulliam, Governor Williams, Senator Fannin, distinguished guests, ladies and gentlemen:

It is a great privilege and pleasure to participate in another meeting of this wonderful organization of professional journalists. I have had several, and I have enjoyed every one, and I am looking forward to this one.

I understand the hour for this occasion was fixed for our meeting not by my Press Secretary, not by the networks, but rather in order to ensure the attendance of all of the late strays from the Lazy R and G Ranch party which Gene Pulliam put on last night. [*Laughter*] Gene is not only a great host but a great publisher. And I am sure I will neither be the first nor the last speaker at this convention to salute him as one of the founders of Sigma Delta Chi, the Society of Professional Journalists.

Between Bob Hartmann and Bill Roberts of my own Presidential staff and half of your Washington professional chapter in the White House press room, I am hardly out of sight of one of your members at any time. And I must say, I enjoy their company, and I admire their professionalism—most of the time, anyway. [*Laughter*]

Veto of Freedom of Information Act Amendments

[1.] In doing my homework for this visit, I was browsing through your magazine, the Quill, and I read as follows, quote: "National S.P.J., S.D.X. President Ralph Otwell is asking local chapters to contact their congressmen to urge them to override President Ford's veto of a bill to strengthen the Freedom of Information Act. Otwell criticized Ford's action, saying"—and I quote—" 'For a President who is publicly committed to a more open and honest Administration to oppose significant reforms in Freedom of Information legislation is both startling and disappointing. . . . President Ford's veto suggests his Administration is pursuing a discredited policy of cover-up as usual.' "

First, I want to assure your fine president, Ralph Otwell, that I have not come here today or tonight to argue, but to enlighten. In fact, I may be the first President, probably the first President in history, to come all the way to Phoenix just to hold a press conference. And when I get here, I find out that Dan Rather [1] is going to get the last word anyhow. [*Laughter*]

Before we go to questions, I would like to make two brief observations, if I might, both of which bear on the business of the Congress which will be returning to Washington next Monday.

First, about my veto of the Freedom of Information Act amendments. I think, incidentally, that the veto is a constitutional power given to the President in order

[1] CBS News correspondent.

to require Congress to take a hard, second look at legislation which the President, who is obliged to faithfully execute the law, considers to be unwise or unworkable in whole or in part.

I really don't think my veto suggests "a discredited policy of cover-up as usual." Uncovering coverups has to be done without the help of any law but by tough reporters and tough editors.

However, before you write all your Congressmen to override my veto, I would like to tell you my side of the story.

I do support the Freedom of Information Act and most of the reforms contained in the current amendments. There are, however, three amendments that bother me both on principle and practicality, and these were the basis of my veto.

I have written the leaders of both the House and Senate to express my hope that when Congress returns, instead of trying to override the veto, they will make three small but very significant changes in these three sections and send me another bill which I can and will sign.

My first objection is to that section that would allow any Federal judge to examine privately or *in camera* the classified records of any Government agency, including our most sensitive national security and diplomatic secrets, and remove the agency's classification if he found the plaintiff's position to be reasonable. In other words, no credibility was given to the Government's initial decision. I think that is wrong. As a matter of fact, this change in the proposed law would overturn a 1973 Supreme Court ruling which limited judicial review to the determination of whether or not in the initial classification there was, in fact, a classification according to law.

With all due respect, I do not believe many Federal judges are experts in the complex weighing of defense and intelligence needs for security or secrecy. I also think that the transfer of this judgment from the executive to the judicial branch of Government may be unconstitutional. My proposed modification, which I think is reasonable, would accept judicial review, but require judges to uphold the original classification if there is a reasonable basis to support it.

My second objection is far less dramatic. In my view, one section sets unrealistic time limits on the Government's response to a request for a specific document. I have proposed that a 30-day deadline in contested cases be increased to a total of 45 days with extra time for complex cases at the option of the court.

The third reason for the veto was an amendment granting public access to investigatory files such as the so-called raw data reports of the Federal Bureau of Investigation. For example, I am told there was actually pending before the

Department of Justice a request for the entire files accumulated by the FBI in their investigation of the Communist Party. If opening such files had been proposed in the so-called McCarthy era, you would all have denounced it as exposing innocent people to vicious rumor and unproven smears—and you would have been right.

On a practical level, it would have required a brand new bureaucracy and millions and millions of man-hours of the FBI simply to review those files over a period of several decades to determine what now may be safely made public without injuring innocent parties or compromising their sources of information. I have proposed a more flexible and realistic set of ground rules that would preserve what I consider to be the essential confidentiality of investigatory files of law enforcement agencies. I hope that professional journalists will take another look at this section of the freedom of information bill and see if you don't agree that this Pandora's box should remain shut.

The 25th Amendment to the Constitution

[2.] There is a second matter I will discuss briefly before this distinguished society, whose members I know have a strong sense of history-in-the-making as well as an insatiable interest in good government, both of which I applaud. That is the vacancy in the Office of the Vice President.

I suppose I can properly claim to be the world's champion or world's expert on the subject of filling the Vice Presidency under the 25th amendment. When I suddenly found myself nominated for this position on October 12, 1973, I did some research on the debate in the House and the Senate on this important constitutional amendment which was proposed by the Congress in 1965 and ratified by the legislatures of 47 States in 1967. Frankly, I was curious as to what I might have said on the subject, particularly Section 2, which deals with vacancies in the Office of the Vice President.

The fact is I found I hadn't said anything in the debate except to vote "aye." And the main subject of the debate was the matter of dealing with Presidential succession in the event of a President's disability or inability to discharge the duties of his Office. The replacement of a Vice President was incidental to this, but it seems fair to infer that the framers, like the Founding Fathers, considered that Office to be essential to the conduct of the Federal Government and the orderly succession of Executive power in any emergency.

It is implicit in the adoption of the 25th amendment as part of the Constitution that a prolonged vacancy in the second office of the land is undesirable as public policy and that such vacancies should be filled as promptly as careful consideration by the President and the Congress will permit.

In my case, despite one of the most exhaustive investigations ever undertaken of anybody not on the FBI's ten-most-wanted list, the Congress moved expeditiously and confirmed me within 8 weeks of my nomination, although I do have to admit it, it seemed a little longer than that 8 weeks to me.

When I suddenly found myself President on August 9, 1974, and the Nation again without a Vice President, I made it my first or highest priority—aside from the Cyprus crisis, which I walked into—to search out and to select the most capable and qualified person I could find for that high Office.

I finished the task in 11 days and sent to the Senate and to the House the name of Nelson Rockefeller of New York. That was almost 3 months ago, and while I recognize the need of the Congress to take a month off for campaigning—I did it 13 times myself—I believe that the time has come for them to fish or cut bait in this matter.

I have been assured by Speaker Albert and by Senator Mansfield, the majority leader of the Senate, that they will make every effort to bring the nomination to a final floor vote before the 93d Congress adjourns *sine die* probably in late December. I am delighted to have their cooperation, because I believe it is what the Constitution mandates and what the American people want from their representatives. I am as convinced as ever that Governor Rockefeller is the right man for the job, and I am anxious to have him as a working partner in our Federal Government.

For the future, however, I will propose to the next Congress a reexamination of the 25th amendment, which has been tested twice in as many years, to see if the provisions of Section 2 cannot be tightened up either by constitutional amendment or by public law.

There should be, in my judgment, a specific deadline for the President to nominate and for the Congress to confirm a Vice President. If this reasonable period passes without affirmative action, the Congress would then be required to promptly begin confirmation hearings on another nominee.

It has been suggested to me—and I underline suggested—that if, because of a partisan deadlock between the President and the Congress, the Congress fails to act within the deadline, the next constitutional successor, presently the Speaker of the House of Representatives, should be required to actually assume the Office of the (Vice) President. Although I am not prepared to advocate such a step, I must say there is really no way, despite secret briefings and all that, that anyone can even partially be prepared to take over the duties of the Presidency on a moment's notice without all the participation in the Executive process that a President can extend to his Vice President.

In this dangerous age, as the 25th amendment attests, we need a Vice President at all times. And I speak as one who ought to know.

I will be glad to answer your questions.

Questions

ECONOMIC POLICY

[3.] Q. Michael Pakenham of the Philadelphia Inquirer.

Mr. President, on Tuesday the word "recession" made its debut in the official diagnostic language of your Administration. Could you tell us if you are of a mind now to press forward with any significant economic policies that are new, beyond and perhaps including wage and price controls?

The President. At the time we put together the 31-point program that I submitted to the Congress on October 8, 1974, which was a finely tuned program to meet the challenges of a softening economy—and there were definite signs at that time—and on the other hand, to tamp down inflation, we believed then, and I believe now, that the plan is sound, that it is constructive, that it will meet the two problems that we face.

And may I add most affirmatively, putting wage and price controls on in a period of recession would be just the absolute wrong approach to the solution of a weakening economy. I never heard of the proposal to use wage and price controls to stimulate an economy. The only time I have heard of wage and price controls being advocated was when we had inflation as our major problem.

I happen to think we have got two problems—a weakening economy and inflation that is too high. The proposals that I submitted, 31 in number, try to meet both, and at the moment, I see no justification for any major revisions.

VICE PRESIDENTIAL NOMINATION

[4.] Q. Mr. President, Gaylord Shaw with AP [Associated Press].

You said just a few moments ago that in this dangerous age we need a Vice President at all times. My question is this: Would you withdraw Governor Rockefeller's nomination if it is not confirmed before Congress adjourns next month, or to put it another way, are there any conditions under which you would withdraw the nomination and submit another name?

THE PRESIDENT. There are no conditions that I can imagine or know of under which I would withdraw Governor Rockefeller's name. As I said in my prepared remarks, I think he is the most qualified person to be Vice President. I intend to do all I can to see that he gets confirmed, and I hope that the Congress will respond constructively and act before adjournment *sine die* in 1974.

HOUSE MINORITY LEADER RHODES

[5.] Q. Good evening, Mr. President. I am Bill Close from KOOL Radio and Television in Phoenix.

Congressman John Rhodes is seated over there, and my question concerns him. A move is underway in the House to challenge John Rhodes of Arizona as the Republican minority leader. In your opinion, is John Rhodes doing a satisfactory job, or would you rather see someone else in his place?

THE PRESIDENT. John Rhodes, in my judgment, is an outstanding Member of the House of Representatives. He has done a superb job as the Republican leader in the House since he took over when I became Vice President. I see no reason whatsoever for any change in that position in the House of Representatives on the Republican side.

THE ELECTIONS AND THE REPUBLICAN PARTY

[6.] Q. Hampden Smith, Washington and Lee University in Lexington, Virginia.

Another political question, if I may, sir. The Republican Party lost 45 seats in the House of Representatives and 5 in the Senate and 6 Governorships in last Tuesday's election, and further public opinion polls seem to indicate that the percentage of Americans who consider themselves Republicans has been declining for quite a while, even before the Watergate reaction set in.

And my question, sir, is how could you explain this seeming decline in the Republican Party?

THE PRESIDENT. You know, it was bad enough, but it is not quite as bad as the numbers you used. We didn't lose quite as many Republicans in either the House or the Senate, but I concede it was not good from our point of view. But I would also like to add this:

As people have indicated, they are leaving the Republican Party, and you are accurate in that the polls show that. They have not gone to the Democrats, they have gone to the Independent category. The Democrats, as a matter of fact, have either lost a little or maintain only their former numerical position. So, the net result is that more and more people are becoming Independents rather than party affiliates.

I can argue it both ways, but what it really shows—in my judgment, in this last election—that the Republican Party was in the White House at the time where we had 10 or 11 percent inflation, where we had some softening of the economy, and where we had the heritage of Watergate.

Now, those are pretty tough problems to overcome in the political arena. Those are transitory. We are going to solve the inflation. We are going to strengthen the economy. And Watergate is ended. This Administration had no connection with it, so we are going to be strong come 1976.

CHAIRMAN OF THE JOINT CHIEFS OF STAFF

[7.] Q. Mr. President, Helen Thomas, United Press International.

Mr. President, do you plan to retire General [George S.] Brown as Chairman of the Joint Chiefs of Staff? And I have a followup.

THE PRESIDENT. I have publicly disavowed the comments made by General Brown.[2] I had General Brown to the Oval Office this morning at 7:15 before I took the plane, and I indicated to him very directly my strong feeling concerning the statements that he made and reaffirmed to him directly my disavowal of those comments that were recorded at Duke University Law School.

I think it ought to be said that General Brown has publicly apologized to those that might have been involved in the comments that he made. I have no intention of asking General Brown to resign. General Brown has been an excellent Air Force officer; he has been an excellent Chairman of the Joint Chiefs of Staff. He made a mistake; he has recognized it. He is going to continue as the Chairman of the Joint Chiefs of Staff.

Q. Mr. President, do you think that the Defense Secretary was remiss or some of your White House aides, perhaps, in not informing you earlier of General Brown's remarks so that you could have been apprised?

THE PRESIDENT. Well, the truth is that I had about 12 to 15 hours advance notice. I could not have remedied the situation any better than we have tried if I had known a few hours earlier.

I just want to say, very candidly, I disapprove and disavow of what he said. I not only said that publicly but to General Brown directly. It was a mistake,

[2] At a question-and-answer session with students at Duke University Law School on October 10, 1974, General Brown was quoted in subsequent news accounts as referring to "Jewish influence" in Congress, saying: "It is so strong, you wouldn't believe now. We have the Israelis coming to us for equipment. We say we can't possibly get the Congress to support that. They say, 'Don't worry about the Congress. We will take care of the Congress.' Now this is somebody from another country, but they can do it. They own, you know, the banks in this country, the newspapers. Just look at where the Jewish money is."

but he is a fine officer, and he has done a good job. And I don't think he should be fired for that one mistake.

WORLD SUPPLIES OF FOOD AND ENERGY

[8.] Q. Peggy Roberson, the Birmingham News, Birmingham, Alabama.

Mr. President, recently we have seen horrifying pictures of starving people in the world, and we have learned that energy and food are unbreakably linked. Are we prepared to use food as a weapon to force down energy prices so farmers can produce low-cost food to feed these people?

THE PRESIDENT. We are not going to use food as a weapon. We must recognize, however, that food is just as important to the world as oil and that in order to get a better distribution of oil that is held in vast reserves by other nations and food that is produced by us to a greater extent than any other nation in the world, we must get together and cooperate to make sure that that which is available in both cases is spread throughout the world for the benefit of all people.

Dr. Kissinger, the Secretary of State, has put together the group of oil-consuming nations. We expect to work with the oil-producing nations. I believe that there can be an understanding achieved that will be to the mutual benefit of the producers in food and oil and the consumers in both.

POSSIBILITY OF A GASOLINE TAX

[9.] Q. Jules Witcover, Washington Post.

Mr. President, Secretary of Interior Morton told reporters yesterday he is still interested in the possibility of a new gasoline tax as a weapon to fight the energy crisis and inflation. Your Press Secretary on your behalf has repeatedly said that you are not considering it. Can you clear up exactly what the Administration's position is on a new gas tax?

THE PRESIDENT. I certainly will, Jules. I don't know how many times I have to say that we are not considering an additional gasoline tax. I said it the first time, I think out in Sioux City [Falls], South Dakota, and I repeated it many times thereafter.

I thought that others in the executive branch got the word, and I hope this word is conveyed to my good friend, the Secretary of the Interior. [*Laughter*] We are not considering an increase in the gasoline tax.

FOREIGN POLICY FORMULATION

[10.] Q. Norman Dohn, Ohio University. That is where Bill Hess is a football coach, not Woody Hayes.

My question is in regard to foreign policy. Senator-elect John Glenn of Ohio and others have suggested that despite Dr. Kissinger's very fine track record, that perhaps foreign policy is such a complex and delicate matter that the machinery of foreign policy ought to be spread out over a broader base. Do you have any plans to do this under your Administration?

THE PRESIDENT. I have no such plans. I can't imagine someone who really is not an expert in the field of foreign policy giving advice to a man who has conducted foreign policy with great skill and great success. If you have got someone who is doing a good job, I don't understand why anyone in seriousness would advocate that he be taken off part of the job and turn it over to someone who might not do as good a job.

I respect the right of the Senator-elect to make the suggestion, but I don't think it makes very much sense.

WAGE AND PRICE CONTROLS

[11.] Q. Tom Jarriel with ABC, Mr. President.

I would like to follow up the answer you gave on the economy a moment ago. You said that wage-price controls would be the wrong approach to combat inflation. Some of your aides are saying inflation is the cause of recession. Should the recession continue and should you see a need to combat inflation in order to halt the recession, would you then reconsider the possibility of wage-price controls, or is this categorically ruled out?

THE PRESIDENT. I have no intention of requesting the Congress to enact mandatory or standby wage and price controls, and I have been told by the Democratic leaders that there is no prospect of the Democratic Congress enacting wage and price controls. There are no circumstances that I foresee today that would justify the heavy hand of wage and price controls in the present economic circumstances.

INCOME SURTAX

[12.] Q. Have you any tax-raising proposals to replace the 5 percent surtax, should that not be acted on by Congress? Your Press Secretary has said that, I believe, you would have an open mind on it. Have you any other proposals in mind?

THE PRESIDENT. No. I would hope that the Congress would take a serious look at this constructive proposal which would affect only 28 percent of the personal income taxpayers, with 72 percent of the income tax payers not being affected at all. And even a person with a $20,000-a-year taxable income would only have to pay an additional $42, or 12 cents a day. I think somebody making $20,000 a year would be willing to make that kind of sacrifice if that would be helpful in whipping inflation and if that would be helpful in helping the people who are less fortunate who need some help during this transition phase from a recession to a healthier economy. It is a good proposal. I hope the Congress does take affirmative action.

PRESIDENTIAL PARDON AND AMNESTY

[13.] Q. Mr. President, Bernie Wynn of the Arizona Republic.

In light of the GOP disasters at the polls, Tuesday, would you rather have waited maybe until after November 5 to pardon Mr. Nixon, to have granted amnesty to draft dodgers?

THE PRESIDENT. Not at all. I think the timing in both instances was right. I could see no justification for another 2 months of delay in the action in pardoning President Nixon. I did it because I think we had very important business to get on with, both domestically and internationally, in the United States. And it was obvious to me that with the prospective court action and all the controversy that would be stimulated by it, that it was wise for me to exercise the right of pardon when I did, and waiting 2 months would have made no difference.

In the case of earned amnesty for draft dodgers and draft evaders, I think the sooner we acted in that case the better, and I am glad to say that from where I have had an opportunity to examine it, it has worked well, it has not given a free ride to individuals, and it has given those who wanted to earn their way back a second opportunity, and we have had quite a few who have applied.

I think in both instances I acted right, and in both instances the timing was correct.

CHANGE IN AMERICAN LIFESTYLE

[14.] Q. Mr. President, Bob Johnson, WHAS, Louisville.

A number of critics say that the people in this country are going to have to adopt a far simpler lifestyle than they have shown their willingness to do voluntarily, something that goes beyond cleaning their plates, eating a great deal less, driving a great deal less.

Do you agree that this will be necessary, and if so, how is it going to be done? What type of leadership are you going to offer?

THE PRESIDENT. I think we may have to tighten our belts a little bit. I think buyers will have to be better Yankee traders, and salesmen will have to be more aggressive salesmen. In other words, we have got to restore some competition on the one hand and people have to be wiser on the other, saving energy, hopefully, in a voluntary way.

If not, we may have to impose some limitations or restrictions. But I don't see us having to retrogress. I don't see us having to go backwards, which, in my judgment, is so contrary to the philosophy of America. We have got a great country; we can make it grow and prosper. We just have to tighten our belts and get rid of the fat and the excesses, and we will be a lot better off as a country and as individuals.

TRIP TO JAPAN, THE REPUBLIC OF KOREA, AND THE SOVIET UNION

[15.] Q. Mr. President, Norman Kempster of the Washington Star-News. You have spoken of the danger of the Nation being without a Vice President. On Sunday you are planning a trip to Japan, where some violence is threatened. What do you expect to achieve on this trip to Japan that can make it worth the risk?

THE PRESIDENT. There are three very important countries that I am visiting. And I should preface that with a comment that a President has two major responsibilities, one in the field of domestic policy and the other in the field of foreign policy.

And where we have three extremely important countries, two where we have good relationships, treaties, where we are allies—Japan and South Korea—where we want to strengthen that relationship, and the third, the Soviet Union, where we have been trying to achieve a détente and broaden it, where we are going to hopefully lay a broader foundation for SALT Two. When you add up the pluses, I think that there is convincing evidence that I, as President, should go to Japan, to expand our good relations with Japan; go to South Korea, a staunch and strong ally and to work out some differences, if any, and to broaden our relations there; and to go to the Soviet Union to hopefully make some progress in détente, in the reduction of arms.

I think it is a very worthwhile trip.

Q. Mr. President, if I may follow up, what is the urgency that would not permit waiting until Governor Rockefeller is confirmed?

THE PRESIDENT. Well, if I knew the Congress was going to act, there might be some justification for it, but I can't sit and twiddle my thumbs and not do something which I think is important for the benefit of foreign policy of the United States.

We have to do things on an affirmative basis which I think are necessary, and to sit and wait until Congress acts on this—and I think they ought to act a lot more quickly than they have—I think would be wrong.

Some things that we have to achieve here are vitally important, and I think the trip ought to go on, and as far as I am concerned, it is.

FUTURE DIRECTION FOR THE REPUBLICAN PARTY

[16.] Q. Jennifer Schanno, College of St. Catherine in St. Paul, Minnesota.

Mr. President, there seems to be some argument as to what direction the Republican Party should go to avoid another landslide defeat. Some are saying it should go in a moderate direction, some in a more conservative.

In which direction do you feel it should go?

THE PRESIDENT. I think the Republican Party ought to continue to be a middle-of-the-road party, a party that has a strong, internationally oriented foreign policy, a party that has a middle-of-the-road to conservative domestic policy—certainly conservative in the field of fiscal affairs.

I think that is a good policy, and I don't see why we should abandon a good policy just because we took a licking on November 5.

If you go back in history, in 1946 when Mr. Truman was President, the Democrats took a worse beating, and the 80th Congress came in with more Republicans in the House and Senate by a substantial number. Mr. Truman and the Democrats didn't abandon their policies. They went out and fought for them. They went out and made an effort to sell them. And Mr. Truman and the Democrats were successful in November of 1948.

I think that is what we ought to do as Republicans in 1976.

PARTY CONTROL OF CONGRESS

[17.] Q. Mr. President, Lester Schlangen of the Associated Press.

Why do the Democrats seem to have better luck in electing Democratic Congresses than Republicans do? Why can't the Republicans do that? You haven't won in 40 years.

THE PRESIDENT. Well, I am glad you pointed out that the Democrats have controlled the Congress—the House and the Senate—38 out of the last 42 years. So, all of the evils that you have had, you can blame on them, not on us. [*Laughter*]

RELATIONS WITH CONGRESS

[18.] Q. Mr. President, Forrest Boyd, Mutual Broadcasting.

I would like to take that just one step further. Senator Dole suggested that you shed your Boy Scout image and get tough with Congress and, if necessary, go over their heads to the people. What will be your tactics?

The President. Well, let me preface the answer to the one part of your question—I was a Boy Scout. I am proud of that experience. I have no apologies for it. I think they have done a great deal of good for lots of young people, and I am not going to back off from the 5 or 6 years that I enjoyed being a Boy Scout and doing the things that I think are good for America.

Now, to answer your other question. I wish there would be a lot more Boy Scouts.

Now, I am going to try to work with the Congress. It is a Democratic Congress, better than 2-to-1 in the House and, I think, about 62 percent in the Senate. I think we ought to try and work together. They do have some sort of a mandate. They have an obligation, they have a responsibility, but they also have an accountability.

I want to work with them. I hope we can. But if we find that they are going to try and override, dominate with policies that I think are wrong, I will have to disagree with them.

But I am going to start out with the assumption that they are as interested as I am in what is good policy, both at home and abroad, and hopefully that will continue. So, let's wait and see.

ATTITUDE TOWARD THE PRESS

[19.] Q. My name is Tim Rife. I am from the University of Nebraska at Omaha.

Mr. President, does your willingness here—to show up here to a Sigma Delta Chi convention reflect a new attitude in your Administration towards the press?

The President. I don't think coming here is a reflection of any new attitude toward the press on my part. I think most of the press from Washington would agree that I have always been open and candid with the members of the press. The fact that I became Vice President or President I don't think has changed me. I acted in the past as I am acting now. We don't agree on some things, but I have always felt that I should treat them as I would want to be treated, and vice versa. And I think that is a good relationship.

MIDDLE EAST NEGOTIATIONS

[20.] Q. Mr. President, Russ Ward of NBC News.

There has been some recent talk in the Middle East about a possible reimposition of the Arab oil embargo. Do you have contingency plans for dealing with such a move, and might those plans include a possible change in our relations over there, either with Israel or the PLO [Palestine Liberation Organization]?

THE PRESIDENT. Our plans are aimed at trying to get the Israelis to negotiate a settlement or additional settlements with the Egyptians and the other Arab nations. Those are the plans we have which are affirmative and plans that I think, if we continue constructively, can bring about some success.

Until we have failed, and I don't think we will, in trying to get the parties to work together, I don't think it is appropriate to discuss what we will do if we don't achieve success.

Q. Are you suggesting, Mr. President, that Israel should deal directly with the PLO? It has been the Israeli objection all along against recognizing the PLO as a bona fide political organization.

THE PRESIDENT. I didn't say that. I did say that the Israelis should negotiate with the Egyptian and other Arab parties. The Israelis have said they will never negotiate with the PLO. We are not a party to any negotiations. I think we have to let the decision as to who will negotiate to be the responsibility of the parties involved.

THE PRESIDENT'S FIRST HUNDRED DAYS

[21.] Q. Gene McLain, KTAR Television and Radio, Phoenix.

Mr. President, you are approaching your first hundred days in office. How do you size up your pluses and minuses, your major disappointments and successes?

THE PRESIDENT. I think the best things we have done—number one, nominating Nelson Rockefeller; number two, the conducting of the economic summit meetings, I think 12 all over the country, with two in Washington; and the formulation of a good, sound economic plan that meets the problems of a weakening economy and inflation.

I believe that we have laid additional groundwork for success in the Middle East. We have redirected some of our policies in the subcontinent areas. We have, in addition, enhanced the possibility of strategic arms limitation agreement number two, which I think will be enhanced by the meeting I am going to have in Vladivostok in about 12 days, hopefully to be followed by a meeting in Washington some time in the summer of 1975.

Some of the disappointments—we had a few bad breaks. I think the Congress was dead wrong when they handicapped myself and Secretary Kissinger in the efforts that we could make in the settlement of the Cyprus question between Greece and Turkey. I think that was a terrible disappointment, and some of the things we warned about might happen, and it won't be helpful to Greece. That was a bad break.

Another was the failure on the part of the Congress to act more affirmatively on behalf of the nomination of Nelson Rockefeller. It should have been done before the campaign recess. I think the Congress also might have moved ahead more rapidly in some of the economic suggestions.

We have had some pluses, and we have had some minuses, but I believe so far we are a little ahead of the game.

POLITICAL PARTIES IN 1976

[22.] Q. Mr. President, Bob Watkins from the University of Houston.

In response to an earlier question, you said that disenchanted Republicans were becoming Independents and not Democrats. Well, many Democrats are becoming Independents, too. Do you see this desertion as a preface to a large-scale third party movement in 1976?

THE PRESIDENT. I don't see that as a third party movement. I think it does suggest that political parties, the traditional ones, are weakening. I think that is sad, however. I think the two major political parties ought to be strengthened, but nevertheless the trend is just the opposite.

I hope that in the months ahead that we, as Republicans, can regain some of those by the performance both at home and abroad in our policy actions. I don't hope that my Democratic friends improve their situation, but if they do, I still think it would be healthy to have more responsible people in political parties than as Independents.

THE ECONOMY AND UNEMPLOYMENT

[23.] Q. Good evening, Mr. President. Walt Rodgers of the Associated Press.

I am sure you have read newspaper accounts suggesting that perhaps the United States faces another Great Depression similar to 1930. Your Administration has already admitted that we have slipped into a recession and that unemployment will go even higher than the current rate of 6 percent. How much more slippage do you expect in the economy? First, when will the slump bottom out, and specifically, will unemployment go over 7 percent?

THE PRESIDENT. I can't give you categorical answers to those three questions. I think we will have some increase in unemployment, but I do believe that if the Congress cooperates with me, we can reverse that trend in 1975. I believe that we have certain safeguards today that we did not have in the 1930's. I remember the depression, Wally; you're too young.

In those days, we didn't have an unemployment compensation insurance which is a very helpful protection. We didn't have in the 1930's the kind of additional payments that the autoworkers, for example, get from the auto unions to bolster the amounts they get from unemployment compensation.

We have a lot of excellent safeguards that protect our economy today from falling into the depression. I don't think we are going to have one because we have these safeguards.

What we have to do is to prevent reactions that will really be harmful to the economy, restimulating or reigniting inflation which is actually starting to recede at the present time. We have to follow a very narrow path, and the Congress can help, and if they do, we can avoid the pitfalls of more inflation and economic conditions worse than we have today.

Q. By way of a followup, Mr. President, if I could, I would like to try to pin you down on the unemployment figure. Have any of your economists suggested that unemployment might go to 7 percent or do you entertain that possibility?

THE PRESIDENT. I have not heard any of the economists that advise me saying that unemployment would go to 7 percent or over. They do indicate that it may increase above the 6 percent which was last reported.

PROCEDURES FOR SELECTING PRESIDENTIAL APPOINTEES

[24.] Q. John Kolbe from the Phoenix Gazette.

Mr. President, earlier this week you withdrew your nomination of Mr. Gibson as the new energy administrator in the midst of some discussions and some disclosures about his severance agreement from an oil company. The White House reported that apparently you personally knew nothing of that agreement before you made the nomination.

Have you taken or do you intend to institute any new staff-type procedures in the White House that will prevent this kind of embarrassing situation in the future, and if so, what do you intend to do?

THE PRESIDENT. Yes, we have. The procedure we intend to follow in the future is to say that a person is being considered and undertake the FBI or investigation review prior to making any specific announcement that we are sending a name up to the Senate for confirmation, which gives the individual some protection and gives us some protection.

In the case of Andy Gibson, he was an excellent head or director, administrator of the Maritime Administration. He took a maritime industry and an agency in the Federal Government in 1969 that was dead and really made it into an effective Maritime Administration.

He was a first-class administrator. I regret that the circumstances developed, because I asked him to serve in a position which requires a first-class administrator. We have not had that kind of firm direction over in the Federal Energy Administration. Andy Gibson would have been a good one.

I regret very much that he didn't make it, and I regret that our procedure at that time was inadequate. We made a mistake. It won't happen again.

Q. Do some of the disclosures that have come out about Governor Rockefeller fit in that same category as Mr. Gibson?

THE PRESIDENT. None whatsoever. In the case of Governor Rockefeller, prior to the nomination I submitted three names to the FBI and asked them to give me an updating of their files and to let me know whether there was anything whatsoever in the files of the FBI concerning Mr. Rockefeller and two others. I think that was a sound procedure.

The gifts that Governor Rockefeller has given, in my judgment, are the kind of gifts that a person, if you have that much money, ought to have the right to give, and there is no political chicanery involved at all. He was generous to people that he thought ought to be helped, and there is no connection, no relationship between the Rockefeller situation and the Gibson matter.

REPORTER. Thank you, Mr. President. Thank you very much.

NOTE: The President spoke at 6:04 p.m. in the Kino Room at the Del Webb Towne House.

237

Letter Accepting Withdrawal of the Nomination of Peter M. Flanigan To Be United States Ambassador to Spain. *November 16, 1974*

Dear Pete:

I have your letter of November 16 asking that I not resubmit your nomination as Ambassador to Spain. Although I fully understand the selfless reasons which led to your decision it is nevertheless with reluctance and deep regret that I accept your request. In doing so, I want to assure you once again of my confidence in you and my admiration for your abilities.

For the past five years as Assistant to the President and Director of the

Council on International Economic Policy, you have served your nation with the highest distinction. You can be justly proud of the critical role you played in helping to shape our country's vital trade and economic policies under the most challenging circumstances. Your efforts won you the highest respect of your colleagues in government and the esteem of the international community for the substantial contributions you have made. You deserve the heartfelt thanks of your fellow citizens, and I want to take this opportunity to express my own lasting gratitude.

I am also deeply grateful for your generous offer of continuing assistance in the future, and you can be sure if the occasion arises we will not hesitate to take advantage of your talents. In the meantime, Betty joins me in extending to Brigid and you our very best wishes for every continuing happiness and success.

With my warmest personal regards.

Sincerely,

GERALD R. FORD

NOTE: Mr. Flanigan's letter, released with the President's letter, read as follows:

Dear Mr. President:

To serve as your Ambassador to Spain would be a great opportunity to work for the Nation as well as a great honor. For that reason I accepted with pleasure your offer of the post. And also for that reason it is with the deepest regret that I now ask that you not resubmit my name.

During the past weeks I have weighed, on the basis of all the information that could be developed, the prospects for my confirmation by year-end. It had been my belief that five years as Assistant to the President and Director of the Council on International Economic Policy provided a record which would command prompt Senate support. Unhappily the distortion of that record, despite the affirmative report given to the White House by Mr. Jaworski, throws that belief into serious question. Though the false charges and insinuations have already been fully answered, I must now conclude that the confirmation process would not be completed by the end of the year and the 93rd Congress. This long delay in the confirmation of your nominee would not be in the best interest of your relations with the Congress nor the Country's relations with Spain.

I will never forget the continued strong support given to me by you and Secretary Kissinger. My purpose in coming to Washington has been to serve the President—not to burden him. Given the current political climate, I can best do this by asking that you not resubmit my nomination.

I am deeply grateful for the honor you did me in offering me the Ambassadorship to Spain. I look back with satisfaction at the past five years of working with you in the Congress and in the White House. If in the future I can be of assistance to you in any way, you know that I would be very pleased to do so.

With warm personal regards, I remain,

Sincerely yours,

PETER M. FLANIGAN

[The President, The White House, Washington, D.C.]

238

Remarks on Departure for Japan, the Republic of Korea, and the Soviet Union. *November 17, 1974*

LET ME just say a word or two, and at the outset thank all of my friends for coming out to see us off.

I think this trip has great significance, both as to timing and as to substance. We all live in an interrelated world. No longer can we, in the United States, think in the terms of isolationism. What we do overseas has great significance for some of the problems that we have here at home.

This, I think, can be defined as a quest for peace, to broaden it, to strengthen it. And as I said in Arizona earlier this week, I would rather travel a thousand miles for peace than take a single step for war.

We are visiting three great countries. The first is Japan, the first visit of an American President on a state visit to that great country. We have a special relationship with Japan, and although we are separated by the broadest of oceans, we have the closest of friendships.

We also will be stopping in the Republic of Korea, a courageous and brave ally, an ally that joins with us in preserving peace in that part of the world.

The trip to the Soviet Union has special significance. There has been a tremendous effort over the years to broaden an effort of peace throughout the world, and I look forward to participating in an ever-increasing strengthening of our ties with the Soviet Union.

I go with optimism. I think we as Americans can be optimistic about the progress that has been made and will be made. I go with a dedication of service to my fellow Americans and a pride in our great country.

Thank you very, very much.

NOTE: The President spoke at 9:22 a.m. on the South Lawn at the White House.

239

Remarks at Anchorage, Alaska. *November 17, 1974*

General Hill, Secretary Kissinger, Lieutenant Governor, Mayor Sullivan, Mayor Roderick, General Gamble, General Marks:

I guess I am what you Alaskans call a *"chee cha ko,"* a newcomer. But I am no newcomer to the knowledge that this great land within another great land, the

United States, is a great and wonderful partner of all of the rest of us in this great land.

There is something very special, I have observed, very special about the pioneer spirit that is not only alive but is growing in Alaska. Alaska gives all of us an inspiring farewell boost as Secretary Kissinger and I proceed to enhance the quest for peace and improved international relations.

I would like to commend Alaska for its determination to be a leading State in providing the United States with self-sufficiency in energy.

I commend you that Alaska is proceeding, with careful and efficient planning, to produce more oil in harmony with appropriate environmental concerns. This is important for you and for the rest of us.

Personally, I am very proud to stop and visit with you for a few minutes today. It has been my good fortune to be in Alaska on several occasions in the past and travel over a good part of this great State.

Then as now, it brought back the memories in the Congress of the United States where, on more than one occasion, I was called upon to vote on whether Alaska should be given statehood. You wouldn't be familiar with the record, but I am. I was proud then, and I am proud now, to have always voted for Alaskan statehood.

I deeply regret the very severe storm and flood damage that ravaged Nome and the Seward Peninsula area in recent days. It is a sad and tragic story, and at the Governor's request, a major disaster declaration was issued by me in Washington so that the area could and will receive immediate assistance.

That is the least we can do, and with that assistance goes our prayers for the very best under those difficult circumstances.

Quick action in this emergency must be taken to aid those affected and afflicted, the Eskimos and others, and we wish them the best in their hour of need.

The State of Alaska is geographically separated from our other States—it took us 7 hours and 20 minutes, I think, to fly from Washington, D.C.—but let me say with emphasis, Alaska is very close to our hearts, to all of those in the "Lower 48."

The hearty people of Alaska, together with the alert Armed Forces stationed in this very strategic area, are a source of great pride to all of us, all of us Americans.

Let me reassure you today that this Administration is energetically seeking world peace but remains very aware that the best insurance for peace is the maintenance of a first-class military force ready for action for the defense of America and freedom everywhere.

We have strong, ably led, well-equipped, dedicated, superb individuals in the Armed Forces of the United States, and I, as Commander in Chief, am very, very proud of the job that has been done and will be done in defense of our country and freedom throughout the world.

Let me assure you that there will be no lessening in this Administration of my support for a strong Army, Navy, Air Force, and Marines, and the Coast Guard. All of us have an interest in the defense of Alaska. Your defense is our defense.

Just a few weeks ago the Secretary of Defense visited Alaska, and I am deeply interested in his recommendations. And upon my return from this mission abroad, I will discuss with the Secretary his recommendations for the strengthening of our defense forces in all of the United States, including Alaska.

Let me reassure Alaska on another subject. It relates to the depletion of our fishery resources by other nations. You can be sure that this matter is high on the agenda, on the list of priorities for diplomacy as far as I am concerned.

As I said at the beginning, I am departing today as a *"chee cha ko,"* a newcomer, but I hope to return next week on my way home as a "sourdough."

I thank all of you for taking the time on a beautiful Sunday and coming to give me and my party a send-off welcome. I am deeply appreciative and very, very grateful. I can assure you that I and the others will do our best on an important and constructive mission.

I thank you all for the send-off. May God bless our efforts as we go forth from here.

NOTE: The President spoke at 12:15 p.m. at Elmendorf Air Force Base. In his opening remarks, the President referred to Lt. Gen. James E. Hill, USAF, Commander-in-Chief, Alaska; Maj. Gen. Jack K. Gamble, USAF, Commander, Alaskan Air Command; Maj. Gen. Sidney M. Marks, USA, Commanding General, United States Army, Alaska; Lt. Gov. H. A. Boucher of Alaska; and mayors George M. Sullivan of Anchorage and Jack Roderick of the Greater Anchorage Area Borough.

240

Message to the Congress on Legislative Priorities. *November 18, 1974*

To the Congress of the United States:

I regret that commitments which I believe will advance the cause of international understanding prevent my delivering this message personally. On two previous occasions when I returned to the Capitol for formal communication with the Congress, I emphasized my sincere desire for partnership with you in the interests of our country. Nothing has changed that intention on my part.

On August 12, three days after assuming the office of President, I asked the Congress to join with me in a new spirit of action and accommodation in getting America moving again. On October 8, I presented a comprehensive 31-point program to strengthen our economy, share the burdens of inflation and stagnation and significantly reduce this Nation's dependence on outside sources of energy which is both strategically and economically undesirable.

There has been piecemeal criticism of my program and I expected it. But there has been no specific and comprehensive alternative program advanced and time is passing. I do not read any mandate in the recent election so clearly as the American people's concern about our economy and their urgent demand for fiscal restraint and responsible action on the economic front.

I am still ready to meet the Congress more than half way in responding to this call from our constituents. We cannot wait and the country cannot wait until next March or April for needed action.

I will always have a special affection for the 93rd Congress—the last one to which I was elected and in which I served both as Minority Leader of the House and as President of the Senate. But I hope this pride can be more solid than sentimental.

Time is short, but time remains for this Congress to finish its work with a real record of accomplishment. Your leaders have given me their assurance of a desire to do as much as possible.

There is much to be done. I am confident that if we all declare a moratorium on partisanship for the rest of 1974 we can still achieve much for America.

In this message I am listing those legislative actions, among the many I have proposed, to which I attach the highest priority. I respectfully request their careful consideration and resolution before the 93rd Congress takes its place in history.

Nominations

I regret that neither body of the Congress has acted on my nomination of Nelson Rockefeller to be Vice President of the United States.

It has been nearly thirteen weeks since I nominated Governor Rockefeller. Our recent experience with the 25th amendment makes it plain that an incumbent Vice President is essential to continuity in Government. I appreciate the need for a thorough examination of this nomination, but it is in the highest national interest that I urge speedy confirmation.

Forty-three other nominations pending before the Senate lapsed with the election recess. I request that my re-submissions be given expeditious consideration so that vacancies in key executive branch posts may be filled with approval of the Senate at the earliest possible time.

I will also transmit to the Senate the names of other candidates for major Administration positions and urge their speedy confirmation. Good government makes it imperative that all pending nominations be acted upon during this session of the Congress.

Economic Issues

No single issue has a higher priority than the economic health of our country. Prices rise while production lags and unemployment increases. It is a severe problem requiring specific corrective actions to start the recovery and to check inflation.

EXPENDITURES

I am gratified that recent deliberations of the House and Senate have recognized the need to restrain Federal spending for fiscal year 1975. I am confident that this action reflects the strong desire of the American people.

Accordingly, for fiscal year 1975, I will recommend to the Congress next week more budget rescissions and will report on budget deferrals and administrative actions to hold down expenditures. I will also request the Congress to make changes in existing authorizations and in pending appropriation bills. I urge the Congress to support these actions and move quickly to enact the required legislative changes.

I have already reported on a number of budget deferrals totalling more than $23 billion and requested seven rescissions of over $675 million. Failure to support these actions would increase outlays by over $660 million in 1975, $2.2 billion in 1976, and even more in subsequent years. I urge the Congress to accept these deferrals and take prompt action on the over $675 million in rescission proposals that have been submitted.

EMPLOYMENT ASSISTANCE

In addition to Government belt-tightening, I also indicated in my economic message of October 8th that special legislation was needed to assist citizens who are particularly hurt by increases in unemployment. On that same day, I sent to the Congress my proposed *National Employment Assistance Act*. Under this plan, employment assistance programs would be triggered into action whenever the average national unemployment rate rose to six percent for three consecutive months.

In that event, these programs would provide special jobless compensation and work opportunities in those labor market areas where the rate averages six and one-half percent for three consecutive months.

These programs should be enacted immediately, since rising unemployment indicates they will very likely be needed before the 94th Congress convenes. I hope this Congress will recognize its responsibility in this important area.

TRADE

Action is urgently needed on the *Trade Reform Act* which I consider absolutely essential to our economic health. Our trading partners in the industrial and less-developed world are waiting to see whether we can negotiate multilateral solutions to the common economic problems which plague us, as well as make much-needed improvements in the trading system. The unacceptable alternative is economic warfare from which no winners would emerge.

I urge the Senate to move as quickly as possible to adopt the Trade Reform Act, and to forego any encumbering amendments. If the Senate acts promptly—and only if it does—there will be sufficient time remaining in this Congress for both Houses to agree on a final measure.

TAXES

The Congress has before it the tax reform proposals sent up in April 1973; the windfall profits tax proposals submitted in December 1973, and the economy strengthening and stabilizing proposals which I recommended last month.

The economic proposals of last month include surtaxes on all corporations and on individuals with well above-average incomes. They call for change in the investment tax credit and in the tax treatment of certain limited kinds of preferred stock.

My individual surtax proposal, I must emphasize, would apply only to families and single persons whose incomes exceed $15,000 and $7,500, respectively, and only to that portion of their actual income above those levels. It is a very progressive tax proposal which takes much more from high bracket taxpayers than middle income taxpayers. Low bracket taxpayers would be exempt. With a $16,000 income, for example, a family of four would pay a surtax of only $3. On the other hand, a family of four with a $50,000 income would pay $482 of surtax.

I also urge Congress to enact the windfall profits tax proposals so that we will not forever lose the chance to recapture a part of the excessive profits that domestic oil producers realize this year. I reiterate my support for eliminating the foreign depletion allowance.

I have asked the Secretary of the Treasury to work with the congressional committees concerned to develop balanced legislation, including additional tax reductions for low-income individuals.

FINANCIAL INSTITUTIONS

There is great need for action on an Administration proposal to strengthen and revitalize banks and thrift institutions through the elimination of certain Federal regulations which impede efficiency and healthy competition. While retaining appropriate safeguards to assure solvency and liquidity, the proposed *Financial Institutions Act* would allow more competition in our banking system to benefit the small saver as well as the institutions themselves. This could also make additional dollars available to the private citizen and to industry.

Further, this proposal would provide the added incentive of the mortgage interest tax credit for our financial institutions to enable them to devote their resources to home mortgages and thus curb the wide and disruptive swings in home mortgage credit availability.

REGULATION

The Congress has before it my proposal to establish a one-year National Commission on Regulatory Reform to examine the practices and procedures of the independent regulatory commissions. It has become clear that many regulatory activities of the Government are themselves stifling competition and producing higher prices without comparable social benefits. I urge this Congress to complete action on this important legislation. Such a Commission, to be composed of Congressional, Executive, and public members, should start now to formulate realistic proposals for reform of our regulatory system for early consideration by the next Congress.

FOOD

Food prices concern everyone. The Congress must act rapidly to not only increase food production but to remove impediments to the maximum production of peanut and rice crops.

I am also recommending that we amend *Public Law 480*, the Food for Peace program. Additional flexibility is clearly needed to assure that our food aid programs can continue to serve the national interest and humanitarian goals.

COMPETITION

Activities which are illegal under the Sherman Anti-Trust Act disrupt the natural competitive forces in the marketplace and invariably result in higher prices to the American consumer. The Justice Department's antitrust efforts against monopolies and activities which operate in restraint of trade must be strengthened.

The maximum allowable penalties for violation of the Sherman Anti-Trust Act should be increased from $50,000 to $1 million for corporations and from $50,000 to $100,000 for individuals. Maximum prison sentences for individual violations should also be increased to five years.

Current estimates by the Immigration and Naturalization Service indicate that there are some 4 to 7 million illegal aliens in the United States. Prompt action on a pending illegal alien bill would help solve this critical problem by providing sanctions against the hiring of illegal aliens. This would make more jobs available for our own citizens.

STOCKPILING

The General Services Administration has submitted stockpile disposal bills for silver, lead and tin. These would permit sale of stockpile quantities that clearly exceed our national security needs. This additional authority will assure adequate supplies of these commodities and also dampen excessive price fluctuations. The additional disposal authority for silver, lead, and tin would also provide potential budget receipts of $1.4 billion, of which about $150 million could be realized in fiscal year 1975 if legislation is enacted by the end of this year.

HOUSING

I thank the Congress for promptly enacting housing legislation making conventional mortgages eligible for purchase by the Government National Mortgage Association. This is giving the housing and real estate industry much needed support, even though the Act did not cover apartments and condominiums. I urge you to consider legislation to correct this omission.

ENERGY

In addition to my deep concern over the economy, I am committed to resolving the problems of achieving sufficient energy supplies for ourselves and our children. I repeat my earlier requests for action during this session on several energy bills under consideration.

First, we need legislation to help increase the supply of natural gas and permit competitive pricing of these new supplies. Our worsening shortages are directly attributable to more than 20 years of unsuccessful Federal regulation of natural gas. Unless we remove Federal regulatory impediments with respect to new sources, supplies of environmentally clean natural gas will remain in the ground. The shortage of natural gas is already forcing curtailment of service to industry in many areas, resulting in increasing unemployment and greater use of imported oil. New homes are being denied natural gas service, forcing the use of alternative fuels that are more costly and far less clean.

I urge the Congress to complete action quickly on legislation to establish a system of permits for the construction and operation of deepwater ports. This system is a far superior means—from both a cost and environmental point of view—for handling that portion of oil which we cannot avoid importing for some years ahead. I have asked the Secretaries of Interior and Transportation to work with the Senate and House conferees to develop a bill that I can sign within the next few weeks.

Last March, legislation was proposed to speed the licensing and construction of nuclear plants, allow more meaningful public participation at early decision points relating to their design and siting and encourage standardization of new nuclear plants. I urge that the Congress pass this bill to speed the development of domestic energy supplies, reduce dependence on imported oil, and help hold down electrical power costs.

The House and Senate conferees are now addressing the difficult issues in the proposed *Surface Mining Act*. I am still hopeful that the conferees can agree on provisions which strike a reasonable balance between our desire for environmental protection and reclamation and the need to increase the production of domestic coal supplies.

I must emphasize that some provisions of the bills now in conference are not acceptable. I have asked the Secretary of the Interior to continue working with the conferees to develop a bill which I can sign.

As a necessary step toward conserving fuel and saving lives, I urge the Congress to make permanent the 55 mile-per-hour speed limit. I also ask the House of Representatives to approve an extension of the carpooling provisions in the *Emergency Highway Energy Conservation Act* which expires December 31, 1974.

I have asked the Secretaries of Interior, Defense and Navy to work with the Congress in finding satisfactory ways of dealing with our emergency petroleum reserves to balance our domestic energy needs. We must proceed with development of the oil reserves at Elk Hills, California, and with exploration and development of the reserve in northern Alaska. We must not wait for another energy crisis to force action, perhaps too late, on these vital resources.

Appropriations

There are four regular appropriations bills still to be enacted—*Agriculture-Environmental and Consumer Protection, Labor-HEW, Military Construction and Foreign Assistance*—and the important *First Supplemental Appropriations* bill.

Action has not yet been completed in the Senate on the Agriculture-Environmental and Consumer Protection Appropriation Bill for fiscal year 1975. This bill was vetoed by President Nixon on August 8th because it would have substantially increased Federal spending. I urge the Congress to complete action on this appropriation measure as soon as possible within reasonable funding limits.

The Labor-HEW and Related Agencies Appropriations bill is currently in conference. Unfortunately, the totals are excessive. Unless the Congress reduces funding in both the House and Senate versions, I will have no choice but to veto this measure.

Appropriations now pending for Military Construction and Foreign Assistance should be given high priority.

The First Supplemental Appropriation bill has passed the House and is pending on the Senate calendar. However, I am concerned about the inflationary aspects of the Senate version and hope final action will produce an acceptable bill.

Vetoes

During the adjournment, it was necessary for me to pocket veto five bills. Two were private relief measures and three were legislative issues: National Wildlife Refuge System, Farm Labor Contractor Registration, and Rehabilitation Act Amendments.

I have determined on advice of the Attorney General that the absence of my signature from these bills prevented them from becoming law. Without in any way qualifying this determination, I also returned them without approval to those designated by the Congress to receive messages during the adjournment period.

If the Congress should elect to challenge these vetoes by overriding them, there could be a prolonged legal uncertainty over this legislation. However, I would welcome new legislation to replace the measures which were vetoed.

Specifically, while the *Farm Labor Contractor Registration Act Amendments* contained worthwhile provisions to protect migrant farm workers, an unrelated rider arbitrarily would have reclassified and elevated certain Federal employees to important Administrative Law Judge positions, regardless of their qualifications. I, therefore, urge the Congress to pass the essential sections of the vetoed bill without the personnel provision which would create serious pay inequities by legislatively overcompensating a particular class of employees in one executive department.

Similarly, the intent of the *Rehabilitation Act Amendments* section of H.R. 14225 is worthwhile. But the features which would force the creation of new and unnecessary bureaucracies in the Department of Health, Education and Welfare prompted my veto.

I have requested the Secretary of HEW to work with Congressional leaders in an effort to correct the serious difficulties in administration and accountability contained in the vetoed bill.

Although it was necessary to return to the Congress without my approval the *Freedom of Information Act Amendments* on October 17th, the day the Congress adjourned, I continue to endorse the intent of that legislation. I have already submitted to the Congress amendments which would eliminate the national security information problems and the damage to effective law enforcement inherent in the bill which I vetoed. I pledge the full efforts of the Administration in working out a fair, responsible way to increase public access to Federal papers and records without impairing individual rights and essential Government activities.

Just before adjournment, I also vetoed the *Atomic Energy Act Amendments*. I objected to a provision I consider to be unconstitutional. Because of this provision, the bill would not have become effective, even had I approved it, unless a Joint Committee of the Congress subsequently took affirmative action. I urge passage of a new measure removing the constitutional objection to section 12 of the vetoed bill, thereby eliminating the legal uncertainties which would becloud the entire nuclear energy program.

During the adjournment, I signed into law a bill overhauling the *Commodity Exchange Act*. This is an important step to assure full confidence in Federal regulation of commodity futures trading. Nevertheless, there are several provisions which need revision. First is the requirement for concurrent submission to the Congress and to the President of both the new Commission's budget and legislative proposals, and second is the need for Senate confirmation of a non-Presidential appointee. These provisions run contrary to good management of the Executive Branch by the President and the traditional separation of powers. I hope these Constitutional and policy questions can be resolved.

Other Major Legislation

In addition to pending nominations, economic legislation and energy issues, there are a number of other important bills awaiting final action by the Congress.

In today's world, all nations are interdependent. The United States owes it to itself, as well as to others, to provide military and economic assistance which may mean the difference between stability and instability in a global or regional context. Where there is instability, there is danger—danger of conflict which can involve the greatest as well as the smallest.

The *Foreign Aid Authorization* bill before you represents a sincere effort to reflect the realities of today's world. It remains my assessment of the minimum which is needed to sustain our peaceful objectives.

I urge the Congress to move quickly to enact legislation which will help to achieve these objectives and meet our moral, political and security obligations. If such legislation is to enable us to effectively carry forward the foreign policy of the Nation, it must not tie the hands of the President nor restrict his authority and ability to act when action is called for.

Also important to the achievement of our objectives overseas is legislation to enable the United States to contribute its fair share to the various multilateral development institutions and, at the same time, provide continued incentives to other nations to join in these international assistance efforts.

In order for the United States to maintain its strong position in foreign markets, it is important that the Congress pass the Export-Import Bank bill and avoid attaching unnecessary encumbrances.

The Congress is making good progress on the Administration's proposal to improve the regulatory climate in an important portion of the transportation industry. *The Surface Transportation Act*, as reported by the House Committee on Interstate and Foreign Commerce, is a beginning in the overall area of regulatory reform. This bill, with certain modifications to insure greater reliance on competitive market forces, would contribute substantially to the efficiency and vitality of this Nation's railroad system. I urge the Congress to complete its work on this vital legislation without waiting for the establishment of the National Commission on Regulatory Reform.

Earlier this year, legislation was submitted to provide reasonable increases in the size and weights of trucks traveling on interstate highways. These increases were to offset the economic disadvantages to truckers resulting from lower permissible speed and higher fuel costs. The Senate passed a bill containing most of the features of the Administration's proposal while a similar bill did not pass in the House. I ask the Congress for early action on this issue in the interest of economic efficiency and fuel conservation.

I also urge the Congress to act promptly to pass the *National Mass Transportation Assistance Act of 1974*. This bill has been developed through close cooperation between the Congress and the Administration. It will provide the Nation's cities with the Federal financial assistance needed to help them meet priority urban mass transportation needs. This bill establishes a long-term assistance program for mass transit—actually, for six years—and distributes a significant portion of the funds according to a simple and equitable formula. It also provides for an enhanced role for the Governors and local officials in mass transit decisions.

I consider the total dollar level of $11.8 billion over a six-year period to be at the upper limits of fiscal responsibility. The needs of the cities and the uncertainties and delays that would result from waiting until the next Congress for a transit bill make it imperative that this Congress act before adjournment sine die.

In 1972, the Judicial Conference of the United States recommended the creation of 51 additional Federal District Court judgeships in 33 separate judicial districts across the country. Senate hearings on legislation incorporating this proposal were concluded in 1973. To date, however, this legislation has not been scheduled for floor action. The increasing backlog in the Federal courts makes this measure an urgent national necessity of a non-partisan nature—for justice delayed is too often justice denied.

Earlier this session, the House passed a bill to codify, for the first time in our history, evidentiary rules governing the admissibility of proof in Federal courts. This bill is the culmination of some 13 years of study by distinguished judges, lawyers, Members of the Congress and others interested in and affected by the administration of justice in the Federal system. The measure will lend uniformity, accessibility, intelligibility and a basis for reform and growth in our evidentiary rules which are sadly lacking in current law. I strongly urge final action on this important bill prior to the conclusion of this Congress.

With respect to the *Vietnam Era Veterans' Readjustment Assistance Act,* I urge the Congress to reconsider the action it has taken to date and send me instead legislation providing a straightforward 18.2 percent cost of living increase, effective January 1, 1975. Increased payments for our veterans in school are necessary. But while acknowledging our great debt to those who served during the Vietnam era, I must insist on a fiscally responsible bill on behalf of all Americans. I object to the inflationary 22.7 percent rate increase, retroactive to September 1, 1974, the direct loan program which the Congress has added and the extension of educational benefits allowing Vietnam era veterans to attend school for 45 instead of the present 36 months. This extra entitlement goes beyond the standard for World War II and Korea veterans.

The Energy Transportation Security Act of 1974 would require a percentage of imported petroleum to be carried on U.S. vessels. Although I fully support a strong U.S. merchant marine, I am seriously concerned about problems which this bill raises in the areas of foreign relations, national security, and perhaps most significantly, the potential inflationary impact of cargo preference.

Administration officials have testified during congressional hearings on our concerns about the impact of this bill.

The House-Senate conferees adopted new language concerning the waiver provision so that the requirements of this bill "may be temporarily waived by the President upon determination that an emergency exists justifying such a waiver in the national interest." However, the legislative history of the waiver does not expressly demonstrate that the Congress intends it to be broad in scope.

The potential problems which could arise if this bill becomes law require a provision which will permit the President to waive its requirements for economic as well as foreign affairs and national defense reasons. Since the waiver language in the bill is not explicit, the Conference Committee Report should make it clear that the Congress intends to grant broad waiver authority.

Other provisions in the bill which concern me are: the narrowness of the definition of which ships are eligible to participate in this trade, the rebate of oil import fees and the unnecessary anti-pollution requirement that vessels serving certain ports be built with expensive double bottoms.

Another measure on which action is required is comprehensive health insurance. I will continue to seek agreement with the Congress on legislation centered on principles incorporated in the Comprehensive Health Insurance Plan. To keep this program from feeding inflation, however, the Congress will have to join with me in cutting Federal expenditures before we can afford this program.

Included in the *Military Construction Authorization* and *Appropriation* bills now before the Congress are funds for completing projects and initiating new ones at installations in 42 States and the District of Columbia. I reiterate my strong conviction that the limited expansion of facilities on Diego Garcia in the Indian Ocean is of critical importance.

Conclusion

This list of legislative priorities represents a streamlined action program for the Nation. To achieve results will require partnership, not partisanship, on the part of both the executive and the legislative branches. It will mean long days and nights of hard work—of communication, conciliation, compromise, and cooperation between the White House and the Congress, the House and the Senate, and majority and minority within the Congress itself.

But it must be done for one overriding reason: America needs these actions. And the American people rightly expect us to do everything we can to accomplish them.

I pledge my full cooperation with the Congress in the weeks ahead. I am confident that the Congress will respond in the same spirit.

GERALD R. FORD

The White House,
November 17, 1974.

NOTE: The text of the message was released November 18, 1974.

241

Statement on Sugar Imports. *November 18, 1974*

I AM announcing actions designed to (1) insure the continued flow of sugar into this country from abroad and (2) encourage increased production domestically at the same time. The actions I am taking will maintain duties on sugar imports at the lowest permissible rate under the Tariff Schedules of the United States.

The Sugar Act is scheduled to expire on December 31, 1974. If no action is taken, tariffs on imported sugar will rise about 1.3 cents per pound on January 1, 1975. The law provides, however, that the President can continue the current rates in force if his proclamation extending the rates includes a quota on sugar imports. I have, therefore, decided to extend the current tariff rates and will set an annual global quota of 7 million short tons for 1975. That quantity is more than adequate to meet anticipated import requirements. At the same time, it will ensure a degree of stability for our own sugar industry to operate effectively in a period of very tight supplies.

Although there is no risk we will run out of sugar, we may well experience higher prices than we would like until production catches up with demand. Users of sugar can help ease prices by buying wisely, conserving supplies, and consuming less sugar. I urge all Americans to reduce the amount of sugar in cooking and to put in half the amount usually used to sweeten coffee or tea.

The world sugar supply has tightened markedly in recent months. For the past 3 crop years, world sugar production has been rising. But even so, consumption has exceeded production by a small margin. Crop setbacks this year in a number of countries will prevent production from keeping pace with the normal growth of consumption. Since sugar production this year is expected to be about the same as last, worldwide sugar supplies will continue to be tight. Because we in this country import about one-half of the sugar we consume, we are directly affected by this worldwide problem. So far this year, our foreign suppliers have shipped 10 percent more sugar to the United States than last year.

The Council on Wage and Price Stability is working with sugar-using industries to stimulate conservation in the use of sugar. The Council will also hold public hearings to examine the margins charged by sugar processors, refiners, and distributors. The purpose of these hearings will be to ensure that the retail prices of sugar and sugar products are not unduly increased.

In the past, sharp increases in sugar prices have always been temporary, because they stimulated offsetting production increases of sugarcane and sugar beets. I have asked Secretary Butz to ensure that all American farmers are made aware of the excellent market opportunities offered by sugar beets and sugarcane and to make sure that there are no governmental impediments to increased production.

Early season contracting between farmers and processors could be very helpful in 1975, and long-term contracting between U.S. refiners and foreign suppliers could be very beneficial as well. Our traditional foreign sugar suppliers who have benefited from our sugar program in the past are also urged to continue providing sugar to our market.

Finally, I have directed the Economic Policy Board to monitor the sugar situation on a weekly basis and to report to me any signs of speculation or market activity in world and domestic markets that would worsen the tight supply situation we face this year.

The Administration recognized the inconveniences worked on the average American citizen by the current sugar situation. It will continue to do everything it can to improve matters and to remove some of the uncertainties for the future.

NOTE: On November 16, 1974, the President signed Proclamation 4334, providing for the establishment of tariffs and quota on certain sugars, sirups, and molasses.

242

Message to the Congress Reporting on the Balance of Payments Deficit Incurred Under the North Atlantic Treaty. *November 18, 1974*

To the Congress of the United States:

In accordance with Section 812(d) of the Department of Defense Appropriation Authorization Act, 1974 (Public Law 93–155), I am pleased to submit a report to the Congress on our further progress toward offsetting the balance of payments deficit resulting from the deployment of U.S. forces in NATO Europe.

I am now able to provide you with figures for U.S. expenditures in NATO Europe during fiscal year 1974. These figures were compiled by the Department of Commerce in consultation with the Department of Defense and the General Accounting Office. They indicate that in FY 74 the expenditures resulting from the deployment of U.S. forces in fulfillment of our NATO commitments and obligations amounted to $1,983 million (including preliminary fourth quarter data subject to revision). Attached to this report is an appendix showing how this figure was derived and what adjustments were made to conform our normal expenditure data to the letter and intent of Section 812. Minor changes in this data may occur as final quarter fiscal year 1974 figures are confirmed during the next few weeks.

As President Nixon reported to the Congress on May 16, 1974, the offset agreement concluded in April 1974 with the Federal Republic of Germany had a dollar value of approximately $2.22 billion over fiscal years 1974 and 1975. Of that amount, the fiscal year 1974 portion, approximating $1.1 billion, will be directly applicable toward meeting the requirements of Section 812, leaving approximately $883 million to be offset by our other European NATO allies.

As I noted in my report of August 20, 1974, the NATO Economic Directorate, at the direction of the North Atlantic Council, has established a mechanism for identifying allied purchases of military-related items from the United States. This was an essential step to enable us to comply with the requirements of Section 812. Representatives of the Economic Directorate consulted in Washington on October 21–22 with the Departments of State, Commerce and Defense and reported that approximately $1,050 million in purchases by allies other than the Federal Republic of Germany have been identified.

The Departments of Commerce and Defense have sought to confirm this figure by examining the U.S. balance of payments accounts and records in an effort to identify balance of payments receipts reflecting military-related sales and exports to our European NATO allies, on both a government-to-government and commercial category basis. However, this data is still incomplete and the U.S. accounting system in many cases is too aggregated to identify all of the specific purchases and payments made by the European members of NATO. For this reason our calculation of the final offset total will take into account the information being provided through the NATO Economic Directorate by our European NATO allies. On the basis of the foregoing, I continue to expect that the requirements of Section 812 will be met.

GERALD R. FORD

The White House,
November 17, 1974.

APPENDIX

A. U.S. Defense Expenditures Entering the International Balance of Payments in NATO Europe During Fiscal Year 1974, (in millions of dollars):	
Personal expenditures by US Military and Civilian Personnel and their Dependents	815
Payments to Foreign Nationals for direct and contract hire	561
Major Equipment purchased in NATO Europe	81
Construction	75
NATO Infrastructure System Payments	76
Petroleum Products (includes cost of crude oil imported into Europe)	137
Materials and Supplies	148
Payments to US and foreign contractors for contractual services	444
All Other Payments (net)	66
Total for Fiscal Year 1974 (preliminary)	2, 403
B. Deductions Made Pursuant to Section 812 for Expenditures not Resulting From the Deployment of US Forces in Fulfillment of our NATO Commitments and Obligations (in millions of dollars):	
Expenditures for US activities not related to NATO such as US strategic forces in NATO countries	279
Major equipment purchased in NATO Europe and imported into the US and unrelated to US troop deployments in Europe	81
Expenditures in NATO Europe for the afloat operations of the Sixth Fleet for US strategic purposes	60
Total for Fiscal Year 1974 (preliminary)	420
C. Expenditures Less Deductions	1, 983

NOTE: The text of the message was released November 18, 1974.

243

Letter Accepting Withdrawal of the Nomination of Daniel T. Kingsley To Be a Member of the Federal Power Commission. *November 19, 1974*

Dear Dan:

I accept with deep regret your request that I not resubmit your name in nomination as a Commissioner of the Federal Power Commission. I very much appreciate the generous spirit which prompted your decision.

During your time in government, both at GSA and in the White House, you have been admired by your colleagues for the quality and diligence of your efforts. Your performance of difficult duties has earned great respect. I am hopeful that you will find it possible to serve the Administration in some other capacity so that we may continue to benefit from the contributions you can make to government.

With warm regards.

Sincerely,

GERALD R. FORD

NOTE: The letters, dated November 16, 1974, were released November 19. Mr. Kingsley's letter read as follows:

Dear Mr. President:

I am deeply grateful for your continued support of my nomination to the Federal Power Commission. However, I believe the time has now come for me to respectfully request that you not resubmit this nomination. I make this request without any concern whatsoever that I would not be confirmed by the Senate, but with the knowledge that any confirmation hearings of one who has been associated with the White House for the last three years, however spotless his record may be, are subject to the natural controversy that is the unfortunate product of the political climate of the last two years. In my opinion, the importance to the country of your legislative program, the confirmation of your other outstanding nominees, and the general spirit of harmony and cooperation with the Congress does not allow the luxury of the possible controversy that might result from my confirmation hearings.

Mr. President, you have made a remarkable record under the most trying circumstances in your first one hundred days in office. I can assure you that as you continue to seek the objectives of lasting peace and a genuine prosperity at home, you will have my total and enthusiastic support.

Sincerely yours,

DANIEL T. KINGSLEY
Special Assistant to the President

[The President, The White House, Washington, D.C. 20500]

244

Toast at a Luncheon Hosted by Prime Minister Kakuei Tanaka of Japan in Tokyo. *November 19, 1974*

Mr. Prime Minister, Excellencies, gentlemen:

The reception that I received upon arriving in Japan and the warm reception received during the day today is further proof of the great hospitality that the Japanese people have for the Americans.

This very kind and gracious hospitality, this warm reception is typical of the attitude of the Japanese Government and the Japanese people. When I stopped in Anchorage on the way to Japan, the last words I said to my fellow Americans were that although Japan and the United States were separated by the broadest of oceans, they were, on the other hand, the warmest of friends.

Mr. Prime Minister, you spent many years in your parliament, and I spent better than 25 years in the Congress of the United States. I have a great liking for the Congress. I called it my home outside of the home.

I can't speak with any personal relationship to the Congress a hundred plus years ago when they were alleged to be lacking in civilization, but I would have to say in defense of the Congress today: Whether I agree with what they do or not, they are better behaved. [*Laughter*]

Let me assure you, Mr. Prime Minister, that Mrs. Ford deeply regrets that she is not with me on this trip. She had long looked forward to visiting Japan, meeting the Japanese people, and she is terribly disappointed that it is impossible for her to be here on this occasion. I spoke with her on the telephone this morning. That didn't help any, because of her desire to be here. But I can say that she is here in spirit if not in person, and she will come on some other occasion.

Mr. Prime Minister, the United States is a nation of citizens with many backgrounds, many ancestries. Some of our very finest citizens have a Japanese ancestry. We are proud of the tremendous contributions that they make to a better America. We are proud of them because of the significant contributions they have made to our culture, to our industry, to our trade, to our education, and to our government.

Mr. Prime Minister, the dialog that we began in Washington and which we have continued here in Tokyo indicates that we have many, many basic ties and many areas of common purpose. We have many problems, but the frank and open discussions that we have had and will continue to have involving areas of prosperity on a worldwide basis and peace on a global basis are beneficial to your country and to ours and to the world as a whole.

Our two countries, by working together, can significantly contribute to world peace, and we will. Our two nations, cooperating with one another, can make a significant contribution to prosperity in both of our countries and to the world at large.

Mr. Prime Minister, we must discuss and coordinate our economic policies in an era of energy shortages and some international monetary crises. We must work together in order to produce and distribute, make available the need of mankind for food throughout the world.

Mr. Prime Minister, we must join together in helping those nations throughout the world that are less fortunate than we. We have in the past, and we will expand those efforts in the future.

In contemplating these problems, the expansion of peace and the betterment of the world economically, it is good to know that we can discuss the issues and problems in an attitude and an atmosphere of mutual understanding in a spirit of good will.

Mr. Prime Minister, let us join in a toast which honors the friendship and the collaboration between our people and our nations. This is a characterization of what is good for all and in the best interests of each.

To Japan.

NOTE: The President spoke at 2:45 p.m. at a luncheon hosted by Prime Minister Kakuei Tanaka. No transcript was issued of the Prime Minister's toast.

245

Toast at a Banquet at the Imperial Palace. *November 19, 1974*

Your Majesties:

I am honored to be the guest of Your Imperial Majesties, and it is with a very deep sense of this special moment that I speak this evening.

The first state visit of an American President to Japan is an occasion of very great importance to all Americans. Your gracious hospitality symbolically honors the 213 million Americans that I have the honor to represent. I can reassure Japan that the United States is determined to perpetuate the unique ties that link our two nations for the common good.

Though separated by the broadest of oceans, Your Majesty, we have achieved between our two nations the closest of friendships. Our relationships transcend that of governments and heads of state. Each year, the ties binding Americans with Japanese increase in trade, science, culture, sports, and many other areas, including cherished personal contacts between individuals.

We share a common devotion to moral and to spiritual strength. Our paths are not always identical, but they all lead in the same direction—that of world peace and harmonious relations among mankind.

Let us continue to seek understanding with each other and among all peoples, Your Majesty. Let us trade, let us share and perpetuate the prosperity of both nations. Let us work together to solve common problems, recognizing the interdependence of the modern world in which we all live.

America, I can assure you, Your Majesty, is determined to do its part. It is in a spirit of respect, a spirit of admiration for the Japanese nation, in dedication of our continuing collaboration, and with sincere and deep-felt confidence in the future that I offer a toast to the health and to the well-being of your Imperial Majesties.

NOTE: The President spoke at 8:56 p.m. at the Imperial Palace in Tokyo at a dinner banquet hosted by Emperor Hirohito and Empress Nagako.

246

Remarks at a Japan Press Club Luncheon. *November 20, 1974*

AS THE first American President to visit Japan while in office, I greet you on this unprecedented occasion. I thank the Japanese Press Club for inviting me and the national television network of Japan for the opportunity to speak directly to the people of Japan.

I deeply appreciate the excellent coverage of my visit by the exceptional news media of Japan. I have always sought a good working relationship with the American journalists and have the same feeling toward their Japanese colleagues. It has been my objective at all times to treat journalists and all other people in the same manner that I would like to be treated.

I bring the warmest greetings of the American people. Our bipartisan political leadership in the American Congress sends its very best wishes. The distinguished leaders of both of America's national political parties have asked me to tell you of the very high value that all Americans attach to our partnership with Japan.

It is the American custom for the President to make a report every year to the Congress on our state of the Union. In the same spirit, I thought the people in Japan might welcome a report on the state of another union—the unity of American and Japanese mutual aspirations for friendship as Americans see that relationship.

In my hometown of Grand Rapids, Michigan, a Japanese company is now assembling musical instruments. Not only are the instruments harmonious in the melodies that they produce but the labor-management relationship followed by the Japanese created a model of harmony between workers and business.

In a nearby community, Edmore, another Japanese firm is manufacturing small electrical motors. This is yet another Japanese enterprise that has injected new energy, new good will in our industrial life. There are similar examples throughout America, and we welcome them.

The time has long passed when Americans speak only of what we contributed to your society. Today, traffic flows in both directions. We are both learning from each other.

To signify the value the United States attaches to partnership with Japan, I chose this to make my first overseas trip. I also met with your Ambassador to the United States on the first day that I assumed office, August 9.

I have long admired the richness and the diversity of Japan's culture, the products of your industry, the ingenuity, creativity, and the energy of your people, your courage as a fountain of resourcefulness in a very troubled world.

My only regret is that Mrs. Ford could not join me on this visit in response to your very kind invitation. We both hope that she can come at some later date.

Americans are very proud of the way that we and the Japanese have worked together during the postwar period. We have had some disagreements, but we have remained friends and we have remained partners. Together we created conditions under which both nations could prosper. Together we expanded our relations in trade and in travel.

The reality of America's economic, political, and strategic interdependence with Japan is very obvious. America is Japan's greatest customer and supplier. Japan is America's greatest overseas trading partner. Japan is the best foreign customer for America's agricultural products.

The total trade between our two nations has doubled since 1970. It will surpass $20 billion in 1974. American investments in Japan are the largest of any foreign state. Japan's investment in America is growing rapidly and accounts for one-fifth of all Japanese investment abroad.

The flow of Japanese visitors to the United States has grown from some 50,000 in 1966 to over 700,000 in 1974. This is also a two-way street: Over 350,000 Americans visited Japan last year, accounting for nearly one-half of all foreign visitors.

Together we removed the legacies of World War II. The reversion of Okinawa eliminated the last vestige of that war from our agenda. We have made independent but mutually compatible efforts to improve our relations with the Soviet Union and the People's Republic of China. We have devised better channels for open consultation. I particularly want you to know that I understand the dangers of taking each other for granted.

As we talk to each other, we must ask each other what we regard as the central needs of our time.

First, of course, is peace. Americans and Japanese know the value of peace. We want to devote our resources and ourselves to building things, not tearing them down. We do not want to send our sons into battle again.

The alliance between Japan and the United States has helped to secure peace and can contribute to help secure it. That alliance is not directed against any other country. It does not prevent us from improving our relations with other countries.

Our alliance does not signify that both nations subscribe fully to identical attitudes or identical styles. It does signify, however, that we clearly share a common resolve to maintain stability in East Asia, to help in the development of other countries that need our help, and to work together to encourage diplomatic and political rather than military solutions to world problems.

Our alliance was forged by people who saw their national interest in friendship and in cooperation. I am confident that our relations will remain solid and very substantial. I pledge that we shall work to make it so.

Peace, however, cannot be our sole concern. We have learned that there are many international threats and dangers that can affect the lives of our citizens. We face dwindling supplies of raw materials and food. We face international economic problems of great complexity. We must be more stringent in conservation than ever before.

We worked together to solve the problems of the cold war. We succeeded because we worked together. Now we confront these new and even more complicated problems.

The Japanese reformer, Sakuma Shozan, wrote some lines in 1854 that provide an insight for 1974. Sakuma said, and I quote: When I was 20 I knew that men were linked together in one province; when I was 30 I knew that they were linked together in one nation; when I was 40 I knew that they were linked together in one world of five continents.

Now, 120 years later, the links between nations are closer than ever. Modern technology has made the world one. What each man or each nation does or fails to do affects every other.

Some Americans wondered why I decided to accept your invitation to come to Japan at a time when we have unsolved problems at home. I replied to those Americans that many of the problems we have at home are not just American problems but the problems of the world as a whole. Like others, we suffer from inflation. Like others, we face recession. Like others, we have to deal with rising prices and potential shortages of fuels and raw materials.

America cannot solve those problems alone. Nations can only solve those problems by working together. Just as we worked together to maintain peace, we can work together to solve tomorrow's problems.

Our two nations provide the world with a model of what can be achieved by international cooperation. We can also provide a model for dealing with the new difficulties. We both have great technological skills and human resources, great energy and great imagination. We both acknowledge the responsibility to developing states. We envisage the orderly and peaceful sharing of essential natural resources. We can work together to meet the global economic issues.

We believe that we are not just temporary allies; we are permanent friends. We share the same goals—peace, development, stability, and prosperity. These are not only praiseworthy and essential goals but common goals.

The problems of peace and economic well-being are inextricably linked. We believe peace cannot exist without prosperity, prosperity cannot exist without peace, and neither can exist if the great states of the world do not work together to achieve them. We owe this to ourselves, to each other, and to all of the Japanese and the American peoples.

America and Japan share the same national pastime—baseball. In the game of baseball, two teams compete. But neither can play without the other, nor without common respect for each other and for the rules of the game.

I have taken the liberty of giving you my views on the world we live in. Now, let me tell you, the Japanese people, a little bit about the American people. The American people have faced some difficult times in our history. They know they will face others in the future. Their burdens are enormous, both at home and abroad. Some observers, including American observers, say that Americans have lost their confidence, their sense of responsibility, and their creativity. It is not true.

I have traveled over much of my country during the past year. Each time I return to Washington refreshed. Our people are determined and realistic; our people are vigorous. They are solving their problems in countless towns and cities across the country. They continue to understand that history has placed great responsibilities on American shoulders. Americans are ready and willing to play their part with the same strength and the same will that they have always shown in the past.

Americans also know that no nation, however strong, can hope to dictate the course of history by itself. But the ability to understand the basic issue, to define our national interest, and to make common cause with others to achieve common purposes makes it possible to influence events. And Americans are determined to do that for the constructive purposes and in the true spirit of interdependence.

In that spirit, let me make a pledge to you today. As we face the problems of the future, the United States will remain faithful in our commitments and firm in the pursuit of our common goals. We intend not only to remain a trustworthy ally but a reliable trading partner.

We will continue to be suppliers of the goods you need. If shortages occur, we will take special account of the needs of our traditional trading partners. We will not compete with our friends for their markets or for their resources. We want to work with them.

The basic concepts of our foreign policy remain unchanged. Those concepts have a solid bipartisan and popular support. The American people remain strong, confident, and faithful. We may sometimes falter, but we will not fail.

Let me, if I might, end on a personal note. It is a privilege to be the first American President to visit Japan while in office. It is also a very great pleasure. I look forward to seeing Kyoto, the ancient capital of Japan.

Japan has preserved her cultural integrity in the face of rapid modernization. I have never believed all change is necessarily good. We must try to apply the enduring values of the past to the challenges and to the pressures of our times. Americans can learn from Japan to respect traditions even as we, like you, plunge ahead in the last quarter of the 20th century.

I also look forward to another deep privilege. Yesterday, during my call upon His Imperial Majesty, the Emperor of Japan, I renewed our invitation for the Emperor to visit the United States. It would be a great pleasure to be the first American President to welcome the Emperor of Japan to Washington and to show His Imperial Majesty our national shrines and treasures, including the graceful Japanese cherry trees whose blossoms provide a setting for the monuments to the great heroes of our own past.

I hope that my visit shall be the first of many by American Presidents. I hope that the leaders of our two countries will follow the example that our peoples have already set, to visit each other frequently and freely as our nations move together to deal with the many common problems and concerns that will affect the lives of all our citizens and all humanity.

I said in my first Presidential address to the Congress that my Administration was based on communication, conciliation, compromise, and cooperation. This concept also guides my view of American policy toward Japan. We both have much work to do. Let us do it together. Let us also continue the quest for peace. I would rather walk a thousand miles for peace than take a single step toward war.

I thank you.

NOTE: The President spoke at 12:05 p.m. at the Imperial Hotel in Tokyo. His remarks were broadcast live on Japanese television.

247

Toast at a Reception for Members of the Diet. *November 20, 1974*

Mr. Speakers:

I am deeply grateful for the very kind remarks and the toast given to me and to my country. It is very significant that I have an opportunity of joining with the members of your Diet.

I am sure all of you have recognized that I spent a quarter of a century of my political life as a member of our legislative body, the House of Representatives—or your parliament.

This was a great experience for me. I think it is quite significant, in addition, that the first American President who visited your great country was an individual who had spent some time in the parliament or the legislature, the House of Representatives and the United States Senate, as Vice President.

This, in my judgment, gives a President a broad perspective of the problems, of the solutions. It has always been my feeling that a person who has served in a parliament or in a legislative body is extremely well-qualified to understand the views of the people of a country, a person who is well-qualified to seek a consensus or a solution to the problems, whether they be at home or abroad.

One of my very top staff members, a number of years ago—Mr. Rumsfeld—initiated with members from your parliament, an exchange between Japanese parliamentarians and legislators from our Congress. It is my judgment that this exchange is a very, very important way of building a constructive relationship between your country and our country.

I was never privileged to participate in the Japanese-American interparliamentary group or exchange group, as I understand it is called. I did have an opportunity as a Member of the House of Representatives—our Congress—to be a member of the Interparliamentary Union delegation on three or four occasions. And I found this exchange between parliamentarians of great benefit, a tremendous asset, and I hope and trust that in the years ahead this exchange between members of parliamentary groups will broaden, will be more extensive. It will be very helpful to each country, to all countries.

Let me conclude by saying that I am honored to be among a group that I grew up with in politics in my country. I understand your problems, I understand each and every one of you. I was always in the minority in our Congress. We always were trying to challenge the majority. We had many differences, but I have found that in the differences in a parliamentary group in our country—and, I believe, in yours—that you can disagree without being disagreeable, which in my opinion is a true test of the strength and the character of a parliamentary body.

The discussions that I have had with your Government have been constructive in seeking to solve problems—domestic, international.

The great opportunity that I had to meet with your Emperor and Empress, His Majesty and Her Majesty—it has been a great experience for me, and I thank them and the people of Japan for being so warm in their welcome. I will report to my people in the United States that they have great friends in Japan, that our Governments are working together to seek solutions to the problems on a worldwide basis and between us, as two governments.

We are friends, we will work together, and we have a great future—the United States with the Government of Japan. And it is, therefore, my privilege and honor to offer a toast to your Government and to your people on behalf of my Government and the American people.

NOTE: The President spoke at 4:27 p.m. in the Akebono Room at the Hotel Okura in Tokyo. In his opening remarks, the President referred to Shigesaburo Maeo, Speaker of the Diet's House of Representatives, and Kenzo Kono, Speaker of the Diet's House of Counsellors.

248

Toast at a Reception for Nongovernmental Dignitaries. *November 20, 1974*

Mr. Tashiro, distinguished guests, ladies and gentlemen:

It is a very high honor and a very rare privilege for me to have the opportunity of joining with all of you on this occasion.

The trip by me as the first American President in office coming to Japan has been a memorable one—one that I shall never forget. The opportunity to meet with Their Majesties, the opportunity to meet with your high government officials, the opportunity to share some thoughts with the members of the Diet, the opportunity to have a governmental exchange at the highest level is, of course, of great significance.

It has been my experience in 25 years of political life, when I served in the House of Representatives, to work hand-in-glove with other Members of the legislative branch and, of course, in later years as a member of the leadership, to work with the legislative and the executive branch. And of course, in the last 13 or so months, I have had the opportunity of serving in two offices in the executive branch.

I have learned, over a period of 26 years serving in the Federal Government, that all wisdom, all support for policies doesn't necessarily come from government, but primarily from people in nongovernmental organizations and individuals who are not directly connected with government itself.

And as I understand it, this group here on this occasion is a nongovernmental group of Japanese and Americans who have spent a great deal of your time working together in a nongovernmental capacity to support a greater unity between our country, the United States, and your country, Japan. I compliment you, and I thank you. Your contribution is of tremendous significance.

Governments, themselves, can't do it. Decisions can be made at the government level—and in our societies, that is essential. But if those decisions are not supported, if those decisions are not explained by people in positions of responsibility in nongovernmental areas, it is impossible for those decisions to be successful. I learned that early in my career in politics. I always could be more successful in working to find a solution if I had the support not only among politicians but by those people, whether they were in management, in labor, in education, in local government.

So, I am deeply grateful for what you have done in the past, and I strongly urge that you continue these efforts in the future, because the Japanese Government and the United States Government, after the 2 days of talks we have had, yesterday and today, are embarking on a stronger unity, a stronger program of helping both in the maintenance of peace and the stimulation of prosperity. And this is what we want in Japan and in America and what we want for the rest of the world.

And so, what you do is of tremendous significance. What you do in explaining to the thousands of Americans who are here in Japan, what the Japanese who are here can do to explain to the millions of Japanese will not only be better for Japan and the United States but will be better for the world.

And I congratulate you, I thank you, and I wish you well. And may I offer a toast at this point to the Government of Japan and the millions and millions of Japanese.

NOTE: The President spoke at 5:08 p.m. in the Heian Room at the Hotel Okura in Tokyo. In his opening remarks, the President referred to Shigeki Tashiro, chairman of the board of the Toyo Rayon Co., Tokyo.

249

Joint Communique Following Discussions With Prime Minister Tanaka of Japan. *November 20, 1974*

I

President Ford of the United States of America paid an official visit to Japan between November 18 and 22 at the invitation of the Government of Japan. President Ford met Their Majesties the Emperor and Empress of Japan at the Imperial Palace on November 19.

II

In discussions held on November 19 and 20, President Ford and Prime Minister Tanaka agreed on the following common purposes underlying future relations between the United States and Japan.

1. The United States and Japan, Pacific nations sharing many political and economic interests, have developed a close and mutually beneficial relationship based on the principle of equality. Their friendship and cooperation are founded upon a common determination to maintain political systems respecting individual freedom and fundamental human rights as well as market economies which enhance the scope for creativity and the prospect of assuring the well-being of their peoples.

2. Dedicated to the maintenance of peace and the evolution of a stable international order reflecting the high purposes and principles of the Charter of the United Nations, the United States and Japan will continue to encourage the development of conditions in the Asia-Pacific area which will facilitate peaceful settlement of outstanding issues by the parties most concerned, reduce international tensions, promote the sustained and orderly growth of developing countries, and encourage constructive relationships among countries in the area. Each country will contribute to this task in the light of its own responsibilities and capabilities. Both countries recognize that cooperative relations between the United States and Japan under the Treaty of Mutual Cooperation and Security constitute an important and durable element in the evolution of the international situation in Asia and will continue to plan an effective and meaningful role in promoting peace and stability in that area.

3. The United States and Japan recognize the need for dedicated efforts by all countries to pursue additional arms limitation and arms reduction measures, in particular controls over nuclear armaments, and to prevent the further spread of nuclear weapons or other nuclear explosive devices while facilitating the expanded use of nuclear energy for peaceful purposes. Both countries underline the high responsibility of all nuclear-weapon states in such efforts, and note the importance of protecting non-nuclear-weapon states against nuclear threats.

4. The United States and Japan recognize the remarkable range of their interdependence and the need for coordinated responses to new problems confronting the international community. They will intensify efforts to promote close cooperation among industrialized democracies while striving steadily to encourage a further relaxation of tensions in the world through dialogue and exchanges with countries of different social systems.

5. In view of the growing interdependence of all countries and present global economic difficulties, it is becoming increasingly important to strengthen international economic cooperation. The United States and Japan recognize the necessity of the constructive use of their human and material resources to bring about solutions to major economic problems. The establishment of an open and harmonious world economic system is indispensable for international peace and prosperity and a primary goal of both nations. The United States and Japan will, to this end, continue to promote close economic and trade relations between the two countries and participate constructively in international efforts to ensure a continuing expansion of world trade through negotiations to reduce tariff and other trade distortions and to create a stable and balanced international

monetary order. Both countries will remain committed to their international pledges to avoid actions which adversely affect the economies of other nations.

6. The United States and Japan recognize the need for a more efficient and rational utilization and distribution of world resources. Realizing the importance of stable supplies of energy at reasonable prices they will seek, in a manner suitable to their economies, to expand and diversify energy supplies, develop new energy sources, and conserve on the use of scarce fuels. They both attach great importance to enhancing cooperation among consuming countries and they intend, in concert with other nations, to pursue harmonious relations with producing nations. Both countries agree that further international cooperative efforts are necessary to forestall an economic and financial crisis and to lead to a new era of creativity and common progress. Recognizing the urgency of the world food problem and the need for an international framework to ensure stable food supplies, the United States and Japan will participate constructively in multilateral efforts to seek ways to strengthen assistance to developing countries in the field of agriculture, to improve the supply situation of agricultural products, and to assure an adequate level of food reserves. They recognize the need for cooperation among food producers and consumers to deal with shortage situations.

7. For the well-being of the peoples of the world, a steady improvement in the technological and economic capabilities of developing countries must be a matter of common concern to all nations. In recognition of the importance of assisting developing countries, particularly those without significant natural resources, the United States and Japan will, individually and with the participation and support of other traditional aid-donors and those newly able to assist, maintain and expand programs of cooperation through assistance and trade as those nations seek to achieve sound and orderly growth.

8. The United States and Japan face many new challenges common to mankind as they endeavor to preserve the natural environment and to open new areas for exploration such as space and the oceans. In broad cooperation with other countries, they will promote research and facilitate the exchange of information in such fields as science, technology and environmental protection, in an effort to meet the needs of modern society, improve the quality of life and attain more balanced economic growth.

9. The United States and Japan recognize that their durable friendship has been based upon the continued development of mutual understanding and enhanced communication between their peoples, at many levels and in many as-

pects of their lives. They will seek therefore to expand further cultural and educational interchange which fosters and serves to increase such understanding.

10. In the spirit of friendship and mutual trust, the United States and Japan are determined to keep each other fully informed and to strengthen the practice of frank and timely consultations on potential bilateral issues and pressing global problems of common concern.

11. Friendly and cooperative relations between the United States and Japan have grown and deepened over the years in many diverse fields of human endeavor. Both countries reaffirm that, in their totality, these varied relationships constitute major foundation stones on which the two countries base their respective foreign policies and form an indispensable element supporting stable international political and economic relations.

III

The first visit to Japan by an incumbent President of the United States of America will add a new page to the history of amity between the two countries.

NOTE: The text of the joint communique was released at Tokyo, Japan.

250

Toast at a Dinner Honoring the Emperor and Empress of Japan. *November 20, 1974*

Your Majesties:

I am honored to have the privilege of welcoming Your Imperial Majesties to this dinner this evening. It permits me to, in a small way, in a symbolic gesture, to reciprocate the wonderful hospitality so graciously extended to me this week.

It has been a period of enlightenment for me, and I will take home an inspiring impression of the possibilities available for an even greater friendship, greater cooperation, and interdependence of our two nations.

America is now approaching its national Bicentennial. Tonight, I would like to recall another meaningful event that took place 114 years ago, on May 14, 1860. That was the day when the first diplomatic mission ever sent by Japan to another nation arrived in Washington, D.C., our National Capital.

I am very pleased, Your Majesties, to present on this evening to all of our distinguished guests a token of the durability of American-Japanese friendship. It is a medal bearing the likeness of President Buchanan, who had the honor of welcoming the Japanese delegation to the historic East Room of the White House. Since that occasion, the American Government has never ceased to look to the East as well as to the West.

Our visitors then regarded us as Americans, as strange creatures, and observed us in every detail. It was with equal fascination that we viewed our Japanese visitors. We learned from each other then, and we are continuing to learn today.

The most important lesson that I have learned during this visit corresponds with a brilliant insight of one of the Japanese envoys on the first mission to the United States. The occasion was a visit to the New York home of the widow of Commodore Perry. The Japanese envoy expressed a very deep emotion at the realization that he was in the home of Commodore Perry and said, and I quote: The time has come when no nation may remain isolated and refuse to take part in the affairs of the rest of the world.

That concept is even more compelling today. The links between our two nations can serve as a model for a world increasingly aware of the need for greater international cooperation. Accordingly, in recalling that first Japanese delegation to Washington, I pledge that my Government will not isolate itself from the world or from Japan.

On behalf of the Nation that I am privileged to represent, to lead, I reaffirm the spirit of friendship that endures between us. I reaffirm my determination to see that warm relationship continues and grows.

Your Majesties, in that spirit and with a heart filled with faith in the future and appreciation of our guests, I offer a toast to the health and to the well-being of Your Imperial Majesties.

NOTE: The President spoke at 9:40 p.m. in the Banquet Hall at the Akasaka Palace in Tokyo.

251

Remarks to Reporters Following a Visit to Nijo Castle in Kyoto. *November 21, 1974*

WELL, I do want to thank all of the people who have made this afternoon so interesting. It is an afternoon which has given us a special insight into the history and into the traditions of Japan.

And I want to thank the young ladies here and the others who have shown us the several castles.

The culture of Japan certainly is an inspiration. It is different. It is something that by its simplicity inspires you to see what can come from hard work and a feeling of making the most out of what you have available, which was the history of Japan in its early days, and then to see these beautiful instruments and fine playing by the young ladies—the beautiful costumes—I think it is a real inspiration for those of us who have had an opportunity to be here today in Kyoto, traditional capital of Japan.

I thank all of you and thank all of you for your thoughtfulness and your hospitality.

REPORTER. How is the trip going, Mr. President?

THE PRESIDENT. I think it has been a wonderful trip. It couldn't have been better, both substantively and otherwise.

Q. What have you enjoyed most, Mr. President?

THE PRESIDENT. The opportunity to see not only the Government officials but an opportunity to see a great deal of the Japanese history and people. It has been an inspiration as well as a very productive 3 days.

Thank you very much.

NOTE: The President spoke at 3:15 p.m. While in Kyoto, the President also visited the Imperial Palace and Kinkakuji Temple (the Gold Pavilion).

252

Remarks on Arrival at Seoul, Republic of Korea. *November 22, 1974*

Mr. President, Excellencies, ladies and gentlemen:

I am very pleased to return to the Republic of Korea, our faithful ally, on a mission of peace.

Twenty-one years have elapsed since I was last here in Korea. I was then a Congressman, a Member of our House of Representatives. Now I return as the third American President to visit you while in office. President Eisenhower came here in 1952 and again in 1960. President Johnson came in 1966. Those visits as well as mine demonstrate a close involvement of different American administrations over a quarter of a century. They reflect the same reality—our long and friendly ties to the Korean people.

When I came to Korea in 1953, I saw a heartrending scene. The Republic of Korea had been ravaged by war. You had made great sacrifices to repel aggression. Your economy was in ruins. I was deeply saddened by what I saw, but I was inspired by the determination of the Korean people to rebuild.

Today I am very happy to return. I want to see the great progress that so many have described so very vividly. I want to see for myself what you have built upon the ashes of war.

I am here, Mr. President, to reaffirm our friendship and to give it new life and meaning.

Nothing binds nations together closer than to have fought side by side for the same cause. Two times we have stood together, here as well as in Vietnam, to preserve the peace, to preserve the stability of Asia and the world. We can never forget this.

Though we have been together with you in war, America's deepest hope is for a world of peace. Let us now join to preserve peace and to prevent any recurrence of hostilities. That is our continuing commitment which I today reaffirm.

I thank you very much, Mr. President, for this heartwarming welcome. My only regret is that my wife, Mrs. Ford, is not here at my side. She sends her greetings to the great Korean people. She looks forward to hearing in detail from me personally about this visit.

You were most gracious, Mr. President, to invite me. I am proud to come here on this, my first overseas journey as President of the United States.

I thank you very, very much.

NOTE: The President spoke at 10:20 a.m. at Kimpo International Airport, where he was greeted by Korean President Park Chung Hee.

253

Remarks at Camp Casey, Republic of Korea. *November 22, 1974*

LET ME just make one or two observations and comments.

As Commander in Chief, I am very proud of this great division. I am very impressed with the people that I have met and the exhibition that I have seen. This is the kind of strong, vigorous American spirit that has made America in 197 years a country in which all of us have tremendous pride.

We are proud of you. We know you can do the job. Thank you on behalf of 213 million other Americans who have their hearts and their faith and their best wishes with you.

Thank you very, very much.

[The President spoke at 12:53 p.m. at Indianhead Field after attending a football game between members of the United States Army 2d Infantry Division, headquartered at the camp. Following his remarks, the President went to Hanson Fieldhouse where he attended intra-divisional championship matches of *tae kwon do,* a form of Korean karate, and received a plaque marking his visit to Camp Casey. His remarks there, beginning at 1:25 p.m., follow.]

Thank you very, very much for this very thoughtful and really wonderful plaque that I will take back to Washington, give it to Mrs. Ford in the White House, and tell her the story of the 2d Infantry Division, which, in my opinion, is a great story of stimulation, of effort, aims and objectives, and dedication.

I am proud of you as Commander in Chief. I know that you have set a high example, not only for each and every one of you individually but for all others in the United States Army and in the Department of Defense.

What you are doing here is something that is not only good for the Army and good for the others in the Defense Department but it is good for America, it is good for you, and we are very, very proud of everything you are doing.

And Mrs. Ford, I am sure, will have this properly displayed in the White House, because it will touch her heart. It will tell her a great deal of what is being done out here—people on watch for her, for 213 million other Americans.

Your pro-life program is tremendous. This is the kind of esprit de corps, the kind of will to win, the will to do something for yourself and your Government that will make America an even greater and better place for all of us to live.

Thank you very, very much.

254

Toast at a Dinner Hosted by President Park Chung Hee of the Republic of Korea in Seoul. *November 22, 1974*

Mr. President, distinguished guests, ladies and gentlemen:

I am greatly honored by this occasion and appreciate the gracious hospitality you have accorded us this evening.

The warmth shown by the Korean people exceeds even that which I remember from my previous visit to Korea—this very hospitable land.

I am very, very much impressed by the dynamism of the Korean society, the energy and vitality of the Korean people, and the charm and the beauty of the Korean women.

Mr. President, I wish that I had more time to see not only the impressive landmarks of the Korean miracle of material progress but also the famous historical shrines of your great country. On another day perhaps, Mr. President, my wife and myself and our family can come, and certainly we would like to return.

Mr. President, it was a great pleasure to meet the leaders of many sectors of the Korean society here tonight. In particular, I am pleased to see the Speaker and the other members of the National Assembly, including representatives of the various major political parties.

Having spent, Mr. President, a quarter of a century of my life in the parliament, or our Congress, I place a great value in the legislative process of a representative government.

I came to your country, Mr. President, to demonstrate America's continued determination to preserve peace in Korea, in Asia, and throughout the world. Koreans and Americans were friends in war. We will remain friends in peace.

America seeks world peace for the good of all and at the expense of none.

Today, Mr. President, I enjoyed a rewarding and a very inspiring visit with your people. I also drew great encouragement by meeting with the armed forces of our American troops in which all of us take such great pride.

I pledge to you, Mr. President, that the United States will continue to assist and to support you. Our relationship and our dialog will continue.

We live in a time of new international realities and new opportunities for peace and progress in Asia and elsewhere. President Park, your statesmanlike initiative in opening a dialog with the North contributed constructively to efforts to find a peaceful and just solution to the Korean problem. With the perseverance and with the courage so typical of the American (Korean) people, I trust you will prevail in this effort.

Let us recognize the new world in which we all live. Let us envisage the interdependence of all nations—large and small. When we plan for such new international problems as energy shortages and financial crises, the United States considers the interests of all nations. We will continue to consult with you in common interests and in common problems.

America has great confidence in the people of Korea, just as we have great confidence in ourselves in America.

Mr. President, I am here on a mission of peace. It is my deepest hope that the entire world will lift its gaze and broaden its vision. I have said before, but I repeat here tonight, I would rather walk a thousand miles for peace than take a single step for war.

Mr. President, the relationship between our two peoples was first formalized as long ago as May 22, 1882. The preamble to that treaty spoke of permanent relations based upon amity and friendship. We have proven that by more than diplomatic phrases. Our relationship has endured through war and through peace.

The welcome you accorded me today is symbolic of our very close ties. It demonstrated the great strength of the friendship between our two peoples. I was greatly touched, Mr. President, by the outpouring of good will from the countless thousands and thousands of people who greeted me so warmly. Their cheers, I am sure, were not only for me as an individual but for the United States of America and our 213 million of which I have the honor to represent.

I wish to thank every Korean that I saw today on behalf of all of the American people.

Today, I visited a very beautiful cemetery and the monument to the brave Koreans who fell in battle. They fought side-by-side with Americans. And let the continued friendship of our two nations pay tribute to the memory of the supreme sacrifices of your courageous men and our own.

Ladies and gentlemen, I ask you to rise and to join me in a toast to my distinguished host, President Park, and to the great people of the Republic of Korea.

NOTE: The President spoke at 9:12 p.m. in the Banquet Hall at the Capitol Building. No transcript was issued of President Park's toast.

255

Joint Communique Following Discussions With President Park of the Republic of Korea. *November 22, 1974*

AT THE invitation of President Park Chung Hee of the Republic of Korea, President Gerald R. Ford of the United States of America visited the Republic of Korea on November 22 and 23, 1974, to exchange views on the current international situation and to discuss matters of mutual interest and concern to the two nations.

During the visit the two Presidents held discussions on two occasions. Present at these meetings were Prime Minister Kim Chong Pil, Secretary of State Henry Kissinger, Foreign Minister Kim Dong Jo, Presidential Secretary General Kim Chung Yum, Ambassador Richard L. Sneider, Ambassador Hahm Pyong Choon and other high officials of both Governments. President Ford also visited American forces stationed in the Republic of Korea.

President Ford laid a wreath at the Memorial of the Unknown Soldiers. He also visited the grave of Madame Park Chung Hee and expressed his deepest personal condolences to President Park on her tragic and untimely death.

The two Presidents reaffirmed the strong bonds of friendship and cooperation between their two countries. They agreed to continue the close cooperation and regular consultation on security matters and other subjects of mutual interest which have characterized the relationship between the Republic of Korea and the United States.

The two Presidents took note of significant political and economic changes in the situation in Asia in recent years. They recognized that the allied countries in the area are growing stronger and more prosperous and are making increasing contributions to their security as well as to that of the region. President Ford explained that the United States, as a Pacific power, is vitally interested in Asia and the Pacific and will continue its best effort to ensure the peace and security of the region. President Park expressed his understanding and full support for United States policies directed toward these ends.

President Park described the efforts being made by the Republic of Korea to maintain a dialogue with North Korea, designed to reduce tensions and establish peace on the Korean Peninsula, and to lead eventually to the peaceful unification of Korea. President Park affirmed the intention of the Republic of Korea to continue to pursue the dialogue despite the failure of the North Korean authorities to respond with sincerity thus far. President Ford gave assurance that the United States will continue to support these efforts by the Republic of Korea and expressed the hope that the constructive initiatives by the Republic of Korea would meet with positive responses by all concerned.

The two Presidents discussed the current United Nations General Assembly consideration of the Korean question. They agreed on the importance of favorable General Assembly action on the Draft Resolution introduced by the United States and other member countries. Both expressed the hope that the General Assembly would base its consideration of the Korean question on a recognition of the importance of the security arrangements which have preserved peace on the Korean Peninsula for more than two decades.

President Park explained in detail the situation on the Korean Peninsula, and described the threat to peace and stability of hostile acts by North Korea, exemplified most recently by the construction of an underground tunnel inside the southern sector of the Demilitarized Zone.

The two Presidents agreed that the Republic of Korea forces and American forces stationed in Korea must maintain a high degree of strength and readiness in order to deter aggression. President Ford reaffirmed the determination of the United States to render prompt and effective assistance to repel armed attack against the Republic of Korea in accordance with the Mutual Defense Treaty of 1954 between the Republic of Korea and the United States. In this connection, President Ford assured President Park that the United States has no plan to reduce the present level of United States forces in Korea.

The two Presidents discussed the progress of the Modernization Program for the Republic of Korea armed forces and agreed that implementation of the program is of major importance to the security of the Republic of Korea and peace on the Korean Peninsula. President Ford took note of the increasing share of the defense burden which the Republic of Korea is able and willing to assume and affirmed the readiness of the United States to continue to render appropriate support to the further development of defense industries in the Republic of Korea.

President Ford expressed his admiration for the rapid and sustained economic progress of the Republic of Korea, accomplished in the face of various obstacles, including the lack of sufficient indigenous natural resources and continuing tensions in the area. President Park noted with appreciation the United States contribution to Korea's development in the economic, scientific and technological fields.

The two Presidents examined the impact of recent international economic developments. They agreed that the two countries should continue to foster close economic cooperation for their mutual benefit, and that they should guide their economic policies toward each other in the spirit of closer interdependence among all nations. They shared the view that coordination of their policies on new problems confronting the international community is necessary. Both Presidents expressed mutual satisfaction over the continuing growth of substantial bilateral economic relations which have been beneficial to both countries. They agreed that continued private foreign investment in Korea by the United States and other foreign countries is desirable. It was agreed that international efforts should focus on the reduction of trade distortions, establishment of a framework for ensuring stable food supplies, and realization of stable supplies of energy at reasonable prices.

President Park expressed his high expectations and respect for the efforts being made by President Ford to establish world peace and to restore world economic order.

On behalf of the members of his Party and the American people, President Ford extended his deepest thanks to President Park and all of the people of the Republic of Korea for the warmth of their reception and the many courtesies extended to him during the visit.

President Ford cordially invited President Park to visit the United States of America and President Park accepted the invitation with pleasure. The two Presidents agreed that the visit would take place at a time of mutual convenience.

NOTE: The text of the joint communique was released at Seoul, Republic of Korea.

256

Toast at a Luncheon Hosted by L. I. Brezhnev, General Secretary of the Communist Party of the Soviet Union, in Vladivostok. *November 24, 1974*

MR. GENERAL SECRETARY, let me say a few words, if I might, about the very special significance of this, our first official meeting.

The world has been accustomed in recent years to regular meetings between the leaders of the Soviet Union and the American people. Cooperation between our two countries has intensified, both in tempo and, more importantly, in substance during the past few years. As a result, all people, Mr. General Secretary, have a better chance to live in peace and security today.

The fact that these meetings have become more regular testifies to the significance attached to them by both countries. In these meetings, we are able to conduct our discussions in a businesslike and a constructive way. We are able to make important progress on the issues that concern our countries.

Mr. General Secretary, I look forward to continuing the close working relationship developed between the leaders of our two countries.

In my first address to the Congress of the United States, I pledged to the Soviet Union to continue America's commitment to the course followed in the last 3 years.

Mr. General Secretary, I personally reaffirm that pledge to you now. As nations with great power, we share a common responsibility, not only to our own people but to mankind as a whole. We must avoid, of course, war and the destruction that it would mean. Let us get on with the business of controlling arms, as I think we have in the last 24 hours. Let us contribute, through our cooperation, to the resolution of the very great problems facing mankind as a whole.

Mr. General Secretary, the problems of food, population, and energy are not confined to any one country or to countries at an early stage of economic development. They affect people everywhere. If this age is to be remembered favorably in the history books, it will be because we met our responsibilities—your country and my country and our friends and allies throughout the world.

May I propose a toast to our joint search for solutions to the problems facing mankind and a toast to you, Mr. General Secretary, and to those associated with you in your Government and to the people of the Soviet Union and to the people of the world, who will benefit from your efforts and, hopefully, mine.

To the General Secretary.

NOTE: The President spoke at 5:20 p.m. at the Okeansky Sanitarium. No transcript was issued of the General Secretary's toast.

257

Joint United States-Soviet Statement on the Limitation of Strategic Offensive Arms. *November 24, 1974*

DURING their working meeting in the area of Vladivostok on November 23–24, 1974, the President of the USA Gerald R. Ford and General Secretary of the Central Committee of the CPSU L. I. Brezhnev discussed in detail the question of further limitations of strategic offensive arms.

They reaffirmed the great significance that both the United States and the USSR attach to the limitation of strategic offensive arms. They are convinced that a long-term agreement on this question would be a significant contribution to improving relations between the US and the USSR, to reducing the danger of war and to enhancing world peace. Having noted the value of previous agreements on this question, including the Interim Agreement of May 26, 1972, they reaffirm the intention to conclude a new agreement on the limitation of strategic offensive arms, to last through 1985.

As a result of the exchange of views on the substance of such a new agreement the President of the United States of America and the General Secretary of the Central Committee of the CPSU concluded that favorable prospects exist for completing the work on this agreement in 1975.

Agreement was reached that further negotiations will be based on the following provisions.

1. The new agreement will incorporate the relevant provisions of the Interim Agreement of May 26, 1972, which will remain in force until October 1977.

2. The new agreement will cover the period from October 1977 through December 31, 1985.

3. Based on the principle of equality and equal security, the new agreement will include the following limitations:

a. Both sides will be entitled to have a certain agreed aggregate number of strategic delivery vehicles;

b. Both sides will be entitled to have a certain agreed aggregate number of ICBMs and SLBMs equipped with multiple independently targetable warheads (MIRVs).

4. The new agreement will include a provision for further negotiations beginning no later than 1980–1981 on the question of further limitations and possible reductions of strategic arms in the period after 1985.

5. Negotiations between the delegations of the U.S. and USSR to work out the new agreement incorporating the foregoing points will resume in Geneva in January 1975.

November 24, 1974

NOTE: The text of the joint statement was released at Vladivostok, U.S.S.R.

258

Joint Communique Following Discussions With General Secretary Brezhnev of the Soviet Union. *November 24, 1974*

IN ACCORDANCE with the previously announced agreement, a working meeting between the President of the United States of America Gerald R. Ford and the General Secretary of the Central Committee of the Communist Party of the Soviet Union L. I. Brezhnev took place in the area of Vladivostok on November 23 and 24, 1974. Taking part in the talks were the Secretary of State of the United States of America and Assistant to the President for National Security Affairs, Henry A. Kissinger and Member of the Politburo of the Central Committee of the CPSU, Minister of Foreign Affairs of the USSR, A. A. Gromyko.

They discussed a broad range of questions dealing with American-Soviet relations and the current international situation.

Also taking part in the talks were:

On the American side Walter J. Stoessel, Jr., Ambassador of the USA to the USSR; Helmut Sonnenfeldt, Counselor of the Department of State; Arthur A. Hartman, Assistant Secretary of State for European Affairs; Lieutenant General Brent Scowcroft, Deputy Assistant to the President for National Security Affairs; and William Hyland, official of the Department of State.

On the Soviet side A. F. Dobrynin, Ambassador of the USSR to the USA; A. M. Aleksandrov, Assistant to the General Secretary of the Central Committee of the CPSU; and G. M. Korniyenko, Member of the Collegium of the Ministry of Foreign Affairs of the USSR.

I

The United States of America and the Soviet Union reaffirmed their determination to develop further their relations in the direction defined by the fundamental joint decisions and basic treaties and agreements concluded between the two States in recent years.

They are convinced that the course of American-Soviet relations, directed towards strengthening world peace, deepening the relaxation of international tensions and expanding mutually beneficial cooperation of states with different social systems meets the vital interests of the people of both States and other peoples.

Both Sides consider that based on the agreements reached between them important results have been achieved in fundamentally reshaping American-Soviet relations on the basis of peaceful coexistence and equal security. These results are a solid foundation for progress in reshaping Soviet-American relations.

Accordingly, they intend to continue, without a loss in momentum, to expand the scale and intensity of their cooperative efforts in all spheres as set forth in the agreements they have signed so that the process of improving relations between the US and USSR will continue without interruption and will become irreversible.

Mutual determination was expressed to carry out strictly and fully the mutual obligations undertaken by the US and the USSR in accordance with the treaties and agreements concluded between them.

II

Special consideration was given in the course of the talks to a pivotal aspect of Soviet-American relations: measures to eliminate the threat of war and to halt the arms race.

Both Sides reaffirm that the Agreements reached between the US and the USSR on the prevention of nuclear war and the limitation of strategic arms are a good beginning in the process of creating guarantees against the outbreak of nuclear conflict and war in general. They expressed their deep belief in the necessity of promoting this process and expressed their hope that other states would contribute to it as well. For their part the US and the USSR will continue to exert vigorous efforts to achieve this historic task.

A joint statement on the question of limiting strategic offensive arms is being released separately.

Both Sides stressed once again the importance and necessity of a serious effort aimed at preventing the dangers connected with the spread of nuclear weapons in the world. In this connection they stressed the importance of increasing the effectiveness of the Treaty on the Non-Proliferation of Nuclear Weapons.

It was noted that, in accordance with previous agreements, initial contacts were established between representatives of the US and of the USSR on questions related to underground nuclear explosions for peaceful purposes, to measures to overcome the dangers of the use of environmental modification techniques for military purposes, as well as measures dealing with the most dangerous lethal means of chemical warfare. It was agreed to continue an active search for mutually acceptable solutions of these questions.

III

In the course of the meeting an exchange of views was held on a number of international issues: special attention was given to negotiations already in progress in which the two Sides are participants and which are designed to remove existing sources of tension and to bring about the strengthening of international security and world peace.

Having reviewed the situation at the Conference on Security and Cooperation in Europe, both Sides concluded that there is a possibility for its early successful conclusion. They proceed from the assumption that the results achieved in the course of the Conference will permit its conclusion at the highest level and thus be commensurate with its importance in ensuring the peaceful future of Europe.

The USA and the USSR also attach high importance to the negotiations on mutual reduction of forces and armaments and associated measures in Central Europe. They agree to contribute actively to the search for mutually acceptable solutions on the basis of principle of undiminished security for any of the parties and the prevention of unilateral military advantages.

Having discussed the situation existing in the Eastern Mediterranean, both Sides state their firm support for the independence, sovereignty and territorial integrity of Cyprus and will make every effort in this direction. They consider that a just settlement of the Cyprus question must be based on the strict implementation of the resolutions adopted by the Security Council and the General Assembly of the United Nations regarding Cyprus.

In the course of the exchange of views on the Middle East both Sides expressed their concern with regard to the dangerous situation in that region. They reaffirmed their intention to make every effort to promote a solution of the key issues of a just and lasting peace in that area on the basis of the United Nations resolution 338, taking into account the legitimate interests of all the peoples of the area, including the Palestinian people, and respect for the right to independent existence of all states in the area.

The Sides believe that the Geneva Conference should play an important part in the establishment of a just and lasting peace in the Middle East, and should resume its work as soon as possible.

IV

The state of relations was reviewed in the field of commercial, economic, scientific and technical ties between the USA and the USSR. Both Sides confirmed the great importance which further progress in these fields would have for Soviet-American relations, and expressed their firm intention to continue the broadening and deepening of mutually advantageous cooperation.

The two Sides emphasized the special importance accorded by them to the development on a long term basis of commercial and economic cooperation, including mutually beneficial large-scale projects. They believe that such commercial and economic cooperation will serve the cause of increasing the stability of Soviet-American relations.

Both Sides noted with satisfaction the progress in the implementation of agreements and in the development of ties and cooperation between the US and the USSR in the fields of science, technology and culture. They are convinced that the continued expansion of such cooperation will benefit the peoples of both countries and will be an important contribution to the solution of world-wide scientific and technical problems.

The talks were held in an atmosphere of frankness and mutual understanding, reflecting the constructive desire of both Sides to strengthen and develop further the peaceful cooperative relationship between the USA and the USSR, and to ensure progress in the solution of outstanding international problems in the interests of preserving and strengthening peace.

The results of the talks provided a convincing demonstration of the practical value of Soviet-American summit meetings and their exceptional importance in the shaping of a new relationship between the United States of America and the Soviet Union.

President Ford reaffirmed the invitation to L. I. Brezhnev to pay an official visit to the United States in 1975. The exact date of the visit will be agreed upon later.

FOR THE UNITED STATES OF AMERICA
GERALD R. FORD
President of the United States of America

For the Union of Soviet Socialist Republics
L. I. Brezhnev
General Secretary of the Central Committee of the CPSU

November 24, 1974

NOTE: The joint communique was signed in a ceremony in the conference hall at Okeansky Sanitarium.

259

Remarks Upon Returning From Japan, the Republic of Korea, and the Soviet Union. *November 24, 1974*

Mr. Speaker, my very dear friends in the Congress, members of the Cabinet, distinguished guests, my fellow Americans:

I thank you all very, very much for coming out this evening and welcoming us so very warmly.

Since I left Washington 8 days ago, I have traveled some 17,000 miles for the purpose of peace and not a single step toward war. And every one of those miles, in my opinion, was most worthwhile. But as always when we return to our homeland, my companions and myself are very, very happy to be here.

Secretary Kissinger has a few more miles to go on this trip,[1] but I will assure him that this warm welcome includes him as well.

Thursday is Thanksgiving. I cannot help but reflect on the many, many blessings that we Americans have. We do have some very serious problems, but we have much, much more to be thankful for. America is a strong country; Americans are very strong people. We are free, and we are blessed with good friends and allies.

On my trip I talked with the leaders of two of our allies, Japan and Korea. In both nations, I saw how much they value their relationship with us. We will continue to work together to strengthen our ties.

The visit to Japan marked my first trip outside North America since becoming

---

[1] Secretary Kissinger visited the People's Republic of China from November 25 through November 29. A United States-People's Republic of China joint communique, issued November 29, 1974, read as follows:

"Dr. Henry A. Kissinger, U.S. Secretary of State and Assistant to the President for National Security Affairs, visited the People's Republic of China from November 25 through November 29, 1974. The U.S. and Chinese sides held frank, wide-ranging and mutually beneficial talks. They reaffirmed their unchanged commitment to the principles of the Shanghai Communique. The two Governments agreed that President Gerald R. Ford would visit the People's Republic of China in 1975."

President, and it was the first time that a President of the United States has visited that energetic and productive island nation.

Our trip was historic for another reason, for it marked a change in our relationship. In the past the central concern of our alliance was military security. This security relationship has now been broadened to include energy and food. I am particularly hopeful that by working together with Japan, one of the world's most technically advanced societies, we will be able to make a substantial joint contribution to resolving the energy crisis.

Japan emerged from the destruction of war with a deep commitment to peace. In Korea, a sturdy people rebuilt a nation from the ashes of another conflict.

Only a little over 20 years ago, Korea was a battleground. Today, it is a showcase of economic development.

Just over two decades ago, American fighting men were battling over the rugged mountains of Korea. Today, the major burden of Korea's defense is borne by the Koreans themselves. American servicemen are stationed there, but like their comrades in Europe and elsewhere, they are there to help an ally maintain the peace, not to do the job alone.

A highlight of the trip for me was the opportunity to meet with our soldiers in Korea and to have lunch with them in one of their camps. They are outstanding fighting men and women doing a fine job. We can all be very proud of them.

The final stop on our trip was the Soviet Union. The meetings with General Secretary Brezhnev, I am pleased, went very, very well. They represent both a beginning and a continuation. They were the beginning of what I hope will be a productive personal relationship between Mr. Brezhnev and myself. We both, I believe, came away from Vladivostok with mutual respect and a common determination to continue the search for peace.

They were a continuation because we maintained the steady improvement of our relations begun 3 years ago. We talked, as American and Soviet leaders have in the past, about the Middle East, European security, and other bilateral relations. We often agreed, but not always. When we did not, we stated our differences quite frankly.

But on perhaps the most important issue facing the Soviet and American peoples, the further limitation of strategic arms, we found a large measure of agreement. We discussed the issue fully, and in the end we established a sound basis for a new agreement that will constrain our military competition over the next decade. The understanding we reached resulted from an intensive round of give-and-take, the kind of give-and-take negotiations that recognized the legitimate security of both sides.

Many details remain to be worked out by our negotiators, but ceilings on the strategic forces of both nations have been accepted. A good agreement that will serve the interests of the United States and the Soviet Union is now within our grasp. Vladivostok was an appropriate ending to a journey designed to strengthen ties with old friends and expand areas of agreement with old adversaries.

I believe we accomplished what we set out to achieve and perhaps more. And in that process, I pray that we have done all we could to advance the cause of peace for all Americans and for all mankind.

Thank you very much.

NOTE: The President spoke at 7:31 p.m. at Andrews Air Force Base, Md.

260

Statement on the Death of U Thant. *November 25, 1974*

I HAVE learned with great sorrow of the death of former United Nations Secretary General U Thant. Above all, he was a man of peace. His distinguished leadership in the world community for a decade won him wide respect and the gratitude of all who cherish world peace. He gave unselfishly of himself in the highest tradition of service to mankind, and the world is better for the example he set.

U Thant's loyalty was not to any one power or ethnic bloc but to humanity, and it is in this same universal spirit that all men will mourn his passing. On behalf of the people of the United States, I extend condolences to his family.

NOTE: U Thant, 65, died in New York City. He was Burma's permanent representative to the United Nations 1957–61 and United Nations Secretary General 1962–70.

261

Remarks on Signing the National Mass Transportation Assistance Act of 1974. *November 26, 1974*

I APOLOGIZE for being late, but we had a meeting with the joint leadership where I reported on the trip to Japan, to Korea, and to the Soviet Union.

It is a pleasure and a privilege to see all of my old friends in the Congress and some of the mayors and some of the Governors.

On this occasion, the news of the passage of this legislation reached me overseas. And I consider this legislation a top priority of the 93d Congress, and I congratulate the Senate and the House for acting so quickly and so decisively.

This marks a long-term and vital major Federal commitment to mass transportation. This legislation represents a compromise in the best sense of the term. Although different positions were set forth in the beginning—the views of the Administration, the Congress, Governors, mayors, and others—we were able to reconcile our differences and develop legislation to meet our most urgent needs in mass transportation at a cost which is not inflationary.

This legislation is significant in our fight against excessive use of petroleum, in our economic battle, and in our efforts to curb urban pollution and reduce congestion. It assures that $11.8 billion in Federal assistance will be available to States and to cities to meet transit needs for the rest of the decade.

This assurance of steady and predictable support for public transit for the first time will enable localities to plan intelligently for their long-term needs. Also for the first time, this legislation will permit the Federal Government to provide limited assistance toward the operating expenses of transit systems. Provisions of the bill will minimize possible adverse effects of Federal involvement in such deficits. The act contains funds, again for the first time, which can be used for rural public transportation.

Many in the Congress and elsewhere worked very hard to develop this legislation, and I am pleased that so many of you could be here today. Secretary Brinegar, Frank Herringer, John Tower, Pete Williams, Joe Minish, Bill Widnall, Garry Brown, Jim Delaney, John Anderson, Ray Madden—and I could go on—deserve special mention. So do many mayors who made numerous journeys to Washington, all for a good cause.

I am encouraged here and now [by] the use, the excessive use of certain energy; that is, the kind of energy expended to enact this legislation by the Congress and by its supporters around the country. Let us put more and more of this personal energy into the effective solution of the important problems facing the Nation today. We surely will find solutions at a price that is right.

It is with a great deal of personal pleasure that I sign the National Mass Transportation Assistance Act of 1974.

Thank you all again. It is so nice to see so many of you, and I compliment in a personal way the cooperation, the assistance, and the understanding. This is what produces results, and I thank each and every one of you very, very much.

NOTE: The President spoke at 10:40 a.m. in the East Room at the White House. In his remarks, the President referred to Frank C. Herringer, Administrator of the Urban Mass Transportation Administration, Senators John G. Tower and Harrison A. Williams, and Representatives Joseph G. Minish, William B. Widnall, Garry E. Brown, James J. Delaney, John B. Anderson, and Ray J. Madden.

As enacted, the bill (S. 386) is Public Law 93–503 (88 Stat. 1565).

262

Special Message to the Congress on Budget Restraint. *November 26, 1974*

To the Congress of the United States:

Last month I sent a 31-point economic program to the Congress. That program was a balanced one, both dealing with the forces of inflation and anticipating the possibility of recessionary pressures. It was, and remains, my particular concern to help those hardest hit by inflation and by the slack that has developed in some sectors of the economy.

Responsible restraint of government spending is an integral part of my economic program. The Congress has publicly proclaimed its support of restraint. In June the Senate voted 74–12 in favor of legislation to hold Federal spending to $295 billion. In September the Joint Economic Committee unanimously recommended holding spending to $300 billion. Last month the House voted 329–20 for a budget target of the same level.

Soon after I took office I asked the heads of Federal agencies to undertake a thorough review of 1975 expenditures. In my October 8 Message to the Congress, I pledged to forward a package of proposed actions to reduce the 1975 budget. Today I am reporting on the results of this review and presenting my specific recommendations for reducing Federal outlays.

First, it is important to understand what has been happening to the budget. When the current fiscal year began last July 1, budget outlays for the year were estimated at $305.4 billion.

Interest costs for Federal borrowing are now expected to be $1.5 billion more than the estimate last June.

The Congress has also added to 1975 budget pressures. Congressional reductions in some programs have been more than offset by actions it has taken to increase spending in others. Particularly disappointing was the Congressional unwillingness to join with me in deferring for three months a Federal pay raise.

This cost the taxpayers $700 million. Equally discouraging was the passage by Congress over my veto of the Railroad Retirement bill costing $285 million this year and $7 billion over the next 25 years.

There have been some reductions in expected spending levels. The Environmental Protection Agency will spend less than planned because anticipated schedules for sewage treatment construction have not been met.

However, the most significant change is the increased aid to the jobless—including the National Employment Assistance Act I proposed last month—that added $2.7 billion to the budget. This increase is necessary to ease the burden on those who are most affected by current economic stress.

Taking these developments into account, my present recommendations for $4.6 billion of budget reductions will result in a budget total of $299.5 billion before considering $2.7 billion increased spending for aid to the unemployed. These recommendations represent a major effort at budgetary restraint. It would be unwise, in my view, to add additional dollar reductions for each dollar of increased aid to the unemployed.

The fiscal year 1975 budget actions by the Executive and the Congress since July 1, including those I now propose, are summarized and compared to last year's actual expenditures as follows:

CHANGES IN BUDGET SPENDING

[Fiscal years; dollar amounts in billions]

	Defense [1]	Interest on the Public Debt	Payments for Individuals [2]	Other	Total
Actual 1974 expenditures	$78.4	$29.3	$110.1	$50.5	$268.4
1975 Budget (July 1 estimates)	85.8	31.5	130.5	57.6	305.4
Changes (including those proposed)	−2.6	+1.5	+1.0	−3.2	−3.3
Presently proposed levels for 1975	83.2	33.0	131.5	54.4	302.2
1975: Percent change since July 1	−3.0%	+4.8%	+.7%	−5.5%	−1.1%
1975: Percent change over 1974	+6.1%	+12.6%	+19.4%	+7.8%	+12.6%

[1] Department of Defense, Military and Military Assistance. [2] Nondefense.

The 1975 outlay estimates can be affected significantly by variations in income from oil lease sales on the Outer Continental Shelf. This income is treated in the budget as an offset to spending. If the current schedule of lease sales is not met, for environmental or other reasons, or if the bids are significantly less than anticipated, outlays could further increase—possibly by $3 billion or more.

The reductions I propose to the Congress will require a number of changes in basic legislation and in pending appropriations. I am also transmitting proposed rescissions and deferrals, as required by the Congressional Budget and Impoundment Control Act, to reduce programs for which funds have already been appropriated. The rescissions would result in decreased outlays of over $200 million in 1975. Deferrals would reduce 1975 outlays by over $300 million.

Normally, funds are already being withheld when reports on rescissions and deferrals are transmitted to the Congress. Recognizing that these rescissions and deferrals are an integral part of a more far reaching and comprehensive proposal, I will not begin to withhold funds for the affected programs until December 16 although the law permits me to do so immediately.

The reductions I propose focus on programs that have grown rapidly in recent years or that have been increased substantially over budget proposals. In most cases, the level of 1975 outlays will be materially above actual spending last year. Even after the proposed cutbacks, Federal benefit payments to individuals are estimated to be $131.5 billion. This is $1.0 billion above the July estimate, and $21.4 billion, or 19%, above actual spending last year.

While I am recommending further cuts in defense spending, I have taken into account the substantial reductions already made by the Congress. My current expectation for defense spending is $83.2 billion, $2.6 billion below the June estimate. I believe that further cuts in defense spending would be exceedingly unwise, particularly at this time.

In determining which budget programs should be reduced, I have tried to eliminate the less essential and to overcome inequities. I have tried to avoid actions that would unduly add to unemployment or adversely affect those hurt most by inflation.

The $4.6 billion budget outlay reduction I now propose is not large when compared with total Federal spending. Nevertheless, the Congress may find it difficult to agree with all my proposals. I strongly urge the Congress to accept them and join with me in this belt tightening. The reductions are essential to demonstrate to the American people that the Federal Government is working seriously to restrain its spending. They are also a start toward the imperative of gaining control over budgets in the future.

GERALD R. FORD

The White House,
November 26, 1974.

NOTE: A summary of the deferrals and proposed rescissions was also released with the message and is printed in the Federal Register of December 5, 1974 (39 F.R. 42524).

263
Veto of Vietnam Era Veterans' Education and Training Benefits Legislation. *November 26, 1974*

To the House of Representatives:

I am returning today without my approval H.R. 12628, a bill which would provide what I consider an excessive increase and liberalization of veterans' education and training benefits.

Instead, I urge the Congress to send me a veterans' education bill along the lines that I have proposed. By doing so, we can avoid adding another half billion dollar load to the already overburdened taxpayer. Failure to do so will mean that the Congress will in the aggregate—Federal pay deferral, Railroad Retirement and Veterans Education—add over one and a half billion dollars to the Federal deficit in 1975.

This bill which I am returning to the Congress provides benefits that are greater than those granted to World War II and Korea veterans. It would cost the taxpayers half a billion dollars more in fiscal year 1975 than is appropriate in view of the country's current economic circumstances.

The decision not to sign this bill has not been an easy one. But it is necessary if all of us are to operate with essential budgetary restraint. The Nation must reduce Federal spending if we are to stop the inflation spiral.

I have asked the Congress on previous occasions to join with me to hold down Federal spending and help whip inflation. In two important instances, the Federal pay deferral plan and the Railroad Retirement bill, the Congress refused to join with me and the result has added an additional one billion dollars to the Federal taxpayers' burden.

Veterans' benefits should—and can—be improved. I continue to support a responsible increase in education benefits for veterans. I again urge the Congress, as I have on many occasions, to enact a GI Bill providing for an 18.2 percent benefit increase rather than the 23 percent in this bill. Such action would be in keeping with the needs for fiscal responsibility while recognizing the Nation's special debt to our veterans.

Since the Vietnam-era GI bill first went into effect in 1966, the total of veterans' benefit increases enacted through 1972 have substantially exceeded the rise in cost of living. Not including the provisions of this bill, the basic monthly education allowance has increased by a $120 per month or 120 percent since 1966. This compares with an actual rise of 55 percent in the Consumer Price Index.

In addition to the 23 percent benefit increase, this bill extends entitlement for GI bill benefits from 36 to 45 months for undergraduates. I believe the present entitlement of four academic years is sufficient time to permit a veteran to obtain his baccalaureate degree and to enable him to adjust to civilian life.

In addition, the bill contains other objectionable features despite my urging that they be eliminated. It establishes a new direct loan program for veteran students which departs from the sound objective of providing student aid through one department—Health, Education and Welfare—rather than through various Federal agencies. A direct loan program is also inefficient compared to available guaranteed loan programs, which provide substantially more assistance to the veteran at less cost to the Federal taxpayer.

I am returning this bill with reluctance, but it is my earnest hope that the Congress will demonstrate its willingness to join the executive branch in taking the difficult actions needed to hold down spending by the Federal Government while being equitable with our veterans.

GERALD R. FORD

The White House,
November 26, 1974.

NOTE: H.R. 12628 was enacted over the President's veto on December 3, 1974, as Public Law 93–508 (88 Stat. 1578).

264

Veto of Zinc Tariff Legislation Containing Tax Riders. *November 26, 1974*

To the House of Representatives:

I am returning without my approval H.R. 6191, "To amend the Tariff Schedules of the United States to provide that certain forms of zinc be admitted free of duty, and for other purposes."

This bill would suspend until June 30, 1977, the present duties on zinc ores and concentrates and zinc-bearing materials.

Unfortunately, the Congress attached to this desirable provision unacceptable tax riders which would grant windfall benefits to individuals already compensated for property losses resulting from certain disasters in 1972. Moreover, the most costly of these riders was added by the conference committee; and the significance of this rider was not explored during adoption of the conference report by the two houses.

Under current tax law, individuals are generally permitted to deduct casualty losses not otherwise compensated for by insurance, tort compensation, loan forgiveness, or other means. If individuals choose to deduct these losses, however, and are subsequently reimbursed, the reimbursement must be included as income in subsequent tax returns. Otherwise, the individual could receive a tax break for a loss that had not cost him anything.

H.R. 6191 would provide unwarranted and costly exceptions to the present law by allowing certain taxpayers who have already deducted their casualty losses to also exclude from taxable income any amounts received from tort compensation or Federal loan cancellations based on those losses. The cost of these benefits to the Government in terms of revenue loss would be about $130 million.

This would result in favored treatment for a select group of taxpayers relative to others with identical or even larger casualty losses. The individuals benefiting from this bill have already been treated more generously by the Federal Government than the present, more equitable law would allow. Finally, this special tax consideration resulting in a windfall to a limited group of taxpayers would be a very undesirable precedent.

If the Congress were to reenact this bill without the undesirable tax riders, I would be glad to approve it.

GERALD R. FORD

The White House,
November 26, 1974.

NOTE: On December 3, 1974, the House of Representatives sustained the President's veto.

265

Letter Accepting the Resignation of Anne L. Armstrong as Counsellor to the President. *November 27, 1974*

Dear Anne:

It was with the deepest regret that I learned that important family responsibilities have prompted your letter of resignation as a Presidential Counsellor and as a member of my Cabinet.

You will be greatly missed at the White House. I am certain, however, that the same sense of dedication to family that has characterized your dedication to country has made your decision a necessary one.

When I assumed the office of the Presidency on August 9, 1974, it was critically important that I have the immediate assistance and support of highly able, skilled, compassionate and loyal leaders in government. You were one of those key people who helped to fill that urgent requirement.

I thank you not only personally but on behalf of our fellow countrymen for your distinguished service.

Betty joins with me in wishing to you and yours the very best.

Sincerely,

JERRY FORD

[The Honorable Anne Armstrong, Counsellor to the President, The White House]

NOTE: Mrs. Armstrong's letter of resignation, dated November 26, 1974, and released with the President's letter, read as follows:

Dear Mr. President:

Right after you were sworn in as President, I remember telling you that even if we had searched 100 years, we could not have found anyone so well suited as you to give our country the high moral leadership it desperately needed in very difficult days. So, as you know, when you asked me to serve as a Counsellor and member of your Cabinet, I was highly honored and eagerly looked forward to serving you for an extended period.

In your first 100 days as President, you have fulfilled my best hopes. It is, therefore, with the deepest regret that I now must submit my resignation because of unforeseen and pressing family responsibilities which make it necessary for me to return to my home in Texas.

Your strong support for my various areas of responsibility, including the Bicentennial, Federal Property Council, the first White House Office of Women's Programs, and liaison to young people and Hispanic Americans, assures me their progress will continue.

We still face very difficult days, but I have great confidence in my country and in my President. The goals you are setting are the right ones. You have the right qualities to lead us to them—wisdom, integrity, strength of character, and the ability to relate to your fellow Americans. Your leadership offers the single best hope that America will enter its Third Century with its basic principles intact, with a clear vision of its future, with prosperity and peace.

After almost four years in Washington, I leave with a profound appreciation of the responsibility of our leaders not only to protect the public interest, but also to safeguard the public trust. Mr. President, I have every confidence in your ability to do both.

I wish you great success, and to you and Mrs. Ford and your family I wish great happiness.

Respectfully,

ANNE ARMSTRONG
Mrs. Tobin Armstrong

[The President, The White House, Washington, D.C.]

266

Remarks on Signing 18 Executive Warrants for Clemency. *November 29, 1974*

FIRST, let me, before reading the prepared statement, thank the Chairman and all of the members of the Board. It has, I know, been a difficult job and a tough responsibility, but I, for one, am very grateful for what each and every one of you have done.

On September 16, I announced my program of clemency, and I am pleased on this Thanksgiving weekend that I am able to announce my first decisions on recommendations of the Presidential Clemency Board involving 18 individual cases of draft evasion.

I wish to thank each of you here for sharing this ceremonial moment, and I also wish to thank the Clemency Board members for their very hard and effective work.

Signing ceremonies often mark the end of a project, but today these signings represent the beginning of the difficult task of administering clemency. Instead of signing these decisions in a routine way, I wish to use this occasion to underline the commitment of my Administration to an evenhanded policy of clemency.

When I initiated the policy, I detailed the reasons for my decision in this very difficult problem. I consider them as valid today as when I first announced them. We do not resolve difficult issues by ignoring them. There are honest differences that will continue to be discussed, but discussions must not overshadow the need for action and fair and open resolution of the clemency problem.

Of the 18 recommendations the Board has made to me, I have reviewed each one and have personally approved each one. Information on these cases will be made available by the Press Office.

I believe this more detailed information will help to explain the basis for my decision in each instance. Of course, considerable more information was made available to the Board, and to me, on which to base these decisions. But to make public the complete files on each individual would be a negation of his right to privacy.

In each case, however, the law was violated, and each has received punishment. The power of clemency can look to reasons for these actions which the law cannot. Unlike God's law, man's law cannot probe into the heart of human beings. The best way we can do this is to offer clemency and to provide a way for offenders to earn their way back into a rightful place in society.

Last week, I traveled overseas in search for peace. Yet, we cannot effectively seek peace abroad with other nations until we have made peace at home. While America reaches out to those whom we have disagreed with in the past, we must do no less within our own Nation.

Sometimes it seems easier for us to forgive foreign enemies than fellow Americans at home. Let us continue to search for a softening of the national animosity caused by differences over the Vietnam war. We will not forget the sacrifices of those who served and died in Vietnam.

In their honor, America must seek ways to live up to the ideals of freedom and charity that they fought to preserve. These first few decisions do not end the unfinished business of clemency, but the task of formal forgiveness is underway.

I hope it marks the beginning of personal forgiveness in the hearts of all Americans troubled by Vietnam and its aftermath.

I do want to thank you, all of the Board members, not only for the first-class job they have done but the way in which they have approached this very difficult responsibility. I am grateful. I am sure the individuals in the cases that are involved here are grateful. And I think the American people will be grateful for them assuming a difficult responsibility and performing it with very great distinction.

I thank you, Charlie, and each of the Board members on this occasion on behalf of all, including 213 million Americans.

Thank you very much.

NOTE: The President spoke at 1:21 p.m. in the Cabinet Room at the White House. In his remarks, the President referred to Charles E. Goodell, Chairman of the Presidential Clemency Board.

267

Letter Accepting the Resignation of William S. Whitehead as Chairman of the Renegotiation Board. *November 29, 1974*

Dear Bill:

I have your letter of November 29, and I will, of course, accept your resignation as Chairman of the Renegotiation Board, effective December 1, 1974.

The last five years have been difficult and challenging ones for you, and I want you to know that I fully understand the considerations which prompted your decision to resign the Chairmanship prior to your resignation as a member. The Renegotiation Board has a most important and vital role in government, and it is my intention to reinvigorate the Board so as to expand its role in the fight against inflation.

You have my sincere thanks and deep appreciation for your years of service to our Nation. Please know that you take with you my very best wishes for every happiness and success in the years ahead.

Sincerely,

JERRY FORD

[The Honorable William Scholl Whitehead, Chairman, Renegotiation Board, Washington, D.C. 20446]

NOTE: Mr. Whitehead's letter of resignation, released with the President's letter, read as follows:

Dear Mr. President:

It is respectfully requested that I be relieved from the duties as Chairman and activities as a Member of this Agency, effective December 1, 1974. Under such an arrangement I would, however, expect to utilize my present facilities at the Board for purposes of putting my affairs in order until my retirement, on December 31, 1974.

The basic reason for the above request is that the Board is about to become involved in the determination of several major policy areas. Under the circumstances, I believe the continuing Members should have a free hand in making these decisions during this last phase of my transitional period.

Sincerely,

W. S. WHITEHEAD
Chairman

[The President, The White House]

268

Remarks at a Reception Honoring Professional Golfer Lee Elder. *December 1, 1974*

LET ME just make a few observations and comments. It is so nice for me personally to have an opportunity to be here with Lee and Rose and to pay tribute not only to Lee's great prowess and capability, skill, competitive spirit on the golf links but also to pay tribute to a wonderful pair. Between Lee and Rose, I don't think, from my observations, you could find a nicer pair, and I compliment both of them.

I think most of you know that I am a sports buff, a has-been who really reads the sports page first every morning, because you at least get a 50–50 break on the sports page. But nevertheless, to be here and to participate in a small way in paying tribute to Lee and to Rose, I consider a great privilege and a high honor.

I have watched Lee, of course, over the years. I do watch those tournaments. I have some work in my lap, and then I watch the drives and the putts and wish I could do as well. And I get about half the work done and the rest of the time I am envious of all the skill of Lee. I met Jim Colbert here, Jim Weickers, and I met Jim Dent's wife. I don't know whether I met Jim or not.

But anyhow, I think sports, athletics are very important in our American society, and it was a great thrill for me a couple of weeks ago to play 18 with Lee and John Pohanka and Les Arends. Lee gave me a little advice, and that advice was very sound. In fact, it was very good, and the newspapers printed it. It was so good that Henry Kissinger was getting a little worried.

But anyhow, I think that Lee and I have a great deal in common. You won't think so at the outset. We both are in occupations where there is some spotlight. We are both in occupations where there is a lot of competition. We are both in occupations where the press kind of look at you and see whether you make a mistake or not. All I can say is that the goofs that we make really get publicized. The good part of it is that Lee doesn't make as many as I do.

But the thing that really impresses me about this turnout is the fact that all of you people are here—and many from all over the country—to pay tribute to a person who has achieved what we think in the sports world is a great accomplishment—the right to compete in the Master's Tournament at Augusta.

I just watch that. I could never compete in it, but I admire and respect everybody who has accomplished that great objective. Now, you know, next April when Lee is a participant, I am going to be watching on that television set, pulling for Lee to show them that the guy that makes it one year can also win the tournament.

But the reason all of you are here is to contribute to a Lee Elder scholarship fund, a fund that is aimed at giving a better education to one or more young people. And as we look around the world today, I think we have to recognize that better education is one way for not only us, individually, but our country and the world to do better in the future. So, I thank all of you who have come here and have contributed, because you are not only paying a tribute to Lee but you are making a good investment in a better America.

Now, one final comment. I don't think many people will remember 1975 as the year that Jerry Ford was President, but they will remember that 1975 was the year that Lee Elder won the Master's.

Good luck to you, Lee. It is nice to be here. You are a great American and a great tribute to golf. I am going to see you at the Kemper. I am going to see you at Doral—I have been to the Doral several times. And I am going to—there is one other that I have committed—Jackie Gleason in Inverrary. I am honorary chairman of that.

It is nice to be here.

NOTE: The President spoke at 7:05 p.m. at the Washington Hilton Hotel. In his remarks, the President referred to professional golfers Jim Colbert, Jim Weickers, and Jim Dent, and to Washington, D.C., area automotive dealer John Pohanka.

269

Letter Accepting the Resignation of Dean Burch as Counsellor to the President. *December 2, 1974*

Dear Dean:

I have your letter and it is with the deepest regret that I accept your resignation as Counsellor to the President, effective December 31, 1974, as you requested.

For more than five years, you have served our Nation, first as Chairman of the Federal Communications Commission and then here at the White House. In each of your responsibilities, we have come to expect of you not only great dedication and energy, but also an unfailing sense of the needs and well-being of all our people. Needless to say, your services will be greatly missed.

I welcome this opportunity to also express my own personal appreciation for the unhesitating and skillful assistance you have rendered to my Administration these past four months. In particular, I am grateful for your help during those early, critically important days following my assumption to the Presidency when I could with confidence call upon your good counsel as well as your leadership.

Also, I deeply appreciate your very kind comments and good wishes in your letter. In turn, you can be sure that Betty and I extend our warmest best wishes for every happiness and success in the future to you and your family.

Sincerely,

JERRY FORD

[The Honorable Dean Burch, The White House, Washington, D.C.]

NOTE: The President's letter, dated November 30, 1974, was released December 2. Mr. Burch's letter of resignation, dated November 29 and released with the President's letter, read as follows:

Dear Mr. President:

For more than five years, it has been my pleasure to serve in the government, both at the Federal Communications Commission and here at the White House. These have been momentous years for me, at once satisfying, frustrating, rewarding and painful.

It is now time for me to return to the private sector to carry out my non-delegable duties as a father and husband. I therefore submit my resignation effective December 31, 1974.

These past months in your administration have been truly gratifying and the courtesies you have extended will never be forgotten. You have grasped the falling standard and by generous applications of hard work, wisdom and above all, human sensitivity, have restored this country's faith in the constitutional system.

I wish for you and your lovely family all the good things which are so richly deserved.

Sincerely,

DEAN BURCH
Counsellor to the President

[The President, The White House, Washington, D.C.]

270

Message to the Senate Transmitting Agreement on the International Office of Epizootics. *December 2, 1974*

To the Senate of the United States:

To receive the advise and consent of the Senate to accession, I transmit herewith the International Agreement for the Creation at Paris of an International Office of Epizootics, originated in Paris on January 25, 1924.

In the nearly fifty years of its existence, the International Office of Epizootics (OIE) has become the most important organization in international control of animal diseases. Its current 79-nation membership includes most major developed countries other than the United States. The OIE provides timely warnings to its members of animal disease outbreaks, a form of exchange of technical information, and other valuable services. In these times of increased concern about food availability at home and abroad, the United States is obliged to help protect that supply. The cost of participation in OIE is small when weighed against its potential benefits. Also the United States can make its scientific and managerial experience in disease control available through OIE in an effective way to underline our international interest in food supply.

I, therefore, recommend that the Senate grant early and favorable consideration to the Agreement and give its advice and consent to accession.

GERALD R. FORD

The White House,
December 2, 1974.

NOTE: The text of the treaty and accompanying papers are printed in Senate Executive M (93d Cong., 2d sess.).

271

The President's News Conference of *December 2, 1974*

TRIP TO JAPAN, THE REPUBLIC OF KOREA, AND THE SOVIET UNION

OPENING STATEMENT

THE PRESIDENT. [1.] Perhaps I can anticipate some of your questions by summarizing my recent visits to Japan, the Republic of Korea, and the Soviet Union.

In Japan, we succeeded in establishing a new era of relations between our two countries. We demonstrated our continuing commitment to the independence and to the security of South Korea. At Vladivostok we put a firm ceiling on the strategic arms race, which heretofore has eluded us since the nuclear age began. I believe this is something for which future generations will thank us.

Finally, Secretary Kissinger's mission maintained the momentum in China with the People's Republic of China.

My meetings at Vladivostok with General Secretary Brezhnev were a valuable opportunity to review Soviet-American relations and chart their future course. Although this was our original purpose, Secretary Brezhnev and I found it possible to go beyond this get-acquainted stage.

Building on the achievements of the past 3 years, we agreed that the prospects were favorable for more substantial and, may I say, very intensive negotiations on the primary issue of a limitation of strategic arms. In the end, we agreed on the general framework for a new agreement that will last through 1985.

We agreed it is realistic to aim at completing this agreement next year. This is possible because we made major breakthroughs on two critical issues:

Number one, we agreed to put a ceiling of 2,400 each on the total number of intercontinental ballistic missiles, submarine-launched missiles, and heavy bombers.

Two, we agreed to limit the number of missiles that can be armed with multiple warheads—MIRV's. Of each side's total of 2,400, 1,320 can be so armed.

These ceilings are well below the force levels which would otherwise have been expected over the next 10 years and very substantially below the forces which would result from an all-out arms race over that same period.

What we have done is to set firm and equal limits on the strategic forces of each side, thus preventing an arms race with all its terror, instability, war-breeding tension, and economic waste.

We have, in addition, created the solid basis from which future arms reductions can be made and, hopefully, will be negotiated.

It will take more detailed negotiations to convert this agreed framework into a comprehensive accord. But we have made a long step toward peace on a basis of equality, the only basis on which an agreement was possible.

Beyond this, our improved relations with the other nations of Asia developed on this journey will continue to serve the interests of the United States and the cause of peace for months to come. Economy, energy, security, and trade relations were discussed, which will be of mutual benefit to us all.

I would like to repeat publicly my thanks and gratitude for the hospitality extended to me by all of my hosts and, through me, to the American people.

Miss Thomas [Helen Thomas, United Press International], I am glad to respond to your question.

QUESTIONS

[2.] Q. Mr. President, this pact permits the nuclear buildup to go ahead. Since you want to cut Government spending, how many billions of dollars will this cost the American people over the years, and also, do you think that the Russians stalled last July because they knew that Mr. Nixon was doomed in the Presidency and preferred to deal with his successor?

THE PRESIDENT. I would like to correct, if I might, one impression. This does not permit an agreed buildup. It puts a cap on future buildups, and it actually reduces a part of the buildup at the present time.

It is important, I should say, however, in order for us to maintain equality, which is a keystone of this program, to have an adequate amount of military expenditures. But I can say this without hesitation or qualification: If we had not had this agreement, it would have required the United States to substantially increase its military expenditures in the strategic areas.

So, we put a cap on the arms race. We actually made some reductions below present programs. It is a good agreement, and I think that the American people will buy it, because it provides for equality and it provides for a negotiated reduction in several years ahead.

Mr. Cormier [Frank Cormier, Associated Press].

[3.] Q. Mr. President, there are reports that you and Mr. Brezhnev made some progress in maybe fashioning a complementary approach to negotiations in the Middle East. More specifically, perhaps the Soviets would agree to try to persuade the PLO [Palestine Liberation Organization] to acknowledge that Israel has a right to exist, and we then might try to persuade Israel to talk to the PLO. Is there any truth to this?

The President. Mr. Cormier, Mr. Brezhnev and I did discuss at some length our different views on the settlement of the Middle East. There are some differences, but they are not as major as it would appear.

We indicated that, in our judgment, it was important for continuous progress to be made, perhaps with negotiations between Israel and one or more of the other Arab nations.

We also agreed that at a certain point a Geneva conference might be the final answer. So, as we discussed our what appeared to be different views at the outset, I think we came to an agreement that it was in the interest of the nations in the Middle East, the interest of the world at large, that both parties make a maximum effort to keep negotiations going.

We think our step-by-step approach is the right one for the time being, but we don't preclude the possibility of a Geneva conference.

[4.] Q. You say that this is going to reduce a part of the buildup. Does that mean, then, that we are going to spend less on defense next year than we are spending this year?

The President. It does not mean that, because only a part of our total defense program is related to strategic arms research, development, deployment, and operations and maintenance. We do have an obligation within the limits of 2,400 on delivery systems and 1,320 on MIRV's to keep our forces up to that level.

And I think we can, with about the same expenditure level for the next fiscal year, as at the present.

But in the other programs, in our tactical forces and other military programs, there is an inflationary cost. The military has that inflation just like you and I do, so we will probably have to increase our military budget next year just to take care of the costs of inflation.

Q. Just to follow up, we are not quite to that ceiling yet, are we? Do you intend to stay below that ceiling, or are you going to try to reach that ceiling?

The President. I intend to stay below the ceiling. That is the agreement. But we do have an obligation to stay up to that ceiling, and the budget that I will recommend will keep our strategic forces either up to or aimed at that objective.

[5.] Q. Mr. President, since it is widely believed the Soviet Union has larger rockets capable of carrying heavier payloads and being MIRVed, to a larger extent carrying more warheads, can you tell us what the relative position would be between the United States and the Soviet Union in terms of warheads if each side goes to the maximum number of 1,320 on the MIRVed limit?

The President. On delivery systems, we are equal. On the MIRVing, we are equal. I think the question you are asking is throw weight. It is recognized that the Soviet Union has a heavier throw weight, but the agreement does not preclude the United States from increasing its throw weight capability.

A number of years ago, our military decided that we wanted smaller missiles that were more accurate. That has been the decision of our military.

Now, if the military decides at the present time that they want to increase the throw weight, we have that right under the agreement, and I can tell you that we have the capability to do so.

So, if there is an inequality in throw weight, it can be remedied if our military recommended and the Congress appropriates the money.

Q. Mr. President, if you find the Soviet Union leaning, then, toward getting the maximum throw weight or the maximum number of warheads on their MIRV missiles, would you then recommend that the United States accelerate and move from smaller missiles to larger ones?

The President. The Soviet military guidelines were for heavier missiles, heavier throw weight. Our military took a different point of view some years ago. The Soviet Union is limited as to delivery systems and as to MIRV's within the delivery systems. They cannot go beyond those.

The agreement gives us the flexibility to move up in throw weight if we want to. It does not preclude the Soviets from increasing throw weight, but I think for good reasons they have no justification for doing so.

Yes, Mr. Sperling [Godfrey Sperling, Christian Science Monitor].

[6.] Q. Wouldn't your stated accomplishments in Russia have carried more long-range credibility if they had been put initially and then described later on in less sanguine and more modest terms?

THE PRESIDENT. Well, if I understand the question, when I came back a week ago yesterday, we did not have in writing what is called an aide mémoire, which was the specific agreement in writing that General Secretary Brezhnev and I had agreed to verbally. That has now been received.

Until that had been received and we had checked it out, we felt it was wise to speak in generalities. I am giving to you and to the American people tonight the specific figures. They are, I think, constructive. It is a good agreement. It is an agreement—if I might repeat—that puts a cap on the arms race, it makes some reductions, and it gives us an opportunity to negotiate.

So, I don't think a week's delay in the specifics has handicapped our presentation.

[7.] Q. More specifically, what percentage of the state of progress in Russia was yours and how much was Mr. Nixon's?

THE PRESIDENT. Well, I don't really think I ought to get into an evaluation of that. The United States has been working on a strategic arms limitation agreement for 3 or 4 years. I think we made headway in SALT I. I think we have made a real breakthrough in SALT Two.

Q. Mr. President, I would like to get back to the cost of missiles for one moment, if we may. I understand we are now spending about $15 billion a year in strategic arms, and there is an enormous amount of missile building to be done under this agreement over the next 10 years, both in MIRV's and in throw weight. Will our costs continue at about the level they are now for the next 10 years or will it be more?

THE PRESIDENT. My best judgment is that our strategic arms costs will hold relatively the same. It will not be substantially expanded other than for any increase resulting from inflation.

[8.] Q. Mr. President, under the agreement, the United States tactical nuclear weapons at the forward bases in Europe were not included. Do you expect that they will be reduced or eliminated under some future mutual balanced force reduction agreement with the Soviet Union?

THE PRESIDENT. One of the very significant benefits of the agreement from Vladivostok was the fact we didn't have to include in the 2,400 or the 1,320—either the delivery systems or the MIRV's—as far as the forward base systems were concerned.

I am sure you know we are involved in mutual balanced force reductions in Western Europe. When we get closer to an agreement there—and I hope we will; we are presently negotiating in Vienna in this area—it is hopeful that we can make some reductions, both in numbers of military personnel between ourselves and the allies on the one side and the Warsaw Pact nations and the Soviet Union on the other, as well as any arms reductions.

Q. Beyond your hope, is that a commitment that you made to the Soviet leaders in Vladivostok?

THE PRESIDENT. No, we made no agreement concerning the mutual balanced force reductions. We did agree to continue negotiations.

[9.] Q. Mr. President, are you satisfied that the Soviets are carrying out the spirit and the letter of the 1972 arms limitation agreements?

THE PRESIDENT. We know of no violations, either on the part of the Soviet Union or by ourselves. There have been some allegations that the Soviet Union has violated the SALT I agreement. We don't think they have.

There are, however, some ambiguities. When the SALT I agreement was agreed to, there was established a standing consultative commission made up of the Soviet Union and the United States. That commission can meet twice a year to analyze any allegations as to violations of SALT I. It is our intention to call for a meeting of that group—I think in January of next year—to analyze any of the ambiguities that have been alleged. We don't think there have been any violations, but I have a responsibility to find out. And we intend to follow through under the agreed procedure of the 1972 agreements.

[10.] Q. Mr. President, since there is no limit in this agreement on throw weight and since there is no limit on multiple warheads, and since additional multiple warheads could be put on the bigger missiles, more or less ad infinitum, how can you say that this is a lid or cap on the arms race?

THE PRESIDENT. Well, it certainly, number one, puts a limit on the delivery systems—2,400—and as I indicated at the outset, this does result in a cutback as far as the Soviet Union is concerned.

The 1,320 limitation on MIRV's does put a lid on the planned or programed program for ourselves as well as the Soviet Union.

Now, the throw weight problem is one that we can remedy if we want to. Our military took a different point of view some years ago when they designed our ballistic missiles, but we have that flexibility.

Now, if we decide to go to a heavier throw weight, we can add on a MIRVed missile a greater number of individual warheads. That is a choice of flexibility that we have, and I think it is one of the benefits of this agreement.

Q. You wouldn't describe that as an arms race?

THE PRESIDENT. Well, it is an attempt, if our military wanted to achieve an equality in this particular area. We have equality on delivery systems and the right to MIRV from those delivery systems. In the other, if it is our choice, we can go up in throw weight.

Yes, Sarah [Sarah McClendon, McClendon News Service].

[11.] Q. Mr. President, I want to ask you, what about conventional weapons? We have heard from Senator Goldwater and we have heard from Admiral Zumwalt[1] that we are very weak on conventional weapons and we need more of those, rather than the kind that you have in your agreement.

THE PRESIDENT. Well, of course, this agreement, Sarah, was limited to strategic arms. We hope, as I indicated a moment ago, to continue our negotiations for the mutual balanced force reductions in Europe. That, of course, would have a limit on the conventional weapons.

In the meantime, I think it is of mandatory importance for the United States to maintain its conventional capability—the Army, the Navy, the Air Force, the Marines—because the United States, through a responsible military program, can maintain the peace.

If we cut back our defense in conventional weapons, I think we will have weakened our position for the maintenance of peace. I don't intend to propose a budget in that regard.

Q. Mr. President, do you think that we can do both of these, then?

THE PRESIDENT. I think so.

[12.] Q. To follow up on Frank Cormier's question, did you and Mr. Brezhnev discuss some kind of a trade-off whereby Israel would deal with the PLO and the PLO would recognize Israel's right to exist as a state?

THE PRESIDENT. We didn't get into that detail. Israel has indicated that it would not negotiate with the PLO. We have no way of forcing them to do so.

The discussion between Mr. Brezhnev and myself, as far as the Middle East was concerned, was to state our position and their position, and as we discussed it, I think we came to a higher degree of agreement in that our position was understood by them and the prospects of a Geneva agreement was understood by us.

MR. CORMIER. I understand you would like to devote about half of the news conference to domestic affairs, and I think we are about at the halfway point.

THE PRESIDENT. Thank you very much, Mr. Cormier.

---

[1] Adm. Elmo R. Zumwalt, Jr., USN (Ret.), Chief of Naval Operations 1970–74.

THE ECONOMY

OPENING STATEMENT

[13.] I would be glad to talk about both of them a lot longer, but let me make a statement about the economy and then we will have questions on that.

Before turning to domestic questions, which I am sure will concentrate on our economic problems, I would like to say this: We are currently facing three serious challenges—inflation, recession, and energy.

Inflation, which is a deadly, long-range enemy that cannot be ignored.

Recession, which is a serious threat that already has hurt many, many citizens and alarms many, many more. Hopefully, it is a shorter-range evil, but neither can be ignored, nor will it be.

Assuring adequate energy will require our best efforts. The energy crisis also contributes both to inflation and to recessionary pressures.

Much of the program that I recommended to the Congress and the American people on October 8 is still pending before the Congress. It was designed to meet all three of these challenges. It was balanced to deal with an already rampaging inflation and already anticipated recessionary forces.

And make no mistake—it is imperative that we fight both inflation and recession at the same time. The question is one of balance and changing circumstances. At least four measures deserve special and, I think, immediate attention by this Congress. They cannot wait until next March or April.

I have recommended a series of budget-reducing actions totaling $4.6 billion so that the Federal Government can set an example of fiscal restraint.

Furthermore, I urge the Congress not to add any more spending. As you can see from this chart [*indicating*] the Congress has already added, or is about to add, over $1 billion to this year's spending and, I add with emphasis, against my recommendations.

Anticipating rising unemployment 2 months ago, I asked for a national employment assistance act to provide useful work for those who had exhausted their unemployment benefits and others not previously covered. Action on this is essential before the present Congress adjourns.

Action is needed on the Trade Reform Act. This can help immeasurably in fighting both recession and inflation, by creating more jobs and providing more goods as well.

The tax reform bill reported by the Committee on Ways and Means of the House provides needed tax relief for low-income citizens while taxing windfall profits of certain oil companies. I don't support every provision in this committee bill, but on balance it is a good bill and badly needed at this time.

Congress has not only ample time but the clear obligation to complete action on several vital energy proposals before adjournment.

Times are nowhere near desperate enough to paraphrase President F. D. Roosevelt's great rallying cry that "the only thing we have to fear is fear itself." Still it is a good thing to remember. But I do want to say to my fellow Americans that our greatest danger today is to fall victim to the more exaggerated alarms that are being generated about the underlying health and strength of our economy.

We are going to take some lumps, and we are going to take some bumps, but with the help of the Congress and the American people, we are perfectly able to cope with our present and foreseeable economic problems.

But action is more helpful than criticism. And every week that the Congress delays makes the prospects a little bleaker.

I will be glad to answer any questions.

QUESTIONS

[14.] Q. Mr. President, many people feel that the country is ahead of the Government, that people are prepared to sacrifice if they know that everyone is going to be biting the same bullet at the same time. How does this jibe with your information?

THE PRESIDENT. I think the American people are ready to make more sacrifices than maybe the Congress and even the executive branch, including the President, believe they will.

I have a great respect and admiration for the strength and the willingness to sacrifice of the American people. I have tried to give them a program that does require some sacrifice—a 5 percent surtax on 28 percent of the taxpayers—so we could alleviate the problems of the people in the lower income brackets.

I have made some other suggestions, but I believe the Congress, along with myself, have to give some leadership to the American people, who I believe are willing to respond. And I have tried to present a program that would call for that response.

I hope the Congress responds, and if they don't like my program, will come up with one of their own that will equally call upon the American people to make some sacrifices.

[15.] Q. Mr. President, in the absence of an Arab oil embargo this winter, could you please give the American people some indication as to whether they can expect a gasoline shortage this winter; that is, long lines at gas stations comparable to last winter? And also, your predecessor made a firm commitment to the effect that Americans would not, under his Administration, have to pay a dollar a gallon for gasoline. Can you make that same assurance over the next 12 months?

THE PRESIDENT. In 1974 at this point, the use of gasoline has been less than the anticipated growth. In other words, we are using less now than the experts forecast we would use when they were laying out the charts as to the anticipated demand. The net result is that we have more gasoline in storage today than we had a year ago at this time.

Now, that is not enough to carry us through in case there was an oil embargo, but we are in a healthier position today than we were a year ago.

Nevertheless, it is my judgment that we have to keep the pressure on the savings of energy, including a holddown on gasoline consumption. We are trying to reduce our importation of oil from overseas by 1 million barrels per day. We are making headway in that regard.

We haven't achieved it, but the net result is we don't anticipate, at this point, from any foreseeable circumstances, any gas rationing, nor do we foresee any serious shortage.

Q. Mr. President, I don't believe you answered my question about can you make the same assurance that your predecessor did about gasoline not going to a dollar a gallon.

THE PRESIDENT. I don't foresee gasoline going to a dollar a gallon. It is what, 45 to 55 cents a gallon today, depending on where you buy it. I see no prospects of the cost of gasoline going up to a dollar a gallon.

[16.] Q. Mr. President, this question perhaps goes back to the earlier part of the news conference, but it has an economic impact. And that is how much will it cost to reach the ceiling which you negotiated with Mr. Brezhnev, and when do you expect that the United States will reach this ceiling?

THE PRESIDENT. As I indicated in answer to an earlier question, I think we must continue our present strategic research development, deployment, maintenance programs.

And we are going to move into the present program some additional new weapons systems—the B–1 aircraft, the Trident submarine. The net result is that costs will probably go up as we phase out some and phase in some and phase out others.

Now, the total annual cost will be relatively the same plus the cost of inflation.

Q. Is it $18 billion?

THE PRESIDENT. It is in that ballpark.

Q. And for how many years do you expect this to continue, Mr. President?

THE PRESIDENT. Until we are able to negotiate a reduction below the 2,400 delivery systems and the 1,320 MIRV systems.

[17.] Q. Although you have repeatedly said that you will not recommend a gasoline tax increase, your advisers on energy seem to be lobbying for this as if we are going to be in a very bad economic situation, very bad in regard to the drain of our assets overseas. Now, will you reconsider your objection to this?

THE PRESIDENT. I have not been persuaded that a 20-cent increase in the gas tax is the right answer. I was interested in a poll that was published today which indicated that 81 percent of the American people agree with my position.

Well, if 81 percent of the American people agree with my position, I really don't think a 20-cent-a-gallon increase in the gasoline tax will go through the Congress, even if I recommended it.

So, it is my judgment that if we have to, by taxation, cut down on consumption, there must be a better way to do it rather than a 20-cent-a-gallon increase in the gas tax. If 81 percent of the American people agree with me and don't agree with the various people who are advocating this, I think I am on pretty solid ground.

[18.] Q. The American Conference of Mayors has put as their number one priority the renewal and continuance of the revenue sharing program. Do you plan, in your State of the Union Message to Congress, to ask for a renewal of that program on its present basis?

THE PRESIDENT. I have indicated while I was Vice President, since I have been President, that I think the general revenue sharing program has been a good one. It is now provided from the Federal Treasury around $16 billion to State and local units of government. I had an hour-plus meeting with the Domestic Council and others several days ago, and we analyzed the program. I think it ought to be extended.

I think it has produced a great deal of good at the local level as well as at the State level. Now, we are in the process of analyzing any internal changes, but overall, I think the program is good, and I want to work with the mayors and the Governors and the county commissioners to make sure that the Congress extends this sound program.

[19.] Q. Mr. President, does the Justice Department suit to break up AT&T have your full approval, and are you satisfied as to the impact that such a breakup would have on the efficiency and cost of telephone service in the United States?

THE PRESIDENT. I was kept informed, but I don't think I should pass judgment on every antitrust suit that is contemplated by the Department of Justice.

If they think they have a case, I think they ought to take the initiative within broad guidelines that I firmly believe in personally.

Now in this case, as I understand it, it is not a suit aimed at AT&T simply because of its size. It is aimed at AT&T because of its alleged activities that result in noncompetition.

Now the Antitrust Act says, in effect, that the elimination of competition is grounds for antitrust action by the Department of Justice. If that is the basis—and I understand it is—then in my opinion the Department of Justice was acting properly.

[20.] Q. Mr. President, would you continue to favor your national employment assistance act even if Congress did not pass a tax program to raise the revenue necessary to pay for it?

THE PRESIDENT. I would hope the Congress would be responsible and pass legislation that would provide the revenue to pay for the Unemployment Act extension that I recommended and the public service employment program that I recommended.

I think this was a sound balance we proposed, or I recommended, that we ought to tax the wealthier people, the top 28 percent of the American people, to spread the difficulties of a recession and inflation.

I think it would be irresponsible for the Congress to add expenditures and not provide any additional revenues.

Q. Mr. President, a followup, please. If you can get the one without the other, would you take it?

THE PRESIDENT. Well, I will pass judgment on that when that alternative is on my desk.

[21.] Q. Mr. President, is it wise, is it fair to concentrate much of your budget-cutting recommendations on health, education, and welfare, and veterans—what we might call the human fringe suffering from inflation most—while not recommending at all any increased stringency in military weapons?

THE PRESIDENT. I don't think that is a fair challenge to my program. What I did at the time I looked at the budget was to take into consideration the reductions that the Congress had made in the defense budget, and the Congress had already cut the defense budget $2.6 billion. I recommended an additional $400 to $500 million cut, making it roughly a $3 billion total cut in the proposed expenditures of the Department of Defense.

Now, since the Defense Department had already had a sizable reduction by the Congress, I felt we had to go across the rest of the spectrum of the Federal Government to find additional reductions.

Now, what we have done was to require certain individuals, for example, who wanted food stamps to pay slightly more in order to qualify for food stamps. We called upon the Congress to slow down, in some instances, public works projects.

We tried in the $4.6 billion reduction to spread the reductions across the board, and I think if you look at what the Congress did in the first place and what we have proposed in the second, it is a fairly well balanced program.

[22.] Q. To follow up, a question that is reaching but is still in the economic ballpark: If the ceiling works, will there ever be a saving, an actual saving, in expenditures for strategic weapons?

THE PRESIDENT. Very, very definitely, and that is the fundamental question that we have answered. If there had been no ceiling of 2,400 on launchers and 1,320 on MIRV's, we would have had an arms race. The Soviet Union had plans and programs, we believe, to substantially increase the number of launchers and to substantially go beyond 1,320 on the MIRV's.

And we have the capability, and I think if there had been an arms race with the Soviet Union going higher and higher and higher, we as a nation, for our own security, would have been forced to do precisely the same.

So, Mr. Brezhnev and I agreed that we first had to cap the arms race, both in launchers and in MIRV's. We have done that, and I wish to compliment Mr. Brezhnev, because his opening statement, if I can paraphrase it, was that he and I, his country and ours, had an obligation to not indulge in an arms race, to put a cap on the proposed expenditures in both categories.

It was a statesmanlike approach at the outset, and because he believed that, and because I believe it, I think we made substantial progress, and I strongly defend what we did.

MR. CORMIER. Thank you, Mr. President.

NOTE: President Ford's fifth news conference began at 7:31 p.m. in Room 450 at the Old Executive Office Building. It was broadcast live on radio and television.

272

Remarks at the Boy Scouts' Annual Awards Dinner. *December 2, 1974*

Bill, Mark, Rudy, Reid, all of you wonderful ladies and gentlemen, and the fine young people, young boys, young girls as well:

It is a great privilege and a very high honor to be here tonight, and I thank you very much for the award. It is one of those things I, for one, will never forget.

I think they say once a Scout always a Scout, and I can tell you from my own experience that is true. After all these years I still love the outdoors. I still know how to cook for myself, at least at breakfast. And as anyone who saw those pictures of me in Japan will know, on occasion I still go around in short pants. [*Laughter*]

I am particularly grateful for your invitation to be here tonight for a very personal reason. It has recently been said that I am too much of a Boy Scout in the way I have conducted myself as President, and so I reviewed the Boy Scout laws and Boy Scout oath.

They say that a Scout is trustworthy, loyal, helpful, friendly, courteous, kind, obedient, cheerful, thrifty, brave, clean, and reverent. That is not bad for somebody who knew it 46 years ago.

And the Boy Scout oath is, "On my honor, I will do my best to do my duty to God and my country, to obey the Scout laws, to help other people at all times, to keep myself physically strong, mentally awake and morally straight."

Well, if these are not the goals of the people of the United States, what they want their President to live up to, then I must draw this conclusion: Either you have the wrong man or I have the wrong country, and I don't believe either is so.

I happen to believe that the ideals and the aspirations of all Americans and all Boy Scouts are one and the same, and I will continue to use those ideals as a guide and as a compass in all of my official duties. I think our goal ought to be, or should be, more Boy Scouts in government, not less.

Coming here this evening, after an interesting press conference, to receive this coveted award takes me back a good many years to one of the proudest moments of my youth: the day I was awarded the Eagle Scout badge, more than 46 years ago.

I remember the pride I felt then in the court of honor and the pledge that I made to myself never to dishonor that badge. As Betty knows, I still have that badge, by the way. It is a very treasured possession, and over the years it has been,

I think, a good reminder to me. It is a reminder of some of the basic, good things about our country and a reminder of some of the simple but vital values that can make life productive and very rewarding.

A very great American, Dwight D. Eisenhower, once said that his faith in our young people was as unbounded as his faith in America. I share that faith. I believe that the youth and America go hand-in-hand. For it is America's youthful spirit, strength, its idealism that are the keys to our country's greatness—even today as we approach our 200th anniversary as a nation, we are still a very young country, a young people compared to most other nations on this Earth.

The early explorers understood better than they realized the significance of calling the American continent the "New World." For it was here on these shores that millions of people from every branch of the human family were to come and to make a new beginning, were to launch one of the greatest, noblest adventures in the history of mankind.

From the start, even the humblest of those early settlers seemed to understand. As they landed in this new world, they knew that they, too, were beginning a new life, leaving behind the oppressions and the injustices that had darkened old countries and old civilizations.

Of course, this new promised land was not delivered to them upon a silver platter. Each new wave of pioneers and immigrants had to build a place for themselves and add their individual contributions to this new life. It was hard work; it was long work; it took long hours; and it never ended. It still goes on today as we tackle new problems and new challenges.

And that is where Scouting comes in. The teamwork, the self-discipline, and just as important, the sense of adventure that grow out of the Scouting experience are the very things we need today to build a better America.

So often, the deepest, the most profound emotions and ideas are expressed in very simple words. Today, when some people are casting about for new values, new answers, and new outlooks on life, the key to many of our problems lies in the basic values of the Scout laws—in trust, in loyalty, courtesy, thrift, bravery, reverence.

One of the wisest judges of our country, probably one of the wisest we ever produced, was Supreme Court Justice Louis D. Brandeis. Like all great jurists, he understood more than just the law. He knew the human mind, the human heart, and he saw a great deal of each of them in his many years on the bench—both their good sides and their bad. It was an experience that might have made a cynic of him, but it did not. The more Justice Brandeis saw of the American people, the more he became convinced of their basic goodness.

In most Americans, he once said, there is a spark of idealism which can be fanned into a flame. Scouting is one of these things that keeps that spark of idealism alive, that plants it in the hearts of young Americans while preparing them for manhood and for citizenship.

That is why, as an old Scout who still tries to live by the Scout laws and the Scout oath, with no apologies, I am proud and honored to accept this award tonight.

Thank you very much.

NOTE: The President spoke at 10:10 p.m. in the Sheraton Hall at the Sheraton-Park Hotel on receiving the Scouter of the Year award, a gold coin honoring him as the first Eagle Scout to become President of the United States.

In his opening remarks, the President referred to William G. Whyte, president, and Rudy Flythe, Scout executive, National Capital Area Council, Boy Scouts of America; Mark "Evans" Austad, master of ceremonies, and W. Reid Thompson, chairman of the dinner.

273

Letter Accepting the Resignation of William E. Timmons as Assistant to the President. *December 3, 1974*

Dear Bill:

It is with the deepest regret, but also with immense gratitude for your many years of dedicated service to our Nation, that I accept your resignation as Assistant to the President, effective December 31, 1974, as you requested. In so doing, I want you to know that I fully understand the personal concerns which prompted your decision.

For more than twenty-two years, you have made outstanding contributions to the public service through your skillful, energetic leadership, sound judgment and a confident sense of our national well-being. Your years as Assistant to the President for Legislative Affairs have been ones of great challenge but also high achievement as decisions have been made and legislative programs molded which will assure a peaceful, prosperous future for all our fellow citizens. You will be missed here at the White House, and I know I can speak for my former colleagues in Congress in saying they too will miss you as the President's liaison with Capitol Hill.

I particularly want to take this opportunity to express my personal appreciation for the unhesitating, loyal and highly capable assistance you have given my Administration since I assumed the Presidency last summer. Your certain support and wise counsel were, throughout those early, critically important days, a constant source of strength and confidence for me. You have my thanks and my lasting gratitude.

Betty joins me in wishing you and your family the very best in the years ahead.

Sincerely,

JERRY FORD

[The Honorable William E. Timmons, The White House, Washington, D.C.]

NOTE: Mr. Timmons' letter of resignation, released with the President's letter, read as follows:

Dear Mr. President:

I respectfully submit my resignation as your Assistant for Legislative Affairs effective December 31, 1974.

My decision to leave public service after twenty-two years has not been easy, but pressing personal affairs now require my attention. I will depart your service with immense gratitude for being given the opportunity to participate in our national Government.

I regret I will be unable to share the many exciting challenges and opportunities the future holds for you. However, I will leave with the greatest confidence in your leadership, comforted by firsthand knowledge of your abilities, and with warm affection for you, the First Lady and family.

Your character, philosophy and commitment will remain a source of inspiration and strength to me. Best wishes for the accomplishments I know you'll enjoy.

Sincerely,

WILLIAM E. TIMMONS
Assistant to the President

[Honorable Gerald R. Ford, The President, The White House, Washington, D.C.]

274

Remarks to the American Conference on Trade. *December 3, 1974*

Distinguished members of the Cabinet, public officials, dedicated American citizens, ladies and gentlemen:

It is a great privilege and a very high honor to have the opportunity of participating in this American Conference on Trade. And at the outset, let me assure you that I thank you and I congratulate you on the magnificent efforts that you have made during the day and previously, and I exhort you to continue your efforts until we are successful in the achievement of the objective that has been determined, which is in the best interest of our country.

Within the last several weeks, I traveled about halfway around the world. I met leaders of Japan, Korea, and the Soviet Union, and I am here tonight to call on you, my fellow Americans, to come with me on an even greater journey, a journey that could be, without a question of a doubt, the most important in our lives, yours and mine, and will affect countless of Americans for many, many years to come.

It is, very simply put, to redefine, to reshape the role of the United States in world trade. Those of you who are serious and cognizant—and all of you are—

about the problems we face on this globe, you know that it is a new world out there. We are witnessing today a worldwide economic revolution.

New, acute economic problems and concerns have moved onto the world scene with startling swiftness. Nations—large as well as small—are redefining their national interests. Some talk in terms of economic bloc or area advantages. And there are those who face the increasing threat of a simple, very stark reality—survival.

The United States and most nations face the most serious economic challenge of the postwar period. Problems of energy, food, inflation, recession pose unprecedented threats in all parts of the world. They threaten employment; they threaten income; they jeopardize international economic cooperation; and they menace political and security relationships that the United States has taken a generation to construct.

Unless we approach these problems constructively and cooperatively with our principal trading partners, we in the world may face a crisis of the most serious proportions.

These times call for positive, constructive American leadership. The United States cannot afford to drift in a sea of international uncertainty at a time when its highest economic interests call for very decisive actions. We cannot honestly claim leadership of the free world if we do not influence—with practical policies and real purpose—greater economic cooperation.

We must be under no illusion that we can go it alone. I think that is why all of you are here tonight and why I am here. And that is the reason the journey we undertake here must go on vigorously, effectively, and constructively. The word must go out from here tonight to the American people and to the people of other nations and especially our friends in the Congress, that America has made a very serious decision: We must pass the trade reform act—*now*. It is essential to the future of the United States trade policy and that of the world as well. The health of our domestic economy and the strength—yes, the very structure—of our international economic relations are deeply involved.

The Congress must act—and I say this with the utmost seriousness—or its inaction will gravely affect my efforts or anybody else's efforts to turn our economy upward. It will severely limit my ability, or the ability of anybody else, to work for international economic cooperation abroad.

You and I know that this legislation will, in all probability, be long delayed, possibly stymied forever, if it is not passed in the current session of this Congress. From a very practical point of view, it means that for the next year or more when the economic situation calls for decisive decisions, I will serve as your President without the power to fulfill my responsibilities in the crucial area of our Nation's trade.

This vital bill, the trade reform bill, has been pending before Congress for nearly 2 years. Actually, no President of the United States has had the authority to negotiate international trade matters since 1967. International trade relations have not been really revamped since that time. It has been 40 years, as we look back over the pages of history, since passage of the Nation's historic and fundamental Trade Agreements Act of 1934.

The central issue of trade reform is the close interrelationship between our domestic economy on the one hand and our economic international relations. And let us look at this important interrelationship for just a moment.

Admittedly, the American economy is in a recession at the present time. Inflation pressures are many. Fear of unemployment is increasing among our people.

The highest priority of this Administration in the weeks and months ahead, as has been said since I took office 4 months ago, will be to attack these growing and changing economic problems. And one of the most effective ways to start is to pass the trade reform legislation in our national self-interest. Obviously, I will need the full cooperation of the Congress. That is essential for all 213 million Americans. And I have certainly welcomed the comments by the Senate majority leader, Mike Mansfield, for bipartisan cooperation. I commend the Senate Committee on Finance and Chairman Russell Long for acting with restraint and not attaching unrelated amendments.

The international economy faces very similar difficulties. Inflation is a worldwide problem. Most of the economies of the industrialized world have swung into a downward cycle, partly as a consequence of inflationary distortions.

International cooperation is absolutely essential if the world is to conquer this twin illness of global recession and global inflation. We in the United States must develop a coordinated domestic and international approach to inflation and to recession. Trade is vital, essential, critical to that program.

Two-way trade for America amounted to $163 billion for the first 10 months of this calendar year. Those are the latest figures. This leaves our current trade balance at a deficit of some $2.3 billion. This is due chiefly to the huge increase in the cost of imported oil. In the first 10 months of this year, oil imports cost us $20.1 billion compared to $7.8 billion for all of 1973. Thus, without the enormous increase in oil costs, we would have a good-sized surplus this year. The United States enjoyed a $1.3 billion surplus last year. This is important to note: Our exports, for the first 10 months of this year, are running at an annual rate of 36 percent above 1973.

These exports add up to many jobs for Americans in all parts of our country and in all sectors of our society. Some 3 million American workers owe their livelihood to our American exports—from stevedores to aircraft machinists to white collar workers staffing American corporations.

Even the smallest of our business organizations in this country—three out of five successful American exporters have fewer than 100 employees. More than 20 percent of American farm income derives from sales abroad.

Trade—everybody in this room knows—is the bread and butter issue to workers and businesses in our communities, large, small, in all parts of our 50 States. That means farms on the one hand, business on the other, and industry as a whole.

Over the years the effect of trade on our economy has been highly favorable. The U.S. economy—consumers, workers—benefits from imports as well as exports. The explanation is relatively simple: Our total imports for the first 10 months of this year amounted to approximately $83 billion. About $37 billion of that figure were essential to American production—metals, foods, chemicals, minerals, including oil.

Many American businesses are heavily dependent on imported materials. Let me offer just a couple of specific examples of how imports help us as an industrial nation.

We are almost entirely dependent on foreign countries for such vital materials as chromium, platinum, titanium, manganese. More than 85 percent of our aluminum comes from overseas; so does most of our bauxite.

When we add the vigor from these imports to the strength of exporting, we can see the significance of trade to America's economic health. Trade adds to the income, the income of the American labor force, and to our economic preeminence in the world at large.

There will be no plus in our balance of trade this year because of the severe, high cost of importing oil. Otherwise, we could be and would be very much in the black.

Naturally, I consider the price we are paying for oil as much too high. It is raising havoc on our domestic economy. If you deduct the increased cost of oil imports, the U.S. exhibits a favorable trade balance of nearly $8 billion during the first 6 months of 1974.

Oil price increases are upsetting the entire international economic system. The adjustments, the answers must come from international bargaining, from international cooperation, and that is the top priority of this Administration.

The overall effect of our trade is highly favorable, but the trade reform act makes specific provision to assist those who might be adversely affected by imports. No sectors of our economy will be left to face serious disruptions. The legislation clearly states—and I will vigorously support such provisions—that we will assist workers, firms, communities adversely affected by imports.

In these very difficult times, it may be tempting for some in our great country to turn inward. Powerful forces in this country are not only thinking but actually urging an inward course on legislation, not only in the trade reform act but in many other pieces of legislation. This, in my judgment, would reverse American postwar trade and other policies and would be enormously harmful to us as to the rest of the globe, our allies as well as our adversaries.

It is my strong feeling—and I say this with the deepest conviction—let us turn outward to view the complex picture of international trade. Our Nation lives and acts in the world community within a very intricate framework. It is the framework of political, security, and economic ties that binds nations everywhere together.

There are those in the world who believe that unilateral and bilateral action, promoting their own self-interest, is the quickest and the most promising solution to their problems. I categorically reject that view. We must believe—and I certainly do—that this policy can only lead to conflict, an unending series of flareups and disputes in all parts of the world.

In contrast, the United States believes—and I am committed to this policy if the Congress will urgently let me negotiate—that the only real answer is the long-range solution of total world cooperation. I seek multilateral solutions to common problems that will benefit all nations, but I need the trade reform act, and I need it now, if the President of the United States is to have any voice in the international scene.

Let me spell out, if I might, some of the consequences if I do not obtain this legislation from this Congress before it adjourns.

The coming GATT [General Agreement on Tariffs and Trade] international trade negotiations involving 105 members would be dealt a crippling setback. I would lack the necessary legislative authority to implement my accords or any accords; therefore, it would be virtually impossible to arrive at any substantial trade agreements.

The United States international, political, military, economic commitments would be seriously undermined. This, in my opinion, would encourage unrest and would certainly encourage world instability.

But let's be even more precise, if I might. In energy, Secretaries Kissinger and Bill Simon are working diligently on international cooperation. But this cooperation cannot be one in a world involved with increasing strife in trade.

The international monetary system needs significant improvement. If we slide back into trade wars, we undermine our honest efforts to keep the international monetary system functioning effectively. Friendly trade is a must if we are to improve our market imbalances.

Trade is necessary so that developing countries can pay back various forms of outside assistance. Some of the developing nations are directly involved in our own growth. They own raw materials and other commodities in short supply, essential to our development.

The trade reform act offers me sufficient negotiating authority to achieve a substantial reduction in tariff levels on a worldwide basis. It would allow me to work toward greater market access for U.S. products abroad, adding innumerable thousands of jobs in our own 50 States.

This means jobs for Americans. That means a healthier economy. That means Congress has a duty and an obligation to pass this legislation now.

Let me use one other fact, if I might. I can assure you from my recent experiences that the Soviets are not sitting back. They are not looking for a seat as a spectator. They want and they will get part of the action.

The Soviets are ready to trade—politically, economically—but it will take time. It will take negotiation on the one hand, some very hard bargaining on the other. We have made a good beginning politically, a breakthrough on controlling the latest generation of nuclear weapons, a breakthrough for peace. Let us make the same breakthrough for trade essential for détente and progress around the world.

In 1973, the United States achieved a trade surplus of more than $1 billion from the Soviet Union. Another $900 million surplus came from other Communist countries around the world. Trade with these nations was, therefore, a very crucial factor in our overall trade surplus of $1.7 [$1.3] billion in 1973.

The Soviets will not deal unless we work to achieve mutually beneficial economic policies, including the elimination of discrimination against their trade, and unless we are willing to provide appropriate levels of credit within the framework established by the Congress.

Let's be very clear about this. Our competitive trading partners of Western Europe and Japan are issuing credits to Communist countries with which they are now trading. Their record shows that the Soviet credit is good. The credits we issue are small compared to our Western trading partners.

53-528 O - 76 - 47

The world today looks to the United States of America for leadership. We have provided this since the end of World War II. We did not provide it prior to World War II. Therefore, I would find it inexcusable, as would many Members of Congress and many Americans, if this legislation were to die as a result of delay and procrastination.

The Congress and the executive branch have cooperated more closely—and I might say, at a greater length—on this bill than in any other single piece of legislation in the past 6 years. I can recount in the 4 months that I have been President a number of meetings with various Senators, various other Members of the Congress, in trying to find a reasonable, constructive compromise on how we might move this legislation forward. And I can assure you that I will personally continue these efforts in the remaining weeks of this session of the Congress.

And let me add this, if I might. And I see how many members of my Cabinet are here—three, four. They are being told tonight, and everybody in their departments, that this is the job of highest priority to get this legislation through between now and adjournment.

And I will add a P.S. If they don't get it through, they are at fault, and you are, too. [*Laughter*]

Well, let me just conclude with these observations and comments.

I would find it inexcusable if this legislation were to become encumbered with nonrelated or nongermane amendments. This is somewhat technical, but those of us who have struggled in the Congress for some time know precisely what it means. These would be unrelated amendments, not related to the fundamentals of trade legislation under any circumstances.

They would be amendments that had no prior consideration at all in the Senate Committee on Finance. They would be extraneous to the subject matter that has brought all of you to the Nation's Capital.

I think the time has come; it is far too serious for this important legislation to be encumbered by these nonrelated or nongermane amendments. So, as you go through the halls and into the offices on Capitol Hill, make the point strongly, effectively, that this legislation must stand on its own and should not be overwhelmed with amendments that have no relationship to trade per se.

At this critical moment in our legislative history on this legislation, I don't think we can afford the gamesmanship of nonrelated, nongermane amendments.

I see some former colleagues of mine in the House of Representatives. In the main, we were able to keep nongermane amendments out of the House version of the bill. The burden is now on the United States Senate to do exactly the same.

And let me conclude with these final observations, if I might. I happen to believe that a society is great if its people think greatly, if its people act greatly, and this is a moment for greatness in America.

The journey which we together have started here tonight has no end, for the labor we undertake will never be complete: to help build a world economy that will contribute to the health and prosperity of people everywhere throughout this globe.

Every nation must carry its share of that great burden to uplift itself on the one hand and others as we move ahead.

Every nation must reach out, out to others, to work together, to share in sweat and in sacrifice, secure in the knowledge that none will have to go it alone. This truly, as I see it, could be one of the world's finest hours. With your help, with our cooperation, and with the dedication of everybody, we can make it so.

Thank you very, very much.

NOTE: The President spoke at 8:42 p.m. in the Sheraton Hall at the Sheraton-Park Hotel. The conference in support of enactment of the trade reform act was sponsored by a number of business, agriculture, consumer, and civic organizations.

275

Remarks at the Rockefeller Public Service Awards Luncheon. *December 4, 1974*

Mr. Rockefeller, distinguished guests, ladies and gentlemen:

At the outset, let me congratulate Mr. Rockefeller again for his generosity and support of a very, very worthwhile program.

Secondly, let me compliment Princeton University and the Woodrow Wilson School of that great university for its participation in this program.

Naturally, I am very pleased and honored to have a part in this awards program and to join in your salute to the five outstanding public servants who are being rewarded here today.

For as long as there has been government—government among men, I should say—it has been fashionable to attack bureaucracy and bureaucrats, sometimes for good and sufficient reason. And I have to confess that in the over 25 years that I served in the House of Representatives, I have, on occasion, joined in that fray, obviously, when I thought the issues and facts were right. I suspect, on occasion, they weren't, but nevertheless, if I did, I apologize.

But the fact remains that career public servants who do keep the vital and highly essential day-to-day business of Government moving year after year—a vast and a very loyal group of good people doing good work for their country.

Now, sometimes the pace is a little too slow for my taste. But when you consider the complexity and the sensitivity of modern government, the question may not be why does government move so slowly, but rather, how does government happen to move at all?

Commenting on public apathy and its effect on government, Adlai Stevenson once joked that our public servants serve us right. Today, we are proud to honor five public servants who have done more than just serve us right. They have served us with great, great distinction.

Each one in his own way has made an important and lasting contribution to our free way of life. The fields these men represent—aeronautics, social welfare, and a range of other areas in the Government related to our economy—but the ability and the dedication which each has brought to his work is the very same.

Fortunately, I have known some, not all. They represent in the best tradition, the best, long tradition of outstanding public servants, and they are among the unsung heroes of millions of men and women who, over a long period of time, have served our Government well and have made it work, despite problems and complexities that few people understand.

So, on behalf of the American people, I wish to thank you, each and every one of you who are being rewarded here today, for a job well done. Your example is an inspiration. It does give a guiding hand to others, those who are your fellow workers. And I hope this ceremony today, like those in the past, will give an inspiration to others, your associates in all departments. And I hope that it will in some way give the American people the proper respect and admiration for those who have excelled, those who have excelled in service to their fellow men in our country.

Thank you very much.

NOTE: The President spoke at 12:49 p.m. in the Grand Ballroom at the Mayflower Hotel. The Rockefeller Public Service Awards program was instituted in 1951 by John D. Rockefeller III to honor career public servants and was administered by Princeton University, Mr. Rockefeller's alma mater. The recipients of the awards were:

JAMES B. CARDWELL, Commissionor of Social Security, Department of Health, Education, and Welfare—award for human resource development and protection;

GEORGE JASZI, Director, Bureau of Economic Analysis, Department of Commerce—award for professional accomplishment and leadership;

GEORGE M. LOW, Deputy Administrator, National Aeronautics and Space Administration—award for administration;

ROBERT M. WHITE, Administrator, National Oceanic and Atmospheric Administration, Department of Commerce—award for physical resource development and protection; and

MAURICE J. WILLIAMS, Chairman, Development Assistance Committee, Organization for Economic Cooperation and Development—award for intergovernmental operations.

276

Letter to the President of the Senate and the Speaker of the House Transmitting Proposals To Establish New National Wilderness Areas. *December 4, 1974*

PURSUANT to the Wilderness Act of September 3, 1964, I am pleased to transmit herewith proposals for thirty-seven additions to the National Wilderness Preservation System.

As described in the Wilderness Message that I am concurrently sending to the Congress today, the proposed new wilderness areas cover a total of over nine million primeval acres. In addition, the Secretary of the Interior has recommended that Congressional action on five other areas which include surface lands suitable for wilderness be deferred for the reasons set forth below:

A. Three areas which are open to mining might be needed in the future to provide vital minerals for the Nation, but these areas have not been adequately surveyed for mineral deposits. The areas are the Kofa Game Range, Arizona; Charles Sheldon Antelope Range, Nevada and Oregon; and, Charles M. Russell National Wildlife Range, Montana.

B. One area is subject to withdrawals for power purposes and additional study is needed of the West's potential energy needs before a wilderness decision can be made. This is Lake Mead National Recreation Area, located in Arizona and Nevada.

C. Certain parts of one area are subject to selection by the village of Mekoryuk under the terms of the Alaska Native Claims Settlement Act and a wilderness recommendation should be made only after the completion of the Native selection process. The area in question is the Nunivak National Wildlife Refuge in Alaska.

Four other possibilities considered by the Secretary of the Interior in his review of roadless areas of 5,000 acres or more were found to be unsuitable for inclusion in the Wilderness System: Deer Flat National Wildlife Refuge, Oregon and Idaho; Blackwater National Wildlife Refuge, Maryland; Mammoth Cave National Park, Kentucky; and, Upper Mississippi River Wildlife and Fish Refuge, Minnesota, Wisconsin, Iowa and Illinois. I concur in this finding and in the other recommendations of the Secretaries of the Interior and Agriculture, all of which are transmitted herewith.

Wilderness designation of both of these new wilderness areas and those already submitted that are pending before the Congress would dramatically demonstrate our commitment to preserve America's irreplaceable heritage, and I urge the Congress to act promptly in this regard.

Sincerely,

GERALD R. FORD

NOTE: This is the text of identical letters addressed to the Honorable James O. Eastland, President pro tempore, of the Senate, and to the Honorable Carl Albert, Speaker of the House of Representatives.

277

Message to the Congress Proposing Establishment of New National Wilderness Areas. *December 4, 1974*

To the Congress of the United States:

Ten years ago, acting with great wisdom, the Congress enacted and President Johnson signed into law the historic Wilderness Act of 1964.

That act declared it to be the policy of this Nation to secure for all Americans the benefits of an enduring resource of wilderness. Some 9.1 million acres were officially designated as part of the National Wilderness Preservation System, and the Executive Branch was charged with the responsibility of surveying the rest of the country and proposing additions to that system which seemed appropriate.

In the intervening years, there have been some 40 additions, so that the Wilderness System now covers 12.9 million acres and extends into many different States.

Today we reach another milestone in this unfolding story. The Executive Branch has now completed the initial, decade-long review prescribed by law in 1964, and as a result of this survey, I am hereby proposing 37 new additions to the Wilderness System. If accepted by the Congress, these recommendations would add an additional nine million primeval acres to the system.

Wilderness areas are, of course, well suited for low density recreation use that does not involve motorized vehicles or equipment, such as hiking, backpacking, primitive camping, and canoeing. They also lend themselves to scientific and educational uses which do not alter their pristine character. But beyond these uses, I believe that the Wilderness System serves a basic need of all Americans, even those who may never visit a wilderness area—the preservation of a vital element in our heritage.

As we approach the Nation's two hundredth birthday, it is well to remember that we are a pioneering people. For our ancestors, the ability to live in rugged, undeveloped countryside was often a matter of survival. The influential American historian Frederick Jackson Turner considered the frontier—the invisible but very real barrier between civilization and wilderness—to be the dominant force in shaping the American character. American writers from James Fenimore Cooper to Ernest Hemingway and William Faulkner have recognized and depicted the almost religious regard which Americans have for their wild places and creatures. Throughout our history, we have felt a need for rugged interaction with nature, for the solitude and the self-reliance that a wilderness experience can foster.

We have tamed and developed much of our original wilderness endowment, but a surprisingly large amount of it is left. The preservation of wilderness areas across the country today enables us to recapture a vital part of the national experience: like our forebears, we can journey into primeval, unspoiled land. The Nation as a whole is enriched by the availability of the wilderness experience to those who are able and willing to seek it. Wilderness preservation insures that a central facet of our Nation can still be realized, not just remembered.

Briefly described, the additions to the National Wilderness Preservation System which I am proposing today are:

(1) Mount Rainier Wilderness, Mount Rainier National Park, Washington—210,700 acres. The ice-clad, dormant volcano after which this park is named towers above the landscape. The park serves as a habitat for deer, bear, elk, and mountain goats.

(2) Kenai Wilderness, Kenai National Moose Range, Alaska—829,000 acres. This is a diverse area near Anchorage which contains scenic mountains, glaciers, lowland lakes, forests, muskegs, and rivers. The range's wide variety of wildlife includes black and brown bear and the Kenai moose.

(3) Cloud Peak Wilderness, Bighorn National Forest, Wyoming—150,490 acres. This proposed wilderness stretches some 27 miles along the backbone of the Bighorn Mountain Range and includes the rugged Cloud Peak and Black Tooth Mountain.

(4) Agassiz Wilderness, Agassiz National Wildlife Refuge, Minnesota—4,000 acres. Located on prehistoric Lake Agassiz, this area provides nesting grounds for the Canada goose and several species of ducks, as well as a habitat for moose, white-tailed deer, and elk.

(5) Sheldon Wilderness, Sheldon National Antelope Refuge, Nevada—20,100 acres. This refuge in the high sagebrush desert of the northern Great Basin is devoted primarily to the preservation of antelope but also supports deer, bighorn sheep, coyotes, bobcats, mountain lions and burros.

(6) Monarch Wilderness, Sequoia and Sierra National Forests, California—30,689 acres. This proposed area is located on the west slope of the Sierra Nevada Mountain Range, contiguous to Kings Canyon National Park. The landscape is characterized by steep ridges, deep canyons, and multicolored geological formations.

(7) Santee Wilderness, Santee National Wildlife Refuge, South Carolina—163 acres. This area is composed of coastal plains which protect such threatened species as the wood ibis, bald eagle, peregrine falcon, red-cockaded woodpecker, osprey, and American alligator.

(8) Everglades Wilderness, Everglades National Park, Florida—1,296,500 acres. A remarkable blending of climates makes this proposed area at the southernmost tip of the Florida mainland hospitable to pine trees as well as mangroves, panthers, and alligators.

(9) Salmon River and Idaho Wildernesses, Boise, Challis, Payette, Salmon, Bitterroot, and Nezperce National Forests, Idaho—1,143,487 acres. Bighorn sheep, deer, and elk abound in this region of deep gorges and lofty peaks.

(10) Parker River Wilderness, Parker River National Wildlife Refuge, Massachusetts—3,110 acres. This recommended area on the north shore of the State, about 35 miles from Boston, is one of the few natural barrier beach-dune areas remaining in the northeastern United States.

(11) Hawaii Volcanoes Wilderness, Hawaii Volcanoes National Park, Hawaii—123,100 acres. Two major active volcanoes, Kilauea and Mauna Loa, are the focal points of this park. Kilauea erupts frequently and is readily accessible at protected vantage points. Thus, this area is particularly rich in the scientific and educational opportunities envisaged by the Wilderness Act.

(12) Big Lake Wilderness, Big Lake National Wildlife Refuge, Arkansas—1,818 acres. Believed to be the product of an earthquake in the 1800's, the lake supports a peak population of 30,000 waterfowl during the winter. The proposed wilderness is a cypress-timbered area that has remained in its natural state.

(13) Aleutian Islands Wilderness, Aleutian Islands National Wildlife Refuge, Alaska—1,395,357 acres. Located among the islands that stretch from the Alaska mainland along a thousand-mile chain toward the Soviet Union, this

area is the principal home of the sea otter and a habitat for large numbers of pelagic birds (those which have the furlike outer coat of a mammal).

(14) Beartooth Wilderness, Custer, and Gallatin National Forests, Montana—542,437 acres. This area is characterized by spectacular river canyons and treeless tundras at elevations of about 10,000 feet. Moose, bighorn sheep, mountain goats, and black and grizzly bears are among the area's wildlife.

(15) Swanquarter Wilderness, Swanquarter National Wildlife Refuge, North Carolina—9,000 acres. In addition to accommodating more than 200 species of birds, this island refuge serves as the northernmost range of the endangered American alligators.

(16) Dinosaur Wilderness, Dinosaur National Monument, Utah and Colorado—165,341 acres. This national monument is the site of the most extensive concentration of dinosaur fossils found anywhere in the world and serves as a habitat for mountain lions and bighorn sheep.

(17) Lacassine Wilderness, Lacassine National Wildlife Refuge, Louisiana—2,854 acres. Among the striking birds and animals which use this refuge, located some 25 miles from the Gulf of Mexico, are ibises, roseate spoonbills, armadillo, otter, white-tailed deer, and alligators.

(18) Popo Agie Wilderness, Shoshone National Forest, Wyoming—81,820 acres. This area consists of deep, narrow valleys and canyons set along a 25-mile stretch of the lofty Southern Wind River Range. Elk, moose, mule deer, bighorn sheep, black bear, and a variety of smaller mammals and birds inhabit the area.

(19) Mattamuskeet Wilderness, Mattamuskeet National Wildlife Refuge, North Carolina—590 acres. Consisting of a lake, islands, and marshy shoreline about 50 miles northwest of Cape Hatteras, this refuge is operated for such birds as the bald eagle, red-cockaded woodpecker, and osprey.

(20) Organ Pipe Cactus Wilderness, Organ Pipe Cactus National Monument, Arizona—299,600 acres. The cactus forests and creosote-bush flats of this rugged, Sonoran desert area support 43 species of mammals, 39 species of birds, and nearly 50 species of reptiles.

(21) J. N. "Ding" Darling Wilderness, J. N. "Ding" Darling National Wildlife Refuge, Florida—2,735 acres. Sanibel, a tropical island in the Gulf of Mexico, is the site of this refuge, which provides habitats for several endangered birds, mammals and reptiles.

(22) Trinity Alps Wilderness, Klamath, Shasta-Trinity, and Six Rivers National Forests, California—267,561 acres. At the highest reaches, permanent

snowfields and small glaciers dominate the landscape; at lower elevations dense stands of trees and patches of wild flowers clothe the mountain ridges. Black bear, mountain lions, and black-tail deer are the area's major animals.

(23) Assateague Island Wilderness, Chincoteague National Wildlife Refuge and Assateague Island National Seashore, Maryland and Virginia—1,740 acres. The dunes and marsh lands of this area serve a variety of wildlife, including the endangered Delmarva Peninsula fox squirrel, the white-tail deer, red fox, raccoon, sika deer, and the Chincoteague pony.

(24) Death Valley Wilderness, Death Valley National Monument, California and Nevada—1,908,000 acres. Despite the seeming barrenness of this area, where rainfall averages less than 2 inches a year, life flourishes here in a tribute to nature's adaptability. Even fish have managed to cling to life in the parched valley: two species of pupfish inhabit desert springs.

(25) Cedar Island Wilderness, Cedar Island National Wildlife Refuge, North Carolina—180 acres. The salt marsh and islands here constitute a developing habitat for waterfowl.

(26) Fort Niobrara Wilderness, Fort Niobrara National Wildlife Refuge, Nebraska—4,635 acres. The high grazing lands and rolling plains of this refuge are managed primarily to support herds of American bison, elk and Texas longhorns.

(27) Medicine Lake Wilderness, Medicine Lake National Wildlife Refuge, Montana—11,366 acres. A large portion of this refuge consists of lakes and ponds; the peak fall population of waterfowl using the area frequently exceeds a quarter of a million birds.

(28) Great Smoky Mountains Wilderness, Great Smoky Mountains National Park, North Carolina and Tennessee—390,500 acres. Beneath the smoke-like haze that envelops these mountains and gives them their name lies an impressive array of unspoiled forests. Among the animals found in the park are black bear, white-tailed deer, wild hogs, and 27 different kinds of salamanders.

(29) Big Blue, Courthouse Mountain, Dolores Peak, Mount Sneffels and Mount Wilson Wildernesses, San Juan and Uncompaghre National Forests, Colorado—80,130 acres. This area is characterized by high, jagged peaks and deep, narrow canyons interspersed with forested and alpine grassland ridges. The largest wildlife species indigenous to it include elk, mule deer, bighorn sheep, bear and mountain lion.

(30) Lake Woodruff Wilderness, Lake Woodruff National Wildlife Refuge,

Florida—1,106 acres. This proposed area is located along the flood plain of the St. Johns River, one of the few large northerly-flowing rivers in the United States. Among the remarkable variety of wildlife found here are threatened species such as the Everglades kite, Southern bald eagle, Florida sandhill crane, manatee, Florida panther, and American alligator.

(31) Anaho Island Wilderness, Anaho Island National Wildlife Refuge, Nevada—747.73 acres. The island is a sanctuary for a multitude of birds, including the largest nesting colony of white pelicans on the continent.

(32) Noxubee Wilderness, Noxubee National Wildlife Refuge, Mississippi—1,200 acres. Consisting of flat and slightly rolling hardwood and pine lands, the refuge provides habitats for the Canada goose, such rare birds as the endangered red-cockaded woodpecker and southern bald eagle, and a good-sized herd of white-tailed deer.

(33) UL Bend Wilderness, UL Bend National Wildlife Refuge, Montana—19,693 acres. Located along the Missouri River's Fort Peck Reservoir, this refuge is primarily a habitat for migratory waterfowl. Among the land birds found here is the unique burrowing owl, which nests in abandoned "dwellings" in prairie dog towns..

(34) Pea Island Wilderness, Pea Island National Wildlife Refuge, North Carolina—180 acres. A part of the Cape Hatteras National Seashore, this refuge is a winter spot for greater snow geese, Canada geese, brant, and many species of duck.

(35) Bombay Hook Wilderness, Bombay Hook National Wildlife Refuge, Delaware—2,000 acres. This salt marsh estuary serves as a habitat for migratory waterfowl and such other birds as the endangered southern bald eagle and peregrine falcon.

(36) Back Bay Wilderness, Back Bay National Wildlife Refuge, Virginia—2,165 acres. A focal point along the Atlantic Flyway, the refuge is the winter home of up to 40,000 Canada geese per year and the rare Ipswich Savannah sparrow.

(37) In addition, the first wilderness area—the Gila Wilderness—in New Mexico, would be enlarged by the addition of 115,648 acres.

Three other areas—Kofa Game Range, Arizona; Charles Sheldon Antelope Range, Nevada and Oregon; and Charles M. Russell National Wildlife Range,

Montana—contain surface lands suitable for wilderness designation. However, because the areas are open to mining and may contain minerals vital to the national interest and because they have not been subjected to thorough mineral surveys, I am recommending that action on these proposals be deferred pending the completion of such surveys.

In addition, Lake Mead National Recreation Area, contains surface lands suitable for wilderness designation. However, virtually the entire area is subject to withdrawals for power purposes. In view of the potential energy needs of the West, I cannot recommend that any part of the area be designated wilderness at this time. I have directed that the area be given additional study and that a further recommendation be submitted within three years.

Finally, Nunivak National Wildlife Refuge also contains surface lands suitable for wilderness designation. Because of the uncertainties of land ownership and their future management which is peculiar to Nunivak, I cannot recommend that any part be designated wilderness at this time. I have directed that future recommendations be guided by native land uses and native land selections pursuant to the Alaska Native Claims Settlement Act.

After a review of roadless areas of 5,000 acres or more and roadless islands, the Secretary of the Interior has concluded that four areas are not suitable for preservation as part of the National Wilderness Preservation System. These are: Deer Flat National Wildlife Refuge, Oregon and Idaho; Blackwater National Wildlife Refuge, Maryland; Mammoth Cave National Park, Kentucky; and Upper Mississippi River Wildlife and Fish Refuge, Minnesota, Wisconsin, Iowa, and Illinois. As to the latter two areas, however, I am directing that a wilderness reevaluation be conducted at such time as management prerogatives and other prospective uses of the areas are better defined.

In addition to this message, I am transmitting herewith to the Congress letters and reports from the Secretary of the Interior and the Secretary of Agriculture regarding these proposals. I concur with the recommendation of the respective Secretary in each case.

As noted above, the Executive Branch has now carried out the original provisions of the 1964 Wilderness Act. Additional surveys will be undertaken on a case-by-case basis, but the Congress now has before it the major recommendations of the Executive Branch, as compiled over a 10-year period. I urge the Congress to give early and favorable consideration to all of these proposals.

Concurrent with the wilderness proposals, I am also transmitting the Tenth

Annual Report on the Status of the National Wilderness Preservation System which covers calendar year 1973.

GERALD R. FORD

The White House,
December 4, 1974.

278

Toasts of the President and Prime Minister Pierre Elliott Trudeau of Canada. *December 4, 1974*

Mr. Prime Minister and gentlemen:

Let me say at the outset, we are delighted to have you as our guests. I must say on behalf of my wife, she made a very special effort. This is the first opportunity she has had to have this room for this purpose, and she said she hoped that you would enjoy the atmosphere and setup. And if you say yes, I will tell her.

Let me, on a more serious note, say that we are delighted to have you here because of our deep respect and affection for you as the leader of one of our great friends and allies.

Let me add, if I might, that we in the United States know of no other country where the United States has some 4,000 or 5,000 miles of border, when you consider not only the north and south but also Alaska. And so, there is a great reason for us to have a rapport and a particular affection, people to people and country to country.

I might say the first trip that I ever took out of the United States—I was quite young and quite thrilled—was the trip that I took from Detroit to Windsor. [*Laughter*]

They didn't preclude me from going to Windsor, and I had no trouble getting back. [*Laughter*]

But that was a thrill to me, and it was my first trip out of our country and to a foreign country.

But my memories of that trip left me with a great remembrance of the relationship that our country has with yours. The truth is, of course, good friends often have many differences, and among friends, differences fortunately can be better debated or discussed than they can when a different relationship exists.

I have heard it said many times—and Rog Morton who formerly served in the Congress and Gale McGee and George Aiken and Bob McEwen [1]—I hope I haven't missed any of the Members of Congress—we often say in the Congress that you can disagree without being disagreeable. And that is the way I think our relations between your country and ours has proceeded in the past, and I hope will proceed in the future.

We do have some differences. I felt that our meeting today was one of the most constructive, one of the most friendly, and with each of us expressing where we had some differences, it was a point of view and an understanding. If you have an understanding, I think you can come to reasonable and rational conclusions.

I look forward to subsequent meetings with you to broaden our personal friendship and to expand our two national relationships. It has been a pleasure for me to get to know your Ambassador. He did present to me about a week or 10 days ago a very thoughtful gift on behalf of your Government, commemorating the 1976 Olympics, which are to be held in Montreal.

It brought to my mind the fact that in 1976 we are celebrating our 200th anniversary. I hope that the people that come to your Olympics—and I hope to come if you will invite me, Mr. Prime Minister—I like that snow, you know—and that some of the visitors that come to the United States will go to Montreal and Canada and vice versa.

But, speaking of Montreal, I have had the privilege a long time ago of skiing at Mont Tremblant and St. Jovite, which I thought were tremendous and I still do. And that was another experience that gave me a great affection and admiration for the people of Canada.

So, with my personal affection for you and the Canadian people and the United States' strong conviction about our relationship, to you and your country, if I might, I would like to offer a toast to you, Prime Minister of Canada, and to the Canadian people and to the Queen.

NOTE: The President spoke at 9:15 p.m. in the Blue Room at the White House. Earlier in the day, the President and Prime Minister Trudeau held discussions at the White House. Prime Minister Trudeau responded to the President's toast as follows:

Mr. President, gentlemen, and friends:

When Canadians travel abroad, Mr. President, they spend lots of time explaining to other people how they are different from the Americans. There is a great belief in other lands that Canadians and Americans are exactly the same. I am particularly distressed to find this when I am dealing with the Common Market. We are different, and we have different problems and different economic requirements.

But it does happen that we have to show how similar we are and how close our two peoples are. And the best example I can find, when I have to explain that kind of thing, is to talk about in summer, in the baseball stadium in Montreal where tens

[1] Senator Gale W. McGee of Wyoming and Representative Robert C. McEwen of New York.

of thousands of Canadians get together to cheer for the Canadian team against the visiting American team when every one of the players on both sides is American! [*Laughter*]

When I have stayed in some of your American cities, it is another story. In winter at your hockey forums, they cheer for the local team, and probably 95 percent of the players on both sides are Canadians—and the best ones.

And this, I think, shows really how close the people are in their goals, in their ways of living, in their love of sports, in their values, even in standards of their own lives.

And that makes your job and mine, Mr. President, so much easier when we meet. We find that most of the subjects which have to be discussed between heads of governments or heads of states when they meet, in our case, have been settled by the people themselves. The figure I was giving you this afternoon of 66 percent of the trade between our two countries being free trade, tariff free, and it will be 81 percent if that trade reform bill gets passed in the form that it went to the Senate committee.

So much of this is done by the people themselves in the trade area, in the cultural area, and the knowledge of each other by the constant visits across the border, that when we meet it is always a pleasant occasion.

As you said, and I realized this afternoon, we can talk to each other in complete candor. We know how the electorates and the press and the House of Representatives or the Senate or the House of Commons will react to various situations. And it is so much—we talk the same language—it is so much easier to deal with problems in this context.

You, Mr. President, have been exposed to the electorates much more frequently than I have. I dare say that I have walked in the valley of the shadow and feel a little more closer than you have. But I think we would both agree that our peoples, Canadian and the American peoples, would cease to support us overnight if they thought that we were embarking on courses which were not friendly, which were not based on cooperation and understanding, on the desire to solve any differences that arise in that spirit of friendship rather than the spirit of hostility.

We, as your neighbors, realize the importance of the leadership that the United States is giving to today's world. Your great success in Vladivostok is something that was received in Canada with immense satisfaction. We know that in matters of Atlantic security, détente, and disarmament—we know that we can follow your lead because the principles on which your policies are based are the same as ours.

And I think you know that you can trust us to support those principles in areas we consider essential.

For these reasons, I must say our tasks are much easier, and I think we should renew the resolve that we mentioned to each other earlier that we will continue this type of meeting on an informal, nonprotocol, or the minimum protocol.

It has a great advantage for us to gather around a table such as this, a very beautiful one. Mrs. Ford will be told that we were struck by its beauty and the warmth of this room and the repast. Did she do the cooking? [*Laughter*]

Insofar as the Olympics are concerned, we very much hope you will come—I hope you will come before that, and that perhaps, perchance, we will find some way of being the forerunners in some ski race——

The President. I'm too young! [*Laughter*]

The Prime Minister.——prepared to test for the winter Olympics whenever and wherever they happen.

Mr. President, we hope you will come before that, that you will find it convenient, as your predecessor did, to talk on a very informal basis even by phone or by quick visits in-and-out which do away with all formality, permit us to come to the point right quickly, and to solve whatever small problems we might have.

So, with this in mind and in the hopes that our friendship of which we talked and the candor with which we talked will be brought out in the spirit of cooperation and understanding and the fairness with which all our meetings together are inspired, I would ask our guests here to raise their glasses in a toast to the President of the United States.

279

Remarks of Welcome to Chancellor Helmut Schmidt of the Federal Republic of Germany. *December 5, 1974*

Chancellor Schmidt, gentlemen:

I am delighted to welcome you here in Washington, our Nation's Capital, on behalf of the American people.

This is your first visit, Mr. Chancellor, to the United States as the leader of the German Federal Government. It comes at an historic time for both of our countries.

We in the United States are on the eve of our Bicentennial. One of the things that we are particularly aware of is the prominent role played by men and women of German descent in the building of America over the past two centuries. They have made tremendous contributions in fields as widespread as education and science, culture and the arts.

A few months ago the Federal Republic of Germany marked its own 25th anniversary. During this quarter century, the Federal Republic has become one of the world's leading political and economic powers, and also one of its most responsible.

Throughout this entire period of relations between our two countries, it has been marked by a very close friendship and a very close cooperation, and we are particularly proud of that association.

Mr. Chancellor, we live in demanding times. In the effort to solve the formidable economic and political problems confronting us today, close cooperation and mutual help have become infinitely more important than ever. Only by working together can we overcome the current difficulties facing our economies and international economy.

I believe we can do it, and speaking for the American people, I appreciate the support your Government has shown for strengthened economic cooperation in the international field.

We also recognize your international contributions in dealing with the problems of energy, food, and financial pressures.

A keystone, of course, of our present and future cooperation is the Atlantic Alliance. At a time when all members of the alliance confront budgetary difficulties, difficult choices for all of them, we applaud and endorse your country's positive attitude toward maintaining the strength of NATO.

We also appreciate, Mr. Chancellor, your cooperation in helping to assure that no nation bear an unfair burden of the cost of our common defense.

We will have many important issues to discuss today and tomorrow, Mr. Chancellor. I look forward to those discussions in full confidence that these talks will contribute significantly to our efforts in creating more stable political and economic conditions throughout the world. I know that your visit will further strengthen the already close friendship and partnership between the Federal Republic and the United States.

Mr. Chancellor, America bids you and your party a most cordial welcome.

NOTE: The President spoke at 10:41 a.m. on the South Lawn at the White House where Chancellor Schmidt was given a formal welcome with full military honors. The Chancellor responded as follows:

Mr. President, ladies and gentlemen:

Thank you, Mr. President, very much for your warm welcome and for the kind words, regardful words addressed to me and my party.

As you said, this is not my first visit to the United States, but the first time that I have come to this country as the head of government of the Federal Republic of Germany.

I am particularly glad to have this opportunity so soon after you, Mr. President, have assumed your office in order to exchange views on the main questions which do concern us both.

In today's world, we are faced with a multitude of difficult problems whose solutions will make unprecedented demands on our countries and will require us to harness our strength in the common effort.

The world is threatened by severe economic disruption. The Middle East conflict, whose settlement your Administration is working so hard to bring about, and the energy crisis which followed in its wake, have suddenly opened our eyes to the fragile nature of the foundations on which our economic and social and political stability does rest.

The strengthening of these foundations is a task which does concern us all and which we can only master through broad international cooperation, as you said.

We in Germany are conscious of this challenge, and we are preparing ourselves to meet it. In this search we do attach specific importance to close cooperation and consultation between the United States of America and Europe and my own country.

The partnership between the United States and Europe has stood the test. It has existed for more than 25 years in the Atlantic Alliance, which was strengthened by the Declaration of Ottawa in the middle of this year. It has also reflected our common efforts to promote détente in Europe and in the world.

We are resolved to do everything within our capability to strengthen and to further develop this partnership.

The untroubled friendship between the United States and the Federal Republic of Germany seems to be an excellent basis for this, and it is my firm conviction that our meeting, Mr. President, will bring us closer to this goal.

Thank you very much.

280

Statement on Signing the Joint Funding Simplification Act of 1974. *December 5, 1974*

I HAVE today signed into law the Joint Funding Simplification Act of 1974.

This is significant legislation. It is a further step in our continuing effort to simplify and streamline grant administration. I am pleased that the legislation had strong bipartisan support in both Houses of Congress.

The act will simplify funding and other procedures in cases where a grantee receives assistance from two or more different agencies or programs within an agency. It provides a means by which funds, procedures, and administrative requirements of related programs can be brought together simply and speedily to support a particular project or group of projects for which Federal assistance is being sought.

More specifically, it provides a basis for:

—meeting interrelated needs with one comprehensive plan for receiving grants from several Federal agencies through one Federal funding source;

53-528 O - 76 - 48

—receiving Federal funds at the same time as the grantee's own planning and funding cycles;
—simplifying and standardizing administrative requirements;
—simplifying paperwork and recordkeeping;
—reporting progress to one Federal agency rather than several;
—replacing separate Federal agency audits with a single audit by only one agency.

The procedures which this act provides have been tested in a number of pilot projects throughout the country with most encouraging results. Not only are the recipients of grants in a better position to apply Federal assistance more effectively but taxpayers will be able to expect more from each tax dollar thus expended.

However, we must not rest here. The explosive growth of Federal grants in recent years makes it imperative that we continue an unrelenting effort towards further improvement in grant administration.

NOTE: As enacted, the bill (S. 2299), approved December 5, 1974, is Public Law 93–510 (88 Stat. 1604).

281

Remarks to the Lilly Endowment Continuing Conference for the Liberal Arts. *December 5, 1974*

Dr. Bell, Dr. Trotter, distinguished college and university presidents, I think some of my former colleagues in the House as well as the Senate, students, and others:

It is a privilege and a pleasure to be here, and I welcome you on not only my behalf but on behalf of the White House Staff, and I certainly hope that your trip here is worthwhile and will be very beneficial.

As a former member of the board of trustees of one of the participating colleges here, Albion College, I appreciate the important relationship between liberal education and professions and the need to understand that relationship better.

Since the early Middle Ages, colleges have been sheltered, almost cloistered communities set apart from general society. Unfortunately, this has caused a certain amount of suspicion and, in some cases, unfortunate distrust. And I don't think, in the current environment, we can afford that today.

Benjamin Disraeli once said, and I quote: A university should be a place of light, liberty and of learning.

In a free society like our own where education is open to many, not just the few, the university's light, liberty, and learning must not be abstract but rather must relate to reality. A sound liberal education can and should be the key to preparing young people, men and women, for a full life beyond their student years that is, as I see it, at least a creative, productive member of our greater community.

This is not just a democratic ideal, it is a practical necessity, one on which we are working at this time in the preparation of our domestic policy recommendations for the State of the Union.

I met this week, earlier this week, with Secretary Weinberger, Dr. Trotter, and Ted Bell. We focused on maximizing available Federal resources to improve opportunities for and the quality of postsecondary education.

In addition, Secretaries Dent, Weinberger, and Brennan are working to build a better relationship and a better balance between the world of work on the one hand and education on the other.

This is vitally important to our young peoples' search for meaningful and satisfying careers. It is equally vital to our Nation's continued requirements for well-educated and well-qualified manpower.

I am hopeful that the National Institute of Education will play an important part, an important part in research and development role in meeting these two important goals. Changing population trends and the emotional aftermath of the turbulent 1960's have contributed to the problems facing liberal education today.

And as I see it, with two sons in college and one about to enter next year and a daughter also about to enter a year from now, the problems remain serious. However, I deeply believe that they can be overcome.

Part of the reason for my belief is programs like yours, programs that articulate and strengthen the bonds between learning and living, between the world of books, philosophy, and ideas and the world of human problems and human solutions.

Dr. Samuel Johnson recognized the need for this link, this vital interrelationship. He urged his readers to pause a while for learning to be wise, to take time to understand and apply the lessons of the classroom to the conditions of the world.

As I understand it, that is what you are doing, developing human and humane insights that only a liberal education provides and applying them to the many professional jobs that must be done in a modern society.

In looking over the list of participants and the events for this conference, I see that you have pursued well your goal of focusing attention on the social responsibility of professionals and the role of the liberal arts college in preparing people for these professions.

The range of your agenda is impressive, including figures from business, the professions, and the communications media as well as the academic community. I am always an optimist, and I happen to believe that you will succeed.

Your basic product and your basic methods of looking at the problem are sound. I believe that the liberal arts college can cope with the change without injuring its roots or its purpose. Your institutions are a much needed part of the modern education system and, of course, of our society.

The ties you are building with business, with the professions, and with the media will help to create a better future for your colleges, your students, and I think, our country.

In the months ahead, because of my interest in the subject and my concern for a solution, I will be following your work with a personal interest. You do have my support, and you certainly have my best wishes for a continued success.

Thank you very, very much.

NOTE: The President spoke at 3:53 p.m. in Room 450 at the Old Executive Office Building. In his opening remarks, the President referred to Terrell H. Bell, Commissioner of Education, and Virginia Y. Trotter, Assistant Secretary for Education, Department of Health, Education, and Welfare.

282

Toasts of the President and Chancellor Schmidt of the Federal Republic of Germany. *December 5, 1974*

MR. CHANCELLOR, it is a great privilege and a pleasure for me and our people to have you and your Foreign Secretary, Mr. Genscher, and the others from your party visiting us in Washington on this occasion.

We, of course, feel that this gathering is a reaffirmation of the longstanding friendship of your people as well as ours, your Government as well as ours, a friendship that has a very broad base in military security, economic relations, people-to-people relations.

Of course, the pages of history in the United States are filled with contributions made over the 200 years of our Nation's history, contributions made by people from your country.

It goes back as far as Baron von Steuben, who was probably the finest military training officer as well as a fighting officer, who took a pretty ragged American outfit at Valley Forge and made it capable and competent to meet the challenges in the next spring.

And of course, Abraham Lincoln had a very outstanding German who was a member of his Cabinet, who contributed significantly to our history in that day and that era.[1]

Of course, the contribution by people from Germany to our country also includes the arts, it includes science, it includes literature, and as Larry Brown[2] and I know, there are some outstanding Germans who have contributed to our proficiency in athletics. One who may come to mind for some of us in the older age group, Lou Gehrig, was probably a legendary baseball player in our athletic history, and his ancestry, of course, was that of your country.

But with the people who have helped to make America great and those that are working with us today in the field of the military, the economic areas, the rapport I think is good for not only each of us but for the world at large.

Twenty-five years of your history has been a period of 25 years of close personal relationship to the United States, and vice versa.

We seem to have the same philosophical views, the same ideological opinions as to how you can move ahead. We tend to subscribe in America to the views of one of Germany's greatest minds—one of the world's greatest, I am told, as I read history—Goethe. He once wrote that we can only earn our freedom and our existence by struggling for it every day.

For 25 years, day in and day out, the Federal Republic and the United States have worked together for a freer, better world in a spirit of mutual friendship and great mutual respect.

So, it is my privilege, Mr. Chancellor, in the spirit of our friendship and cooperation and mutual interest, to offer a toast to you and all that you embody and that of your great country.

To the Chancellor and to the Federal Republic and its people.

NOTE: The President spoke at 10 p.m. in the State Dining Room at the White House. Chancellor Schmidt responded as follows:

Mr. President, Mrs. Ford, ladies and gentlemen:

I would like to thank you, Mr. President, for the kind and warm words you have addressed to my party and to me. I think one of the two of us has to confess to this distinguished gathering that, despite the fact that we did not intend to solve any bilateral problems between ourselves, because we don't have any bilateral problems—[*laughter*]—nevertheless we did make a bilateral agreement just tonight

[1] The President was referring to Carl Schurz, Minister to Spain and Union Army general in the Lincoln administration, and Secretary of the Interior 1877–81.

[2] Running back for the Washington Redskins professional football team.

insofar as we agreed to put away the speeches which were made for us. [*Laughter*]

And so, the President did, and I am going to do it, but we allowed for just one quotation from the speeches. You will later on detect me, or observe me looking to my paper once, but before so doing, I would like to point out that I think you were especially generous, Mr. President, in talking of the last 25 years of our really very good and ever-improving relationship, a relationship between your great country and ours.

You were very gracious not to mention periods of history before that I will not dig into it. But I would like to say that my compatriots and I, myself, we are really thankful for the great help which we received from your people immediately after the war and that we also are thankful for having had your assistance, your standing firm on matters vital for our own sake; for instance, for your standing firm on Berlin all these years.

You have just come back to the United States from a meeting with the number one man of the Soviet Union. From what I understand from your report to us, you have clearly added one step further in the policy of bringing about balance in the world and the stability of that balance, and bringing about détente, if you wish to call it that, a policy which we have followed—both of our nations, both of our Governments, parallel to each other—as we have all these long decades followed in common the policy of making ourselves capable, if need should arise, to defend ourselves against threats or pressures from outside.

It seems to me that so far, we have been very successful together with our other partners within the Atlantic Alliance. In the meantime, new problems have come up which we did not foresee 10 years ago—referring to the Middle East or referring to the oil price explosion; I think one might call it an explosion—and all our economies so far have not adapted to that enormous change, whether it is in the field of real incomes, whether it is in the field of balance of payments, whether it is in the field of aggravating the process of inflation.

We have talked at length today, and also your Secretaries and aides and my party have talked at length about economic problems. We have exchanged our analyses, we have exchanged our attitudes, our plans for future actions. Advice was given freely and taken from both sides—this is the point where I have to look to my paper—[*laughter*]—because I wrote down in my own handwriting a little quote.

I think it is from some American. He is not as famous as Goethe. Nevertheless, it reads: "Free advice is the kind that costs you nothing unless you act upon it." [*Laughter*] So, I warn you, Mr. President, to be careful in acting upon our advice, and we will be careful on our side as well.

But coming back to a more serious aspect of the matter, I think I could say on behalf of my party, especially my colleague, Genscher, and the rest, that we were very thankful for this free exchange of analyses and thoughts and of the plans we might put into operation in the next time; because we do really feel that your great country, five times as big—I mean in economic size—than ours, and our second biggest in terms of foreign trade, we do really feel that both our responsibilities, vis-a-vis the world's economy as a whole and the other partners in the free world economy, request from us that we try as much as one can to coordinate our economic policies as we have coordinated our defense policies, as we have coordinated our détente policies, as we tried to coordinate our policies all over the globe.

Now, at this present stage, I think, in the economic field there lies a great part of our faith, not only of your people, also of ours, also of other peoples in the world.

If the economic future becomes bleak and uncertain, economic uncertainty and economic failure can lead to economic unrest not only, but also social unrest and also domestic political unrest in a number of countries, not in the first instance in the United States of America, not in the first instance in our country, but we might be infected in the course of time.

I think all of my compatriots heard with great satisfaction what you said this afternoon about you would not permit an aggravation of the downward trend of the economy, which at present is characterizing all our economies.

I am not going to too much dig into that field. I only wanted—using this as an example, the economic exercise of ours as an example—to express again, sir, our gratitude for this really free and frank and candid exchange of views and to express our gratitude for the endeavor on both sides to coordinate and harmonize our policies which, in fact, does not mean that both of our parts have to exactly operate along the same lines, but means that we will have to follow complementary policies in order to achieve the same goal that we have in common.

Ladies and gentlemen, I would like to rise and drink to the President of the United States and our charming hostess.

283

Letter Accepting the Resignation of Leonard Garment as Assistant to the President. *December 6, 1974*

Dear Len:

I have your letter of December 2 and it is with deep regret that I accept your resignation as Assistant to the President, effective December 31, 1974.

In so doing, I welcome this opportunity to express my personal appreciation for your dedicated service to the Presidency and to our Nation. In particular, I want you to know of my gratitude for your highly capable assistance and unhesitating support during the early, critically important period of transition. Yours is an exceptional record of public service and one in which you can always take great pride and personal satisfaction.

You have my admiration and warmest best wishes for every happiness and success in the years ahead.

Sincerely,

JERRY FORD

[The Honorable Leonard Garment, The White House, Washington, D.C.]

NOTE: The President's letter was dated December 5, 1974, and released December 6. Mr. Garment's letter of resignation, dated December 2 and released with the President's letter, read as follows:

Dear Mr. President:

I herewith submit my resignation as Assistant to the President effective December 31, 1974. I do so with particular appreciation for your personal thoughtfulness to myself and other members of President Nixon's staff during the transition period.

It has been a pleasure knowing you through these years in Washington and a privilege working for you during the past few months.

You and Mrs. Ford have my warmest regards and best wishes.

Sincerely,

LEONARD GARMENT

[The President, The White House, Washington, D.C.]

284

Joint Statement Following Discussions With Chancellor Schmidt of the Federal Republic of Germany. *December 6, 1974*

THE PRESIDENT of the United States of America Gerald R. Ford and the Chancellor of the Federal Republic of Germany Helmut Schmidt met in Washington on December 5 and 6, 1974. They reaffirmed the relationship of friendship and trust and confidence between the United States and the Federal Republic of Germany, and they held wide-ranging talks embracing international and economic problems, security and defense policy, and current East-West discussions. Secretary of State and Assistant to the President for National Security Affairs Henry A. Kissinger and Foreign Minister Hans Dietrich Genscher participated in the discussions between the President and the Chancellor and held complementary talks. In the economic talks, the President was joined by members of his Economic Policy Board and the Chancellor was accompanied by representatives of labor and business.

The President and the Chancellor reviewed the world economic situation in depth and explored effective solutions for current economic problems. They were agreed that international energy problems, the sharp increases in world prices, the contraction of economic activities, and large-scale payments imbalance constitute a severe threat to political and social stability in many countries. A creative new effort to coordinate economic policies between the United States and the Federal Republic of Germany, together with its partners in the European Community, will be required to master these difficulties.

The United States of America and the Federal Republic of Germany recognize the responsibility which falls to them for ensuring a prosperous international economy and safeguarding world trade. In this context they attach great significance to the upcoming multilateral trade negotiations. They reaffirmed their international pledges to avoid trade and payments restrictions which adversely affect other countries.

The President and the Chancellor agreed that in current circumstances they both have a responsibility to manage their domestic economic policies so as simultaneously to strengthen output and employment and to avoid new inflationary impulses. They affirmed that both countries have a need to encourage investment, to combat rising unemployment, and to act to increase confidence in the financial and the economic outlook. They recognized that the two countries are at different points in their fight against inflation, and that policies will take that fact into account. They are determined not to permit a serious deterioration in their economies to occur. If necessary, they will step in with adequate measures to prevent it.

The United States and the Federal Republic of Germany agreed that determination and cooperation are also necessary in dealing with energy-related problems. They underlined the importance of the International Energy Agency set up within the framework of the Organization for Economic Cooperation and Development to coordinate the energy policies of the industrialized countries. They attach particular importance to measures to reduce dependence on imported energy through conservation, more economic use of energy, and opening up of alternative sources. They stressed the need for cooperation in the field of research, notably in relation to coal processing and gasification.

Despite cooperative efforts to reduce dependence on energy imports, the President and the Chancellor recognized that in the coming year there will continue to be large scale imbalances in trade among nations and a corresponding necessity for large international flows of funds. They recognized that these flows for the most part have been, and in all probability will continue to be, handled by existing private and official channels. At the same time they agreed on the necessity of close cooperation among the financial authorities to insure the continued safe and orderly functioning of financial institutions in their expanding international roles. They agreed on the importance of the International Monetary Fund and other multilateral financial agencies being in a position in 1975 to provide flexible responsive financial assistance to any member nation facing international payments difficulties arising from the rapidly changing world economic situation. In addition, to insure that industrial countries which follow prudent and cooperative economic and energy policies have access to adequate financial resources in case of need, the President and the Chancellor agreed that early consideration should be given by these nations to the establishment of a supplementary financial safety net in the framework of the OECD.

The President and the Chancellor also stressed their determination to improve cooperation with the oil-producing countries. They expressed the conviction that further economic progress in the world, both in the developing and the developed countries, can only be resolved by means of world-wide cooperation.

The United States and the Federal Republic of Germany recognize the necessity of international cooperation to improve the international food situation. They will undertake prompt discussions on an international system of nationally-held grain reserves, increased global food production and substantial growth in food output in developing countries in order to prevent the recurrence of major food problems in the future. Both recognize the need for cooperation between food producers and consumers to ensure equitable adjustment to shortages and deficits.

The discussions on political questions centered on the North Atlantic Alliance, the evolution of East-West relations, and the situation in the Mediterranean and in the Near East.

The President and the Chancellor reviewed the progress of matters before the Alliance on the eve of the NATO Ministerial meeting to be convened next week in Brussels. They agreed on the continuing importance to the Allies of maintaining their political cohesion and strong defenses as the indispensable prerequisites for continued efforts to advance the process of East-West détente. Against the background of current challenges to their strength and solidarity, they reaffirmed their support for the principles of the Declaration on Atlantic Relations signed by Allied Heads of Government in June 1974.

The President and the Chancellor reiterated their resolve to contribute to the process of détente and the growth of cooperation between East and West. President Ford reviewed the SALT negotiations in the light of his talks with General Secretary Brezhnev in Vladivostok. They noted with satisfaction that it has been agreed to aim for limitations on strategic nuclear weapons on the basis of equality. The Chancellor expressed his appreciation for the progress achieved in Vladivostok which he considered most important for the pursuit of the policy of détente and safeguarding peace. President Ford and Chancellor Schmidt agreed that the understandings of Vladivostok would have a salutary effect on the overall development of East-West relations.

The two delegations also discussed the state of negotiations in Vienna on mutual and balanced force reductions in Central Europe. They confirmed their shared view that the aim of MBFR should be to arrive at a common ceiling for forces of both alliance systems.

Both sides expressed the hope that the Conference on Security and Cooperation in Europe would soon complete its initial consideration of texts dealing with all items on the agenda. It would then be possible to enter into the final stage of the negotiations. They agreed that certain progress had recently been made in reaching agreement on such areas as family reunification and improved access to printed information. They noted, however, that important texts still remain to be agreed, especially with regard to the Declaration of Principles governing Relations between States.

The President and Secretary of State Kissinger reviewed the United States' efforts to contribute to progress toward the achievement of a just and lasting peace in the Middle East. Both sides emphasized the importance of the disengagement agreements and of further results in the negotiating process.

As to developments in the Eastern Mediterranean, both sides stressed the responsibility of the parties immediately concerned. They stated their readiness to encourage Greece, Turkey, and Cyprus in the search for a mutually acceptable settlement of the dispute on the basis of the independence and territorial integrity of the Republic of Cyprus.

The German side reviewed the state of the relations of the Federal Republic of Germany with the GDR [German Democratic Republic] and of the issue of foreign representation of West Berlin by the Federal Republic of Germany.

Both sides were agreed on the importance of maintaining and developing the ties between the Federal Republic of Germany and West Berlin as well as full and complete implementation of all other parts of the Quadripartite Agreement.

The President and the Federal Chancellor reaffirmed the attachment of their Governments and peoples to the high purposes of the United Nations. They reviewed the proceedings of the current General Assembly and expressed their hope that the spirit of cooperation would prevail over divergencies and divisions so that the cause of international harmony, cooperation and a sound and enduring peace would be furthered.

The President and the Chancellor agreed to remain in close touch with one another, and to consult on all matters of mutual interest as might be required in the future.

285

Statement on Signing the Departments of Labor, and Health, Education, and Welfare Appropriation Act, 1975. *December 9, 1974*

I HAVE signed H.R. 15580, the 1975 appropriations act for the Departments of Labor and Health, Education, and Welfare and related agencies.

The Congress intended that the appropriations provided in H.R. 15580 should not exceed the fiscal year 1975 budget. Nevertheless, amounts included in the bill for mandatory Federal payments for public assistance are $1.2 billion below the estimates in the budget. The conferees' report on the bill, however, explicitly states that the "Conferees are acutely aware of the need to control inflation and of the need to restrain spending as one means to achieve this objective." The report further states: "The Conferees have no intention of approving new budget (obligational) authority which will ultimately result in spending in excess of the total budget estimate for the bill." In conclusion, the conferees expressed the willingness of the Congress to consider fully deferrals and rescissions submitted by the President to achieve these objectives.

I commend the Congress on this responsible approach to reducing inflationary pressures. I believe, however, that further review of mandatory public assistance spending will confirm the need for significantly higher spending than provided for in H.R. 15580. In the meantime, I will submit, as expected by the report of the conferees, deferrals to restrain spending for discretionary programs under this bill.

NOTE: As enacted, H.R. 15580, approved December 7, 1974, is Public Law 93–517 (88 Stat. 1634).

286

Statement on Signing the Farm Labor Contractor Registration Act Amendments of 1974. *December 9, 1974*

IN THE DECADE since enactment of the Farm Labor Contractor Registration Act of 1963, it became apparent that the law did not adequately protect migrant farm workers from various abuses. For about a year, the Administration has worked with the Congress to develop legislation to improve the act. There has been give-and-take on all sides. I am pleased that this cooperation has greatly strengthened the act.

On October 29, 1974, I vetoed a similar bill, H.R. 13342. It contained an objectionable rider entirely unrelated to improving the working conditions of migrant workers. The rider would have changed the classifications of certain Department of Labor administrative law judges, members of the Benefits Review Board, and other persons in no way involved with migrant workers. At that time, I urged the Congress to reenact this legislation without the objectionable rider. I am very pleased that it has done so.

This legislation, S. 3202, makes a number of improvements in the act, including the following:

—The act's coverage is expanded. Under existing law, a crew leader has to be recruiting migrant workers on an interstate basis—10 or more workers at any one time—before being required to register as a farm labor contractor. This bill removes these restrictions except with respect to those operating within a 25-mile intrastate radius of their homes and for 13 weeks a year or less. This provides protection for many more migrant workers under the act.

—Sanctions against violators are expanded. The only penalty which may be imposed against crew leaders who violate the present law is a $500 fine. It has been relatively ineffective against violations. This legislation adds a jail sentence of up to 1 year to the present $500 criminal fine, and a maximum fine of $10,000 as well as a maximum 3-year jail sentence for subsequent violations—including unregistered crew leaders who knowingly recruit illegal aliens. The Labor Department is now authorized additionally to seek injunctions and assess administrative civil money penalties. Private individuals also have the right to bring civil suits. Those discriminated against are offered means to exercise their rights under the act. The Labor Department is also given increased investigatory authority. In short, crew leaders now have greater responsibilities toward the migrant workers they recruit.

—Other leaders' responsibilities are increased. Under this legislation, crew leaders must obtain increased vehicle insurance coverage and provide transportation and housing which satisfy State and Federal health and safety requirements. Crew leaders must make a complete employment disclosure to the migrant workers they recruit. This disclosure must now be written, and in a language in which the workers are fluent.

—The act prohibits use of unregistered crew leaders and calls for improved recordkeeping.

I strongly believe that these and the other amendments to the Farm Labor Contractor Registration Act will go a long way toward improving the working conditions of our Nation's migrant farm workers. I therefore am pleased to have signed into law the Farm Labor Contractor Registration Act Amendments of 1974.

NOTE: As enacted, S. 3202, approved December 7, 1974, is Public Law 93–518 (88 Stat. 1652).

287

Remarks at the Unveiling of a Portrait of Representative George H. Mahon, Chairman of the House Committee on Appropriations. *December 10, 1974*

Thank you very much, Jamie. Helen and George, Mr. Speaker, the distinguished leadership of the House, my former colleagues and friends:

You don't know how honored and wonderful I feel about coming up here to say the things that come from the heart concerning George Mahon.

I am proud to say to George and his lovely wife Helen that I consider them among the very best friends that I have ever had in the Government of the United States.

In the House, according to the titles, George sat on the other side of the aisle, but that is one of the things that I think are great about this Government, that it doesn't really make much difference where Republicans or Democrats sit on so many, many issues, and of course, the friendships that you develop over the years do transcend the aisle. The relationship, we all know that have served in the House, goes well beyond the handshake. The relationship, really, as I found it, was an abiding trust, a total understanding, a person-to-person relationship that bridged the gap of partisanship or any of the other things that we hear or read about so often.

You know, it is an interesting fact that the second week after I became President—I should say the second weekend—George Mahon, Les Arends, Mel Laird, and I played golf together out at Burning Tree. I won't say how I did on that day, but I think it was a veto-proof foursome. [*Laughter*]

A lot of people subscribe to the theory that when you play golf with the President you don't try too hard to win. I have some news for you. I don't think George Mahon ever heard of that theory. But come to think of it, I haven't found anyone that I have ever played with that did either. [*Laughter*]

But my respect and my admiration for George Mahon goes far, far beyond the golf course. George may have an interlocking grip on his putter, but he has a hammerlock grip on unnecessary Federal spending.

I was blessed in the House to have the opportunity of serving 14 years on the House Committee on Appropriations with George Mahon. We all know that George Mahon has served 10 years as chairman of that great committee. And from my perspective as a Member of the House, as a Republican leader, as Vice President and President, I know that George Mahon has done a super job.

Now, I have to concede he is not quite like Clarence Cannon or John Taber.[1] Many of you didn't have the privilege of knowing those stalwart characters. But let me assure you that although his style is different, he learned a great deal from both of those historic characters.

I think we know from the record that George has devoted his total energies, his boundless resources, to keep America morally, militarily, and fiscally strong. He is one man that I have found in my years in the Congress and elsewhere who, in all sincerity and with deep conviction, did put his country above his party.

If I were to describe somebody that I served with who would deserve the accolade of a statesman, I certainly would pin that label on George Mahon.

I can't tell you how many countless hours I spent with George, not only in the full Committee on Appropriations but on the Defense Subcommittee on Appropriations and various other subcommittees of the Committee on Appropriations. But I don't think I can think of a single person that I served with who was

[1] Clarence A. Cannon, United States Representative from Missouri 1923–64, and John Taber, United States Representative from New York 1923–63.

more decent, more honorable, more dedicated, more loyal, more careful, and when the issues were down and the going was tough, could be more forthright. And to me, those are the kind of characteristics that, in my judgment, determine a great Member of the Congress more than any of the others.

So, George's service, his leadership, and all of the other things he has done for his district, his State, and his Nation, I think will go down in history and will always be on the record books for all other Members of Congress to try and emulate and to follow.

Texas, we all know, has been known for its bigness. In George Mahon it has lived up to its reputation.

Thank you very much.

NOTE: The President spoke at 11:29 a.m. in the Rayburn Room at the Capitol. In his opening remarks, the President referred to Representative Jamie L. Whitten of Mississippi.

288

Statement on the Senate's Confirmation of Nelson A. Rockefeller To Be Vice President of the United States. *December 10, 1974*

I AM gratified by the action of the Senate today in voting for confirmation of Nelson A. Rockefeller to fill the vacancy in the office of Vice President of the United States.

Few Americans have ever been more closely scrutinized or more thoroughly investigated by the Congress than Governor Rockefeller. The Senate's overwhelming vote of approval, after probing so meticulously into every aspect of his public and private life, speaks eloquently for his character and outstanding qualifications for public office.

The Senate vote brings us much closer to the day when the constitutional office of Vice President will be filled. I trust that similar action will be taken as rapidly as possible by the House of Representatives before final adjournment of the 93d Congress. Governor Rockefeller would then be able to put his experience and energy to work for all the people of the United States in our efforts to deal with the great challenges ahead.

NOTE: The statement was released at New York, N.Y.

289

Remarks on Presenting the National Football Foundation and Hall of Fame's Distinguished American Award to Bob Hope in New York City. *December 10, 1974*

Chris, Your Eminence, President Dick Kazmaier, distinguished guests:

It is a very high honor and a very great privilege to have the opportunity of participating in this program this evening, and may I at the outset congratulate the new inductees as well as the scholar-athletes.

Bob Hope and I were commenting, as all of these fine young athletes were being introduced, we never saw such a packaging of brains, appearance, and skill, and I congratulate each and every one of you.

Let me thank you, Chris, for that introduction. It is kind of the routine introduction that comes with this office. [*Laughter*]

You know, since I became President, I am usually introduced in a more dignified and stately manner. On some occasions there is a variation, however. But there was one dinner a few weeks ago when I was introduced by a former teammate of the University of Michigan back a good many years, and frankly I will never forget that introduction.

He said, "Ladies and gentlemen, it might interest you to know that I played football with Jerry Ford for 2 years, and it made a lasting impression on me. I was a quarterback, Jerry Ford was a center, and you might say it gave me a completely different view of the President." [*Laughter*]

If you stopped to think about it, there are many similarities between football and government. For instance, in both areas nothing is ever done without discussing it first; in football you call it a huddle, in Washington you call it a debate. And sometimes the talk goes on for many, many hours without really saying anything; in Washington it is called a filibuster, in football it is called Howard Cosell.[1] [*Laughter*]

You know, Howard Cosell takes a lot of kidding, but in all fairness, someone once said, "To me, Howard Cosell will always look 10 feet tall." I don't know who said it, but I think it was Abe Beame.[2] [*Laughter*]

It is a real honor to be here tonight, because football has meant so much to me for a good many years. You might be interested to know that I have put together

---

[1] An ABC sportscaster.

[2] Abraham D. Beame, mayor of New York City.

over the years a small collection of memorable football quotations, and I would like to share with you tonight two of them.

The first quotation is from Grantland Rice, who was a great, great sportswriter many years ago, and he said: "When the one Great Scorer comes to write against your name, he marks not that you won or lost, but how you played the game." And the other is from Woody Hayes: "Bah, humbug!" [*Laughter*]

Incidentally, I wish Woody Hayes—he is an ex-Big Tenner—and the Ohio State Buckeyes good luck in the Rose Bowl. But as a former Michigan football player and a 12-term Congressman from Michigan, I think that is about as far as I ought to go. You know, I may cook my own breakfast, but I am not about to cook my own goose. [*Laughter*]

Well, obviously, the Michigan Wolverines are not the only team I root for. In fact, back in the Capital we have a professional team we are very, very proud of—the Washington Redskins, more affectionately known as the Over-the-Hill-Gang.

You know, it is always exciting to watch the Redskins play, because you are never quite sure what they are going to reach first—the playoffs or social security. [*Laughter*]

And the Redskins have one of the most colorful quarterbacks in the history of the game, Sonny Jurgensen. And isn't George Allen lucky to have two great quarterbacks like Billy Kilmer and Sonny Jurgensen?

Well, earlier I was saying a word or two about my good friend Woody Hayes. I think it is well known that Sonny Jurgensen has a much more relaxed attitude toward the game. I can remember back in 1968 when Sonny, throwing with a very, very sore arm, scored five touchdowns passes against the Chicago Bears. And as he came off the field at the end of the game, Otto Graham, who was then the coach of the Redskins, asked him, "Sonny, how's your arm?"

Sonny said, "It hurts me awful."

Graham looked worried. He said, "It is going to be a problem."

Sonny said, "It is. Did you ever try to drink left-handed?" [*Laughter*]

Well, somewhere between Sonny Jurgensen and Woody Hayes I think there is a little room for compromise.

In my lifetime I have attended a lot of sports dinners, and it has been something of a ritual to honor the exercise, the sportsmanship, the teamwork, the good fellowship that we all receive and have received from football. And that is as it should be.

But what about winning? How about a good word for the ultimate reason

53-528 O - 76 - 49

any of us have for going into a competitive sport? As much as I enjoyed the physical and emotional dividends that college athletics brought me, I sincerely doubt if I ever suited up, put on my helmet—and yes, I did wear a helmet—[*laughter*]—without the total commitment of going out there to win, not to get exercise, gold, or glory, but simply to win.

To me, winning is not a shameful concept. I would like to think that winning is in the great American tradition. Two hundred years ago we fought for our freedom, and we won; and for the next hundred years we challenged a continent, and we won.

But somebody once said the problem with winning is you have to keep on doing it. And so today, we Americans face another historic struggle to maintain our strength as a nation, as a people, and our economic well-being for all of us. And believe me, in this battle against inflation, or recession, there are no playoffs, and there is no "wait till next year." It is winner take all, or loser have nothing.

As I see it—"win"—it is a very small word, but let's be careful not to lose it.

Tonight I have come to New York for a very, very personal reason, and it also has something to do with winning. I have come to do honor and to pay tribute to a man who has won the admiration, the affection, and the everlasting gratitude of all Americans—a superstar before the term was ever thought of.

Bob Hope has consistently brought to our lives the warm glow and the sustaining lift of that precious gift of laughter. And to those of us who served in the Armed Forces, Bob's eagerly awaited visits brought home an awful lot closer.

But Bob Hope is more than a superlative entertainer—much, much more. His dedication to the needs and the welfare of Americans has made him a leader in humanitarian activities. It would be a monumental task to list all of the charities and causes that have said "thanks for the memory" of Bob Hope's helping hand.

Throughout the years I have always looked forward to sharing a head table, a foursome, and many a memorable hour with Bob Hope. I am proud to call him my friend.

And so, it gives me a great deal of personal pleasure to present tonight the Distinguished American Award of the National Football Foundation and Hall of Fame to Bob Hope—patriot, ardent sportsman, indomitable, courageous, unselfish American whose lifetime credo is the lifting of the human spirit.

Gentlemen, Bob Hope.

NOTE: The President spoke at 9:26 p.m. in the Grand Ballroom at the Waldorf-Astoria Hotel. Also honored at the annual awards dinner were Gerald B. Zornow, chairman of the board of the Eastman Kodak Company, who received the Foundation's Gold Medal; 10 new members of the Hall of Fame; and 11 scholar-athletes receiving graduate fellowships.

In his opening remarks, the President referred to ABC sportscaster Chris Schenkel, who was master of ceremonies; His Eminence Terence Cardinal Cooke, Archbishop of New York; and Richard W. Kazmaier, Jr., president of the National Football Foundation and Hall of Fame.

290

Remarks at a Meeting of the Business Council. *December 11, 1974*

Dave, Anne, members of the Business Council, and guests:

I don't have to tell you I deeply appreciate the opportunity to meet with you tonight as leaders of commerce and industry, to discuss some very serious economic problems that we all face.

The mutuality of our problems was never more clearly stated than when I was introduced at a business conference quite recently. The moderator said, and I quote: The greatness of America is that anyone can grow up to be president of an auto company, president of an airline, president of a utility, or President of the United States.

Then he took a long, long pause and added, "That's just one of the chances you have to take!" [*Laughter*]

Four months ago, in my first words as President, I promised my fellow citizens from time to time "a little straight talk among friends."

I hope I am among friends tonight, because we are all in the same business, trying to keep this country politically and economically stable and strong, and to bring about better lives for more and more people through the genius of our American system.

Businessmen are not the only Americans working toward these goals, but it is very certain they cannot be reached—these goals—without you.

Now for a little straight talk. The economy is in difficult straits. All the statistics, or most of them, prove that quite conclusively. We are in a recession. Production is declining, and unemployment, unfortunately, is rising. We are also faced with continued high rates of inflation greater than can be tolerated over an extended period of time.

There is some good economic news, but I can concede much or most of it is bad. Nevertheless, our country is not in an economic crisis.

A crisis—in the sense of a national crisis—is something that demands immediate and drastic action. A national problem is something that demands widespread understanding and carefully deliberated solutions—cures that are not worse than the disease.

In my 25-plus years in this Capital, our economy has gone through at least five recessions—five in 25 years. And the facts are that we have recovered from every one of them. And I predict without any hesitation that we will recover from this one also. The question is not when, but how. And your question to me as President is what am I doing about it? What am I doing about it as President?

I cannot and will not promise you a sudden change for the better. There is no prospect that I can discern for instantaneous improvement in the economy. Without enumerating them, you and I know that today's difficulties stem from policies and developments of past years. The effect of policies adopted today would not be felt for months to come.

Nor do I believe that confidence in the American economy can be restored with rhetoric—mine or that of other political players or sideline sitters. I do not believe it can be restored by Federal Government activity alone. I do believe it can be restored by the effective teamwork and enlightened self-interest of all elements of our American free enterprise economy and our representative, free political system.

Long-term success is not assured by short-term panaceas. There appears to be a tendency these days to focus only on the immediate needs or effects of any proposed economic remedy and not to examine its long-term effects. Speaking only for myself, I do not buy that.

Not just the President, not just the Congress, not just business or labor or consumer, but all of us must act to renew and invigorate our economy and everybody's faith in that economy.

Hopefully we will do most things right and only a few wrong things—maybe some of you have done that in business or had the same experience. But I can assure you this Government, as far as I am concerned, will do nothing deliberately wrong. But just because doing something—yes, it might perk up political opinion polls, but I think the facts are in some instances that course would be the worst course of all.

Men survive by instinct but make progress by intelligence. Perhaps we could survive by merely following our instincts now—an immediate return to wage and price controls, as some demand; immediate and mandatory gasoline rationing, as others advocate; the enactment of other compulsory programs that treat the symptoms but retard the cure.

I happen to believe that instincts must be overruled by intelligence and politics must yield to principles if we are to make reasonable economic progress that can honestly be sustained in the future, whether it is short-term or long-term. And let me say without any hesitation or qualification, that is what I intend to do.

Today I met with the bipartisan leaders of the House and Senate at the White House in the Cabinet Room. The campaign is over, the voters have spoken, and the present Congress is about to adjourn. At that meeting there was a spirit of concern for the country in that representative roomful of responsible Democrats and responsible Republicans which I wish I had the eloquence to describe. Really, you would not believe how well we all get along when the doors are closed.

So, I asked my former colleagues how well we all could get along, and I think most of them sincerely agreed that it would be wise if we could have a sort of an informal moratorium on partisan economics, at least until the next Congress convenes in January. Could not we sort of bite our tongues when tempted to say things that might further weaken confidence in the economy and compound the confusion in many Americans' minds about their future?

I was encouraged by the meeting this morning—I thought it was wholesome, beneficial, and I think it will have an impact. But, for a start, let me say this: Do not believe I have made any economic decisions unless you hear those decisions from me personally. There can be only one person that makes those decisions. And when I make them, I'll announce them.

I intend to keep my experts working over the holidays, translating into specifics a number of new or alternative measures to augment and update the economic package that I will place before the Congress within the next 2 months. We will meet the changing priorities of our present based on future realities.

I will have new proposals on the desks of the new Members of Congress when they convene in mid-January, if not sooner. In the few days left before this Congressional session, I assured the leaders that I would communicate, conciliate, compromise, and cooperate to the outer limits of my fundamental principles in order to assure prompt enactment of the most urgent economic measures.

Among these are long-delayed trade reform legislation as well as legislation to make sure that unemployed workers receive temporary assistance, including public service jobs and extended unemployment compensation to protect their buying power. If these measures reasonably approximate the criteria I set 2 months ago, I will support adequate dollar amounts now indicated by worsening employment statistics, especially in some industries.

Tomorrow I intend to meet with the leaders of the automotive industry—Roy Chapin of American Motors, Lee Iacocca of Ford, Tom Murphy of General Motors, Lynn Townsend of Chrysler, and Leonard Woodcock of the UAW. This will be a face-to-face discussion of the industry's very special problems, but problems that affect our economy on a very broad basis.

My door has been open, and remains open, to the responsible spokesman of any segment of our economy which has been unduly damaged by our present economic difficulty.

I will continue to press for legislation and regulatory policies providing increased incentives and assistance for industrial modernization, replacement, and expansion to assure a sound industrial base now and for future generations, so that new jobs will be created.

Increased productivity lies at the heart of our free enterprise system which made America what it is today. And I have been a firm believer in that very important ingredient all of my adult life, and I will say without any hesitation I am not going to change that conviction as President of the United States.

In short, what I am saying is quite precisely this: that insofar as I can prevent it, the fundamental rules of the economic game are not going to be changed every month or every other year in the short or the long haul. But I am also saying that insofar as I can achieve it, the programs and the policies of the Federal Government will be responsive to changed circumstances and our best available economic forecasts.

Some factors—especially fuel and food production—contribute formidably, as you well know, to our current economic problems. And when I fly to meet the President of France this weekend, I will be by no means neglecting our domestic difficulties if I improve the climate of cooperation among the fuel-consuming industrial nations by a common effort to ensure adequate food and fuel supplies at acceptable prices.

Just as all of your businesses depend upon enough energy, they also depend upon enough customers. "Customers" is a lovely word to you, and "consumers" sounds like an organized pressure group. The facts are that they are interchangeable. And consumers in America are concerned about the economy as employees and stockholders—in fact, they are one and the same people.

This Administration, I can assure you, is pledged to protect the consumer buying power, or customer purchasing power, as an essential element of sustaining and strengthening the free enterprise system. This is where the voluntary part of my economic program comes in—primarily in each individual's purposeful determination to reduce conspicuous waste and to spend wisely.

The WIN campaign—a volunteer, nonpartisan citizens' effort—is yet an unexploited success. It has my full support, and it deserves yours.

I can tell you this: I have received more than 200,000 pieces of mail in support of the WIN program, by far the largest amount of favorable public response to anything that I have done since taking office.

Now personally, I don't care whether WIN spells "Whip Inflation Now" or "Work Is Needed." America needs the winning spirit to surmount its present economic difficulties. Whatever the challenge, Americans like to win. If there are any among you who want me to take a 180 degree turn from inflation fighting to recessionary pump priming, they will be disappointed.

The fact of the matter is I am deeply concerned about all three domestic devils—inflation, recession, and energy. They are all part of the same economic torment that now afflicts every industrial nation. I will continue to treat this general economic ailment with a balanced program. We have not, should not, and will not concentrate exclusively on any single aspect of our complex economy. I think it is wise, and I intend to concentrate on the total picture.

Heretofore I have emphasized the distortions of inflation, because price increases must be blunted before we can realistically expect to restore employment gains and capital investment. There are now early signals that price pressures are beginning to ease. I expect inflation will move steadily down from the intolerable double-digit level.

The facts are, conditions are changing rapidly. Only by acting in a responsible manner can we strengthen confidence and move toward recovery without destroying the accumulated anti-inflation pressures that are just now beginning to work.

I know that the Business Council can rise to this challenge, and I will tell you why. I remember a little history. You and your predecessors were a very key factor in helping the Government mobilize the economy for World War II, and what an incredible record that you wrote—in top managerial posts in Government, in industry, and in the war itself.

Gentlemen, you have to—and we need you to—mobilize again. This Administration will do its part. I will personally do my part. The country needs your full cooperation and your full support.

What is needed is to unite our entire American leadership in this effort, not to divide ourselves with self-defeating pessimism.

As a most perceptive Washington veteran news columnist recently wrote under the heading "The Calamity Howlers," he said the following, and I quote:

"Now the situation is awkward, and in the automobile towns it is alarming, but the calamity howlers are adding to the depression psychology and making things even worse than they need be.

"For example, many companies now seem to be holding back on essential purchases for fear of what might happen in 1975, and there is upward pressure on both prices and wages in the belief that President Ford will finally be forced to adopt wage and price controls. In short, many people are beginning to act on their fears, which are worse than the facts.

"Washington," he went on to say, "is a little jittery, too. Because everybody has a pain sooner or later and comes here to complain about it, the capital has a tendency to think everybody has a pain. . . .

"So things are a little mixed up," he went on to say, "and everybody is looking for painless solutions and hoping to get back to where we were before, with cheap gas and 96 fancy new models to choose from. But it's not on, folks. That world is gone," he said. "We're going to have to make do and mend for a while, but this is a very strong country and it will get along if we don't talk ourselves into a mess."

As Mr. Reston rightly concluded, this is a very strong country. It started weak and disunited, but two centuries later our free economic system and our free political system are both the strongest and the most enduring in the world. And as long as I am President, I propose to keep them that way.

Thank you very much.

NOTE: The President spoke at 9:06 p.m. in the State Room at the Mayflower Hotel. In his opening remarks, the President referred to David Packard, president of the Business Council, and Anne L. Armstrong, Counsellor to the President.

James B. Reston was a syndicated columnist for the New York Times.

291

Memorandum on the Minority Business Development Program. *December 12, 1974*

MEMORANDUM FOR
THE SECRETARY OF STATE
THE SECRETARY OF THE TREASURY
THE SECRETARY OF DEFENSE
THE ATTORNEY GENERAL
THE SECRETARY OF THE INTERIOR
THE SECRETARY OF AGRICULTURE
THE SECRETARY OF COMMERCE
THE SECRETARY OF LABOR
THE SECRETARY OF HEALTH, EDUCATION AND WELFARE
THE SECRETARY OF HOUSING AND URBAN DEVELOPMENT
THE SECRETARY OF TRANSPORTATION

I want to stress that an important objective of my Administration will be assistance to disadvantaged minorities to further allow their participation in the economic benefits of the private enterprise system. Too little attention has been given to this objective in certain sectors of the Federal Government. I am, therefore, seeking improvements in the Government's minority business development program.

Although the Office of Minority Business Enterprise in the Department of Commerce and the Small Business Administration have had primary responsibility for minority business programs, their success to date in these efforts has been due in large measure to the support of other Federal agencies. Your strong backing of this objective is essential to a meaningful Federal effort, and I ask that you undertake a reexamination of your agency's commitment to assisting the creation of successful minority businesses and of the effectiveness of your program. Please submit a report of your findings to me by January 31, 1975.

During this difficult economic period, many minority businesses are particularly vulnerable. They need every help the Government can reasonably provide. It is especially important, therefore, that your agency look for every appropriate opportunity for minority businesses to participate in Government programs as contractors, subcontractors, bankers, etc., and that management, technical and financial assistance be provided whenever feasible.

I am confident of your support of this important effort.

GERALD R. FORD

NOTE: The text of the memorandum, dated December 11, 1974, was released December 12.

292

Message to the Congress Transmitting Annual Report of the Council on Environmental Quality. *December 12, 1974*

To the Congress of the United States:

I am pleased to transmit to the Congress the Fifth Annual Report of the Council on Environmental Quality.

When future historians look back on the pursuit of environmental quality in our era, they will recognize it as a positive turning point.

As I stated in an Earth Day speech in 1970, "the day is gone when concern for the land, the air and the water was sole province of the conservationist, the wilderness enthusiast, the bird watcher, and the environmental scientist."

Instead, today, millions of our citizens share a new vision of the future in which natural systems can be protected, pollution can be controlled, and our natural heritage will be preserved. The crusade to improve the quality of our human environment has begun—a crusade which has already led to great accomplishment over the past five years.

Another valuable lesson was learned during the energy crisis last winter when, in trying circumstances, it became clear that we cannot achieve all our environmental and all our energy and economic goals at the same time. Had our commitment to the environment not been ingrained, we might have reacted to this situation by discarding our environmental goals. Had our commitment to the environment not been mature, we might not have recognized the need for balance to accommodate other social and economic goals as well. By rejecting the extremes—by accepting the need for balance—we held fast to the accomplishments of the past and looked with new perspective toward the imperatives of the future. This, in my judgment, is the course we must continue to follow.

The need to move toward greater self-sufficiency in energy is one of the major challenges of the decade ahead. We can and must meet our needs for energy, and in ways that minimize damage to the environment.

The conservation of energy provides an essential common ground between our need for energy and our desire to protect the environment. By eliminating waste in the use of energy, and by increasing the efficiency of the energy we use, we can move toward both goals simultaneously. Our experience this year has shown that there are major opportunities to conserve energy. And we are coming to understand that actions which temper our growing use of energy contribute to self-sufficiency as well as actions which increase our domestic supply.

We must also recognize that, even with a strong conservation program, we will still have to mine more coal, drill for more oil and gas, and build more powerplants and refineries. Each of these measures will have an impact on the environment. Yet this can be minimized, and the last five years have shown that we have the capacity and the willingness to do so. Science and technology, in which America excels, provides one means of limiting environmental damage; careful analysis and planning, with broad public participation, offers another.

Let us also be guided by our increased recognition of the interdependence of all nations of our globe and the fundamental relationship between population, resources, economic development, world stability, and the environment.

No longer is concern for the environment the dream of a few. Instead, it is reflected in countless actions by many citizens, by industry, and by government at all levels every day. The environmental movement has matured, and the nation and its environment have benefited in the process. Looking to the future, we can expect further accomplishment in enhancing our environment and, along with it, further improvement in our quality of life.

GERALD R. FORD

The White House,
December 12, 1974.

NOTE: The report is entitled "The Fifth Annual Report of the Council on Environmental Quality—December 1974" (Government Printing Office, 597 pp.).

293

Remarks on Awarding the Congressional Medal of Honor to WO Louis R. Rocco and S. Sgt. Jon R. Cavaiani, United States Army. *December 12, 1974*

Secretary Schlesinger, Secretary Callaway, our distinguished recipients, ladies and gentlemen:

It is, of course, a great blessing that the last American soldier is home from the battlefields of Vietnam. Our landing ships again, fortunately, have long since departed those distant shores. And our planes have long ago flown their last mission on the war across those faraway jungles.

Let us, individually and collectively, fervently pray that Vietnam was, indeed, the last—our last war.

We are, however, reminded of Vietnam today—of that long and painful time—by two men who lived it and whose actions will never die in the annals of the United States military history. For the Nation they served bestows on them today the Congressional Medal of Honor for their acts of courage above and beyond the call of duty.

United States Army Warrant Officer Louis Rocco—Sergeant First Class in Vietnam—and Army Staff Sergeant Jon R. Cavaiani, by the courage of their acts, carried forward the long and very proud military tradition of selfless dedication to the cause of freedom.

Army Warrant Officer Louis Rocco distinguished himself on May 24, 1970. He volunteered to help evacuate eight critically wounded South Vietnamese troops under attack. His helicopter crashlanded at the evacuation site under intense enemy fire. Ignoring a fractured wrist and broken hip and severely bruised back, Warrant Officer Rocco pulled the unconscious survivors from the burning wreckage. His hands were severely burned, causing him excruciating pain. He nevertheless carried each of his unconscious comrades more than 20 yards through enemy fire to friendly positions. Trained in first aid, he administered to them before collapsing into unconsciousness.

Warrant Officer Rocco's bravery was directly responsible for saving three of his fellow soldiers from certain death. His gallantry, disregarding his own pain and injuries, is in the highest tradition of self-sacrifice and courage in our military service.

And I say to his family here today, you also walk in the respect and admiration of your country and of your President.

Sergeant Cavaiani was believed to have been killed in action when recommended for the Medal of Honor. It was only later learned that he had been captured. He was a prisoner of war for more than 2 years and was repatriated on July 10, 1973.

On June 4 and 5, 1971, he served as a platoon leader, providing security for an isolated radio relay site within enemy-held territory. The Sergeant's unit was attacked by a superior enemy force. For those 2 days, firing with different weapons, Sergeant Cavaiani directed the evacuation of some of his platoon by helicopter while ordering the others to escape. Many were able to do so. He remained, however, exposing himself to heavy enemy fire. Sergeant Cavaiani was wounded numerous times, finally falling to his captors.

We are honored that the Sergeant's family is here with us today. The President of the United States wishes to tell them in person that Sergeant Cavaiani is an American of extraordinary heroism, and his valor reflects well on all of them.

This day is witness to the fact that the bravest of the brave still rise from among our people, that freedom and that justice have survived and will survive, that peace is still our most precious and enduring goal, and that we the American people will forever cherish the noble deeds, the noble ideals entrusted to us these past two centuries by our forefathers.

These ideals do not sleep. They are not silent. They live among us here today in the presence of Jon Robert Cavaiani and Louis Richard Rocco and their families.

The Secretary of the Army will now read the citations.

[At this point, Secretary of the Army Howard H. Callaway read the citations. The President then resumed speaking.]

Thank you very much, Secretary Callaway, Secretary Schlesinger, ladies and gentlemen. I thank you all for being here.

It is a very wonderful occasion paying tribute and honor to two very gallant and wonderful soldiers in the very highest and the very best traditions of the United States military service.

I suggest now that we all might go into the State Dining Room and have some refreshments.

NOTE: The President spoke at 3:09 p.m. in the East Room at the White House. The texts of the citations follow:

The President of the United States of America, authorized by Act of Congress, March 3, 1863, has awarded in the name of The Congress the Medal of Honor to

WARRANT OFFICER LOUIS R. ROCCO
UNITED STATES ARMY

for conspicuous gallantry and intrepidity in action at the risk of his life above and beyond the call of duty:

Warrant Officer (then Sergeant First Class) Louis R. Rocco, United States Military Assistance Command, Vietnam, Advisory Team 162, distinguished himself on 24 May 1970, northeast of Katum, Republic of Vietnam, when he volunteered to accompany a medical evacuation team on an urgent mission to evacuate eight critically wounded Army of the Republic of Vietnam personnel. As the helicopter approached the landing zone, it became the target for intense enemy automatic weapons fire. Disregarding his own safety, Warrant Officer Rocco identified and placed accurate suppressive fire on the enemy positions as the aircraft descended toward the landing zone. Sustaining major damage from the enemy fire, the aircraft was forced to crash land, causing Warrant Officer Rocco to sustain a fractured wrist and hip and a severely bruised back. Ignoring his injuries, he extracted the survivors from the burning wreckage, sustaining burns to his own body. Despite intense enemy fire, Warrant Officer Rocco carried each unconscious man across approximately twenty meters of exposed terrain to the Army of the Republic of Vietnam perimeter. On each trip, his severely burned hands and broken wrist caused excruciating pain, but the lives of the unconscious crash survivors were more important than his personal discomfort, and he continued his rescue efforts. Once inside the friendly position, Warrant Officer Rocco helped administer first aid to his wounded comrades until his wounds and burns caused him to collapse and lose consciousness. His bravery under fire and intense devotion to duty were directly responsible for saving three of his fellow soldiers from certain death. His unparalleled bravery in the face of enemy fire, his complete disregard for his own pain and injuries, and his performance were far above and beyond the call of duty and were in keeping with the highest traditions of self-sacrifice and courage of the military service.

The President of the United States of America, authorized by Act of Congress, March 3, 1863, has awarded in the name of The Congress the Medal of Honor to

STAFF SERGEANT JON R. CAVAIANI
UNITED STATES ARMY

for conspicuous gallantry and intrepidity in action at the risk of his life above and beyond the call of duty:

Staff Sergeant Jon R. Cavaiani, United States Army Vietnam Training Advisory Group, distinguished himself by conspicuous gallantry and intrepidity at the risk of life above and beyond the call of duty in action in the Republic of Vietnam on 4 and 5 June 1971 while serving as a platoon leader to a security platoon providing security for an isolated radio relay site located within enemy-held territory. On the morning of 4 June 1971, the entire camp came under an intense barrage of enemy small arms, automatic weapons, rocket-propelled grenade and mortar fire from a superior size enemy force. Sergeant Cavaiani acted with complete disregard for his personal safety as he repeatedly exposed himself to heavy enemy fire in order to move about the camp's perimeter directing the platoon's fire and rallying the platoon in a desperate fight for survival. Sergeant Cavaiani also returned heavy suppressive fire upon the assaulting enemy force during this period with a variety of weapons. When the entire platoon was to be evacuated, Sergeant Cavaiani unhesitatingly volunteered to remain on the ground and direct the helicopters into the landing zone. Sergeant Cavaiani was able to direct the first three helicopters in evacuating a major portion of the platoon. Due to intense increase in enemy fire, Sergeant Cavaiani was forced to remain at the camp overnight where he calmly directed the remaining platoon members in strengthening their defenses. On the morning of 5 June, a heavy ground fog restricted visibility. The superior size enemy force launched a major ground attack in an attempt to completely annihilate the remaining small force. The enemy force advanced in two ranks, first firing a heavy volume of small arms automatic weapons and rocket-propelled grenade fire while the second rank continuously threw a steady barrage of hand grenades at the beleaguered force. Sergeant Cavaiani returned a heavy barrage of small arms and hand grenade fire on the assaulting enemy force but was unable to slow them down. He ordered the remaining platoon members to attempt to escape while he provided them with cover fire. With one last courageous exertion, Sergeant Cavaiani recovered a machine gun, stood up, completely exposing himself to the heavy enemy fire directed at him, and began firing the machine gun in a sweeping motion along the two ranks of advancing enemy soldiers. Through Sergeant Cavaiani's valiant efforts with complete disregard for his safety, the majority of the remaining platoon members were able to escape. While inflicting severe losses on the advancing enemy force, Sergeant Cavaiani was wounded numerous times. Staff Sergeant Cavaiani's conspicuous gallantry, extraordinary heroism and intrepidity at the risk of his life, above and beyond the call of duty, were in keeping with the highest traditions of the military service and reflect great credit upon himself and the United States Army.

294

Letter Accepting the Resignation of Kenneth R. Cole, Jr., as Assistant to the President for Domestic Affairs. *December 13, 1974*

Dear Ken:

It is with deepest regret that I accept your resignation as Assistant to the President for Domestic Affairs and Executive Director of the Domestic Council effective in March, 1975, as you requested.

Needless to say, you will be greatly missed here at the White House, where you have served so admirably for the past six years. Since the earliest days of the Nixon Administration, you have played a leading and vital role in shaping the direction of national domestic policy. From revenue sharing, welfare reform and health care, to anti-crime legislation, drug-abuse prevention planning and energy policy, your sweep and scope have been across the board. As the President's representative with the Nation's Governors and other local government officials, you have performed superbly. Their praise and universal respect for you should be a special source of satisfaction to you.

Beyond this, however, I want to express my personal appreciation for your contributions to my Administration in its first days and throughout the transition. I am especially grateful for your selflessness in temporarily setting aside your plans to return to the private sector in order to assist in the transition and completion of the 1974 legislative program. Also, your guidance and counsel in helping to shape and establish this Administration's domestic agenda have been immensely valuable.

You may be sure you and your family have Mrs. Ford's and my warmest best wishes for every success and happiness in the years ahead.

Sincerely,

JERRY FORD

[The Honorable Ken Cole, The White House, Washington, D.C.]

NOTE: Mr. Cole's letter of resignation, dated December 12, 1974, and released with the President's letter, read as follows:

Dear Mr. President:

When President Nixon asked me to join the White House staff six years ago, I came with the personal conviction that the Federal Government had grown so big as to be unresponsive to the people's needs and with the personal desire to help in the restoration of power and responsibility to the people themselves. Through such historic initiatives as General Revenue Sharing, I believe that process of restoration has begun. Your own role has been an indispensable part of the process from the beginning, and your continuing leadership will carry it forward to completion.

Serving my country has always been of the highest importance to me, and the opportunity to participate at the highest levels of government will always be the most meaningful and the most rewarding experience of my life. You and your predecessor gave me the opportunity to serve in a way I never envisioned, even in my wildest dreams, and my gratitude for the confidence reposed in me is literally beyond expression.

Now, I believe, it is time for me to pursue my career in the private sector. With mixed feelings of regret and thanks and anticipation, I ask therefore that you accept my resignation as Assistant to the President for Domestic Affairs and Executive Director of the Domestic Council, effective March 2, 1975.

We are fortunate to have you as our President. We need your leadership to restore confidence in government. But more importantly we need your leadership to restore confidence in ourselves. Government cannot do everything for everybody, but individual Americans, working together, can meet and beat the toughest of challenges. I believe you are setting the example for us to follow, and that the people will respond. I consider it an honor and a privilege to have been able to work with you. If as a private citizen I can be of help, please know that you can count on me.

Marilyn and I wish you great success in the future and wish for you, Mrs. Ford and your family all the happiness that life can bring.

Very respectfully,

KENNETH R. COLE, JR.

[The President, The White House, Washington, D.C.]

295

Letter Accepting the Resignation of William B. Saxbe as Attorney General of the United States. *December 13, 1974*

Dear Bill:

I have your letter of December 12 and, for the purpose of keeping the records straight, I will, of course, accept your resignation as Attorney General of the United States, effective upon the appointment and qualification of your successor or your own appointment and confirmation as Ambassador to India, whichever occurs earlier.

Nearly a year ago, you assumed the duties of Attorney General under the most difficult circumstances. At that time you wisely set as your goals the rekindling of public confidence in the law and the rebuilding of morale within the Department of Justice. You offered then as your watchwords a verse from the Book of Micah, "To do justice and love mercy and walk humbly with thy God."

The impressive record you have compiled as Attorney General has in large measure brought fulfillment of those goals, adding new luster to your already distinguished career and further testifying to your superb leadership and unswerving devotion to the public good. You have truly earned the admiration of your colleagues in government and the thanks of your fellow citizens throughout the Nation.

It is with these high qualities in mind that I look forward to your continued service to this Administration and to our Nation as my Ambassador to India. I am wholly confident you will bring to your new responsibilities the same skills, energy and dedication to responsible government that you have demonstrated throughout your public life.

Betty joins me in wishing Dolly and you our best wishes for every continued happiness and success.

With my appreciation and warmest personal regards.

Sincerely,

JERRY FORD

[The Honorable William B. Saxbe, The Attorney General, Washington, D.C.]

NOTE: Attorney General Saxbe's letter of resignation, dated December 12, 1974, and released with the President's letter, read as follows:

Dear Mr. President:

I hereby submit my letter of resignation as Attorney General of the United States of America so that I may accept the new responsibility which you have assigned to me as United States Ambassador to the Republic of India, subject to confirmation by the Senate of the United States.

As we agreed, it is my intention to make my resignation effective upon my appointment as Ambassador, or, in the alternative, upon the appointment of my successor as Attorney General, whichever occurs earlier.

I want to take this opportunity to express to you, Mr. President, my appreciation for the opportunity to serve as Attorney General. A strong Department of Justice is vital to our country, and I can assure you that the officials of this Department will cooperate in every way with my successor in order that the interests of government and the people may best be served.

Respectfully,

WILLIAM B. SAXBE

[The President, The White House, Washington, D.C.]

296

Statement on the Canonization of Elizabeth Bayley Seton. *December 13, 1974*

THE ANNOUNCEMENT by Pope Paul VI that Elizabeth Bayley Seton will be canonized in 1975 as the first American-born saint of the Roman Catholic Church is a milestone in our Nation's diverse spiritual history. The fact that a woman is the first native-born American named to sainthood by the Holy See is all the more historic since women have never made a greater contribution to America's national life than today.

It is fitting that we recall at this time another woman—Mother Cabrini, who was born in Italy—who was named a saint by the Holy See after devoting much of her life to religious work in the United States.

Mother Seton's singular honor is a tribute to all American women who have entered the religious life to serve in schools, hospitals, and charitable work. She died in 1821, but today there are thousands of Sisters of Charity—the religious order she founded—carrying on the important service which Mother Seton began. I congratulate them on this most joyous occasion and wish them well in their future endeavors.

297

Remarks on Arrival in Martinique, French West Indies, for Meetings With President Valéry Giscard d'Estaing of France. *December 14, 1974*

Mr. President, Madame Giscard d'Estaing, ladies and gentlemen:

Thank you for your most gracious welcome to this beautiful, gorgeous island. I am delighted to be here.

Mr. President, this is an opportunity for us to become personally acquainted

53-528 O - 76 - 50

and to discuss the serious issues which confront our two countries. Our meeting vividly demonstrates the importance we attach to working together.

General Lafayette stopped here on his way to assist America to achieve its independence. The friendship of our two countries spans the oceans as well as the centuries. It is fitting that you and I, both given responsibilities for leadership in our respective countries this year, are taking this early opportunity to address problems of common interest and common concern.

We must combine our efforts with those of our friends and our allies if we are to meet the challenges of the last quarter of the 20th century. The list of the challenges is long, including such vital issues as food, energy, finance, and of course, the fundamental security of our people and the quest for further reductions in international tensions.

Just as our talks mark the beginning of a personal relationship, I am confident that our nations will reaffirm the tradition of Franco-American cooperation in great endeavors.

I look forward to our meetings for the exchanges they will permit and our resulting understandings. In meeting here, we, of course, will be mindful not only of American and French interests but the contributions our efforts can make toward a more peaceful, stable, and prosperous world.

NOTE: The President spoke at 4:57 p.m. at Lamentin Airport in response to President Giscard d'Estaing's remarks of welcome.

President Giscard d'Estaing spoke in French. His remarks were translated by an interpreter as follows:

Dear Mr. President:

It is a great honor for this French land of the West Indies to welcome the President of the United States of America.

It is a real pleasure for me to extend to you, and to all those accompanying you, a most cordial welcome. As soon as you came into office, we both felt that we should establish a direct and personal contact. Such a contact is in keeping with the traditional relations between France and the United States. And in the present circumstances, we thought this would be especially useful.

Faced with the enormous changes taking place throughout the world, our two countries have, in different capacities and to various degrees, responsibilities to bear.

Belonging to the community of liberal democracies, their personality and their situation leave them sometimes—quite naturally, I would say—to assume different stands in the face of such changes. However, too old are their ties of friendship for them not to wish to harmonize such stands whenever necessary, and they are too deeply attached to the same ideal of freedom, progress, and peace not to be determined to succeed.

All this points to the importance of our meeting, as stressed by our partners in the European community, hence also the frankness and cordiality with which I trust our talks will start and be concluded.

Mr. President, France of the Martinique offers to you, and all those accompanying you, its charm and its beauty. From the bottom of our heart, I wish you an excellent stay.

Welcome, Mr. President.

298

Statement on the Death of Walter Lippmann. *December 14, 1974*

WITH the death of Walter Lippmann, we have lost a great American. As a newsman, political analyst, and author, Walter Lippmann played a major role for more than half a century in the development of public dialog and in shaping a new standard of journalism.

Mr. Lippmann's contributions to the good society which he envisioned for his country will long be remembered.

NOTE: Mr. Lippmann, 85, died in New York City. He wrote a nationally syndicated newspaper column, Today and Tomorrow, from 1931 to 1967, for which he received Pulitzer Prizes in 1958 and 1962. The statement was released at Martinique, French West Indies.

299

Statement Following Senate Action on the Trade Act of 1974. *December 14, 1974*

ON BEHALF of all Americans, I would like to thank the United States Senate for approving the foreign trade bill. The House has already passed the bill. We are especially grateful to the leaders of both parties. Thanks to their strong, bipartisan efforts we are now in a position to launch a trade program that will strengthen our economy and further our efforts for peace. The Senate has demonstrated a willingness to set aside party differences when the interests of our Nation are at stake.

With this sort of continued compromise and cooperation between the executive and legislative branches of Government, I am more confident than ever that working together we will continue to develop comprehensive programs to meet all our Nation's needs.

NOTE: The bill passed the Senate on December 13, 1974, and was signed by the President on January 3, 1975, as Public Law 93–618 (88 Stat. 1978). The statement was released at Martinique, French West Indies.

300

Toasts of the President and President Giscard d'Estaing of France at a Dinner in Martinique. *December 14, 1974*

MR. PRESIDENT, the hospitality extended to me has reflected in the warmth of the climate of this most remarkable island and the spirit of your kind words of welcome, and I am deeply grateful.

I am very, very proud to be the first American President in office to visit this part of the Caribbean, and I would like to express again my appreciation to you personally for suggesting Martinique as the location of our first meeting.

The United States and France, we all know, have been very, very close. We have been extremely close friends for over two centuries. From our American Revolution through the darkest days of World War II, our countries have stood together in moments of crisis. And today, of fundamental importance to our countries and to the West, a strong Atlantic Alliance safeguards our security.

As old friends and allies, Mr. President, we have much to talk about. On many, many points we shall agree; on others we may differ. But it is of the greatest importance, in my judgment, that we will talk with full candor, since we share the same ideals. A relationship of confidence is absolutely essential. It is only through such a relationship, Mr. President, that our common objectives can best be served and our differing views reconciled.

As in the past, we jointly face, Mr. President, major challenges. This time the immediate danger is not war but the problems of peace: inflation, balance of payments deficits, energy shortages, and for many throughout the world, shortages of food itself. These problems unfortunately accentuate the interdependence of nations and the need for communication and cooperation.

At stake is the stability of every economy, the welfare of every nation. Unilateral measures, Mr. President, can no longer suffice in solving problems of such universal dimension.

Mr. President, you recently described this situation very vividly when you said the world is unhappy. Indeed, the world is troubled. But if we are to transcend our difficulties and successfully meet our challenges, we, France and the United States, must cooperate.

We face a major problem in the field of energy. In dealing with it on the basis of consumer solidarity, we seek constructive dialog, not confrontation. The United States is convinced that cooperation and solidarity among the consumer nations mark the surest way to reach understanding with the producer nations, which we all desire.

I am also looking forward, Mr. President, to exchanging impressions on East-West relations and on our recent meetings with General Secretary Brezhnev. I am sure we will all agree that all of us in the West will benefit from close relationships as the policy of détente continues to develop.

Our interdependence requires that we—together with our friends and our partners—join in concerted measures or responses to the dangers which confront us all. Let us continue our historic relationship with renewed spirit and redoubled effort, as good and responsible friends.

Our common heritage gives me confidence that we will continue our joint endeavors for peace and stability in the world. Mr. President, it is with this objective that I look forward to our discussions tomorrow. I have every hope that our talks will strengthen the friendship between us, both in a bilateral sense and also as members of the alliance which Americans regard as the cornerstone of our foreign policy.

Ladies and gentlemen, in the spirit of strengthening our historic ties, I ask all of you to stand and to raise your glasses in honor of the President of the French Republic and his lovely wife.

NOTE: The President spoke at 10:05 p.m. at the Prefect's Residence in Fort-de-France, Martinique, in response to President Giscard d'Estaing's toast. The dinner was hosted by the French President.

President Giscard d'Estaing spoke in French. His remarks were translated by an interpreter as follows:

Mr. President, a meeting between France and the United States is always a rendezvous of freedom and friendship. And what could be a better place for it than this island of Martinique which cherishes the proud memory of having served as a naval base for the French Fleet during the American War of Independence; and in 2 years' time, we will be celebrating together the successful outcome of that event.

It was in the name of freedom that our friendship was born, and we shall celebrate its 200th anniversary at the same time as the Bicentennial of American independence.

It was also in the name of freedom that twice in the course of this century the active solidarity of the United States enabled France to preserve or to regain her independence.

Different as we may be, what appeals so much to us, the French, is all that in the United States symbolizes and means freedom: your vast spaces, your openness to new ideas and bold endeavors, your mastery of technology, which gives man his power over nature and lightens his burden.

Freedom and friendship have stamped their mark on the relations between our two countries. Freedom allows for their frankness and independence; friendship demands mutual understanding and cooperation.

This spirit of free dialog and trust between partners who recognize the equality of their rights and duties, even if they are not equal in terms of resources or power, is characteristic of Franco-American relations, and there is nothing to prevent that the same spirit be applied to solving the major problems of the world today.

For our part, we express the wish that this spirit inspire the relations between the United States and the Europe that we are striving patiently and, we are bound to say, slowly to build.

It is only on condition that it can exist by its own accord that Europe will be for the United States a firm and reliable partner and for the world a factor of balance and peace.

We also wish that this spirit of dialog should govern our thinking on the profound changes in the world scene.

As you were mentioning, you yourself, Mr. President, on your arrival here, the path of consultation—which is as far removed from that of confrontation as it is from that of capitulation—is the only one which is in keeping with the political, economic, and human needs of our time.

It is the path we followed when it was time to emerge from the cold war and, on our war-torn continent, to organize détente, entente, and cooperation, while maintaining actively our desire for independence in safeguarding our security. It is the path we recommend be followed in the Middle East where, in spite of the remarkable efforts of American diplomacy and the useful progress it has achieved, the situation remains a threatening one.

A just and lasting settlement must, in our view, take into account the three legitimate aspirations of all parties concerned: those of the State of Israel, to live in peace within secure and guaranteed boundaries; those of the Arab States, to recover their territorial integrity; and those of the Palestinian people, to have, as all peoples, a homeland.

It is also through consultation that we shall succeed in finding a solution to the problem caused by the increase in oil prices. This in no way excludes a prior harmonization of the positions within each of the major categories involved.

It, however, presupposes that the purpose of this harmonization process be to prepare the meeting at the same table and at a fixed date of countries willing to reconcile their respective points of view in the peaceful interests of the world.

Mr. President, we shall be having talks in a climate of mutual trust on all these subjects of concern to the world today. These talks will once again demonstrate that the frankness of our discussions draws us together much more than it divides us, as should be between partners and allies when they have for each other, as I have for your country, a sense of their dignity and their sovereignty.

Mr. President, we all deeply regret the absence of Mrs. Ford, and I would like to ask you to be kind enough to convey to her our very warm and respectful wishes for a prompt recovery.

I drink this toast in your honor, Mr. President, as well as to the great people of the United States, to whom the French people, through me, extend their greetings in testimony of our two-centuries-old and ever young friendships like our two countries.

301

Toasts of the President and President Giscard d'Estaing of France at an Informal Dinner Honoring the French President. *December 15, 1974*

Mr. President, Madame Giscard d'Estaing, our distinguished guests:

Let me say with great personal conviction and strong feelings, we have enjoyed being here in a part of France. The warmth of the welcome of the people, the superb atmosphere created by the beauties of nature have made this trip a wonderful experience for all of us.

Mr. President, the United States within a relatively few months is going to be celebrating our 200th anniversary. Whenever we think about that anniversary, we can't help but feel the participation that France played in the achievement of our independence. July 4, 1976, will bring back many, many memories of the help and assistance that France gave to our country at a very difficult and controversial period in our early history in America.

It is my understanding, Mr. President, that one of your ancestors, Admiral d'Estaing, did have an interest in and did help us at a period when we, the United States, were in our formative years. For that we thank you, and for all of the other great Frenchmen who were assisting America in our early days.

It is my understanding, Mr. President, that France is making a very meaningful contribution to our 200th anniversary with the "sight and sound" program that will be a highlight in Washington for the many, many thousands who will visit the Nation's Capital. We thank you for this contribution, and we are grateful for your feeling that France should participate in this way.

If I might now turn to our own personal relationship, which I say without any hesitancy or qualification—it was a pleasure to meet you and to have the opportunity of broadening a relationship and developing a friendship. It seems to me this can be meaningful in our relations between France and the United States, but even more meaningful on a far broader basis, I am grateful for your statesmanship; I am most appreciative for your views that we have exchanged here on this occasion in a part of France.

And so, Mr. President, may I offer a toast to you and Madame Giscard d'Estaing and to the Republic of France. It is a pleasure and a privilege.

NOTE: The President spoke at 9:38 p.m. at the Swimming Pool Terrace of the Meridien Hotel, Martinique. In his remarks, the President referred to the "sound and light" show to be installed at Mount Vernon as France's gift to the American Bicentennial celebration.

President Giscard d'Estaing spoke in French. His remarks were translated by an interpreter as follows:

Mr. President, ladies and gentlemen:

Mr. President, we have both come into office very recently, only a few months ago, and so—this is a source of deep satisfaction—we are both extremely young. Indeed, one can say it is a secret of youth, in fact, to be elected President.

Now, we are, however, young Presidents of countries whose relations are very longstanding, indeed, as you yourself have just mentioned. And indeed, all you have to do is to look behind you at Fort-de-France—Fort-de-France, which has carried that name for three centuries and, two centuries ago, harbored the French Fleet that sailed off the coast of the then young and new United States.

I would add that the relations between France and the United States are not merely a matter of what you might call the picturesque side of history, or simply a matter of stories on the subject. No, it is something which reflects a deep and reciprocal mutual interest; it is something which has been borne out in numerous circumstances. For instance, when at the time of the First World War the United States came to the defense of France, the landing of the Americans on French territory was met with tremendous enthusiasm on the part of the French population.

And so, when at the end of the Second World War, I myself was involved in the last stages of the war, the unit that I served in was a part of the First French Army which, itself, was under the Seventh United States Army.

But the great problems of our times—even to those of us who, like ourselves, are deeply attached to tradition—the big problems of our time, I say, are in fact ahead of us and will call for considerable imagination and action. And that is why it was very important for me, Mr. President, to know whether these new problems and tasks could, in fact, be tackled with the very great country that you represent in a spirit of openness and mutual understanding.

And so, it was important for me to establish this personal contact with you yourself, sir, and the distinguished persons accompanying you. And yesterday morning, when I was meeting you at the airport, it occurred to me that during these 2 days we were, in fact, going to, perhaps, take initiatives and perform actions which would lead to solutions which could well have a lasting effect, not only on our own relations but also, perhaps, on world affairs.

The results of our talks will be embodied in a communique which will be issued at the end of tomorrow morning, and if I were to divulge right now what the results of our talks have been, this would deprive the members of our staff from the pleasures of the late evening and early morning during which they would engage in the arduous task of preparing the suitable form of words.

But what I can say something about is the atmosphere of our talks, and what I would like to mention is their very cordial nature, the very simple way in which our talks have proceeded, the great frankness and the clarity of your positions, and the great competence with which you have led our discussions.

Now, on international gatherings or occasions

such as this, people tend to wonder, in fact, who won, who came out on top, who gave the concessions, who, in fact, was the victor. But at the very outset, you will recall that I said it was my hope that, in fact, there would be neither a matter of concessions nor victors in a case like this, but we should both emerge from these talks with the feeling that we had, in fact, achieved something useful, realistic, and worthwhile in furthering the solutions of the problems that we are, in fact, discussing.

And could I say very sincerely, Mr. President, how very much Madame Giscard d'Estaing and myself deeply regret the absence of Mrs. Ford. We had been looking forward very much to meeting her here on this occasion, and I may say that some of the arrangements that had been made had been made precisely in anticipation of the pleasure of, for instance, having her with us today at lunch.

Now, there is one great advantage of this situation, and that is that the rights of international affairs dictate that one cannot, twice running, invite the same head of state. That means, therefore, that despite the great pleasure that this would afford us, it would not be possible for us to invite you, sir, again so soon. But we could, of course, invite Mrs. Ford. And we would very much hope that she would accept, and that you would be kind enough to accompany her.

Now, people in this world of ours very often ask themselves all sorts of questions, and indeed, one of the things they often wonder about, apparently, is why statesmen, in fact, are statesmen and why they accept to sacrifice many aspects of their existence to the responsibilities of state.

Now, as far as you are concerned—and I have seen this during our talks—and as far as I am concerned, the reason, perhaps, for which we do so is that we feel that we have, perhaps, a contribution to make in furthering the affairs of the world.

Now, the fact that the responsibilities that we have to shoulder at this particular time in history are particularly heavy at the same time means that our contribution will be a significant contribution.

Now, it is clear, however, that the affairs of mankind and the peace of the world do not depend solely on the action or the efforts of one country alone—however big that country may be—but will always depend on the combination, on the conjunction of the efforts of several. And I now know that it is quite clear that we will be able to work together.

Mr. President, when the French Fleet left these waters two centuries ago for the North American Continent, there were doubtless, at the time of departure, great festivities on board. And I can well imagine that my ancestor may well have offered a toast on that occasion which would probably have had something to do with the wishes that he would have expressed concerning the continent that they were about to discover and would have expressed their hopes and their expectations.

Now, this evening, today, the situation to some extent is the other way around in that it is we who are hosting you here in Martinique. But the French Martinique of two centuries ago and the French Martinique of today, Mr. President, are deeply proud of having here the visit today of the President of the United States. Our friend, the President.

302

Communique Following Discussions With President Giscard d'Estaing of France. *December 16, 1974*

THE PRESIDENT of the United States, Gerald R. Ford, and the President of the French Republic, Valéry Giscard d'Estaing, met in Martinique December 14–16, 1974, to discuss current issues of mutual concern. They were joined in their discussions by the Secretary of State and Assistant to the President for National Security Affairs Henry A. Kissinger and Minister of Foreign Affairs Jean Sauvagnargues, and by Secretary of the Treasury William Simon and Minister of Finance Jean-Pierre Fourcade. The Ministers also held complementary side talks.

The meeting took place in an atmosphere of cordiality and mutual confidence.

President Ford and President Giscard d'Estaing welcomed the opportunity to conduct detailed substantive discussions on the whole range of subjects of mutual concern. As traditional friends and allies, the two nations share common values and goals and the two Presidents expressed their determination to cooperate on this basis in efforts to solve common problems.

They reviewed the international situation in the economic, financial and monetary fields.

The two Presidents agreed that the Governments of the United States and of the European Community, in the name of which the French President spoke on this subject, must adopt consistent economic policies in order to be effective in avoiding unemployment while fighting inflation. In particular, they agreed on the importance of avoiding measures of a protectionist nature. And they decided to take the initiative in calling additional intergovernmental meetings should they prove necessary for achievement of the desired consistency of basic economic policies among industrial nations.

In the light of the rapid pace of change in international financial positions in the world today, the Presidents were in full agreement on the desirability of maintaining the momentum of consideration of closer financial cooperation both within the International Monetary Fund and through supplementary measures. As one specific measure to strengthen the existing financial framework, the Presidents agreed that it would be appropriate for any Government which wished to do so to adopt current market prices as the basis of valuation for its gold holdings.

The two Presidents considered in depth the energy problem and its serious and disturbing effects on the world economy. They recognized the importance for the USA, the EEC and other industrialized nations of implementing policies for the conservation of energy, the development of existing and alternative sources of energy, and the setting up of new mechanisms of financial solidarity. They stressed the importance of solidarity among oil importing nations on these issues.

The two Presidents also exchanged views on the desirability of a dialogue between consumers and producers and in that connection discussed the proposal of the President of the French Republic of October 24 for a conference of oil exporting and importing countries. They agreed that it would be desirable to convene such a meeting at the earliest possible date. They regard it as important that all parties concerned should be better informed of their respective interests and concerns and that harmonious relations should be established among them in order to promote a healthy development of the world economy.

The two Presidents noted that their views on these matters are complementary and, in this context, they agreed that the following interrelated steps should be taken in sequence:

—They agreed that additional steps should be taken, within the framework of existing institutions and agreements to which they are a party, and in consultation with other interested consumers, to strengthen their cooperation. In particular, such cooperation should include programs of energy conservation, for the development of existing and alternative sources of energy and for financial solidarity.

—Based on substantial progress in the foregoing areas, the two Presidents agreed that it will be desirable to propose holding a preparatory meeting between consumers and producers to develop an agenda and procedures for a consumer/producer conference. The target date for such a preparatory meeting should be March 1975.

—The preparatory discussions will be followed by intensive consultations among consumer countries in order to prepare positions for the conference.

The two Presidents agreed that the actions enumerated above will be carried out in the most expeditious manner possible and in full awareness of the common interest in meeting this critical situation shared by the United States and France and all other countries involved.

President Ford and President Giscard d'Estaing reviewed current developments in East-West relations. They discussed their respective meetings with General Secretary Brezhnev, and Secretary Kissinger reported on his discussions with leaders of the People's Republic of China. They exchanged views on developments in East-West negotiations, including the Conference on Security and Cooperation in Europe. They expressed their conviction that progress in easing tensions was being made.

The two Presidents exchanged views on the present situation in the Middle East. They agreed on the importance of early progress toward a just and lasting peace in that area.

President Giscard d'Estaing described current efforts by France and other members of the European Community to further the process of European unity. President Ford reaffirmed the continuing support of the United States for efforts to achieve European unity.

The two Presidents discussed the situation in Indochina. They noted that progress in Laos toward reconciliation and reunification was encouraging.

The two Presidents agreed on the need for all parties to support fully the Paris

Peace Agreements on Vietnam. Regarding Cambodia, they expressed the hope that the contending parties would enter into negotiations in the near future rather than continuing the military struggle. They expressed the hope that following Laos, Cambodia and Vietnam might also find their political way towards civil peace.

The two Presidents renewed the pledges of both Governments to continue close relations in the field of defense as members of the Atlantic Alliance. They agreed that the cooperation between France and NATO is a significant factor in the security of Europe.

They noted with satisfaction that the positive steps in negotiations on SALT taken during the Soviet-American meeting at Vladivostok have reduced the threat of a nuclear arms race. The two Presidents explored how, as exporters of nuclear materials and technology, their two countries could coordinate their efforts to assure improved safeguards of nuclear materials.

The President of France indicated that his Government was prepared to reach a financial settlement in connection with the relocation of American forces and bases committed to NATO from France to other countries in 1967. The French offer of $100 million in full settlement was formally accepted by President Ford.

The two Presidents concluded that the personal contact and discussion in this meeting had demonstrated accord on many questions and expressed their determination to maintain close contact for the purpose of broad cooperation in areas of common concern to the two countries.

NOTE: The text of the communique was released at Martinique, French West Indies.

303

Letter Accepting the Resignation of Roy L. Ash as Director of the Office of Management and Budget. *December 17, 1974*

Dear Roy:

Although I have known for some time of your plans to return to private life, nevertheless it is with deepest regret that I have received your letter and accept your resignation as Assistant to the President and Director of the Office of Management and Budget, effective on a date to be determined.

Throughout the past two years, you have served the Presidency and our Nation with high dedication and exceptional ability. You have had the tremendous task of keeping the Federal budget within reasonable proportions while at the same time enabling our government to meet its responsibilities to the American people. No one knows better than you how difficult a challenge this has been and continues to be.

With your assistance, however, I believe we have been able to shape effective, workable Federal budgets. I am particularly and personally grateful for your unhesitating support over the past four months and for your willingness to see through to completion our budget for 1976. I am confident it, too, will be responsive to the needs of our citizens and to their desire for fiscal restraint.

Your leadership and sound judgment will be sorely missed but it is some consolation to know we can call on your expertise again when the occasion arises. In the meantime, please know that Betty joins me in sending to Lila and you our warmest best wishes for every success and happiness in the future.

Sincerely,

JERRY FORD

[The Honorable Roy L. Ash, The White House, Washington, D.C.]

NOTE: Mr. Ash's letter of resignation, dated December 10, 1974, and released with the President's letter, read as follows:

Dear Mr. President:

In just four months, you have gone a long way toward restoring the faith of the American people in their system of government and confidence in its executive leadership. As our great country nears the finish of its second century and begins the third with a need for renewed inspiration and strength, it is fitting that it do so under the exemplary leadership you provide.

I am grateful for the opportunity to have been a part of the Administration you lead. As we discussed shortly after you took office, it has been my intention to serve two years in government, which time is now concluding. As a matter of fact, those two years are completed this very day. Thus, I am hereby submitting my formal resignation to take effect at your convenience.

Mr. President, you will have my continued support. With it goes my personal admiration for you, Mrs. Ford and your wonderful family.

Sincerely yours,

ROY L. ASH

304

Christmas Message. *December 17, 1974*

MRS. FORD and I send our warmest holiday greetings to all our fellow citizens. We hope that each of you will share the traditional joys of this Holy season with your family and friends. And we pray that the Christmas spirit of generosity and renewal will be with you throughout the coming year.

We begin 1975 in the midst of many serious challenges. As we work to resolve them, let us be encouraged by counting the blessings we have gained from those who have met similar challenges in the past. Let us draw strength from our unity of purpose and hope from our past resourcefulness. And let us work together to ensure that the good which we have achieved will be strengthened and preserved for our children and future generations.

GERALD R. FORD

NOTE: The text of the message was issued by the White House.

305

Statement on Signing the Safe Drinking Water Act. *December 17, 1974*

I AM pleased to have signed the Safe Drinking Water Act (S. 433). Much effort has gone into the development of this legislation as much as for any enacted in this session of Congress.

This Administration proposed a Safe Drinking Water Act, and several others were introduced by Members of Congress. All of these bills had the same objectives: to increase protection of the public's health. Many compromises had to be made before this bill reached my desk. Yet it is a strong bill, reflecting the combined efforts of the Congress and the Administration.

This legislation will enhance the safety of public drinking water supplies in this country through the establishment and enforcement of national drinking water standards. The Environmental Protection Agency has the primary responsibility for establishing our national standards. The States have the primary responsibility of enforcing them and for otherwise ensuring the quality of drinking water. In some situations where States fail to enforce the standards, the Federal Government could. I believe this will seldom be necessary. During the extensive consideration of this legislation, spokesmen for the Administration opposed extensive Federal involvement in what has traditionally been State and local regulatory matters and unnecessary costs to the Federal Government. Even with the compromises that were made, I still have reservations about those two aspects of this bill, and I intend that it be administered so as to minimize both Federal involvement and costs.

The bill enhances the ability of the Federal Government to conduct research into the health effects of contaminants in drinking water. Recent news stories have highlighted several potential drinking water problems that can only be resolved through research. I am pleased to say that we are already moving ahead on these problems.

Nothing is more essential to the life of every single American than clean air, pure food, and safe drinking water. There have been strong national programs to improve the quality of our air and the purity of our food. This bill will provide us with the protection we need for drinking water.

NOTE: As enacted, S. 433, approved December 16, 1974, is Public Law 93-523 (88 Stat. 1660).

306

Remarks at the Lighting of the National Community Christmas Tree. *December 17, 1974*

Thank you very, very much, Secretary of Interior Rogers Morton, Mayor Washington, Mr. Hoffman, my fellow Michiganders from the University of Michigan Chorus, my fellow Americans:

Obviously, I am very delighted to participate in this celebration tonight, to light and to share with you the Nation's Christmas tree.

As a former National Park Service ranger a good many years ago, I have been and am concerned with conservation. I am pleased to know, of course, that this tree has a heritage from Colorado but was transplanted here from the great State of Pennsylvania. But this tree will be the National Community Christmas Tree and will be so for many, many years to come.

As a President vitally concerned with the saving of energy, I also want you to know that the electricity consumed, as the Secretary of Interior has said, is a considerable reduction of what has been used in years past. And that is the way it should be, and that is the way that it must be.

The glow of Christmas, however, should come from a power source which we will never run short of, our abiding faith and our love of God.

The true spirit of this season can best be seen in our faces. The children here tonight, like millions of children around the world, reflect the wonder and the excitement of anticipation. Those of us who are older look forward to the warmth of reunions with families and with friends.

Traditions, treasured memories, shared hopes—these are the ties that bind families together and nations together. The tree before us is a part of our national tradition, and as such, it has seen both triumphs and tragedies.

Christmas and the New Year have always been a time to reflect on the past and then look ahead to the future. I firmly believe that 1975 will be a brighter year for all America, but it must also be a brighter year for the world around us, the entire globe, if we as a nation are to prosper.

And so, I would like to share with you my personal list of Christmas wishes. At the top of my list are peace, economic well-being for all, and a caring climate that will permit everyone to achieve the fullest potential of their human gifts. And I wish this Nation a strong future out of a very proud past. And I wish every one of us the realization of love and belonging.

Billions of words over the years have been written, have been sung, have been spoken about the true meaning of Christmas. None have ever said it more eloquently than "on earth peace, good will toward men." And that is my final Christmas wish for all of us.

Thank you very kindly.

NOTE: The President spoke at 5:55 p.m. at the 21st annual Pageant of Peace ceremonies on the Ellipse near the White House.

In his opening remarks, the President referred to Walter E. Washington, mayor of the District of Columbia, and Edwin K. Hoffman, vice-chairman of the 1974 Christmas Pageant of Peace Honorary Committee.

The President's remarks were broadcast live on radio and television.

307

Veto of Willow Creek, Oregon, Flood Control Project Legislation. *December 18, 1974*

To the United States Senate:

I have withheld my approval from S. 3537, "To modify section 204 of the Flood Control Act of 1965."

This bill would authorize a revised Willow Creek Project in Oregon and provide for advance payment of the Federal share of the cost to relocate the water system of the nearby town of Heppner.

The Department of the Army, on behalf of the Administration, opposed this bill in committee on the grounds that it raised unresolved issues relative to the general principles and standards governing the evaluation of water resources projects.

These departures include:

—Re-evaluation of the project by using questionable methods for calculating benefits.

—Coupled with these methods of computing benefits, retention of an interest rate of 3¼ percent provided for in the original 1965 project authorization, compared to the present rate of 5⅞ percent now being used.

—Authorization for advance payment of the Federal share of the costs to relocate the town's water system, as compared to the standard approach—to await the actual beginning of construction of a project.

While I fully understand the desire of the town of Heppner to obtain Federal assistance in financing its water system, I cannot, in good conscience, accept the departures which S. 3537 would make from the established principles and standards that are employed in the evaluation of other water resources projects.

In my judgment, the Willow Creek Project should be considered for construction on the basis of current evaluation principles and standards. Any other course would be indefensible at a time when the Congress is being asked to defer funding for numerous other water resources projects.

GERALD R. FORD

The White House,
December 17, 1974.

NOTE: The text of the veto message was released December 18, 1974.

308

Letter Accepting the Resignation of Claude S. Brinegar as Secretary of Transportation. *December 18, 1974*

Dear Claude:

I have your letter of December 17, and it is with deep gratitude for your dedicated service to our Nation that I accept your resignation as Secretary of Transportation, effective February 1, 1975, as you requested.

In doing so, I want you to know of my personal appreciation for the many improvements in the Nation's transportation system that have occurred in your tenure as Secretary. The Regional Rail Reorganization Act of 1973 and the National Mass Transportation Act of 1974 are but two of many legislative achievements of truly historical significance. Under your capable leadership, we have for the first time since the creation of the Department articulated a National Transportation Policy, and I particularly want to commend you for this important achievement.

As you now return to the private sector, I am confident you will continue your interest in government. It is only through the willingness of people such as you to serve that our system can receive its needed breadth of views and talents.

Betty joins me in extending to you and to your family our warmest good wishes for continued success and happiness in the years ahead.

Sincerely,

JERRY FORD

[The Honorable Claude S. Brinegar, Secretary of Transportation, Washington, D.C. 20590]

NOTE: Secretary Brinegar's letter of resignation, dated December 17, 1974, and released with the President's letter, read as follows:

My dear Mr. President:

I would appreciate it if you would accept my resignation as Secretary of Transportation, effective February 1, 1975. In the interest of a smooth transition, I would be willing to serve for a brief time longer if my successor is not confirmed by that date.

My two years as the third Secretary of Transportation have been exciting, educational, and, at times, hectic. I believe that, on balance, I have made progress in a number of ways toward improving the Nation's transportation system, although I well recognize that it's a job that will never be finished. But now it is necessary for me to return to the private sector.

I would like to add that I have especially enjoyed serving under you. Please accept my very best wishes for good health and continued success.

Respectfully,

CLAUDE S. BRINEGAR

[The President, The White House, Washington, D.C. 20500]

309

Letter Accepting the Resignation of Tom C. Korologos as Deputy Assistant to the President. *December 18, 1974*

Dear Tom:

It is not only with the deepest regret but also with a personal sense of loss that I accept your resignation as Deputy Assistant to the President, effective December 31, 1974, as you requested.

For more than three years, you have served as the President's representative in the Senate with brilliance, loyalty and the kind of political acumen that is the hallmark of the true Washington professional. I know from my own long experience in the Congress that your understanding of the complexities of our legislative system and your ability to work with and within that system is unsurpassed. On numerous occasions in recent months I have greatly valued your sound counsel and assistance on the difficult legislative issues which have come before us. You have given me your full, unhesitating support throughout the period of transition. For this and for your many, many contributions to my Administration and to our Nation you have my unqualified admiration and heartfelt gratitude.

I deeply appreciate your kind comments and expression of confidence as you prepare to depart the White House staff. I know that in the months and years ahead you too will be devoting your skills and energies to the future strength and prosperity of our Nation.

Betty joins me in extending to your family and to you our very best wishes for every future success and happiness.

Sincerely,

JERRY FORD

[Mr. Tom C. Korologos, The White House, Washington, D.C.]

NOTE: Mr. Korologos' letter of resignation, dated December 12, 1974, and released with the President's letter, read as follows:

Dear Mr. President:

After almost four years in the Congressional Relations office in the White House, personal considerations require that I submit my resignation as your Deputy Assistant for Legislative Affairs effective December 31, 1974.

I will always be grateful for your asking me to continue in my position the same day you were sworn in as President of the United States.

To serve as the President's representative in the Senate has been an incomparable experience which I shall always cherish; likewise, it has been a distinct privilege to serve on your White House staff. I shall remember fondly our personal relationship through the years when you were Minority Leader, Vice President and now as President. I also thank you for your many kindnesses, professionally and personally to me and my family.

I regret that I will not be able to share the many accomplishments that are ahead for you both domestically and internationally. I leave the White House, however, with the fullest confidence that you will achieve the goals you have set for our Nation. And, in your efforts, I wish you every success.

Warm best wishes to you and the First Lady.

Sincerely,

Tom C. Korologos
Deputy Assistant to the President

[The President, The White House, Washington, D.C.]

310

Letter Accepting the Resignation of W. Eugene Ainsworth, Jr., as Special Assistant to the President. *December 18, 1974*

Dear Gene:

I have your letter of December 9, and your resignation as Special Assistant to the President, effective as you requested December 31, 1974, is accepted with deepest regret. While I fully understand the personal and professional considerations which led to your decision, I want you to know that your superb services in the White House Office of Legislative Affairs will be greatly missed.

As an able, dedicated member of our Congressional liaison staff, no one better appreciates than you the vital importance of sound, effective working relationships between the White House and the Congress. Time and again, in fulfilling the special trust and responsibilities of your position, you have demonstrated that major legislative successes can be achieved even under the most difficult circumstances. This has been due in very large measure not only to your thorough understanding of governmental processes, but also to your exceptional ability to work within these processes and do so with utmost integrity and commitment to the greatest good for the American people. You have earned their thanks, the respect and friendship of your colleagues on both sides of the political fence, and my own lasting admiration and gratitude.

Now, as you prepare to depart, I am confident the same outstanding skills you brought to the White House will serve you well in your new career in the private sector. Certainly, you have my warmest good wishes for all of life's blessings in the years ahead.

With kindest personal regards.

Sincerely,

JERRY FORD

[The Honorable W. Eugene Ainsworth, Jr., The White House, Washington, D.C.]

NOTE: Mr. Ainsworth's letter of resignation, dated December 9, 1974, and released with the President's letter, read as follows:

Dear Mr. President:

Because of very pressing personal and professional demands which no longer can be postponed, I have regretfully concluded that I must submit my resignation as Special Assistant to the President effective December 31, 1974.

To represent the President with Members of the United States House of Representatives is a unique responsibility and a special trust. I have had the good fortune to serve you in this capacity as you seek the objectives of domestic prosperity and a lasting world peace. I will always be grateful for your confidence and many acts of personal kindness.

Your special relationship with the Congress will be vital to the Nation in the years ahead and I assure you of my continuing support in your efforts to develop the programs necessary for the good of our Nation. It has been an honor to serve you and your Administration.

Sincerely yours,

W. EUGENE AINSWORTH, JR.

[The President, The White House, Washington, D.C.]

311

Remarks at American Freedom Train Ceremonies in Alexandria, Virginia. *December 19, 1974*

Thank you very, very much, John Warner, Don Kendall:

Let me say at the outset I am most grateful for the participation by the Jefferson High School Band and the T. C. Williams High School Band, and I thank very deeply those who have participated and made it possible for this Freedom Train to undertake its journey throughout the United States.

Obviously I am tremendously pleased to participate in the official ceremony recognizing the American Freedom Train as a major Bicentennial effort.

When this train begins its 17,000-mile journey through 48 of our 50 States this spring, the Freedom Train will serve as one of the focal points for our Bicentennial commemoration. It will visit 76 cities and give Americans a once-in-a-lifetime opportunity to view some of the most historic national documents—documents which relate directly to our history for the last 200 years.

I strongly urge parents and teachers to make sure that your children and students take advantage of this wonderful opportunity. The cargo on this train represents much of our Nation's past history and our hopes for the future.

This exhibit touches virtually every phase of the American experience. The train will carry, for example, George Washington's personal copy of the Constitution. It will contain the handwritten draft of President Kennedy's inaugural address. There will be Moon rock samples, the first Bible printed in America, Paul Revere's saddlebags, as well as exhibits representing the Nation's culture, technological progress, professions and trades, sports, and the arts.

During the next year and a half, 40 to 50 million Americans are expected to view these exhibits as we near our 200th birthday as a nation.

I sincerely hope that every American, as he or she contemplates these historical reminders, will reflect on how far we have come in the short span of 200 years. And as we take a long look back, let us also take a long look forward. If we do, we will be able to see the problems facing us today in a much clearer perspective.

Our problems are serious ones—especially our energy problems and those of our economy. But think of the problems our forefathers had. Think of those 13 tiny colonies taking on the mightiest nation, the mightiest empire in the world. And think of them winning their liberty as well as ours.

Very few people back in 1776 would have thought that in just 200 years, those 13 colonies would provide the jumping off spot from which, eventually, 50 united States would span a vast continent and beyond, tame a mighty wilderness, construct a technological society of enormous scientific complexity, and then set out to explore space itself. But as we look back over this span of time and see what we have today, that is exactly what took place and transpired.

As we reflect on these historic accomplishments, let us also look ahead to the future that we are building. Let us reaffirm our faith in the American spirit.

As one of the great nations of the world—spiritually, militarily, diplomatically, and economically—we in America have the best of many worlds. We have nearly all of the resources which we desperately need. We have the technological resources. We have the human resources. Now, what we need in this period of—a critical time, we must have the will to resolve those problems, the will to win and the will we will win with in the months ahead.

By the year 2000, I see a people living in a community of peace with other nations, with a standard of living still the highest in the world, with disease greatly conquered, with individual liberties secure for everyone, with wide opportunities for good education and good housing, and with our national will and spirit still climbing as we move toward celebration of our tricentennial.

I see the Bicentennial of 1976 as a rebirth as well as a birthday—a rediscovery of our strength and of our potential. It will strengthen our resolve to fulfill the promises of our forefathers. It will fortify our determination to continue to build a freer, more just, and more humane society.

This American Freedom Train will be a fitting symbol for what the Bicentennial really represents. Since the day the golden spike was driven, the railroad has symbolized our unity as a nation.

On behalf of all Americans, I thank the American Freedom Train Foundation and the corporations that have provided grants for this Freedom Train. I know that your contributions will inspire others to participate in the Bicentennial. I would like to say a very special word, a special word of thank you to the people of Portland, Oregon, who provided the "iron horse" that will actually pull this Freedom Train.

I look forward to the Freedom Train to provide a unifying symbol of the heritage that made America's great past a great one and will make its future an even greater one.

Now if I might, I would like to pick up this and present it to the Freedom Train for display, which is a document of tremendous historical significance, symbolic of what America really stands for—freedom.

NOTE: The President spoke at 10:45 a.m. at the Alexandria Railway Station. In his opening remarks, the President referred to John W. Warner, Administrator of the American Revolution Bicentennial Administration, and Donald M. Kendall, chairman of the national advisory board of the American Freedom Train Foundation.

Following his remarks, the President presented George Washington's personal copy of the Constitution to Mr. Kendall.

312

Remarks at a Ceremony Marking the Retirement of Gen. Andrew J. Goodpaster as Supreme Allied Commander, Europe. *December 19, 1974*

LET ME just say I have known General Goodpaster, well, I guess, since 1951 or thereabouts, and all of you know better than I his long and distinguished record, 35 years or more in the military, a wide variety of commands and responsibilities.

Somebody told me that you were a real triple threat operator in the services, General, and as I looked at the record I am very, very impressed with that broad area of responsibility and achievement.

I certainly congratulate you on this fine, fine record.

Those who have served with you in the military of course know infinitely better than I the things that you have done and the achievements that you have accomplished. And I share with them the pride that I have as Commander in Chief. And I can assure you that we look upon people such as yourself as the epitome of achievement in the military, representing all of us who are civilian.

And I congratulate the services. And I congratulate you. And I thank your wife and family for, I am sure, the many hours that you were gone, and the difficulties they had in holding the fort, so to speak, while you were serving your country.

And I congratulate you, and thank you, and wish you the very, very best.

NOTE: The President spoke at 12:45 p.m. in the Cabinet Room at the White House before presenting the Defense Distinguished Service Medal to General Goodpaster. General Goodpaster had served as Supreme Allied Commander, Europe, since May 1969.

313

Statement on Signing the Presidential Recordings and Materials Preservation Act. *December 19, 1974*

I HAVE signed S. 4016, the Presidential Recordings and Materials Preservation Act. This measure provides the following:

Title I: governs the possession, security, and accessibility of tape recordings and other materials of the former President. Included are virtually all documents produced within the White House during the previous Administration. The Administrator of General Services is charged with obtaining "complete possession and control" of the tape recordings and materials which would be made available immediately, subject to any rights, defenses, or privileges which may be asserted, for "subpoena or other legal process."

The Administrator is also directed to issue protective regulations "at the earliest possible date" governing the possession, security, and custody of the tapes and materials. Finally, the Administrator shall draft regulations governing general public access to the tapes and materials, taking into account a series of specified needs: (1) to provide the public with the "full truth" on the abuses of governmental power incident to "Watergate"; (2) to make available the tapes and materials for judicial proceedings; (3) to guarantee the integrity of national security information; (4) to protect individual rights to a fair trial; (5) to protect the opportunity to assert available rights and privileges; (6) to provide public access to materials of historical significance; and (7) to provide the former President with tapes or materials in which the public has no interest.

Title I also provides for the expeditious judicial review of challenges to the "legal or constitutional validity" of the statute or of any regulation issued under its authority, and any action or proceeding involving "the question of title, ownership, custody, possession or control" of any tape recording or other material. In the event it is determined that the former President has been deprived of personal property under the provisions of title I, "just compensation" shall be paid to him.

Title II: establishes a "Public Documents Commission" to study problems with respect to the control, disposition, and preservation of records produced by or on behalf of "Federal officials." These are defined to include elected Federal officials and any officer of the executive, judicial, or legislative branch of the Federal Government. The Commission is directed to make specific recommendations for legislation and other recommendations for rules and procedures as may be appropriate regarding the documents of such officials. A final report fulfilling their mandate is to be submitted to the Congress and the President by March 31, 1976.

It has been my consistent policy toward the records of the former President to protect both the records themselves and the legal rights of all parties involved. Following the release of an opinion of the Attorney General of the United States to the effect that the tapes and materials of the former President constituted his personal property, an agreement was entered into by Mr. Nixon and Mr. Sampson, the Administrator of General Services, on September 6, 1974. This agreement was intended to govern the possession, security, and accessibility of the tapes and materials and it secured them from destruction or alteration during the periods when they might be needed in court and grand jury proceedings. Since then, a great deal of litigation and public attention have centered on that agreement. Although I believe it would not be appropriate to comment on the various issues, constitutional or otherwise, which are presented by pending cases or by the subject bill, I do want to mention that, by agreement made November 9, 1974, the interests of the Watergate Special Prosecution Force for access to the tapes and materials were fully accommodated.

It is my understanding of the intent of the Congress that this act will provide the former President and others with the opportunity to litigate any right or privilege which may be asserted relevant to the tapes or materials.

The Administrator of General Services will move promptly to obtain complete possession and control of the tapes and materials and to discharge his other duties under the law.

I will name the Presidential appointees to the "Public Documents Commission" as quickly as possible. I am hopeful that the Commission will suggest even-handed and uniform rules governing the documents of all Federal officials.

NOTE: As enacted, S. 4016, approved December 19, 1974, is Public Law 93–526 (88 Stat. 1695).

314

Statement on the Confirmation of Nelson A. Rockefeller To Be Vice President of the United States. *December 19, 1974*

I AM delighted that Nelson Rockefeller has been duly confirmed today to be the 41st Vice President of the United States. I congratulate him and look forward to his participation and assistance in the Administration.

I commend the House of Representatives for its confirmation vote today and the Senate for its vote earlier. Members of the 93d Congress have rendered a service to the Nation by filling the constitutional office of the Vice President before adjournment. All Americans will benefit from the distinguished and devoted public service of the new Vice President.

NOTE: Following the confirmation vote in the House of Representatives on the evening of December 19, 1974, the President and Mrs. Ford accompanied Governor and Mrs. Rockefeller to the Senate Chamber at the Capitol where Governor Rockefeller took the oath of office as Vice President.

315

Remarks at a Birthday Party for Senator John J. Sparkman. *December 20, 1974*

THANK YOU very, very much for the opportunity of coming to your birthday party, John. It was not on the program as such, but I knew that you were having a party, and I knew I wanted to come.

So, we are here because of the great respect and admiration I have, not only for you personally but for the fine and outstanding job I know firsthand you have done in the Congress.

A 75th birthday is quite a landmark and a milestone. Let me put it in football terms: John, you may be too old for the University of Alabama, but I think you could be too young for the Washington Redskins. [*Laughter*]

Thirty-eight years in the Congress is something that I never achieved. I, under no circumstances, could have made it.

I do respect those who have served six terms in the House of Representatives and the remainder of that long and constructive record in the United States Senate.

I think the people of Alabama have benefited tremendously from the work that you have done for that State. But those of us who know the record, that come from different States, can honestly say that your contributions have been national. And I would go one step further—and I know this firsthand—your contributions have been international, for the objectives and the goals and the aims that all Americans want: peace and a good and happy life for all of us.

So, I thank you, as a former colleague of yours in the Congress and now as President, and wish you and your wonderful family the very, very best for another good many years.

NOTE: The President spoke at 1 p.m. in the Senate Caucus Room at the Capitol.

316

Statement on the Ninety-third Congress. *December 20, 1974*

INASMUCH AS I was elected to the 93d Congress and was part of it for half its term, any assessment I make of its accomplishments upon adjournment *sine die* cannot be entirely objective. But I will always be grateful for the personal friendship and courtesies Members of this Congress have shown to me in three different official capacities and for the confidence they have demonstrated in confirming both me and my subsequent nominee for the Vice Presidency.

The legislative accomplishments of the 93d Congress have been less than I had hoped, but perhaps that is the perspective of everyone at this end of Pennsylvania Avenue, and certainly this has been far from an ordinary session. Among the measures for which I do commend and congratulate the Congress are trade reform, pension reform, housing and community development, mass transit, assistance for the temporarily jobless, deepwater ports, creation of the new Energy Research and Development Administration, and strengthening the antitrust laws.

In my first message as President, I told the Congress that "we have work to do." Much has been done, but much more remains. I wish the departing Members a warm farewell and all a happy holiday season. I look forward to the coming Congress and the New Year with the mixture of challenge and hope that the always-unfinished agenda of our Nation inspires in those who serve it in all its branches.

317

Statement on Signing the Antitrust Procedures and Penalties Act. *December 23, 1974*

I HAVE signed S. 782, the Antitrust Procedures and Penalties Act, which will strengthen significantly antitrust laws and the ability to enforce them.

This legislation is the first major reform of the Nation's antitrust laws in nearly 20 years. It changes such antitrust violations of the Sherman Act as price fixing from misdemeanors to felonies; increases the maximum sentence from 1 year to 3 years; and raises maximum allowable fines from $50,000 to $1 million for corporations and from $50,000 to $100,000 for individuals.

In my economic message to the Congress on October 8, 1974, I called for legislation which would give us the tools to fight inflation. Increased penalties, as those in S. 782, are some of those tools.

The bill also amends the Expediting Act, permitting appeals of civil antitrust cases directly to the Supreme Court *only* upon a finding of the district court that the case is of national economic importance. This will halt the practice of clogging the Supreme Court docket by taking all antitrust appeals directly to that tribunal, thus denying it the wisdom and advice of the U.S. Circuit Courts of Appeals.

Finally, S. 782 provides for closer scrutiny and greater participation by the public in the consent decree process. This is used by the Government in the pretrial settlement of its civil antitrust cases.

The time is long overdue for making violations of the Sherman Act a serious crime, because of the extremely adverse effect which they have on the country and its economy. S. 782 will provide a significant deterrent to potential violators and will give the courts sufficient flexibility to impose meaningful sanctions. Moreover, the bill will serve the public interest by expediting cases that have a profound influence on American industrial organization and allowing the courts to do other important work at the same time.

I called for further antitrust legislation in my October message, and I hope that the new Congress will carry that forward. It includes an amendment to the Antitrust Civil Process Act allowing the Department of Justice to take testimony in antitrust investigations—as the Federal Trade Commission has done for years—rather than simply relying on routine document subpoenas.

This Congress recognized that antitrust violations injure both our economy and individual consumers, and I commend it on enacting S. 782. I assure you that with this new legislation, this Administration will continue to create a strong antitrust record. In times like these, we cannot afford to do less.

NOTE: As enacted, S. 782, approved December 21, 1974, is Public Law 93–528 (88 Stat. 1706). The statement was released at Vail, Colo.

318

Statement on Signing Budget Rescission Legislation. *December 23, 1974*

I HAVE signed H.R. 17505, a bill to rescind $131 million budget authority that is not needed for five Federal programs. This is the first such bill to come to me under the new provisions established by the Congressional Budget and Impoundment Control Act of 1974. In that respect, I take pleasure in signing this bill because its passage demonstrates that the new procedures will work.

However, at the same time, I am dismayed that the Congress failed to include in this bill rescissions I proposed of $85 million for the so-called "REAP" [Rural Environmental Assistance Program] program and $456 million for the Rural Electrification Administration. By failing to include my proposals in this bill, the Congress has, in effect, insisted that $541 million of the taxpayers money be spent, even though there is no demonstrated need.

Instead of accepting its responsibilities as a full partner in the struggle to keep Federal spending under control, the Congress has yielded to the pressures of special interest constituencies and provided unneeded benefits at the expense of the fight against inflation and the welfare of the taxpayer. For the Nation's sake, this kind of action must not set the pattern for the future. I urge the Congress to reconsider this matter.

NOTE: As enacted, H.R. 17505, approved December 21, 1974, is Public Law 93–529 (88 Stat. 1710). The statement was released at Vail, Colo.

319

Memorandum of Disapproval of Health Revenue Sharing and Health Services Legislation. *December 23, 1974*

I HAVE withheld my approval from H.R. 14214, the "Health Revenue Sharing and Health Services Act of 1974."

H.R. 14214 conflicts with my strong commitment to the American taxpayers to hold Federal spending to essential purposes. The bill authorizes appropriations of more than $1 billion over my recommendations and I cannot, in good conscience, approve it. These appropriation authorizations are almost double the funding levels I have recommended for Fiscal Year 1975 and almost triple the levels I believe would be appropriate for 1976.

As part of my effort to see that the burden upon our taxpayers does not increase, I requested the Congress last month to exercise restraint in expanding existing Federal responsibilities, and to resist adding new Federal programs to our already overloaded and limited Federal resources. These recommendations reflect my concern with both the need to hold down the Federal budget and the need to limit the Federal role to those activities which can make the most necessary and significant contributions.

In H.R. 14214, the Congress not only excessively increased authorizations for existing programs but also created several new ones that would result in an unjustified expenditure of Federal taxpayers' funds. Although the purposes of many of the programs authorized in this bill are certainly worthy, I just cannot approve this legislation because of its effect upon the economy through increased unwarranted Federal spending.

Finally, it should be pointed out that the Federal Government will spend almost $20 billion in 1975 through Medicare and Medicaid for the financing of health services for priority recipients—aged and low-income persons. These services are provided on the basis of national eligibility standards in Medicare and State eligibility standards in Medicaid and therefore are available to individuals in a more equitable and less restrictive manner than many of the programs authorized in H.R. 14214.

GERALD R. FORD

The White House,
December 21, 1974.

NOTE: The text of the memorandum was released December 23, 1974, at Vail, Colo.

320

Memorandum of Disapproval of Tennessee Valley Authority Legislation. *December 23, 1974*

I HAVE withheld my approval from H.R. 11929, "To amend section 15d of the Tennessee Valley Authority Act of 1933 to provide that expenditures for pollution control facilities will be credited against required power investment return payments and repayments."

This bill would permit TVA to defer or offset its repayment obligations to the United States Treasury about $85 million per year for 5 years because of expenditures required to install pollution control equipment—and thereby enable TVA to postpone some rate increases otherwise required.

The people who are provided with electric power by the Tennessee Valley Authority have been subjected to substantial increases in power rates in recent months. I must point out, however, that consumers of electricity throughout the Nation have experienced similar rate increases for essentially the same reasons—the rising prices of fuel and materials, the cost of installing air pollution control equipment, and the rising cost of labor.

Nevertheless, TVA customers still pay among the lowest power rates of any region in the Nation—about 30 percent of rates in New York, 64 percent of Chicago, and 78 percent of Louisville, Kentucky.

No one likes to pay higher electric bills. But we must not allow this simple fact to result in new legislation which violates the fundamental principle that electricity should be priced to reflect its cost of production, including the cost of pollution abatement and control. My environmental advisers as well as my economic advisers agree with me that this principle must be upheld.

I see no basis in equity or in logic for departing from this principle in the case of the TVA, and for asking the general taxpayer to make up the difference in TVA power rates. To do so would be unfair to power consumers elsewhere in the Nation who do not have the benefit of Tennessee Valley Authority power facilities and who are required to bear the costs attributed to pollution control in their power bills.

GERALD R. FORD

The White House,
December 21, 1974.

NOTE: The text of the memorandum was released December 23, 1974, at Vail, Colo.

321

Letter Accepting the Resignation of William D. Eberle as Special Representative for Trade Negotiations. *December 24, 1974*

Dear Bill:

I have your letter of December 17, and it is with deep regret that I accept your resignation as Executive Director of the Council on International Economic Policy, and as my Special Representative for Trade Negotiations.

For more than three years, you have served our Nation with the greatest devotion and distinction. You can be very proud of the vital role you played in helping to develop and carry out our country's international economic and trade programs, often under the most demanding circumstances. Your skills in the area of trade negotiations have won you the respect of your colleagues throughout the Government as well as the esteem of the economic and business community for the many substantial contributions you have made in advancing America's position in the world marketplace. You deserve the heartfelt thanks of your fellow citizens, and I want to take this opportunity to express my own admiration and gratitude.

I am grateful, too, for your offer of assistance in the future. You can be sure if the occasion arises we will not hesitate to take advantage of your talents. You have my best wishes for success and happiness in the years ahead.

Sincerely,

JERRY FORD

[The Honorable William D. Eberle, The White House, Washington, D.C.]

NOTE: Mr. Eberle's letter of resignation, dated December 17, 1974, and released with the President's letter at Vail, Colo., read as follows:

Dear Mr. President:

It is my personal desire to return to the private sector after more than three years of Government service, and am therefore submitting my resignation as Executive Director of the Council on International Economic Policy and as your Special Representative for Trade Negotiations. I hardly need say that I came to the decision only after considerable thought. It has been a privilege and a most rewarding opportunity to have served the Government of the United States, and I take this decision with a sense of regret.

I want to thank you, Mr. President, for the honor of serving our country that has been given me and to wish your Administration the very best. I will stand ready as a private citizen to continue to assist you in any way that I can.

W. D. EBERLE

[The President, The White House, Washington, D.C.]

322

Telegram to Mrs. Jack Benny About the Death of Her Husband. *December 27, 1974*

MY FAMILY and I were deeply saddened to learn of the passing of your devoted husband. For the past half century, Jack Benny brought joy and laughter not only to us but to millions of other Americans.

Jack's service to his country, his charitable works, and his genuine enjoyment of the humor of others are accolades that he wore with modesty, grace and charm. If laughter is the music of the soul, Jack and his violin and his good humor have made life better for all men.

We will remember you in our family prayers.

GERALD R. FORD

NOTE: Jack Benny, 80, died on December 26 in Beverly Hills, Calif. The text of the telegram was released at Vail, Colo.

323

Statement on Signing Legislation Establishing a Commission on Federal Paperwork. *December 27, 1974*

I AM pleased to have signed H.R. 16424, a bill creating a temporary Commission on Federal Paperwork to study paperwork generated by various Government reporting requirements. To the public, the burden of filling out Government applications, reports, and other forms of various kinds is not pleasant, frequently annoying, sometimes overwhelming, and often costly and time-consuming. To the Government, adequate information is vital if it is to have responsible policymaking and effective operation of agency activities.

For over 30 years, we have had a public policy of holding Government reporting and recordkeeping requirements to a minimum. These efforts have achieved substantial results, but have not stemmed the increasing tide of Government reporting requirements.

Two main features set the new Commission on Federal Paperwork apart from earlier attacks on the paperwork problem.

It has a broader scope. It will look at laws, regulations, rules, policies, procedures, and practices relating to the gathering, processing, and dissemination of information as well as at the management and control of these activities.

No less important is the composition of the Commission. It brings together representatives of the legislative and executive branches of the Federal Government, representatives from State and local governments, and members from industry and the public. All are involved in the paperwork problem in one way or another. It is fitting that we all share the opportunity and responsibility of reexamining our present policies and procedures and recommending new ways to obtain more effectively the information the Government needs without unreasonably burdening the public.

I look forward to seeing the results of the Commission's work.

NOTE: As enacted, H.R. 16424, approved December 27, 1974, is Public Law 93–556 (88 Stat. 1789). The statement was released at Vail, Colo.

324

Statement on Signing Legislation Establishing the Cuyahoga Valley National Recreation Area in Ohio. *December 28, 1974*

I HAVE approved H.R. 7077, which establishes the Cuyahoga Valley National Recreation Area in Ohio. The establishment of this area paves the way for the preservation of thousands of acres of unspoiled land for the enjoyment of present and future generations.

In signing this bill, I want to express my reservation about a provision of the bill which authorizes the Secretary of the Interior to provide Federal police and fire services to the area, or reimburse local agencies which perform these services. I ask the Congress to amend this legislation to remove this provision so that police and fire services are provided by local agencies, without reimbursement, as in other such Federal recreational areas.

NOTE: As enacted, H.R. 7077, approved December 27, 1974, is Public Law 93–555 (88 Stat. 1784). The statement was released at Vail, Colo.

325

Statement on Signing the Foreign Assistance Act of 1974. *December 30, 1974*

I HAVE signed S. 3394, the Foreign Assistance Act of 1974, with some reservations, but with appreciation for the spirit of constructive compromise which motivated the Congress.

I sought a bill which would serve the interests of the United States in an increasingly interdependent world in which the strength and vitality of our own policies and society require purposeful and responsible participation in the international community. Foreign assistance is indispensable in exercising the role of leadership in the cooperative and peaceful resolution of conflicts, in pursuing political stability and economic progress, and in expressing the American spirit of helping those less fortunate than we are.

In most respects, the Foreign Assistance Act of 1974 will serve those ends. It includes, however, several restrictions that may pose severe problems to our interests. I must bring them to the attention of the Congress as matters which will be of continuing concern and which may require our joint efforts to remedy if circumstances require.

First, are the numerous and detailed limitations on assistance to Indochina. The economic and military assistance levels for Cambodia, particularly, are clearly inadequate to meet minimum basic needs. Our support is vital to help effect an early end to the fighting and a negotiated settlement. This is also the objective of the United Nations General Assembly which approved a resolution calling for a negotiated settlement. I intend to discuss this critical issue with the Congressional leadership at the earliest possible time.

In South Vietnam, we have consistently sought to assure the right of the Vietnamese people to determine their own futures free from enemy interference. It would be tragic indeed if we endangered, or even lost, the progress we have achieved by failing to provide the relatively modest but crucial aid which is so badly needed there. Our objective is to help South Vietnam to develop a viable, self-sufficient economy and the climate of security which will make that development possible. To this end, the economic aid requested represented the amount needed to support crucial capital development and agricultural productivity efforts. The lower amount finally approved makes less likely the achievement of our objectives and will significantly prolong the period needed for essential development.

I appreciate the spirit of compromise which motivated the Congress to extend to February 5, 1975, the period during which military assistance to Turkey may continue under specified circumstances. I regret, however, that the restriction was imposed at all. Turkey remains a key element of U.S. security and political interests in the eastern Mediterranean. The threat of cutoff of aid, even if unfulfilled, cannot fail to have a damaging effect on our relations with one of our staunch NATO allies whose geographic position is of great strategic importance. This, in turn, could have a detrimental effect on our efforts to help achieve a negotiated solution of the Cyprus problem.

I regret the action of the Congress in cutting off the modest program of military assistance to Chile. Although I share the concern of the Congress for the protection of human rights and look forward to continuing consultation with the Chilean Government on this matter, I do not regard this measure as an effective means for promoting that interest.

Finally, the Congress has directed that during the current fiscal year no more than 30 percent of concessional food aid should be allocated to countries which are not among those most seriously affected by food shortages—unless the President demonstrates that such food is required solely for humanitarian purposes. I understand and share the spirit of humanitarianism that prompted a statement of Congressional policy on this subject. But that policy could unduly bind the flexibility of the United States in an arbitrary way in meeting the needs of friendly countries and in pursuing our various interests abroad.

As with other differences which the Congress and the executive branch worked out in consideration of this bill, I look forward to working with the 94th Congress in meeting and solving the problems that are still before us. We share the common goal of best serving the interests of the people of the United States. Working together, we shall continue to serve them responsibly.

NOTE: As enacted, S. 3394, approved December 30, 1974, is Public Law 93–559 (88 Stat. 1795). The statement was released at Vail, Colo.

326

Memorandum of Disapproval of Surface Mining Control and Reclamation Legislation. *December 30, 1974*

I AM withholding my approval from S. 425, the Surface Mining Control and Reclamation Act of 1974.

S. 425 would establish Federal standards for the environmental protection and reclamation of surface coal mining operations, including the reclamation of orphaned lands. Under a complex procedural framework, the bill would encourage the States to implement and enforce a program for the regulation of surface coal mining with substitution of a federally administered program if the States do not act.

The Executive Branch submitted to both the 92nd and 93rd Congresses legislation that would have established reasonable and effective reclamation and environmental protection requirements for mining activities. Throughout this period, the Administration made every effort in working with the Congress to produce a bill that would strike the delicate balance between our desire for reclamation and environmental protection and our need to increase coal production in the United States.

Unfortunately, S. 425, as enrolled, would have an adverse impact on our domestic coal production which is unacceptable. By 1977, the first year after the Act would take full effect, the Federal Energy Administration has estimated that coal production losses would range from a minimum of 48 million tons to a maximum of 141 million tons. In addition, further losses which cannot be quantified could result from ambiguities in the bill, forcing protracted regulatory disputes and litigation. In my judgment, the most significant reasons why such coal losses cannot be accepted are as follows:

1. Coal is the one abundant energy source over which the United States has total control. We should not unduly impair our ability to use it properly.
2. We are engaged in a major review of national energy policies. Unnecessary restrictions on coal production would limit our Nation's freedom to adopt the best energy options.
3. The United States uses the equivalent of 4 barrels of expensive foreign oil for every ton of unproduced domestic coal—a situation which cannot long be tolerated without continued, serious economic consequences. This bill would exacerbate this problem.
4. Unemployment would increase in both the coal fields and in those industries unable to obtain alternative fuel.

In addition, S. 425 provides for excessive Federal expenditures and would clearly have an inflationary impact on the economy. Moreover, it contains numerous other deficiencies which have recently been addressed in Executive Branch communications to the Congress concerning this legislation.

In sum, I find that the adverse impact of this bill on our domestic coal production is unacceptable at a time when the Nation can ill afford significant losses from this critical energy resource. It would also further complicate our battle against inflation. Accordingly, I am withholding my approval from S. 425.

In doing so, I am truly disappointed and sympathetic with those in Congress who have labored so hard to come up with a good bill. We must continue to strive diligently to ensure that laws and regulations are in effect which establish environmental protection and reclamation requirements appropriately balanced against the Nation's need for increased coal production. This will continue to be my Administration's goal in the new year.

GERALD R. FORD

The White House,
December 30, 1974.

NOTE: The text of the memorandum was released at Vail, Colo.

327

Memorandum of Disapproval of United States Tanker Preference Legislation. *December 30, 1974*

I AM withholding my approval from H.R. 8193, the Energy Transportation Security Act of 1974.

The bill would initially require that 20 percent of the oil imported into the United States be carried on U.S. flag tankers. The percentage would increase to 30 percent after June 30, 1977.

This bill would have the most serious consequences. It would have an adverse impact on the United States economy and on our foreign relations. It would create serious inflationary pressures by increasing the cost of oil and raising the prices of all products and services which depend on oil. It would further stimulate inflation in the ship construction industry and cut into the industry's ability to meet ship construction for the U.S. Navy.

In addition, the bill would serve as a precedent for other countries to increase protection of their industries, resulting in a serious deterioration in beneficial international competition and trade. This is directly contrary to the objectives of the trade bill which the Congress has just passed. In addition, it would violate a large number of our treaties of Friendship, Commerce, and Navigation.

Although this bill would undoubtedly benefit a limited group of our working population, such benefit would entail disproportionate costs and produce undesirable effects which could extend into other areas and industries. The waiver provisions which the Congress included in an effort to meet a few of my concerns fail to overcome the serious objections I have to the legislation.

Accordingly, I am not approving this bill because of the substantial adverse effect on the Nation's economy and international interest.

I wish to take this opportunity to reiterate my commitment to maintaining a strong U.S. Merchant Marine. I believe we can and will do this under our existing statutes and programs such as those administered by the Maritime Administration in the Department of Commerce.

GERALD R. FORD

The White House,
December 30, 1974.

NOTE: The text of the memorandum was released at Vail, Colo.

328

Statement on Signing Emergency Jobs, Unemployment Assistance and Compensation Legislation. *December 31, 1974*

TODAY I signed into law H.R. 16596, the Emergency Jobs and Unemployment Assistance Act, and H.R. 17597, the Emergency Unemployment Compensation Act. These are important measures which provide much needed help to our unemployed fellow citizens.

On October 8, when I outlined to Congress my proposals to fight inflation and unemployment, I pointed out that the Conference on Inflation had made us all aware of the undue burden being carried by those who lost their jobs during this period of worsening economic conditions. I proposed a temporary program to expand unemployment assistance and create jobs.

The Emergency Unemployment Compensation Act provides an additional 13 weeks of benefits to persons who are now covered by unemployment compensation laws. This makes it possible for workers who have lost jobs to receive up to one full year of protection if they are unable to find employment.

Title II of the Emergency Jobs and Unemployment Assistance Act creates a temporary unemployment insurance program for jobless workers not now eligible for payments under any other State or Federal programs, including State and local government employees, farm workers, domestic workers, and others not now covered.

Designed to respond to changing economic conditions, these two programs providing urgent, added protection for workers will automatically expand when unemployment is high and contract when it recedes.

Expenditures under existing law of at least $10 billion are projected in fiscal year 1975 for unemployment compensation. The urgent supplemental appropriations bill which I will sign shortly provides $2.75 billion for these two new temporary programs to be used as needed for direct aid to workers.

Title I of H.R. 16596 authorizes a temporary expansion of funding for jobs in the public sector. This action provides up to 100,000 new jobs in addition to the 170,000 financed by funds currently available under existing law.

At my request, the Secretary of Labor has already urged the State Governors to move quickly in making assistance available to the jobless. The Secretary is also working with the States and localities to develop all available resources for the immediate and effective creation of jobs.

With regard to Title III of H.R. 16596, I believe that its provisions would create an unnecessarily complex and unwieldy administrative mechanism involving program and project reviews by all Federal agencies, regional commissions, and units of general government. I will, therefore, request that the Congress transfer appropriations from this title to title I of the act so that needed employment can be provided as quickly and efficiently as possible.

In sum, however, I commend the 93d Congress for its action on these two vital measures and am confident that the spirit of cooperation and conciliation which marked their passage will carry over into the new year and the new Congress.

NOTE: As enacted, H.R. 16596 and H.R. 17597, approved December 31, 1974, are Public Law 93–567 (88 Stat. 1845) and Public Law 93–572 (88 Stat. 1869), respectively. The statement was released at Vail, Colo.

329

Statement Announcing Presidential Clemency Decisions. *December 31, 1974*

I HAVE signed pardons under the clemency program for 18 civilians who have never served in uniform—nine of these effective immediately, and nine of them conditional upon the recipients earning their way back into society by alternate service. In addition, I have formally approved the [Presidential Clemency] Board's recommendations for clemency for 29 former servicemen, including 26 whose pardons will be conditional on their completing alternate service.

These former servicemen still have available to them military appellate mechanisms for review of their earlier convictions. Since I do not intend to impair or prejudice their access to that legal process, I have not signed the formal instruments of clemency at this time. I will not do so until and unless the convictions will have become final, and the resulting punitive and undesirable discharges will have been executed.

Each of these cases involves an individual—a judgment of his past and a determination of his future. The responsibility in each decision is a grave one. The Board and I have carefully considered each case on its individual merits. I believe we have acted with both justice and mercy.

NOTE: The statement was released at Vail, Colo.

Appendix A—Additional White House Releases

NOTE: This appendix lists those releases which are neither printed as items in this volume nor listed in subsequent appendixes. If the text of a release was printed in the Weekly Compilation of Presidential Documents, the page number is indicated below. Page references are to Volume 10 of the Compilation unless otherwise indicated.

August		*Page*
9	Appointment: J. F. terHorst as Press Secretary to the President	1025
9	Appointment: Robert T. Hartmann as Counsellor to the President	1026
9	Biographical data: members of the Presidential transition team (Donald H. Rumsfeld, Rogers C. B. Morton, John O. Marsh, Jr., and William W. Scranton)	...
10	Appointment: John O. Marsh, Jr., as Counsellor to the President	1027
12	Advance text: address to a joint session of Congress	...
13	Nomination: Jack B. Kubisch to be United States Ambassador to Greece	1036
13	Nomination: Richard L. Sneider to be United States Ambassador to the Republic of Korea	1036
14	News briefing: on the President's meeting with the Executive Committee of the National Governors' Conference—by Governors Calvin Rampton of Utah, chairman, and Daniel J. Evans of Washington, past chairman of the executive committee	...
14	News briefing: on their meeting with the President to discuss urban problems—by mayors Tom Bradley of Los Angeles, Calif., E. J. Garn of Salt Lake City, Utah, Ben Boo of Duluth, Minn., and Joseph D. Alioto of San Francisco, Calif	...
15	Appointment: Philip W. Buchen as Counsel to the President	1037
15	News briefing: on their meeting with the President to discuss trade reform legislation and an amendment to the legislation providing for free emigration from Communist countries—by Senators Abraham A. Ribicoff of Connecticut, Henry M. Jackson of Washington, and Jacob K. Javits of New York	...
15	News conference: on his appointment as Counsellor to the President—by John O. Marsh, Jr	...
15	News briefing: on the President's meeting with representatives of the National Association of County Officials—by Commissioner Stanley M. Smoot of Davis County, Utah, and county executives Ralph G. Caso of Nassau County, N.Y., and Alfred D. Del Bello of Westchester County, N.Y	...
16	Appointment: John W. Hushen as Deputy Press Secretary to the President	1038
16	Appointment: Paul A. Miltich as Assistant Press Secretary to the President	1038
16	Appointment: James R. Holland as Assistant Press Secretary to the President	1039
19	Nomination: Richard L. Roudebush to be Administrator of Veterans Affairs	1050
19	Advance text: remarks to the Veterans of Foreign Wars annual convention, Chicago, Ill	...
19	Text: additional remarks to the Veterans of Foreign Wars annual convention	...
20	Nomination: Shirley Temple Black to be United States Ambassador to the Republic of Ghana	1052
20	Appointment: Richard T. Burress as White House liaison with the Vice President-designate	1053
20	News briefing: on the selection of a Vice Presidential nominee—by Counsellor to the President Robert T. Hartmann	...
21	Nomination: William R. Crawford, Jr., to be United States Ambassador to the Republic of Cyprus	1055
21	Fact sheet: Education Amendments of 1974	...

Appendix A

Appendix A

Appendix A

September — Page

17 Nomination: H. Tyler Marcy to be an Assistant Secretary of the Navy....... 1163

17 Nomination: Gary Dean Penisten to be an Assistant Secretary of the Navy.... 1163

17 Nomination: James Leonard Pate to be an Assistant Secretary of Commerce.. 1164

17 Nomination: Kay McMurray to be a member of the National Mediation Board 1164

17 Biographical data: Paul W. McCracken, Special Consultant to the President to assist in the Conference on Inflation.... ...

18 Advance text: address to the 29th Session of the General Assembly of the United Nations.................... ...

20 Appointment: William E. Casselman II as Counsel to the President.......... 1175

20 Nomination: Daniel Minchew to be a member of the United States Tariff Commission 1176

20 Appointment: Clyde S. DuPont as a Commissioner of the Postal Rate Commission 1176

20 Appointment: Ron Nessen as Press Secretary to the President............ 1178

20 Fact sheet: Executive order on inspection of tax returns by the President and White House employees............ ...

20 Fact sheet: budget deferrals and proposed rescissions.................. ...

20 News briefing: on budget deferrals and proposed rescissions—by Roy L. Ash, Director, Office of Management and Budget ....

23 Announcement: disaster assistance for Louisiana 1187

23 Advance text: remarks to the Ninth World Energy Conference in Detroit, Mich ....

24 Appointment: Donald H. Rumsfeld as Assistant to the President.......... 1189

24 Appointment: Thomas P. DeCair as Assistant Press Secretary to the President 1189

September — Page

24 Advance text: remarks to the annual convention of the International Association of Chiefs of Police.......... ..

24 Nomination: Peter C. Dorsey to be United States Attorney for the District of Connecticut.................... ...

24 Nomination: George Beall to be United States Attorney for the District of Maryland ....

25 News briefing: on the President's meeting with the Presidential Clemency Board—by Charles E. Goodell, Chairman, Presidential Clemency Board.... ..

25 Appointment: Bruce H. Hasenkamp as Director of the President's Commission on White House Fellowships..... 1194

26 Nomination: Philip Edward Coldwell to be a member of the Board of Governors of the Federal Reserve System........ 1196

26 Nomination: three members of the National Commission on Libraries and Information Science................ 1196

26 Announcement: transfer of additional lands for park and recreational use under the Legacy of Parks program.... 1197

26 Nomination: Gen. Frederick C. Weyand to be Chief of Staff, United States Army 1197

26 Nomination: David K. E. Bruce to be United States Permanent Representative on the Council of the North Atlantic Treaty Organization......... 1198

27 Statement: on the President's designation of AID officials to assess relief efforts in Honduras—by Press Secretary Ron Nessen...................... 1204

27 Advance text: remarks opening the summit Conference on Inflation....... ...

27 Advance text: remarks at groundbreaking ceremonies for the LBJ Memorial Grove.................. ...

27 Text: informal remarks at a reception for participants in the Conference on Inflation ....

27 Statement: on Mrs. Ford's hospitalization and surgery—by Press Secretary Ron Nessen...................... ...

Appendix A

Appendix A

October		*Page*
15	Nomination: Charles W. Robinson to be Under Secretary of State for Economic Affairs	1284
15	Fact sheet: Federal Election Campaign Act Amendments of 1974	...
15	Advance text: remarks to the annual convention of the Future Farmers of America in Kansas City, Mo	...
16	Advance text: remarks at a breakfast for Republican candidates in Kansas City	...
16	Advance text: remarks in Sioux Falls, S. Dak. (2 releases)	...
16	Advance text: remarks at Lincoln, Nebr	...
16	Advance text: remarks in Indianapolis, Ind	...
16	News briefing: on their meeting with industry representatives on energy matters—by Secretary of the Interior Rogers C. B. Morton, and Secretary of Commerce Frederick B. Dent	...
17	News briefing: on the President's meeting with Hispanic American leaders—by Special Assistant to the President Fernando DeBaca; Luis Alvarez, director of Aspira; Edward Valenzuela, president of Image; Jose Casanova, National Hispanic Assembly; and Antonio Morales, American G.I. Forum of the United States	...
18	Reappointment: Clyde S. DuPont as a Commissioner of the Postal Rate Commission	1322
18	Fact sheet: Emergency Home Purchase Assistance Act of 1974	...
18	News briefing: on the Emergency Home Purchase Assistance Act of 1974—by Secretary of Housing and Urban Development James T. Lynn	...
18	News briefing: on trade reform legislation and the agreement reached on emigration from the Soviet Union—by Senators Henry M. Jackson of Washington and Jacob K. Javits of New York, and Representative Charles A. Vanik of Ohio	...
19	Advance text: remarks at the dedication of the Anderson Independent and Anderson Daily Mail Building in Anderson, S.C	...

October		*Page*
19	Advance text: remarks in Greenville, S.C	...
19	Advance text: remarks at Greensboro, N.C	...
21	Advance text: remarks at the United States-Mexican border, Nogales, Mexico	...
21	Advance text: toast at a luncheon for Mexican President Luis Echeverría Alvarez in Tubac, Ariz	...
21	Statement: on the agreement concerning Soviet emigration and trade legislation—by Press Secretary Ron Nessen	...
22	Advance text: remarks at a rally in Oklahoma City, Okla	...
22	Advance text: remarks in Cleveland, Ohio	...
22	News briefing: on the President's meeting with representatives of the cattle industry—by Senator Henry L. Bellmon of Oklahoma, John Dunn, president of the Oklahoma Cattlemen's Association, and Wray Finney, first vice president of the National Cattlemen's Association	...
23	Appointment: seven members of the President's Committee on Mental Retardation	1357
24	Advance text: remarks at the Iowa State House, Des Moines, Iowa	...
24	Advance text: remarks at a luncheon for Republican candidates in Des Moines	...
24	Advance text: remarks at the United Republican Fund dinner in Chicago, Ill	...
25	Appointment: five members of the National Advisory Council on Adult Education	1372
25	News briefing: on the President's meeting with black civil rights leaders—by Special Assistant to the President Stanley S. Scott; Vernon E. Jordan, executive director, National Urban League; Rev. Jesse Jackson, Operation PUSH; Leon H. Sullivan, chairman of the board, Opportunities Industrialization Centers of America; Clarence M. Mitchell, Jr., director of the Washington bureau, NAACP; Dorothy Height, president, National Council of Negro Women; and Bayard Rustin, director, A. Philip Randolph Institute	...

Appendix A

Appendix A

November	Page
26 Fact sheet: the President's message to Congress on actions to reduce 1975 spending	...
26 News briefing: on the President's message to Congress on actions to reduce 1975 spending—by Roy L. Ash, Director; Frank G. Zarb, Associate Director for Natural Resources, Agriculture, Energy and Science; Donald G. Ogilvie, Acting Associate Director for National Security and International Affairs; and Paul H. O'Neill, Deputy Director-designate, Office of Management and Budget	...
27 Nomination: Jack J. Valenti to be a member of the Board of Directors of the Corporation for Public Broadcasting	1504
27 Nomination: Neil P. Spiers to be a member of the Railroad Retirement Board	1504
27 Nomination: Wilson K. Talley to be an Assistant Administrator of the Environmental Protection Agency	1505
27 Appointment: four members of the Citizens' Advisory Committee on Environmental Quality	1505
27 Nomination: James P. Churchill to be United States District Judge for the Eastern District of Michigan	...
27 Nomination: H. Dale Cook to be United States District Judge for the Northern, Eastern, and Western Districts of Oklahoma	...
29 Nomination: Kathryne Ford Vachon to be a member of the National Credit Union Board	1506
29 News briefing: on the signing of 18 executive warrants for clemency—by Charles E. Goodell, Chairman, Presidential Clemency Board	...
29 Nomination: James M. Fitzgerald to be United States District Judge for the District of Alaska	...
30 Announcement: disaster assistance for Texas	1511
30 Announcement: disaster assistance for Puerto Rico	1511

December	Page
2 Appointment: William N. Walker as Director of the Presidential Personnel Office	1513
2 Announcement: transfer of additional lands for park and recreational use under the Legacy of Parks program	1513
2 Statement by the President: on his trip to Japan, the Republic of Korea, and the Soviet Union (included in the President's news conference of December 2)	...
2 Statement by the President: on the economy (included in the President's news conference of December 2)	...
3 Nomination: Richard B. Parker to be United States Ambassador to the Democratic and Popular Republic of Algeria	1521
3 Appointment: Max L. Friedersdorf as Assistant to the President for Legislative Affairs	1522
3 Advance text: remarks to the American Conference on Trade	...
3 News briefing: on their meeting with the President to discuss task force studies concerning the relation of education and career planning—by Secretary of Commerce Frederick B. Dent, Secretary of Labor Peter J. Brennan, and Secretary of Health, Education, and Welfare Caspar W. Weinberger	...
4 Fact sheet: the President's message to Congress on proposed additions to the National Wilderness Preservation System	...
4 News briefing: on the President's message to the Congress on proposed additions to the National Wilderness Preservation System—by Rogers C. B. Morton, Secretary, E. U. Curtis Bohlen, Deputy Assistant Secretary, Fish and Wildlife and Parks, Department of the Interior, and John R. McGuire, Chief, Forest Service, Department of Agriculture	...
4 Advance text: toast at a dinner honoring Canadian Prime Minister Pierre Elliott Trudeau	...
4 News briefing: on the President's meeting with Prime Minister Trudeau—by Arthur A. Hartman, Assistant Secretary of State for European Affairs	...

Appendix A

Appendix B—Presidential Documents Published in the Federal Register

NOTE: The texts of these documents are also printed in title 3A of the Code of Federal Regulations. Texts of the proclamations and Executive orders are printed in the Weekly Compilation of Presidential Documents for the period covered by this volume.

PROCLAMATIONS

Proc. No.	*Date 1974*	*Subject*	*39 F.R. page*
4308	Aug. 20	Columbus Day, 1974	30333
4309	Aug. 22	Women's Equality Day, 1974	30819
4310	Sept. 4	National Hispanic Heritage Week, 1974 [1]	32317
4311	Sept. 8	Granting pardon to Richard Nixon [2]	32601
4312	Sept. 12	Citizenship Day and Constitution Week, 1974	33197
4313	Sept. 16	Announcing a program for the return of Vietnam era draft evaders and military deserters [3]	33293
4314	Sept. 17	National Employ the Handicapped Week, 1974	33661
4315	Sept. 19	Johnny Horizon '76 Clean Up America Month, 1974	34259
4316	Sept. 26	National School Lunch Week, 1974	35101
4317	Sept. 27	Imports of petroleum and petroleum products	35103
4318	Sept. 27	National Hunting and Fishing Day, 1974	35315
4319	Sept. 28	Enlarging boundaries of Cabrillo National Monument, Calif	35317
4320	Oct. 2	Fire Prevention Week, 1974	35779
4321	Oct. 3	Leif Erikson Day, 1974	35781
4322	Oct. 5	Child Health Day, 1974	36107
4323	Oct. 7	Veterans Day, 1974	36313
4324	Oct. 7	National Farm-City Week, 1974	36315
4325	Oct. 10	General Pulaski's Memorial Day, 1974	36561
4326	Oct. 12	Country Music Month, October 1974	36951
4327	Oct. 14	National Legal Secretaries' Court Observance Week, 1974	36953
4328	Oct. 18	Drug Abuse Prevention Week, 1974	37473
4329	Oct. 21	Immunization Action Week, 1974	37629

[1] Proclamation 4310 is printed in full on p. 81 of this volume as an example of the proclamations issued by President Ford in 1974.

[2] Proclamation 4311 is printed in full on p. 103 of this volume.

[3] Proclamation 4313 is printed in full on p. 138 of this volume.

Appendix B

Proc. No.	*Date 1974*	*Subject*	*39 F.R. page*
4330	Oct. 28	American Education Week, 1974	38217
4331	Oct. 28	National Parkinson Week, 1974	38219
4332	Nov. 5	Emergency Medical Services Week, 1974	39425
4333	Nov. 11	Thanksgiving Day, 1974	40003
4334	Nov. 16	Imports of sugars, sirups, and molasses	40739
4335	Nov. 16	Imports from Canada of cattle, beef, veal, swine, and pork	40741
4336	Nov. 27	Wright Brothers Day, 1974	41497
4337	Dec. 3	Bill of Rights Day, Human Rights Day and Week	42335
4338	Dec. 5	National Day of Prayer, 1974	42671
			40 F.R. page
4339	Dec. 30	March of Dimes Birth Defects Prevention Month, 1975	749

EXECUTIVE ORDERS

E.O. No.	*Date 1974*	*Subject*	*39 F.R. page*
11798	Aug. 14	Administration of export controls	29567
11799	Aug. 17	Suspension of maximum percentage of certain Navy and Marine Corps officers who may be recommended for promotion	30101
11800	Aug. 17	Delegation of Presidential authority related to aviation career incentive pay	30103
11801	Aug. 21	Display of flag at half-staff on the death of Ambassador Rodger P. Davies	30335
11802	Sept. 4	Display of flag at half-staff on the death of Gen. Creighton W. Abrams, Chief of Staff, U.S. Army	32111
11803	Sept. 16	Establishment of the Presidential Clemency Board	33297
11804	Sept. 16	Delegation of Presidential authority to the Director of Selective Service to administer alternative service program for Vietnam era draft evaders and military deserters	33299
11805	Sept. 20	Inspection of tax returns by the President and certain employees of the White House Office	34261
11806	Sept. 25	Continuation of the National Commission for the Observance of World Population Year	34641
11807	Sept. 28	Occupational safety and health programs for Federal employees	35559
11808	Sept. 30	Establishment of the President's Economic Policy Board	35563
11809	Sept. 30	Establishment of the President's Labor-Management Committee	35565
11810	Sept. 30	Administration of export controls	35567
11811	Oct. 7	Civilian pay increase	36302
11812	Oct. 7	Military pay increase	36307
11813	Oct. 7	Career or career-conditional appointments for cooperative education students	36317

E.O. No.	*Date 1974*	*Subject*	*39 F.R. page*
11814	Oct. 11	Activation of the Energy Resources Council	36955
11815	Oct. 23	Delegation of Presidential authority to the National Capital Planning Commission for establishment of metes and bounds of the National Capital Service Area	37963
11816	Oct. 23	Delegation of Presidential authority to the Secretary of the Treasury of reporting functions under the Foreign Assistance Act of 1961	37965
11817	Nov. 5	Designation of U.S. Civil Service Commission to concur with agency determinations of age limits for appointments of law enforcement officers and firefighters	39427
11818	Nov. 5	Administration of export controls	39429
11819	Nov. 16	Enlargement of membership of the Energy Resources Council	40743
11820	Nov. 27	Bicentennial year meeting of the International Council on Archives	41499
11821	Nov. 27	Inflation impact statements	41501
11822	Dec. 10	Designation of certain officers of the Treasury Department to act as Secretary of the Treasury	43275
11823	Dec. 12	Abolishment of the National Commission for Industrial Peace	43529
			40 F.R. page
11824	Dec. 28	Exemption of Whitney Gillilland from mandatory retirement	751
11825	Dec. 31	Gold transactions by U.S. citizens	1003
11826	Dec. 31	Exemption of Willard Deason from mandatory retirement	1004

PRESIDENTIAL DOCUMENTS OTHER THAN PROCLAMATIONS AND EXECUTIVE ORDERS

Date 1974	*Subject*	*39 F.R. page*
Aug. 14	Presidential Determination: Sale of wheat to Egypt	30473
Sept. 20	Special Message to the Congress: Budget deferrals and proposed rescissions*	34222
Oct. 4	Special Message to the Congress: Budget deferrals and proposed rescissions*	36214
Oct. 29	Presidential Determination: Sale of defense articles and services to Kenya, the Malagasy Republic, and Mauritius	39863
Oct. 29	Presidential Determination: Military assistance and sales to Turkey to help peace negotiations on the Cyprus conflict	39865
Oct. 31	Special Message to the Congress: Budget deferrals and proposed rescissions*	39230
Oct. 31	Special Message to the Congress: Deferral of funds appropriated for the Family Practice of Medicine Act*	39255
Oct. 31	Presidential Determination: Sale of wheat to Egypt	39431
Nov. 4	Presidential Determination: Sale of wheat and rice to Syria	40005
Nov. 13	Special Message to the Congress: Budget deferrals and proposed rescissions*	40702
Nov. 26	Special Message to the Congress: Budget deferrals and proposed rescissions*	42521

*Printed in full only in the Federal Register.

Appendix B

Date 1974	*Subject*	*40 F.R. page*
Dec. 27	Special Message to the Congress: Budget deferrals and proposed rescissions*	1638
Dec. 30	Memorandum: Funds from the Atomic Energy Commission for salaries and expenses of the Energy Research and Development Administration	1221
Dec. 31	Presidential Determination: Military assistance and sales to Turkey to help peace negotiations on the Cyprus conflict	4257

*Printed in full only in the Federal Register.

Appendix C—Presidential Reports to the 93d Congress, 2d Session

NOTE: The following is a listing of those Presidential reports required by statute to be transmitted to the Congress.

Subject	*Published*	*Sent to the Congress*	*Date of White House release*
Special International Exhibitions (11th annual)		Aug. 13	Aug. 13
Balance of payments deficit incurred under the North Atlantic Treaty:			
3d quarterly	H. Doc. 271	Aug. 20	Aug. 20
4th quarterly	H. Doc. 388	Nov. 18	Nov. 18
National Traffic and Motor Vehicle Safety Act of 1966 and the Highway Safety Act of 1966 (1973)	H. Doc. 343	Sept. 4	Sept. 4
Federal Coal Mine Health and Safety Act of 1969 by Department of the Interior (1973)		Sept. 6(H) Sept. 9(S)	
Federal Prevailing Rate Advisory Committee (1st annual)	H. Doc. 359	Sept. 19	
United Nations (28th annual)	H. Doc. 360	Sept. 19	Sept. 19
National Heart and Lung Institute (1st annual)		Sept. 24	Sept. 24
Advisory Council on Intergovernmental Personnel Policy (final)		Sept. 25	Sept. 25
Food for Peace Program under Public Law 480, 83d Congress (1973)	H. Doc. 362	Sept. 25	Sept. 25
Farmers Home Administration Contract Activities		Sept. 26	Sept. 26
Economic Stabilization Program (final quarterly)		Oct. 1	Oct. 1
National Advisory Council on Economic Opportunity (7th annual)	H. Doc. 367	Oct. 9	
National Advisory Council on Extension and Continuing Education (8th annual)	H. Doc. 368	Oct. 10	Oct. 10
Automotive Products Trade Act of 1965 (8th annual)		Oct. 23	
National Cancer Advisory Board (2d annual)		Oct. 23	Oct. 23
National Cancer Program (2d annual)		Nov. 4	Nov. 4
National Capital Housing Authority (fiscal year 1973)		Nov. 13	Nov. 13
Upland Cotton (3d annual)		Nov. 19	
National Wilderness Preservation System (10th annual)	H. Doc. 402	Dec. 4	Dec. 4
Department of Transportation (7th annual)		Dec. 9	
Council on Environmental Quality (5th annual)		Dec. 12	Dec. 12
National Growth and Development, 1974 (2d biennial)		Dec. 17	
National Housing Goals (6th annual)		Dec. 31	

Appendix D—Interview in Newsweek Magazine: "How It Looks to Ford"

NOTE: Following is the transcript of an interview with the President reprinted from the December 9, 1974, issue of Newsweek. The interview was conducted the previous week in the Oval Office by Newsweek editor Osborn Elliott, managing editor Edward Kosner, and Washington bureau chief Mel Elfin. (Copyright 1974 by Newsweek, Inc. All rights reserved. Reprinted by permission.)

Q. *We would like to start with your recent trip and what kind of man you found Mr. Brezhnev to be.*

A. Let me say at the outset, I spent a great deal of time in preparation for the trip, particularly in preparation for the negotiations with Mr. Brezhnev on SALT. I had three National Security Council meetings . . . and we had various options prepared, and we discussed them.

I listened and asked questions. In addition, I spent a great deal of time with Henry [Kissinger] going over the original proposal we submitted to the Soviet Union, their counterproposal, and then I refined it, working with Henry on our counterproposal to them.

Of course, Henry went over and discussed in some depth the conceptual approach that we thought would break the deadlock, which actually did break the deadlock. Then I should say, in addition, I did a lot of reading on the background for SALT I.

The net result was that when I first met Brezhnev, I had a good appraisal of him as a person, his style, his negotiating techniques, and, of course, I was extremely well-informed on their position, our position, and any variations that might develop.

It was, I would say, a tough negotiation. The fact that I had done this background work was extremely helpful because he is a person who can be alternately very jovial, very pleasant, he will kid a lot, and then he can get deadly serious and be extremely firm, and the net result was we worked from 6 to a little after midnight the first time. I guess it was almost 12:30 or 1 o'clock.

We had planned to have a dinner after a relatively short meeting, but it just kept going on and on so when we got through, we broke up in complete deadlock the first night. We had narrowed the issues, but had not—well, we just had a firm difference of opinion on a very important point.

So, then we agreed to come back the next morning, and they came up with a proposal which was a change in their position that had to a substantial degree caused the deadlock.

Q. *Can you specify, Mr. President?*

A. I really don't think so.

Q. *You mentioned earlier it was a conceptual mode that you brought to this which caused the breakthrough.*

A. What we really were trying to do was to achieve what both Henry and the Defense Department felt was vitally important, not only substantively, but perceptively: equivalence. So, you had to take the number of launchers, the number of MIRV's, and you had to make sure that we did get an equivalence, which meant basically that they had to come down from not their present status but their planned or programed status, and it had to fit into our plans and our programs.

As you know, I am sure, in SALT I there was some give and take. We accepted a lesser figure in launchers and took a bigger figure as far as MIRVing because we were ahead and they were behind. So, the conceptual breakthrough was really on the basis of equivalence and then, of course, what you included within the equivalence.

Q. *But you suggested, Mr. President, that they came back the next day with a new perception of their own, or new suggestion.*

A. Well, they offered a figure which we felt was a reasonable area of—actually, it was more or less the numbers we finally agreed on.

Q. *Mr. President, do you think that this concession was the result of the American side's firmness on the first night?*

A. I think so, yes.

Q. *Do you think you were being tested on that first night?*

A. I think that is a fair conclusion. This was a new negotiator across the table, and they raised a number of questions about alleged violations, and you have read some of these alleged violations, some of our own people have raised about them. And they, in turn, of course, made allegations that we had made some violations.

So it was a pretty good give and take. And I think they were probing and testing to see how eager we were, whether we would capitulate, whether our appetite was so whetted for an agreement that we would agree to almost anything.

But I will say this in their behalf. It is my judgment they likewise genuinely wanted to make an agreement. That does not mean they wanted to make an agreement that would be harmful to them, but they did not come there with their position so firmly set in concrete that they had no maneuvering room. The net result was we did maneuver. We did negotiate. And we gave some, and they gave some.

Q. *How about the probing and testing on your side, Mr. President?*

A. We suggested several alternatives which they did turn down. We, I think, for tactical reasons, wanted them to know that we had some positions that we thought were valid. I also think we knew they would not accept them, but that is part of the negotiating. It is to some extent like you negotiate up on the Hill. You have to take some extreme positions on occasion to get what you want.

Q. *This happens at* NEWSWEEK *sometimes.*

A. I am sure. I know it happened in labor-management negotiations when I was practicing law. Why, you have to start out up here, and you end up at a reasonable compromise.

Q. *It has been suggested that you and Mr. Brezhnev have certain similarities in personality. How do you think he would do as a politician in this country?*

A. I think he would do very well. I was impressed with him. He is a strong person. He has some qualities that I like in a person. He is very friendly.

And none of the experiences I have had with him indicate that he is a person who is mean or vindictive. None of that attitude at all. He was firm in what he wanted, and yet he could understand our point of view.

He is very pleasant to be with. Very enjoyable, both not only when we were negotiating, but in the luncheon and the automobile ride we took at the end where we spent an hour driving around Vladivostok, where I sat with him in the back seat. Very pleasant, very amiable in his discussion, very generous in the way he talks.

Q. *You never felt like Kennedy did with Khrushchev in 1961?*

A. I had no feeling like that. At least the atmosphere in my judgment was friendly to start with, and there was no effort on their part to put us down, as we certainly did not have any view of trying to put them down. He started out almost at the beginning in saying that we had a serious—speaking of them as well as ourselves—a serious obligation to try and reach an agreement to stabilize the problems between the two major nuclear powers. He took a very broad view.

Q. *Did he take a comparable attitude toward the Mideast when you got around to that discussion?*

A. They have strong feelings there.

Q. *Your critics say that while it was very important to conclude a SALT treaty, more time should have been devoted to the urgent problem of war possibly breaking out in the Middle East.*

A. We spent, I would say, better than two hours [on the Mideast], and I think we got a better understanding of our view and their view. They, of course, want to go to the Geneva Conference, get everything in a package and try to solve Israel and Egypt, Israel and Jordan, Israel and Syria, Israel and the PLO at one time. That is their approach.

We think that may be a final step, but in the meantime I think our view is we have to do some step-by-step negotiating, and it was important for us to get some understanding of their views and vice versa. I think we spent enough time on that.

After all, we cannot negotiate, the Soviet Union and ourselves, Mr. Brezhnev and myself, on where the line should be, if the line should be in the Sinai Peninsula. We cannot negotiate for Israel and Syria if there is to be any further give in the Golan Heights. It is not for us to decide that Israel has to negotiate with the PLO.

Q. *Do you think that is a likely eventuality, Mr. President?*

A. That Israel will negotiate?

Q. *Ultimately have to negotiate with the PLO.*

A. I think it is very premature to make any judgment on that. I think some other things have to develop, and only time will tell on that.

Q. *What kind of diplomatic contact do you think the United States should have with the PLO, if any?*

A. At this point I don't think we should have any diplomatic contacts. Again, I think it is premature. A lot depends on their actions, how they are going to get involved in the Middle East itself.

This is a very delicate circumstance right now, and for us to make any precipitous decision is premature.

Q. *Do you think the United Nations advanced the cause of peace by its gesture of recognition to the PLO, or do you think that complicated the situation?*

A. I think it has complicated the situation.

Q. *Mr. President, having just returned from what seems to have been quite a successful summit meeting with Mr. Brezhnev, you have come back to find a number of your critics saying you should not have gone in the first place.*

A. A lot of them said it before I left.

Q. *They said you should be sitting here in Washington and coping with the economic problems and solving economic difficulties that the country is in. How do you respond to that sort of criticism?*

A. It was vitally important to go to Japan ~~for~~, I think, understandable reasons; to Korea for equally understandable reasons, and certainly to go to Vladivostok to see Mr. Brezhnev. The question then is what did I not do here while I was gone.

Appendix D

Before I left, I spent a great deal of time carrying out a commitment I had made for the submission of this package for the reduction of expenditures in the current fiscal year. I cannot give you the precise figure, but I must have spent at least twelve hours or more in detailed analysis with Roy Ash and his people.

They had to put the package together, predicated on my decisions. There was not any need for me to be here to make any other decisions. The decisions were made. The mechanics were in their hands.

When I came back, of course, I had to approve it in its final form. So, from that point of view, there was no need for me to be here.

We had prepared and submitted, or I had prepared and approved the message to the Congress for the lame-duck legislative program. We had outlined about 40 some items that we had refined, that I felt the Congress had to do in this five or six weeks that it is going to be here, so that work was done.

The burden was really on the Congress to get moving. I had made a number of personal contacts, individually, and also by letter on something that I felt was of most urgent necessity, and that was getting Nelson Rockefeller confirmed, and I think my phone calls, my personal letters, plus part of the message, I think, has gotten that off dead center.

I just finished talking to [House Judiciary Committee Chairman Peter] Rodino before you came in, and Pete pretty well assures me as best he can that in the week, I think, of Dec. 16—they will vote probably on the 20th of December—so I had done everything that I felt could be done to get the Congress going again, and that was all done before I left.

So, the question is, what more could I have done by staying here?

Q. *The focus of much of the criticism has to do with what people perceive as being an inadequate leadership role on the energy front, in particular.*

A. On that we have had two Cabinet meetings where we went around the table, and we had them at a two-week interval. As you recollect, I sent up on Oct. 8 a 31-point program which included the things we felt were needed and necessary for the energy program, as well as the economic program.

What I have started with the Cabinet is a scorecard, and every member of the Cabinet has to report when they come to the Cabinet meeting on what has been done in their field of responsibility and whether it is the economic front or the energy front, and we have a scorecard up there where the bills are, and a progress report.

And on the energy front, of course, [Interior Secretary Rogers] Morton is now the chairman of the Energy Committee. [Treasury Secretary William] Simon was moved from that over to the Economic Committee, so Rog has the principal responsibility to give us at these meetings a rundown on every bill that we think is necessary, every administrative action, and quite frankly—I said it directly to them—their performance on this is going to be the basis on whether—to put it quite bluntly—whether they stay or not. It is a scorecard.

Q. *We have heard reports that you were planning a speech either for the beginning of December or in January which will take a much tougher line than you have taken in the past on the whole subject of energy and conservation. We hear among those things that may be proposed is a 20 per cent cut in domestic consumption. Is that in the works?*

A. Let me add one thing. Prior to my departure, I made the decision to withdraw Andy Gibson's name as head of the Federal Energy Administration, for reasons that are unfortunate, but be that as it may, I made that decision and decided that Frank Zarb should be transferred from the Office of Management and Budget over to FEA.

So, we do have an organization now because I am sure Frank will be confirmed. I don't foresee any problems as far as Congress is concerned.

I think you have been misled as to rumors—inaccurate—about a speech of that kind. What we do intend to do is on the basis of this scorecard procedure, if we find that our voluntary program, which is a reduction of 1 million barrels per day, is not successful, we certainly have a fallback position, which we will not hesitate to implement, which is a mandatory embargo on the importation of 1 million barrels a day of foreign crude oil.

And we also have the capability of moving into a mandatory allocation system, allocation of the 5 million barrels per day [we import] plus our domestic of about 10 or 11 million barrels a day, which we produce here. So, the actions we take will be based upon the success of the present program.

Q. *What is the deadline you gave yourself for the testing of the voluntary program, Mr. President?*

A. We are having a Cabinet meeting next week . . . That will give us a much better feel on whether or not the voluntary program is proceeding satisfactorily. Of course, we run into a couple of paradoxical circumstances.

For various reasons, we have more gasoline and more fuel oil in storage today than we had a year ago. I was talking to a man who is an expert in this field, a nongovernmental expert. He tells me that as of a couple of days ago, we have 45 million more barrels in storage today than we had a year ago. So, you are in a difficult situation.

You want to talk about conservation and yet you have got more crude oil on hand and gasoline stocks on hand than you had a year ago. So, it is pretty hard to sell that individual who goes to a gasoline station or to a distributor and say, "You have to use less," when you have more on hand than you had a year ago.

Q. *Would you argue for the gas tax that your namesake [Henry Ford II] is recommending?*

A. I don't foresee that as a possibility. I do get arguments or I do get people who advocate it. I do have to say to them—not only the substantive arguments that I think are reasonable, equally balanced—but most of the people who argue for it do not realize the vigorous opposition on the Hill to any program.

You may recollect when the program was first discussed there was the inference, I think, from John Sawhill or maybe John and two or three others that this was going to be recommended by me at the time we were going through the [economic] summit process.

Bill Timmons, our legislative liaison, tells me he got more telephone calls from Capitol Hill, Democrats, Republicans, leaders, troops, saying, "Don't, under any circumstances, recommend that because it will not go anyplace, period."

Is that important? Well, you have to be realistic. Is there any point in submitting something where you get substantive arguments from both sides that at least in the environment that existed in late October there was absolutely no possibility of any affirmative action on Capitol Hill?

Q. *Did the same conditions apply to your surtax?*

A. No, because the surtax—I think if Congress understood it or made an effort to understand it, or if we had sold it better—and I must confess, I don't think I, and others, sold it as well as we should—is a far more equitable, less regressive, tax than a tax of say 10 or 20 cents per gallon additional on gasoline. Now, maybe the vigor with which it was opposed in October was predicated on the election or the prospective election.

But my judgment at that time was clear. A gas-tax increase would have fallen like a lead balloon up on Capitol Hill. And this word came from people whose judgment I really respect, not only on substance, but on the political realities.

So, I still think the surtax at that time, and even today, was a good approach. Maybe it ought to have been [set at an income level of] $20,000 to make it more applicable to a greater degree on higher-income people, but even at the figure we used it was applicable only to 28 per cent of the tax returns, so that is hitting a very narrow part of the spectrum.

But I just wish Congress, if it does not like what we propose, comes up with a plan of their own, and I have not seen any plan yet.

Q. *Mr. President, the polls show that while you yourself remain personally popular, the American people would like to see a greater sense of urgency in meeting the energy problems and in meeting the economic problems in this country. Do you see truth in the polls, and how do you intend to respond?*

A. Let's take the energy problem as a whole. Even before I took this office there were a dozen or more bills up there that President Nixon had recommended for action that did involve the energy problem and the solutions. We submitted some extra ones. The scorecard on the Hill is really minor league on passing bills related to energy.

Q. *By minor league, you mean Michigan's field-goal kicker?*

A. [Laughter.] Don't pick on that poor kid. He missed two last year. He did not go to the Rose Bowl, and he missed one this year. That kid must have had nightmares every night.

No. How much more can a President do than to recommend legislation, have his people do their very best to talk to committee members, to chairmen, to the leaderships?

I have talked to them. I have met with the leadership. There are just roadblocks up there that are apparently unbreakable until we get a real crisis.

And I am being very practical now. I do not think you are going to get a breakthrough in legislation in the field of energy until you get a brownout or a blackout. I think it is just that pragmatic.

You won't get deregulation on natural gas until the cutbacks in natural gas in Washington and in New York and New England start to hurt people or hurt jobs. That is a bad commentary on our system, perhaps, but that is the way we act, right or wrong.

Q. *Is the Congress out of step in this case? Do you think the people would be more open to initiatives than the Congress is willing to show?*

A. Very definitely. I really think so.

Q. *Would that include gasoline rationing? The polls show people would approve gasoline rationing.*

A. In this case, I think the Congress is showing better judgment than the people who have been polled. Most people who have been polled I suspect never went through gasoline rationing.

Many members of Congress remember it, and it was not a very satisfactory system. Of course, the circumstances are different today than they were in World War II.

Q. *In terms of the economy, would you sketch for us what kind of crisis stage would perhaps force Congress to act? Or that you yourself might recommend additional action other than what you already recommended?*

A. I think we have a plan that we submitted in October that fitted the circumstances as we saw them then and as we envisaged them over the horizon. I must confess that there has been a more rapid deterioration in the economy since Oct. 8.

In the last two months unemployment has risen more rapidly. The deterioration in the automotive industry has been far more serious. So, the plan we submitted in light of this deterioration may have to be modified some. But I think we probably have another month or so at the most before we would have to make any major changes.

The Congress has done very little on the plan we submitted. The only bill they have really passed is the housing bill.

Q. *Is your suggestion of a $4.6 billion budget cut instead of your earlier proposal for a larger reduction a reflection of your new appraisal of the economy, and in effect, a beginning of pump priming?*

A. No, no. There were several, I think, significant things that ought to be pointed out. We put them in the message. You see, we started out with $305.4 billion. Then for various reasons it had gotten up to $306.9 billion, primarily because of the increase in interest of about $1.5 billion, the increase in interest cost.

What we did was—and this took an awful lot of time—department by department we made a reduction of $4.6 billion. Now, actually we are below $300 billion, except for an increase of $2.6 billion in unemployment compensation which has taken place or will take place because of the deterioration in the employment situation.

Now, I rationalize by saying at the time I made the commitment of $300 billion we did not anticipate that extra $2.6 billion in unemployment compensation. So, we took $4.6 billion and we took credit for a change in circumstances of $2.6 billion because of increased unemployment, plus I reminded the Congress that if they had deferred the Federal employees' pay increase for six months it would have saved $700 million this fiscal year.

I reminded them I had vetoed a railroad retirement bill that took an extra $284 million out of the Federal Treasury, not out of the retirement funds. And I also said that I was vetoing the veterans' education bill. That added $502 million to expenses over and above what we had anticipated when we thought of the figure of $305.4 or $306.9 billion.

Now, that is a lot of words, but if you sit down and analyze it, we really maintained our credibility substantially, but had to take into account the Congress's failure to cooperate in cutting back on the items I mentioned on expenditures, plus the increase in unemployment, which we did not foresee at the time.

Q. *What kind of numbers would it take to lead you to think that it was time to begin pump priming? What level of unemployment, what rate of GNP fall-out?*

A. Well, I think a substantial increase. The last figure of unemployment was 6 per cent. It had gone from 5.7. Previous to that it was 5.4, I think. So, there has been a steady climb. The jump to 6 was a signal. In the interim, we have had the additional layoffs in the automotive industry. I would say 6.5, a half per cent, would be indicative of a very serious added deterioration.

Now, we could have cranked into it short-term problems, though. We are going to have less employment at the next count because of the coal strike. Now that really is not unemployment, but if you have less jobs at the top and you have the same amount of unemployment or increased unemployment, the percentage of unemployment gets distorted.

Q. *What sort of modification in your economic policies would be triggered by a 6.5 per cent unemployment rate?*

A. Well, I would not want to make any definitive comment in that regard, but I do have my top economic people reviewing so that they are prepared for any alternatives in case this deterioration continues.

As a matter of fact, I have asked them to come back in the next week or ten days with some choices for me in case these unemployment figures, the GNP figures, show a circumstance quite different from when we had the summit and when we made the decision on Oct. 8.

But I have not seen the options they are working on. I simply know that they have been told by me to come up with some option papers in case there is a significant change.

Q. *Have you ruled wage and price controls out of their option thinking?*

A. Yes.

Q. *They are still ruled out?*

A. Yes. The encouraging thing we see—now the drop in the increase in the cost of living from 1.3 per cent to .9 per cent in the figures that came out while we were overseas is significant; .9 per cent is not good by any standards, but the drop and the areas of reduction within the .9 per cent from the previous level are very encouraging.

Now, if you are making headway in holding the line, not that you have achieved what you want, but if you are making headway in getting a handle on inflation, and you are beginning to have not shortages, but surpluses, I just do not see the need for wage and price controls.

You are sort of getting away from conditions that would, in my judgment, from an economy point of view, justify wage and price controls. Now, the other side of the coin, if we get a runaway in wage settlements, which I hope is not going to be the case—that is why the wage-price policy board is on board, why they are working, what they hope to do through advice—I just think it is less and less needed at the present time, when you are talking about wage and price controls.

I cannot help but note what the Congress is not doing. They are not going to do it in the lame-duck session, period. They do not want to do it by mandatory action. All they want to do is, if they do anything, is to give the President the option to impose them.

So, I do not think they are needed now. Apparently the Congress does not think that they are needed now, and I do not find many advocates today—although the polls show that there is 60 percent or thereabouts—the public thinks they are needed.

Q. *You have been accused of moving too slowly in putting your own stamp and personality on this Administration. You have talked about the standards by which you are going to judge members of the Cabinet. Do you plan, other than what you have mentioned before about the Cabinet, to move more quickly in making this a Ford Administration, rather than a Ford-Nixon Administration?*

A. I think that the most important job for me to do at the outset was to put a Ford Administration into the White House. That is about 99 per cent achieved at the present time. Nobody in the old Administration who at the top level had any responsibility is still here.

Q. In light of the information that has come out in recent weeks in the Watergate cover-up trial, would you reiterate that your decision was correct in pardoning President Nixon when you did it?

A. I am more convinced than ever, and I have thought a good deal about it. I have tried to analyze where we would be today if I had not done it. And it is my judgment now that the decision I made then, Sept. 9, is more right now than it was then.

Q. *Where do you think we would be, Mr. President, had you not done it?*

A. I think that the divisiveness that was evident then, pros and cons, the clash that was there then, would be even more so now. I think Mr. Nixon's devoted friends—and he has a lot of them—in light of his health, would be really up in arms if they tried to subpoena him and if they tried to prosecute him.

I think the people who hated Mr. Nixon would have no sympathy, regardless of his health. So, you would have this constant clash, which I think was bad then and I think it would be worse now.

Q. In the last month or so you have been subjected to an increasingly vituperative kind of attack, which is probably uncharacteristic of your whole political career. A magazine in New York recently portrayed you as Bozo the Clown.

A. I just read about that . . .

Q. *Do you think some of this approach is getting out of bounds, that you are now being subjected to the kind of attack that is malicious and destructive rather than constructive?*

A. I learned a long time ago in athletics, and in rigors of the political arena, that you just cannot concentrate on the job if you worry about those kinds of articles, whether it is newspaper or cartoon or anything else.

Sure, you don't like them, but I don't sit and moan and groan about them. Just like in a ball game, if you miss a pass, the fans boo you. It does not help to catch the next one, if you wring your hands and get frightened about it. If you think you are right, I think you have to keep on doing what you have decided to do, and you cannot let people who are critical affect your judgment on what you have decided.

Now, to some extent I think here is a way to illustrate it. I have some friends, as well as some critics, up on the Hill, who say I should not veto something if I know in advance it is going to be overriden. That is no way to judge from this office whether a piece of legislation is good or bad.

They have their obligations. I have mine, and if I predicate my decision on the basis of their responsibility or irresponsibility, I am not carrying out the function of this office.

So, I have told every member of the Cabinet that we are not going to decide what we do on legislation because of critics out there or on the basis of whether they are going to sustain or override the veto.

Q. *Yet, Mr. President, you are citing that kind of Congressional resistance in rejecting any thought of a gas tax?*

A. Yes. I think it is a little different, though, than whether you veto a bill—that is one circumstance. The other is whether you send something up there that you know is going to fall flat. Maybe it is not as clear a distinction as it should be, but at least I can see the difference.

Q. In general, Mr. President, do you think you, have been getting a fair shake from the press?

A. I think I am. I really do. Even if I did not think so—

Q. *You would not say so.*

A. . . . No. As a matter of fact, I think I have gotten a fair shake, but I am not going to worry about it even if I don't think I get a fair shake. It is not going to interfere with my personal relationship with members of the press, even if I thought I was not getting a fair shake. That does not help any.

Q. *You have said that a top priority was for Congress to confirm Nelson Rockefeller, which they are about to do. What particular role do you see for him in this Administration?*

A. I want him to be a full partner, and that means obviously being in on the foreign policy, but I would say his main emphasis would be on the domestic side. Nelson, I think, has a particular and maybe peculiar capability of balancing the pros and cons in many social programs, and I think he has a reputation and the leadership capability.

I want him to be very active in the Domestic Council, even to the extent of being chairman of the Domestic Council. I do think we have to have some real leadership and strength there, and I think he is peculiarly equipped for that responsibility.

Q. Do you expect him to be helpful in attracting new and good people into the Administration?

A. I think he can be very helpful. You know, he has always had good people. At least I think he has.

He has attracted them, I think, because of his personality and the dedication he has to the job, and I think we can get more good people with him here. He has many, many connections, of course, over the years, academic, business, financial. I think his presence here will help to draw people.

Thank you, Mr. President.

Appendix E—Rules Governing This Publication

NOTE: These rules are reprinted from the Federal Register, vol. 37, p. 23607, dated November 4, 1972. and title 1 of the Code of Federal Regulations.

TITLE 1—GENERAL PROVISIONS

Chapter 1—Administrative Committee of the Federal Register

PART 10—PRESIDENTIAL PAPERS

SUBPART A—ANNUAL VOLUMES

AUTHORITY: 44 U.S.C. 1506; sec. 6, E.O. 10530, 19 FR 2709; 3 CFR 1954–1958 Comp. p. 189.

SUBPART A—ANNUAL VOLUMES

§ 10.1 *Publication required.*

The Director of the Federal Register shall publish, at the end of each calendar year, a special edition of the FEDERAL REGISTER called the "Public Papers of the Presidents of the United States." Unless the amount of material requires otherwise, each volume shall cover one calendar year.

§ 10.2 *Coverage of prior years.*

After consulting with the National Historical Publications Commission on the need therefor, the Administrative Committee may authorize the publication of volumes of papers of the Presidents covering specified years before 1957.

§ 10.3 *Scope and sources.*

(a) The basic text of each volume shall consist of oral statements by the President or of writings subscribed by him, and selected from—

(1) Communications to the Congress;
(2) Public addresses;
(3) Transcripts of news conferences;
(4) Public letters;
(5) Messages to heads of State;
(6) Statements released on miscellaneous subjects; and
(7) Formal executive documents promulgated in accordance with law.

(b) In general, ancillary text, notes, and tables shall be derived from official sources.

§ 10.4 *Format, indexes, and ancillaries.*

(a) Each annual volume, divided into books whenever appropriate, shall be separately published in the binding and style that the Administrative Committee considers suitable to the dignity of the Office of the President of the United States.

(b) Each volume shall be appropriately indexed and contain appropriate ancillary information respecting significant Presidential documents not printed in full text.

§ 10.5 *Distribution to Government agencies.*

(a) The Public Papers of the Presidents of the United States shall be distributed to the following, in the quantities indicated, without charge:

(1) *Members of Congress.* Each Senator and each Member of the House of Representatives is entitled to one copy of each annual volume published during his term of office, upon his written request to the Director of the Federal Register.

(2) *Supreme Court.* The Supreme Court is entitled to 12 copies of each annual volume.

(3) *Executive agencies.* The head of each executive agency is entitled to one copy of each annual volume upon application to the Director.

(b) Legislative, judicial, and executive agencies of the Federal Government may obtain copies of the annual volumes, at cost, for official use, by the timely submission of a printing and binding requisition to the Government Printing Office on Standard Form 1.

§ 10.6 *Extra copies.*

Each request for extra copies of the annual volumes must be addressed to the Superintendent of Documents, to be paid for by the agency or official making the request.

INDEX

[Main references are to item numbers except as otherwise indicated]

[Main references are to item numbers except as otherwise indicated]

Index

[Main references are to item numbers except as otherwise indicated]

[Main references are to item numbers except as otherwise indicated]

Index

[Main references are to item numbers except as otherwise indicated]

[Main references are to item numbers except as otherwise indicated]

Index

[Main references are to item numbers except as otherwise indicated]

[Main references are to item numbers except as otherwise indicated]

[Main references are to item numbers except as otherwise indicated]

[Main references are to item numbers except as otherwise indicated]

Index

[Main references are to item numbers except as otherwise indicated]

[Main references are to item numbers except as otherwise indicated]

[Main references are to item numbers except as otherwise indicated]

[Main references are to item numbers except as otherwise indicated]

Index

[Main references are to item numbers except as otherwise indicated]

[Main references are to item numbers except as otherwise indicated]

[Main references are to item numbers except as otherwise indicated]

[Main references are to item numbers except as otherwise indicated]

[Main references are to item numbers except as otherwise indicated]

[Main references are to item numbers except as otherwise indicated]

Index

[Main references are to item numbers except as otherwise indicated]

Index

[Main references are to item numbers except as otherwise indicated]

Index

[Main references are to item numbers except as otherwise indicated]

[Main references are to item numbers except as otherwise indicated]

[Main references are to item numbers except as otherwise indicated]

Index

[Main references are to item numbers except as otherwise indicated]

[Main references are to item numbers except as otherwise indicated]

[Main references are to item numbers except as otherwise indicated]

[Main references are to item numbers except as otherwise indicated]

U.S. GOVERNMENT PRINTING OFFICE : 1975 O—53-528